CAIRO
SECURITIZED

The Middle East Urban Studies series
Deen Sharp and Noura Wahby, series editors
This series explores new research from a progressive and critical lens on the wide-ranging implications of urban transformation in the Middle East. It engages with the intensifying processes of urbanization across the region, from large-scale infrastructure projects to the construction and destruction of new cities and urban regions.

CAIRO
SECURITIZED

RECONCEIVING URBAN JUSTICE AND SOCIAL RESILIENCE

EDITED BY
PAUL AMAR

The American University in Cairo Press
Cairo New York

This paperback edition published in 2025 by
The American University in Cairo Press
113 Sharia Kasr el Aini, Cairo, Egypt
420 Lexington Avenue, Suite 1644, New York, NY 10170
www.aucpress.com

First published in hardback in 2024
ISBN 978 1 649 03436 6

Library of Congress Cataloging-in-Publication Data applied for

1 2 3 4 5   29 28 27 26 25

Designed by Adam el-Sehemy

CONTENTS

List of Illustrations   ix

Contributors   xi

Acknowledgments   xxi

Introduction: Cairo Securitized: Can Another World Be Made?   1
    Paul Amar

Section 1. Vernacular Mediascaping: Beyond the Binary of Digital/Virtual Space versus Street/Real Space

1   The Crime of Shamelessness: TikTok Women, the Principle of Bodily Integrity, and Independence without Regrets   35
      Sara Soumaya Abed

2   Securitized Consolidation, or How the State Co-opted Private Media   55
      Mohamed Elmeshad

3   The City and the Jungle: Africa and Blackness in the Egyptian Interwar Cinematic Imagination   69
      Ifdal Elsaket

4   Viral Visualities, Image Cycles, and Mosireen's Revolutionary Archives   81
      Mark R. Westmoreland

5   Queer Digital Activism: Street Media and Subversion of Digital Securitization   95
      Afsaneh Rigot and Nora Noralla

Section 2. Reversing Social Cleansing and Depathologizing Justice: Beyond the Binaries of Sociability versus Social Cleansing, Value versus Waste, Abled versus Debilitated, Medicine versus Magic

6   Toilets for the People? Hygiene in the City and
     Depathologizing Popular Sanitation   109
     Tina Guirguis

7   Cairo's Sexuality Infrastructures: Securitizing Abortion,
     HIV, and Gender-affirming Surgery   125
     Miguel A. Fuentes Carreño

8   Road to the Future: Infrastructure and Landscape Sanitized
     of Trees and People, Viewed from "God's Eyes"   143
     Mohamed Elshahed

9   The Khaki Color of Football: Digitized Militarization
     and Social Sanitization of Egypt's Most Popular Game   159
     Rania Ahmed

Section 3. Anti-enclave Densityphilia: Beyond the Binary of Working-class Slum versus Elite Gated City

10   Urban (Counter)Revolution against Gentrification:
     Shadow Security Networks, *Baltagiya* Subjectivities,
     and Community Densities   177
     Omnia Khalil

11   Urbanizing Dreams: The Struggles of Attaining "New"
     Social Contracts for the Middle and Upper Middle Classes
     at Cairo's Desert Edge   191
     Momen El-Husseiny

12   Military Capitalism: The Economic and Security Logics
     of Egypt's New Administrative Capital   205
     Roberta Duffield

13   Gulf Investment, Megacontractor Projects, and Urban
     Isomorphism: The Imposition of a New Way of Life   221
     Maïa Sinno

Section 4. Convivial Sociabilities: Beyond the Binaries of Street Mobility versus Family Domesticity, Public versus Private

14   Cairo Up! Infrastructures of Security and Desire   233
     Aya Nassar

15   The Curious Cases of the Disappearing Maids: Mobilization
     and Precarity among Foreign Domestic Workers in Cairo   247
     Sabrina Lilleby

16 Cruising Ethics in Cairo: Queer Street Socialities against
    Fear Regimes   259
    Ahmed Awadalla

17 South Sudanese Refugees and Community Schools in Cairo:
    A Home Away from Home   273
    Amira Hetaba and Elena Habersky

18 Entangled in the City: Interstitial and Queer Urbanism
    through the Eyes of a Second-generation Nubian   285
    Yahia Saleh

Section 5. Participatory Futurity: Beyond the Binary of Informal versus Planned

19 Seeing Like a City-state: Behavioral Planning and Governance
    in Egypt's First Affordable Gated Community   295
    Nicholas Simcik Arese

20 Peripheralization and Infrastructural Violence:
    "Haussmannization" in Managua, Nicaragua and
    Cairo, Egypt   309
    Ahmad Borham

21 Statizing Informality and Unbundling Rights: Neoliberal
    Infrastructure in Cairo's *'Ashwa'iyat*   317
    Deena Mahmoud Sobhy Khalil

22 Al-Asmarat: Managing Informality, Reproducing Precarity,
    and Dislocating Workers   327
    Mostafa Mohie

23 *Pacta Sunt Servanda?* Exercising Possession in an
    Informalized Cairo   339
    Yahia Shawkat

Section 6. Enforcement Sovereignties: Beyond the Binary of Thugs versus Police

24 Gestures of Territorialism: *Baltagiya*, Land Anxieties,
    and Securitizing Squatting   353
    Hatem Hassan

25 Cairo Militarized: Army Economies, Security Industries,
    and Surveillance Geographies   367
    Zeinab Abul-Magd

26 Thuggery, Urbanity, and Enforced Sovereignties:
    Competing Universes of the *Baltaga*   377
    Aly El Raggal

27 Deconstructing Thuggery: Riots, Prison Breaks,
    and the Criminal Subject of (Non)Violent Street Politics   389
    Mohamed Ahmed

28 Sectarian Politics? Securitization, Urban Development,
    and Coptic Advocacy in Cairo   401
    Amy Fallas

Section 7. Abolitionist Desecuritization: Beyond the Binary of "Crime from Below" versus "Security from Above"

29 Security from Within: The Case of the Informal Policing of
    al-Matariya Neighborhood   413
    Bassem Al-Samragy

30 Challenging Urban Militarization in Post-2011 Downtown
    Cairo: Walls and Checkpoints   423
    Laura Monfleur

31 Becoming a Man in Cairo: Sudanese and South Sudanese
    Refugees, Gangs, and Structural Violence   433
    Paul Miranda

32 Policing Women's Sexual Economies in Downtown Cairo:
    Students and Their Brothel Friends in Colonial Times   449
    Hanan Hammad

Index   463

ILLUSTRATIONS

Figures

1.1 Solidarity demonstration in Berlin. Source: Photograph by Mariam Mekiwi. Reproduced with permission.

5.1 Sarah Hegazy, waving a flag at a Mashrou' Leila concert in summer 2017. Photo credit: Amr Magdi/@ganobi Twitter.

10.1 Maspero Triangle before the demolitions in 2018 (left) and after the demolitions in 2020 (right). Drawing by author.

20.1 Peripherization. Drawing by author.

20.2 Peripheralization. Drawing by author.

27.1 Khanufa's wedding picture. Sources: *al-Ahram*, "Khanufa: akhtar baltagi," August 27, 2011; and Mahmud Abd al-Sami', "Suqut Khanufa," *al-Ahram*, August 24, 2011.

30.1 Ammar Abo Bakr's graffiti representation of Khaled Said, one of the martyrs of the revolution. Photo by author, February 2015.

Tables

12.1 Proposed Projects and Credentials of the New Administrative Capital

32.1 The distribution of police sections in Cairo in the 1920s

32.2 Major sex-work establishments in Azbakiya in 1940

32.3 Registered sex workers and licensed brothels in Azbakiya

32.4 Fees collected by the police from licensed sex workers

CONTRIBUTORS

Sara Soumaya Abed is a researcher on the project Feminist Leading Voices in Africa Fellowship Programme at the African Leadership Centre (ALC), King's College London, and an alumni fellow of the ALC's Peace, Security and Development Fellowship Programme for African Women. Sara holds an MA in Human Rights from University College London (UCL), and was part of Operation Anti-Sexual Harassment & Assault (OpAntiSH), which confronted the rising tide of gender-based violence against women in Cairo's Tahrir Square during the January 25, 2011 revolution. Sara is interested in researching the intersections of queer theory and feminist political economy, social movements and cyberfeminism, and performance studies and sex work through the lens of labor rights.

Zeinab Abul-Magd is a professor of Middle Eastern history at Oberlin College. She received a PhD in history and political economy in 2008 and an MA in Arab studies and Islamic law in 2003, both from Georgetown University. Her books include *Militarizing the Nation: The Army, Business, and Revolution in Egypt* (Columbia University Press, 2017) and *Imagined Empires: A History of Revolt in Egypt* (Berkeley: University of California Press, 2013).

Mohamed Ahmed is an Egyptian historian with an MA in political science and Arab studies.

Rania Ahmed is a Cairo-based researcher interested in the economics and politics of sports, nationalism, and public space. She holds an MA in political science.

Paul Amar serves as a professor in the Global Studies department at the University of California, Santa Barbara (UCSB), and as director of the Orfalea Center for Global and International Studies. He is a political scientist and anthropologist with affiliate appointments in feminist studies, political science, sociology, comparative literature, Middle East studies, and Latin American and Iberian studies. A three-time Fulbright Fellowship winner who speaks six languages, Professor Amar served as founding director of the PhD program and subsequently as department chair in Global Studies; he was a cofounder of the AreaGlobal Institute and of the Center for Feminist Futures at UCSB, as well as the Center for Middle East Studies at the Fluminense Federal University in Rio de Janeiro and the Center for Global Studies at the State University of Rio de Janeiro. Before he began his academic career, he worked as a journalist in Cairo, a police reformer and sexuality rights activist in Rio de Janeiro, and a conflict-resolution and economic development specialist at the United Nations. His books include *Cairo Cosmopolitan* (2006), *New Racial Missions of Policing* (2010), *Global South to the Rescue* (2011), *Dispatches from the Arab Spring* (2013), *The Middle East and Brazil* (2014), and *The Tropical Silk Road* (2022). His book *The Security Archipelago* was awarded the Charles Taylor Award for Best Book of the Year in 2014 by the Interpretive Methods Section of the American Political Science Association. In 2019, he was awarded Mentor of the Year by the Latin American Studies Program at UCSB.

Nicholas Simcik Arese is an assistant professor of architecture and urban studies at the University of Cambridge and a research affiliate in the PEAK Urban program at the University of Oxford's Department of Anthropology. He is an ethnographer and architect who combines economic anthropology and legal geography to understand how people repurpose planned cities. His monograph on the political creativity of squatters in suburban Cairo and an edited volume titled *Experimental Properties* are forthcoming.

Ahmed Awadalla is a writer, artist, and health practitioner who grew up in Egypt and is currently based in Berlin. Their writing and research foreground the intersections between health, migration, and radical sexual politics. Their blog *Rebel with a Cause* has been one of the leading online spaces addressing these issues in Egypt. Awadalla's work around these themes in Egypt and Germany has ranged from grassroots community building to international advocacy.

Ahmad Borham is an independent urban researcher, a practicing design architect and lecturer, and an assistant professor of practice at the Arab Academy for Science and Technology and the Nile University in Cairo. He earned an MS in architectural engineering for a master's thesis entitled "Resilient Rules: Culture and Computation in Traditional Built Environments." He is the cofounder of the Cairo from Below and Madd initiatives, which share the aim of encouraging inclusive urbanization in Cairo. He is also affiliated with a number of other urban initiatives in Cairo such as the Built Environment Collective (Megawra) and Tadamun.

Miguel A. Fuentes Carreño was born and raised in Mexico City and is pursuing a PhD in the Global Studies Department at the University of California, Santa Barbara. He has been the chief of staff at Arab Week in Mexico, the largest scholarly space fostering the study of MENA in Mexico. He is currently exploring interregional comparisons of human rights regimes, with a particular focus on MENA and Latin America.

Roberta Duffield is a freelance researcher currently living in Cairo, Egypt. She holds degrees from the University of California, Santa Barbara and Oxford University. Her research focuses on urbanism, public space, and the politics of technology and infrastructure.

Mohamed Elmeshad is a journalist and researcher who received his PhD from SOAS University of London. His research has focused on political economy, and he has worked extensively on Egypt, Bahrain, West Africa, the UK, and the US. He has written for various publications and outlets including *Sada* (Carnegie Endowment), *The New Arab*, and *Egypt Independent*. He is a contributor to the book *Attacks on the Press: Journalism on the World's Front Lines*, published by The Committee to Protect Journalists.

Ifdal Elsaket is assistant director of Arabic and Islamic Studies at the Netherlands-Flemish Institute in Cairo. Her work focuses on film, cinema culture, and audiences. Ifdal has published in the *International*

Journal of Middle East Studies and *Arab Studies Journal*. She is coeditor (with Daniel Biltereyst and Philippe Meers) of the book *Cinema in the Arab World: New Histories, New Approaches* (Bloomsbury, 2023).

Mohamed Elshahed is a curator and architectural historian focusing on modernism in Egypt and the Arab World. After completing his undergraduate studies at the College of Architecture and Design (NJIT), he earned a master's degree from MIT's Aga Khan Program for Islamic Architecture and a PhD from NYU's Department of Middle Eastern Studies. His work spans architecture, design, and material culture. He is the curator of the British Museum's Modern Egypt Project and curated Egypt's winning pavilion, "Modernist Indignation," at the 2018 London Design Biennale. In 2019, *Apollo Magazine* named him among the "40 under 40" influential thinkers and artists in the Middle East.

Amy Fallas is a PhD candidate in history, working across the fields of modern Middle East and late Ottoman history, religious studies, archival studies, and the Latin East (Middle East–Latin American studies). Her research focuses on modern Egypt, religious minorities in the Middle East, missions and global Christianity, and comparative empires. She is also a freelance writer on religion and politics in Egypt, the United States, and Central America.

Tina Guirguis is a PhD candidate in global studies at the University of California, Santa Barbara. She holds previous degrees from the University of California, Irvine and the American University of Beirut. Her research examines the biopolitical and bioeconomic dimensions of contemporary sanitation infrastructure megaprojects, hygiene campaigns, wastewater surveillance, and excremental politics in China, India, and Egypt.

Elena Habersky is the current project manager of the Egyptian Migration Hub (EHUB), which is a network on migration in Egypt, and the former project manager of the Refugee Entitlements in Egypt Project, both of the Center for Migration and Refugee Studies at the American University in Cairo. She holds an MA in migration and refugee studies from AUC and a BA in international studies from the University of Scranton. She has spent the past decade working in the MENA/SWANA region with urban refugee populations.

Hanan Hammad is a professor of history and director of Middle East studies at Texas Christian University. She is a social and cultural historian whose work on gender, sexuality, working classes, and popular culture has received prizes from the National Women's Studies Association, the Association for Middle East Women's Studies, MESA, Middle East Political Economy Book Award, the Arab American Book Awards, and the *Journal of Social History*. She is the author of many academic publications, most notably *Industrial Sexuality: Gender, Urbanization, and Social Transformation in Egypt* (UT Press, 2016) and *Unknown Past: Layla Murad, the Jewish-Muslim Star of Egypt* (Stanford University Press, 2022).

Hatem Hassan is an urban ethnographer, editor, senior researcher, and organizer focusing on policies disproportionately affecting working-class youth in Cairo and beyond. His work has been published with Oxford University Press and *International Sociology*, among other journals, news outlets, and magazines. He has lectured on ethnography and political sociology at the Fayette State Correctional Institution and the University of Pittsburgh while successfully organizing to ban solitary confinement in Allegheny County (Pennsylvania). He currently designs surveys for tens of thousands of ballot initiatives with the aim of reforming the world of criminal justice. He was born in Cairo, Egypt.

Amira Hetaba holds a master's degree in law from the University of Vienna (Austria) with specializations in the law of international relations; international legal practice and language; and *culture juridique francophone européenne et internationale*. After completing her LLM degree in international and comparative law at the American University in Cairo, she joined the Center for Migration and Refugee Studies (CMRS-AUC), where she worked as a legal researcher at the Refugee Entitlements in Egypt Project from 2018 until 2020 and copublished a comprehensive report on the project's findings. Currently she is pursuing a career as a civil servant with the government of Lower Austria and serving as a lawyer at the Administrative Court of Lower Austria.

Momen El-Husseiny is an assistant professor of architecture and urbanism at the American University in Cairo. He holds a PhD in architecture from the University of California at Berkeley with a designated emphasis in global metropolitan studies. He is a registered architect and a trained ethnographer whose research falls at the intersections of critical urban theory, massive urbanization, and gated communities, exploring the constant profusion of fragments, fictions, and factions since postcolonial times and their role in remaking Cairo's extended urbanization and its desert surrounds.

Deena Mahmoud Sobhy Khalil is a development planner and urban researcher, currently working as a lecturer and postdoctoral fellow in the School of Humanities and Social Sciences, American University in Cairo. She holds a PhD in development planning from University College London (UCL) and an MA in the economics of international development from AUC.

Omnia Khalil is a PhD candidate in the cultural anthropology program at the City University of New York (CUNY). Her research and writings focus on city, violence, political economy, and redevelopment as they intersect with the anthropology of revolution. Since 2008, Khalil, as an urban researcher, has focused on community participatory action planning, and she has led many projects in Cairo, working with local communities.

Sabrina Lilleby is a doctoral candidate at the University of Texas, Austin. Her work focuses on mental health, the urban, violence, and work in Cairo. She holds an MA in gender and women's studies from the American University in Cairo.

Paul Miranda received his MA in law and diplomacy from the Fletcher School at Tufts University in 2019, focusing on humanitarian studies and human security. Previously, he lived in Egypt for five years, where he worked for a refugee assistance organization, focusing on refugee resettlement, protection, and legal aid provision for refugees and asylum seekers in Cairo. Paul speaks Arabic and earned a B.A. in history from the University of Delaware.

Mostafa Mohie is a PhD student in the Anthropology Department of Rice University. Formerly, he worked as a journalist for the bilingual news website *Mada Masr* in Egypt, focusing mainly on the urban transformations of Cairo. He participated as a researcher in two documentary films, one about the Alexandrian trade unionist Fathallah Mahrous and the leftist movement in the second biggest city in Egypt, and the other on the struggle of the residents of the Izbat Khairallah neighborhood in Cairo to contest the government order to demolish that dense urban area. He holds an MA in cultural anthropology from the American University in Cairo. In 2021, Cairo Papers in Social Science published his monograph, *Biographies of Port Said: Everydayness of State, Dwellers, and Strangers*, an ethnography of the city of Port Said and its spaces and how they were mutually produced and transformed through the practices of both dwellers and the state.

Laura Monfleur is a PhD candidate in geography at the University François-Rabelais of Tours, working in partnership with the CEDEJ (Centre d'études et de documentation économiques, juridiques et sociales). Her research focuses on the production and reception of authoritarian space-times in Cairo after 2011, exploring securitization, performance, and megaprojects. She teaches the geography and history of the Middle East and Maghreb at the National Institute of Oriental Language and Culture (INaLCO) in Paris.

Aya Nassar is an interdisciplinary political and urban geographer. She has taught human geography at the universities of Royal Holloway (London), Durham, and Sussex. Her research covers understanding elemental geography, the materiality of cities, fragments of space, and storytelling on the politics of the postcolony. She has published on memory, geopoetics, and materiality of the city with a focus on concrete and dust and their intertwining with memorialization, archives, and subjectivity—all in the context of Cairo.

Nora Noralla is an Egyptian human rights researcher and consultant focusing mainly on issues of sexual and bodily freedoms in the MENA region. Her engagement with the human rights field started in the wake of the January 25, 2011 revolution in Egypt. She holds a master's degree in international human rights law from the Central European University and is currently the executive director of Cairo 52 Legal Research Institute and a research fellow at the Information Society Law Center of the University of Milan.

Aly El Raggal is a political sociologist completing his PhD at the Scuola Normale Superiore in Florence, Italy. His MA in peace, development, security, and international conflict transformation was completed at the University of Innsbruck, Austria, under the supervision of Professor Wolfgang Dietrich. His MA thesis title is "The Weak Revolution: Revolution under a Society of Control: The Case of the Egyptian

Revolution." He writes regularly in the news outlets *Assafir* (Lebanon) and *Mada Masr* (Egypt). His published work includes "Police and Modernization in Egypt," "The Weak Revolution," "The Transformations of the Universes of Thugs and the Egyptian Society," "De-securitizing Egypt," "Police and Neoliberalism in the Mubarak Era," and "The Permanent Society of Suspicion: A Short History of the Contentions and Integration between the Law State and Police State in Egypt."

Afsaneh Rigot is a researcher with years of experience covering law, technology, and LGBTQ, refugee, and human rights issues. Currently she is a senior researcher at ARTICLE 19 on Middle East and North Africa (MENA) regional issues, an affiliate at the Berkman Klein Centre (BKC) at Harvard University, a 2020–21 Technology and Public Purpose Fellow at Harvard Kennedy School's Belfer Center for Science and International Affairs, and an advisor for the Cyberlaw Clinic at Harvard University.

Yahia Mohamed Saleh is an activist engaged in issues concerning ethnic minorities, queer identities, and political participation. Together with other Nubian youth activists who have worked to raise Nubian issues to the political sphere after decades of marginalization, he has advocated for cultural recognition and land rights. Faced with the combined challenges of race, ethnicity, and sexuality, he advocates for these different identities in a variety of contexts. He is currently based in Malmö, Sweden, where he is working to obtain a master's degree in international migration and ethnic relations at Malmö University.

Bassem Al-Samragy is a researcher in political science who received an MA from the American University in Cairo, with a thesis entitled "Politics on the Margins: A Case Study of Neoliberal Subject Formation in the Popular Quarters of Cairo."

Yahia Shawkat is an advocate and researcher of equitable housing and spatial policies and strategies. He is a cofounder of the Cairo-based research studio 10 Tooba and edits its Built Environment Observatory, publishing investigations, including "Who Owns Cairo?" Yahia authored *Egypt's Housing Crisis: The Shaping of Urban Space* (American University in Cairo Press, 2020), and coedited *Nashtari kul shay'* (We Buy Everything) (Dar al-Maraya, 2022). He is currently a PhD candidate at Technische Universität Berlin.

Maïa Sinno works as an urban planning consultant on a state-developed program for reducing land artificialization processes and promoting a more inclusive urban model in French territories. Her research focuses on the influence of Gulf countries' investments in the political regimes during the period of the 2011 Egyptian Revolution, and their consequences for the urban planning model adopted for Cairo. She holds a PhD in geography and urban planning from Paris I Sorbonne.

Mark R. Westmoreland coordinates the visual ethnography specialization at Leiden University and is a former coeditor of *Visual Anthropology Review* before cofounding the *Writing with Light* journal for anthropological photo essays. His work engages both scholarly and practice-based approaches at the intersection of art, ethnography, and politics.

ACKNOWLEDGMENTS

The brilliant, innovative, brave, and illuminating contributions that constitute this volume—and the community of scholars that generated them—came together during a ten-year period (2012–22). This was a time where exhilaration morphed into horror and revolution into coup. Subsequently, trauma-driven depression for many gradually receded and, for some, vision and creativity blossomed. Patterns of dispersion and exile gradually turned toward reunion and homecoming. This volume acknowledges, in its subtitle, the remarkable resilience of social advocacy and transformative engagement in and around Egypt throughout this wrenching period, led by urban social movements, community organizations, policy actors, and scholars researching in this area, many of whom became targets of the degrading and repressive logics of securitization and criminalization that they study.

The backstory to this volume begins in 2012, when I (the editor, Paul Amar) was living in Cairo while doing urban research on processes of urban violence and city-wide attempts to reimagine alternatives to repressive security practices. I had the pleasure of engaging with researchers, leaders, and thinkers that constituted a new generation of innovative Egyptian or Egypt-specialist anthropologists, feminists, community organizers, political scientists, human rights champions, new media/social media innovators, and visionary artists. Between 2010 and 2013, large-scale mobilizations to reimagine urban social justice and civic participatory democracy demanded thorough restructuring, reimagining, and (at times) even abolishing of certain practices and institutions within overlapping sectors. Such sectors include policing, public safety, areas of criminalized public health, and a host of security institutions (military, state, surveillance) and norms (class, race, gender, and sexuality). And in the years that followed 2013, conversations launched previously continued to mature and proliferate in other countries, media, communities, and spaces.

In this context, I felt it would be crucial to generate a necessary sequel to the volumes *Cairo Cosmopolitan* and *Cairo Contested* that Diane Singerman and I had created with our teams of colleagues and contributors (that we, in 2006, collectively dubbed the "Cairo School of Urban Studies") for the AUC Press in the 2000s. This sequel would zero in on questions of urban violence, security, repression, and criminalization, as well as spotlight the resilience of urban alternative conceptualizations, public organizations, and progressive policy visions emerging from the grassroots and from diaspora and exiles in these tough times. This book would be called *Cairo Securitized* to emphasize the processes of transformation the city had endured and the dynamics of resilience it had generated since the events of 2013.

Together, a set of exciting, innovative, and unique scholarly contributions were brought together. Particularly during the drafting and editing phase of 2020–21, we passed through many challenging phases of political uncertainty and two years of extreme pandemic isolation. But we shared moments of celebration as well, as several contributors finished their PhD programs or enrolled in graduate programs. Our contributors launched major new initiatives at their arts centers, NGOs, or humanitarian organizations or became department chairs or field leaders at the universities.

We are profoundly grateful to the Carnegie Corporation and the incredible Security in Context international network that generously funded, nurtured, and provided constant feedback and a safe home for our contributors. Specifically, I would like to thank our astute and visionary program director Hillary Wiesner and the generous guidance and support of our always available and brilliant program analyst Nehal Amer, both at the Carnegie Corporation. I would also like to thank Prof. Omar Dahi at Hampshire College, whose leadership of the Security in Context network has been our intellectual, policy-making, and public engagement role model and generative space of operations throughout the process of conceiving, developing, and launching this book. Also, I am profoundly grateful to Dr. Omnia Khalil, who as a contributor, advisor, and Security in Context program assistant served as a valued colleague to me during crucial times negotiating the more sensitive moments of drafting while she also served as project assistant at the Orfalea Center at UCSB.

When I drafted this book proposal and discussed it with the enthusiastic team at the AUC Press, we knew we wanted this to be a comprehensive and comprehensible collection, designed to embody twenty-first-century concerns and appeal to contemporary students and scholars, policymakers and the general public. We also knew that each chapter needed to be tightly written and edited so that a member of the general public, or an undergraduate student just beginning their educational journey, could navigate through the book easily and enjoy each chapter and be captivated by the story it tells. In this way, we carefully introduce each reader to this rich intersection of Middle East Studies, Urban Studies, Gender/Sexuality Studies, and Security Studies, with chapters that are short but substantive, punchy, and captivating. Each chapter introduces new concepts through an empirical case study; each speaks with a voice articulated clearly at the intersection of evolving social research frameworks, justice concepts, and methodological models. In order to maintain an accessible, impactful, and consistent format for each chapter of this book, a brilliant team of associate editors and project co-managers came together.

The work of project management to generate a volume that aspires to include the work of thirty-two diverse and cutting-edge scholars requires a combination of multidisciplinary fluency, logistical acumen, diplomatic nuance, and interpersonal skills. In this context, I would like to especially thank Dr. Hatem Hassan, my associate editor of this collection, who also performed repeated rounds of developmental editing with almost all of the contributions, made the texts sing with his careful line editing and restructuring, and fixed countless reference inaccuracies. And most importantly, he believed in and loved the contributors' perspectives and ensured that their integrity, conceptual uniqueness, and empirical rigor shined through. Without Hatem, the book would not have made it through all the stages of revision and polishing necessary to make it the extremely high-quality product it is today. I would also like to thank Dr. Miguel Fuentes Carreño, who served as project co-manager and research/editing assistant during the tough years of 2020–21 as he completed his own fantastic PhD dissertation in Global Studies at UC Santa Barbara and served as a research fellow at the Orfalea Center for Global & International Studies that I direct at USB. All of the contributors will remember Miguel's lucid and inspiring guidance as he identified and recruited certain authors, wrangled up original drafts, and juggled diplomacy and networking across multiple continents, time zones, personalities, and technologies. His hard work, ingenious coordination skills—and his advocacy for a book that centers health, sexuality, safety, and security economies—improved the collection in vital ways. I also want to thank Prof. Thaddeus Blanchette, my lifelong colleague and translating/writing role model in Brazil, who as co-assistant editor meticulously pored through chapter drafts to suggest moments where the chapters could better speak to each other. His work was crucial to the art of weaving the chapters into a fabric of conversations, adding up to more than the sum of their parts.

I would like to thank the team at the American University in Cairo Press for taking on this ambitious project and bringing this book to life in such a beautiful way that exceeded our expectations. First, I want to thank Neil Hewison, my dear friend and esteemed writer and editor role model, who served in the past as associate director for editorial programs at the AUC Press and gave tentative approval to the concept note for this volume, "Cairo Securitized," back in 2012. He offered crucial guidance and generous leadership as the proposal was relaunched in 2020. I would also like to thank the editors of the Urban Studies Series at the AUC Press, my dear colleagues Dr. Deen Sharp and Dr. Noura Wahby, for believing in our project and shepherding the manuscript through. And I would like to thank the brilliant team of acquisition editors and editing specialists from the AUC Press, including Nadia Naqib, Miriam Fahmi, Johanna Baboukis, and our incredible, meticulous indexer David Prout. I would like to offer very special thanks to Anne Routon, our acquisitions editor at the AUC Press, who believed in us from the start and who worked so hard, with creativity, patience, vision, and diligence, to guide us through this long process. It has been such a joy to work with Anne and the whole AUC team, along with all of my esteemed contributors. I acknowledge the passion, hard work, and intelligence of all of these people, particularly during this era of multiple intersecting crises. Without them, this groundbreaking volume would never have made it into the hands of the students, publics, and change-makers. We hope these readers and publics will find value and usefulness in this book to help transform Cairo and catalyze processes of worldmaking in a range of contexts and fields.

I would like to thank my team of inspiring, loving, and hard-working colleagues at the University of California, Santa Barbara, without whom this book would never have existed. My pod of friends who sustained each other during the pandemic: Bishnu Ghosh, Lisa Hajjar, Bhaskar Sarkar, Constance Penley, Mireille Miller-Young, Terrance Wooten, and Abdulhamit Arvas. My dear friends and inspiring leaders in the Center for Middle East Studies at UCSB: Sherene Seikaly, Shiva Balaghi, Walid Afifi, Dwight Reynolds, Laila Sherene Sakr, Vladimir Hamed-Troyanski, and many others. To the comrades and constant inspiration of my colleagues in the Department of Global Studies. And special thanks to Dean Charles Hale, who works tirelessly in support of engaged and collective scholarship. And I owe a deep debt of gratitude to the team at the Orfalea Center for Global & International Studies at UCSB, my home base of operations for these past five years, especially to Center founder and constant inspiration Mark Juergensmeyer; benefactor and cherished supporter Paul Orfalea; Academic Coordinator Dr. Melissa Bator; Public Education Academic Coordinator Omar Mansour; Executive Director Dr. Manaira Athayde; Financial Officer Bashar Tarabieh; and Media/Technology Producers CY Xiu and Weihao Qiu. This team together implemented the Carnegie Corporation grant and gave me the infrastructure to run such a large-scale exercise in the co-production of knowledge.

Finally, a huge shout-out to all of the contributors, the brilliant authors who are the real stars of this volume and whose diligent research, conceptual innovation, and scholarly bravery animates every page of this volume. I have been honored to work with each and every one of you and continue to learn more from you each day.

INTRODUCTION

CAIRO SECURITIZED: CAN ANOTHER WORLD BE MADE?

PAUL AMAR

Questions of the Epoch

Our age is one of environmental crisis, viral pandemics, authoritarian politics, and criminalized inequality. In this context, is it even possible to think of a densely populated megacity as a space of justice, sustainability, safety, and voice?

Ours is also an age of spatially expressed emancipation. Cities are nurturing zones for mobilizing peoples, articulating alliances, and challenging systemic racial and sexual violence. Cities are incubators for transformative housing, health, ecology, and education agendas. They are test sites for abolitionist and demilitarized responses to crime and punishment—intersections that can bypass binaries of gender and challenge the ontological divides between technology and nature. Given this, we feel that the time has come to listen to the megacities of the global south so that we can learn to think—and make new worlds—in new ways.

These are also times of paradigm shifts and revolutions of consciousness. The megacities of the global south are leading the way, forging sets of new tools for building idea systems and analytics, for prying open stereotypes and generating empowering representations of bodies, identities, communities, states, and futures. One of the most generative productive sites in the global south has been Egypt, particularly in the first two decades of the twenty-first century, in the exhilarating and agonizing years of collective creativity and transformation around the January 25,

1

2011 Revolution. Egypt has given the world a new generation of ingenious activist-scholars, visionary leaders, and sociopolitical models that has precipitated, in part, a new global age of shifting paradigms. From these creative contexts and social laboratories, real-world projects were launched and lived in, prerogatives of security and fear were challenged, and frameworks for being were reimagined. This generation's perspectives and tools will circulate and illuminate questions and struggles in other regions, across the cities of the Americas, Africa, Asia, and beyond.

To comprehend and acknowledge the role of Egypt in global paradigm shifts, we ask the reader to consider reversing their preconceptions about how new ideas emerge and travel. At first glance, certain readers might be concerned that some of this volume's authors may seem to be importing "Western" notions or terms for capturing the sexuality, racial, ecological, or social fabric of social change and urban transformation. Can a book about Cairo by scholars of Cairo utilize English-language terms that are so engulfed in "culture wars" in the US and Europe— Blackness, queer, thug, and so forth—in ways that translate, transmit, and provoke new appreciation for deeply rooted issues of security and insecurity and critical questions of social justice in Egypt? This volume's contributors do not shy away from engaging with and repurposing these terms and tools, not in order to import "foreign" ideas nor to legitimize perspectives by attaching fashionable labels, but to launch from Egypt a new vocabulary for understanding security and society that rearticulates, retranslates, and resignifies these terms and many more that have become hot spots for struggles around cultural relativism and appropriation. In this way, ideas and assertions originating in Egypt launch alternative projects aimed at global publics and planet-scale concerns. The worlds and terms conveyed here reflect a set of deeply committed and contextualized conversations generated by scholars, artists, and social investigators either born and raised in Cairo or who have spent years making the city their home and reference point.

By focusing on Cairo, this volume addresses global and epochal questions around the spatial and political origins of violence, inequality, and marginalization, identifying alternative practices of emancipatory worldmaking—shaping spaces and futures concretely, through action and via reconceptualization. This book utilizes twenty-first-century and global-south-originating approaches for tackling these questions. With these aims in mind, *Cairo Securitized* articulates seven new thematic areas, and creates a new agenda at the intersection of security studies, global studies, human geography, urban sociology, media and surveillance studies, and political anthropology. We make the case for taking seriously Cairo's status as a laboratory for global change and as a site for shifting paradigms and innovative concepts. Each chapter in this volume provides useful and accessible tools for teaching, policy making, research, and activism.

In recent years, scholars have pushed to the side "urban studies" and the "spatial turn" in the social sciences and cultural theory fields, which peaked in the 1990s–2000s. Focus has shifted to the critical interventions of "new materialism" and infrastructure studies. Alternative lenses of technology studies and new media studies have been crafted. In these ways, place-based and built-form research has been vastly enriched by recognizing nature, the environment, and the nonhuman as agents of space-making and world-building. But in departing from humanist preoccupations, these interventions have sometimes flattened the realm of the social and reduced the complexities of class, caste, race, sect, and sexuality. Certain epistemological binaries have been reestablished even as they were decolonized. The realms of Indigenous or vernacular alternatives can be evoked in monolithic or romanticizing terms. *Cairo Securitized* intervenes in these debates, generating a framework for teaching and publicly engaging in and with cities, provisionally (re)centering the figures of "urban" and "space."

At the recent launch of the magazine *Arab Urbanism*, Deen Sharp (2020) reminded us that "the Arab world is undoubtedly an urban one. Home to some of the oldest continuously inhabited cities in the world and to a number of the newest, the Arab region is a critical but neglected research site for scholars trying to grapple with our urban age." Adding to the chorus of scholars attempting critical intervention, Mohamed Elshahed (2020) notes that "modern Cairo was positioned at the intersection of cultural, political, and artistic networks that produced a dynamic, heterogeneous city that embraces change and the new" (Elshahed 2020, 31). The importance of grounded empirical ethnographies and urban research continues the legacy of the volume *Cairo Cosmopolitan* (Singerman and Amar 2006) that launched the book series that also spawned this volume. The introduction to *Cairo Cosmopolitan* specified its objectives.

We aim to survey the landscape of globalizing power and socio-political contestation in the Middle East . . . to engage and appreciate classes of people, economies, and institutions at work, even if they only rarely attract the attention of those scholars and media outlets that generate familiar profiles of extremism, dictatorship, and violence in the region (Singerman and Amar 2006, 10).

Building on that tradition, this successor volume, *Cairo Securitized*, challenges conventional misconceptions about urban space that are amplified when applied to megacities of the global south. Conventional assumptions have generated a set of approaches that "securitize" urban worlds. By examining "securitization," we mean we pose and answer key questions about specific processes that render densely populated megacities into landscapes of fear, surveillance, paranoia, criminalization, overpolicing, and surveillance. We ask: Are fear, crime, and violence the perverse nature of the large metropolis? Are the inherent social, environmental, and infrastructural attributes of the big city criminogenic? Do population density, public mobility, and functional complexity render urban safety unattainable? Do large agglomerations of the urban "poor" chronically foster criminality, health insecurity, social insecurity, gender violence, and moral panic? Is the only way to imagine urban safety and security through increased policing, intensified searches and surveillance, "quality of life" crackdowns, and the banning of open public spaces, free public protests, and unpoliced public pleasures?

This inclusive and conceptually innovative work of collective scholarship presents contemporary Cairo as a world laboratory for rethinking justice, safety, and equality—creating lenses through which to reassess the dynamics of any twenty-first-century global city. *Cairo Securitized* generates cutting-edge intersectional research and transformative academic praxis. Breaking with academic tradition in both urban and security studies, we do not relegate questions of gender, race, and the new media to the end of the volume as gestures of "diversity" or "curiosity." Instead, we have developed a thoroughly nonbinary, anti-patriarchal, and queer methodology that we deploy throughout this book.

Questions of race, sectarianism, and class formation are interrogated systematically from decolonial and historically grounded perspectives. Our research and findings present alternative epistemologies and notions of "desecuritized" praxis. Rather than drawing from international relations debates and the "Copenhagen School" of security studies (Howell and Richter-Montpetit 2020; Buzan et al. 1998; Wæver 1995), we define "securitization" by drawing upon Stuart Hall et al. (1978), Jacqui Alexander (1994), Egyptian revolutionary feminisms and community organizing traditions (El Said, Meari, and Pratt 2015; Amar 2011, 2013), and the African Negritude surrealist movement (Rabaka 2016; Césaire 2001). We understand *securitization* to mean the repressive saturation of public spheres and media, governance and policing practices, and social and political worldviews informed by waves of criminalization, fear politics, race/sex panics, and surveillance technologies. In this context, we define our approach to securitization as rigorously abolitionist. In this context, the "abolitionist" stance refers to the fact that we posit acts of criminalization, repression, fear, and incarceration—and the actors and cultures that deploy and enforce them—to be autocratic, extractive, cruelly punitive, and exploitative in form and intent, rather than providing any kinds of long-term, substantive protection or justice.

Cairo Securitized systematically weaves together fresh urbanist conceptualizations of sexuality politics, racialization histories, class embodiments, military political economies, policing and parapolicing technologies, surveillance and social media, and the systemic violence of urban infrastructure, biomedicine, housing, and sanitation. This collection provides a twenty-first-century handbook for critical security studies in the context of global and everyday authoritarianism. It conveys the agency and specificity of a courageous city of scholar-activists who apply, in new ways, rich and revolutionary traditions of urban and security studies, providing a set of resources for emancipation and transformation, a methodological and epistemological tool kit for thinking beyond securitization and toward an inclusive and empowering urban social order. The principal aims of this volume are to generate public conversations and teaching tools that: (1) bring a new generation of security, crime, and media studies to the center of urban debates; (2) center a new generation of young activist and publicly engaged scholars in dialogue with field leaders; and (3) highlight methodological and epistemological innovations from global south perspectives and grassroots knowledge production.

Destabilizing Regimes of Inquiry: Themes and Concepts

This volume pushes back against the aforementioned assumptions and presents a new generation of engaged perspectives and desecuritizing outlooks. In order to clarify our alternative approaches, we have distilled them into a set of paradigm-changing questions and concepts. These questions challenge a set of seven governing binaries that have propped up popular misconceptions of the city and social science regimes of inquiry. *Cairo Securitized* articulates a set of alternative questions and concepts, summarized in seven lines of inquiry.

Section 1 of this volume is entitled "Vernacular Mediascaping." It asks: *How can we see the city in new ways that challenge the binary between digital/virtual space and street/real space?* In this first section of the volume, our contributing authors provide a comprehensive analysis of the radical shifts in media, technology, and surveillance, and their intersecting apparatuses of control, and representation. These have remade the social practices and virtual spaces of Cairo in innumerable ways. For many local and international observers, Cairo's Tahrir Square in 2011 evoked a utopia where the progressive potential for social media and digital communications intersected with and amplified real-time, in-person experiments in remaking social solidarity practices, promoting cross-class encounters and sociabilities, recoding experiences of gender/sexuality and racialized embodiments, performing new kinds of religious and sectarian conviviality, and developing alternative practices of community security and approaches to policing or security-state rule. But by the 2020s, this utopia had become a techno-dystopia of hardened surveillance, entrapment, paranoia, skyrocketing rates of moral panic, police harassment, and jailing of youth, dissidents, creatives, and sexual minorities. Our notion of "vernacular mediascaping" faces the dystopian turn, but insists on underlining its vernacular character. By vernacular, we mean the popular or people-level, often working-class, street-level, and community-grounded urban social media and social space campaigns that create "scapes." These scapes include new landscapes of sociability, sexuality, media culture, and alternative economies and community institutions as well as virtual-scapes, transcendent-scapes, and escape routes. Drawing upon the work of L.L. Wynn (2018, 36–39), we challenge the labels generated by respectability politics in Egypt, seeing "love and desire as highly moralized cultural domains" (37).

The second section of our volume is entitled "Reversing Social Cleansing and Depathologizing Justice." It asks: *How can we transcend the colonial–modernist assumptions that prop up urban designs and infrastructure projects that sanitize under the assumption of health, purity, and hygiene, and secure a binary between value and waste, abled and debilitated, and normal and diseased?* In this section, we turn from the urban questions of surveillance and mediation to questions of health and sanitation and to broader struggles around who is to be marked as physiologically diseased or socially pathological. In this section, our unique researchers build frameworks for seeing social action and spatial change as they renarrate modern histories of pathologization, sanitization, and security. Our shared normative perspective here is that social justice cannot be pursued through lenses of pathologization of the body and social difference. Access to reproductive and sexual health–related pharmaceuticals should not be a route for criminalizing women or trans people; struggles to access public toilets and proper water and sanitation should not be twisted in order to limit or police women's movements through public space; notions of youth pathology or adolescent delinquency shouldn't be deployed to "cleanse" sports culture of popular agency and voice; and urban planning models should not be elaborated and sold to investors based on their efficiency in "sanitizing" the city of its popular masses and even of trees, which supposedly obscure the view of the state and socially pollute the landscape.

Section three of our volume is called "Anti-enclave Densityphilia," and leads to the question: *How can we theorize inequality of access and investment in the urban framework without resorting to the binary language of working-class slum versus elite enclave?* In this section, our contributors bring years of case-study fieldwork to bear on analysis of the "enclaving" phenomenon that has rendered Cairo utterly unrecognizable (and "unseeable" as a whole by its own residents) in the past twenty years. Middle- and upper-class residents have largely moved into luxury desert enclaves, gated communities, and speculative developments on the city's periphery. Meanwhile the majority of the popular-class and working-class populations have continued to settle or resettle into unplanned, informal "slum" *(ashawiyyaat)* neighborhoods. During the same period, the longstanding, socially diverse, and historically significant central urban neighborhoods and zones of Cairo's urban core have been gentrified, meeting strong resistance from residents. Our concept of "densityphilia" may sound a bit clumsy, but it is one way to convey our methodological insistence on the social value of cross-class sociabilities and pluralized modes of inhabiting public space. Our analytic privileges proliferating modes of gender, sexuality, class, and racial embodiment, and prioritizes the need to spatially cultivate dense modes of socioeconomic, cultural, and affective interactions that are unmediated by security technologies, moral panic campaigns, or the imposition of carceral, criminalizing, or social sanitation norms.

The fourth section of our volume is entitled "Convivial Sociabilities," and asks: *How can we encourage city dwellers as well as policymakers to think beyond the binary of urban mobility ("public") versus family domesticity ("private")?* In this section, our brilliant contributors push back against "family values" notions of the naturalized, heteropatriarchal notion of the domestic or private sphere. This group of interventions generates alternative analytics that challenge the public/private binary, describing how the domestic is generated through women migrant laborers, and how African refugees or Nubian exiles create alternative home spaces in streets and schools. We see how the securitized air above Cairo can become a space for desire and home-projection through drone infrastructures, while some of its riskiest streets can be recoded as cruising zones where fear culture is challenged by bold modes of sociality and intimacy, and affirmation of alternative racially and sexuality-inflected experiences of conviviality and everyday cooperation.

Our fifth section is entitled "Participatory Futurity." It asks: *How can we imagine just and inclusive cities beyond the notions of informal versus planned, shanty versus condominium?* In this section, our contributors unleash our imaginations of the future, both globally and in the Egyptian context. Like so many megacities of the global south, Cairo is imagined as a city with two futures, two faces—one "informal" (the "slums" where the majority of the city's population and popular classes reside), and one "formal" (the "gated cities" and enclaves of the privileged Egyptian upper 10 percent, the foreign investors, and the second-home owners). In this section our contributors challenge this binary of formal/informal and offer an integrated analysis of urban realities and social cartographies. These chapters build on the work of scholars such as David Sims (2012) and Mona Fawaz (2009), who have insisted that "informal slums" in the Middle East and throughout the global south are much more "formally" state-planned and top-down coordinated by state-linked corporate and military elites than their seemingly chaotic street life may indicate, and that gated cities and elite enclaves are also much more "informal," avoidant of regulation and planning regimes, corrupt or rogue in their speculative profiteering, and often more lacking in infrastructure, sanitation, and public services than the much-maligned "slums." In this section, our contributors enable urbanists and readers to finally break free from this informal/formal, planned/spontaneous binary and to imagine integration and even utopian potentials in this megacity landscape of inequality.

The sixth section of this volume, "Enforcement Sovereignties," uses as its guiding question: *How can we map the operations of social coercion, community protection, gendered safety, vigilantism, working-class direct action/dissent, and racketeering without resorting to the binary that poses "thugs" as the opposite of "police," or "bandits" versus "heroes," particularly in terms of exercising state dominion and popular sovereignty?* In this section, we trace the multiple institutions and practices of norm enforcement, hierarchy protection, and legal and extralegal coercion that proliferate in the contemporary megacity, riddled with multiple military and paramilitary, uniformed and plainclothes "security" forces. We also offer an integrated analysis of forms of alternative security practices, popular sovereignty assertions, and vigilantism self-generated by communities—in league with the state or in opposition to it (or both). Our contributors offer a social history and political geography of the figure of the "thug" that has risen to such prominence in the counterrevolutionary era after 2013, and they do so by in-depth and in-person ethnographies that span the years prior to and following this watershed moment. We tie these social shifts to, or differentiate them from, enforcement logics and practices within the military economies behind new security industries, in both the public and private sectors. This section also articulates the agency of Coptic Christian youth in their alternative safety mobilizations and community preservation initiatives, which is so often excluded from analysis of securitization, desecuritization, and informal/formal sources of such processes.

In this volume's seventh and final section, we focus on visions of "Abolitionist Desecuritization" and bring the reader to another overarching question: *How can we challenge the all-consuming binary of "crime from below" versus "security from above" in an age of "defunding, disarming, and demilitarizing" movements, worldwide?* In this section, we return to the concept of "securitization," or the notion of a city monopolized by security fears, social paranoia, surveillance practices, socially sanitizing constructions, pathologizing geographies, media monitoring, and police proliferation. How can we imagine, map, and analyze practices that transcend or abolish the security-obsessed matrices of control that have shaped Cairo? How can we imagine the lifting of the city's walls and checkpoints? What alternative social organizations might, imperfectly, serve as alternatives to policing? What histories of gender, sexuality, and labor can provide a socially just and economically inclusive model of the future?

In each of the seven concept-themes elaborated above, we challenge binary ways of thinking by drawing upon global-south-specific scholarship, inspired by the concepts and lessons offered by researchers, activists, and communities in Cairo. In this way, the present volume provides the tools for engineering a set of paradigm shifts.

Scholars more committed to conventional research methods or bounded disciplinary traditions often repeat the same tiresome complaint: innovative researchers are "negative," critiquing without proposing solutions or fixing policies. Yet when critical scholars do propose new concepts or solutions, they are dismissed once again, accused of trafficking in jargon or neologisms. Many of this volume's collaborators and contributors have faced these complaints. We reject this dismissive conservatism and embrace an agenda that is simultaneously critical and solution-oriented, unafraid of thinking in new ways. We are happy to twist social-science languages and urban policy discourses in order to generate new meanings and destabilize previously dominant signifiers.

Another City Is Possible

With this careful selection of new voices and perspectives, *Cairo Securitized* presents a range of empirical findings and analytically revealing concepts that prove that urban insecurity is made, not born. City crime, violence, and fear are created by specific means of extraction, production, and control. This means that they can be reversed, reengineered, and/or replaced. Another kind of city can live again, but "security," as we have been led to understand it, is never the answer. Insecurity can be deconstructed and replaced by an equitable urban order through justice, participation, and redistribution—a transformative redesign process we call "desecuritization."

To be clear, we are not focusing on top-down regime and state security apparatus-driven solutions. Instead, we introduce a bottom-up approach, centering public space, social imaginaries, and media infrastructures as intersecting engines of insecurity and laboratories of struggle. Part of the reason for this approach is that many of the authors have lived through such struggles and dangers, triumphs and discoveries, and continue to do so in Cairo and across Egypt. And despite the repressiveness of so many of the processes depicted here, we argue that many of the tools and models for desecuritization of the megacity are already unleashing powerful new alternatives and lifeworlds. However, these alternative movements, concepts, models, and their advocates are relentlessly targeted and misrepresented by suffocating governmental policies and debilitating disregard. To expose these control regimes, the chapters below trace how apparatuses for producing the monstrous megacity are generated and in whose interest they are imposed.

Even in these difficult circumstances, we demonstrate that the density and dynamism of public urban sociability offers its own solutions and ways of being, alternatives to the security urbanisms advocated by gated cities, enclave isolation, and urban sprawl. Redefined to include agrarian urbanism (forms of city development that favor local agriculture for community use), urban density creates room for rural justice to counter plantation agrobusiness models that hoard land and unleash paramilitary forces. The forms of "justice urbanism" and "desecuritization" introduced here are inherently linked to disrupting and dismantling the extraction projects that devastate rural areas.

Here, we highlight the politics of urban public health, including pandemic protection, accessibility, gender/sexuality/reproductive rights, social well-being, and labor safety. Healthy social mobility and public transportation can be distinguished from stressed hypercirculation and pollution and from privatized fossil fuel–burning transportation providers. Case studies underline how medical universalism in the urban context can be liberated from the monopolistic regime of the global pharmaceutical industry in which profits are channeled to a handful of large Western corporations who own the premier drug patents. We prioritize housing and property redistribution rather than fear-engineered enclave elitism, and we recognize the role that popular and vernacular religiosity plays in social emancipation, collective celebration, and community vitalization while distinguishing these forms of religious sociability from toxic practices of moral policing, sectarian demonization, and dogmatic patriarchy.

Why Securitization?

"Securitization" is an intentionally estranging concept, thus a "queer" notion, in the most multivalent sense. In one etymology, the term dates to 1990s critical security studies debates within political science. Another etymology traces the term to the discourse around commodification of financial holdings that are labeled "securities." The scholars gathered here are interested in establishing yet another conceptual history for securitization and security studies. Our genealogy of securitization references a different set of perspectives, including:

(1) Critical criminology, radical penology, "decrim"[1] activism, and anti-carceral abolitionism;

(2) Anti-colonial surrealism, cultural studies of "monster technologies" of abjection and fear-making, and studies at the intersection of race, media, and political economy;

(3) Long histories of theorizing the imbrication of police violence, para-militarism, social violence, and security privatization, and how these processes stem from unequal land ownership, property regimes, and racial and gendered political economies;

(4) Sexuality, gender, feminist, and biopolitical studies approaches to the fabrication of sex panic, moral panic, social debility, and gender violence;

(5)   Anthropological and sociological approaches to "violence actors," phobogenic subjects, and control regimes;

(6)   Studies of counterinsurgency and counterrevolution in the urban context; and

(7)   Subaltern urban studies perspectives that have brought to life material questions of infrastructure and built space.

We extend these interventions through the new theories, concepts, and findings of scholars, activists, creatives, and dissidents within Egypt and those with long-term commitments to the Middle East and the global south—individuals and collectives who think and write using the tools of distinct or emergent epistemologies and worlding practices. These include: new theories of violence actors (Savci 2021; Seigel 2018; Mbembe 2003); militarization and paramilitarization (Marshall 2015; Abul-Magd 2017; Sayigh 2011); urban social movements, youth and gender/sexuality (Ali 2018; Amar 2011; Sharp 2018); and studies of thugs, criminalization, and street organization (Ezzeldin 2014; El-Meehy 2012; El-Hamalawy 2011; Hassan 2015, 2019; Khalil 2019; Ismail 2006; Abdelhameed 2015).

Why Cairo?

Over the last two decades, Cairo—whose greater metropolitan region hosts a population of over twenty million individuals— has become a security laboratory. The revolution of 2011, portrayed locally and internationally as a utopia of social media progressivism, youth agency, and on-the-ground labor and community mass mobilization, morphed into a counterrevolution characterized as a dystopia of surveillance, militarization, and mass incarceration. The dynamic urban intersectionality and intimacy of Cairo as a megacity was replaced with a fragmented sprawl spawning more and more gated enclaves on its periphery, with its governing institutions displaced to a distant New Administrative Capital, far from public access, protest spaces, and accountability structures. Technological change swept through social and cultural life, not with the "liberalizing" effects predicted by many of its inventors, but providing tools for criminalization, horrific purges and entrapment campaigns, and censorship that unleashed tsunamis of "dreams" that flooded beyond the virtual world and into the streets, squares, cafés, and once-beloved public spaces of Cairo. The megacity became a captive dark site, transformed by its governing regimes and economic elites from a model of safety and conviviality into a horrified conglomeration of political terror, carnage, and grotesque wealth concentration. These elites intentionally unleashed catastrophic levels of unrelenting daily assault against women, children, "outsiders," religious people, public cultures, dissidents, journalists, community organizers, and those targeted as LGBTQ+.

How Did This Happen?

Relatively recently, until the year 2000, reports by experts agreed with general public perceptions: Cairo was a model megacity, relatively crime-free, safe, and public-facing. Even in the wake of occasional terrorist incidents, the grand city featured a thriving public culture and street life, a vibrant sense of well-being, and a famously mischievous sense of humor and confidence. The city was well known for its twenty-four-hour pulsing conviviality, where men and women, working and middle classes, Muslims and Christians, all mingled. In that Cairo, it was a wonderfully useless endeavor to disentangle the Mediterranean from the African and the Arab, the public from the private.

But around the year 2000, the structural and spatial impact of imposed transformations became acute and their sinister effects began to cascade. The last half of the thirty-year Mubarak presidency reflected the sociopolitical hegemony of the IMF, the United States, and the Gulf oil monarchies. In this phase, the Egyptian state accelerated a wholesale dismantling of public education and public-sector jobs, and reversed the modest land reforms of the Nasser era. Health, education, and housing became privatized in the 1990s Mubarak era, radically increasing forms of marginalization and erasing the structural supports that had kept citizens interconnected. This meant that most of Cairo's people were forcibly deprived of rights, social benefits, and educational capital. Their jobs were de-skilled and their tillable plots were seized in land grabs. Meanwhile, the tiny population of privileged elites who maintained their social rights and capital were encouraged to invest in environmentally devastating desert enclaves, automobile-centered lifestyles, and gated cities. These elites were encouraged to believe that it was necessary and prestigious to shut themselves off from the majority of their fellow citizens and, moreover, to fear and distrust them as thugs and terrorists. The privileged few supported the transformation of the state into a vast policing apparatus and regime of explicit as well as shadowy formations of brutality and intimidation. In parallel, the economy was restructured into a military oligopoly that established partnerships with the titans of the contracting sector and privatized security, intelligence, and policing corporations.

These processes of brutalization and dispossession did not extinguish the other kinds of world-making and urban agency that continue to animate Cairo, however. The resilient and dissident ways of urban worlding in Cairo were conveyed by Diane Singerman, myself, and our contributing authors in *Cairo Cosmopolitan* (2006) and by the Cairo School of Urban Studies that we collectively inaugurated at that time. *Cairo Cosmopolitan* captured the first signs of the country's popular movements against brutality, exclusion, gender intimidation, crony governance, and class segregation that would eventually take center stage in the global consciousness. The scholars, activists, creatives, and dissidents in this volume reveal the continuing vitality and urgency of this alternative Cairo.

Although the centrality of the social lenses of urban studies may have been displaced in some circles by the new materialist turn, this is not the case for scholarly communities focused on the Middle East, who have introduced a set of spectacular contributions orbiting around certain themes: urban history and literature (Sluglett 1998; al-Attar 2018; Hayek 2014); urban planning and development (Yarwood 2011; Kilinç and Gharipour 2019; Alraouf 2018; Elsheshtawy 2011); social landscapes and culture (Gharipour 2016; Weidmann and Salama 2019; Rieker and Ali 2008; Fawaz, Garbieh, and Harb 2018; Low 2016); urban violence (Freitag et al. 2015; Fuccaro 2016; Bou Akar 2018); urban modernity and spectacle (Molotch and Ponzini 2019; Elsheshtawy 2009; Kanna 2011; Weidmann and Salama 2013); urban informality, slums, and precarity (Elsheshtawy 2019; Sims 2012; Naeff 2018; Bogaert 2018); mobility and rights to the city (Fawaz 2006; Samara, He, and Chen 2013; Monroe 2016); grassroots counter-urbanisms (Sim 2019; Montgomery 2013; Simone 2018); and people as infrastructure and emancipatory urban movements (Nucho 2016; Chattopadhyay 2012; Simone 2004; Sharpe and Panette 2016).

In addition to these resources, the contributions of *Cairo Securitized* build upon research and innovations coming out of the Arab Council of the Social Sciences and the continuing conversations of the networks that comprise the Cairo School of Urban Studies and the Beirut School of Critical Security Studies. This volume offers a set of conceptual innovations and teachable case studies clustered around seven interventions, each offering nonbinary answers to questions that have been posed conventionally in rigidly binary fashion. Collectively, we have generated a new set of analytics while experimenting with new or adapted terminologies to express them. The seven sections mentioned earlier in this introduction are covered in more depth in the following section, where such collective generations of analytics are offered to the readers and to fellow scholars, activists, and dissidents.

Structure of the Book

In the paragraphs below, we will review the contributions gathered here in more detail, after having introduced the seven thematic concepts above.

"Vernacular Mediascaping"

How can we see the city in new ways that challenge the binary between digital/ virtual space and street/real space?

"Vernacular Mediascaping" begins with a moving analysis of the sexual-security crackdown on TikTok users in Egypt in 2019 and 2020. Sara Soumaya Abed generates a new set of critiques of respectability politics and the use of surveillance media to target and arrest working-class women media influencers. In particular, new media and an emerging generation of feminists attack class privilege and the state's investment in protecting rapists and perpetuating systematic sexual violence under the guise of securitizing the "Egyptian family." This chapter is followed by Mohamed Elmeshad's groundbreaking analysis of "media statism," or how the security and intelligence sector took over or coopted private media and news outlets. The contribution traces how this propagandistic apparatus—which aims to merge the surveillance, propaganda, and information sectors—portrays and manipulates the vernacular "street politics" of economic and social dissidence.

Ifdal Elsaket continues by tracing media manipulation and imaginaries. In her extraordinary exploration of racializing media, she examines the cinematic representation of Cairo as a city and "jungle" where colonial notions of Blackness and Africa are projected as somehow external to but essential for producing Egyptian Arabness and urban civilization. Race haunts the postcolonial urban imagination of class, danger, sexuality, and security. The filmic portrayal of domestic workers, servants, and working-class laborers in the service sectors in Cairo illuminates the real history of the city's relationship to Sudan, which continues to define and racialize the security sector today.

Mark Westmoreland then offers an alternative to the state-security media and national(ist) cinema, spotlighting vernacular, street-generated media. He outlines the practices that emerged during the 2011–12 uprisings, which successfully created, for an important period, an alternative model for portraying and recording distinct social, class, and race/gender representations of the people, social contestations, and political predicaments of Cairo. These alternative media and archives gave dignity to and decriminalized a set of issues and struggles that subsequently became highly securitized and demonized by both state media and national cinema. Afsaneh Rigot and Nora Noralla address the community-forming functions of cruising apps and their use by the state since 2011 for operations of online entrapment and surveillance. Their contribution focuses particularly on attacks against queer communities and same-sex social networks, and the impact of these crackdowns on physical urban spaces of sociability and circulation across the city. Like the other contributions in this section, Rigot and Noralla do not simply critique the acts of repression, but also provide a roadmap for resistance and highlight the ingenuity of social actors who combine digital and real-world action.

"Reversing Social Cleansing and Depathologizing Justice"

How can we transcend the colonial–modernist assumptions that prop up urban designs and infrastructure projects that sanitize under the assumption of health, purity, and hygiene, and secure a binary between value and waste, abled and debilitated, normal and diseased?

This section begins with T. Guirguis's revealing and often hilarious analysis of new "toilet politics" and social sanitation regimes in Egypt. This author investigates sanitation politics and its ability to reproduce gender and class-specific notions of respectability, paternalism, and human waste. The resulting study combines an analysis of international sporting events (where visitors need public toilets) and of the everyday struggles of women commuting to work or circulating throughout the city where such facilities have been removed. Here, the degraded, vanishing restroom represents a casualty of the state's security takeover, the results of which include the closure of mosques (which previously provided free restrooms) and a shutdown of public restrooms over fears of same-sex intimacy and sexual violence.

Extending reterritorialized landscapes, Miguel Fuentes Carreño exposes the relationship between pharmaceutical state capitalism and sexuality politics. He offers a groundbreaking notion of "pill politics" and a concept of "chemical sexualities." Both help explain how abortion pills, antiretroviral HIV drugs, and transgender hormone therapies are deployed and controlled as extractive and policing technologies, intended to control, profit from, and generate public territories for sexually criminalized social groupings and dissident gender/sexuality communities.

Examining the relationship between physical, symbolic, and historic infrastructures, Mohamed Elshahed's chapter reconceptualizes how a storm of urban interventions at every scale has radically transformed Cairo in the decade following 2011. These include such heavy-handed interventions as demolishing large swaths of the city, a city-wide campaign of pathologizing and eliminating trees, the securitization of public spaces, and the rapid construction of anti-pedestrian road networks and bridges bisecting residential districts. This capacity to quickly alter nature and create new development arteries in previously inaccessible sections of the Egyptian landscape has been widely celebrated as a monumental accomplishment. Beyond the optics of sleek roads bisecting rough terrains, however, there is total lack of transparency when it comes to labor conditions, the real economic costs and benefits of such projects, and the greater vision inherently assumed within such plans. To accomplish such projects, the military has secured a near-monopoly on certain technologies of landscape surveying, such as the use of explosives and a massive, conscripted labor force. Control of the republic and its landscapes has thus been linked by infrastructure in ways unprecedented in Egypt.

Many of the city's recent political events as well as its complex social structures have been made illegible through a rearticulation of its past. The result is a hyper-policed urban environment that forecloses the potential for mobilization, memory, and democratic reforms for urban governance. In the final chapter in this section, Rania Ahmed traces the pathologization of soccer/football fans and the military's push to own, socially sanitize, and control soccer stadiums and to technologically monitor and identify fans, who have a long legacy of organizing resistance to police repression and military rule. Ahmed's exceptional case study centers global sports capitalism and its relationship with military-authoritarian social control as well as the new forms of persistent youth resistance that persevere under the regime's extreme securitization.

"Anti-enclave Densityphilia"

How can we theorize inequality of access and investment in the urban framework without resorting to the binary language of working-class slum versus elite enclave?

"Anti-enclave Densityphilia" first focuses on gentrification. Omnia Khalil reimagines the resilience and value of urban density and the struggles against luxury enclaves in urban Cairo. This novel conceptualization helps readers better understand the political economy and social strategies of criminalized housing struggles and anti-brutality mobilizations. Bulaq Abu al-'Ila is a district subjected to major urban transformations due its highly valued land located on the western periphery of the banks of the Nile. Its residents have been dispossessed by business capital and the government, especially since 2017. The shadow state-security network at Bulaq Abu al-'Ila is not restricted to those who take the side of the state against the interests of the people. Many of those involved in these shadow networks have also worked against forced evictions in ways which would appear to make them revolutionaries. At other times, they took part in counterrevolutionary actions. Khalil's elucidation of territorialism helps better explain ostensibly contradictory and ambivalent relationships between residents, the state, and the land.

Gradual growth and the massive development of the "Egyptian Dream" are further explored by Momen El-Husseiny in three phases: the rural second home, the totalizing experience, and the suburban world-city. Privatized housing compounds have expanded during the last few decades, becoming part of a larger urban political ecology in Egypt and the MENA region. In contrast to previous work on Cairo's gated communities, El-Husseiny argues that the neoliberal project of privatized housing falls within global-south urbanisms and worlding practices characterized by informality as a way of life, temporal improvisation, and interferential planning. The rescaling of Cairo's compounds defines a homegrown neoliberalism that treats the suburban desert edge as an experimental free laboratory. This initiates a new social contract that is itself indefinite, undefined, and in constant reconstruction.

Accompanying experimental and peripheral forms of neoliberalism is the emergence of a new kind of super-enclave and the totalistic abjection of urban density and of the city's population itself. By 2022, the government of President al-Sisi permanently relocated Egypt's seat of national authority to a new capital city, currently under construction forty-five kilometers east of Cairo. Roberta Duffield's contribution contextualizes the New Administrative Capital megaproject and its proposal to tackle issues of overcrowding and pollution, theoretically alleviating strain from Cairo through the relocation of certain sectors of its inhabitants and workplaces. The new capital is being promoted as a global city to represent contemporary Egypt: a powerhouse fit for modern government, international business, and the "good life," as written in glass towers, air-conditioned interiors, and smart urbanism. Duffield outlines the New Administrative Capital project as a cipher for the contradictory "populism" of the al-Sisi administration. Claims to improve quality of life through the generative properties of global city status obscure the state's responsibility to locate solutions to poverty and exclusion. This is underpinned by the reasserted primacy of the Egyptian Armed Forces as the nation's premier political and economic author—a force that continues to capitalize on its ownership and development of Egypt's surplus desert land.

What emerges is a form of military capitalism whereby free-market principles of privatization and foreign investment are tempered by closed networks of military and business nepotism. The implications of this network have inspired regional and global alliances. In the last chapter of this section, Maiä Sinno focuses on the decisive influence of investors, designers, contractors, and new residents from the Persian Gulf region—particularly Saudi Arabia, the UAE, and Kuwait. She conceptualizes how this new "Gulf way of life" and its attendant security panics, ecological catastrophes, enclave gated-city elitisms, and consumer leisure concepts have transformed the megacity and further demonized the urban-density model wherein the vast majority of Cairo's populace reside. In twenty-first-century Cairo, the goal is not to copy what is thought of as "religious Saudi Arabia," but rather the prosperous United Arab Emirates. The adaptation of Egyptian traditional values to the Gulf way of life is influenced by Gulf real estate projects as well as Egyptian and international companies that reproduce this model. Cairo compounds like Uptown Cairo and the new capital fashion themselves as the Gulf cities of Egypt. Like their Gulf counterparts, these developments aim to exclude those who cannot afford such a lifestyle or who refuse to abide by it. Exclusion is vertical, seen through golden towers that represent unattainable wealth, but also horizontal—embodied by the rich gated communities that undermine informal areas and erase fears of a new popular uprising.

"Convivial Sociabilities"

How can we encourage city dwellers as well as policymakers to think beyond the binary of urban mobility ("public") versus family domesticity ("private")?

"Convivial Sociabilities" opens with a conceptually generative examination by Aya Nassar of the state's crackdown on kite flying as a pastime during Cairo's 2020 COVID-19 pandemic lockdowns. Cairenes took to flying kites over one of Cairo's bridges in the few hours before curfew time, attaching their cell phones to the kites to take snapshots of the city from above. Within a couple of months, however, kites were banned and seized and their owners were fined. The pretexts for grounding the kites were personal safety as well as national security, marking yet another crackdown on joy. This chapter proposes a framework through which to think about urban (in)security in terms of materiality and infrastructure—specifically, through thinking about air, skylines, bridges, and the other "fantastic things" that populate Cairo's skies.

Discussions on the livelihoods of Cairo's inhabitants often disregard the attempts of noncitizens and recent immigrants to attain a higher quality of urban life. Sabrina Lilleby reveals urban sociabilities and public circulation patterns that provide spaces for resistance and quotidian collective solidarity for domestic workers. These laborers are expected to produce a "private/family" sphere as a natural and noneconomic entity, even as they are inserted into a global care market organized according to racialized and gendered hierarchies of affect and effort. Stereotypes based on nationality, race, and gender make these migrants attractive to employers in Cairo, where women from Asia, in particular, are seen as more docile and desirable. Human rights groups often portray Asian workers employed in the Gulf states and Lebanon as "modern-day slaves," since they work under highly precarious conditions. However, this study shows how migrant domestic workers in Cairo engage in alternative forms of labor mobilization, oftentimes made possible by the specific spatial and nondomestic sociabilities enabled by the makeup of the city.

Turning to the lives of working-class men, Ahmed Awadalla's boldly original chapter explores how class identification queers Cairo's urban spaces and communities. Mapping the sociabilities, dangers, and policed checkpoints arrayed around downtown cafés and bathhouses, Awadalla's contribution compares multiple temporalities of residence and class among members of different queer communities that circulate through the city's downtown area. This chapter sheds light on how forms of conviviality and anonymous encounters in public spaces are configured by and configure classed interactions. The author deploys "cruising" as an analytical lens and model of relational ethics and cross-class sociability. These ethics of contact can forge new solidarities and alliances in the face of fear regimes.

The racialized experiences of some Cairenes not only determine the quality of life of new migrants but may also create the impetus for alternative spaces to thrive. In their chapter, Amira Hetaba and Elena Habersky analyze the rich sociabilities of South Sudanese refugee communities in Cairo as they struggle with racialization, respectability, and the policing of "street" and "family" as urban spatial formations. Because of racial (specifically, anti-Black) and class divisions within the host community—manifesting in targeted harassment and bullying—Sudanese and South Sudanese parents are more likely to send their children to local community-based schools that often organically develop within their own social networks. In this way, parents and caregivers provide a safe space apart from students' homes, and children's exposure to the safety concerns they encounter whenever they enter the public space is minimized. Utilizing ethnographic interviews with Sudanese and South Sudanese refugee and migrant teachers and parents in the working-class neighborhood of Ain Shams, Hetaba and Habersky shed light on two communities adapting to the challenges of protecting children while offering them life in a familiar environment.

Since the beginning of the twentieth century, many Nubians have moved to Cairo from Upper Egypt in hopes of a better life in the aftermath of displacement by the infrastructure megaprojects that have wiped out their ancestral communities. For example, the building of the Aswan High Dam destroyed the main sources of many of these people's livelihoods and submerged their villages under the newly created super-reservoir lakes. In this historical context, Yahia Mohamed Saleh provides an intersectional epistemology for apprehending the interconnected and disjointed spaces of the megacity and the ways a Nubian queer-identified youth finds mobile convivialities and generates alternative erotic sociabilities. Attacks on Saleh's Blackness reveal a perilous form of respectability in the borderlands between the middle and working class, as well as the simultaneously securitized and eroticized public spaces that generate both revolutionary political consciousness and a historical embrace of the racial consciousness within himself. Here, Saleh examines Cairo's Maadi and Hada'iq al-Maadi neighborhoods, which host some of the largest Nubian populations in Cairo along with Abdin (Downtown) and Imbaba.

"Participatory Futurity"

How can we imagine just and inclusive cities beyond notions of informal versus planned, and shanty versus condominium?

In "Participatory Futurity," Nicholas Simcik Arese launches a conversation around how community residents, with grassroots participation, can generate urban futures that challenge the notion of a "dual city," the spatial apartheid that splits urban space into zones of informal urbanism versus more privileged zones of planned development.

This urban binary has served to criminalize and infantilize popular neighborhoods and working-class settlements as it condescendingly grants agency to the "self-generating" areas of the city, which remain highly securitized and are viewed as inherently alien to law, sovereignty, property rights, and norms of civility. Meanwhile, those neighborhoods deemed "properly planned"—often elite, gated condominium or villa developments—are also colonies of another kind of securitization and respectability politics. Arese explores how this binary operates through a case that challenges it, focusing on Haram City, Egypt's first "affordable" gated community, hosting both aspirational middle-class homeowners and resettled poor urban residents. Amid the legal ambiguity of Egypt's 2011–13 revolutionary period, the management team of this public–private partnership was tasked with creating a "fully self-sufficient" city. Arese uses ethnography of management techniques that aim to "upgrade behavior" (that is, to police middle-class norms and property values) to theorize that a private entity, in a strategically indeterminate relationship with the state, reconciles future-oriented planning and storied prejudices by merging two visions of governance. Imitating the repertoire of urban law, managers transform top-down urban planning into bottom-up dispute resolution processes to consolidate "consensus."

Activism organizers have emerged in response to this new city–state localized governance model. Ahmad Borham, a leading housing activist, theorizes on the infrastructural violence, peripheralization, and Haussmannization of Cairo, focusing on the highways, overpasses, ring roads, and grand avenues that have plowed through and around the city. These emerging designs and developments have been used to justify a process of isolating or bulldozing "informal" quarters to grant access and circulation to and between the new, formal, planned enclaves. Borham offers a uniquely comparative perspective, bringing the history of infrastructural violence in Cairo and Managua, Nicaragua into dialogue while tracing how urban activists in Cairo strive to generate a model of participatory futurity by challenging the fetishization and violence of grand highway infrastructures and advocating more humane and mixed models of "non-Haussmannized" urbanism.

Also focusing on infrastructure projects, Deena Mahmoud Sobhy Khalil details the implications of state electricity and water provision in order to challenge the notion that "informal" or "slum" areas are outside the state, external to the central processes of capital accumulation that favor Egypt's elites. Khalil explores how the state-owned utility companies have changed the way in which they deal with nonmetered connections and how the *ashwa'iyat* (informal or slum communities) are implicated in the discourse surrounding these practices. This study concentrates on the discourses employed by the water and electricity companies, particularly directed toward informal areas with nonmetered connections. It describes the sudden spread of numerical and prepaid technologies within the utility infrastructure, suggesting a reimagined form of urban citizenship within the specific context of Egypt and amid global processes of sectorial neoliberal reforms of securitization. While monitoring technologies have been framed by the state as a necessary evil—resorted to by the utility companies to deal with illegal transgressions and "urban informality"—some critical perspectives depict such technologies as mechanisms for increased capital accumulation and modes of extraction from communities.

Mostafa Mohie's chapter explores another urban experiment that aims to challenge the binary of planned versus informal, enclave versus slum, all while reproducing models of classphobia and securitization. Mohie's contribution analyzes the construction and inhabitation of model planned residential blocks in al-Asmarat enclave, built by the state to house residents displaced from their "informal" or slum communities as the result of speculative luxury developments. For various legal and economic reasons, the residents of al-Asmarat have continued to live in precarious conditions that recreate the sense of unsafety and reinforce dependency on the still-standing, supposedly self-built or "informal" neighborhoods. Al-Asmarat serves two ends: ensuring social control over segments of the residents of self-built neighborhoods so that they do not participate in making decisions about their own futures, and redistributing Cairo's population in a way that enables the government to profit from the land of the evicted neighborhoods.

Working-class residents, of course, fight back after being displaced from their "informal" neighborhoods, and then are tricked by unscrupulous entities into signing up for already occupied or uninhabitable units in "planned developments." Yehia Shawkat concludes this section by documenting the exploitation of tenure informality by the government against individuals and communities. He examines how this practice manufactures the gray spectrum of informality that it claims to be eliminating. Shawkat aims to shed light on the lesser-known practices employed by individuals and small private enterprises against other individuals—although still within the government's efforts to implement a consistent urban political economy of "manufactured informality." In this scheme of things, the government gains by exploiting and manufacturing informality in order to commodify housing and then exploits the rent gap. Additionally, Shawkat focuses on how non-state actors in the private sector—from individuals to large corporations— have been profiteering through fraud. Since three-quarters of urban Egyptians are homeowners, this profiteering claims millions of low-income victims across the city and the country.

"Enforcement Sovereignties"

How can we map the operations of social coercion, community protection, gendered safety, vigilantism, working-class direct action/dissent, and racketeering without resorting to the binary that poses "thugs" as the opposite of "police," or "bandits" versus "heroes," particularly in terms of exercising state dominion and popular sovereignty?

"Enforcement Sovereignties" is introduced by Hatem Hassan's extraordinarily generative analysis of "thugs" *(baltagiya)*—urban parasecurity actors that operate as territory creators, space protectors, and vernacular-sovereignty enforcers. Previous ethnographic and anecdotal accounts suggest the *baltagi* was simply a neighborhood criminal, a bastion of masculinity, or an extension of government violence—all of which reified the idea of a unified, easily located thug and his corresponding violence. By contrast, this chapter conceptualizes and details the nuances, contradictions, and persistent instability in the *baltagi*'s moral and political motivations and, consequently, their oscillating proximities to both popular and state interests. The contribution captures oral histories, debates, and government portrayals that have contributed to forming the *baltagi* in the popular imaginary of five Cairo neighborhoods: Talbiya, Misr al-Qadima, Ard al-Liwa', Dokki, and Maadi. Hassan captures the central regulatory power of the *baltagi*: to reaffirm the importance of vernacular/formal territory and habituate extralegal enforcement regardless of its beneficiaries. Practices of circulating *baltagiya* force the fear of instability into confronting varying (moral, political, economic, urban) securitizations. As Hassan puts it in his chapter here (p. 354), "This is effective precisely because the *baltagi* is nonideological, disloyal to political agendas, especially as one's analysis moves beyond one specific event or neighborhood."

On the other end of the enforcement spectrum, Zeinab Abul-Magd focuses on the armed forces of Egypt and how they ensure and profit from limitless claims to sovereignty over land and state resources. Abul-Magd tracks donations from Gulf states—particularly the UAE— which have led to the construction of thousands of military-contracted apartment buildings in desert areas on the outskirts of Cairo. Military bureaucrats hastily moved the inhabitants of the *'ashwa'iyat* into these new structures. Interestingly, Emirati real estate developers have taken control of many of the evacuated lands, asserting sovereignty over these economic and security-oriented urban projects alongside that of the Egyptian military. Displaced inhabitants of the slums are confined in ghetto-like communities that suffer from heavy securitization and a lack of jobs and basic services. Military contractors are building numerous bridges and toll highways across the congested city in order to connect newly developed upscale areas to each other and facilitate the mobility of consumerism. Military ruling elites are gentrifying Cairo in the image of another Dubai.

Synthesizing the overlapping military and bottom-up production of securitization, Aly El Raggal returns to the figure of the *baltagi*, this time as woven into the fabric of police and military enforcement, extraction, and territorialization regimes. El Raggal reveals, in vivid detail, how the police and military deployment of thugs and thuggery have reconstructed the imagination of the city and its policing. Through the securitization of thugs, a newly expansive set of security practices has descended upon most of Cairo's poor and middle-class population. Thuggery has, in this process, both reterritorialized and deterritorialized the city. The former occurs through the occupation of public spaces—a physical presence within different spots and areas of neighborhoods—using spatiality as territory for enforcing sovereignty. The latter provides thug services upon request—physical assaults during parliamentary elections, the destruction of property and moral frameworks, and repression (both physical and sexual) on behalf of the state. These permanent processes of territorialization and deterritorialization have transformed thugs into omnipresent ghosts of the city, located in the slums and popular quarters, who can strike at any moment in any place. The ghost of thug enforcement occupies a huge place in the ways different people imagine and visualize the city and govern their movement within it.

Continuing the discussion of violence and nonviolence in their varied constructions, Mohamed Ahmed reflects upon the role of "slum communities" in the uprisings of 2011 in Egypt, critically challenging notions of nonviolence as a mantra of politics and effective mobilization. This study shifts the analytical focus from middle-class protests in Tahrir Square to working-class mobilizations in the *'ashwa'iyat*. Politicians' statements, TV talk shows, newspaper columns, and popular discourse stirred up a panic around thuggery, described as exploding out of working-class slums and terrorizing the city. Reactionary commentators framed the 2011 revolution as a wave of chaos, looting, and indiscriminate violence ostensibly committed by irrational, criminal subalterns and residents. This contribution focuses on Izbat Abu Qarn, a place which served as a projection screen for this discourse during the early twenty-first century. This case study dismantles the instrumental understanding of urban violence that depoliticizes and reduces it to a mere reaction to economic impoverishment, denying it any political significance or revolutionary potentiality. In this context, one could argue that the riots in the slums were not merely expressions of "depoliticized criminality."

Telling another story of criminalization, Amy Fallas highlights the relationship between securitization, sectarianized sovereignty, and advocacy through Coptic encounters with state intervention, security, and surveillance—with a particular focus on the northern Cairo neighborhood of al-Warraq. Egypt's Coptic Christian community is often examined through a sectarian lens that does not interrogate questions of class, generational differences, and how Coptic youth have been targeted by newly evolving practices of state security and intracommunal security deployed by the Church itself. Fallas examines the aftermath of the high-profile attacks against Copts in 2017. After these attacks, churches in al-Warraq—an island neighborhood in the heart of Cairo, rapidly being gentrified—began recruiting their laity to serve as "scouts" to protect the Christian community from possible security threats. More recently, the sizable Coptic community that resides in the area is under threat of displacement due to a public–private development project seeking to transform the area's "informal settlements" into a new district of residential, commercial, and retail spaces. Resistance to this development, among other issues, contributed to the detention of Coptic activist and founder of the Maspero Youth Union (MYU) Ramy Kamel in 2019. These events underscore how social, economic, and political issues are central to Coptic advocacy priorities alongside religious concerns in the shadow of the state's growing security and enforcement apparatus.

"Abolitionist Desecuritization"

Our volume concludes by posing the following question: *How can we challenge the all-consuming binary of "crime from below" versus "security from above" in an age of "defunding, disarming, and demilitarizing" movements, worldwide?*

"Abolitionist Desecuritization" reimagines notions of community self-security, reconceptualizes street organizations and gangs, and offers practical and epistemological tools for "desecuritizing" or challenging the "security necessity" of the particular logics of policing, checkpoints, and gendered surveillance programs. Bassem Al-Samragy opens this section with a new set of concepts that undermines the "security from above and criminality from below" framework. He analyzes how criminality "from below" is being appropriated, employed, and encouraged by the state *(al-hukuma)* as part and parcel of neoliberal policing techniques. Through the examination of the neighborhood of al-Matariya, this chapter examines the hybrid network used to discipline people in public spaces. In this neighborhood, policing is carried out by both the local police station and the neighborhood's prominent clan networks. An important source of the power wielded by the police in the neighborhood is their relationship of exchange with these social notables, whereby both collaborate in illegal activities and share in the resulting revenues. The police and the clans, together, constitute a power mesh, or grid, which governs the public space and the neighborhood economy. The "security" of al-Matariya is not criminality per se, but the popular use of the neighborhood's public space outside this all-penetrating mesh of power networks.

Revisiting Downtown Cairo's securitization, Laura Monfleur exposes the urban and material *dispositifs* of securitization in Downtown between 2013 and 2020. Until 2016, this securitization took the shape of brutalist physical interruptions—walls, checkpoints, and barbed-wire fences set up to protect Downtown's political institutional structures (e.g., ministries, the People's Assembly, courts, media headquarters, etc.) from the turmoil of street contestations. Since the relocation of most political institutions (including the dreaded Ministry of Interior) from Downtown to the new desert enclaves on the peripheries of Cairo, the militarization of Downtown seems to be less materially visible, brutalist, and permanent. Instead, temporary and mobile checkpoints have become common in particular temporalities, such as the anniversary of the revolution. While artistic appropriations of downtown walls have created temporary safe spaces for revolutionaries during events, other forms of mobile sociability and tactical mobility are staged during times of heightened security with the appearance of checkpoints in Downtown. Mobility becomes a way to ensure the everyday safety of working populations but also the provenance of activists wishing to challenge the material and temporal control of the regime's securitized urbanism.

Securitization, of course, is not simply spatial—as we have seen from the aforementioned contributions—and tends to operate across nationalist and racial lines. Paul Miranda centers Blackness in Cairo, and the mobilization of community and transnationally linked alternatives to policing. Miranda tells the story of South Sudanese and Nubian–Sudanese youth in al-Hayy al-'Ashir, Arba'a wa-Nus, Ain Shams, and Hada'iq al-Maadi. The findings presented here map the forms of racism, anti-Blackness, social exclusion, and structural violence that these youth face in different settings in Cairo. This chapter contextualizes these experiences by analyzing how experiences of war and displacement from their home countries and social exclusion from their own communities further influence their identities and destabilize binaries such as those of migrant/refugee. A particular form of gang masculinity has developed in Sudanese and South Sudanese communities in Cairo, bringing to the fore patterns of gendered racialization from within and outside of the community. This study highlights how these forms of masculinity are reproduced through the everyday social practices of men and women, the social environment they inhabit in Egypt, and the history of conflict in the Nuba Mountains and South Sudan. Despite the tragic effects of gang violence in these neighborhoods, Sudanese and South Sudanese engage in considerable grassroots organizing to prevent violence and develop alternatives to policing, criminalization, and anti-Black biases.

At the conclusion of this volume, Hanan Hammad invites us to travel historically back into the British colonial era of the early twentieth century. In order to remind the reader of the colonial and Victorian-era legacies that continue to profoundly shape how class, gender, sexuality, race, and urban sociability are policed, Hammad considers how challenging securitization in the megacities of the world requires contextualizing contemporary nationalisms, authoritarian discourse, or moral-sectarian campaigns. Such an analysis centers colonial investments in the founding of police forces and methods of extracting wealth and power from poor people's land, work, and cultures. This contribution focuses on policing downtown Cairo against the backdrop of hosting both the country's largest brothel industry and the political turmoil of the first half of the twentieth century. Between politically motivated violence and oppressive imperial forces, "policing downtown Cairo proved a challenging task that authorities pursued on the backs of working women's bodies," Hammad argues. The government closed the Cairo brothels in 1949 and criminalized sex work altogether two years later. The criminalization of women's bodies continues to this day, demonstrating that this type of oppression is actually a means of preserving the security regime itself.

Together, these analyses weave together a set of alternatives—analytical, political, and tactical—to enable "desecuritized" world-making in a place where security logics are spiraling. This book offers seven themes, coining new concepts and featuring innovative approaches. These studies locate and identify the processes and apparatuses that generate fear and social injustice in the urban context, while offering inspiring models for change in part by clearing the space of stagnant conversations overly focused on outdated binaries (state vs. non-state, security vs. insecurity, formality vs. informality, law vs. outlaw, etc.). Its contributors' intimate knowledge and lived experiences in Cairo offer empirical rigor, reaching far beyond case studies to launch worlds of new perspectives and possibilities.

Notes

1   Decrim is an abbreviated term for the decriminalization of sex work, various drugs used recreationally or medicinally, and houselessness—and was inspired by organizers against inequitable criminalization of queer, poor, and people of color (Micallef 2021).

Works Cited

Abdelhameed, Dalia. 2015. "Ultras Ahlawy and the Spectacle: Subjects, Resistance and Organized Football Fandom in Egypt." Master's thesis, American University in Cairo. https://fount.aucegypt.edu/cgi/viewcontent.cgi?article=1139&context=etds.

Abul-Magd, Zeinab. 2017. *Militarizing the Nation: The Army, Business, and Revolution in Egypt*. New York: Columbia University Press.

Alexander, M. Jacqui. 1994. "Not Just (Any) Body Can Be a Citizen: The Politics of Law, Sexuality and Postcoloniality in Trinidad and Tobago and the Bahamas." *Feminist Review* 48: 5–23.

Ali, Zahra. 2018. *Women and Gender in Iraq: Between Nation-building and Fragmentation*. New York: Cambridge University Press.

Alraouf, Ali A. 2018. *Knowledge-based Urban Development in the Middle East*. Hershey, PA: IGI Global.

Amar, Paul. 2011. "Turning the Gendered Politics of the Security State Inside Out? Charging the Police with Sexual Harassment in Egypt." *International Feminist Journal of Politics* 13, no. 3: 299–328.

———. 2013. *The Security Archipelago: Human-security States, Sexuality Politics, and the End of Neoliberalism*. Durham, NC: Duke University Press.

Al-Attar, Iman. 2018. *Baghdad: An Urban History through the Lens of Literature*. New York: Routledge.

Bogaert, Koenraad. 2018. *Globalized Authoritarianism: Megaprojects, Slums, and Class in Morocco*. Minneapolis: University of Minnesota Press.

Bou Akar, Hiba. 2018. *For the War Yet to Come: Planning Beirut's Frontiers*. Stanford, CA: Stanford University Press.

Buzan, Barry, Ole Wæver, and Jaap de Wilde. 1998. *Security: A New Framework for Analysis*. Boulder, CO: Lynne Rienner Publishers.

Césaire, Aimé. 2001. *Discourse on Colonialism*. New York: Monthly Review Press.

Chattopadhyay, Swati. 2012. *Unlearning the City: Infrastructure in a New Optical Field*. Minneapolis: University of Minnesota Press.

Elshahed, Mohamed. 2020. *Cairo since 1900: An Architectural Guide*. Cairo: American University in Cairo Press.

Elsheshtawy, Yasser. 2009. *Dubai: Behind an Urban Spectacle*. New York: Routledge.

———. 2011. *The Evolving Arab City: Tradition, Modernity and Urban Development*. New York: Routledge.

———. 2019. *Temporary Cities: Resisting Transience in Arabia*. New York: Routledge.

Ezzeldin, Mohammed Saaid. 2014. *The History and Memory of Banditry in Modern Egypt: The Controversy of Adham Al-Sharqawi*. Washington, DC: Georgetown University.

Fawaz, Mona. 2006. *Urban Heritage and Politics of the Present: Perspectives from the Middle East*. Beirut: AUB Press.

———. 2009. "Contracts and Retaliation: Securing Housing Exchanges in the Interstice of the Formal/Informal Beirut (Lebanon) Housing Market." *Journal of Planning Education and Research* 29, no. 1: 90–107.

Fawaz, Mona, Ahmad Garbieh, and Mona Harb. 2018. *Refugees as City-Makers*. Beirut: Social Justice and the City Program, American University of Beirut.

Freitag, Ulrike, Nelida Fuccaro, Claudia Ghrawi, and Nora Lafi. 2015. *Urban Violence in the Middle East: Changing Cityscapes in the Transition from Empire to Nation State*. New York: Berghahn Books.

Fuccaro, Nelida. 2016. *Violence and the City in the Modern Middle East*. Stanford, CA: Stanford University Press.

Gharipour, Mohammad. 2016. *Contemporary Urban Landscapes of the Middle East*. New York: Routledge.

Hall, Stuart, Chas Critcher, Tony Jefferson, John Clarke, and Brian Roberts. 1978. *Policing the Crisis: Mugging, the State and Law and Order*. London: Macmillan.

El-Hamalawy, Hossam. 2011. "Egypt's Revolution Has Been 10 Years in the Making." *The Guardian*, March 2, 2011. https://www.theguardian.com/commentisfree/2011/mar/02/egypt-revolution-mubarak-wall-of-fear.

Hassan, Hatem M. 2015. "Extraordinary Politics of Ordinary People: Explaining the Microdynamics of Popular Committees in Revolutionary Cairo." *International Sociology* 30, no. 4: 383–400.

———. 2019. "Thugs in Revolution: Transforming the Criminal Body amidst Political Transition in Egypt, 2011–2016." PhD diss., University of Pittsburgh.

Hayek, Ghenwa. 2014. *Beirut: Imagining the City Space and Place in Lebanese Literature*. New York: Blackwells.

Howell, Alison, and Melanie Richter-Montpetit. 2020. "Is Securitization Theory Racist? Civilizationism, Methodological Whiteness, and Antiblack Thought in the Copenhagen School." *Security Dialogue* 51, no. 1: 3–22.

Ismail, Salwa. 2006. *Political Life in Cairo's New Quarters: Encountering the Everyday State*. Minneapolis: University of Minnesota Press.

Kanna, Ahmed. 2011. *Dubai: The City as Corporation*. Minneapolis: University of Minnesota Press.

Khalil, Omnia. 2019. "The State as an Urban Broker: Subjectivity Formation, Securitization, and Place-making in Post-revolutionary Cairo." *Urban Anthropology and Studies of Cultural Systems and World Economic Development* 48, no. 1/2: 85–128.

Kilinç, Kivanc, and Mohammad Gharipour. 2019. *Social Housing in the Middle East: Architecture, Urban Development, and Transnational Modernity*. Bloomington: Indiana University Press.

Low, Setha. 2016. *Spatializing Culture: The Ethnography of Space and Place*. New York: Routledge.

Marshall, Shana. 2015. "The Egyptian Armed Forces and the Remaking of an Economic Empire." Carnegie Middle East Center, April. Washington, DC: Carnegie Endowment for International Peace.

Mbembe, Achille. 2003. "Necropolitics." *Public Culture* 15, no. 1: 11–40.

El-Meehy, Asya. 2012. "Egypt's Popular Committees.'" *Middle East Report* 42: 265.

Micallef, Max. 2021. "You Need to Know about Decrim." *An Injustice! Magazine*. https://aninjusticemag.com/you-need-to-know-about-decrim-545020245102, viewed July 15, 2021.

Molotch, Harvey, and Davide Ponzini. 2019. *The New Arab Urban: Gulf Cities of Wealth, Ambition, and Distress*. New York: New York University Press.

Monroe, Kristin V. 2016. *The Insecure City: Space, Power, and Mobility in Beirut*. New Brunswick, NJ: Rutgers University Press.

Montgomery, Charles. 2013. *Happy City: Transforming Our Lives through Urban Design*. New York: Farrar, Straus, and Giroux.

Naeff, Judith. 2018. *Precarious Imaginaries of Beirut: A City's Suspended Now*. New York: Springer.

Nucho, Joanne Randa. 2016. *Everyday Sectarianism in Urban Lebanon: Infrastructures, Public Services and Power*. Princeton, NJ: Princeton University Press.

Rabaka, Reiland. 2016. *The Negritude Movement: W.E.B. Du Bois, Léon Damas, Aimé Césaire, Léopold Senghor, Frantz Fanon, and the Evolution of an Insurgent Idea*. Boulder, CO: Lexington Books.

Rieker, Martina, and Kamran Ali. 2008. *Gendering Urban Space in the Middle East, South Asia, and Africa*. New York: Palgrave.

El Said, Maha, Lena Meari, and Nicola Pratt. 2015. *Rethinking Gender in Revolutions and Resistance: Lessons from the Arab World*. London: Zed Books.

Samara, Tony Roshan, Shenjing He, and Guo Chen. 2013. *Locating Right to the City in the Global South*. New York: Routledge.

Savci, Evren. 2021. *Queer in Translation: Sexual Politics under Neoliberal Islam*. Durham, NC: Duke University Press.

Sayigh, Yazid. 2011. *We Serve the People: Hamas Policing in Gaza*. Washington, DC: Brandeis University, Crown Center for Middle East Studies.

Seigel, Micol. 2018. *Violence Work: State Power and the Limits of Police*. Durham, NC: Duke University Press.

Sharp, Deen. 2018. "The Urbanization of Power and the Struggle for the City." *Middle East Report* 287: 2–5.

———. 2020. "Testimonials: Deen Sharp." Arab Urbanism, n.d. https://www.araburbanism.com/testimonials.

Sharp, Deen, and Claire Panette. 2016. *Beyond the Square: Urbanism and the Arab Uprisings*. New York: Urban Research.

Sim, David. 2019. *Soft City: Building Density for Everyday Life*. Washington, DC: Island Press.

Simone, AdbouMaliq. 2004. "People as Infrastructure: Intersecting Fragments in Johannesburg." *Public Culture* 16, no. 3: 407–29.

——. 2018. *Improvised Lives: Rhythms of Endurance in an Urban South.* Cambridge, UK: Polity.

Sims, David. 2012. *Understanding Cairo: The Logic of a City Out of Control.* Cairo: American University in Cairo Press.

Singerman, Diane, and Paul Amar. 2006. *Cairo Cosmopolitan: Politics, Culture, and Urban Space in the New Globalized Middle East.* Cairo: American University in Cairo Press.

Sluglett, Peter. 1998. *The Urban Social History of the Middle East, 1750–1950.* Syracuse, NY: Syracuse University Press.

Wæver, Ole. 1995. "Securitization and Desecuritization." In *On Security*, edited by Ronnie D. Lipschutz, 46–86. New York: Columbia University Press.

Wiedmann, Florian, and Ashraf M. Salama. 2013. *Demystifying Doha: On Architecture and Urbanism in an Emerging City.* New York: Routledge.

——. 2019. *Building Migrant Cities in the Gulf.* New York: I.B. Tauris.

Wynn, L.L. 2018. *Love, Sex, and Desire in Modern Egypt: Navigating the Margins of Respectability.* Austin: University of Texas Press.

Yarwood, John. 2011. *Urban Planning in the Middle East.* Newcastle upon Tyne, UK: Cambridge University Press.

1

THE CRIME OF SHAMELESSNESS
TIKTOK WOMEN, THE PRINCIPLE OF BODILY INTEGRITY, AND INDEPENDENCE WITHOUT REGRETS

SARA SOUMAYA ABED

Between April and July of 2020, the Egyptian state cracked down on a group of women, including belly-dancer Sama El Masri and nine women who had gained fame on TikTok.[1] They were all charged with inciting immorality. The crackdown coincided with a larger wave of repression against women and queer Egyptians. It also occurred in the context of a resurgence of feminist organizing against sexual violence across the country in 2020 in the wake of new revelations and renewed debates—particularly in online Egyptian feminist blogs and social media postings—that brought public attention to an alleged gang rape at the Fairmont Hotel in Cairo involving high-profile attackers in 2014 (*Mada Masr* 2021d), that reinvigorated a commemoration of "Black Wednesday" public sexual assaults in Egypt in 2005 (Nazra for Feminist Studies 2020), and that successfully mobilized citizens to ensure passage in August 2020 of new laws protecting the identities of victims and those who report sexual assault or harassment to authorities (Arab Weekly 2020). However, these successful feminist efforts for accountability and visibility were overshadowed by draconian intimidation campaigns and arbitrary arrests that brought tragedy—for example, precipitating the death by suicide of communist, queer, feminist activist Sarah Hegazy and the state kidnapping and detention of activist Sanaa Seif. Here I focus on the state attacks on female influencers, often simply labeled "TikTok women," who came largely from rural working-class and lower-middle-class origins, moving to Cairo as single ambitious women, where they attained a degree of fame online. I compare how these women were perceived in contrast with more privileged female social media influencers. I also examine how women influencers have energized and shaped the concerns, discourses, and strategies of the previously existing feminist movement in Egypt. As Elmeshad reports in their chapter in this volume, Egyptian media is heavily moderated by state influence, following directives to "protect public morality." And Rigot and Noralla, in this volume, also demonstrate how, in recent years, this censorious impulse has been extended to social media as well and integrated with morality policing operations.

Rana[2] is an upper-middle-class former sex worker in her thirties, based in Cairo. In a conversation we had, she recalled that "when I was still at university, I always wanted to become an actress. When my professor in English literature once said that most of us were going to become teachers, I immediately told her I would rather be a prostitute. She laughed, but it was true."[3] Rana utilized the word in English, rather than Arabic, well aware that the term is more provocative than other options, like "sex worker." I first met Rana in 2014, and then again in 2016. We got together at her apartment in central Cairo, where we discussed ways to navigate non-normative and marginalized sexual practices and how these are informed by economics and morality. Diving into her early experiences with online sexuality and desire, Rana told me:

I would always go online and look up fetish stuff. This was my entrance into the virtual world. It was a space where I could indulge my fantasies safely. But it's just virtual. You start to crave something that's actually physical. I started to think of using this [virtual] space to provide escorting services. For me, the virtual world is a safe space. No one will know what's happening. I can learn about people before meeting any of them through chatting, and we can agree on the terms and conditions beforehand. It was a space where I lingered like a sniper; a lone-wolf. This is why it's my favorite space.[4]

Although Rana still had to hide her identity via a mask, a few years later—under the 2018 cybercrime law—her relatively safe space was weaponized against all women. It is my belief that the state has made our bodies a battlefield to silence us.

In the chapter below, I take an intersectional approach to my analysis, weaving class, gender, sexuality, and age into an investigation of the politics of moral panic. I attempt to address state rhetoric, official legal institutions, and pro-state media outlets in order to queer our perceptions of power—that is, to highlight and challenge exclusionary normativity and hypocritical moralism. I argue that the politics of respectability operate through gender, sexuality, morality, and social class discourses that are monopolized by the Egyptian state. An intersectional approach offers a more nuanced understanding of sexual oppression in Egypt, allowing one to move beyond the simplistic classist assumptions about public mobility and the visibility of class-differentiated women's bodies that currently permeate Egyptian security culture and media debates.

I utilize the concept of "erotic labor," and define it as a type of performative labor that is centered on one's sexuality and/or gender. In my attempt to locate and frame the TikTok women's struggles within debates around political economies of erotic and sex work, my aim here is not to ask whether these women who were criminalized for posting sexy TikTok videos perceived their working identities as being sexual. Rather, I focus on these women's efforts to oppose the state's moralizing attitudes and surveillance. Audre Lorde reminds us to recognize the erotic as a creative source of power through which we reclaim "our language, our history, our dancing, our loving, our work, our lives" (Lorde 1984, 55). The "erotic" continues to be used against women, and so I join Lorde and many others (e.g., Sayegh 2015) in their quest to disrupt respectability politics and the moral panics that have reoccupied the erotic sphere. I intend to uncover the motives behind state panic toward the "TikTok women" and to allow their stories to shape queer feminist histories. The intention, as Dima Kaedbey puts it, is "to root these terms in local histories of difference" (Kaedbey 2016, 63).

#If_The_Egyptian_Family_Permits

The systematic crackdown of 2020 started when a male lawyer and a group of YouTubers filed cases against working-class and middle-class women who had become prominent on TikTok, attracting millions of followers on social media. After being trolled by male YouTubers (e.g., Naser Hekaia), the state arrested and publicly humiliated Haneen Hossam, Mawada al-Adham, Menna Abdelaziz, Sherry Hanem and her daughter Zomorroda, Manar Samy, Renad Emad, Hadeer Alhady, and Bassant during the spring and summer of 2020.[5] Most of these women were charged under Article 25 of the 2018 cybercrime law for "violating Egyptian family values" (*Bawabaa News* 2020; Al Haq 2021; see Rigot and Noralla, this volume, for a more in-depth discussion of the scope and content of Article 25).

The ambiguity of Article 25 enables limitless surveillance. The article violates both basic freedoms of expression and the Egyptian constitution, which stipulates the drafting of precise laws (Masaar 2020). The constitution also requires articles to comply with international human rights conventions[6] such as CEDAW and ICCPR, of which Egypt is a signatory. Like many on social media, I asked several questions while examining such articles. What are the state's proposed family values? Who gets to decide what these values are? Which model of the family do we follow? What is the geographic and cultural scope and scale of these values? How do these articles affect certain bodies more than others, depending on class and other factors?

In early July 2020, multiple women and men flooded Instagram with assault and rape stories specifying a common perpetrator, identified as ABZ (Walsh 2020). This sparked a widespread movement against sexual violence, opening up essential discussions on bodily rights that extended beyond women's and human rights organizations (El-Rifae 2020; Al Haq 2021). Sexual violence became a spark that reignited the feminist movement, whose existence represents one of the few gains of Egypt's January 25, 2011 revolution (see Saad and Abed 2020).

The earliest documentation of the feminist movement in Egypt dates back to the nineteenth century,[7] which, although it overlapped with the national liberation struggle, was aligned with a larger international feminist perspective. Put differently, women's movement organizers built national, regional, and international solidarity networks and alliances to pursue social change. An Egyptian delegation went to Rome in 1923 to participate in the Women's Congress.

Since the twentieth century, the feminist movement (in Egypt and more generally) has both directly and indirectly tackled sexuality and bodily autonomy, among other issues. Leading up to the first decade of the twentieth-first century, the number of feminist and human rights NGOs increased. These tended to focus on issues around sexuality rights, sexual violence against women, and personal and human rights of LGBTQI+ citizens. Their efforts can be seen as a continuation of the issues discussed during the 1994 United Nations International Conference on Population and Development (ICPD). This conference, hosted in Cairo, represented a breakthrough, propelling women's rights onto the "national agenda" and promoting gender issues within Egyptian civil society. Sexual rights were integral to the ICPD Program of Action agenda, as were women's bodily rights (Kamal 2016).

Two critical events further highlighted the importance of amending the laws and the urgent need to move questions of sexual violence to the forefront of the feminist movement's agenda. The first was Black Wednesday in 2005.[8] A second event arose in 2008, when filmmaker Noha Elostaz became the first woman to take her harasser to court and win her case. Groups such as Operation Anti-Sexual Harassment (OpAntiSH) were formed against the rising tide of sexual violence in Cairo's Tahrir Square (see Westmoreland, this volume, for more information regarding this uprising). OpAntiSH promoted emancipatory language and a model that challenged demeaning attitudes toward sexual violence.[9] In 2014, around two years after OpAntiSH's founding, an anti-sexual harassment law was passed (Saad and Abed 2020; El-Rifae 2020; Zaki 2021). By the end of the decade, discourse had moved beyond victim blaming (Kirollos 2016; Saad and Abed 2020; HarassMap 2014). Women in cyberspace not only exposed their assaulters but also made videos that highlighted issues of consent/coercion, slut-shaming/accountability, and various sex education topics.[10] In particular, women focused on issues of bodily integrity, connecting past sexual violence to ongoing crackdowns against women in the virtual world. This conversation around bodily integrity revealed how authoritarian heteropatriarchal systems obsessively police sexuality and bodies, particularly through classphobic discourse (presuming inherent immorality or criminality among working-class communities) ideologically masked as an effort to protect "families." This is not a new phenomenon.

On July 13, 2020, an anonymous group of feminist women created a petition with the satirical hashtag[11] "#if_the_Egyptian_family_permits" (#ba'ad_izn_el-osra_el-masriya) in an attempt to emphasize the interconnectedness of the general movement against sexual violence and the specific crackdown on TikTok Women arrested for "degrading family values" under the new Article 25 (TikTok Women 2020). Haneen, Mawada, and Manar received harsh sentences in July 2020,[12] just as a public outcry burst into the social-media spotlight around an alleged gang rape that had taken place years earlier at the Fairmont Hotel (Egyfeminist 2020). The state's arresting of feminist activists and the police harassment of working-class women influencers seemed to be echoing or redoubling the violence against women's bodily integrity in ways that resonated with the alleged assaults and rapes. This mix of issues fueled anger on social media platforms and began a campaign to humanize the women criminalized for their TikTok postings (see fig. 1.1). In solidarity, Egyptian women and their allies in Berlin came together in a mass demonstration on August 14, 2020. Another of their banners (not pictured here) featured an image of

Figure 1.1. Solidarity demonstration in Berlin.

Mawada and powerfully mocked the absurdity of the cybercrime law, pro-claiming "The Crime: a shameless woman; independent with no regrets."[13] Some also shared dancing videos with the hashtag #alraqs_msh_gareema (#dance_isn't_a_crime).[14] Mawada al-Adham was sentenced in June 2021 to six years in prison for "human trafficking" because her TikTok videos were supposedly "exploiting girls through video-sharing apps for money."[15] Despite the demonstrations and online mobilizations of support for the arrested TikTok influencers, on August 17, 2020 the Egyptian National Council for Women (NCW) launched a moral critique that aimed to expose and shame the convicted women. In a campaign called "Do you know that . . . ?"[16] they posted information defending the importance of "Family Values Law" Article 25 on their Instagram and Facebook pages while publicly condemning the TikTok women.

Intersectionality and TikTok Women

Intersectionality theory uncovers multiple forms of oppression and reveals how multidimensional experiences are constructed and maintained, disclosing the "structural, disciplinary, hegemonic, and inter-personal dimensions of power" (Carastathis 2014, 307). For example, to be both Black and a woman offers an intersectional experience distinct from both women who are not Black and Black men. As the black femi-nist Deborah King puts it, intersectionality springs from "the necessity of addressing all oppression" (as cited in Carastathis 2014, 308). In pursuing the intersectional approach, social scientists and organizers have found the simultaneity, complexity, irreducibility, and inclusivity central to the lives of those they wrote about. The importance of intersectionality—as explained by Kimberlé Crenshaw (1989) and Angela Harris and Zeus Leonardo (2018), among others—stems from its ability to make social locations and lived experiences noticeable rather than remaining obstructed and sealed within "essentialist and exclusionary constructions."

Within an intersectional view, class is a significant vector of power that intersects with race, gender, and sexuality, and is critically important in the analysis of moral securitization in Egypt.[17] Essentialist theorization fails to apprehend the complexity and fluidity of social structures and the complexity of subjective lived experiences. It reduces simultaneous oppressions and treats categories of identification as additive classifications rather than being co-constitutive. When reading intersectionally, it is nearly impossible to separate "who people are" from "the way things work" (Nash 2019, 75). The dichotomy between social structures and subjective experiences often disregards the fact that "experiences of embodiment, projects of self-making and self-performing, sensations of pleasure, pain, injury, desire, and so on" are constantly reshaped and "constituted by social locations, experiences of power and disempowerment" (Nash 2019, 75). The Egyptian regime targeted the TikTok women because these unmarried, publicly visible working-class women presented themselves as fully comfortable with their bodies and sexuality, accentuating their femininity beyond the accepted norms of "traditional family values." Although their social media content (video clips) is performed in a style almost identical to unsanctioned videos posted by many other upper-middle-class influencers in Egypt, the videos of these working-class women, who had migrated from smaller cities or villages into Cairo on their own, were demonized and strongly securitized by a wave of legal and moral panic.[18] The interplay of gender, class, and sexuality positions triggered multiple vectors of simultaneous oppression.[19]

To humanize and validate their actions, we must see these nine TikTok women through their "internal differences as much as by commonalities" (Carastathis 2014, 311–12). Their social locations and their sexual oppression are related to other cases of sexualized violence against women and queer bodies in Egypt. In the Fairmont Hotel rape incident, for instance, the victim/survivor belonged to Egypt's upper middle class, but her socioeconomic position did not protect her from sexual oppression (Michaelson 2020). In comparing the TikTok women and the Fairmont incident, one can grasp how sex- and gender-based violence has "ensnared us all, even as we are ensnared in different and socially contingent ways" (Nash 2019, 75). Unlike an essentialist and determinist perspective, an intersectional view of these cases allows us to see how the sex/gender axis of exclusions and privileges persists even as it is modulated by class and other factors.

Morality and respectability are influenced by a perpetrator's social-class location and associated power, which are also related to state interests. In discussing the highly sexualized policing tactics of the ironically named "human-security state," Amar (2011, 309) points out that

In the 2000s, Egyptian feminists generated plans to publicly deploy gender and class-specific protests in order to resist the performative cultivation of terroristic hypermasculinity by the Egyptian security state . . . . The state responded by shifting its aims from using demonized masculinity in order to delegitimize political opposition to using state-imposed sexual aggression in order to undermine class respectability. Women who protested were sexualized and had their respectability wiped out: not just by innuendo and accusation, but literally, by sexually assaulting them in public and by arresting them as prostitutes, registering them in court records and press accounts as sex criminals and then raping and sexually torturing them in jail.

In this way, the Egyptian state polices the bodies they deem dangerous, rendering them hypervisible and portraying them as sexualized security risks. Inspired by this analysis of securitized bodies, the following section aims to look at how varying social statuses and intersecting identities are inconsistently affected by the politics of moral panic and the policing of bodies.

A Classic Moral Panic?

Gayle Rubin (1987, 171) defines sexual panic as a variant of moral panic: moments where "diffuse attitudes are channeled into political action and from there into social change" and "fears attach to some unfortunate sexual activity or population. The media become ablaze with indignation, the public behaves like a rabid mob, the police are activated, and the state enacts new laws and regulations" (1987, 171). In the example we analyze here, a broader moral panic was constructed through discourses that targeted "sexual deviants" in Egypt. The crackdown on the TikTok women was part of a tsunami of moral panics launched by the state in league with state-controlled media and religious elites. State-sponsored media exacerbated anxiety by deploying a language of resentment and morality, while the police systematically arrested and punished individuals and groups in accordance with the new 2018 Cybercrime Law. Carreño's and Guirguis's chapters in this volume demonstrate the enormous degree of societal penetration this sexual panic has had, affecting even questions of basic health and hygiene infrastructure in Cairo. With every wave of moral panic, the state has expanded its governance of erotic labor and behavior. As Rubin (1987, 171) shows us, criminalization discourses claim that erotic labor is a threat to "health and safety, women and children, national security, the family, or civilization itself." In Egypt, these sorts of discourse were clearly on display as the TikTok influencers were accused of endangering the "Egyptian family."

Other state entities deployed somewhat contradictory responses to the TikTok controversy. For a moment, it seemed that Parliament listened to social media feminist activists. On August 16, 2020, the People's Assembly in Egypt approved Article 113(bis) to the Code of Criminal Procedure, which protects the anonymity of victims/survivors of sexual violence and rape in response to social media activists' appeals (Sadek 2020). The state-sanctioned National Council for Women represented themselves as allies in this struggle, encouraging women to report rapes and sexual assaults. The NCW stopped short of protecting witnesses in the Fairmont incident, however. Nevertheless, media personalities such as Amr Adib delivered dramatic public statements defending women who report rapes and sexual violence, leading to conversations about sexual consent during his TV show *Al Hekaya* under the theme of "No means No" (Mokhtar 2020; Lotfi 2020).

However, once again, the working-class TikTok women influencers were not regarded or treated in the same way as the Fairmont incident victim. Menna Abdelaziz, for example, was recast from a victim into a criminal during her quest for justice. In May 2020, she was arrested after posting a video calling for justice after she had been raped. She had been filmed during the attack and then blackmailed with the footage. Although her assaulters were sent to trial, she was charged with inciting debauchery and sent to a rehabilitation center; she was released in September 2020 (El-Rifae 2020; Al-Amar 2020; Al Haq 2021). Likewise, the TikTok cases discussed above tend to be reported as cases of prostitution by the conventional media (Eskandar 2020). The media has weaponized the leaked private pictures of Mawada and Manar (fig. 1.1; Amnesty International 2020). They have slut-shamed them and also violated their personal and private rights, depicting them as working outside the boundaries of social norms and morality, and thus deserving punishment.[20]

Under Egyptian law, rape is not defined in a gender-neutral way, but is limited to nonconsensual vaginal rape between a man and a woman. Nonconsensual anal, oral, and object-based sexual coercion—as well as marital rape—are not included (Saad and Abed 2020). Existing legislation does not cite rape specifically, but instead forbids anyone from "perform[ing] a sexual act without a woman's consent" (Egyptian Public Prosecution 2020). The Egyptian penal code includes historically vague notions of "inciting debauchery" and "sex offenses" that can be deployed against individuals in a wide variety of cases of sexual assault and unlawful but also consensual erotic behavior such as same-sex intimacy, consensual sex work, or simply being publicly queer and/or trans to some degree (Dupret et al. 2021). More specifically, Article 9 of Law 10/1961 of Egypt's Court of Cassation[21] state criminalizes

(a) any person who hires or offers in any possible way a place that serves debauchery or prostitution . . . ; (b) any person who owns or manages a furnished flat or room or other place open to the public that facilitates the practice of debauchery or prostitution . . . ; (c) any person who usually practices debauchery or prostitution is condemned to imprisonment for a period of no less than three months and no more than three years, and to a fine of no less than five pounds and no more than ten pounds, or to one of these two penalties. When the person is arrested in this last situation, he or she may be subjected to a medical examination and, if it appears that he or she suffers from an ordinary venereal disease, to confine him or her in a medical institution until he or she has recovered (Arab Republic of Egypt 1961, Article 9).

In the Queen Boat case (Amar 2013, 71–77), a May 2001 police raid on a riverboat nightclub in Cairo led to the arrest of fifty-two men who were portrayed in the media as gay and by the law as "debaucherous." During the ensuing trial, the judge specified debauchery as follows:

The crime designated in [this text] is only committed when a man or a woman fornicates [mubasharat al-fahsha'] with people without distinction, habitually. When a woman fornicates and sells her virtue to whomever asks for it without distinction, she commits prostitution [da'ara] . . . ; fujur occurs when a man sells his virtue to other men without distinction (11).[22]

Queer people are targeted and scapegoated using these codes, and police wield enormous discretionary power and control over the process. Likewise, the state was able to effectively target the TikTok women since their case was specifically not framed as being about freedom of expression or sexuality rights. The state's focus on employing vaguely defined morality laws portrayed these women as aggressors who attacked Egyptian family values—the very apparatus of respectability that legitimizes the structure of grossly inequitable forms of class and gender-based hierarchies in Egypt (Michaelson 2020).

Nicola Smith (2016) asserts that commercial sex work is often misrepresented through moral binary language: victimhood versus agency and violence versus pleasure. These binaries erase issues of political economy, class position, and economic or labor issues. Social media is an important labor sector as well as a space for upward economic mobility for underprivileged content producers. Social media applications are increasingly utilized for earning a living and, in other cases, for organizing activists and linking members of social movements. As an economy and set of public spaces, the virtual world is consequently becoming as real as the streets, especially in a country where street protests are outlawed (TIMEP 2017). In the context of the authoritarianism implemented in Egypt since 2013 and the 2020 COVID-19 pandemic lockdown—both of which led people to become increasingly reliant on virtual spaces— the TikTok women challenged the traditional dichotomy between the physical and virtual worlds. They defined new urban realities, work opportunities, and routes for social/physical/virtual mobility to and from major cities.

Bassant, for example, blurred the lines between her virtual and street-based network (based in Alexandria and Cairo). Likewise, via her TikTok content/videos Mawada was able to operate both in Cairo and in her neighborhood in Matruh. Nevertheless, as much as this new intertwined space advanced these women's economic livelihoods, it simultaneously increased the surveillance and incrimination of their bodies. After all, the Egyptian penal code (the Prostitution Law of 1961) still prohibits sexual commerce (Abed 2016), the broad and limitless definition of which can be stretched to cover any kind of "sexy" renumerated social media—a huge part of social media!

Outlawing bodies in virtual space and deeming them immoral constitutes a larger effort to maintain a system of surveillance. State anxiety over the moral–political economy and the deployment of a moral security regime incentivizes repression against the TikTok women's sexuality. These women's ability to establish "celebrity, influence, and financial" independence offered them some autonomy from the state (Eskandar 2020). When Haneen posted on Instagram, for instance, she suggested it was "a way out" in order to earn a living.

She did this by calling other women to join her on the photo- and video-based platform, like during a time where "the gig economy" was hit hard by the COVID-19 pandemic. She was accused subsequently of human trafficking for that call. Although Haneen was originally acquitted and Mawada's prison sentence was rescinded, in January 2021 she was condemned to pay a fine of LE 300,000 (approximately $18,780 at the time) (Abuelsoud 2020; Al Haq 2021; Mada Masr 2021a). Haneen, like Mawada, was sentenced in absentia in June 2021 to ten years in prison for "human trafficking." She was retried after posting a video on Instagram stating she had not wronged anyone, and requesting a pardon from President al-Sisi. She then was sentenced to three years in prison by the same court, in addition to a fine of LE 200,000 (approximately $10,800 at the time) (BBC 2022).

State-sponsored moral–security frameworks still require sexual behavior in Egypt to be "heterosexual, between married individuals, monogamous, reproductive, and non-commercial" (Rubin 1987, 171). This goal is encouraged by campaigns policing respectability and morality, reinforcing the subordination of the second-class citizenship of working-class Egyptians and mostly preserving male domination over women and queer bodies. Women's liberation movements are often aligned and interlinked with anti-racist, queer, and feminist movements (El-Rifae 2020) precisely because sexual behavior is analyzed in narrow moral terms rather than on the "presence or absence of coercion" (Rubin 1987, 171). Sex-related laws severely limit free expression, whether it includes forms of erotic labor or queer ways of life.

[W]ars over [sexuality] are often fought at oblique angles, aimed at phony targets, conducted with misplaced passions, and are highly, intensely symbolic. Sexual activities often function as signifiers for personal and social apprehensions to which they have no intrinsic connection. During a moral panic, such fears attach to some unfortunate sexual activity or population. The media become ablaze with indignation, the public behaves like a rabid mob, the police are activated, and the state enacts new laws and regulations. When the furor has passed, some innocent erotic group has been decimated, and the state has extended its power into new areas of erotic behaviour. (Rubin 1987, 171)

The criminalization of sexuality, led by state- and media-sponsored discourse, has severe implications that not only endanger queer ways of living and seeing the world, but also imperil the very communities and lives that attempt to challenge normative frameworks.

Conclusion: Prospects of Queering the TikTok Case

Rendering visible the question of class in our analysis of the TikTok case dovetails with a need to queer our reading of these cases. I use Amar's (2013) definition: "By 'queering' I do not mean [only] the policing of lesbian, gay, bisexual, transgender (LGBT) or non-heteronormative populations ... [instead 'queering' refers to] a set of security-state practices that generate sexualized, criminalized, and sanctioned subjects of social and moral panic" (Amar 2013, 209–10). Although I ventured to situate these women's stories within the literature on the feminist political economy of commercial sex work, state media continues to focus on heterosexual women in this group of cases, creating separate silos for sex panics against cisgendered, supposedly heterosexual TikTok influencers, while other simultaneous instances of sex panics and social media surveillance violently monitor and police queer and trans Egyptians.

In these TikTok cases, women are presented as "prostitutes," and sex workers are presumed to be cisgendered women, while their clients are presumed to be cisgendered men. Queer theory has challenged this general tendency to frame sex work as heteronormative. The perspectives of queer theory denaturalize the concept of sex value and hierarchy, showing the moral and policing tactics used against commercial sexual exchange (Smith 2016). Queer theory disrupts the simplified binaries that depict women as always losing and men as usually benefiting. I contend that a queering of these questions along with a class-sensitive approach is particularly helpful. Women's experiences and power relations in Egypt are complex and sometimes contradictory, revealing "agency, multivalent meanings, and fluctuating situations" (Cabezas 2009, 117; Stardust 2015).

Within a framework that appreciates fluid identifications, the TikTok women's videos have a vast and diverse fan base. For instance, Sherry Hanem's content once discussed menstrual cycle etiquette and mockingly challenged the notion of facial hair shaving. Her relationship with her daughter Zomorroda underscores and challenges heterosexist, married, and monogamous relations.[23] Although uneven power relations can suppress and control women's bodies, they cannot "erase" their agency (Cabezas 2009), nor do they determine a single lived experience. The TikTok women, in this light, are active creators of their content and livelihoods.

Most of the TikTok women received stiff prison sentences and ended up behind bars, punished for threatening "Egyptian family values." On June 13, 2021, Sherifa Refaat (known as Sherry Hanem) and her daughter Nora Hashim (known as Zomorroda) were sentenced to five years in prison (*Mada Masr* 2021b). On June 20, 2021, Haneen Hossam and Mowada al-Adham were sentenced by the Cairo Criminal Court to ten and six years, respectively (*Mada Masr* 2021c). In Egypt, legislation policing feminist and queer bodies and their media innovations continues to proliferate and to generate a steadily intensifying state of recurring moral panic, suppressing the production and circulation of erotic knowledge and sexual bodily integrity and dignity. The TikTok women were punished for embodying and transmitting this knowledge and integrity. Although the class dimension may seem to shield some more privileged women from facing a similar fate, the freedom of all is bound together. Audre Lorde (1984) teaches us to recognize that our differences do not separate us, but rather deepen the importance of shared struggles.

To remember and support Mawada, Sherry Hanem wore a long blonde wig filter and told her audience: "Mawada al-Adham did not die. If Mawada al-Adham is arrested, millions of Mawada al-Adhams will rise again."[24] In our fight against authoritarian, heteropatriarchal, classphobic state violence—disguised by concepts like "the Egyptian family"—we should always remember how the TikTok women reignited public discussion and demonstrated how to transcend notions of deviance, passivity, and narrow conceptions of bodily integrity.

Notes

1   An online social media application and platform that allows its users to post short videos.
2   Pseudonym—verbal consent was given to quote her for this chapter.
3   Rana, personal correspondence with the author, December 2016.
4   Rana, personal correspondence with the author, December 2016.
5   Haneen (in her early twenties) studies archaeology at Cairo University, while Mawada (also in her early twenties) is based in 6th of October City and originally from Matruh. Sherry Hanem and Zomorroda are mother and daughter, both based in Greater Cairo. Menna was seventeen years old at the time of her arrest and also based in Greater Cairo. Manar is based in Banha city, while Bassant is based in Alexandria (*Bawabh News* 2020; *Egyptian Streets* 2020).
6   Article 93 of Egypt's Constitution of 2014.
7   There are earlier documented historical accounts of women protesting taxation and cost of living increases during the Ottoman Empire and during the French Expedition. Even though historical accounts documenting women's participation were mostly linked

to the national cause, Egyptian women participated in the Rosetta Women's Conference in 1799, in which its gender dimension was noticeable (Kamal 2016).

8   During an anti-Mubarak protest, women were assaulted by "plain clothes" security officers and National Democratic Party thugs, members of Egypt's former ruling party, at the Press Syndicate Building (Saad and Abed 2020).

9   OpAntiSH's websites include https://twitter.com/OpAntiSH and https://www.facebook.com/opantish.

10   Instagram accounts such as @catcallsofcairo, @dantillaspeaks, and @thisismotherbeing.

11   Hashtags refer to keywords preceded by the "#" (pound) sign, and usually refer to a particular subject matter. For example, "#me_ too" began as a hashtag that reflected a movement against sexual violence by cisgendered men.

12   In the first court ruling, Haneen, Mawada, and Manar were sentenced to two to three years in prison and a fine of LE 300,000. Manar Samy's appeal was denied, while Sherry Hanem and Zomorroda were sentenced to six years in prison each and a fine of LE 100,000 (Egyfeminist 2020).

13   The translation from Arabic to English is my own.

14   Hashtag link: https://tinyurl.com/2txwxn9f

15   "Egypt Female TikTok Star Jailed for Three Years for Human Trafficking," BBC News, April 18, 2022. https://www.bbc.com/news/world-middle-east-61139566

16   You can find this campaign on the NCW twitter page: @ncwegypt

17   For more on the concept of moral securitization, see Amar 2013, 101, 176, 219.

18   Mawada al-Adham's account provides context: https://www.tiktok.com/@mawadaeladhm?source=h5_m

19   It is important to highlight the point that gender can act as a precedence factor in other settings—for example, the indiscriminate mob assaults against women in Tahrir Square or the prevalent and everyday sexual harassment and mob assaults during feast vacations (Kamal 2016).

20   Comparably, the Fairmont witnesses were made out as criminals and subjected to virginity tests, and their private pictures and videos were also leaked (Michaelson 2020).

21   For a translation of Law 10/1961, see EIPR 2017.

22   For a translation of Law 10/1961, see EIPR 2017.

23 Sherry's menstrual video: https://www.youtube.com/watch?v=L
    spNvDWLPhw; facial hair shaving video: https://www.youtube.
    com/watch?v=AjKbKZiCFKQ
24 Sherry's video on Mawada: https://www.youtube.com/
    watch?v=8YKMc_wWN9s

Works Cited

Abed, Sara. 2016. "How Do Sex Workers Perceive their Working Iden-
    tity? Case Studies in Egypt." *Kohl: A Journal for Body and Gender
    Research* 2, no. 2: 245–61.
Abuelsoud, Nana. 2020. "An Open Letter to the Egyptian Family." *Resurj*,
    October 2. http://resurj.org/post/open-letter-egyptian-family.
Al-Amar, Maya. 2020. "'TikTok' wa-Misr wa-l-fatayat: ayy 'alam nahnu
    fih?" *Khateera*, June 1. https://tinyurl.com/yyye3584
Amar, Paul. 2011. "Turning the Gendered Politics of the Security
    State Inside Out? Charging the Police with Sexual Harassment in
    Egypt." *International Feminist Journal of Politics* 13, no. 3: 299–328.
———. 2013. *The Security Archipelago: Human-security States, Sexuality Poli-
    tics, and the End of Neoliberalism*. Durham, NC: Duke University Press.
Amnesty International. 2020. "Egypt: Survivors of Sexual Vio-
    lence and Online Abuse among Prosecuted Women TikTok
    Influencers." Amnesty International Press Release, August
    13. https://www.amnesty.org/en/latest/press-release/2020/08/
    egypt-survivors-of-sexual-violence-and-online-abuse-among-
    prosecuted-women-tiktok-influencers/
Arab Republic of Egypt. 1961. On the Combating of Prostitution. Law
    No. 10. Adopted 1961. Accessed October 23, 2023. https://cairo52.
    com/egypt-law-no-10-1961-on-the-combating-of-prostitution/
Arab Weekly. 2020. "Egyptian Law Shields Identity of Harassment
    Victims." *The Arab Weekly*, August 18. https://thearabweekly.com/
    egyptian-law-shields-identity-harassment-victims
al-Bawabh News. 2020. "Ta'arraf 'ala al-qa'ima al-kamila wa-l-tasalsul
    al-zamani li-l-qabd 'ala fatayat TikTok." July 12. https://bawabaa.org/
    news/419147?fbclid=IwAR0N51esbiSaTp4vJwdgQPMRWsoyV5
    TlNbK7SbjpBUyhdOcjBFJtW2Wlibc (accessed July 15, 2021).
BBC. 2022. "Egypt Female TikTok Star Jailed for Three Years for
    Human Trafficking." *BBC News*, April 18. https://www.bbc.com/
    news/world-middle-east-61139566
Cabezas, Amalia L. 2009. *Economies of Desire: Sex and Tourism in Cuba and
    the Dominican Republic*. Philadelphia: Temple University Press.

Carastathis, Anna. 2014. "The Concept of Intersectionality in Feminist Theory." *Philosophy Compass* 9, no. 5: 304–14.

Crenshaw, Kimberlé. 1989. "Demarginalizing the Intersection of Race and Sex: A Black Feminist Critique of Antidiscrimination Doctrine, Feminist Theory and Antiracist Politics." *University of Chicago Legal Forum*, vol. 1989, iss. 1, art. 8. http://chicagounbound.uchicago.edu/uclf/vol1989/iss1/8

Dupret, Baudouin, Samer Ghamroun, Youmna Makhlouf, Marième N'Diaye, Ayang Utriza Yakin, and Alexis Blouët. 2021. "Playing by the Rules: The Search for Legal Grounds in Homosexuality Cases—Indonesia, Lebanon, Egypt, Senegal." In *Legal Rules in Practice: In the Midst of Law's Life*, edited by Baudouin Dupret, Julie Colemans, and Max Travers, 255–82. New York: Routledge.

Egyfeminist. 2020. "Freedom for Egypt's Women." Support Women in Egypt. https://supportegyptswomen.carrd.co/

Egyptian Public Prosecution. 2020. Notice via Facebook, September 20. https://www.facebook.com/ppo.gov.eg/photos/a.2579366742171212/3341248985982980/

Egyptian Streets. 2020. "From TikTok to Jail: Popular Egyptian Influencer Arrested for 'Violating Family Values.'" May 16. https://egyptianstreets.com/2020/05/16/from-tiktok-to-jail-popular-egyptian-influencer-arrested-for-violating-family-values/

EIPR. 2017. "The Trap: Punishing Sexual Difference in Egypt: Law No. 10/1961." Egyptian Initiative for Personal Rights, November 22. https://eipr.org/en/content/law-no-101961

———. 2020. Egyptian Initiative for Personal Rights, Press Release, September 17. https://eipr.org/en/press/2020/09/after-menna-abdel-aziz%E2%80%99s-release-and-prosecutions-decision-there-are-no-grounds

Eskandar, Wael. 2020. "Egypt: No Country for All Women." *Open Democracy*, July 24. https://www.opendemocracy.net/en/north-africa-west-asia/egypt-no-country-all-women/

Al Haq, S. 2021. "From Behind the Screens: Feminism and Hope in 2020." *Mada Masr*, January 19. https://www.madamasr.com/en/2021/01/19/opinion/u/from-behind-the-screens-feminism-and-hope-in-2020/

HarassMap. 2014. "Towards a Safer City. Sexual Harassment in Greater Cairo: Effectiveness of Crowdsourced Data." HarassMap.org. https://s3-eu-west-1.amazonaws.com/harassmap/media/HarassMap%20Egypt/Towards%20a%20Safer%20City_full%20report_EN.pdf

Harris, Angela, and Zeus Leonardo. 2018. "Intersectionality, Race-Gender Subordination, and Education." *Review of Research in Education* 42, no. 1: 1–27.

Kaedbey, Deema. 2014. "Building Theory across Struggles: Queer Feminist Thought in Lebanon." PhD diss., Ohio State University.

Kamal, Hala. 2016. "A Century of Egyptian Women's Demands: The Four Waves of the Egyptian Feminist Movement." In *Gender and Race Matter: Global Perspectives on Being a Woman*, edited by Shaminder Takhar, 3–22. Bingley, UK: Emerald Group Publishing.

Kirollos, Mariam. 2016. "The Daughters of Egypt Are a Red Line: The Impact of Sexual Harassment on Egypt's Legal Culture." *Kohl: A Journal for Body and Gender Research* 2, no. 1: 50–70.

Lorde, Audre. 1984. "Uses of the Erotic: The Erotic as Power." In *Sister Outsider: Essays and Speeches*, 53–59. Berkeley, CA: Crossing Press.

Lotfi, Fatma. 2020. "Draft Law on Protecting Identities of Sexual Abuse Survivors Initially Approved." *Daily News*, August 4. https://dailynewsegypt.com/2020/08/04/draft-law-on-protecting-identities-of-sexual-abuse-survivors-initially-approved/

Mada Masr. 2020. "The Public Prosecution's Crusade against Social Media." October 3.

———. 2021a. "Fi al-nashra." January 14. https://www.facebook.com/557202771003530/posts/3914499258607181/?d=n

———. 2021b. "5 Years for Violating 'Family Values,' 'Promoting Prostitution' Upheld against 2 TikTok Influencers." June 14. https://www.madamasr.com/en/2021/06/14/news/u/5-years-for-violating-family-values-promoting-prostitution-upheld-against-2-tiktok-influencers/

———. 2021c. "Court Sentences TikTok Influencers to 10 and 6 Years in Prison on Human Trafficking Charges." June 20. https://www.madamasr.com/en/2021/06/20/news/u/court-sentences-tiktok-influencers-to-10-and-6-years-in-prison-on-human-trafficking-charges/

———. 2021d. "Witnesses Arrested and Intimidated: How the Fairmont Rape Case Fell Apart." September 2.

Masaar. 2020. "Masaar tadfaʿ bi-ʿadam dusturiyat garimat al-iʿtida' ʿala qiyam al-usra al-misriya." Masaar.net, August 17. https://tinyurl.com/y42jkpxu

Michaelson, R. 2020. "Hope Turns to Despair as Egypt Arrests Witnesses to Alleged 2014 Gang Rape." *The Guardian*, September 7. https://www.theguardian.com/world/2020/sep/07/hope-turns-to-despair-as-egypt-arrests-witnesses-to-alleged-2014-gang

Mokhtar, Weam. 2020. "Muga misirya gadida min 'ana aydan': hal hana waqt al-'adala?" *Khateera*, August 22. https://tinyurl.com/y5mtysye

El-Nadeem Center. 2004. "Days of Torture: Women in Police Custody."

———. 2006. "Torture in Egypt: 2003–2006." El-Nadeem Center for the Management and Rehabilitation of Victims of Violence and Torture. https://archive.org/details/TortureInEgypt 2003-2006English

Nash, Jennifer C. 2019. *Black Feminism Reimagined: After Intersectionality*. Durham, NC and London: Duke University Press.

Nazra for Feminist Studies. 2020. "Background Paper: Violence against Women in Egypt: From Black Wednesday to the Pandemic." Report, n.d. https://nazra.org/en/2020/07/background-paper-violence-against-women-black-wednesday-pandemic

El-Rifae, Yasmine. 2020. "Inherent Guilt: Menna Abdel Aziz and the Victims of Ahmed Bassam Zaki." *Mada Masr*, July 20. https://mada25.appspot.com/madamasr.com/en/2020/07/20/opinion/u/inherent-guilt-menna-abdelaziz-and-the-victims-of-ahmed-bassam-zaki/

Rubin, Gayle S. 1987 [2007]. "Thinking Sex: Notes for a Radical Theory of the Politics of Sexuality." In *Thinking Sex: Notes for a Radical Theory of the Politics of Sexuality*, edited by Richard Parker and Peter Aggleton, 150–87. London and New York: Routledge.

Saad, Radwa, and Sara S. Abed. 2020. "A Revolution Deferred: Sexual and Gender Based Violence in Egypt." In *Gender, Protests and Political Change in Africa*, edited by Awino Okech, 81–106. London: Palgrave Macmillan.

Sadek, George. 2020. "Egypt: Parliament Approves Draft Law Concealing the Identity of Victims of Sexual Violence Crimes during the Pretrial Investigative Stage." Library of Congress, September 8. https://www.loc.gov/item/global-legal-monitor/2020-09-08/egypt-parliament-approves-draft-law-concealing-the-identity-of-victims-of-sexual-violence-crimes-during-the-pretrial-investigative-stage/

Samir, Marina. 2020. "The Women of TikTok: Their Freedom Is My Freedom." *Kohl: A Journal for Body and Gender Research* 5, no. 3: 21–28.

Sayegh, Ghiwa. 2015. "The Erotic, the Exotic, and the Space(s) In Between: The Race for Feminist Waves." *Kohl: A Journal for Body and Gender Research* 1, no. 2: 1–5.

Smith, Nicola. 2016. "The Global Political Economy of Sex Work." In *Handbook on Gender in World Politics*, edited by Jill Steans and Daniela Tepe-Belfrage, 370–77. Cheltenham, UK: Edward Elgar Publishing.

Stardust, Zahra. 2015. "Critical Femininities, Fluid Sexualities and Queer Temporalities: Erotic Performers on Objectification, Femmephobia and Oppression." In *Queer Sex Work*, edited by Mary Laing, Katy Pilcher, and Nicola Smith, 67–78. New York: Routledge.

TikTok Women. 2020. "Free Egypt's TikTok Women" Change.org petition, n.d. https://www.change.org/p/free-egypt-s-tiktok-women

TIMEP. 2017. "TIMEP Brief: Protest and Freedom of Assembly in Egypt." The Tahrir Institute for Middle East Policy, October 18. https://timep.org/reports-briefings/protest-and-freedom-of-assembly-in-egypt/

Tisdall, S. 2006. "Egypt Finds Democracy Can Wait." *The Guardian*, May 16. http://www.guardian.co.uk/commentisfree/2006/may/16/world.egypt

Twitter. 2020. Twitter hashtag thread (reproduced with permission from the Egyptian family), July 13. https://twitter.com/hashtag/بعد_اذن_الاسرة_المصرية.

Walsh, Declan. 2020. "Accusations of Serial Rape Push Egypt Toward a Reckoning." *New York Times*, July 8. https://www.nytimes.com/2020/07/08/world/middleeast/egypt-metoo-rape-assault.html.

Zaki, Hind Z. 2021. "How Egyptian Women Have Broken the Stigma around Sexual Violence." *Mada Masr*, January 21. https://mada29.appspot.com/madamasr.com/en/2021/01/21/opinion/u/how-egyptian-women-have-broken-the-stigma-around-sexual-violence/

2

SECURITIZED CONSOLIDATION, OR HOW THE STATE CO-OPTED PRIVATE MEDIA

MOHAMED ELMESHAD

In 1991, a decade into the presidency of Hosni Mubarak—Egypt's fourth and longest-serving president (1981–2011), who was deposed after the 2011 Revolution—and with the signing of agreements with the IMF and World Bank, the Egyptian government began to implement the liberalization policies prescribed by the Economic Reform and Restructuring Programme (ERSAP) and also to undertake some political liberalization. The agreements sparked fundamental changes in how the state approached development, class, and resource distribution as well as neoliberal policies, freedom of speech, and democratization, topics that are extensively covered elsewhere in this volume in the chapters by Elshahed, El-Husseiny, Duffiels, Sinno, Arese, and Khalil, among others.

The status of the Egyptian media fell at the peculiar intersection of political and economic liberalization. Allowing for private ownership of the media promoted the private sector while also ostensibly allowing more space for freedom of thought, expression, and the flow of information. For practically the first time since the 1960s, the new policies transformed the ability of private individuals to own and manage broadcast and print media. And since they were among its principal beneficiaries, these media outlets would also become some of the main champions of the state's new policies.

In the case of broadcast media, one can claim that the private outlets were allowed to develop as a "reactive" measure, mostly in response to the state's shifting policies (Sakr 2007). Another view sees developments in Egyptian mass media as being symptomatic of an "adaptive authoritarianism" looking to maintain its grip on society in ways that prolonged the regime's survival and control over public spaces (Webb 2014). Through successive transformations in the country's power dynamics since the introduction of private media, the state has never fully embraced freedom of information as absolute. The media has not been entirely disconnected from the regime's goals, but rather, has continued to be viewed as instrumental to national security. Since Egypt had been under a de facto "state of emergency" since 1960, regulating the media sector remained within the purview of the security establishment.

This chapter explores the ways in which the state has securitized private media despite dramatic political transformations. Private and state-run media entities have occupied areas emblematic of "liberalization" and the symbolic roles they have been allowed, or expected, to play in Egyptian life. Some outlets were launched outside of this paradigm. Most of those were unable to sustain themselves for more than a few years in operation, and were either unable to survive financially or were shut down through a variety of legal mechanisms constricting media operations. Outlets that survived, such as the rigorous and independent journalism outlet *Mada Masr*, did so despite consistent backlash from the state. *Mada Masr*, however, has been banned from being accessed in Egypt since 2017, and despite operating fully from within the country, its website cannot be accessed from within its borders (Human Rights Watch 2022).

The EMPC: An Enclosed Broadcast Suburb

Changes to broadcast mass media in Egypt began in 1990 with a plan to revamp the aged Egyptian Radio and Television Union (ERTU).[1] That same year, construction began on the Egyptian Media Production City (EMPC), originally meant to be one of the largest state-of-the-art studio complexes in the world. It was built on 3.5 million hectares of land in 6th of October City, one of the new and sprawling Cairene suburbs to which wealthy Egyptians had begun moving to escape the city's congestion—a broader trend within Egyptian urban development, as documented by Elshahed and El-Husseiny in this volume. The EMPC stands in stark contrast to the earlier monument of Egyptian broadcasting, the Maspero Building, housing the ERTU. As Khalil reminds us in their chapter in this volume, that imposing Nile-facing edifice, built in 1960 to house the ERTU, was jarring even for the usual bustle of downtown Cairo. It came to represent Gamal Abd al-Nasser's (president of Egypt from 1956 to 1970) brand of socialist urbanism, offering both a communication epicenter and a visible example of one of his grand "national projects." The spectacle of such a building was almost as important as its functionality, as grandiose projects have been a hallmark of every Egyptian president since the dawn of the republic. Similarly, Abd al-Fattah al-Sisi (since 2014, Egypt's sixth president) has made the building of shiny new cities and infrastructure projects the centerpieces of his regime, meant to reflect new beginnings for Egypt under his leadership. The EMPC, on the other hand, was built in an area that would come to symbolize the expansion of the private sector under Mubarak, as well as the relocation of wealth to the outskirts of Cairo by the few who enjoy privileged access to capital.

The EMPC megaproject became a showpiece for the liberalization era and eventually became the incubator for private Egyptian satellite television, which was not part of the original plans. The EMPC, designated a free enterprise zone for media in 2000, was regulated by the General Authority for Investment and Free Zones (GAFI), which also issues licenses to television stations. Ultimately, the state (via the ERTU) had the final say as to who could operate within the city's limits, guided by the security-minded ethos of the regime. The area's distance from other areas of Cairo and Giza provides a sense of detachment, which serves to secure it from any external factors and to isolate it from societal influence.

Champions of Neoliberal Transition: The First Private Broadcasters

The first satellite television broadcasters out of the EMPC were restricted to operating within 6th of October City (after gaining highly scrutinized security clearances) and to using the government-owned Nilesat company. The first Egyptian broadcaster to operate within these confines was DreamTV, owned by US-based businessman Ahmed Bahgat, to whom Mubarak personally had reached out to return to Egypt. Bahgat launched DreamTV as part of his broader "Dreamland" project, which was a major suburban development meant to cater exclusively to upper-middle-class Egyptians.

DreamTV had been engaged in airing relatively controversial subjects on seemingly critical talk shows. However, the station's true value to its owner and the state lay in how it showcased a liberalizing Egypt. Amr Khafaga, who held the positions of executive producer and head of programming for DreamTV (2002–2007), claimed that there was "a top-down decision by the government to establish private television stations."[2] Rather than attempt to engineer the private broadcasting sector in any way that would institutionally rein in the sector, the walled-in studio location reflected its intended containment. As a handful of other private "current affairs" stations emerged between 2000 and 2010, the state appeared content to use them for window-dressing purposes, showcasing ostensible liberalization (Nasser 2012), or as a safety valve (Webb 2014), allowing for the release of pent-up angst in an overly controlled political environment.

The first private broadcast owners, like Bahgat, maintained positive relations with the Mubarak regime or were directly involved with the revamped (ruling) National Democratic Party, which attempted to present the group as a progressive and pro-business cohort led by Mubarak's son and heir apparent, Gamal (Saleh 2004). In the case of the very first few private media outlets—Dream, al-Mehwar, al-Hayat—the ERTU was an obligatory shareholder.

Private Media: Early Growth, New Connections

In the absence of vibrant political parties in Egypt, the pressures of globalization and the penetrative effects of technological innovations meant that there was a heightened appetite for diversified flows of information. Blogs, which predated the pro-democracy street demonstrations occurring between 2005 and 2011, had become preeminent sources of information, especially on opposition activity, free speech suppression, and the documenting of cases of injustice.

The politicization of mass media spaces in Egypt greatly expanded with open-access online and media platforms. Networks were not allowed to launch news stations, but they did provide talk shows that delved into topics previously considered taboo by the political leadership, such as growing poverty and local government corruption. Access to these satellite networks was initially limited for the poorer areas of the country, which reduced their impact.

Restrictions placed on private broadcasters and limited state attempts to circumscribe the sector made traditional outlets subject to rapid technological innovations. Internet usage nearly tripled after 2005, gravitating toward 30 percent in 2011 (Atallah and Rizk 2011), while access to satellite television reached 90 percent by 2010 (Dubai Press Club 2012). Private print news outlets such as *Al-Masry Al-Youm* (est. 2004) legitimately competed with the century-old, state-owned *al-Ahram*.

The state's absolute control over the flow of information had loosened considerably by 2011. Current affairs content became more populist. Private television and print outlets were offering content pertaining to social and human rights issues while mostly steering clear of known "red lines"—mainly criticism of the president and the military.

Social media helped lead the way in driving public discourse toward discussing issues concerning social justice, and the private mass media outlets followed suit. Some looked to capture that portion of the market previously underserved by state media, whose focus remained the presidential palace. One study highlighted the divergent coverage between the various newspapers (Mabrook 2010), stating that "the front page of Egyptian newspapers in mid-September 2009 ran different stories . . . . The government-run *al-Ahram*'s online page had as its first story President Mubarak's comments on Jerusalem capturing the hearts and minds of all Muslims. . . . The front page contained none of the articles that were prominently covered in its independent counterparts . . . [that were] less flattering to the government, such as Cairo's mounting garbage problem" (Mabrook 2010, 5). The 2011 uprising helped propel private media into the epicenter of the industry, enabling alternative news sources to reach an all-time high readership. Newspapers such as *Al-Masry Al-Youm* and *ElDostor* had built a track record of reporting topics and protests that helped fuel public sentiment leading to the uprisings and became part of the national discourse.

The role of private outlets was not lost on demonstrators. In 2011, protesters huddled together to read private newspapers and made a display of tearing apart state-owned ones, which had initially ignored the events. The Mubarak regime quickly moved to control the information flow in the country by shutting down internet networks between January 28 and February 3, 2011. Nonetheless, most private outlets actively covered the developments.[3]

Return of the Securitized State amid Counterrevolution

For seventeen months following February 2011, the Egyptian state was run by the Supreme Council of the Armed Forces (SCAF). While they were in power, the SCAF attempted to restructure the management of the media to reflect the quickly shifting public sphere after the massive Tahrir Square uprisings and increasingly dynamic public media engagements. New television outlets were granted licenses, although the mechanisms through which they were licensed or regulated did not change. Sixteen new channels—representing varying institutional, political, and business-related backing—were licensed in the immediate aftermath, almost all of which remained located within the media city's confines.

In 2012, the administration of President Mohamed Morsi, of the Muslim Brotherhood party, elected in June of that year, made attempts to stifle opposition media, including pushing Naguib Sawiris to sell ON TV.[4] Many of the tactics used during the Mubarak era to suffocate opposition media were continued by the new minister of information under Morsi, who preserved around seventy articles of Mubarak-era laws related to media (ANHRI 2013; ANHRI 2020).

Field Marshal Abd al-Fattah al-Sisi announced his candidacy for the presidency in March 2014 after coming to power nearly one year after the ouster of Mohamed Morsi[5] and a subsequent massacre of nearly a thousand Muslim Brotherhood supporters who had been involved in a month-long sit-in, mostly in Rabaa Square, protesting Morsi's ouster. Plurality of content quickly withered away as part of this transition.

Broadly speaking, the first five years of al-Sisi's presidency and its relationship with the shift to privately owned mass media can be divided into two periods. The first was an attempt by the president to court the existing (non–Muslim Brotherhood sympathizing) private media outlets and owners. The second phase was a direct consolidation, requiring all media to rally behind the state's grand projects—most prominently, a massive plan to build a new administrative capital adjacent to Cairo. Yosri Fouda, a prominent talk show host, expressed the military leaders' expectations that all media, including the privately owned, be explicit allies of the state and commit to dutifully advancing its goals.[6] Al-Sisi appeared in a leaked video before becoming president confirming that one of his goals would be to co-opt the media. He told a group of officers in uniform, "Building a state-wide alliance takes a long time and effort . . . . It takes a very long time until you possess an appropriate share of influence over the media" (Kirkpatrick 2013).

One of the first orders that al-Sisi gave after Morsi was deposed in July 2013 was to shut down two newspapers and all nine privately owned pro-Morsi television stations airing out of Egypt (Yasin 2013). Many of the employees and owners were subsequently jailed on terrorism-related charges, as the Muslim Brotherhood and all its affiliates were declared terrorist organizations by the Ministry of Justice (*BBC News* 2013). These stations were never allowed to reopen.

Al-Sisi's alliance-building became clear during his first year in power. Within four months of being named president, he held meetings with journalists and media organizations, often asserting (in an instructive manner) their duty to "unify the nation." The only other cohort al-Sisi met with more than media were members of the armed forces. Yosri Fouda recalled one instance during one of these meetings when a fellow broadcaster proposed to al-Sisi that he declare the day of the Rabaa massacre a national holiday. To Fouda's shock, the proposal was not dismissed, although it wasn't taken up either. That interaction led Fouda to believe that only journalists who praised the military and new president would be tolerated and that there was no hope in the immediate future for independent journalism in Egypt, prompting him to end his show on ON TV and leave the country.[7] He was not the first among his colleagues to leave their positions or be forced to resign.

The consolidation of media behind al-Sisi began early on during the campaign for the 2014 presidential election. CBC and ON TV aired a joint broadcast of a highly edited, reverential interview with al-Sisi to introduce his campaign platform on May 5, 2014. During the interview, al-Sisi openly chastised the hosts for their choice of words when referring to the military. Five days later, his main opponent on the ballot, former MP and long-time labor activist Hamdeen Sabahy, was offered only a live interview with CBC in which he was heavily challenged by combative hosts. Many popular television hosts who came to prominence afterward or as a result of the January 25, 2011 Revolution, or who were less-than-enthusiastic supporters of al-Sisi, were purged from the airwaves during the first portion of al-Sisi's presidency, most through internal organizational decisions.

Ahmed Ragab—formerly an executive producer of Yosri Fouda's show *Akhir kalam* (Final Words) and a managing editor at *Al-Masry Al-Youm*—noted that many private outlets made the changes willingly in response to the "general atmosphere."[8] According to Ragab, the lack of objective media stemmed from a combination of social "hysteria" regarding terrorism and the threat of political instability and commercial interests that drove media outlets to toe the government line. Enough of the public either believed the Muslim Brotherhood was steering the country toward becoming a fanatic theocracy or, alternatively, that Egypt was an embattled nation being targeted by various global conspiracies so that "the market for neutral level-headed news shows, like Fouda's, was decreasing while the market for sensationalist nationalism was on the rise."[9] These sentiments were fomented by the palpable instability in Egypt. Political factions were in constant open conflict—a very uncommon situation for a country that had been under autocratic rule for so long. Furthermore, the police were noticeably less involved in maintaining public order and obedience than they had been under Mubarak, as Hassan, El Raggal, Fallas, and Ahmed document in their contributions to this volume.

Fourth-generation Warfare

In time, the state veered toward more direct forms of control. Media systems were once again regarded by the government as an element of national security, as many of the major figures in the field found themselves being assessed by the state under a strict "with us or against us" framework.[10] The new information minister, Usama Haikal,[11] opined that the media space was a battleground for sovereignty. He claimed the country was fighting a "fourth-generation war,"[12] representing nothing less than an existential threat, with the media at the epicenter of global and regional conspiracies to foment a state of chaos in Egypt (Haikal 2015). Following his initial appointment as minister of information in 2011, Haikal moved to manage the media production city with a de facto mandate to regulate all private television. He was also the head of the Media and Culture Committee in Parliament until December 2019, when he was reappointed as minister of information (*Egypt Independent* 2019).

Consolidation

Political power during Abd al-Fattah al-Sisi's presidency has become increasingly more centralized over time. The initial expansion of the role individuals with military backgrounds played in the government betrayed hopes of civilian leadership. At the time, only eight of Egypt's twenty-seven provinces were run by civilians. Investigative journalist Hossam Bahgat has detailed how, prior to that, the General Intelligence Service interfered directly in order to place loyalist candidates in the 2015 parliamentary elections. By 2018, al-Sisi's consolidation of power looked complete, and oppositional political activity became extremely hazardous and increasingly rare.

Similarly, the first few years of al-Sisi's presidency saw power in private media slowly change hands, as the role of the military and security organizations continued to noticeably expand. The regime believed that the media had played a critical role in fomenting the 2011 protests. Their approach changed from allowing easily manipulated businessmen to control the private media space to controlling the sector more directly.[13] The interest taken by al-Sisi in private media and the prompt elimination of all Muslim Brotherhood allies or sympathizers from the airwaves and newspapers proved to be a precursor to a more direct involvement of the armed forces in the private media.

In November 2015, al-Sisi lambasted media coverage of his presidency in a keynote speech delivered at an Armed Forces Cultural Seminar (*Masrawy* 2015). His tirade ended with an everyday phrase for Egyptians, *"ma yisahhish kida"* (that is not right). Some witnessed the spectacle and concluded that he had in fact lost patience with the sector. News presenter Dina Abdelrahman noted that this speech synthesized the president's outlook and revealed that even mere questioning of al-Sisi's policies or actions would not be tolerated.

The wheels had, in fact, already been set in motion for what Yazid Sayigh has described as a hostile takeover of media by the Ministry of Defense (MoD) and allied agencies (Sayigh 2019). The introduction of a heavily funded DMC television network in 2015 represented one of the early forays of the MOD into private media. One of the DMC network's stations, DMC News, became the first privately owned 24-hour Egyptian news network. Other attempts to create a 24-hour news channel by private media owners, such as Mohamed Gohar, were repeatedly met with refusal on national security grounds.[14] Tarek Ismail, the DMC channel's founder, was seen as a direct front for military intelligence. According to *Mada Masr* (2018), DMC was the brainchild of al-Sisi and his chief of staff, Abbas Kamil, both of whom had emerged from Egypt's military intelligence sector. They had envisioned that DMC would become a competitor to other regional news outlets like Al Jazeera, Al Arabiya, and Sky News Arabia (*Mada Masr* 2018).

Conglomeration and Militarization

Another group to burst onto the media scene was the Egyptian Media Group, headed by businessman Ahmed Abou Hashima, owner of Egyptian Steel Group. He had initially acquired *Youm7* newspaper in 2011 and began his expansion in the media through the Egyptian Media Group in 2016. It very quickly became the largest media conglomerate in Egypt. According to Hossam Bahgat, who chronicled the rise of the group in detail for *Mada Masr* (Bahgat 2017), while Abou Hashima was always seen as the group's owner, his stake in the company paled in comparison to that of the majority owner, the General Intelligence Directorate. The Egyptian Media Group initially expanded in print media, acquiring several major online and print publications in 2016: DotMasr, *Sout al-Omma*, *Youm7*, *Egypt Today*, and *Business Today*. The group expanded into television as well, first acquiring ON TV in 2016, and then Al Hayah

TV Network in 2018. They also acquired a majority share of Future Media Holding, the owner of CBC (Media Ownership Monitor 2020).

In addition to these private but state-favored companies, the state itself, in the form of the military intelligence branch, continued to aggressively engage directly in the media sector. According to Yazid Sayigh, "In January 2017, al-Asimah television network came under the management of the Cheri Media company, whose deputy head is a former Egyptian Armed Forces (EAF) spokesperson. In August, al-Asimah and its subsidiaries were acquired by Falcon Group International, a front for Military Intelligence, which established Tawasol for Public Relations to handle its growing media portfolio" (Sayigh 2019).

Other media owners who were not bought out, such as Salah Diab, the owner of *Al-Masry Al-Youm*, found themselves at the center of significant legal battles. In 2015, Diab faced major prison time over an illegal weapons charge (ANHRI 2013; ANHRI 2020). Most pro-revolution media professionals and journals who had come to prominence during the Arab Spring of 2011 had all but disappeared from the scene, either opting out of the sector or—as one television producer put it—"choosing to stay quiet, because there is no option other than being on the side of the state."[15] By six years into al-Sisi's presidency, the military had gained a nearly complete stranglehold on the sector. The private media sector only nominally existed and expanded. Much of this expansion, however, was by companies with ownership links to branches of the security institutions.

Conclusion

Egyptian private media has been effectively securitized despite the dramatic political transformations that have taken place in the country over the past decade. Private and state-run media entities played highly symbolic roles in the "liberalization" of Egyptian life during this period. Independent media outlets were even launched outside of the state-run paradigm. Most of these, however, were unable to last more than a few years. Outlets that did survive, did so in the face of state scrutiny, and many of these have been effectively banned from the country.

After 2018, private media in Egypt no longer resembled the sector in its early days and now certainly does not resemble the aspiring, pluralistic sector that was systematically dismantled in the immediate aftermath of the Arab Spring. The spaces that private media occupied remained, but changed due to the state's attempts to rein them in as a sensitive sector of national security. The composition of the cohort controlling or owning private media changed to mainly include those that enjoyed good relations with the state. The regime appears to have completely securitized the private media space, effectively disconnecting those areas from the strata of society that had momentarily felt connected to a more populist media. Even newspapers that have migrated completely online have to contend with new restrictive laws being passed. Since 2017, the government has resorted to blocking hundreds of these websites either for failure to obtain a license or, later on, for committing publishing crimes under the 2018 Press Regulation Laws. That law brought all online publications and social media pages with over five thousand followers under the purview of the same media licensing and regulation guidelines. Some, like *Mada Masr*, have had their attempts to adhere to the letter of that law inexplicably rebuffed. For the most part, the state has attempted to block any online path through which unsanctioned (critical) independent journalistic content can be accessed within Egypt.

Privately held media has resembled state-sponsored media when it has discussed some of the large-scale projects that al-Sisi has undertaken. When the president unveiled the new mosque–church complex in his administrative capital, private media outlets covered the day's events in a tone that was just as zealous and obsequious as the coverage given by state-owned media. State plans to gentrify and clear out areas within Cairo designated as "slums" have been referred to as "development plans." Despite mass opposition by both civil society groups and residents,[16] very few outlets (relative to 2005–13) give voice to dissenters or allow for vibrant conversation on the matter. Private media itself exists in theory, but both the structural underpinnings of the sector and its editorial direction seem to have reverted to the state for all intents and purposes.

Notes

1   The organization that governs all state broadcasting.
2   Amr Khafaga, interview by the author, October 24, 2015.
3   This assertion is based on personal experience as both a reporter for *Al-Masry Al-Youm* English and an activist.
4   Naguib Sawiris, Founder of ON TV, Chairman/CEO, Orascom Telecom Holding, Cairo, October 5, 2015.
5   Morsi was removed from office on July 3, 2013 after mass protests, backed by both the military and police.
6   Yosri Fouda, several interviews with the author during 2015.
7   Yosri Fouda, several interviews with the author during 2015.

8   Ahmed Ragab, several interviews with the author during 2015.

9   Ahmed Ragab, several interviews with the author during 2015.

10 Yosri Fouda, several interviews with the author during 2015.

11 Haikal was chief editor of *al-Wafd* and had been a military corre-
    spondent.

12 A defining characteristic of fourth-generation warfare is when a
    country chooses to bypass an opposing military force and strike
    directly at cultural, political, or population targets (Vest 2001).

13 Hesham Kassem, interview by the author, October 18, 2015.

14 Mohamed Gohar, several interviews with the author during 2017.

15 From an interview conducted by the author in 2019. The inter-
    viewee insisted on anonymity.

16 Most notably, in 2017 the state demolished dozens of homes on
    al-Warraq Island, in Cairo, to make way for plans to create a high-
    end real estate project.

Works Cited

ANHRI (Arab Network for Human Rights Information). 2013.
    "Report: The Crime of Insulting the President, a Crime of an
    Authoritarian Regime." http://www.anhri.net/en/?p=10908
——. 2020. "Report: Untold, Unforgotten . . . Nine Pending
    Cases that Need Answers and Justice." https://www.anhri.
    info/?p=17140&lang=en
Attalah, L., and N. Rizk. 2011. "Egypt's Evolving Media Landscape:
    Access, Public Interest and Control." Chapter 7 (pp. 118–35) of the
    Ford Foundation report, *A New Frontier, an Old Landscape*, edited
    by A. Puddephatt, D. Hawtin, L. Zommer, J. Brant, L. Attalah, N.
    Rizk, R. Bhat, M. Lim, G. Githaiga, and R. Zausmer, November.
    New York: Ford Foundation. https://www.gp-digital.org/wp-
    content/uploads/2013/10/Egypt.pdf
Bahgat, H. 2017. "Looking into the Latest Acquisition of Egyptian
    Media Companies by General Intelligence." *Mada Masr*, Decem-
    ber 21. https://madamasr.com/en/2017/12/21/feature/politics/
    looking-into-the-latest-acquisition-of-egyptian-media-companies-
    by-general-intelligence/
BBC News. 2013. "Egypt Brotherhood 'Terrorist Group.'" https://www.
    bbc.co.uk/news/world-middle-east-25515932
Davison, John, and Ahmed Tolba. 2018. "Egypt's Sisi Wins 97 Per-
    cent in Election with No Real Opposition." *Reuters*, April
    2. https://www.reuters.com/article/us-egypt-election-result/

egypts-sisi-wins-97-percent-in-election-with-no-real-opposition-idUSKCN1H916A

Dubai Press Club and Deloitte. 2012. "Arab Media Outlook 2011–2015." Dubai Press Club, Dubai, United Arab Emirates. https://www.slideshare.net/cbakir/arab-media2015

Egypt Independent. 2019. "Profile: Osama Heikal Returns as Minister of Information." https://egyptindependent.com/profile-osama-heikal-returns-as-minister-of-information/

Haikal, U. 2015. *Hurub al-gil al-rabiʻ.* Cairo: Sama Publishers.

Human Rights Watch. 2022. "Egypt: Prosecution of Mada Masr Journalists." Human Rights Watch, September 8. https://www.hrw.org/breaking-news/2022/09/08/egypt-prosecution-mada-masr-journalists

Iskandar, A. 2013. "Free at Last? Egypt's Media after the Revolution." In *Mediating the Arab Uprisings*, edited by A. Iskandar and B. Haddad. Washington, DC and Beirut: Tadween Publishing.

Kirkpatrick, D. 2013. "In Leaked Video, Egyptian Army Officers Debate How to Sway News Media." *New York Times.* https://www.nytimes.com/2013/10/04/world/middleeast/in-leaked-video-egyptian-army-officers-debate-how-to-sway-news-media.html

Mabrook, M. 2010. "Changing the Channel: Egypt's Evolving Media Landscape and Its Role in Domestic Politics." Brookings Institute Report, May 20. Washington, DC: The Brookings Institution. https://egypt.mom-rsf.org/uploads/tx_lfrogmom/documents/12-1456_import.pdf

Mada Masr. 2018. "Sources: Head of DMC Network Dismissed, Plans to Launch DMC News Scrapped." October 7. https://madamasr.com/en/2018/10/07/news/u/sources-head-of-dmc-network-dismissed-plans-to-launch-dmc-news-scrapped/

Masrawy. 2015. al-Sisi li-l-misriyin: ma yisahhish kida, ana hashki li-l-shaʻb minkum. https://www.masrawy.com/news/news_egypt/details/2015/11/1/686178/%D8%A7%D9%84%D8%B3%D9%8A%D8%B3%D9%8A-%D9%84%D9%84%D8%A5%D8%B9%D9%84%D8%A7%D9%85%D9%8A%D9%8A%D9%86-%D9%85%D8%A7%D8%B5%D8%AD%D8%B4-%D9%83%D8%AF%D9%87-%D8%A3%D9%86%D8%A7-%D9%87%D8%B4%D9%83%D9%89-%D9%84%D9%84%D8%B4%D8%B9%D8%A8-%D9%85%D9%86%D9%83%D9%85-

Media Ownership Monitor. 2020. "Egyptian Media Group." https://
egypt.mom-rsf.org/en/owners/companies/detail/company//
egyptian-media-group/

Nasser, M. 2012. "Private Satellite Channels in Egypt: The Relationship
between Ownership and Editorial Policy." *Arab Media & Society* 15,
no. 1.

Sakr, N. 2007. *Arab Television Today*. London: I.B. Tauris.

———. 2013. *Transformations in Egyptian Journalism*. London: I.B. Tauris.

Saleh, H. 2004. "Egypt's Rulers Struggle with 'New Thinking.'" BBC
News, September 21. http://news.bbc.co.uk/1/hi/world/middle_
east/3676256.stm

Sayigh, Y. 2019. *Owners of the Republic: An Anatomy of Egypt's Military Economy*. Washington, DC: Carnegie Endowment for
International Peace. https://carnegie-mec.org/2019/11/18/
soldiers-and-businessmen-pub-80339.

Vest, J. 2001. "Fourth Generation Warfare." *The Atlantic*, December. https://www.theatlantic.com/magazine/archive/2001/12/
fourth-generation-warfare/302368/

Yasin, S. 2013. "Egyptian Army Shuts Down Media Outlets." Index on
Censorship, July 4. https://www.indexoncensorship.org/2013/07/
egyptian-army-shuts-down-media-outlets/

Webb, E. 2014. *Media in Egypt and Tunisia*. New York: Palgrave
Macmillan.

THE CITY AND THE JUNGLE

AFRICA AND BLACKNESS IN THE EGYPTIAN INTERWAR CINEMATIC IMAGINATION

IFDAL ELSAKET

The murder of George Floyd in 2020 precipitated a flurry of discussion about race in the Arab world.[1] Public personalities expressed horror on social media, tutting at what they saw as an inherently American problem. Whereas long-established solidarity movements were reanimated, producing insightful discussions about race in the Arab world, so were deeply entrenched feelings of unaccountability. In one case, the singer Tania Saleh posted an image of herself in blackface, musing: "I wish I was black, today more than ever" (Osman 2020). Black Palestinian filmmaker Maryam Abu Khaled took to social media to lay out the insidious anti-Blackness that takes place within Arab countries (Reuters 2020). In the present volume, the contributions of Miranda, Hetaba and Habersky, and Hammad remind us that Egyptians' views of blackness as Other have not only a long history, but also deep consequences for the lives of black Egyptians and immigrants.

As many critics have argued, the sudden focus on support for Black lives in the US, or the BLM movement, has obscured a longer tradition of anti-Blackness within the Arab world. There has been a pervasive silence about this history of anti-Blackness, which is only recently changing with the rise of a new cohort of scholars engaging with questions of race and racialization in the Middle East (Watson Institute for International and Public Affairs 2020). Even as attention to anti-Blackness and race expands, there continues to be little academic reckoning with the twentieth-century mediascape and cinematic cultures in which anti-Blackness has proliferated (Powell 2000; Powell 2001; Powell 2003; Gordon 2008).

This chapter explores specific historical iterations of anti-Blackness with a focus on the early Egyptian cinema's experiments with what film scholars refer to as the "jungle" genre (Robinson 2007, 296–98). At the heart of the jungle genre is an imagining of Africa that is both an expression of Egypt's own imperial fantasies and an undeniable reproduction of widespread Hollywood tropes already proliferating in cinemas across the country. There is no doubt that Egypt's relationship to race (and, specifically, the rise of a derisive attitude to Blackness) derives from a complex set of historical circumstances specific to its own history (Powell 2000; Powell 2003; Gordon 2008; Cuno and Walz 2010; Daly 1991). We cannot understand the rise, development, and ever-changing nature of anti-Black sentiment without exploring the sub-Saharan slave trade, racialized forms of domestic labor, colorism, Egypt's imperial expeditions into Sudan and other territories, and highly racialized rhetoric—or the "layering of race," to use Razan Idris's term (Watson Institute for International and Public Affairs 2020)—that have cultivated it. We must recognize the incredible power of a global flow of racialized images and cinematic motifs, which can be traced from Hollywood and that have flowed into Egypt filmmaking.

I will analyze two films, *Wadi al-nugum* (1943) and *Naduga* (1944), to show how, through a fusion of nationalist fantasies of imperial grandeur and Hollywood inspiration, Egyptian filmmakers have helped cultivate stereotypes of Africans as barbaric, violent primitives, and in doing so, seek to enhance the modernity and sophisticated urbanity of Egyptians. In both films, the city is deployed as a central motif of Egyptian modernity, while Africa provides the "other" against which Egyptian urbanity is drawn into sharp focus. The categorization of Egypt as a "country of cities"—with buildings, courthouses, and motorized transport—sits at the very heart of the films' claims to Egyptian modernity. To be "modern" on screen entailed a visual dissociation of Egyptians from Black Africans as well as a conversion of Egyptians into pith-helmet-wearing, gun-strapped conquerors from the city.

By representing Egyptians as imperial adventurers, *Wadi al-nugum* and *Naduga* blurred the lines between the colonized and the colonizers. To be sure, Egyptian cinema-goers were meant to identify not with the African characters, but with the safari-suited, Egyptian imperialists (Powell 2001, 30). This is not surprising. To a large extent, middle-class

Egyptian filmmakers historically have not presented radical cinematic visions of the class and racial underpinnings of power. African characters were the oppositional visions against which Egyptians asserted their claims to modernity, international prestige, and independence. When Black characters were portrayed in the city, it was in less threatening roles: servants, doormen, and butlers. In their representations of Africa, *Naduga* and *Wadi al-nugum* reveal visions of a postcolonial order that was fundamentally racialized in nature. While efforts were made in the 1950s and 1960s, amid a political milieu of African solidarity, to offer the cinema-going public alternative images of Black people, this trend did not last. In the second half of the twentieth century, there has been a reemergence and normalization of lampooning Black characters that continues today.

Africa on the Egyptian Screen

Released in 1943, *Wadi al-nugum* (Valley of the Stars) was the first Egyptian jungle film. Fusing together animal scenes, tribal drumming, and pith-helmeted scholars, the film follows anthropologist 'Adli (played by Mahmud Dhul-Faqar) as he conducts field research in Wadi al-nugum, a fictional island off the coast of northeastern Africa. With camera, notebook, and gun in hand, 'Adli encounters an African ceremony in which a tribe is sacrificing a woman to a sorcerer. 'Adli enthusiastically photographs the event for his research. Suddenly, the woman being sacrificed, Zaynab (played by 'Aziza Amir), begs for mercy in Egyptian Arabic. Upon hearing her Arabic cries for help, 'Adli swells with nationalist passion and saves her. His intervention incites the fury of the sorcerer and tribesmen, who give chase. Through a clever escape plan, 'Adli leaves the Valley of the Stars and takes Zaynab back with him to Cairo, where the film takes on a melodramatic story of love and revenge.

While *Naduga*'s plot differs somewhat—and can be described more as an adventure comedy—it also depicts a quest for a lost Egyptian woman in the African jungle. Featuring tribal scenes, wild animals, and bare-chested Black porters, the film follows Murad, who sets off into the jungle to find Nadya, the long-lost daughter and sole heir of Murad's late employer, Khurshid Pasha. Nadya was lost during her father's stint in Africa as a physician. Murad is accompanied by two clumsy assistants, comically named Khamis (Thursday) and Jum'a (Friday). When, during his journey into the jungle, Murad notices a photograph of a "white girl" (*bint bayda*)—note the immediate racialization—he insists it must be Nadya. Soon Murad encounters Naduga, a feisty woman clad in a fashionable floral swimming costume and protected by a gorilla named Cheetah. Murad realizes that she is, in fact, Nadya, and falls in love with her. But her greedy cousins, who covet her father's inheritance, thwart his efforts to bring her back to Egypt. After foiling her cousins' plans, Nadya/Naduga returns to Egypt, inherits her father's fortune, and lives happily with Murad, a trope centralizing family at the heart of sexual/affective morality, which Abed's chapter of the present volume reminds us is still very much a part of contemporary Egyptian imaginaries.

If the storylines and motifs seem familiar, there's a good reason why. Both *Wadi al-nugum* and *Naduga* adapted an already popular American jungle-film genre, of which Tarzan was the most successful iteration. Certain scenes from *Wadi al-nugum*, especially the tribal scenes, appear strikingly similar to scenes from the 1932 American film *Birds of Paradise*. *Naduga*'s title, and parts of its plot, were also similar to the American film *Nabonga* and even featured a similar gorilla character. Both films were released around the same time and indicate a global exchange of plots, motifs, and title names. Although it is unclear how this exchange functioned, what is clear is that Egyptian cinema-goers throughout the twentieth century consumed American films and were exposed to American racial tropes of white superiority and African barbarity.

At the time of their release, very little debate appeared in the press about the issue of race in films or in broader visual culture. In fact, during the 1930s, magazines often published racist cartoons depicting Black people as servants and lacking the smarts and sophistication of Egyptians. Tarzan films continued to be among the most popular films screened in Egypt, with Tarzan becoming a recognizable cultural icon. Johnny Weissmuller was a household name; his face and Tarzan poses regularly appeared in newspapers and magazines. In 1933, the back cover of the fan magazine *al-Kawakib* featured a bare-chested Weissmuller in a pose that alluded to the interwar primitivist fantasies of virile white men (*al-Kawakib* 1933). But *Wadi al-nugum* and *Naduga* not only deployed Hollywoodesque visual cues; they also relied on nationalist imaginings of Africa that were plugged into a global "dark continent" discourse central to imperialist discourse.

The idea of "Africa," as it was elsewhere, has historically been central to constructions of modernity and claims to civilization in Egypt, as Hammad's comments (this volume) on the ethnic organization of brothel hierarchies in the 1910s to 1940s illustrate. Middle-class reformers and politicians have desperately sought to fight imperial claims of Egyptian backwardness by asserting their modernity and racial superiority. A growing film industry expanded the possibilities of these claims, promising a global platform for the circulation of images of modern Egypt. In the 1920s Talaat Harb, the industrialist economist who headed Egypt's national bank and who, under its auspices, established the national film company, the Misr Company for Acting and Cinema, even argued that films could dispel any misconceptions that Egyptians were like "people of Central Africa" (Hasan 1986: 90–92). In Harb's imagination, Central Africa was the antithesis of the modern, and the embodiment of barbarism. The very idea of "Africa" functioned as a rhetorical tool in Harb's attempts to claim modernity for Egypt on the international stage. It is this image of Africa that *Wadi al-nugum* and *Naduga* elucidate and elaborate.

In *Wadi al-nugum* and *Naduga*, "Africa" is depicted as a perilous jungle-dense terrain. Ethnographic archival footage of wild animals (whether or not native to Africa, including large snakes, monkeys, bats, alligators, and tigers) reinforces the image of Africa as untamed, as does footage of dense jungle and sturdy vines from which to swing. Drumming and dancing take place around a fire, as characters played by Black actors (and others clearly in blackface) chant and drop recognizable terms like "Congo" and "Africana." In *Wadi al-nugum*, Black men menacingly point spears at the camera as others frantically drum and dance.

In both *Wadi al-nugum* and *Naduga*, the local Black characters, aside from the loyal servants and the tribal leaders, are voiceless. While ethnic classifications remain ambiguous, fusing Polynesian and African tropes, Egyptian characters simply refer to the locals as "*wuhush*" (savages). In *Naduga*, Khamis and Jum'a plead with Murad not to fight the natives after they had threatened to kill him, because "they are nasty, they would do it." In *Wadi al-nugum*, 'Adli described the locals as *wuhush* during his nationalist-inspired rescue of Zaynab. In response to pleas from his adventure sidekick not to interfere in the tribe's affairs, 'Adli, with a gun in hand, retorts: "Should I leave my sister in the hands of *wuhush*?"

References to the alleged cannibalism of the Black characters are scattered throughout *Wadi al-nugum* and *Naduga*, and work to further distance them from Egypt's claims to civilization. In *Naduga*, Murad's goofy aides, Khamis and Jum'a, repeatedly express fear of being eaten in the jungle. In one scene, the loyal African guide, Cougar, joins in the Egyptians' jokes about his own cannibalism. In jest, Khamis and Jum'a describe what they would do to the greedy cousin should they get their hands on him: they speak of undressing him, cleaning him, marinating him, cooking him, then handing him over to Cougar, who at this point replies in a thick Arabic accent, "and Cougar will eat his flesh and suck his bones," to rapturous laughter. Later in the film, during a confrontation between Murad and the angry tribes, Khamis expresses fear of being eaten by the tribes when he cries: "They will make *mulukhiya* [an Egyptian dish made from jute leaves] from our stock." In *Wadi al-nugum*, Zaynab's association with Africa makes her a target for cannibalism claims. When she bites 'Adli's assistant on the ship, 'Adli asks: "Are you planning to have us for lunch or what?" When 'Adli's assistant tells friends about their trip, she claims that inhabitants of the island "eat people. I saw them with my own eyes roasting a man." In both films, cannibalism and allusions to it further position African characters outside the realms of modern living and humanity.

Country of Cities

In these films, images of "Africa" and "Africans" attempted to bring into sharp relief Egypt's modernity, in which the city's luxuries and security are central. "We are not in the jungle any more, we are going to Egypt, a country with laws and police," 'Adli remarks in *Wadi al-nugum*. From at least the early 1930s, representations of the city have functioned as a key motif with which Egyptian characters have laid claim to superiority and power. Filmmakers especially gravitated to a broader trend that equated modern life to city life and argued that the very production of films introduced Egypt onto the global stage as an urban, sophisticated nation. A recurring theme in early Egyptian film criticism was whether a film fulfilled its "duty" to represent Egypt as a modern nation and effectively counter negative representations of Egyptians. The duty of representation in early film criticism hinged on a broader nationalist attempt to prove Egypt's worthiness for independence (Mitchell 1988).

Niazi Mustafa, the director of *Wadi al-nugum*, expressed similar beliefs in the power of the cinema to represent Egypt positively abroad, arguing that it constituted "a weapon to refute all that the biased/prejudiced foreigners" say about Egypt (Mustafa 1933, 8, 10). It is no surprise, then, that *Wadi al-nugum* dwelt on Egypt's modernity—see Sinno, this volume, for more contemporary iterations of this trope. The Africa scenes in *Wadi al-nugum* only take up the first twenty-four minutes of the film, after which scenes take place in the modern facilities of the ship transporting the main characters back to Egypt. During the trip, the antics of Zaynab, referred to as "Tarzan's daughter," both horrify and amuse the civilized Egyptians, as she bites, growls, and gobbles down food without using utensils. Of course, 'Adli is there to coax her back to civilization. When Zaynab cries out that she saw the sorcerer, 'Adli rebukes her with the line: "We are not in the jungle any more. We are going to Egypt, a country with laws and police."

In *Naduga*, while far more action takes place in the jungle, modern life in Cairo appears cyclically at the start, repeating as a repose and a safe space at the end. The film also constructs the courtroom and the concept of justice as underpinning the entire trip into the jungle; it is a space of bureaucracy and law. It is only after being granted time, by a judge, to search for the lost Nadya that Murad pursues her.

In *Wadi al-nugum*, as the returned adventurers happily drive through Cairo, Zaynab is stunned and afraid of what she sees: tall buildings, trams, trucks. She fearfully ducks in the front seat, amusing her modern friends. The car scene, shot in downtown Cairo, includes footage of the high court, neo-modernist buildings, and street scenes. After a dinner party—ruined after Zaynab bites a guest—Zaynab insists that she is "*bint nas*" (the expression literally means "a daughter of people" but is referring to a certain type of middle/upper-class woman). The dialogue points again to a deep dichotomy that necessitates a distance from the "jungle people." "Why do they laugh at me and fear me? Am I not a human being like them? I am also a *bint nas*." Zaynab insists on her identity, only to be replied to by 'Adli's mother: "You call those people in the jungle 'people'?" In disbelief and sadness, Zaynab snaps back, "I am not from the jungle. I am from Egypt, and my mother and father are Egyptians, like you exactly." Zaynab fights against any presumption that she is anything other than Egyptian, and in doing so concedes to the dehumanization of "jungle people."

Naduga similarly sets up Egypt as an urban oasis. When Murad describes life in Egypt to the fascinated and naive Naduga/Nadya as they sit by a river (surrounded by plastic alligators), he exuberantly comments, "Egypt is far, far away. We must ride a ship to arrive in Egypt . . . Egypt, filled with people, roads, cities, buildings, cars—hoot hoot hoot— trams—clang clang clang—and [newspaper] vendors [yelling]: "*al-Ahram, al-Muqattam, al-Musawwir, al-Ithnayn*. Egypt! Long live Egypt!" When Naduga/Nadya's guardian is paid off by the cousins to get rid of Murad and his friends, he tells Murad, "You have defiled this pure/good land, O son of modernity/civilization (*ya wilad al-madaniya*). Leave immediately, you and your devils." In trying to convince Naduga of the vileness of city life, the same guardian expresses distaste with what had earlier been called the "hell of modernity/civilization" (*jahim al-madaniya*). He chides Naduga for wanting to "go to the country of cities (*bilad al-madayin*) and live in the clamour with a people who worship money, and who are like fish: the large one eats the small, the brother kills his own brother, the friend betrays his friend." He then asks, "Will you leave, O Naduga, the beauty of nature, and the love of nature, and replace love with remorse-lessness . . . and freedom for slavery?" Taken out of context, such lines may express an underlying primitivism and a condemnation of the moral bankruptcy of urban living. But despite the perceived profundity of the film's anti-modern attacks, an unlikeable character who hypocritically accepted the bribes—a bag of gold—from the cousins, is the one to artic-ulate them. Indeed, expressions such as "son of modernity/civilization," "country of cities," and "hell of modernity/civilization" further position Egypt as a rational, industrial, and fundamentally urban nation. Any hint of primitivism is offset by the glitter of the modern, the urban, and the dizzying love for the luxuries of city life.

Blackness in the City

In *Wadi al-nugum* and *Naduga*, Black characters who move in urban spaces are relegated to the role of servants or butlers—tame, servile, and unthreatening. The characters are often said to be Nubian or Suda-nese—reflecting a continued stereotype of domestic labor in Egypt. In *Wadi al-nugum*, 'Adli's nationalist-inspired impulse to save the Egyptian woman from the "*wuhush*" (barbarians) comes after his butler pleads with him not to interfere in the affairs of the tribe, arguing that the woman might "just be a Sudanese girl." Indignant, 'Adli snaps back: "The Suda-nese woman is my sister exactly like the Egyptian. The one Nile unites us, and if I do not defend her when she is in trouble, I would be a coward . . . and I would not deserve to be an Egyptian."

'Adli's claims to both masculinity and Egyptianness rest on his res-cue of the potentially Sudanese woman. It is important to note that 'Adli's sidekick is his Sudanese servant (played by Mohammad Kamil, who was typecast in this role). It takes an Egyptian to remind his Suda-nese counterpart of their unity. 'Adli's reprimand of his Sudanese servant and his ironic insistence on their unity embodies the tension that has underlined cinematic representation of Sudan. In Egyptian films, while Black characters were indeed part of the nation, they were not equal compatriots, but servants. Sudanese and Nubian characters (identified by their accents) played the role of domestics, butlers, or doormen. Countless Egyptian films have incorporated Sudanese or Nubian ser-vants. They include *Rabha* (1943), *Qalbi dalili* [My Heart Is My Guide] (1947), *Layla bint madaris* [Layla the Schoolgirl] (1941), *Layla* (1942), *Si 'Umar* [Mr. 'Umar] (1941), and *Layla bint al-akabir* [Layla, Daughter of

Aristocrats] (1953). Cinematic depictions of the Sudanese or Nubians as servants were not new to the Egyptian entertainment industry, but can be traced back to late nineteenth-century and early twentieth-century Egyptian theatrical productions (Powell 2003, 64–104, 168–216). The effects the deep penetration these tropes have had in Egyptian popular culture can be seen in the prejudices faced by Sudanese immigrants and refugees in Egypt today, as documented by Hetaba and Habersky and Miranda's chapters in this volume.

Following the analysis of Cedric Robinson, we can clearly see here that depictions of the Black servant and the Black tribesperson are closely related (Robinson 2007, 298). *Naduga* and *Wadi al-nugum* teased the boundaries between melodrama and jungle films in a way that unites the two images of Black characters. In both films, the jungle remains untamed. Black people there remain a threat to be killed or co-opted. In Egypt, Black characters exist as domestic tools, slotted into the hierarchies of home and further alienated from urban life. If the jungle genre depicted the racial struggle between Egyptians and Africans, then the shift to a melodramatic genre declared victory in the domesticated finale.

Postrevolutionary Representations

Representations of Africans changed after the 1952 revolution as the new regime propagated a strict anti-colonial ideology (Gordon 2008, 67–90). From around the mid-1960s, the Ministry of Culture even banned American-produced Tarzan films because they reflected a "colonialist outlook" (Pace 1968, 115.) The ministry lifted the ban in 1968, with stern warnings that such films would remain under the watchful eye of the censorship board.

Egyptian filmmakers dramatically shifted film representations of Sudan and dropped older stereotypes of Black Africa. The Sudanese–Egyptian Niazi Mustafa, who directed *Wadi al-nugum*, used the new political milieu after the revolution to overturn the negative images he previously had produced. In 1958, Niazi Mustafa directed his second jungle film, *Isma'il Yasin Tarazan*, which represented a more modern image of Sudan, reflecting a new phase in the Egyptian–Sudanese relationship (Gordon 2008, 147–51). In the film, the traditional motifs of the jungle genre—the tribal dancers around a fire and threatening Black people—did not appear. By revolving around the quest to find the lost heir to an Egyptian millionaire's fortunes, *Isma'il Yasin Tarazan* defined the Egyptian character's journey to Sudan as one motivated by economic greed, and by doing so, it took a subtle swipe at the real motivations of Egyptian excursions into Sudan. But in comparison to Mustafa's previous jungle film, *Wadi al-nugum*, *Isma'il Yasin Tarazan* functioned as a powerful critique of the power dynamics that had informed older Egyptian cinematic representations of Africa.

While the 1952 revolution and the end of British colonialism did not entail a radical rejection of anti-Black stereotyping in Egyptian cinematic culture, they did open up the possibility of reinventing Egypt's relationship with Africa through a reconsideration of the colonialist image. However, nothing changed structurally. Problematic Tarzanesque images persisted in Egyptian popular culture. Perhaps the apotheosis of this persistence was an image on the cover of *al-Musawwir* in February 1954 depicting Free Officer Salah Salim in shorts swinging from a tree in the "jungles of the South" and his Egyptian companion, the colonel Gamal Thabit, clasping his hands around his mouth in a Tarzan war-cry pose. The caption read: "An Egyptian Tarzan in Sudan" (*al-Musawwir* 1954). In 1953, while Muhammad Naguib bolstered Sudanese–Egyptian unity, child star Fayruz and one of the biggest male stars of the time, Anwar Wagdi, engaged in an offensive blackface scene in one of the year's biggest movies. Although there were efforts to curb the trend, and throughout the 1960s critics paid particular attention to race in films, anti-Black images and the marking of Africa as a site of adventure, danger, and comic relief continued to shape visual practices throughout the twentieth and twenty-first centuries.

Conclusion

Anti-Blackness has manifested in various ways in Egyptian cinematic culture, whether through blackface performances, jokes about Blackness, or the promotion of white standards of beauty. This chapter explores one iteration of anti-Blackness by examining the jungle–city dichotomy that was at the heart of Egyptian imagining of Blackness and of Egypt as representative of urban modernity. Central to interwar Egyptian claims to modernity and urban sophistication were images of "Africa" as wild, untamed, and in need of conquering. Early Egyptian representations of Blackness played into these notions, functioning at the intersection of global visual tropes inspired by dominant Hollywood images. *Wadi al-nugum* and *Naduga* overturned representations of Egypt's colonial dependency with fantasies of imperial power. Using the same representational motifs that governed Egypt's own colonization—crude stereotypes, binaries between barbarian natives and sophisticated white-collar adventurers—*Wadi al-nugum* and *Naduga* constituted affirmative celebrations of Egyptian civilization and modernity. The films provide important case studies for the role of race in the making of a modern Egypt, calling attention to how cinema was deeply implicated in histories of anti-Blackness that continue today. The films also invite us, by way of widening the scope of research, to interrogate more seriously the role that representations of Africa and anti-Blackness have played in visions of national liberation.

Notes
1   This chapter is a revisiting, expansion, and adaptation of Elsaket 2017.

Works Cited

'Abd al-Fattah, Muhammad. 2005. *Sinima Niazi Mustafa*. Cairo: al-Hay'a al-'Amma li-Qusur al-Thaqafa.

Ahmad, Anwar. 1952. "Al-Sudan fi aflamina." *Al-Kawakib*, December 9.

Cuno, Kenneth M., and Terence Walz, eds. 2010. *Race and Slavery in the Middle East: Histories of Trans-Saharan Africans in Nineteenth-century Egypt, Sudan, and the Ottoman Mediterranean*. Cairo: American University in Cairo Press.

Daly, M.W. 1991. *Imperial Sudan: The Anglo-Egyptian Condominium, 1934–1956*. Cambridge: Cambridge University Press.

Elsaket, Ifdal. 2017. "Jungle Films in Egypt: Race, Anti-Blackness, and Empire." *Arab Studies Journal* 25, no. 2: 8–33.

Fawzi, Husayn. 1944. *Naduga*. Cairo: Nahas Films.

Gordon, Joel. 2008. "River Blindness: Black and White Identity in Early Nasserist Cinema." In *Narrating the Nile: Politics, Cultures, Identities*, edited by Israel Gershoni and Meir Hatina, 67–90. London: Lynne Rienner Publishers.

Hasan, Ilhami. 1986. *Mohammad Talaat Harb: ra'id sina'at al-sinima al-misriya, 1867–1941*. Cairo: al-Hay'a al-Misriya al-'Amma li-l-Kitab.

Husayn, Uthman. 1952. "Nasib al-Sudan fi al-aflam al-misriya." *Al-Kawakib*, October 14, 11.

Jacob, Wilson Chacko. 2005. "The Masculine Subject of Colonialism: The Egyptian Loss of the Sudan." In *African Masculinities: Men in Africa from the Late Nineteenth Century to the Present*, edited by Robert Morrell and Lahoucine Ouzgane, 153–69. New York: Palgrave Macmillan.

al-Kawakib. 1933. June 5 issue, back cover.

Lopez, Shaun. 2009. "Football as National Allegory: *Al-Ahram* and the Olympics in 1920s Egypt." *History Compass* 7, no. 1: 297–300.

Mitchell, Timothy. 1988. *Colonising Egypt.* Berkeley: University of California Press.

Al-Musawwir. 1954. February 5 issue, photographs on pages 9, 14, and front cover.

Mustafa, Niazi. 1933. "Al-Sinima fi khidmat al-umma." *Fann al-sinima*, December 23.

———. 1943. *Wadi al-nugum.* Cairo: Sharikat Aflam 'Aziza Amir, Isis Films.

Osman, Nadda. 2020. "'Blackface' Arab Stars Spark Backlash over Tasteless Solidarity with US Protests." *Middle East Eye*, June 3.

Pace, Eric. 1968. "Cairo is Willing to Let Tarzan Films Return." *New York Times*, November 24, 115.

Powell, Eve Marie Troutt. 2000. "Egyptian Concepts of Race and Ethnicity: 1895–1910." In *The Nile: History, Cultures, Myths*, edited by Haggai Erlich and Israel Gershoni Boulder, 171–81. London: Lynne Rienner Publishers.

———. 2001. "Burnt-cork Nationalism: Race and Identity in the Theatre of 'Ali al-Kassar." In *Colors of Enchantment: Theatre, Dance, and the Visual Arts of the Middle East*, edited by Sherifa Zuhur, 27–38. Cairo: American University in Cairo Press.

———. 2003. *A Different Shade of Colonialism: Egypt, Great Britain and the Mastery of the Sudan.* Berkeley: University of California.

———. 2012. *Tell This in My Memory: Stories of Enslavement from Egypt, Sudan, and the Ottoman Empire.* Redwood City, CA: Stanford University Press.

Reuters. 2020. "Black Arab Women Confront Racist Beauty Ideals." *The National*, June 23. https://www.thenationalnews.com/world/mena/black-arab-women-confront-racist-beauty-ideals-1.1038168

Robinson, C.J. 2007. *Forgeries of Memory and Meaning: Blacks and the Regimes of Race in American Theater and Film before World War II.* Chapel Hill: University of North Carolina Press.

Watson Institute for International and Public Affairs. 2020. "Racialization and Racism in the Middle East: Historical Perspectives." Webinar, October 30. https://www.youtube.com/watch?v=OzwUn b73ghQ&feature=youtu.be

4

VIRAL VISUALITIES, IMAGE CYCLES, AND MOSIREEN'S REVOLUTIONARY ARCHIVES

MARK R. WESTMORELAND

As many authors of this collection relate (Khalil, Ahmed, Awadalla, and Fallas, among others), the uprisings and downfalls across the Arab world that began to unfold at the end of 2010 marked a watershed moment in Egyptian history for the growth of all sorts of popular movements and initiatives.[1] They also provided fertile territory for citizen journalists and activist filmmakers to document both the assembling of mass protests and the atrocities of state violence. In Egypt, images played an unprecedented role during the initial uprising—from the frenetic scenes of spectacular violence to the online circulation of vernacular images, to the rescreening of protest videos on the streets, to the handmade posters that provided English captions for foreign viewers of the events. Most of the people drawn to these street protests with their cameras had been neither politically active nor skilled in newsmaking beforehand. And yet, the videos they shot and shared provided the main source of information for people across the globe before the major news outlets arrived on the scene (Nanabhay and Farmanfarmaian 2011). The dominant narrative in global media quickly became about "Revolution 2.0" (Ghonim 2012) and the capabilities of new mobile, interconnected digital technology. Cellphone cameras enabled an unaffiliated network of filmers to easily document and upload their videos—both for viewers only a few blocks away and for audiences watching thousands of miles from the scene, although only a small number of these videos went truly viral. However, the collective recording of these events—producing thousands of videos from a multiplicity of perspectives—provided momentary street-level glimpses of mass movements (Westmoreland 2016).

Although the videos circulating on social media and televised on satellite networks bore witness to the unprecedented events unfolding from a variety of vantage points, the shared exhilaration of these rebellious images often gave way to fleeting sensationalism. This mediated phenomenon mistakenly decontextualized images from the spontaneous and improvised practices that created, collected, curated, and continued to care for them in the weeks, months, and years ahead. Despite being largely uncoordinated acts, the process of shooting video and uploading it online is an important context for thinking through the range of filmmaking practices needed to create and sustain an unaffiliated record of the revolution (Westmoreland 2020). As Alisa Lebow (2018c) notes, "It was crucial not only that there were cameras there to document it but that there was a place where that material would be stored, to be used to contest the government claims." Disconnecting these practices from celebratory discourses about social media helps bring the mundane features of the revolutionary archive into focus.

The Street View

Many activists in Egypt risked their lives to empower "the voice of a street-level perspective" (Aboubakr 2013). The streets of Cairo provided the stage for the carnivalesque aspects of the uprisings (Mehrez 2012) and became the site of the subsequent formation of a new public culture (Abaza 2014) that was potentialized by the relative democratization of the Egyptian media, social and otherwise, of previous years, as Abed documents in her chapter in this book. The street was also the scene of horrific battles in its role as "the modern urban theater of contention par excellence" (Bayat 2013). These were not the riotous mob of the "Arab Street," but were indicative of "those with enough of a cause to put their life at risk."[2] As the chaotic street is something that the elite wish to conceal—as both a symptom and symbol of social inequality— the hypervisibility of the street in times of protest makes image-making practices both threatening and powerful. Drawing upon the notion of "everyday cosmopolitanism," in which people must negotiate difference on a routine basis, the street becomes not merely a space or platform for politics, but "a complex entity wherein sentiments and outlooks are formed, spread and expressed in a unique fashion" (Bayat 2003). While indicative of the everyday sphere where people work and perform their routines, the street is simultaneously a public sphere where people negotiate resources and ideas, a hostile zone filled with human and non-human refuse, a site of contempt from which privileged classes retreat into malls (Abaza 2006) and coffee shops (Koning 2006), and (whether evoked as the "Arab Street" or the revolutionary multitude) also a political subject in itself.

Among the various encampments occupying the middle of Tahrir Square in 2011 (Mollerup and Gaber 2015), a makeshift structure emerged called the Media Tent. Here, witnesses could pool their records with the ambition of collecting visible evidence for future trials (Raoof 2011). Various practitioners, journalists, and media activists congregated here to compile video clips and testimonies. Among various forms of collective action mobilized in this liminal moment, the Media Tent became a site to channel the photos and videos being collectively produced in the square (and beyond). This initial archive of collective action provided materials to international media producers absent from some of the most important events. But following the ouster of entrenched President Hosni Mubarak, when most of the global news coverage had moved on despite the regime continuing to violently suppress dissent, those who had connected in the Media Tent realized that the continuing revolution would need to be documented by the people participating in it (Abdalla 2018).

Many activists gained resolve in the turbulent months that followed, with varying efforts to reoccupy the streets (Abdalla 2018). Among a variety of citizen journalist efforts and activist collectives, Mosireen proved to be one of the more significant for their well-organized, multifaceted, and coordinated efforts (Stuhr-Rommereim 2011). Brought together around a shared belief in the basic tenets of the revolution ("bread, freedom, and social justice") and that "media should always be confrontational toward power," the Mosireen media collective was constituted around fifteen core members within a larger network of contributors and supporters (Gaber 2018c). Mosireen's "first mission was to collect and preserve of [sic] as much digital memory of the initial 18 Days as possible" (Hamilton 2017). On the scene during the army's horrifying massacre outside the Maspero state television headquarters, Mosireen's first edited film—uploaded to YouTube as "The Maspero Massacre" (Mosireen Collective 2011)—crystallized their imperative to cover the politics of the street (Mosireen Collective 2017d).

Mosireen (meaning "determined ones," and a play on the Arabic word for Egyptians, *misriyin*) provided a key example of media activism committed to radically new political formations. Devoted to horizontal structures of nonhierarchical authorship and management, they refused outside funding or sponsorship, and found local support to offer training and equipment to anyone interested in contributing to the demand for camera-mediated activism. Their vision of social change remained resolutely revolutionary as they focused on documenting street protests, worker strikes, and mass sit-ins. From their crowdsourced material, the collective produced dozens of short videos covering different issues and events specifically from the perspective of the street, many of which featured in mainstream news.

As Mosireen's video archive grew, so too did their membership and initiatives, from producing and uploading videos to training programs for activists elsewhere in Egypt. By January 2012, Mosireen briefly became the most viewed nonprofit YouTube channel in the world and generated a significant online following with their video coverage of major battles and massacres (Trew 2012). It was arguably more effective when redirecting the power of digital media to more public spaces. They emphatically placed their emphasis on addressing the local population, the street, holding impromptu public screenings in Tahrir Square and elsewhere (Mollerup and Gaber 2015; Westmoreland 2016). By taking digital material back to the street, activist groups like Mosireen and Askar Kazibun could address people directly and thus transcend, in small measure, some of the impediments of the digital and literacy divides. During the July 2011 sit-in, which would be forcibly dispersed by military police on August 1, activists realized that many protesters had never seen "the iconic images from the initial 18 days of uprising across Egypt" (Mollerup and Gaber 2015). They set up a projector and started screening that footage.[3] Drawing revolutionary footage out of the ephemeral cloud of social media, they replayed it back on the streets. Mosireen "disseminated [their] images through flash drives, CDs, and Bluetooth connections in an attempt to use new methods to get our images into different spaces: living rooms, coffee shops, university dorms, or further street screenings" (Rizk 2013). As with the Media Tent in Tahrir Square during the initial protests, these screenings also facilitated the donation of footage to be screened and incorporated into Mosireen's growing digital archive. The circular movement between online and offline activism still maintains "the centrality of street activism" (Aboubakr 2013). Emphasizing the street as the site of viewing also spoke to the crucial task of getting people on the street through the protracted revolutionary period that extended into the summer of 2013.

Unlike the packaged analysis of news coverage or the aerial perspective that became iconic of Tahrir (Westmoreland 2016), activist street screenings typically featured either visceral footage of street protests and battles or personal testimonies of "military trials, torture and mistreatment at the hands of security forces" (Taher 2011). By accepting "open submissions" from people on the street, "Tahrir Cinema informed and raised discussion among demonstrators" (Schoene 2012). Noting the "difference between watching TV and seeing something that has been filmed by someone just like you," the initiative provides "a feeling of possession" (Stuhr-Rommereim 2011). These screenings often offered moments of personal recognition, "when a clip from the morning of 10 April showed young men displaying the bullet casings they found on the ground after the military cleared the square the night before, one spectator was prompted to stand up and tell his parallel story" (Stuhr-Rommereim 2011).

The dialogic dimension also allowed for "heated debate," however (Enders 2012). One activist recounted to me the way provocative scenes generated discussions about the veracity and possible manipulation of footage. The corporeally shared experience of danger and resistance enabled these street screenings to harness a transformative power (Mollerup and Gaber 2015). These screenings of "sensuous struggle" apparently had the ability to provoke spontaneous marches, enacting what Jane Gaines calls "political mimesis" (1999), in which "people go from unresponsive bystanders to active participants in a political demonstration in the course of a screening" (Mollerup and Gaber 2015). The impromptu and spontaneous nature of these images, combined with their shared assembly and collective identity, added to the sense of potentiality that anything was possible, until it wasn't.

The Weight of the Revolution

Online attention and public outreach led to an exponential growth in Mosireen's donations, and the initial collection from the Tahrir Media Tent quickly grew by several terabytes (spread over a series of hard drives). With only a small portion of the archive materials available in their online videos, the ambition to make the archive fully accessible (online) emerged early in the group's formation. But the magnitude of the collection, combined with a host of complicated ethical issues, saddled Mosireen with a monumental burden as the custodians of the so-called archive of the revolution.[4] Inexperienced with managing large data collections and facing a continual influx of new material, Mosireen struggled to implement best practices in data management. Initially, a simple date and author folder structure enabled some level of organization, but these efforts had to be completed piecemeal as they were constantly responding to an unstable and dynamic political context. When editing their own videos or trying to provide content upon request, they had to rely on the distributed memory of the collective to identify the correct hard drive and file. While committed to tagging and indexing the materials, they recognized the messiness as integral to the conditions of this archive and sought ways to "preserve the disorderliness" (Gaber 2018a).

Furthermore, they did not want the archive to serve simplistic purposes of merely depositing material into a repository. Rather, they critically engaged the collection "as a tool in the struggle" to understand the events within a broader context of rapidly shifting political conditions (Gaber 2018b). One of the affordances of having such a massive collection was the ability to imagine different kinds of engagements. They aspired to activate an online archive in which user-generated annotations would form the basis of generative queries that could help rethink the problem. They began with extremely granular concrete variables that can be traced through the archive irrespective of conventional organizational schemes. This analytical approach to the archive enacts a "cybernetic storyteller" as a generator of narratives and arguments, new political situations, and analytical agencies without prefigured connections. This model flips the YouTube and Google algorithm, "which organizes material in ways that prioritize the new and the sensational, making it difficult if not impossible to find artifacts from the past, even the recent past" (Lebow 2018b).

Unlike a repository hidden in the stacks where documents collect dust, Mosireen's ideal for the archive required open access. This demonstrated their commitment to deliver stories and images entrusted to them by the people of the street. And yet, Mosireen felt burdened by their collection of images and the magnitude of their responsibility to bring the images back to the people—not specific individuals, but a more collective sense of those revolutionaries that took to the streets to fight for justice, many losing life or limb. Access also presents infrastructural challenges to address the demands of delivering thirty days of footage to the servers in an organized manner, not to mention designing an interface to facilitate jumping down the euphemistic rabbit holes. The pernicious and multifaceted issues with access remain at the core of this and other archives of the Arab uprisings.

Furthermore, giving the archival footage an online Creative Commons license means that it can be freely appropriated for counter-revolutionary purposes. Access by nefarious parties can expose people to persecution, particularly in the wake of what Elmeshad describes, in their chapter above, as the effective re-statization of the Egyptian media and the expansion of its control into digitalized social media spheres (Abed, this volume). In fact, the viability of the archive required hiding it from authorities, making duplicates to be stored in different locations, and restricting access "on the basis of networks of trust that seem . . . to be frail and unreliable" (Lebow 2018d). As Alisa Lebow has argued in her Filming Revolution project,[5] the various unofficial efforts to produce "a people's archive of the revolution" present the same dilemma on an official level. This is evident even in the effort to create an official archive of the revolution, headed by historian Khaled Fahmy, in which "access to any official State archive in Egypt . . . requires that the researcher get permission from State security" (Lebow 2018c). While imagined to be an archive for the people, it became clear that the information gathered therein would likely be used by the state against those who participated in the revolution (Lebow 2018a).

This question of how to balance their commitment to free access with the protection of people's identities grew increasingly difficult. After years had passed and different regimes moved through power in Egypt, the notion of consent presented another problematic issue to address. Nothing has remained static or stable. Someone's politics at the time of donating footage may have radically shifted. This is even more challenging when considering those imaged in the footage. Mosireen recognized that these issues cannot be completely resolved. They place the burden on others to contact them with requests for removal. That said, part of the arduous process of preparing the footage for public accessibility meant sorting through it, culling and withholding material that would clearly put people at risk. While the footage may reveal compromising evidence, it was commonly understood that everything was being recorded at the time. Furthermore, as often demonstrated, "the State in Egypt does not seem to need hard evidence in order to detain or imprison those it deems dangerous, and thus it might not make much sense to worry about providing them with such evidence" (Lebow 2018a).

Already exhausted and losing focus, the upswell of popular support for the army to remove the Muslim Brotherhood in 2013 left those critical of both ruling parties without a defensible position. Though many of the Mosireen members may not have known it at the time, inertia had already sealed their fate (Mosireen Collective 2017b). After the Rabaa massacre in August 2013, where hundreds of Muslim Brotherhood supporters were murdered on live television, Mosireen was silent. The filmmakers reported, "we had no response. We were not there, we had not risked our lives to film it. We had fallen out of the equation of power in the stand-off between the Army and the Brotherhood. We were powerless and yet we felt complicit. We were racked by a confusion and guilt and impotence. We sat stunned in our office day after day, smoking, silenced" (Mosireen Collective 2017c). While committed to radically new political formations, the collective had to change tactics under the Abd al-Fattah al-Sisi regime. And as the revolutionary period collapsed, Mosireen became even more burdened by the custodial responsibility of what had become ostensibly the largest video archive of the revolution, particularly for its now silenced perspective from the street protests.

Facing Posterity

In the subsequent years, Mosireen struggled to maintain momentum. All their strategies up to that point lost traction. Energy in the collective dissipated. The exhilaration of witnessing something truly emancipatory with real potential for change confronted sentimental nostalgia, leading them to begin asking themselves if "what happened meant anything at all?" (Gaber 2014). While the group tried to reconcile its "post mortem" state vis-à-vis a failed revolution, researchers and journalists continued to laud Mosireen for its achievements as a success story. Following the publication of its final video in February 2015 (Mosireen Collective 2015), one laments, "this video feels, to me, like little more than a symptom of a moment of desperation as we became lost in the endless swamp of the judiciary's counter-revolution" (Mosireen Collective 2017a). Filming on the streets was no longer viable and releasing new videos on social media became senseless.

The unrealized burden of delivering the archive to the people of the street in many ways epitomized the larger sense of failure. Procrastination and neglect became understandable responses to the tedious tasks of organizing and viewing thousands of videos of people and events that no longer remained, not to mention having to relive horrific scenes of violence. But these circumstances did not absolve Mosireen of their promise to make the archive accessible based on a shared expectation that the archive with all its parts is not merely a repository, but an "arsenal" that must be activated. In those hopeless years, the fate of their archive, now 12TB in size with over thirty continuous days of footage, provided a faint beacon of hope in the throes of defeat: "soon the full archive, the raw, unedited archive will be online and open for anyone, for everyone, to step in and make the next [film]" (Mosireen Collective 2017a).

The story of the Mosireen archive may ultimately be a testament to the perseverance of noble ideals and the hope for political reactivation. The idea of publishing the Mosireen archive languished, progressing slowly in fits and spurts. After struggling for seven years to make the archive accessible, a half dozen or so members organized archiving retreats in 2016 and 2017 to force themselves to sit down and work through the materials. With technical support provided by members of the Pad.ma open-source video archive, they designed front- and back-end elements of an archival platform to actualize their long-awaited goals.

But another and ultimately more abstract question that confronted the collective turned on defining the archive. Despite the common idiomatic reference to the "Mosireen archive," its members did not want to impose their claim to it. If it is an archive of the revolution, then it belongs to the street (Westmoreland 2016). Whether the street can access online platforms is another matter. But if the revolution is framed in nationalistic terms as the Egyptian Revolution, then it reproduces the framework of the nation-state, which goes against the widespread spirit of revolution emboldened across the Arab world and part of the global phenomena of public protests. Reflecting the hopes and dreams of these borderless revolutions and unifying causes, the collective launched "858: An Archive of Resistance," noting its inevitable limitations. Offering a humble pretext, they reminded users that "858 is, of course, just one archive of the revolution. It is not, and can never be, 'the archive.' It is one collection of memories, one set of tools we can all use to fight the narratives of the counter-revolution, to pry loose the state's grip on history, to keep building new histories for the future."[6]

The platform featured 858 hours of footage completely indexed and tagged with an interface that encourages crowdsourced annotation. It encourages multivariate journeys through "thousands of histories of revolt told from hundreds of perspectives." The platform also allows further submissions—indeed, encourages them. The 858 aspires "to make public all the footage shot and collected since 2011." Now that the archive has finally been released online, how does its disconnect from the streets begin to reconcile the critiques of Revolution 2.0 for overemphasizing technology at the expense of on-the-ground work? For now,

the fate of this archive remains uncertain. It is unlikely that these documents will be used to incriminate leaders guilty of human rights abuses
or compel protesters to return to the streets, but they may serve as an
important resource for future revolutionaries.

After 2013, the revolutionary period in Egypt that began in early
2011 came to an abrupt halt. Starting in 2013, the prohibition of public image-making was forcefully reasserted. As Elmeshad has shown
(this volume), there is an urgent need to understand the significance of
these images for future political imaginaries. By enacting new forms of
media practice in the making, sharing, and screening of images of street
politics, activists did cultivate new aesthetic possibilities for political
subjectivity and collectivity during the Egyptian uprisings. A decade
later, the archive is now available, accessible to whoever would like to
utilize it. And yet, it may still be too soon to really face it. In the present
moment, nobody may possess the ability to activate these images with
revolutionary potential. If the images of the Egyptian revolution have
become bankrupt, lifeless, or otherwise inaccessible, what hope can we
anticipate for them in the future?

Notes

1   This text is composed of revised portions of two previously
    published articles: Mark R. Westmoreland, "Street Scenes: The
    Politics of Revolutionary Video in Egypt," *Visual Anthropology* 29,
    no. 3 (2016): 243–62; and Mark R. Westmoreland, "Time Capsules
    of Catastrophic Times," in *The Arab Archive: Mediated Memories
    and Digital Flows*, ed. Donatella Della Ratta, Kay Dickinson,
    and Sune Haugbolle, 20–34 (Amsterdam: Institute for Network
    Cultures, 2020). The corresponding research was part of the
    "'Resistance-by-Recording" project based in the Department of
    Media Studies (IMS), Stockholm University, and made possible by
    Riksbankens Jubileumsfond Reference No. P14–0562:1.
2   The author has conducted several interviews with members of the
    Mosireen collective, but has opted to remove direct references for
    the purposes of this publication.
3   These screenings continued in Tahrir during subsequent sit-ins,
    but were not limited to Cairo. "Mosireen has held regular public
    screenings that have taken place in 15 of the country's 27 governor-
    ates" (Enders 2012).
4   For an in-depth self-reflection on the ethical challenges see
    Mosireen_Soursar 2020.

5   Lebow's meta-documentary is an archival project in itself that combines textual commentary with interviews about the creative process of filmmaking in Egypt during the Arab uprisings. Lebow uses a nonlinear structural framework that makes it possible to trace different constellations of relations and to move through themes and topics in an organic manner or by following prescribed curated conversations.

6   https://858.ma

Works Cited

Abaza, Mona. 2006. "Egyptianizing the American Dream: Nasr City's Shopping Malls, Public Order, and the Privatized Military." In *Cairo Cosmopolitan: Politics, Culture, and Urban Space in the New Globalized Middle East*, edited by Diane Singerman and Paul Amar, 193–220. Cairo: American University in Cairo Press.

———. 2014. "Post January Revolution Cairo: Urban Wars and the Reshaping of Public Space." *Theory, Culture & Society* 31, no. 7–8: 163–83. https://doi.org/10.1177/0263276414549264

Abdalla, Khalid. 2018. "The Advent of Mosireen 25 February 2011." In *Filming Revolution*, edited by Alisa Lebow. A Stanford Digital Project. Stanford, CA: Stanford University Press. https://filmingrevolution.supdigital.org/clip/37/the_advent_of_mosireen_25_february_2011

Aboubakr, Randa. 2013. "New Directions of Internet Activism in Egypt." *Communications—The European Journal of Communication Research* 38, no. 3: 251–65. https://doi.org/10.1515/commun-2013-0015

Bayat, Asef. 2003. "The 'Street' and the Politics of Dissent in the Arab World." *Middle East Report* 226: 10–17.

———. 2013. *Life as Politics: How Ordinary People Change the Middle East.* 2nd ed. Stanford, CA: Stanford University Press.

Enders, David. 2012. "A Year after Tahrir." *The Indypendent*, January 24. https://indypendent.org/2012/01/23/year-after-tahrir

Gaber, Sherief. 2014. "Mosireen and the Battle for Political Memory (1/4)." AUC New Cairo, February 19. Video, 16:22. https://www.youtube.com/watch?v=qR00cgaHoR8

———. 2018a. "Organising the Archive." In *Filming Revolution*, edited by Alisa Lebow. A Stanford Digital Project. Stanford, CA: Stanford University Press. https://filmingrevolution.supdigital.org/clip/81/organising_the_archive_

——. 2018b. "The Archive." In *Filming Revolution*, edited by Alisa Lebow. A Stanford Digital Project. Stanford, CA: Stanford University Press. https://filmingrevolution.supdigital.org/clip/80/ the_archive

——. 2018c. "The Mosireen Collective." In *Filming Revolution*, edited by Alisa Lebow. A Stanford Digital Project. Stanford, CA: Stanford University Press. https://filmingrevolution.supdigital.org/clip/79/ the_mosireen_collective

Gaines, Jane M. 1999. "Political Mimesis." In *Collecting Visible Evidence*, edited by Jane M. Gaines and Michael Renov, 84–102. Minneapolis and London: University of Minnesota Press.

Ghonim, Wael. 2012. *Revolution 2.0: The Power of the People Is Greater than the People in Power: A Memoir*. Boston: Houghton Mifflin Harcourt.

Hamilton, Omar Robert. 2017. "Six Moments from a Revolution: A Mosireen Video Timeline." Ibraaz, July 4. https://www.ibraaz.org/ channel/169

Koning, Anouk de. 2006. "Cafe Latte and Caesar Salad: Cosmopolitan Belonging in Cairo's Coffee Shops." In *Cairo Cosmopolitan: Politics, Culture, and Urban Space in the New Globalized Middle East*, edited by Diane Singerman and Paul Amar, 221–33. Cairo: American University in Cairo Press.

Lebow, Alisa. 2018a. "Archive." In *Filming Revolution*, edited by Alisa Lebow. A Stanford Digital Project. Stanford, CA: Stanford University Press. https://filmingrevolution.supdigital.org/theme/75/archive

——. 2018b. *Filming Revolution*. A Stanford Digital Project. Stanford, CA: Stanford University Press. http://www.filmingrevolution.org/

——. 2018c. "Mosireen." In *Filming Revolution*, edited by Alisa Lebow. A Stanford Digital Project. Stanford, CA: Stanford University Press. https://filmingrevolution.supdigital.org/article/226/mosireen

——. 2018d. "Sherief Gaber." In *Filming Revolution*, edited by Alisa Lebow. A Stanford Digital Project. Stanford, CA: Stanford University Press. https://filmingrevolution.supdigital.org/article/234/ sherief_gaber

Mehrez, Samia. 2012. *Translating Egypt's Revolution: The Language of Tahrir*. London: I.B. Tauris.

Mollerup, Nina Grønlykke, and Sherief Gaber. 2015. "Making Media Public: On Revolutionary Street Screenings in Egypt." *International Journal of Communication* 9: 2903–21.

Mosireen Collective. 2011. "The Maspero Massacre 9/10/11." Video, 9:01. https://www.youtube.com/watch?v=oot-oNEwc3E&feature=youtu.be

———. 2015. "A Brief History of the Shura Council Trial so Far." Video, 4:03. https://www.youtube.com/watch?v=4UzXqfeA6lQ&fea ture=youtu.be

———. 2017a. "Six Moments from a Revolution: A Brief History of the Shoura Council So Far." Ibraaz, July 4. Video, 4:03. https://www. ibraaz.org/channel/175

———. 2017b. "Six Moments from a Revolution: A Coup or a Continuation of the Revolution?" Ibraaz, July 4. Video, 6:58. https://www. ibraaz.org/channel/173

———. 2017c. "Six Moments from a Revolution: Prayer of Fear." Ibraaz, July 4. Video, 4:25. https://www.youtube.com/ watch?v=vIXAFkXHHRs

———. 2017d. "Six Moments from a Revolution: The Maspero Massacre: October 2011." Ibraaz, July 4. https://www.ibraaz. org/channel/170. Video, 9:01. https://www.youtube.com/ watch?v=oot-oNEwc3E

Mosireen_Soursar. 2020. "No Archive Is Innocent: On the Attempt of Archiving Revolt." In *The Arab Archive: Mediated Memories and Digital Flows*, edited by Donatella della Ratta, Kay Dickinson, and Sune Haugbolle. Amsterdam: Institute of Network Cultures.

Nanabhay, Mohamed, and Roxane Farmanfarmaian. 2011. "From Spectacle to Spectacular: How Physical Space, Social Media and Mainstream Broadcast Amplified the Public Sphere in Egypt's 'Revolution.'" *The Journal of North African Studies* 16, no. 4: 573–603. https://doi.org/10.1080/13629387.2011.639562

Raoof, Ramy. 2011. "About the Media Tent in Tahrir Square." *Egyptian Blog for Human Rights* (blog), May 4. http://ebfhr.blogspot. se/2011/05/media-tent-in-tahrir-square.html

Rizk, Philip. 2013. Interview by Shuruq Harb. https://www.monabaker. org/2015/09/20/interview-with-philip-rizk-by-shuruq-harb/

Schoene, Dorothea. 2012. "Art in a Revolution: A Conversation with Lala Baladi." *Afterimage* 39, no. 5: 19.

Stuhr-Rommereim, Helen. 2011. "Tahrir Cinema Displays Revolutionary Power of Archives." *Egypt Independent*, July 20. http://www.egypt independent.com/news/tahrir-cinema-displays-revolutionary-power-archives

Taher, Menna. 2011. "Egyptian Cinema in 2011 between Activism and Art." *Ahram Online*, December 27. http://english.ahram.org.eg/ NewsContent/1/114/30336/Egypt/-January-Revolution-continues/ Egyptian-Cinema-in--between-activism-and-art.aspx

Trew, Bel. 2012. "Egyptian Citizen Journalism 'Mosireen' Tops YouTube." *Bel Trew: Freelance Journalist* (blog), January 20. http://beltrew.com/2012/01/20/egyptian-citizen-journalism-mosireen-tops-youtube/

Westmoreland, Mark R. 2016. "Street Scenes: The Politics of Revolutionary Video in Egypt." *Visual Anthropology* 29, no. 3: 243–62. https://doi.org/10.1080/08949468.2016.1154420.

———. 2020. "Documentary Film Making." In *The Routledge Encyclopedia of Citizen Media*, edited by Mona Baker, Bolette B. Blaagaard, Henry Jones, and Luis Pérez-González. London and New York: Routledge.

5

QUEER DIGITAL ACTIVISM
STREET MEDIA AND SUBVERSION OF
DIGITAL SECURITIZATION

AFSANEH RIGOT AND NORA NORALLA

The clampdown on online queerness in Egypt has been well documented. As Abed has discussed in her chapter in this volume, there was a considerable shift in queer and other nonhegemonic forms of sexual existence after the introduction of the internet. Upper- and middle-class Egyptians, in particular, had better and earlier access (in the 1990s) to this new technology. From these Egyptians came the first groups to congregate online and to begin what came to be known as the "modern wave of queerness" in Egypt. Online space provided much-needed freedom for the LGBTQ+ community to connect and to create safe spaces in Egypt. With this, the battle over cyberspaces began between Egyptian authorities and the new wave of queer Egyptians, reforming the queer urban landscapes of Cairo, as described by Awadalla and Saleh in their chapters in this volume.

Stories of Egyptian police officers "sexting" on apps like Grindr to entrap and arrest queer folks are common news that rightly garners international attention (Jankowicz 2017). The nuances and contextual background of these stings rarely survive editorial cuts, however. What are the parameters and structures that allow for this method of criminalizing queer communities? What is the history of the queer shift to online spaces and the corresponding shift in policing these spaces? More importantly, what has been the response of queer communities in the protection of their virtual and community spaces?

With further social and legal pressures on LGTBQ+ communities in Egypt and a rise in arrests (especially after Abd al-Fattah al-Sisi came to power in June 2014), the switch to digital spaces to connect, work, meet, have sex, or fall in love has steadily increased. There is a complex legal and social infrastructure that allows for ongoing cat-and-mouse policing methods in these virtual domains. More recently, we have seen the further establishment of structures that allow for the criminalization of queer lives and the digitization of prosecution. These methods have become further operationalized by laws criminalizing vague notions of "publicizing" and "inciting" debauchery, as well as laws that criminalize online behavior that is deemed harmful to Egyptian national "morals." Police methods are ever changing as technologies and ways of online existence themselves change. Likewise, with the operationalization of anti-queer police tactics in the digital realm have come new, coordinated strategies and moves by queer communities to gain the upper hand while keeping each other safe. In this chapter, we will look at the history of Egypt's online anti-queer arrests, the laws that enable them, and how Egypt's queer communities continue to resist and exist in the ways pointed to by Awadalla, in this volume.

They Came for the Apps

Online vice police operations under the General Directorate for Protecting Public Morality began to be conceived of following the growth of queer dating apps in Egypt around 2013–14. The Egyptian Initiative for Personal Rights (EIPR) identified 2015 as "the beginning of when the Morality Police began its systematic electronic campaign on LGBTQ dating and social applications and websites as we have come to know it now" (Abdel Hamid 2017). The same document indicates a consistent, fixed message in most police reports that recommended action "based on the directions of the Deputy Minister for Social Security and the Head of the General Directorate for Protecting Public Morality to intensify efforts to combat all crimes that affect the values and morals of Egyptian society and to combat the sinful activities of international prostitution rings that target the nation's youth, particularly the recent emergence of pornographic websites and social media platforms."

Having worked with queer communities in different capacities, the authors of this chapter understand that the role of digital tools in these contexts remains vital. Queer dating apps, for example, have always been crucial for communities living under laws that criminalize sexuality (Article 19 2018). Such platforms connect these communities and represent our most intimate and fragile interactions with technology. Over the last few decades, the increase in "queer cyber spaces" has been accompanied by a shift in Egyptian vice police campaigns against "issues of morality," as Sara Abed has documented in her chapter in this volume. "Innovative" ways of restricting, surveilling, and investigating these online spaces have begun to be employed, including the now infamous online entrapments that are still being used to this day—more specifically, queer dating app entrapments.

Having queer dating apps such as Grindr or Hornet on one's phone has come to represent a confession of one's "unacceptable" sexuality—and thus criminality—in the eyes of police officers. Officers use fake profiles on these dating apps to conduct long conversations with individuals, encouraging them to have explicit sexual chats, asking for nude or sexual photos, offering money as gifts, and employing an array of other tactics in orchestrated conversations. In an interview conducted by the Cairo 52 Legal Research Institute, one targeted individual reports, "I went on Grindr, as I do every day. I was bored, and suddenly someone texted me, telling me he is from the Gulf, and we started talking. Soon I found myself sending him nudes and him offering me a 'gift' if I came to spend the night with him."[1] Then, as it goes with any dating app situation, a plan is made to meet somewhere in public. Once the user arrives, the police make an immediate arrest. The suspects are arrested, searched, and then detained at a regular police station or often in the morality police section on Gamat al-Dowal Street in the Muhandisin neighborhood of Cairo. The arrested individuals are then often convicted based on recorded conversations. This is evident in numerous documented cases and dozens of case files, including those by NGOs on the ground who have reviewed the situations of the victims of these entrapments.

What is entrapment? Black's Law Dictionary provides a baseline definition of entrapment as "a law enforcement officer or government agent's inducement of a person to commit a crime, by means of fraud or undue persuasion, in an attempt to later bring a criminal prosecution against that person" (Garner 2004). This definition fits the Egyptian cases analyzed here. As it stands, Egypt does not have any particular law that frames a defense for victims of entrapment: all methods used by the police fall under the rubric of "necessary investigative powers."

There is some debate as to whether it is the officers and vice police that conduct these entrapments or whether they are conducted by paid or coerced "informants." In the case files, the prosecuting teams and courts always refer to these individuals as the police's "informants" or "consultants." This helps the police bypass self-incrimination laws since, if the information is gathered through informants, the accused are less likely to be able to claim self-incrimination. This is a common method in the United States, where information from an "informant"—for example, in a drug case—clears police of entrapment accusations (HRW 2018). Of course, it is unclear if this is the reason why the police in Egypt frame these cases and the information gathered by "informants" when there are no legal restrictions on entrapment in Egypt.

These sting operations are not some hidden, arbitrary method of targeting individuals, which one might expect from a country that has routinely denied having laws that prosecute LGBTQ people. The Egyptian media, in its increasingly state-controlled form (see Elmeshad, this volume) has been at the forefront of glorifying these police operations. From 2015 on, numerous conservative and tabloid-type outlets began to glorify and legitimize online entrapment, employing fearmongering and (as Abed documents in the case of female "immorality" in this volume) stoking moral panic by using homophobic stereotypes to justify the raids. Although we cannot claim that there is a correlation between increased international scrutiny and lower numbers of entrapments, since 2019 the number of arrests via entrapment has decreased. However, this may only represent a temporary decrease due to the COVID lockdown of 2020. Unfortunately, although online entrapment is the main element of the arrests that gain international attention, the Egyptian police have numerous other methods at their disposal to target the queer community. All of these ultimately rely on phone searches and access to photos, chats, and dating apps—any elements of digital life that, to the police and prosecutors, indicate queerness.

In addition to surveillance of digital apps, one of the other methods the police use is the monitoring of so-called "LGBTQ meeting spots" in real social space. They focus on certain squares, streets, and coffee shops where members of LGBTQ communities often meet. Police will raid these spots and arrest the people in them—a tactic particularly practiced against trans individuals and those perceived as gender nonconforming. The raids are often set up through a secret informant who works with the police and accompanies them on patrol to locate queer people they know. A less commonly employed police tactic involves arresting people at home or in a hotel. In the latter case, police are notified by someone who works at the hotel that there's a guest who looks "suspicious." In the case of home arrests, the police generally receive a similar tip-off from a neighbor. According to the arrest data gathered by the NGO Bedayaa from 2018 and 2019, there has been a large spike in the arrests of those perceived as gay or trans in public spaces and so-called "gay" hangouts: 87 percent of cases in 2018 and 69 percent of cases in 2019 (Bedayaa 2019).

International news outlets began to cover, in particular, the cases of online entrapments in Egypt in 2014–16, but the coverage did not always highlight the mobilization of support in Egypt for those arrested, local challenges to the police entrapment practices, and the insistence, by Egyptian activists and organizations, on ensuring the safety of LGBTQ+ people. Many international reports allotted little room for the history and richness of activism and contestation in Egypt and instead focused overwhelmingly on the "geolocation" features of apps (Brandom 2018), the feature that allows for a user to see the location of and the distance to another user, for example, or to speak to people closest to them through GPS ("Grindr: A Chronicle" n.d.). Though the conversation around the threats to privacy posed by GPS locators on dating apps is a valid one, this was not actually how people were being arrested, since most were either lured into meeting in person somewhere outside the home or arrested in a public hangout space. The GPS-focused coverage infuriated the groups working on these cases and providing legal support to victims because most threats to queer users have come from street arrests through informants and entrapments, leading to the confiscation of their phones (facilitated by the new law Article 19 of 2018 that gives sweeping powers to the state to police online activity, journalism, and social media) [Article 19 2018]). There have been zero geolocation-related arrests in any Middle Eastern or North African (MENA) countries. Due to the international focus on geolocation, queer dating apps changed their geolocation options for Egypt (SBS The Feed 2014). Users' and local groups' needs are very much unrelated to this feature change, however, and many queer users in Egypt and the region want and need the feature as it originally was constructed.

History of Other Targetings

In 2001, during the presidency of Hosni Mubarak, one of the biggest attacks on sexual and bodily freedom took place in Egypt. In May 2001, police arrested and the courts tried fifty-two men (accused of debauchery and described as "gay" in the press) during a party in Cairo on a riverboat nightclub, referred to as "the Queen Boat case" (HRW

2004, 13). The trials led to a flurry of homophobic press coverage and intensified the pressure on and intimidation of the LGBTQ community. The Queen Boat case is important because many of those who were arrested were not the lower-middle- or working-class men who previously had been more likely to suffer criminalization. In the Queen Boat case, many of the arrestees came from well-connected families of Egypt's upper class. With this operation, the state made a clear statement: it doesn't matter what status you have when it comes to enforcing "morality" in Egyptian society.

The incident increased the wave of moral panic that already had been underway in Egypt since the 1990s. This zeitgeist came into direct conflict with forms of social liberalism or the laissez-faire attitudes that flourished during the end of former president Anwar al-Sadat's era, which during the 1970s and early 1980s had opened Egyptian society to a diversification of sexual values. In the 1990s. the Egyptian state reversed this trend and began presenting itself as the protector of Egyptian family traditions and values. Police authorities increasingly targeted, persecuted, and marginalized groups deemed unfit according to the "conservative ideals" of Egyptian society (e.g., queer people, sex workers, and even heavy-metal music lovers) (Noralla 2020; Cairo 52 2020). The harassment of LGBTQ+ individuals, particularly of gay men and trans individuals, had been occurring long before the Queen Boat case. Prior to that case, however, arrests rarely led to prosecution.

In this increasing atmosphere of fear, more and more LGBTQ+ individuals began to use virtual platforms to connect. Many used personal ad pages ("personals") to find and email other queer people. Others employed newly developed instant-messaging apps to communicate (HRW 2004). With LGBTQ peoples' move to online communications came the first shifts in methods of police targeting of these groups in Egypt. The first case of arrest through online entrapment took place in January 2001, predating the Queen Boat case. The second case was published in the Egyptian tabloid *al-Naba'*, which announced the arrest of two men who had responded to online personal ads in March 2001 (HRW 2004).

By the end of 2001, there were increasing reports of "Internet monitoring units" within the Ministry of Interior being employed in combating the LGBTQ community's growing online sphere. In May 2002, General Abd al-Wahab al-Adli, head of the vice squad within the Ministry of Interior, announced: "We are dealing with a different type of criminal and the spread of new crimes . . . This requires security and technical expertise to be able to patrol the Internet the same way we patrol Egyptian streets" (Abou el-Magd 2002). Tactics and laws have since been optimized. Trans queer activist Nora recalls "growing up using phones like Nokia N72 with apps like Manjam and Nimbuzz to meet other queer people."[2] Through these communication technologies, Nora and others built and rebuilt the spaces queer people pioneered in the pre–Queen Boat days. Despite the increase in the types of methods police used to come after LGBTQ communities, the queer community continues to build meeting spaces and resist oppression.

In recent years, the crackdown on gender and sexual identity has rapidly increased. According to the Egyptian Initiative for Personal Rights, between 2000 and 2013 there were 189 arrests of LGBTQ people, with an average of fourteen people being taken into police custody each year (Abdel Hamid 2017). This number dramatically increased fivefold between 2013 and 2017, with a total of 232 LGBTQ people arrested and prosecuted—an average of sixty-six people per year. These numbers do not give us the full picture of what is happening on the ground, however. Human rights organizations working on the issue do not have enough resources to cover every case coming through the system and many go undocumented. During coauthor Nora Noralla's work providing legal aid for the LGBTQ+ community, her team documented cases for over two hundred people during 2017 and 2020.

The Rainbow Flag Incident

What has now become known as the "Rainbow Flag" incident signaled a new commitment by the Egyptian authorities to shut down any public or private shows of queerness. In the summer of 2017, Mashrou' Leila, a hugely popular Lebanese indie rock band, held a concert in Cairo. Mashrou' Leila is known not only for their sexy, cool, genre-bending music, but because Hamed Sinno, the lead singer, is one of North Africa and the Middle East's (MENA) first openly gay musicians (Krause 2019). The band's lyrics often encompass ideas about sexual liberty from a regional perspective. Wherever Mashrou' Leila plays, a large contingent of queer people from the area

Figure 5.1. Sarah Hegazy, waving a flag at a Mashrou' Leila concert in summer 2017.

show up. It was no different in Egypt where—even if one wasn't a fan of the group's music—the symbolism of the concert was enough to draw many to the show.

During the concert, a group of people raised the rainbow flag, including and most notably Sarah Hegazy (fig. 5.1). Pictures of the flag and public outrage about the concert spread throughout Egyptian social media. Pictures of concertgoers such as Hegazy went viral not only in Egypt, but around the region. The Egyptian state realized that what had just happened was technically not illegal. Even so, the Egyptian general attorney at the time, Nabil Ahmed Sadiq, commissioned State Security prosecutors to conduct a serious investigation into the incident (*Masrawy* 2017). Keep in mind that State Security Prosecution is an exceptional prosecutory body established to investigate only the most dangerous crimes against the Egyptian state. Seventy-five people, including Hegazy, were arrested.

The Egyptian LGBTQ organization, Bedayaa, reported that the seventy-five were charged with "habitual debauchery," "incitement to debauchery," and/or "public indecency" under Law 10/1961 on Combating Prostitution—largely used against queer individuals in Egypt (see below) (Bedayaa 2020). Many of those arrested, including Hegazy, suffered torture and degrading treatment while in prison. After her initial release, Hegazy faced penalties of up to fifteen years' imprisonment (Article 19 2020) and fled the country. Following the State Security investigation, several MPs drafted three new bills, criminalizing homosexuality even more directly. The most significant of these three contained articles that punish homosexuality with a minimum of one year and maximum of three years imprisonment for first-time offenders and five years for repeat offenders (Sadek 2017).

The image of Hegazy waving a rainbow flag in Egypt (Walsh 2020) became a symbol of existence and resistance for the country's queer communities. "I was declaring myself in a society that hates all that is different from the norm," Hegazy declared. The same image was used as part of a homophobic public outrage campaign that led to the massive crackdown. It was also used as part of the evidence presented against Hegazy in court. On June 14, 2020, while still in exile in Canada, Hegazy took her own life (Younes 2020). On the one-year anniversary of her asylum in Canada, she had written: "Even after my release, fear of everyone, family, friends, and the street continued to haunt me" (Hegazy 2018). Yet, with familiar defiance, she declared, "a year after [Egypt's] biggest security attack against gay people, a year after I announced my difference (yes, I am a gay), I have not forgotten my enemies. I have not forgotten the injustice that left black and bleeding spots carved in my soul; spots that doctors have never been able to treat" (Younes 2020).

Institutionalized Homophobia

Egypt never directly criminalized homosexuality or any form of gender expression. The legislation of the 1950s and 1960s, however, created a de facto criminalization. These laws mobilized vague terms such as "morality" and "debauchery" to criminalize any act that did not fit the state-approved heteronormative narratives. To understand where this system came from, we need to look at Egyptian lawmakers' decision to punish "victimless crimes" and to restrict the country's sexual freedoms. In 1951, this process began when an Egyptian lawmaker decided to go after another moral issue in order to establish a system that later evolved to cover all sexual moral issues: sex work. Sex work had been legalized and regulated as a trade until 1951, when Law No. 68/1951 was passed. Following this, many other "moral" crimes were subsequently criminalized.

Law No. 68/1951 is more or less identical to the currently operative law that was passed in 1961: Law No. 10/1961 on the Combating of Prostitution. In 1959, Egypt (then the United Arab Republic) joined the Convention for the Suppression of the Traffic in Persons and of the Exploitation of the Prostitution of Others and commenced work on new legislation in compliance with the requirements of the convention. In 1961 a final bill was passed, becoming Law No. 10/1961 on the Combating of Prostitution. This law is still in effect in both Syria and Egypt and is a primary tool employed in persecuting the queer community (Noralla 2020).

The current legal infrastructure continues to reflect the outlines set in the 1960s and 1970s. Today's authorities, however, have optimized the basic framework to target queer Egyptians (and activists) online. To date, the main law used to prosecute the LGBTQ community is Law No. 10/1961, often referred to as the "anti-debauchery law." The most important article of this law is the infamous Article No. 9(c), which specifies punishment "by imprisonment for a period not less than three months and not exceeding three years and a fine of not less than 25 LE and not exceeding 300 LE (in the Egyptian administration) or not less than 250 Lira and not exceeding 3,000 Lira (in the Syrian administration). One of these two punishments applies against whoever habitually engages in debauchery or prostitution." The article is only one of many debauchery-related articles, including an even broader Article 14(a), which states that "whoever publicizes in any form an invitation which includes inducement to debauchery or prostitution, or draws attention to this, is to be punished by imprisonment for a period not exceeding three years and a fine not exceeding 100 LE (in the Egyptian administration) and 1,000 Lira (in the Syrian administration), or one of the two punishments." Importantly, when the physical crime of "practicing debauchery" under Article 9(c) cannot be proven, the court relies on digital evidence found in an individual's social media, chats, and photos—frequently, anything on the arrested person's mobile phone. In entrapment cases, one also finds the evidence the "informant" has gathered in chats. In these cases, the charge will be for the crime of incitement or publicity (persuasion or seduction) of debauchery according to Article 14(a) (Rigot 2020).

Homosexuality was de facto criminalized in 1975 through the Court of Cassation, the highest court in Egypt. Appeal No. 683/Year 45 of May 12, 1975, and Appeal No. 977/Year 47 of January 29, 1978, contrary to judicial custom of the time, struck down the clause that considered debauchery as a charge necessarily related to financially compensated sex work. The court stated that there are two forms of debauchery: habitual and indifferent (with regard to sexual partners) (Rigot 2020, 13). With these two verdicts—which lay down a precedent—the doors were opened to the de facto criminalization of homosexuality. This, combined with the law's use of vague terms such as "debauchery" and "morality" in its rulings, granted lower courts and the police a judicial mandate to arrest any "male" who "habitually and indifferently" slept with another "male."

Since the shift of digital-based cases to the Economic Courts, these charges have been combined with charges based on Egypt's Telecommunication Law: specifically, the Telecommunication Regulation Law of 2003 (10/2003) and its Article 76. This article stipulates that "Without prejudice to the right for suitable indemnity, a penalty of confinement to prison and a fine not less than five hundred pounds and not exceeding twenty thousand pounds, or either penalty, shall be inflicted on whomever: 1. Uses or assists in using illegitimate means to conduct telecommunication correspondence; 2. Premeditatedly disturbs or harasses a third party by misusing Telecommunication Equipment." The vaguely worded concept of "misuse of Telecommunication Equipment" under the Telecommunications law is often used in arrests of political activists and in governmental clampdowns on speech. This article is frequently cited as "misuse of social media" in digital expression cases and is sometimes combined with debauchery and cybercrime laws to charge LGBTQ individuals. The impact of having their case transferred to the Economic Courts is drastic for those being persecuted. The laws are vague and broadly applied. Queer people who used to be faced with two charges under the "debauchery law" now face five charges under the debauchery, telecommunications, and cybercrimes laws, leading to lengthier sentences.

In 2018, the Egyptian parliament passed the new Cybercrime Law #175/2018, which contains several vague articles currently being used to prosecute the LGBTQ community. The main one is Article 25, which criminalizes "anyone who violates the values and principles of the family in Egyptian society." Punishment is stipulated as jail time of at least six months and a minimum fine of LE 50,000 (maximum of LE 100,000).

In August 2019, a decree was passed granting jurisdiction over the 2018 Anti-Cyber and Information Technology Crimes Law ("Cybercrime Law") to the Egyptian Economic Courts. Since their inception in 2008, the Economic Courts have been given legislative power for the 2003 Telecommunication Law and other financial and economic laws (Ali 2019). These have since become part of the tool kit that the Egyptian authorities employ in policing online "morality" and surveilling people's everyday lives. This was notoriously the case in the 2020 TikTok arrests, where Haneen Hossam and Mawada al-Adham were sentenced for "violating family values" (Kataya 2020). In practice, this tool kit allows for the application of charges under the Cybercrimes Law and Telecommunications Regulations, and entails further digitization of the prosecution of LGBTQ+ individuals.

Since March 2020, our research has shown a rapid and concerning shift of LGBTQ+ persecution charges from the Misdemeanors Courts, where these cases were normally heard, to the Economic Courts in Egypt. There, people will often be charged under three different pieces of legislation and with higher sentences. All of this is mainly employed against those being charged with digital crimes (Rigot 2020; HRW 2020).

And Yet They Persisted

All these legal and social frameworks have not stopped the LGBTQ+ community from evolving and becoming more powerful. Nora Noralla's work is testament to this. The community is not getting bigger; it always has been big. Yet it is becoming more visible and better connected. This strong community cannot be dismissed by homophobic heteronormative policies a government like Egypt's might enact. It refuses to be erased despite surviving numerous attempts to eradicate it through hostile governmental and social policies. At the end of the day, Egypt's LGBTQ+ rights movement and community is here to stay. Through new social media tools and other technological advances, the movement continues to thrive. Many initiatives and networks exist to support the community: international/national strategies, digital security training, and legal aid support. On the digital side, companies have introduced better security measures in response to what users and groups on the ground have wanted, including efforts to introduce changes to dating apps (such as Grindr) in order to make them harder for the police to use. This work will need to continue. Until fundamental changes are made to Egypt's queer-phobic laws, activists and queer community members will strive to resist the authorities and to increase the safety of members of the LGBTQ community.

Notes

1　The full interview was conducted by Cairo 52 Legal Research Institute. https://cairo52.com/
2　Anonymized personal interview by author Rigot.

Works Cited

Abdel Hamid, Dalia. 2017. "The Trap: Punishing Sexual Difference in Egypt." Report, November 22. Egyptian Initiative for Personal Rights, Cairo, Egypt. https://eipr.org/en/publications/trap-punishing-sexual-difference-egypt

Abou el-Magd, Nadia. 2002. "Cyberspace-scouring Cops Accused of Suppressing Online Expression." Associated Press, May 21. https://wwrn.org/articles/10377/

Ali, Noor. 2019. "Nanshur nass qanun al-mahakim al-iqtisadiya ba'd tasdiq al-ra'is wa-nashrihi bi-l-garida al-rasmiya." *Youm7*, August 13.

Article 19. 2018. "Apps, Arrests and Abuse in Egypt, Lebanon and Iran." London: LGBTQ Online. https://www.article19.org/wp-content/uploads/2018/02/LGBTQ-Apps-Arrest-and-Abuse-report_22.2.18.pdf

———. 2020. "Article 19 Pays Tribute to Queer Egyptian Activist Sarah Hegazy." June 25. https://www.article19.org/resources/article-19-pays-tribute-to-queer-egyptian-activist-sarah-hegazy/

Bedayaa. 2019. Legal Aid Project in Egypt. Bedayaa Organization (Egypt and Sudan). https://bedayaa.org/publications/

———. 2020. Bedayaa Organization Statement on Sarah Hegazy's Death. June 18. https://drive.google.com/file/d/1-MqGiuhw53HG kLWloIKrv3s9aWxKUL7G/view

Brandom, Russell. 2018. "Designing for the Crackdown." *The Verge*, April 25. https://www.theverge.com/2018/4/25/17279270/lgbtq-dating-apps-egypt-illegal-human-rights

Cairo 52. 2020. Cairo 52: Legal Research Institute, Cairo, Egypt. https://cairo52.com/wp-content/uploads/2020/11/ElKarakhana_English.pdf

Garner, Bryan A., ed. 2004. *Black's Law Dictionary*. 8th ed. Eagan, MN: Thomson Reuters.

"Grindr: A Chronicle of Negligence and Irresponsibility." n.d. https://grindrmap.neocities.org/

Hegazy, Sarah. 2018. "'Am 'ala mawqi'at 'al-rainbow': nizam ya'taqil wa-l-islamiyun yusaffiqun." *Mada Masr*, September 24.

HRW (Human Rights Watch). 2004. "In a Time of Torture: The Assault on Justice in Egypt's Crackdown on Homosexual Conduct." https://www.hrw.org/report/2004/02/29/time-torture/assault-justice-egypts-crackdown-homosexual-conduct

———. 2018. "Dark Side: Secret Origins of Evidence in US Criminal Cases." https://www.hrw.org/report/2018/01/09/dark-side/secret-origins-evidence-us-criminal-cases

———. 2020. https://www.hrw.org/news/2020/06/08/pride-month-shame-you-exposing-anti-lgbt-government-strategies-mena

Jankowicz, Mia. 2017. "Jailed for Using Grindr: Homosexuality in Egypt." *The Guardian*, April 3. https://www.theguardian.com/global-development-professionals-network/2017/apr/03/jailed-for-using-grindr-homosexuality-in-egypt

Kataya, Abed. 2020. "The TikTok Case: A New Platform to Oppress Women in Egypt." SMEX, August 28. https://smex.org/the-tiktok-case-a-new-platform-to-oppress-women-in-egypt/

Krause, Ryan Killian. 2019. In Conversation with Hamed Sinno. *V Magazine*.

Masrawy. 2017. "The Public Prosecutor Assigns State Security to Investigate the Incident of Raising Gay Flags in al-Taggama' al-Khamis." September 25. Masrawy.com

Mecky, Mariam. 2018. "State Policing: Moral Panics and Masculinity in Post-2011 Egypt." *Kohl: A Journal for Body and Gender Research* 4, no. 1: 94–105.

Noralla, Nora. 2020. "ElKarakhana: History of Sex Working in Modern Egypt between Legalization and Criminalization." Cairo 52. https://cairo52.com/2020/11/05/elkarakhana-eng/

Rigot, Afsaneh. 2020. "Egypt's Dangerous New Strategy for Criminalizing Queerness." *Slate*, December 30. https://slate.com/technology/2020/12/egypt-lgbtq-crime-economic-courts.html

Sadek, George. 2017. "Egypt: Draft Law Criminalizes Homosexuality." Global Legal Monitor, Library of Congress. https://www.loc.gov/item/global-legal-monitor/2017-11-01/egypt-draft-law-criminalizes-homosexuality/

SBS The Feed. 2014. "Grindr Security Flaw Exposed." *The Feed*, September 10. YouTube video. SBS, Sydney, Australia. https://www.youtube.com/watch?v=rTC4p_YHntw

Valentine, Paul W. 2009. "To Catch an Entrapper: The Inadequacy of the Entrapment Defense Globally and the Need to Reevaluate Our Current Legal Rubric." *International Law Review* 1, no. 2: 22–35.

Walsh, Declan. 2020. "Arrested for Waving Rainbow Flag, a Gay Egyptian Takes Her Life." *New York Times*, June 15. https://www.nytimes.com/2020/06/15/world/middleeast/egypt-gay-suicide-sarah-hegazi.html

Younes, Rasha. 2020. "For Sarah Hegazy: In Rage, in Grief, in Exhaustion." *The New Arab*, June 16. https://www.newarab.com/opinion/sarah-hegazy-rage-grief-exhaustion

6

TOILETS FOR THE PEOPLE?
HYGIENE IN THE CITY AND DEPATHOLOGIZING POPULAR SANITATION

TINA GUIRGUIS

Introduction

In January 2009, I arrived as a study-abroad student at the American University in Cairo. On my second night, I took a moonlit camel ride around the Pyramids of Giza as part of the international student orientation week. After spending time in traffic, we arrived at the camel stables to begin our excursion. (I've since learned of the animal cruelty involved in these enterprises and would now never participate in or recommend them). Another student and I inquired about restrooms before our camel ride. The student organizers spoke with the people running the stable, who consulted with random residents walking on the street and concluded that there weren't many publicly accessible toilets in the area. A woman emerged upon hearing the commotion, however, and, taking me by the arm, led me and my bewildered classmate through a maze of narrow streets into someone's apartment to use their toilet. The resident did not seem surprised by our request; it apparently happened all the time.

The apartment was part of an *'ashwa'iyat:* one of Cairo's informal, unplanned settlements, which house more than 50 percent of the city's 20 million inhabitants (Bell 2009). These settlements largely lack access to proper state-sanctioned sewage and sanitation systems. In the absence of state-established planning in these densely populated neighborhoods, informal waste management systems (including much-neglected septic tanks) have been established, often leading to several structural, health, and environmental issues.

Thinking through this experience and many other instances of failed attempts to find a toilet in Cairo, I noticed two major issues. The first was a lack of public toilet infrastructure throughout the Egyptian capital. According to a Cairo government media spokesman, in 2018 there were only forty-four working public toilets in the entire city (Al-Iraqi 2018). Second, the lack of sanitation infrastructure is not limited to public toilets; it extends to an absence of state sanitation and waste management provisions to connect informal housing and many other homes to sewage systems in general. According to the 2006 Egyptian Census of Population and Living Conditions, only 46 percent of households in Egypt were connected to the public sewage network, while 41 percent used septic tanks, 9 percent used informal networks, and 4 percent had no connection to any sewage system. The absence of proper infrastructure as well as improper septic tank usage and maintenance has led to building collapses and preemptive evictions as groundwater levels rise, causing structural damage to buildings. Additionally, the absence of proper waste management services exposes Cairo's population to potentially deadly pathogens, often leading to illness or even death, particularly among children (10 Tooba 2016).

Many communal facilities—hospitals, schools, mosques, public toilets, and bathhouses—were initially established and operated through a system of religious endowments known as *awqaf*. Through this system, based in Islamic law, a donor can establish a charitable endowment that provides public utilities to the community. Under Mohammed Ali, the *awqaf* system began to undergo nationalization, bringing endowments under the control of the government and of al-Azhar, the most prominent Sunni university and arbiter of Islamic culture. Nationalization continued under President Nasser and subsequent Egyptian presidents, leading to the accumulation of a massive system of public land and utility endowments managed by the Ministry of Religious Endowments. As a result, particularly before the advent of indoor plumbing, all social classes used these public facilities—established through religious endowments rather than the state—as their primary access to toilets and bathing. In the early nineteenth century, Cairo had 130 bath houses, but by the 1880s, this number was reduced by half due to the introduction of plumbing to residential buildings in middle- and upper-class parts of the city. The remaining public bathhouses and toilets continued to be used by much of the population who did not have access to indoor plumbing. By 2012, however, there were only sixteen public bathhouses left in the city (El-Gergawi 2012).

The closure of bathhouses and their accompanying public toilets is often blamed on the prevalence of indoor household plumbing, although these public services were still (and are) very much in demand by a large portion of the population. However, many bathhouses have been reported as having been abandoned by their owners, seized, or pronounced "disreputable" by the state as spaces to "commit obscene deeds and sins" (Sherief 2012). The closure of these facilities is due to the perception that public bathhouses are outdated places for the poor, as well as immoral spaces for practicing sexual perversions (El Kerdany 2008). As recently as 2014, one of the few remaining Cairo bathhouses was raided by Egyptian security forces and accompanying media under the guise of serving the public interest by clamping down on homosexuality and raising awareness of the spread of AIDS. The raid led to the arrest and public humiliation of dozens of men suspected of homosexuality, who were later released (Cunningham 2014). The coverage of the raid in the media reiterated associations between bathhouses and queer sexualities, reinforcing these spaces' reputation as disreputable and deterring their use for fear of accusations of being a homosexual. The transformation of sexual moralities into a focus for public security, outlined in this volume by Abed, Rigot and Noralla, Awadalla, and Saleh, has unexpected collateral effects. One of the least discussed has been the ongoing impact on public health and sanitation in Cairo (and Egypt more generally) through the elimination of public restrooms. Additionally, access to toilets and water services in churches and mosques has also been hampered in recent years. Religious sites have been further securitized to curb and monitor Islamic extremism, restricting access to religious buildings (and their bathrooms) to service hours only.

Informal communities have risen to fill the infrastructural void, not only by establishing informal sanitation and waste management infrastructure in the 'ashwa'iyat, but also by providing much-needed public toilet infrastructure as random tourists and workers make their way into homes to use private toilets. This infrastructure challenges the dichotomy between the state, as the provider of infrastructure, and the citizen as its end user. The state is not always responsible and accountable for "public good" infrastructure, such as sanitation systems, raising the question of what motivates the state to undertake or neglect infrastructure projects? How do these projects or their lack work to add value to the state in its assertion of control as the city is further securitized? What role does the community play in establishing an informal toilet infrastructure or in enforcing social cleansing in the process of gentrification?

To pathologize someone is to diagnose or characterize them as medically or psychologically abnormal. Similarly, justice is often pathologized, meaning that criminality is linked to abnormality or depicted as a societal aberration rather than a result of systemic inequality. This research aims to depathologize justice by looking at the ways in which measures and discourses of criminality, deviance, hygiene, and morality replace state infrastructural responsibility in the pursuit of the modern urban international city. Infrastructural neglect of public toilets has been co-opted and reworked as a productive tool for the state through human security discourse(s), employed to justify the increased securitization of Cairo under the guise of an urban physical and social cleansing for the public good—an unexpected side effect of the securitization of Cairo, as described by Hassan and Abul-Magd in their chapters in this volume. Community endorsement and enforcement of social cleansing efforts and criminality measures are partially achieved through the linking of hygiene and cleanliness etiquette to the moral and religious duties of maintaining a clean body and clean shared environment. When public toilet initiatives have been announced or attempted, they have been motivated by aspirations for modernity and international prestige prior to the hosting of international mega-sports events.

Where to Pee?

Anyone who has been to Cairo has experienced the lack of public toilets in the city. Upon returning to Cairo in summer 2019 to begin this research, I set out to find public toilets based on their reported locations in media reports, press releases, and social media posts. I posted inquiries in Cairo housing groups, women's neighborhood groups, and expatriate groups on Facebook, looking for local suggestions and recommendations as to where people relieve themselves while navigating the city and, in particular, asking if they had come across or heard of any public toilets. The post received nearly a hundred responses, with the bulk coming from a "women in Cairo" group. The responses mostly advised others to avoid public toilets at all costs and to try to use a restroom in a coffee shop, department store, or restaurant, with the disclaimer that they would still be dirty. Some women were very specific about which toilets they used and in which neighborhoods. One woman (the only one who recommended a public toilet) suggested a restroom behind the GoBus ticket office in Tahrir Square, which she described as acceptable for one or two pounds, but not as clean as home. Another woman, dismayed by the GoBus ticket office suggestion, stated that when she is in Tahrir Square she always uses the Nile Ritz Carleton bathroom, which she described as five stars and accessible to anyone. The comments reflected the diversity in toilet usage and accessibility based on class as well as nationality, with many expatriate women suggesting the use of private toilets, which may require you to make a purchase to use the facilities. Even if a purchase is not required, these toilets would not be available to a street vendor, for example, as they are very much limited in access, based on the perceived socioeconomic and national status of the bathroom patron. The comments I received also reflect the respondents' (and their socioeconomic cohorts') imaginings of what is public. For a wealthier toilet seeker, a hotel bathroom might be considered "public," while for someone working on the street, "public" refers to an uncommodified space.

Overall, four public toilets were mentioned in the posts, each with their accompanying horror stories. There was one self-cleaning toilet behind the Almaza bus station, which repeatedly malfunctioned, soaking the user. There was the adequate public toilet behind the GoBus ticket office near Tahrir Square. There was a reported "dirty hole" behind the main mosque in Khan al-Khalili. Lastly, the fourth toilet was a new self-cleaning toilet recently built near the Heliopolis Cathedral, which despite being self-cleaning was not, in fact, clean.

While combing through newspaper articles that mentioned public toilets around the city, time and time again I found these facilities described as spaces run by thugs and as places where vice took place, including drug use and prostitution. A media piece (Kassab 2018) described a Cairo public toilet as not only neglected and unhygienic, but also as covered in advertisements for sex workers with phrases like "beware of AIDS" written on the walls. One user interviewed in the piece, who comes to Cairo twice a week for work, stated that he uses the public toilet because he has no other option, although upon a recent visit someone there tried to sell him drugs. Articles also mentioned dirty syringes and empty vials on the floors. A list of public toilets mentioned in the articles was compiled and included public toilets in Ramses Square, on Tahrir Street, at the Muslim Youth Association, in Abd al-Munʿim Riyad Square, on Muʿizz Street, and in Bab al-Luq, by Ammonite Square. After searching for the ten public toilets reported in the Facebook group thread and in newspaper articles, nearly every toilet either could not be found or was closed or neglected beyond repair.

Who Gets to Pee?

The persistent lack of public toilets in Cairo plagues tourists and locals alike, but poses heightened challenges for women, the elderly, the sick, and those who work on the street with no access to facilities (Al-Iraqi 2018; Kotb 2014). The lack of access to a toilet to relieve oneself is linked to socioeconomic status. In general, one must be able to blend in and be read as "of the right class" while walking into a coffee shop, hotel, or restaurant, or one must be able to make a purchase in order to access a bathroom. Those who cannot afford to spend money in order to use the toilet throughout the day, such as street vendors, are left with few options. Public toilets are rarely available. When they are, a vendor must consider spending money to urinate in a toilet filthier than a street corner. The vendor is then left with four options: hold it, find a nearby toilet in the home or shop of someone they know, go to a mosque, or pee in the street. The first option is not sustainable. The second option is viable only if one can find someone to watch one's cart while one relieves oneself. Toilets in mosques used to be accessible to the general public, but recent laws aimed at curbing extremism have required mosques to close when not holding services, greatly limiting this option. The last alternative—peeing in the street—emerges as the most convenient option but is primarily available to men.

Due to the lack of public toilet infrastructure, there has been a growing issue with male public urination in Cairo, which has led to new forms of surveillance, shaming, and criminalization. In an initiative coordinated by local authorities and civil society groups, shame is deployed as a tactic to clean up the city and deter public urination. Signs have been posted in certain affluent neighborhoods in New Cairo and Heliopolis that warn public urinators that CCTV surveillance footage of people caught publicly urinating will be uploaded to YouTube in order to expose them. Several social media users were outraged at the appearance of these signs, criticizing the state for punishing citizens fulfilling a bodily function instead of providing public toilets (Diab 2018; Nabbout 2018).

There has also been an increased effort to enforce penalties for public urination under Article 278 of the Egyptian penal code, which references public indecency—a rather vague and flexible concept outlined by Rigot and Noralla and Abed in their chapters in this volume. According to this, offenders can be imprisoned for at least six months and/or be fined up to 5,000 Egyptian pounds (around $300) (Diab 2018). Men who urinate in public are pathologized as abnormal or indecent. They are also criminalized as the state deflects infrastructural neglect in providing basic services to its citizens, leading to the contamination of the urban environment. Additionally, the fine serves as a poverty tax. It disproportionately targets and burdens men of the lower socioeconomic classes who have nowhere else to relieve themselves throughout their workday. The lack of public infrastructure and the failure of the state to maintain existing public facilities thus becomes the plight of the pathologized, criminalized poor. The focus on policing low-level signs of visible disorder—loitering, graffiti, and public urination—is reminiscent of the "broken window theory" of urban disorder, which became popular in New York City in the early 1980s. The theory suggests that cracking down on low-level types of crimes prevents more serious crimes from occurring. Variations of these policies have been adopted by police forces in many cities around the world. Proponents have suggested that the presence of vandalism, public urination, or "broken windows" indicates the breakdown of the community, leaving it vulnerable to criminal invasion. The theory also pathologizes those who commit these low-level offenses by presuming that they are more likely to commit (or to attract those who would commit) more serious crimes, with pre-emptive arrest being cast as an effective means of preventing social disorder and delinquency (Kelling and Wilson 1982). These policies have often led to the biased policing of marginalized communities and massive numbers of arrests.

At the same time, the continued rhetoric of the Egyptian state and media depicting toilets as places of vice and uncleanliness, allegedly abused by citizens, becomes a rationale for the state and dominant classes for not building and maintaining more public toilets. The provision of infrastructure is thus transformed from a state-provided service to one provided by an informal network of toilet providers, creating an infrastructure from below. Likewise, the securitization of urination and the maintenance of social cleansing is carried out through surveillance from below, as neighborhood groups become enforcers of decency through shaming practices in coordination with state criminalization and policing efforts.

Infrastructure, Security, and Urban Social Cleansing

Over the last two decades, Cairo authorities have announced numerous initiatives to build public toilets in an effort to address these issues. The use of security discourse to distract from infrastructural neglect or to justify interventions of physical and social cleansing have been addressed by few authors.

Jennifer Bell and Mohammed Rafi Arefin have both written on the ways in which the Egyptian state has used environmental and security discourses to recast infrastructural neglect. Lack of proper infrastructure in Cairo's 'ashwa'iyat, particularly with regard to sanitation and waste management, can be re-narrated by the state as an environmental threat to the public good (Bell 2009). This environmentalist discourse is then used as a justification for the physical and social cleansing of an area through evictions, demolitions, and the surveillance of marginalized communities in order to make way for urban development and securitization of the city. Over the last few decades, the Egyptian state has focused its efforts on evacuating and demolishing many informal settlements, particularly those located near the heart of the city, in favor of developing private real estate projects, building roads, tourism, and other forms of urban development and gentrification.

The state has been motivated to deal with these informal settlements in order to reassert control over large swathes of the city that state actors fear would otherwise succumb to Islamist control. The often violent political struggles between 'ashwa'iyat residents and the state during the 1990s to early 2000s were often cast as environmental in nature, as the informal settlements largely do not have access to proper sanitation and waste management infrastructure. The use of environmentalist discourse as a justification for mass evictions provides political cover for the state in its claim to preserving the environment as a public good.

Rather than connect these settlements to proper infrastructure, the Egyptian state uses environmentalist discourse to clear an area, attempting to relocate residents to the outskirts of the city. The state thus reframes infrastructural neglect as environmental threat in order to justify gentrification and securitization (Bell 2009). Lack of infrastructure can also be used as a political tool, as the state reframes narratives through security discourses to further justify intervention in and control of the city (Arefin 2019). Heavy rainstorms in Alexandria in 2015 overwhelmed the city's sewage and drainage infrastructure systems and led to the deaths of seven people. The Egyptian state reframed these events to indicate that they were not due to state failure, a lack of proper urban and environmental governance, or climate change, but instead due to terrorism. The minister of the interior, as well as the director of Egypt's sanitation system, put out statements indicating that the flooding of the city was caused by terrorists who had attacked Alexandria's sewage infrastructure in order to create social unrest and encourage anti-government sentiments. Using security logic as a master discourse, the Egyptian state thus managed to obfuscate the infrastructural neglect of Alexandria's sewage system (which had previously been acknowledged as needing maintenance and modernization) and environmental issues, while justifying the increased securitization of the city. Following the incident, arrests were made of three Muslim Brotherhood members who had allegedly attacked the sanitation infrastructure. It was later revealed, however, that the men had been forcibly "disappeared" before the floods took place, and were already in custody. State violence often operates through the management of urban and environmental disasters, where deteriorating infrastructure and subsequent disasters are depicted as highly political threats that require an increase in policing, state presence, and urban security (Arefin 2019).

In both Bell's and Arefin's case studies, neglected or inadequate sanitation infrastructure has served as a productive tool for the state, justifying the physical/social surveillance and cleansing of the city and, in particular, aiding in efforts to crackdown on Islamist movements. Similarly, the coordinated decision of local authorities and community groups to install cameras and signage to deter urination through shaming practices capitalizes on the lack of available public infrastructure and the community's desire to rid itself of a public urination epidemic. This creates an empowered "neighborhood-pee-watch" security regime that endorses the state's social and physical cleansing of the city, resulting in the targeting of residents of lower socioeconomic status who lack access to toilets as they navigate or work in the city.

A Moral Duty to be Clean
An integral part of pursuing the securitization of the city under the guise of physical and social cleansing initiatives for the public good is attaining community support and engagement. In addition to working in coordination with community groups to monitor and punish public urination, the Egyptian and Cairo governments have also made efforts to link hygiene etiquette and bodily and urban cleanliness with moral and religious duties.

After President Morsi's ouster, interim president Adly Mansour issued a law in 2014 regulating sermons in an effort to stamp out extremist or Muslim Brotherhood messaging in mosques. The Egyptian Ministry of Endowments (*Awqaf*) became the government's means of regulating religious discourse through state-approved sermons and imams. President Abd al-Fattah al-Sisi continued these efforts and began working with the Ministry of Endowments to issue government-scripted sermons at Friday mosque prayers (Radwan 2015). The third government sermon delivered by Minister Mohamed Mokhtar Gomaa in July 2016, entitled "Cleanliness is a Civilized Human Behavior," linked Islamic requirements for cleansing and caring for the physical body *(tahara)* with spiritual purification of and responsibility for the cleanliness of the community. Gomaa stated that in developed societies, cleanliness and hygiene are practiced as routine behaviors and that Islamic law mandates this cleanliness as well. He explained in detail how Islam requires that cleanliness be a habit that touches every aspect of life: body, food, clothes, home, work, street, and public space. He specifically stated that Islam forbids people from urinating in public spaces where others rest, congregate, or walk, and that it is considered a contamination of the city that causes others harm. He also added that all were responsible for protecting the environment, particularly water resources, avoiding river and groundwater contamination. Gomaa questioned, if we know that Islam mandates cleanliness of the body and the environment and it is our duty to practice these requirements, why there was such a difference between our lived reality (and the pollution of our environment) and the teachings of the Prophet? He concluded that it is our duty as individuals to be personally clean and to participate in the cleanliness and maintenance of our society and environment. This, according to Gomaa, would truly reflect Islamic teachings and make Egypt a civilized, advanced society (Gomaa 2016).

Security logic has been reconfigured through new forms of sexualized and moralized governance in cities like Cairo and Rio de Janeiro by forming "human security states" (Amar 2013). As Duffield points out in this volume, security and redevelopment interventions by elites and the state are framed around the discourse of "humanitarian protection or securitized humanization," which is amplified and reified through dominant religious rhetoric. This Global South variant of the humanitarian rescue doctrine serves two purposes: a coerced protection and moral rehabilitation of society to bring dignity to communities, and the securing and policing of public spaces and the population. Rio de Janeiro's campaigns to redevelop and securitize the city in anticipation of hosting the 2014 World Cup and the 2016 Olympic Games offers an excellent illustration of this shift in discourse. Prior to 2011, security rhetoric in Rio was framed around the war on drugs. However, as plans were made to revamp the city prior to the mega-sports events, discourse shifted to human security. Protecting the population became a justification for mass social purification and urban cleansing efforts "to protect, rescue, and secure certain idealized forms of humanity identified with a particular family of sexuality, morality and class subjects" (Amar 2013, 5–6).

Sifr al-Mondial

The major impetus behind building public toilets in Cairo has been the desire to host international mega-sports tournaments, which signal international prestige and demonstrate the achievement of national aspirations to modernity. In January 2000, Egypt's Football World Cup organizing committee launched the nation's bid to host the 2010 World Cup, which was promised by the FIFA selection committee to be held in an African nation for the first time. The decision was linked to a modernization discourse regarding which African nation would be capable enough to host the event (Lopez 2009). In 2004, FIFA announced that South Africa had secured the bid for the 2010 World Cup with fourteen votes. Morocco received the second highest number of votes with ten. To the shock of Egyptians, Egypt had received zero votes (FIFA 2004). Despite the country's best-laid plans, and the fact that Egypt's national football club is Africa's oldest, its massive bidding campaign had drawn zero votes. A scandal ensued, referred to as *sifr al-mondial* (zero votes), trying to lay blame on various officials or FIFA corruption (which, indeed, was later exposed). One of the reasons given by FIFA for their lack of confidence in Egypt's ability to host the games was the absence of public toilets available throughout the country (Shahba 2018; al-Iraqi 2018). "*Sifr al-mondial*" became a popular Twitter hashtag (صفر_المونديال#) as well as a colloquial catch phrase to refer to all the government's failings (*Daily News Egypt* 2009).

Following the zero-vote scandal, Dr. Abd al-Azim Wazir, who was the governor of Cairo at the time, announced the launch of a new project to build electronic self-cleaning public toilets throughout the city that people could use for fifty piasters. These toilets were never built. A few years later, in 2007, another initiative—"Smart Toilets"—was announced. These plans included the installation of thirty-six electronic public toilets around various parts of Cairo. Most of these toilets were never built. The few that were constructed were removed by the state during the Egyptian Revolution, cited as security risks (Shahba 2018; al-Iraqi 2018).

The next public toilet initiative was announced in 2019 by Cairo governor Ali Abd al-'Al, who stated that, by the start of the 2019 Africa Cup of Nations (hosted in Egypt), there would be at least thirty eco-friendly public toilet units built in Cairo's various districts. These units would conserve water and have three separate stalls for men, women, and people who are differently abled. The facilities would also sell snacks and beverages, have two TVs, and be secured by round-the-clock video surveillance (*Egyptian Streets* 2019). A few of these for-pay toilet units were seen in proximity to stadiums during the African Cup: most could not be found, however. It is unknown if any still remain functional.

In 2018, Egypt's minister of youth and sports, Ashraf Sobhy, announced that Egypt would be bidding to host the 2030 World Cup and 2032 Olympics (*Ahram Online* 2018). After the announcement, Egyptians expressed concern over the expense to prepare for these efforts, and also the fear of potential humiliation and embarrassment, recalling the "zero vote" scandal of 2004 (Galal 2018). According to FIFA's guide to the bidding process, infrastructure accounts for 70 percent of a city's overall score in the evaluation process. The host government is also evaluated for its ability to maintain the safety and security of the event (FIFA 2017). Given the importance of infrastructure and security in the bidding process, one must ask, how will Cairo be physically and socially cleansed in its bid to host these international mega-events? As Amar highlights, Egypt already embodies the authoritarian, exclusionary, and debilitating logics of the so-called "human security state." How will this discourse shape the development of sanitation and other infrastructure, as well as the securitization and moralization of these public goods in the state's attempt to project the image of a clean modern city, and a physically and morally clean citizenry?

Conclusion

The lack of public toilets in Cairo has made it a challenge for anyone to relieve oneself while navigating or working in the city. This has led to a growing reliance on personal networks to access an informal toilet infrastructure, as well as the growing issue of public urination. Rather than build public toilets to meet these infrastructural challenges, the Egyptian state has focused on the social cleansing and securitization of the urban environment through community-coordinated surveillance, shaming strategies, and punitive measures, and by linking hygiene and urination etiquette to the religious and moral duty to maintain a clean body and environment. The infrastructural neglect of public toilets has thus been co-opted as a productive tool by the state through the use of a human security discourse to justify social cleansing and securitization efforts. The lack of public toilets is perpetuated by a narrative that they are dirty, immoral dens of vice that pose a threat to security, offering justification for not providing more public toilets. This leads to more public urination, which then justifies the further use of cameras, shaming tactics, and criminalization that disproportionately target the poor. The state has thus pathologized and criminalized behaviors rooted in poverty and a dearth of public services, rather than filling systemic infrastructural gaps.

Over the last two decades, the impetus to build public toilets in Cairo has been largely a response to Egyptians' desire to host international mega-sports events such as the Olympics and World Cup as part of an effort to project a modern and international image of the nation and cultivate patriotism. The public toilets built to accommodate these events are also a part of the surveillance and social cleansing of the city, equipped with cameras and attendants to monitor public spaces. As Egypt prepares its bids for more mega-events, discourse around human security and morality will continue to play a crucial role in the development or neglect of infrastructure in the process of cleansing and modernizing the urban environment and its inhabitants.

Works Cited

10Tooba. 2016. "Built Environment Deprivation Indicators: Access to Improved Sanitation." Built Environment Deprivation Indicators (BEDI), September. http://10tooba.org/bedi/en/water-sanitation/

Ahram Online. 2018. "Egypt Aims to Host 2030 World Cup and 2032 Olympics: Minister of Sports." *Al Ahram*, July 11. http://english. ahram.org.eg/NewsContent/1/64/306708/Egypt/Politics-/Egypt-aims-to-host--World-Cup-and--Olympics-Minist.aspx

Amar, Paul. 2013. *The Security Archipelago: Human-security States, Sexuality Politics, and the End of Neoliberalism*. Durham, NC: Duke University Press.

Arefin, Mohammed Rafi. 2019. "The State, Sewers, and Security: How Does the Egyptian State Reframe Environmental Disasters as Terrorist Threats?" *Annals of the American Association of Geographers* 109, no. 2: 412–21.

Article 19. 2018. "Egypt: 2018 Law on the Organisation of Press Media and the Supreme Council of Media." https://www.article19.org/wp-content/uploads/2019/03/Egypt-Law-analysis-Final-Nov-2018.pdf

Bell, Jennifer. 2009. "Land Disputes, the Informal City, and Environmental Discourse in Cairo." In *Cairo Contested: Governance, Urban Space, and Global Modernity*, edited by Diane Singerman, 349–71. Cairo: American University in Cairo Press.

Brandom, Russell. 2018. "Designing for the Crackdown." *The Verge*, April 25. https://www.theverge.com/2018/4/25/17279270/lgbtq-dating-apps-egypt-illegal-human-rights

Central Agency for Public Mobilization and Statistics (CAPMAS). 2008. "2006 Egyptian Census of Population and Living Conditions: Household Access to Sanitation." https://egypt.open dataforafrica.org/EGSNS2006/egypt-census-2006

Cunningham, Erin. 2014. "Cairo Bathhouse Raid Spreads Fear in Egyptian Gay Community." *Washington Post*, December 14. https://www.washingtonpost.com/world/middle_east/cairo-bathhouse-raid-spreads-fear-in-egyptian-gay-community/2014/12/13/2b332d96-7fc8-11e4-b936-f3afab0155a7_story.html

Dahir, Abdi Latif. 2016. "Egyptian Mosques Are Being Forced to Read Government-written Sermons." *Quartz*, July 29. https://qz.com/africa/739756/egypts-secular-government-is-making-mosques-read-government-written-sermons/

Daily News Egypt. 2009. "More about Hosni." *Daily News Egypt—Hidden Cities*. https://hiddencities.wordpress.com/tag/daily-news-egypt/

Diab, Nadim. 2018. "Urine Trouble! Cairo Campaign Threatens Public Shaming for Public Urination." *CGTN*, March 2. https://news.cgtn.com/news/3055544f35677a6333566d54/share_p.html

Egyptian Streets. 2018. "Cameras Installed in One of Cairo's Main Streets to Prevent 'Public Urination.'" *Egyptian Streets*, February 27. https://egyptianstreets.com/2018/02/27/cameras-installed-in-one-of-cairos-main-streets-to-prevent-public-urination/

———. 2019. "Egypt Will Introduce Eco-friendly Public Toilets around Cairo by the Summer." *Egyptian Streets*, March 31. https://egyptian streets.com/2019/03/31/egypt-introduces-eco-friendly-pub lic-toilets-around-cairo-by-the-summer/?fbclid=IwAR1-RZiRd3v YnspMEthXy7mvFJU2T56R-vuMrxdaWwPFonJsOPV3Nn3xH9c

FIFA. 2004. "2010 FIFA World Cup™—News—Host Nation of 2010 FIFA World Cup™—South Africa—FIFA.com." https://www.fifa.com/worldcup/news/host-nation-2010-fifa-world-cuptm-south-africa-92544

———. "Guide to the Bidding Process for the 2026 FIFA World Cup." https://img.fifa.com/image/upload/hgopypqftviladnm7q90.pdf

Galal, Rami. 2018. "Egyptians Brace for Disappointment as Cairo Makes Play for 2030 World Cup." *Al Monitor*, July 24. https://www.al-monitor.com/pulse/originals/2018/07/egypt-bids-for-2030-world-cup.html

El-Gergawi, Sherry. 2012. "A Surviving Tradition of Public Bathing in Egypt." *Ahram Online*, June 11. http://english.ahram.org.eg/ NewsContent/32/98/44502/Folk/Folk-Arts/A-surviving-tradition-of-public-bathing-in-Egypt.aspx

Gomaa, Mohamed Mokhtar. 2016. "al-Nazafa suluk insani mutahaddir." Awkaf Online. http://tinyurl.com/367bmdum

Greenberg, Andy. 2016. "Gay Dating Apps Promise Privacy, but Leak Your Exact Location." *Wired*, May 28. https://www.wired. com/2016/05/grindr-promises-privacy-still-leaks-exact-location/ #:~:text=Researchers%20in%20Kyoto%20demonstrate%20 for,features%20meant%20to%20hide%20them

HRW (Human Rights Watch). 2020. "Egypt: Spate of 'Morality' Prosecutions of Women." Human Rights Watch, August 17. https://www.hrw. org/news/2020/08/17/egypt-spate-morality-prosecutions-women.

Al-Iraqi, Reham. 2018. "Hammam 'umumi li-kul 757 alf muwatin: 'al-muhafazat maznuqa.'" *Al-Masry Al-Youm*, October 29. https:// www.almasryalyoum.com/news/details/1337734

Kassab, Mahmoud. 2018. "Suwar: 'Marahid al-shawari': sabbuba yudi-ruha baltagiya fi ghiyab al-riqaba." *Akhbar el-Yom*, August 12. https:// tinyurl.com/yypbc53b

Kelling, George L., and James Q. Wilson. 1982. "Broken Windows." *The Atlantic*, March. https://www.theatlantic.com/magazine/ archive/1982/03/broken-windows/304465/

El Kerdany, D. 2008. "The Reproduction of Popular Hammam: Applied on Tanbali, Bab El Shareyah." In *The Traditional Hammam: A Gift from the Past for the Future*. Damascus: n.p.

Khalaf, Rayana. 2018. "Egypt Wants to Host the World Cup and People Are Cracking Jokes." *Stepfeed*, July 13. https://stepfeed.com/egypt-wants-to-host-the-world-cup-and-people-are-cracking-jokes-3115

Kotb, Amr. 2014. "Public Urination: A Cairo Problem." *Ahram Online*, October 2. http://english.ahram.org.eg/NewsContent/1/0/112169/ Egypt/Public-urination-A-Cairo-problem.aspx

Krause, Ryan K. 2019. "In Conversation with Hamed Sinno." *V Magazine*, October 25. https://vmagazine.com/article/ in-conversation-with-hamed-sinno/

Lopez, Shaun. 2009. "Football as National Allegory: Al Ahram and the Olympics in 1920s Egypt." *History Compass* 7, no. 1: 282–305.

Al-Masry al-Youm. 2019. "Egypt to Establish Eco-friendly Toilet Units in Cairo Streets." *Egypt Independent*, March 28. https://egyptindependent. com/egypt-to-establish-toilet-eco-friendly-units-in-cairo-streets/

Nabbout, Mariam. 2018. "Egypt Installs Camera in Street to Catch People Who Pee in Public." *Stepfeed*, February 28. https://stepfeed.com/egypt-installs-camera-in-street-to-catch-people-who-pee-in-public-3085

Radwan, Tarek. 2015. "Egypt's Ministry of Endowments and the Fight against Extremism—Atlantic Council." Atlantic Council, July 23. https://tinyurl.com/25fe6vyu

Rigot, Afsaneh. 2020. "Egypt's Dangerous New Strategy for Criminalizing Queerness." *Slate*, December 30. https://slate.com/technology/2020/12/egypt-lgbtq-crime-economic-courts.html

Shahba, Alyaa Abo. 2018. "'The Egyptians Are Holding "It" In': One Public Toilet for Every 1/4 Million." *Medium*, October 5. https://medium.com/@alyaashahba_63413/the-egyptians-are-holding-it-in-one-public-toilet-for-every-%C2%BC-million-8b7b280a956b

Sherief, Abdel-Rahman. 2012. "The Ancient Tradition of Cairo's Bath Houses." *Daily News Egypt*, October 11. https://dailynewsegypt.com/2012/10/11/the-ancient-tradition-of-cairos-bath-houses/

Younes, Rasha. 2020. "For Sarah Hegazy: In Rage, in Grief, in Exhaustion." *The New Arab*, June 16. https://www.hrw.org/news/2020/06/16/sarah-hegazy-rage-grief-exhaustion

7

CAIRO'S SEXUALITY INFRASTRUCTURES
SECURITIZING ABORTION, HIV,
AND GENDER-AFFIRMING SURGERY

MIGUEL A. FUENTES CARREÑO

Research in the Middle East and North Africa can enrich the field of urban studies by looking at how the "street" and the "clandestine" can be re-territorialized from the perspective of sexuality and reproduction. News outlets and ethnographies have covered how police officers forced 170 inmates to get HIV testing after one man, arrested for alleged debauchery, was outed as living with HIV (Magid 2016). This harassment and stigmatization extends to the fever hospitals in the Cairo neighborhoods of Abbasiya and Imbaba, where people living with HIV (PLHIV) get their medicines. People I have met over the last few years often recall officers interrogating those who looked "effeminate" as they came out of these hospitals, checking their bags for condoms and antiretroviral treatments (ARV). The police assumed these men engaged in male-to-male intercourse or sex work.

Following similar prejudices, pharmacists in certain neighborhoods restrict the sale of misoprostol—"abortion pills"—to women they deem "unrespectable." This has led to such widely covered scandals that the current government has decreed that only hospitals, and not pharmacies, can sell misoprostol (Abd al-Salam 2014). Furthermore, Egypt, which allows gender reassignment surgery and provides hormonal treatment for trans people in hospitals, stalled such procedures between 2016 and 2019. A new system requiring the approval of the al-Azhar Islamic Research Academy is restricting how doctors may or may not "treat" an already pathologized "disorder" (Michael and Fam 2020). The sexual panics described by Abed, Rigot and Noralla, and Awadalla elsewhere in this volume cannot only be thought of in terms of arrests and legal repressions; they are also expressed in the literal infrastructural fabric of the city.

Access to certain treatments related to sexuality and reproduction does not come easily in Cairo. These include abortions, antiretroviral (ARV) treatments for HIV, hormone therapy, and gender reassignment surgery. Hospitals, laboratories, and pharmacies have become infrastructural intermediaries that must "authorize" the distribution of prescriptions, circulation of medication, and provision of healthcare. They also compete, however, with each other's and users' contradictory moral systems and the capitalist interests around sexuality and reproduction. Cairo's urban health infrastructure has become a regulatory force exerting control over free and autonomous bodies. It is inhabited by healthcare providers who replicate the moral panics and heteronormative systems of values around patients and nonpatients. Building on the research on reproductive and sexual pharmaceuticals in Egypt and the Middle East by Wynn and Foster (2016), in this chapter I examine the attempts of Egyptian administrators to establish a human-security governance regime that protects, rescues, and secures certain idealized forms of humanity identified with a particular group of sexualities, moralities, and class subjects (Amar 2013, 1–19) by pathologizing, commoditizing, and biomedicalizing sexuality and reproduction.

The public healthcare infrastructure in Cairo—understood in the present context as the spatial embodiment of "accessible" services and medications to either undergo an abortion,[1] carry on with HIV treatment, or go through hormone suppression/replacement therapy and/ or gender-reassignment surgery—needs to be understood differently than through the present pathologization and securitization of bodies. Epidemiologist Joseph Amon suggests we take an "epidemiological" approach to HIV that goes beyond the current biomedical and ethnographic approaches to infections. Scholars in the 1990s debated the epidemiological dimensions of abortion, mainly those surrounding abortion care advances in abortifacient chemical compounds, but also centering on the biomedical definition of the procedure (Blumenthal 1992, 506). Amon (2014) invites us to imagine the broad influence of education, drugs, criminal justice, laws, policies, and enforcement practices on health. Political epidemiology highlights not only the laws and police harassment noted in the introduction of the present chapter, but also how the laws, violence, and policies that deny prevention information and services impact upon vulnerability to HIV infection, access to treatment, and AIDS mortality. In other words, to understand what is happening in Cairo's health care system, we must go beyond pathologizing bodies as medical subjects, and look at the social and political practices that make these bodies vulnerable.

Here, I take an urban epidemiological approach where the location, construction, and organization of Cairo's buildings, streets, and centers impact upon vulnerability to HIV infection, treatment, and mortality, and upon induced-abortion care and maternal mortality. The urban epidemiology of healthcare infrastructure in Cairo reveals the dominance of the private sector and the informal circulation of medication in the last couple of years. It contextualizes restrictions on the supply of medication and healthcare that public hospitals and their pharmacies may offer. It also sheds light on: a) how people circulate and are displaced across cities in order to feel safe while accessing services that might otherwise heighten moral panics in their localities; b) how pathology in physical healthcare infrastructures can cement stigmas around sexual practices and reinforce inaccessibility to certain treatments; and c) how such infrastructure reinforces tropes of immorality and licentiousness, ignoring the need for imagining sexualities and sexual behaviors outside of and in transit from Cairo.

Methodologically, I look at material infrastructure and how it serves as the means to pathologize sexual and reproductive behaviors while de-centering medical infrastructures as the only spaces where these behaviors circulate and are embodied. I discuss the neighborhoods, streets, and unregulated centers that provide healthcare outside official hospitals. I consider not only the political, but also the infrastructural determinants that serve the securitizing and pathologizing political drive against people living with HIV, those seeking abortions, and those seeking hormonal treatment or gender reassignment surgery.

Following Abourahme's (2015) ethnography of concrete, and Hamdy's (2012) ethnography of biotechnologies, I map different healthcare centers and pharmacies in multiple neighborhoods in Cairo that have become more securitized since 2011. This is an integral part of a reworking of healthcare and its urban geography (sometimes as responses to emergencies; sometimes as responses to economic interests). I base my analysis on field work I conducted from 2016 to 2018, complementing this with participant observation in hospitals, pharmacies, and other spaces in the city where medical services and goods are found. Finally, I compare and contrast these sources with archival analysis of the official reports of the National AIDS Committee Officer published since 2011, UNFPA Egypt figures, and chronicles and reports from media outlets and other researchers' ethnographies.

Locating Cairo's History of Healthcare

As Hammad reminds us in their discussion of policing prostitution in the early twentieth century (this volume), Cairo has a long history of government-supported hospitals and clinics dedicated to sexual health. The centralization of HIV treatment, abortion procedures, hormone therapy, and sex reassignment surgery (SRS) in hospitals —be they fever or gyneco-obstetric hospitals— has similarly been ongoing in Cairo for a very long time. Public hospitals in the teeming popular neighborhoods of Imbaba, Abbasiya, al-Kasr al-'Aini, al-Husayn, and Ain Shams maintain a tight grip on the city with respect to sexual and reproductive affairs. Centralization creates new imaginations within and outside of Cairo regarding how to undergo certain sexual practices and reimagine networks of solidarity in order to keep oneself from dying within a debilitating healthcare system. Cairo's urban grid of healthcare infrastructure isn't limited to the top-down goals of government-led hospitals, but also is part of a complex of simultaneously competing markets and moral systems.

Although not the only place where abortions were provided, al-Kasr al-'Aini's School of Medicine has regulated midwifery and abortion care since the 1820s, when the school's predecessor was established in the industrial–military area of Abu Za'bal, after which it moved in the 1830s to downtown Cairo, and then moved once again in the 1990s to the edge of the upper-middle-class neighborhoods of Garden City and Manial. In 1789, Sultan Selim III forbade physicians and pharmacists from selling drugs that induced abortion (Demirci and Somel 2008, 377), demonstrating that pharmacies were already present in Cairo at that time and that private transactions already faced competing obstacles and freedoms around sexuality and reproduction.

Abbasiya Hospital came into being around 1840, just a couple of decades before the British Mandate. Labeled a fever hospital, it was one of the first of its kind in Egypt. We can find records dating to 1908 of "Cairo's Fever Hospital" treating cases of typhoid fever (Phillips 1910, 969). Abbasiya remained the only hospital treating infections that caused fevers of unknown origins until the 1940s. The report of the USA Typhus Commission noted the founding of Imbaba's fever hospital in 1943–44, and described it as a way to deal with the rising number of typhus cases in Cairo during the Second World War (Ecke et al. 1945).

Hospitals in charge of hormone therapy and gender reassignment surgery in Egypt date back only to the late twentieth century. Sally Mursi was the first person to undergo such treatment in Egypt in 1988, but the hospital where she underwent her procedure has remained anonymous (Skovguard-Peterson 1995). Mahmud Hashim's PhD thesis on female epileptic patients in 1987, however, reported trans patients in al-Husayn Psychiatry Hospital, Bab El Shariaa Hospital, and El Zahra Hospital (Ibrahim Abd el Atti 2009, 67). Since the Egyptian Medical Syndicate modified their Code of Ethics in 2003 to allow for surgery on intersex people, al-Kasr al-'Aini and al-Husayn University Hospital of al-Azhar became the public hospitals where these procedures could be undergone for free. Although the Egyptian Medical Syndicate hasn't yet made available their 2013 Code of Ethics (Egyptian Medical Syndicate 2003), several activists and news outlets report that it has medicalized and authorized treatment for "gender identity disorder" in the country (Amin 2020; Islam 2015; Magid 2015).

Postrevolution Urban Infrastructures of HIV

Various news articles, along with official reports from the National AIDS Program (NAP), constantly claim an insufficiency of coverage of ARV treatment for people who need consistent access to their medication. Cairo centralized the distribution of ARV medications until 2010, when it expanded coverage to six more governorates (Ministry of Health and Population (Egypt) 2010, 14). Despite this alleged increase in access and distribution, in 2015 people still generally went to Abbasiya and Imbaba in Cairo (although some also preferred Tanta in the Delta) to get their treatment, mainly because of the degree of anonymity permitted there in contrast with smaller provincial hospitals (W. Hassan 2015, 52). This means that Cairo's urban healthcare landscape remains the main governing body over HIV care in Egypt.

Although Wessam Hassan argues that people prefer Cairo's hospitals (W. Hassan 2015, 52), since 2011 there has been a significant shortage and irregular distribution of treatment in them. Centralization has led people who want access to ARV treatment to receive it late or in an incomplete form, or to buy it from abroad. Class and gender differences become evident in the processes of the rigid yet inconsistent healthcare system surrounding HIV. Hassan's ethnography of mothers from working-class neighborhoods in Cairo revealed how social workers regard them differently from upper-class women. The former are seen as naive and "simple," unaware of what the virus entails. Islam Khalid Hassan's work sheds light on the patronizing treatment these women receive, labeling them "culturally or morally 'inadequate for treatment'" based on social class (I.K. Hassan 2015, 56). On the other hand, middle- and upper-class men I've encountered since 2016 who are diagnosed with HIV tend to be treated as having been infected "abroad" due to their constant traveling as professionals. They have access to healthcare consultation in Europe, as well as to (expensive) ARV treatments outside Egypt.

Despite these examples, healthcare providers have told me that quality of healthcare is not determined by class, as they've known people, both rich and poor, getting sent to the fever hospitals and receiving their treatment for free. A specific case these professionals have mentioned involves an Egyptian man with dual European citizenship. He was an injected drug user, and instead of getting his treatment in Europe, he received it at Abbasiya's Fever Hospital without any problem. However, I wish to highlight the intersections of class and gender at play in this example and also how sexuality doesn't play a central role in the story of this man, who never lost the option of traveling abroad for medication. Without discounting the reality that not everyone is treated violently or is discriminated against in these hospitals, sexuality has become a central variable in how people interact with these structures and those who inhabit them. In this way, the sexual panics described by Abed, Rigot and Noralla, and Awadalla in this volume have had a profound impact on healthcare in Egypt.

Kabbash et al. conducted a study in 2018 that reaffirms this trend. They found that urban infrastructure has effects on seeking consultation, adhering to treatment, and reinforcing stigma. The specific urban location of certain facilities that dispense ARVs has become stigmatized by healthcare workers, hospital patients, and their visitors as "the place for drugs for HIV/AIDS patients." Within these structures, patients with complications related to AIDS are isolated in a "ward for AIDS patients." Finally, pharmacy workers in the hospitals' pharmacies speak loudly when talking about drugs being used for HIV treatment, publicly disclosing people's diagnoses (Kabbash, Zidan, and Shehata 2019, 63–64).

This story isn't isolated. Imbaba is perceived as a working-class neighborhood that serves the many refugees and migrants from Upper Egypt that inhabit the area. In its fever hospital, the area testing and treating PLHIV is accessible only through a small corridor at the back of the building. The HIV ward is not easily found nor publicly announced. In it, people are crammed into a small room (Mesahat Foundation for Sexual and Gender Diversity 2020, 25). When asked about it, healthcare providers and security guards are secretive and judgmental. This neglect of the physical space around which HIV is discussed is replicated in other government-run spaces. Voluntary and Confidential Counseling and Testing Centers (VCCTs) are usually hidden in residential buildings and their neighbors stigmatize them. People are reluctant to use them because the actual spaces enact a culture of stigma against giving away condoms, as if this encouraged "vice" and "illegal sex" (Bakhoum 2015, 190).

The physical construction of these spaces is thus a vital element in subject formation. The criminalization of certain sexual practices, such as those among sex workers and men who have sex with men, raises tensions and contradictions in its codependence with restrictions in healthcare services for things like HIV treatment. Nardine, a trans woman living with HIV, tells how the doctor at Abbasiya yelled, "Oh, shame!" when she disclosed that the cause of her infection was "same-sex intercourse." She demanded to be treated respectfully when trying to get her ARVs, but she was kicked out and transferred to Imbaba after fighting with the doctor, who responded, "I know what I need to know" (Mesahat Foundation for Gender and Sexual Diversity 2020, 22–23).

Abortion and Private/Public Divisions

Reproduction and birth can present an intersecting point to look at differentiated treatment based on sexual and reproductive performativities, as well as a way of transitioning toward abortion as a public service. Due to the COVID-19 crisis, UNAIDS Egypt and public hospitals issued reports on how to continue the provision of gynecological services, especially for women living with HIV. Reading between the lines of this report, however, we see that while the title reads "Dedicated Health Interventions to PLHIV in times of COVID-19," the content only covers mother-to-child transmission (UN Egypt 2020, 7). This ongoing "invisibilization" in the public sphere of criminalized sexual behaviors—in this case, those that may lead to abortion—has come about through a long-term process of criminalization and repression in healthcare services post-2011.

Harb and Habil conducted a study in 2013 on induced abortion in the two largest public hospitals in Cairo and one in Alexandria. Their study shows that women in Cairo report that they induced abortion at a rate three times less than those in Alexandria. The authors compared their findings with a study from the 1990s where the national prevalence for induced abortion was around 60 percent. While it appears that a reduction in abortions has taken place in Egypt, in reality, there has been a reduction in aborting women in public hospitals. Looking at Cairo more than a decade later, the low rate of abortions reported in the largest hospitals of the capital allows us to reflect on how these spaces have become feared, resorted to only when no other option seems to be available (Harb and Habil 2013, 160–61).

As is the case with HIV treatment, class divisions circulate through and outside hospitals, reifying how sexuality and reproduction can be affected by class and gender. Like the stories of people getting their ARV treatment for HIV outside Egypt if they can afford to avoid stigma in Cairo's cityscape of moral panic, people seeking an abortion will pay to avoid public hospitals in the city. Lack of a proper healthcare network in the city to provide care for those wanting to get an abortion leads people to seek clandestine abortions from what are known as "stairwell clinics." The main factor involved in this decision is socioeconomic status (Gaddah 2019). According to the EIPR, this translates into women having to "buy safety" in order to conduct an abortion at clandestine clinics or with private gynecologists (EIPR and SRI 2014).

As in the narrow corridors of the Imbaba Fever Hospital, where information regarding HIV is whispered or avoided, secrecy around abortion in the healthcare system leads to a configuration of sexual behaviors around shame and discretion which seeks to hide them "under the stairwell." Consequently, negligence and unsafety reproduce a circle of embodied danger around abortion when it takes place in hospitals. An account from 2015 narrates how a woman affirmed that one can only get abortions in hospitals, but the gynecologist she contacted said he wouldn't do it unless it was performed in a private hospital located in a low-income neighborhood (presumably far away from his usual clientele). Despite the infrastructural association of abortion with sketchy medical facilities, the woman said the doctor agreed to help her because she seemed to be a "reputable girl." Another account in that same article narrates how a private physician performs the same procedure in his clinic, but generally only for middle- and upper-class women who can afford it (Hosny 2015). In another story from 2018, rich people were described as being able to undergo surgical abortions in a safe medical facility, while many others, regardless of their social status, cannot or don't know how to reach doctors and private hospitals (Abazza 2018). Achieving a safe abortion—or any abortion at all—is thus a matter of learning how to circulate through these health-related cityscapes and negotiate their constant capital-based barriers.

A different trend occurring around abortion involves rising costs. That hasn't happened with ARV treatment, due to the low prices of "abortion pills," mainly based on misoprostol.[2] Because misoprostol isn't labeled for abortions, but rather for treating gastric ulcers, this medication can be easily bought in pharmacies across Egypt.[3] However, in the last couple of years, a rise in awareness among government officials and healthcare providers of its use as an abortifacient has resulted in new regulations and surveillance. Pharmacies in Cairo, as sites for private transactions, have become spaces for competing values surrounded by moral panics that extend outside the physical infrastructure of hospitals.

According to the testimonies of both consumers and pharmacists, Cytotec (Pfizer's brand name for misoprostol) was available over the counter in Egypt early in the 2000s. Different pharmacists claim that the government gradually restricted it, causing the price to rise from around LE 11 ($0.60 in 2017) to between LE 50 and LE 200 per blister pack (Abdel Rahman 2017; El-Behary 2016). In 2009, however, the government decided to restrict Cytotec's distribution, allowing only hospitals to prescribe the pills under the supervision of a treating physician (Abd al-Salam 2014).

Pharmaceutical regulations and the threat of getting shut down have led many pharmacists to pretend they do not have the pills, even when they do. One pharmacist, Shadi Abd al-Hafiz, said that Misotac was also available for a very low price in pharmacies, despite the government having banned it. No officials have ever followed up on how many pills he has sold (Abdel Rahman 2017). Wa'il Ahmad, another pharmacist, said that both mifepristone and misoprostol are available in pharmacies, but are not sold to consumers because pharmacists fear that women coming in to ask for it are trying to abort. Moreover, pharmacists assumed that those female customers were unmarried women and sex workers. Another pharmacist, Nuha al-Sayyid, further explained that women came to buy misoprostol pills so regularly that the Ministry of Health, operating under the same assumptions, banned their sale outside hospitals (Abdel Rahman 2017; El-Behary 2016; Shalaby 2013).

Securitization in Cairo has led to the persecuting and public reprimanding of pharmacies as a way to reconfigure the urban landscape of Cairo around sexuality and reproduction. When it shuts down and polices these private spaces, the state forces people seeking an abortion back into the hospitals, over which the government holds more control. There are two cases of pharmacies in Cairo that shed light on how gender and class configure this part of the healthcare infrastructure. In

2016, a pharmacist in Nasr City reported that there had been an increase in demand for abortion pills among high school and college students, as well as among married women (al-Din 2016). He said it had become harder to get Misotac, an Egyptian brand, but that women still managed to get Cytotec, an American brand, through illegal importation. In the second story, five pharmacies in the Basateen district were accused of selling "sexual stimulants" and "abortion capsules," leading to arrests and widespread coverage by the media of "security aspects that affect the daily life of citizens" (Al Gabaty 2015; Marei 2015; Ghaith 2015). In contrast with the description of the pharmacist in Nasr City, the article describes these pharmacies in a slum area between Cairo and Maadi as selling illicit drugs that put people at risk, and which promote both abortion and forbidden sexual behavior.

The urban landscape of working-class neighborhoods includes the criminalization of the activities taking place in it and a harsher description by the media. As a middle-class area, the reporting about the "educated women" of Nasr City seemed to portray the topic with a softer take, even though it is still characterized as illegal. Similarly, it is harder to find news scandals about pharmacies selling abortion pills in Maadi or Zamalek, two affluent neighborhoods in Cairo. The closest I could find to work done in a middle-class neighborhood was reporting about contraception in Dokki (Eickhof 2018, 207). Meanwhile, moral panics around slums as sites of debauchery and sex crimes reproduce an urban landscape where the rich can "buy their safety," as EIPR explained, while poor neighborhoods appear to incubate sex criminals. These cases become examples of what Paul Amar calls "infranationalism," since media coverage naturalizes social, moral, and cultural binaries by building gendered, class, and moral control discourses into the grids, services, and built infrastructural forms of the city (Amar 2013, 32). In this case, pharmacists are reproducing binaries through the physical location of the pharmacies themselves. They are an embodiment of the moral panic over certain people being able to buy "illicit drugs" like abortifacient pills.

Urban Epidemiological Approaches to Hormones and Gender-affirming Surgery

Since 2013, EIPR has tracked a rise in the average number of arrests among men who have sex with men and transgender people in Egypt under a new type of security campaign directed against those considered to have "non-normative sexualities." This campaign was particularly centered in

Cairo, where most arrests took place from 2013 to 2017 (Abdel Hamid 2017, 9). Evidence used against trans people has consisted of "hormonal medication" along with other objects such as wigs, women's underwear, beauty products, condoms, and lubricants (Abdel Hamid 2017, 22). EIPR's report focused on the legal and security dimensions of entrapment of non-conforming sexualities, but it is also important to demystify the urban grid and the government's grip over it in order to break open the "black box" of the state. This involves looking into competition between the differing values of doctors and religious officials; between private and public hospitals; and between hospitals and pharmacies. Ahmed, a transgender man who went public with his life story, explains that "different entities in Egypt don't talk to each other." According to him, even if the government subsidizes gender-affirming surgeries, police officers and the judiciary will refuse to change official documents to match one's gender. Police officers continuously question, ridicule, and abuse transgender people when looking at their documents (Murdock 2016).

Any hormone or surgical treatment for trans people comes with the direct intervention and authorization of al-Azhar's religious authorities. Fatwas by al-Azhar's muftis tighten or loosen control over medical procedures around sex and gender reassignment surgeries. They have provided doctors with autonomy at different points in time, however. In 2013, news outlets and activists reported a shift in restrictions. The Egyptian Medical Syndicate's new Code of Ethics allowed for surgeries as long as they were approved by an ethics committee from the syndicate (Islam 2015; Mounir 2019). This committee is composed of medical specialists and a representative from Egypt's Islamic Advisory (Dar al-Iftaa). The latter stopped attending meetings around 2016, and subsequently procedures and authorizations were halted (Amin 2020; Michael and Fam 2020). In 2017, Dr. Usama Abd al-Hayy, the chair of this committee, stated that no gender reassignment surgery could take place without the committee's approval and that all such surgeries must be performed in "government hospitals" (Abbas 2017b).

Looking at the archives of journal productions regarding medical treatments for trans people, along with public interviews and testimonies, we can identify three stages where Cairo's public healthcare involvement and urban layout shape trans people's medical care, depending on the services they can access at different geographical points of the city. These include: 1) limited psychiatric treatment from the 1980s until 2003 in public hospitals (notably at the al-Husayn and al-Kasr al-ʿAini hospitals) (Amin 2020; Ibrahim Abd el Atti 2009; Skovguard-Peterson

1995); 2) hormone treatment that generally takes place through private pharmacies and surgery, mainly in private hospitals, due to criminalization in the 2000s, with mostly psychiatric and psychological support from Cairo's public hospitals (Murdock 2016; Nader 2019); 3) hormone and surgical treatment in public hospitals since 2013, although some obstructions and suspensions in 2017 led to a return to seeking treatment from the private sector (Magid 2015; Mahmoud 2018; Amin 2020). The strict control and many obstacles over the government-run medical centers has led to people seeking a broader array of private services, dispersed through the city.

These overlapping histories signal a complicated postrevolutionary landscape of institutions and bureaucracies that trans people must learn to navigate. I focus here on three hospitals that offered medical treatment for trans people: al-Kasr al-'Aini, the al-Husayn Psychiatric Hospital of al-Azhar, and Demerdash Hospital (part of the Faculty of Medicine of Ain Shams University). Like al-Kasr al-'Aini and the Abbasiya Fever Hospital, Demerdash Hospital is also located in Abbasiya. The al-Husayn Hospital is part of the al-Azhar complex that mainly manages the psychological and psychiatric dimensions of treatment for trans people (Abbas 2017a). Al-Kasr al-'Aini's first floor contains the psychiatry, addiction treatment, and "gender identity disorder" (GID) clinics. People coming from distant governorates arrive in Cairo mainly for the GID clinic, leaving "not much space for psychiatric or drug addiction patients" (Abbas 2017a). The clinic becomes a space where they end up exchanging phone numbers to "transmit their experiences and help each other," which allows them to "remain a group," "seize their rights," and force the state to "recognize them" so they can "have their operations and confirm their identity." Abbas describes the al-Husayn and Demerdash hospitals as having similar layouts. Within the clinics, trans people express their preferred gender through clothes, demeanor, and voice. Real access to a service now available in public facilities is again limited by social class (to those who can afford travel abroad and paying for surgery without major medical obstacles); gender divisions (more successful surgeries for trans women than for men); geographic mobility within Egypt; and spatial literacy regarding hospitals.

Al-Azhar Husayn Hospital's role in leading research in trans hormone and surgical treatments reaffirms the already powerful role the institution holds in approving the requests that go through the new ethics committee. If patients want (or can only afford) free or low-cost care, then they must travel to Cairo. This does not mean, however, that such care has not existed elsewhere in the country. Around 2013, studies showed that the medical care for GID in Assiut was comparable to the care available in Cairo (Helmy and Mohammed 2014), signaling some decentralization.

Thinking about pharmacies as smaller, less intimidating, and more available sites for treatments involving sexuality becomes increasingly relevant in the urban epidemiology of healthcare infrastructures. Although some healthcare providers, like those in the al-Husayn Hospital, argue that they provide hormones to any trans patient they take care of (Cairoscene Staff 2015), activists and healthcare providers outside the psychiatric world confirm that people buy hormones in local pharmacies without medical prescriptions (Magid 2015). But even within this parallel urban economy, there are gendered differences in hormone access. Estrogen pills are commonly available, as they are usually prescribed by gyneco-obstetricians for women undergoing menopause. However, healthcare providers have informed me that testosterone blockers (used mainly by trans women) are harder to find. Though it is popular, Egypt stopped importing Androcur. Activists weren't able to tell me why, but commercial websites describe it as a sex-drive inhibitor (Samir n.d.) rather than a hormone used for gender-affirming processes.

Reconfiguring Cairo's Cityscape of Sexuality

Understanding sexuality and reproduction in terms of urban infrastructures of health has salience in the realms of abortion, HIV treatment, and trans hormone and surgery treatments—practices that presume illicit sexual behaviors and are forced to operate in a cloud of moral panic. Based on conversations among ARV users, uneven and interrupted access leads to people sharing pills and prolonging treatment for as long as possible. Networks of solidarity in support groups allow shared success stories in accessing necessary care. Similarly, people using abortion pills report getting them from peers when pharmacies won't provide them. Male-presenting people who read as upper-class in certain neighborhoods gain access to misoprostol for those who wouldn't otherwise be helped (Ahmed 2018). Finally, trans people buy hormones from private pharmacies and create their own networks after visiting public hospitals. Informal circulation outside the public and private enterprises of the urban landscape blurs lines that seem rigid in terms of access to healthcare around abortion, HIV, and hormones. Despite the widespread use of this clandestine and porous circulation, the practice still poses risks for people lacking professional consultation with healthcare providers (Inhorn 1994).

The assemblage of human and nonhuman actors linked to a larger political structure consists of biotech corporations, the state, nurses, doctors, engineers, the electrical grid, machines, and the human body itself (Hamdy 2012, 184). Abortion patients are hooked into hospitals when medical abortions go wrong. Similarly, trans people are forced to depend on medical approval and jump through new bureaucratic hoops with regard to ID changes, the labor market, and interactions with the security forces. Patients experience vulnerability at every step through this cityscape. The present text provides alternative ways to imagine Cairo's urban epidemiological healthcare infrastructure through decentralized circulation by showing competing moral and economic value systems and uses of existing and new infrastructure. But there are alternative approaches that account for mobility of bodies, economies, and materialities outside apparently rigid urban grids.

Notes

1   Pills such as misoprostol and methotrexate are less invasive and less expensive than other abortion pills.
2   Mifepristone is banned in Egypt; thus all chemical abortifacients are based solely on misoprostol. Medical studies in the country always cite Pfizer's Cytotec as the most common version, but in the last couple of years, it has been substituted by Egypt's generic versions.
3   For detailed information about reproductive pharmaceutical regimes and availability, see medicationabortions.com, a website authored by Angel Foster and L.L. Wynn.

Works Cited

Abazza, Jihad. 2018. "Tahta bi'r al-sillim: al-ighad ghayr amin fi Misr." *Daraj*, January 24. https://daraj.com/1282/

Abbas, Ibtisam Mahmoud. 2017a. "Idtirab al-huwiyya al-ginsiyya . . . gadwal al-marda: thalathat ayyam bi-l-Qasr al-Aini wa-l-Dimirdash wa-l-Hussayn." *Masr al-Youm*, August 28. https://www.almasry alyoum.com/news/details/1183884.

———. 2017b. "Ra'is tashih al-gins bi-l-atibba': tawassalna li-ittifaq ma'a mufti al-gumhuriya li-'awdat 'amal al-lagna, wa-uhadhir min igra' al-'amaliyyat duna muwafaqatuna." *al-Masry Al-Youm*, August 28. https://www.almasryalyoum.com/news/details/1183931

Abd al-Salam, Walid. 2014. "al-Sayadila tukhatib al-Sihha li-sarf mustahdar Misoprostol bi-l-saydaliyyat al-'amma." *Youm7*, September 9. https://tinyurl.com/y5225e62

Abdel Hamid, Dalia. 2017. "The Trap: Punishing Sexual Difference in Egypt." Cairo: Egyptian Initiative of Personal Rights. https://eipr.org/en/publications/trap-punishing-sexual-difference-egypt

Abdel Rahman, Aya. 2017. "Seeking an Abortion in the Arab World." *Raseef22*, March 28, 2017. http://raseef22.com/en/life/2017/03/28/extortion-possible-death-seeking-abortion-arab-world/

Abourahme, Nasser. 2015. "Assembling and Spilling-over: Towards an 'Ethnography of Cement' in a Palestinian Refugee Camp." *International Journal of Urban and Regional Research* 39, no. 2: 200–17.

Ahmed, Ghadeer. 2018. "Abortion Tales: Women's Work." *Mada Masr* (blog), January 19. https://madamasr.com/en/2018/01/19/feature/society/abortion-tales-womens-work/

Amar, Paul. 2013. *The Security Archipelago: Human-security States, Sexuality Politics, and the End of Neoliberalism*. Durham, NC: Duke University Press.

Amin, Shahira. 2020. "Actor's Revelation about Transgender Son Sends Shock Waves across Conservative Egypt." *Al-Monitor*, May 12. https://www.al-monitor.com/originals/2020/05/egypt-actor-transgender-son-lgbtq-rights.html

Amon, Joseph J. 2014. "The Political Epidemiology of HIV." *Journal of the International AIDS Society* 17, no. 1: 19327. https://www.ncbi.nlm.nih.gov/pmc/articles/PMC4110379/

Bakhoum, Atef Yousef. 2015. "HIV/AIDS, Hepatitis and Sexually-transmitted Infection Prevention among Egyptian Substance Users." PhD diss., University of East Anglia. https://ueaeprints.uea.ac.uk/id/eprint/59677/

El-Behary, Hend. 2016. "Buying an Abortion in the Virtual World of Facebook." *Egypt Independent*, July 26. https://ww.egyptindependent.com/buying-abortion-virtual-world-facebook/

Blumenthal, P.D. 1992. "Abortion: Epidemiology, Safety, and Technique." *Current Opinion in Obstetrics & Gynecology* 4, no. 4: 506–12.

CairoScene. 2015. "Transgender in Egypt: Uncovering the Ugly Truth." *CairoScene*, August 27. https://cairoscene.com/In-Depth/transgender-in-egypt-uncovering-the-ugly-truth

Demirci, Tuba, and Selçuk Akşin Somel. 2008. "Women's Bodies, Demography, and Public Health: Abortion Policy and Perspectives in the Ottoman Empire of the Nineteenth Century." *Journal of the History of Sexuality* 17, no. 3: 377–420.

al-Din, Uthman Jamal. 2016. "Saydaliyyat tabiʻ adwiya li-l-ighad . . . wa-talibat al-gamiʻat wa-l-madaris al-akthar iqbalan." *Al-Fajr Gate*, September 30. https://www.elfagr.org/2293393

Ecke, Robert S., A.G. Gilliam, J.C. Snyder, A. Yeomans, C.J. Zarafonetis, and E.S. Murray. 1945. "The Effect of Cox-type Vaccine on Louse-borne Typhus Fever." *American Journal of Tropical Medicine and Hygiene* 1, no. 6: 447–62.

Egyptian Medical Syndicate. 2003. "Profession Ethics Regulations. Issued by the Resolution of the Minister of Health and Population No. 238/2003." Egyptian Medical Syndicate. http://www.ems.org.eg/rules/sub/27

Eickhof, Ilka. 2018. "Fear and Floating in Alexandria: The Economy, the Pound, and Women's Sexual Health." *Egypte/Monde Arabe* 17, no. 1: 193–216.

EIPR and SRI. 2014. "Joint Submission to the Universal Periodic Review 2014 of Egypt." United Nations Human Rights Council. https://www.upr-info.org/sites/default/files/document/egypt/session_20_-_october_2014/js1_upr20_egy_e_main.pdf

Al Gabaty, Tamer. 2015. "Dabt aqras wa-munashitat ginsiya fi hamla mukabbara 'ala saydaliyyat al-Qahira." جريدة البيان (blog), March 15. https://tinyurl.com/y3hxbdtr

Gaddah, Rasha. 2019. "Abortion in the Arab World." *Ahram Online*, August 3. http://english.ahram.org.eg/NewsContent/1/64/341914/Egypt/Politics-/Abortion-in-the-Arab-world.aspx

Ghaith, Ashraf. 2015. "al-Qabd 'ala mas'ulin 'an khams saydaliyat wa makhazin adwiya bi-l-Qahira." *Al-Masry Al-Youm*, March 14. https://www.almasryalyoum.com/news/details/679555

Hamdy, Sherine. 2012. *Our Bodies Belong to God: Organ Transplants, Islam, and the Struggle for Human Dignity in Egypt*. Berkeley: University of California Press.

Harb, H., and I. Habil. 2013. "Frequency and Profile of Induced Abortions: Hospital Based Study in Tertiary Hospitals in Egypt." *Journal of Preventive Medicine and Hygiene* 54, no. 3: 159–62.

Hassan, Islam Khalid. 2015. "GCC's 2014 Crisis: Causes, Issues and Solutions." Al-Jazeera Centre for Studies, March 31. http://studies.aljazeera.net/en/dossiers/2015/03/20153317262365253l.html.

Hassan, Wessam. 2015. "Cantus Lamentus: Navigating HIV Positive Mothers Subjectivities in Egypt Post 2011." Master's thesis, American University in Cairo.

Helmy, Yasser, and Essam Eldin Mohammed. 2014. "Medico-legal and Ethical Regulations in Management of Sexual Disorders (SD): Assessment of Patients' Satisfaction." *Al-Azhar Assiut Medical Journal* 12, no. 3: 316–28.

Hosny, Farah. 2015. "The Trouble with Abortions in Egypt." *CairoScene*, August 20. https://cairoscene.com/In-Depth/The-Trouble-with-Abortions-in-Egypt.

Ibrahim Abd el Atti, Sameh. 2009. "Systematic Review of Egyptian Studies on Sexual and Gender Identity Disorders." Master's thesis, Ain Shams University Faculty of Medicine, Cairo. http://psychiatry-research-eg.com/texts/ins/HQ2010–10430.pdf

Inhorn, Marcia. 1994. *Quest for Conception: Gender, Infertility and Egyptian Medical Traditions*. Philadelphia: University of Pennsylvania Press.

Islam, Salma. 2015. "The Untold Story of Egypt's Transgender Community." *Egyptian Streets*, July 12. https://egyptianstreets.com/2015/07/12/the-untold-stories-of-egypt-transgender-community/

Kabbash, Ibrahim A., Omar O. Zidan, and Yasser A. Shehata. 2019. "Antiretroviral Therapy in Egypt: Are There Any Barriers to Medication Adherence?" *The Egyptian Journal of Community Medicine* 37, no. 2: 58–65. DOI: 10.21608/EJCM.2019.30916

Magid, Pesha. 2015. "On Being Transgender in Egypt." *Mada Masr* (blog), June 4. https://www.madamasr.com/en/2015/06/04/feature/politics/on-being-transgender-in-egypt/

———. 2016. "What the Decision to Test All Detainees at a Police Station for HIV Reveals about Egypt's Security Services." *Mada Masr*, March 18. https://www.madamasr.com/en/2016/03/18/feature/politics/what-the-decision-to-test-all-detainees-at-a-police-station-for-hiv-reveals-about-egypts-security-services/.

Mahmoud, Ebtsam. 2018. "Transgender in Egypt: Sex Reassignment Surgical Procedures around the World." *Egypt Independent*, January 8. https://egyptindependent.com/transgender-egypt-sex-reassignment-surgical-procedures-around-world/

Marei, Ahmed. 2015. "Dabt arba' mas'uli saydaliyyat bi-dakhilaha alaf al-aqras ghayr al-musarrah bi-tadawuliha bi-l-Qahira." *Youm7*, March 14. https://www.youm7.com/story/2015/3/14/ضبط-4-مسئولى-صيدليات-بداخلها-آلاف-الأقراص-غير-المصرح-بتداولها/2105137

Mesahat Foundation for Sexual and Gender Diversity. 2020. "Medical Violations against LGBTQI++ Community." Meem-oirs 5 (July 26). https://issuu.com/amroos/docs/english

Michael, Maggie, and Mariam Fam. 2020. "In Egypt, Transgender Activist Fights Battle on Many Fronts." *The Times of Israel*, March 30. https://www.timesofisrael.com/in-egypt-transgender-activist-fights-battle-on-many-fronts/

Ministry of Health and Population (Egypt). 2010. "Egypt. National Country Progress Inform. Survey Response Details."

Mounir, Imam. 2019. "Transsexuals Shall Not Inherit — Law vs Society in Egypt." *Raseef22*, November 20. https://raseef22.net/article/1076073-transsexuals-shall-not-inherit--law-vs-society-in-egypt

Murdock, Heather. 2016. "Transgender Operations Stall in Egypt." *Voice of America*, June 15. https://www.voanews.com/middle-east/transgender-operations-stall-egypt

Nader, Aya. 2019. "The Suffering of Egypt's Transgender Community — Letter from Cairo." VOiSS (blog), October 15. http://en.voiss.com/2019/10/15/aya-nader/

Phillips, Llewellyn. 1910. "Typhoid and Paratyphoid Fever in Egypt." *The British Medical Journal* 2 (2596): 969–71. https://www.jstor.org/stable/25292328

Samir, Sahar. n.d. "Androcur, aqras li-'ilag al-raghba al-ginsiya al-shadida lada al-rigal." https://www.al-agzakhana.com/8848/androcur-tablets.html

Shalaby, Ethar. 2013. "Abortion in Egypt: Whose Choice?" *Daily News Egypt*, April 24. https://dailynewsegypt.com/2013/04/24/abortion-in-egypt-whose-choice/

Skovguard-Peterson, Jakob. 1995. "Sex Change in Cairo: Gender and Islamic Law." *Journal of the International Institute* 2, no. 3. http://hdl.handle.net/2027/spo.4750978.0002.302

UN Egypt. 2020. "Egypt COVID-19: Response and Recovery Interventions of the United Nations in Egypt." Cairo: United Nations Egypt. https://www.unodc.org/documents/middleeastandnorthafrica//2020/COVID19/COVID_19_Egypt_Final.pdf.

Wynn, L.L. 2016. "'Viagra Soup': Consumer Fantasies and Masculinity in Portrayals of Erectile Dysfunction Drugs in Cairo, Egypt." In *Abortion Pills, Test Tube Babies, and Sex Toys: Emerging Sexual and Reproductive Technologies in the Middle East and North Africa*, edited by L.L. Wynn and A.A. Foster, 159–71. Nashville, TN: Vanderbilt University Press. DOI:10.2307/j.ctv16758qq.16

Wynn, L.L., and Angel M. Foster. 2016. "Setting the Context: Sexuality, Reproductive Health, and Medical Technologies in the Middle East and North Africa." In *Abortion Pills, Test Tube Babies, and Sex Toys: Emerging Sexual and Reproductive Technologies in the Middle East and North Africa*, edited by L.L. Wynn and A.M. Foster, 1–12. Nashville, TN: Vanderbilt University Press. DOI:10.2307/j.ctv16758qq.4

8

ROAD TO THE FUTURE
INFRASTRUCTURE AND LANDSCAPE SANITIZED OF TREES AND PEOPLE, VIEWED FROM "GOD'S EYES"

MOHAMED ELSHAHED

Military Productions and Aerial Monopolies

Accompanied by a bold masculine voiceover and beginning with a view of planet Earth from space, the camera zooms down through the clouds over Africa and into Egypt, arriving over a spotless highway bisecting agricultural land. An Egyptian flag is waving in the foreground. This is one of the many sleek videos produced by the Egyptian military's Public Relations Division and disseminated through television channels owned by its affiliates (and on YouTube). The video, *Road to the Future*,[1] is part of the powerful propaganda of the Egyptian military, showcasing construction projects of various types—in this case, highways and roadworks. The video utilizes drone photography, a technology that the military has maintained monopoly over (see Aya Nassar's chapter, in this volume), ensuring that the sterile image of a country "getting cleaned up" will maintain its hegemony.

The vantage point is always aerial, with footage of highways, roads, bridges, and flyovers in a variety of landscapes—from agricultural, desert, and mountainous lands to densely populated "informal" urban areas, to planned residential districts. On the one hand, the military has absolute control over this vantage point; because it controls all permissions for aerial photography, it controls the skies. It also controls the landscapes seen from above, as evidenced by the quickly paved roads cutting through Egypt's topography. Due to the scale of highways, they are best

143

photographed from above for the purposes of public relations and propaganda. Street level views are considered too mundane and unlikely to excite an audience, nor are they useful in branding the notion of accomplishment, so prevalent in such media. The language used by these campaigns remains unambiguous, presenting a socially sanitized image of Cairo and Egypt in a post-2011 era, much as an earlier generation of audiovisual production projected a view of Egypt as the shining white hope of African development (see Elsaket, this volume). Encapsulated in this seemingly simple gesture—the visual representation of highways and roads as seen from above—is a growing disparity between the ruler and the ruled. The military plans such interventions in the landscape from the vantage point of gods, with little regard to what exists on the ground. As Elsaket has reminded us in their chapter in this volume, Egypt has long used audiovisual narratives to link itself to the concepts of cutting-edge modernity and civilization, particularly in its portrayal of itself as an emerging Middle Eastern and North African power. As El-Husseiny and Sinno point out, also in this volume, the new frontier for this ever-renewable discourse of the Egyptian future can now be found in the developing urbanism along the desert's edge. We should thus not be surprised to find this dream lavishly portrayed in the infotainment and commercial real estate spheres with the latest video production technologies.

Road infrastructure is presented in these military-produced promotional materials as the manifestation of the Egyptian presidency's vision for economic progress. This notion of progress is introduced in the videos with views of American highways paired with the Egyptian president speaking about the need to create "new veins" across the landscape to facilitate economic growth and development, namely real estate and horizontal urban expansion. The national program for road infrastructure is led by the US Army Corp of Engineers with the cooperation of the Egyptian Ministry of Housing's Central Authority for Development and the Ministry of Transport's agency for road construction. Other projects are carried out by the Ministry of Transport and the Ministry of Local Development.

Together (and in record time), in the second half of the 2010s, these agencies built a series of major roads, including the Regional Ring Road around Cairo—a four-hundred-kilometer eight-lane highway through the periphery of Greater Cairo, running parallel to the city's Ring Road completed in 2001 (Elshahed 2016). The Regional Ring Road is a colossal project that connects various governorates and cuts through kilometers of private land, particularly in the Delta, which were seized sometimes by force or with minuscule compensation. Yet the general narrative built around such widespread and speedy road construction focuses on the economic well-being of the country and the provision of labor opportunities. Despite this, the projects often pave over agricultural land in conflict with Egyptian law, confiscating private property and putting immense economic pressure on small landowners. To add insult to injury, the labor used in the projects can be supplemented by forced labor by military conscripts. If the official narrative around these projects is untrue and the negative consequences are kept hidden, what then is the purpose of this infrastructure?

National road construction projects are currently manifesting all over the capital city. In the decade following the 2011 protests that unseated President Hosni Mubarak, Cairo underwent an aggressive remaking and disfigurement (Elshahed 2015). The already tattered city—the result of decades of dysfunctional municipal management, informal urbanization, and haphazard state interventions—experienced a systematic program of demolition and, most notably, road construction. On the surface, it appears that Egypt's president, set to remain in office at least until 2034, might have taken inspiration from the Eisenhower federal highway system that was touted in the mid-1950s as an engine for economic growth in the United States. However, far from being a system, Cairo's highway, road, bridge, and overpass construction programs are not the outcome of urban plans designed for and aimed at serving the public. Rather, Egypt's roadway projects are often designed in situ, with no prior study. They belong to an opaque military economic apparatus driven by quantity, visibility, and speed—values that make the nation visible within a global economic arena governed by measurable and calculable metrics. This chapter traces some of the ways in which the road, a different kind of monumental endeavor, belongs to a wider vision for the militarization and control of the landscape.

Working Class and Ecological Sanitization

Road and highway construction represents a larger project of reimagining Cairo and the nation as a pristine landscape (Elshahed 2020). This larger project of socially cleansing urban spaces follows a specific sanitizing pattern: "critical geographers have long noted the ways in which New Urbanist principles impart a series of esthetic considerations that can serve to sanitize space and drive out the poor" (Quastel 2013, 701). These roads often aim at connecting this privileged minority while pathologizing the residents of poorer neighborhoods as unorganized, illegal, irresponsible with natural resources (Arefin 2019; Wahby 2021), and/or unsanitary. For instance, Ibrahim Shihata, the governor of Cairo in the late 1990s, argued for transforming informal neighborhoods, insisting that "no one's talking about moving masses of people, just dirty industries" (Bell 2009, 353). To offer another example, when the state wanted to construct roads in Zarayib in the late 1990s, despite growing resistance from the garbage collectors who lived in the area, the state defended itself by suggesting they would remove "nothing but a set of shacks which are a source of environmental pollution, especially as they include pig pens and dumps" (Bell 2009, 355).

Class subjugation thrives by using a sanitizing discourse that aims to "develop" neighborhoods containing largely working-class and poor populations. The goal remains consistent: the "cleansing of the built environment and the streets of the physical and human detritus . . . to make the city over into a pleasant site of and for bourgeois consumption" (Wacquant 2008, 199). This is not a phenomenon that has only recently emerged. Rather, it is something that has preserved and exacerbated class relations and inequalities throughout the modern period, notably in bifurcated colonial cities (Fanon 1961). In a hyperglobalized context, however, mega-events have often ushered in rapid displacement and promoted a "representation of space that does not include visibly poor youth within affluent neighborhoods; the agents of rearrangement employed to align the city's space with its representation were often the police" (Kennelly and Watt 2011, 775). Just as East London's erasure of its poor and homeless youth during the 2012 Olympics marked an attempt to "clean up the streets . . . in order to make the public spaces of East London presentable for inspection by the world's media" (Kennelly and Watt 2011, 776), so do postrevolutionary regimes attempt to project images of social stability, economic development, and "cleansing of the urban environment to maintain a consistent image of a safe, fun, and sanitary city" (Kennelly and Watt 2011, 768). Urban planners, architects, and state officials sometimes genuinely believe they are saving poor and working-class Egyptians from their own unsanitary selves.

In the decade following the 2011 uprising, this sanitizing discourse has not evaporated into the ether. In the 2017 battle between government officials and residents of al-Warraq Island in Cairo, for example, President al-Sisi asked, "Where does [the residential] sewage go? It goes into the Nile water that we drink. We can't allow that and hurt ourselves." The island-based community was deemed to be not only an urbanization obstacle, but a sanitary threat to the rest of the city (*Mada Masr* 2019).

Such projects are aimed at corroborating media-sponsored celebrations of the president's sanitizing initiatives. For example, *al-Gomhuria*'s headline on June 11, 2021 read: "Egypt, al-Sisi, the Road to the New Republic: Years of Building, Development, and Progress" (Magdi 2021). Others have informally renamed Egypt on social media as "the republic of roads and bridges" (Ebrahim and Lewis 2021). But what preceded this "new road" effort and others like it? The pages below investigate the logic of building the new republic through new roads, and describe how residents are sanitized and swept away from the "path toward progress."

Even nonhuman urban populations—in this case, many of the beautiful trees that have long lined the avenues of downtown Cairo and its historic public spaces—have been removed in this sanitizing purge. In the summer of 2021, residents of al-Abbasiya complained about the removal of trees in al-Mohammadi Park by the administration of the Ain Shams Hospital. Mahmud al-Matini, then the president of the well-known hospital, suggested it would instead create "the most beautiful garden in the world" and that "the president granted it [to the hospital]," despite the explicit and subsequent mention that the resulting green space would be privatized (Mamdouh and *Mada Masr* 2021). In the process, the engineers involved in the demolition also removed buildings intended to be orphanages and garden walls lining the nearby children's library. Trees have also been cut down on Gamal Abd al-Nasser Road, Suleiman Guhar Street (in Agouza and Giza), and the Masakin Sheraton area (in Nasr City), despite the Ministry of Environment's simultaneous and seemingly contradictory $200 million pollution management project funded by the World Bank (*Mada Masr* 2021). This seems even more perplexing, considering the state-sponsored media's attempt to promote the Ministry of State for Media's (Wazarat al-Dawla li-l-Iʻlam) "Tree Initiative" in al-Qattamiyya (Taha 2020). However, tree removal and simultaneous replanting represent a central tendency and a logic connected to other forms of (road, highway) construction: a state that wishes to manage its own sanitization projects and define ecological progress by its own metrics.

Tree removal is a strategic process of securitization and simultaneous sanitization of previously public, creative spaces and ecological autonomy (Manaugh 2016). Despite a reduction of crime reported in spaces where old growth exists (Wolf 2010; Marritz 2012), trees are explicitly considered as part of the larger ecological considerations for monitoring city streets: "Depending on the location, the installation of additional street lighting and significant tree pruning may be necessary" (La Vigne et al. 2011, 10).

The trees that have lined the avenues of downtown Cairo and the surrounding areas have provided shade to shoppers, flaneurs, and protesters, and have guarded against Cairo's ever more scorching summer sun. Many of these trees have been hacked down and uprooted, as security fanatics believe the trees block the view of surveillance cameras and the lines of sight of the rooftop snipers deployed by the state during protests. This was how the deputy governor of Cairo's northern and western regions, Mohammad Ayman Abd al-Tawwab, explained tree removal, when he said it was needed "because of the surveillance cameras" (Timraz 2017). Tree cutting in the Upper Egyptian city of Aswan prompted outrage among residents. In response, the director of Hadeyek Aswan (the Gardens of Aswan), Amani Ibrahim, told *Al-Masry Al-Youm* that cutting trees in the city was necessary since they were "a danger to pedestrians and cars" and "obscured the view of the Nile" (Mala 2020).

The regime has consistently married a biopolitical agenda with beautification processes within the city. The trees of an upscale neighborhood, Maadi, have recently been threatened by new military road construction—a development that has sparked outcry by residents and even members of parliament. One resident summarized the general concern of Maadi residents in the following words:

It's the quality of life we are campaigning for, in line with the National Presidential Target, as well as in sustaining and creating a better quality of life for all Egyptians. We are defending our right for this life and preserving a beautiful garden suburb in Egypt, which is considered an icon for sustainability and cultured heritage. (Khaled 2021)

In this formulation, not even trees are safe from the military-sponsored image of Egypt's success, despite its attempt to create an ecological utopia in the New Administrative Capital (Galal 2018; Ayoubi 2021). Tree removal is not an isolated process of objectively beautifying the city, but rather a systematic and comprehensive project to monopolize the means to define, plan, and enforce social-aesthetic sanitization and infrastructural development from above.

Turn Right at October Bridge

Understanding Cairo's road infrastructure and its relationship to the increased militarization of the city begins with the famed October Bridge. During the 2011 uprising, the twenty-kilometer elevated road bisecting Cairo was an instrumental asset for controlling the revolutionary action in Tahrir Square and around the city. During the protests in Tahrir Square, the bridge provided an elevated vantage point from which police forces and pro-regime thugs could attack protesters below. When the military took control in the aftermath of Mubarak's ousting, the bridge provided an easy means for the quick deployment of state security and military vehicles to enforce a city-wide curfew. This element of Cairo's infrastructure thus proved useful to state security and military authorities, as it fulfilled a dual purpose of securitization and control during exceptional times. Since 2015, as Roberta Duffield has pointed out in her chapter for this volume, the military has initiated a massive campaign of expanding Cairo's road infrastructure in unprecedented ways, building a $1 billion cement factory, large churches and mosques, and the tallest building in Africa. These megaprojects are "being implemented at the expense of projects that will bring about tangible economic improvements and contribute to raising the standard of living for ordinary Egyptians suffering under the weight of increasing economic hardship" (Mandour 2019). The history and evolution of the October Bridge provide a precursor to the post-2011 militarization of Cairo through seemingly civilian infrastructure, particularly its relationship to existing communities and monuments.

Initially named Ramses Bridge and built in nine phases over a thirty-year period from 1969, the road is Cairo's east–west spine and a potent symbol of state planning. The construction of the elevated road through the heart of several neighborhoods and once-open public squares was slow, as it required the demolition of several landmarks and compensation paid to some affected properties. The road offers infamous bottlenecks, squeezed in between buildings as it enters Ramses Square, where a colossal statue of Ramses was placed in the 1960s outside the city's main train station. Properties that once lined one of the city's main avenues were now within arm's reach of a high-volume thoroughfare. At eye level with some floors of apartment and office buildings, the bridge significantly devalued those properties, many of which had been already devalued by Nasserist rent laws when the government confiscated them. The state—represented by the figure of the president, with his military background—exerted its authority to reform Cairo's urban landscape, regardless of the impact on private property. This trend has exponentially expanded in subsequent decades, reaching unparalleled growth in the ten years following 2011.

Obstacles that delayed the October Bridge's construction were eliminated through legal adjustments that gave the state uncontested control over private property for the "public good." Additionally, new state bodies were created that do not abide by existing laws and regulations, thus facilitating the construction of megaprojects while funneling large sums of money into the hands of a few state-favored contractors. The funding of these institutions ruined companies not favored by the state and almost entirely removed civilian oversight from major construction projects and their budgets. Needless to say, oversight bodies are entirely linked to the military leadership through an extended network of officers who occupy directorial positions and own the companies that are contracted to undertake the work, much in the same fashion as Elmeshad has described the state cooptation of the public media in their chapter in this volume.

The October Bridge created a precedent in which two trends were solidified—almost two sides of the same coin. On the one hand, construction of road infrastructure became largely dominated by the military. On the other hand, such projects gave (serving and retired) members of the armed forces an opportunity for economic gain by providing services through their private and state companies to facilitate the construction of these projects. The slow pace of constructing the October Bridge ('Afifi 2021) can be contrasted, however, with the pace of construction in the decade after 2011, with entire road systems being built within the span of a few short years. The expediency of military construction—facilitated by violating or changing existing laws—became a major selling point to the masses for military control over such projects during the first two decades of the new millennium. Economic stimulation and markers of state infrastructure represent progress to a large portion of the population who have lost any remaining sense of economic stability. While it's likely that this was not an intention of its designers, by the time of its completion in 1999, the October Bridge stood as a monument to the potential of increased military involvement in civil affairs as mundane as road construction. The results represent an increased intensity in the role of the army in everyday life in the new millennium.

Transforming the Landscape

The expansion of road construction in the decade following 2011 transformed a variety of urban, agrarian, mountain, and desert landscapes in profound ways. With the rapid appearance of new roads, often built by the army in locations parallel to older ones, a distinction appeared between these higher-quality constructions and unmaintained older state roads. A prime example of this is the new north–south highway parallel to the Nile and the old Upper Egypt road. Other roads built by the army create entirely new experiences of moving across Egypt's landscape. The new road network bisecting the mountains of the Red Sea was built rapidly with the wide use of dynamite, creating new vistas previously unseen from the comfort of a moving vehicle. These belong to what proponents have deemed "the new republic" (Ebrahim and Lewis 2021). Al-Sisi himself used this language during a military symposium in March 2021: "the declaration of a new republic and the birth of a new state with the opening of the administrative capital" (Abu al-Alaa 2021). The capacity to quickly terraform—to alter nature and create new development veins in previously inaccessible sections of the Egyptian landscape—has been celebrated widely as a monumental accomplishment. Contrasted with the optics of sleek roads bisecting rough terrains, there is total lack of transparency when it comes to labor conditions, the real economic costs and benefits of such projects, and the greater vision inherently assumed within such plans. To accomplish these projects, the military has secured a sort of monopoly on certain technologies of land surveying (such as the use of explosives) and a massive, conscripted labor force. Control of the republic and its landscapes has been linked by infrastructure in unprecedented ways in Egypt.

In addition to highway projects in desolate locations, other projects bisect more sensitive landscapes, such as archaeological zones and agricultural land. Cairo's Ring Road plan included an unfinished section bisecting the Giza Plateau. Due to the sensitivity of the site, the Ministry of Antiquities suspended construction in the 1990s. It was resumed with a second parallel road further south within the same historic site, fully transforming the Giza Plateau from a desert vista at the edge of Cairo and Giza to a fully navigable archaeological zone surrounded on three sides by urban development (Reuters 2020). The pyramids have been at the center, or more precisely, at the culmination, of another road project that was proposed as part of Vision Cairo 2050—a plan developed during the National Democratic Party's 2005 election campaign and spearheaded by Gamal Mubarak, which included planned relocation of "informal" areas (e.g., Fustat, Warraq, Bulaq al-Dakrour, and Nazlet al-Semman) (El-Mahdawy 2021).[2] The plan called for a massive eleven-kilometer Khufu Avenue to bisect the largely informal and impenetrable urbanization of Giza, extending Arab League Avenue in Muhandisin in a straight line, flanked by plazas and hotels, that would reach the pyramids. Investment opportunities would line the avenue, giving a modern face both to the city and to the regime. However, concealed behind it would remain the dense urbanization that transformed Cairo's once-agrarian surroundings to help house a growing city. While this project has not been implemented and for some time was shelved following criticism of the immense human and economic cost to such an intervention, it is likely to remain on the table.

These highway and road projects must be understood within a larger (albeit ambiguous) vision of modernizing Cairo by creating new spaces largely sponsored by Gulf countries, such as the Kuwaiti investments in the Maspero Triangle (along the Nile waterfront just north of Tahrir Square in central Cairo). This was an area of tenements and working-class homes from the turn of the twentieth century which had been a fundamental part of Cairo's modern development. Talk about demolition has circulated since the late 1980s, but remained off the table due to residents' resistance and the legal complexity of the properties' ownership status. However, demolition finally took place via a rapid process of expropriation in the 2000s. This type of project proliferated in the decade following 2011, in which various zones within the city, marked as unsightly by state planners, were swiftly demolished. Residents consequently moved to the outskirts of the city—in some cases, pushed by force or intimidation— in order to create centrally located and sanitized urban experiences that operate under the full control of foreign investments, state control, and military orchestration. The area along the ancient aqueduct—historically home to the leather tanneries of Ain al-Sira—and the location in historic Fustat (the popular communities of "Old Cairo") of the newly inaugurated National Museum of Egyptian Civilization feature new road networks, rapidly developed to serve Cairo's car-owning minority. This was part of a larger project seeking to "create a void in the center of the city, suitable for tourism and cultural re-investment" (Mohie 2020). These interventions have required the demolition of private residences, and also buildings whose heritage-based value is deeply contested, such as the working-class tenements of Maspero or the numerous mausoleums and tombs in the Northern Cemetery belonging to key twentieth-century figures. Known as City of the Dead, this cemetery and World Heritage Site has been subjected to yet another bisecting road.

Evictions making way for major road and investment projects have also affected two of Cairo's agricultural islands: al-Warraq Island to the north and Qursaya Island in the south. Evictions already implemented on al-Warraq Island gave way to the construction of the Long Live Egypt Bridge, claimed to be the world's widest cable-stayed bridge (Ali 2019). Both agrarian islands host villages, a unique situation for a city the size of Cairo. Since the unrest in 2011, residents of the two islands have been intimidated by sudden and sometimes violent army raids, which use tear gas and riot control methods. The hastily developed projects for these two locations, like nearly all those initiated by the state or various architectural contractors, devote a great deal of energy to socially cleansing prospective developments.

Residents of the Nile island had been shocked that morning [July 16, 2017] to find that security forces were starting to tear down houses while some residents were at work. Demonstrations started in an attempt to prevent the demolition of the homes, and security forces started to use tear gas. After hours of violence between the residents and security forces, one civilian—Sayed—was dead, and 59 people were injured, including 31 members of the police force. Nine residents were arrested and jailed for 15 days, accused of fomenting chaos, possessing weapons, and obstructing roads. . . . Security forces had supposedly been sent to al-Warraq to demolish houses built on state-owned land. The move followed the formation of a commission headed by former Prime Minister Ibrahim Mehleb as a result of Decree No. 57 of 2016 issued by Egyptian President Abd al-Fatah al-Sisi. . . . Members of the commission represent different ministries and government entities because of the complexities of land ownership and to promote coordination among state institutions. . . . But notably absent from these committees is any sort of citizen involvement (Khalil 2017).

The main interest of the state appears to be to gentrify rural communities from the face of the city and to transform the two islands into real estate vistas shaped by a Gulf–military partnership which has, since 2013, transformed the city at large.

Roads not only provide potential security infrastructure and a way for military officers to supplement their income, but to the public they are useful monuments to some sort of future development, but where do the roads lead its population?

Notes

1 https://www.youtube.com/watch?v=uPW92ANdHTI
2 The Cairo 2050 plan disappeared during the 2011 revolution, but has been relaunched several times since then, once under the title "Greater Cairo Strategic Plan" by Prime Minister Mostafa Madbouly's housing ministry (El-Mahdawy 2021).

Works Cited

Abu al-Alaa, Qamar. 2021. "Madha qasada al-ra'is al-Sisi bi-i'lanihi 'an al-gumhuriya al-gadida?" RA Center for Strategic Studies. rcss egypt.com/3901

'Afifi, Yousef. 2021. "Al-Ra'is al-Sisi yuwaggih bi-tatwir wa-tawsi'at mihwar 6 October wa-l-turuq al-sathiya asfaluh." *Masrawy*, April 14. https://www.masrawy.com/news/news_egypt/details/2021/4/14/2005245/-الرئيس-السيسي-يوجه-بتطوير-وتوسعة-محور-كوبري-٦-أكتوبر-والطرق-السطحية-أسفله.

Ali, Aya. 2019. "Egypt Claims New Record for Widest Cable-stayed Bridge." Guinness World Records, June 27. https://www.guinnessworldrecords.com/news/2019/6/egypts-new-bridge-becomes-the-widest-cable-stayed-bridge-580736

Arefin, Mohammed Rafi. 2019. "Infrastructural Discontent in the Sanitary City: Waste, Revolt, and Repression in Cairo." *Antipode* 51, no. 4: 1057–78.

Ayoubi, Nur. 2021. "Egypt: Plans for 'Vertical Forest' Development in New Capital Derided on Social Media." *Middle East Eye*, July 17. https://www.middleeasteye.net/news/egypt-vertical-forest-cairo-new-capital-online-backlash

Bell, Jennifer. 2009. "Land Disputes, the Informal City, and Environmental Discourse in Cairo." In *Cairo Contested: Governance, Urban Space, and Global Modernity*, edited by Diane Singerman, 349–69. Cairo: American University in Cairo Press.

Ebrahim, Nadeen, and Aidan Lewis. 2021. "Egypt's Road Building Drive Eases Jams but Leaves Some Unhappy." Reuters, May 14. https://www.reuters.com/world/middle-east/egypts-road-building-drive-eases-jams-leaves-some-unhappy-2021-05-14/

Elshahed, Mohamed. 2015. "The Prospects of Gentrification in Downtown Cairo: Artists, Private Investment and the Neglectful State." In *Global Gentrifications: Uneven Development and Displacement*, edited by Loretta Lees, Hyun Bang Shin, and Ernesto Lòpez-Morales, 121–42. Chicago: Policy Press.

———. 2016. "Cairo Ring Road: Anthony Hamboussi's Poetic Survey of an Urban Topography." *International Journal of Islamic Architecture* 5, no. 2: 279–300.

———. 2020. *Cairo since 1900: An Architectural Guide*. Cairo: American University in Cairo Press.

Fanon, Frantz. 1961. *Les Damnés de la Terre*. Paris: François Maspero.

Galal, Rami. 2018. "Egypt's Trees Threatened by Urbanization." *Al-Monitor*, November 7. https://www.al-monitor.com/originals/2018/11/egypts-trees-chopped-down-for-roads-residences.html

Kennelly, Jacqueline, and Paul Watt. 2011. "Sanitizing Public Space in Olympic Host Cities: The Spatial Experiences of Marginalized Youth in 2010 Vancouver and 2012 London." *Sociology* 45, no. 5: 765–81.

Khaled, Nadine. 2021. "We Can't Lose More Trees: Egypt's Maadi Road Project Sparks Uproar." *Egyptian Streets*, July 15. https://egyptian streets.com/2021/07/15/we-cant-lose-more-trees-egypts-maadi-road-project-sparks-uproar/

Khalil, Omnia. 2017. "Visions or Illusions? State Development Plans and Violence in al-Warraq." Tahrir Institute for Middle East Policy, August 3. http://tinyurl.com/yrfwqvdx

La Vigne, Nancy G., Samantha S. Lowry, Allison M. Dwyer, and Joshua A. Markman. 2011. *Using Public Surveillance Systems for Crime Control and Prevention: A Practical Guide for Law Enforcement and Their Municipal Partners*. Washington, DC: The Urban Institute Justice Policy Center. https://www.urban.org/sites/default/files/publication/27551/412402-Using-Public-Surveillance-Systems-for-Crime-Control-and-Prevention-A-Practical-Guide-for-Law-Enforcement-and-Their-Municipal-Partners.PDF

Mada Masr. 2019. "Verdict for Warraq Residents' Lawsuit against the Government Set for March 23." *Mada Masr*, January 25. https://www.madamasr.com/en/2019/01/26/news/u/verdict-for-warraq-residents-lawsuit-against-the-government-set-for-march-26/

———. 2021. "Ma' istimrar qat' al-ashgar, al-Bank al-Dawli yumawwil mashru'an li-idarat talawwuth al-hawa' fi al-Qahira. Al-Ta'bi'a wa-l-Ihasa': al-mawga al-thaniya min kuruna fi Misr akthar khutura." *Mada Mas*r, February 25. https://tinyurl.com/hjswuen8

Magdi, No'maat. 2021. "July of the New Republic." *Rose el Yousef*, July 4. https://magazine.rosaelyoussef.com/52622/3-%D9%8A%D9%88%D9%84%D9%8A%D9%88-%D8%A7%D9%84%D8%B7%D8%B1%D9%8A%D9%82-%D9%84%D9%84%D8%AC%D9%85%D9%87%D9%88%D8%B1%D9%8A%D8%A9-%D8%A7%D9%84%D8%AB%D8%A7%D9%86%D9%8A%D8%A9-%D8%A7%D9%84%D8%B7%D8%B1%D9%82-%D9%88%D8%A7%D9%84%D9%83%D8%A8%D8%A7%D8%B1%D9%89-%D8%AA%D8%B1%D8%A8%D8%B7-%D8%A7%D9%84%D9%82%D8%A7%D9%87%D8%B1%D8%A9-%D8%A8%D8%A7%D9%84%D9%85%D8%AF%D9%86-%D8%A7%D9%84%D8%AC%D8%AF%D9%8A%D8%AF%D8%A9-%D8%B4%D8%B1%D8%A7%D9%8A%D9%8A%D9%86-%D8%A7%D9%84%D8%AA%D9%86%D9%85%D9%8A%D8%A9-%D9%81%D9%89-%D8%A7%D9%84%D8%AC%D9%85%D9%87%D9%88%D8%B1%D9%8A%D8%A9-%D8%A7%D9%84%D8%AB%D8%A7%D9%86%D9%8A%D8%A9

El-Mahdawy, Hadeer. 2021. "Cairo Eye: Will the Great Wheel of History Keep Turning?" *Mada Masr*, February 11. https://www.madamasr.com/en/2021/02/11/feature/politics/cairo-eye-will-the-great-wheel-of-history-keep-turning/

Mala, Mahmoud. 2020. "Istimrar taqlim al-ashgar 'ala kurnish Aswan, wa-muwatinun: tariqa ga'ira." *Al-Masry Al-Youm*, April 8. https://www.almasryalyoum.com/news/details/1892269

Mamdouh, Rana, and *Mada Masr*. 2021. "Ba'd qat' ashgar 'Arab al-Mohammadi: ra'is gami'at Ain Shams: dummat li-mustashfayatuna wa-sanag'aluha agmal hadiqa fi-l-'alam." *Mada Masr*, July 24. tinyurl.com/yy9c2wv4

Manaugh, Geoff. 2016. "How Aerial Surveillance Has Changed Policing—and Crime—in Los Angeles." *New York Times*, March 23. https://www.nytimes.com/2016/03/27/magazine/panopticops.html?ref=todayspaper

Mandour, Majid. 2019. "Mashari' al-Sisi al-kubra al-'aqima." Carnegie Endowment for International Peace, August 6. https://carnegieendowment.org/sada/79629

Marritz, Leda. 2012. "Trees for Public Safety: Reducing Crime Rates." *Deep Root* (blog), March 30. https://www.deeproot.com/blog/blog-entries/trees-for-public-safety-reducing-crime-rates

Mohie, Mostafa. 2020. "'Ala anqad magra al-'uyun: mashahid min agmal madina fi al-'alam." *Mada Masr*, March 19. https://www.madamasr.com/ar/2020/03/19/feature/مجتمع/على-أنقاض-مجرى-العيون-مشاهد-من-أجمل/.

Quastel, Noah. 2013. "Political Ecologies of Gentrification." *Urban Geography* 30, no. 7: 694–725.

Reuters. 2020. "Egypt Cuts Highways across Pyramids Plateau, Alarming Conservationists." *The Guardian*, September 15. https://www.theguardian.com/world/2020/sep/15/egypt-cuts-highways-across-pyramids-plateau-alarming-conservationists

Taha, Mohamed. 2020. "Mubadarat 'Shaggarha': zira'at ashgar muthmira fi 'adad min shawari' al-Qahira." *Al-Masry Al-Youm*, December 1. https://www.almasryalyoum.com/news/details/2101381

Timraz, Majid. 2017. "'Alashan kamirat al-muraqaba: taqlim ashgar shari' Champollion." *Sout al-Omma*, November 21. https://tinyurl.com/hd2fp5u8

Wacquant, Loïc. 2008. "Relocating Gentrification: The Working Class, Science, and the State in Recent Urban Research." *International Journal of Urban and Regional Research* 32, no. 1: 198–205.

Wahby, Noura M. 2021. "Urban Informality and the State: Repairing Cairo's Waters through Gehood Zateya." *Environment and Planning E: Nature and Space* 4, no. 3: 696–717. https://doi.org/10.1177/25148486211025262

Wolf, Kathleen L. 2010. "Crime and Fear—A Literature Review." In *Green Cities: Good Health*. College of the Environment, University of Washington, June 28. https://depts.washington.edu/hhwb/Thm_Crime.html

9

THE KHAKI COLOR OF FOOTBALL
DIGITIZED MILITARIZATION AND SOCIAL SANITIZATION OF EGYPT'S MOST POPULAR GAME

RANIA AHMED

Introduction
The twenty-ninth episode of the highly celebrated, state-sponsored Ramadan telenovela miniseries, *al-Ikhtiyar* (The Choice),[1] focused on the role of the police in revealing, tracing, and stopping a planned terrorist attack on a stadium during the 2019 Africa Cup of Nations (AFCON), hosted by Egypt. While the first season of the series in 2020 highlighted the bravery and victories of the military in Egypt—particularly in Sinai against al-Qaeda and ISIS-linked militants—the theme for the 2021 sequel was police and their role in protecting Egypt against terrorism and Islamist conspiracies. The twenty-minute segment[2] starts with a meeting attended by different police agencies during which they discuss intelligence received about an imminent attack. The police in the drama utilize technologies such as tapping into the encrypted Telegram phone app, surveillance via drone cameras, and GPS tracking chips to identify and arrest three young suspects. One of the suspected terrorists nabbed in the stadium during the Africa Cup had slightly long curly hair and a disheveled short beard, and wore a cap—a look that is strongly asso-ciated with the revolutionary youth, including Ultras members (young soccer fans who, since 2007, often organized to support local teams and had a strong enmity for the police).

In the Ramadan episode of the telenovela, we follow one of the alleged terrorists as he enters the stadium, wearing his fan ID around his neck, and chooses a bench in the second-class seating area. As he sits down, we overhear two fans in front of him speaking about their predictions for the match and their wishes for the Egyptian national team to win. One of them talks about being overjoyed to be back at the stadium after ten years: "Back then, we were jumping over the fence to enter the stadium." "This time we have fan IDs hanging around our necks," the second fan replies. We also see a small family of three with the father speaking to his young son about all the famous players they are about to watch as they take a selfie in the stadium. We then see how the police go through the footage from the stadium's closed-circuit security cameras and manage to identify the "terrorist," who is subsequently arrested by plainclothes police officers (ON TV 2021).

This scene summarizes how the Egyptian state imagines ideal fans, what kind of cheering is sanctioned, and what kind of team spirit is prohibited and pathologized. In this chapter, I trace how the state promotes and justifies the hyper-securitization of football stadiums. An intermittent ban of football fans has been in force since 2012, after the tragic Port Said massacre where at least seventy-four Ultras Ahlawy's (UA07) members were killed in Port Said Stadium during a match between the al-Ahly and al-Masry teams in February of that year. The ban on match attendees became permanent in 2015 after a second massacre of youth fans from the second-biggest Ultras group, the Ultras White Knights (UWK), which took place at the Air Defense (or 30 June) Stadium in Nasr City. The only exceptions to this ban on fans are the regional and international matches, where FIFA and the Confederation of African Football (CAF) rules are obligatory. These organizations insist on the right of fans to attend.

As we have seen in the chapters by Elmeshad, Elsaket, and Westmoreland in this volume, fictional and nonfictional portrayals of Egypt in electronic media have long been used to create the country's sense of self, and the media field itself has almost always been subject to intense oversight to ensure that it produces the proper narratives regarding "Egyptianness." Sports, of course, is a highly mediated spectacle that has not escaped this controlling and social engineering impulse.

This chapter is based on two periods of fieldwork in Egypt, in 2014 and in the summer of 2019. Using AFCON as a case study, it focuses on the systematic securitization and militarization of football in Egypt throughout the past decade. The chapter argues that this securitization is evident through three processes: the militarization of football stadiums and infrastructure, digitization of the football ticketing system, and state control over sports media. Through these strategies, the Egyptian state has managed to (partially) dismantle Egypt's organized football fandom—specifically the Ultra groups—and to socially "sanitize" the stadiums by foregrounding an ideal image of the docile, middle-class fan. It was precisely the ability of low-income men and boys to exist within the stadium that came under attack. Using Raymond Williams's (1977) theory of "the emergent, dominant, and residual," the chapter argues that the strong and tight social organization of the Ultras will continue to exhibit vestiges of resistance even after years of imprisonment and oppression. Despite their rarity, their acts of defiance reveal the autocratic nature of the current football administration in Egypt. Before delving into those three areas, I will review the recent history of Egypt's organized football fandom, including their revolutionary role in the events of 2010–13, and their longstanding vendetta against the police and army.

Ultras' Tumultuous History: Bans, Batons, and Alternative Families

Contrary to the popular belief that the Arab Spring was a bolt from the blue, social scientists and local activists both recognize that the first decade of the new millennium, which was the last ruling decade for many Arab dictators, including Mubarak, witnessed the emergence and flourishing of many forms of youth and political organizations. Most prominent was the Kefaya Movement, a liberal, leftist, and Islamist alliance resisting Mubarak's long reign and his attempts to transfer power to his son Gamal Mubarak (Shorbagy 2007; Clarke 2011; Oweidat et al. 2008). These social movements also included the April 6 Youth Movement, which was a key player in the buildup before the Egyptian Arab Spring (Lim 2012, Sika 2012), There were also the National Association for Change, led by the former director-general of the International Atomic Energy Agency, Mohamed ElBaradei, and "We Are All Khaled Said," the Facebook page group that organized thousands of Egyptian youth against police brutality and torture in police stations. On a more serious level of organization, albeit for different ends, was the rise of organized groups of football fans in Egypt in 2007, known as the Ultras. The first two fandom groups that came into being were those who supported the capital-based al-Ahly and Zamalek teams: Ultras Ahlawy (UA07), supporting the former, and Ultras White Knights (UWK), rooting for the latter. Many other Ultra groups in different Egyptian governorates followed the lead of UA07 and UWK.

By the time of the Arab Spring around 2011, more than ten major organized superfan groups were active in the football scene in Egypt. The fun-seeking and pleasure-oriented organizations managed to attract thousands of young men (and some women, but mostly men), who enrolled in a tightly knit organization based on residential neighborhoods and engaged in activities like organizing choreographed *tifo*s (highly stylized and synchronized singing in the terrace), graffiti spraying, and traveling with their teams inside and outside of Cairo and Egypt (Ibraheem 2015). The persistence of the groups can be attributed to their complicated organizational structure. For all the attention they receive, stadiums are not the only organizing threads. Each Ultras group is divided into residential sections, and the leaders of sections (called *actives*) are not always cheerleading in the crowd. True to their mantra "Ultras is a lifestyle," the daily lives of young men intersect beyond attending matches. The members of the group are usually study mates or videogame buddies and sometimes become one another's alternative family. A young UA07 leader told me in an old interview, "You do not plan it, but once you join the entity [the Ultras], you find your whole life is being reoriented. You are either organizing something for the next match, thinking of an idea for graffiti, or hanging out with other people from the group."[3]

This description echoes many queer scholars' analysis of how queer people perform their kinwork to create alternative families and support networks (Zengin 2019)—in other words, families by choice. The familial ties in the case of the Ultras are fraternal. The neighborhood, street, and stadium-level family networks illuminate why the state might have cracked down on the Ultras even before the 2011 uprising. This alternative mode of sociality, as in many queer experiences, tends to undermine the legitimacy of the state and its patriarchal notions of family and youth.

From their early years, Ultras had a deep rivalry with the police forces, who cast fans as deviant youth who use flares and swear words. The fans' capacities to organize and their competence in street fights threatened police control over the stadiums (Ennarah 2017; Rommel 2016). Clashes between the fans and police, with police arresting groups' leaders before or after significant matches, were regular occurrences in the years between 2007 and 2010. Analysts and commentators have analyzed the Ultra–police saga as a battle over public space and the right of youth to have fun (El-Sherif 2012). Hence, it came as no surprise to those who closely followed the Ultra groups, especially in Cairo, that these groups were part and parcel of the revolutionary masses during the 2011 uprising. The Ultras' presence in Tahrir and other revolutionary places was both audible and visible; their competence in street fights and deep enmity for the police pushed them to the front lines in clashes with security forces. Moreover, their song repertoire added a carnivalesque and colorful strand to the otherwise gloomy protest music (Close 2019).

Both the Ultras and wide sectors of demonstrators believe that the aforementioned massacres were part of an orchestrated revenge tactic against the fans for their participation in the 2011 uprising. Military and police neglect was reported in the aftermath.

The police investigation of the Port Said incident was flawed. Security forces collected poor forensic evidence and there were no arrests of potential suspects made at the football stadium at the time, nor later that day. Forty forensic examinations were referenced during the court case, but only four full-body autopsies were performed on UA07 victims. . . . Numerous security officials and riot officers were present at the stadium when violence erupted against al-Ahly fans, but they failed to prevent the mayhem. . . . Ultras Ahlawy stated that the attack was not a manifestation of football hooliganism but, rather, was carefully calculated revenge, orchestrated by pro-Mubarak forces against them. They considered the ambush to be retribution for their prominent role in the 2011 uprising, which occurred almost exactly one year prior to the Port Said massacre. (Close 2019, 37, 44)

In addition to subsequent trials of fans thought to be complicit in the massacre, one senior military officer was sentenced to fifteen years in prison while only two police officers (including the chief of the Port Said police station) were found guilty (Close 2019, 53).

The efficiency of the policy banning fans was remarkable in curbing the Ultras' cohesion and influence. It not only spared the police all potential confrontations with fans but, more importantly, deprived Ultras of their raison d'être—supporting their teams at the stadium. This undermined the strength of the organization without managing to completely eradicate it. The initial ban was followed by a ruling in May 2015 by the Cairo Court for Urgent Matters declaring Ultra groups to be terrorist organizations. The ruling outlawed "any association, organization, group or gang that practices, aims at or calls for destabilizing public order, endangers society's well-being or its safety interests, or endangers social unity by using violence, power, threats or acts of terrorism to achieve its goals" (Linn 2015). The ruling paved the way for a legal offensive adopted by the state from 2016 to 2019, which included a 2017 draft law that was approved with ninety-five articles. Among them, Article 84 outlawed behavior that is "spoken or reproduced in signs, defames or insults a natural or legal person, or incites feelings of hatred or racial discrimination by any means of publicity, during or as a result of a sporting activity," and provided for imprisonment for one year (Hamam and Mamdouh 2017). Ahmed Hamed, a renowned human rights lawyer, stated in an interview that three major court cases were mobilized against UA07 and UWK in the aforementioned years. The first was against UA07 in July 2016, when the police arrested more than eighty fans after an al-Ahly vs. Moroccan Wydad match in Borg al-Arab Stadium. The second and biggest episode was the arrest of around three hundred UWK members after a Zamalek vs. Libyan al-Ahly match. Again, in July in Borg al-Arab Stadium, dozens of UWK fans were arrested and this time tried in front of a military court. The final chapter, Hamed added, was the police arrest of more than forty fans belonging to the UA07 in the aftermath of the March 2018 al-Ahly vs. Gabonian Mounana game in Cairo International Stadium. "What can you do with all of your close friends constantly being arrested?" the lawyer asked rhetorically.

Turned into fugitives and with many friends either dead or behind bars, the leaders of the two biggest Ultras groups announced their dissolution in May 2018. UA07 first issued a statement through their Facebook page, where they mentioned that their sole purpose was to support al-Ahly and prevent the group from being exploited by any party. The UWK subsequently burned down their group's banner in front of the Zamalek Soccer Club (SC), stating that their Facebook page had been hacked and that the banner burning represented the end of the group.

The aftermath of the dissolution coincided with the 2018 CAF Champion League, the fifty-fourth Africa Premier Club's tournament. It was also a heated year for Egyptian football. After the army's restoration of the military to power over the state in 2013, the influence and presence of Saudi Arabia became dramatically more prominent in many arenas of public life—drama, cinema, songs, and sports. The Saudi business tycoon and minister of the general authority for entertainment in the Kingdom of Saudi Arabia, Turki Alshikh, started to invest heavily in football in Egypt by 2017, particularly in the al-Ahly Club. However, the honeymoon between the Saudi money and al-Ahly administration was short-lived, as the club administration started to resist the Gulf businessman's recurrent and heavy-handed interventions in the club's decisions. Trying to prove that wealth can easily create another huge sports club to rival al-Ahly, al-Sheikh bought an inglorious club, renamed it Pyramids Sporting Club (or Pyramids SC), spent millions of dollars in players' deals and hiring coaches, and made it one of the main competitors of al-Ahly and Zamalek.

Motivated by hyper-chauvinistic sentiments and an absolute devotion to al-Ahly, a group of Ultras Ahlawy—meaning the Ultra-fans of the Ahly team, also known as UA07—took advantage of their ability to be in the stadium's terrace during al-Ahly and Guinean Houria SC game and chanted in unison, "Turki Alshikh, you motherf***er." The chants and profanity took the police by surprise. Seven members of UA07 were arrested and accused of joining a terrorist organization. The business mogul resigned from his honorary presidency of al-Ahly over the incident. The Turki Alshikh incident proved that imprisoning huge numbers of Ultras, or banning the fans from most of the matches, would not grant police full control over the stadiums. Subversive, tongue-in-cheek tactics were still powerful techniques. Labeling the incident as an act against capitalism or a full re-emergence of a social movement (Shafick 2018; Hassan 2018) would be an over-simplistic explanation that overlooks how tight the grip of securitization is and also how complicated the Ultras politics are. By the time CAF granted Egypt the right to host AFCON 2019, the state and the Egyptian Football Association (EFA) had developed a multifaceted strategy to guarantee that the Ultras would be completely barred. As Asef Bayat eloquently explains:

Fun also presupposes a powerful paradigm, a set of presumptions about self, society, and life that might compete with and undermine the legitimizing ideology of doctrinal power when these ideologies happen to be too narrow, rigid, and exclusive to accommodate ethics of fun. It is particularly this aspect of fun that causes fury among the Islamist moral-political authority. (Bayat 2013, 126)

What scared the state was not the mere use of profanity, but that the profanity was chanted by a collective. The persistence of the organization after the systematic crackdown was what took the state and police by surprise in the Turki Alshikh incident. The threat cannot be reduced to their capacity to organize, but lies rather in the radical potentialities of "playfulness" and indiscipline inherent to the acts of those young men (Amar 2016).

AFCON 2019: The Beginning of a New Era of Football in Egypt

Since 2013, hosting sports mega-events (SME) has been considered an important step in legitimating military rule in Egypt and is, generally speaking, a reminder that SMEs foster international recognition for developing nations (Grix 2012). Seeking international legitimacy and constructing national consent are plausible explanations for the state's simultaneous policies against fans and extravagant SMEs. Samer Ayman, an economist and journalist, commented on the motives of Egypt to host AFCON 2019. He stated that "throughout history, organizing big sports events was used by authoritarian regimes to whitewash their image. This has happened in Germany in 1936 with the summer Olympics and with Argentina in the 1978 World Cup" (EG 2019).

AFCON catalyzed and crystallized the securitization and militarization processes that existed previously and intensified them by the time of the tournament. As mentioned previously, three strategies employed by the police and state created an airtight security system to filter Ultras members and give the state full control over the stadium. The first gradual and insidious strategy is related to owning the physical infrastructure. For decades, the army has used its military stadiums and larger sports complexes to host tournaments between various military groups. Even when the military started to have football teams that would compete in the civilian premier league, the military stadiums were usually used to host military teams' matches and training. In fact, it was not until 1980 that the Cairo Military Academy Stadium became one of the premier league's hosting pitches. Almost a decade and a half later, the army expanded by opening new stadiums and renovating older ones to host SMEs.

This fever of building military stadiums was gaining momentum in 2006 when the military renovated the Border Guards (Haras al-Hudud) Stadium and the Max Stadium in Alexandria to serve as hosting stadiums for AFCON 2006. During the following year, the army constructed the largest stadium in Egypt and one of the biggest in the Middle East and Africa, Borg al-Arab stadium. Also known as the Egyptian Army Stadium, this structure offered a seating capacity of eighty-six thousand spectators, ten thousand more than Cairo Stadium. In 2009, the military inaugurated two new stadiums: the Military Production Stadium (al-Salam Stadium), located in al-Salam City at the far east side of Cairo, and the Military Stadium in the Suez Governorate (previously known as Mubarak International Stadium until 2011). In that same year, Egypt hosted the FIFA U-20 World Cup, where four out of the eight hosting venues belonged to the army. Experts interviewed for this chapter emphasized that we should differentiate between the army's investments in football infrastructure before and after 2011. Two sports journalists, Tamir Shawqi and Mohamed Soliman, asserted that the construction of military stadiums before 2011 was purely motivated by economic incentives. By becoming a major player in football infrastructure in the country, the army was competing for the profits of renting the stadium as well as from tickets, merchandise, and advertising.[4]

This enthusiasm for building new military stadiums continued after the Arab Spring of 2011, yet for different ends. In 2012, the army inaugurated the Air Defense Stadium, whose name was changed to the 30 June Stadium, marking a national holiday celebrating the army's usurpation of power, removing the elected president, in 2013. The succeeding years also witnessed the renovation of some older military stadiums. Tamir Shawqi, a journalist covering football and investments, explained in a 2019 interview that economic profit cannot be the only reason behind the army's expansion in stadium building after 2011. On the one hand, fans are rarely allowed in the stadium, so tickets are no longer a revenue source. On the other hand, most of the clubs are financially struggling and are unable to pay rent. "I can't call this [a] military investment in football; I call it [an] expenditure," he emphasized. As for this expenditure, he noted that the army pumps in money to gain more control over the infrastructure and to control the fans even if this would not lead to any financial profit. Interestingly enough, the overtly militaristic names of many of these stadiums started to fade out after the Air Defense Stadium massacre, with mostly geographically oriented names replacing them. Cairo Military Production Stadium became al-Salam Stadium, while Borg al-Arab Stadium became the more common name of the Egyptian army stadium. No statements or explanations were issued to justify these changes.

Four Tournaments, Three Military Strategies

Military stadiums have had an ever-increasing presence in hosting SMEs in Egypt since the first decade of the new millennium. AFCON 2019 represented the pinnacle of the shift from state-owned stadiums to military ones. Egypt has hosted five AFCONs throughout its history, in 1959, 1974, 1986, 2006, and 2019. For the purpose of this analysis, I will only focus on the last four, since the 1959 tournament was particularly small and almost insignificant. The percentage of military stadiums that hosted these tournaments jumped from 0 percent in 1974 and 1986 to 33.33 percent in 2006 and 50 percent in the latest AFCON. One can see the military's interest in investing in football and sports infrastructure as part of the wider militarization of all aspects of business and civil life that intensified in the aftermath of 2013. Yet human rights lawyers have pointed out a different angle through which we can analyze this militarization: turning the stadiums into military zones. In an interview in 2019, Ahmed Hamed, a human rights lawyer, told the author,

These stadiums, according to the law, are military establishments. The presence of a military unit in each stadium is something stipulated by law. The walls of these stadiums, their portals, their pitches, the terraces, the tracks . . . everything there must be secured by the army. That is different from who might be responsible for organizing and securing the matches. The entrance, presence in, and exit of the fans and players might be the responsibility of the police or private security companies but the whole stadium remains a military zone. More importantly, if for any reason, riots erupted in the stadium, the arrested fans would be, by law, subjected to military trials. It is within the powers of the military judiciary, though, to give up their rights in trying the defendants to civil courts.[5]

In the years between 2015 and 2019, most of the international and regional matches were played in military-owned stadiums. This made it easier for the security forces to further intimidate Ultra groups whenever they decide to chant or speak out. The scariest moment was in 2017, when the police arrested more than 230 UWK members after riots during the Zamalek vs. Libya's Ahli Tripoli match in the Borg al-Arab Stadium during the CAF Champion League tournament. The 237 fans were all subjected to military trials before being released after five months of detention. Borg al-Arab's military case made it clear that these new military zones radically changed the nature of the game and posed grave risks for football fans. Regime propagandists and state-loyal sports anchors have repeatedly encouraged the use of military trials against football fans, especially the members of Ultras groups, after any riots in military-owned stadiums. Since the 2015 ruling that deemed the Ultras a terrorist group, the military and police have continued monitoring and regulating the behaviors of Ultras, and sometimes arresting them. The Port Said Massacre served as a narrative that transformed the Ultras themselves into security risks for the public to fear.

While Ultras previously contested the control of the state in public spaces, ironically, violence against them came to justify the role of the state in these spaces. Indeed, even

many Ultras agreed that renewed law and order was needed in public space but argued that such order would be impossible without police reforms. (Jerzak 2013, 252)

Just as Diane Singerman (2009) describes narratives built against young men in the *'ashwa'iyat*, so too were the Ultras later "portrayed as 'backward' thugs, terrorists, troublemakers, and agitators" (Singerman 2009, 116) who ostensibly exhibit "passionate" and "animalistic" primordial traits (Singerman 2009, 120). The military prosecution accused the 237 fans from the Borg al-Arab case of "preventing state institutions from operating, acquiring and possessing explosives, using them to threaten and endanger the lives of persons which led to injuries" (Egyptian Organization for Human Rights 2017). The Ultras were portrayed as vulgar and disrespectful terrorists and threats to the nation—at least, in the eyes of the state.

Yet the real game-changer in securitizing stadiums and its fans was the full digitization of the ticketing system with the help of the private sector. By May 2019, the EFA announced that an online platform, created by a corporation called Tazkarti, which means "my ticket" in Egyptian Arabic, would be responsible for selling the tickets to the tournament. To purchase a ticket, one must complete an online registration that includes one's data (e.g., national ID number) to obtain something called a Fan ID. After acquiring the Fan ID, people can proceed to purchase the tickets they want online and then collect the tickets from assigned outlets. Many sports commentators suspected that this was a way to screen previous Ultra members and exclude and ban them from attending the matches. The premonition was very much accurate, as Tazkarti banned many Ultra members who had been previously involved in court cases, even if they had been acquitted. In a recent interview, a famous Ultra member who did manage to get his fan ID issued without a problem reported:

I was with a group of friends who all were Ultras leaders and we successfully registered through the website and bought some tickets as well. We collected the Fan IDs and the tickets shortly after. Before the match, we tried to log in again but we were notified that our Fan IDs were revoked. I still went to the stadium but as the Tazkarti employee was checking my fan ID through the electronic portal, it showed that I was blocked and he politely told me that I cannot attend the match.[6]

The leader, who spoke on condition of anonymity, said that this happened to him along with many other Ultras leaders.

The process of digitizing the ticketing system was anything but transparent. Those who were denied the Fan ID were never offered any explanation. In addition, many fans were surprised to find that the tickets of many games were sold out hours after they were made available on the website. This stood in stark contradiction to the empty terraces in most of the matches. Some journalists and sports experts have explained that they suspect that the government sold tickets en masse to some corporations, like the mobile internet companies and petroleum companies, and an eminent employee in a mobile internet company has confirmed this to the author. Since 2019, Egypt has hosted many regional and international sports mega-events, even amid the 2020 COVID pandemic. Tazkarti handled the ticketing of most of these tournaments, especially the ball games. The Egyptian government has repeatedly boasted of its organizational skills and its ability to host SMEs during a health crisis.

Tazkarti turned out to be a multipurpose weapon. On the one hand, it enabled the state to filter out unwanted fans through registration; on the other hand, Tazkarti functioned as a class filter and social sanitization technology. This is part of a larger effort specific to mega-events under authoritarian jurisdiction. In such spaces, working-class individuals are either pathologized as terrorist-fans or made to disappear altogether—or appear only as working in, or building, the stadiums that they cannot afford to attend. They are effectively excluded by the new ticketing system under the assumption that the poor might pose a threat and, in any case, they exist outside the state's standards of sanitized "respectability." Both the internet literacy required for the registration process and the high prices of the tickets exclude those Egyptians with low incomes and poor accessibility (and deter those who do not want to sign up for the surveillance implied by completing the online registration system). A third-class ticket costs more than $5. Accordingly, an Egyptian family of four would need more than $20 to attend a single match. Such prices are out of reach for millions of families in a country where, according to CAPMAS, more than 30 percent of its population lives in poverty (Moneim 2020). It is hard to gauge to what degree these filtering processes were intentionally planned by the regime, but dozens of articles in the press and sports news programs on television have called for sanitizing the stadiums and attracting more presentable spectators. Since AFCON 2006, the state media have celebrated a docile middle-class fan base while demonizing loudly enthusiastic organized fan groups like the Ultras.

Televised sports media in Egypt has always functioned as a megaphone for the regime, and the relationship of sports journalists with the Ultras was always strained. In 2015, a state-owned company assumed the rights to broadcast football. The details of state ownership and its exclusive rights to broadcast football matches through the ON Sports Channel are all well documented in an investigation written by George Mikhail for al-Monitor in early 2019 (Mikhail 2019). The piece also follows the increased influence and intervention of Presentation Sports (a media company) in the selection and decisions of national coaches. Prior to the 2019 AFCON, AFE announced the launch of Time Sports, which would exclusively broadcast championship matches. This was part of Egypt's propaganda to foster competition with a Qatari-owned channel, BeIN Sports, which maintained a monopoly over regional and international tournaments at the time. Apart from the intervention in the clubs' internal politics, the state (and the intelligence services in particular, who had purchased many television stations) monopolized most sports media—at least, the outlets that broadcast local tournaments. This represented a powerful push to dominate and shape the discourse on almost all sports. State media often vilified the Ultras groups even before the uprising, using the widely accepted discourse of thuggery. This discourse discredits young men based on their class background and lack of middle-class mannerisms (Rommel 2016; Amar 2016; Hassan 2015). The use of a discourse that equates Utras to *baltagiya* (thugs) has only intensified since 2013, justifying the recurrent arrests and the constant bans from entering the stadium.

Conclusion

Despite all the forms of securitization of AFCON-2019 and efforts to silence and arrest unruly fans, certain fans have managed to send some oppositional messages during games. In this case, fans on the terrace used their cellphone flashlights to express solidarity with the victims of the two massacres against the Ultra groups (the Port Said and Air Defense Stadium massacres). At each match, mobile lights would shine on the stadiums at minutes 20 and 74 of each game to commemorate the number of the victims, while the fans chanted "Rest in heaven, O Martyr." They used the same technique to support the legendary retired football player Aboutrika, whom the state considers to be sympathetic to the Muslim Brotherhood.[7] The policemen were relatively lenient with commemorating the Ultra massacres' victims, although supporting Aboutrika deeply angered them. Police routinely began to screen the terraces before the twentieth minute of each game to identify and arrest those who were wearing national team shirts bearing the player's number. Although dozens of fans were arrested because of their support for Aboutrika, their detention was always brief and almost all of them were released shortly after their arrest. It might be the case that the police stopped a potential terrorist attack on the stadium during the last AFCON, but what we know for sure and what was omitted from the TV series is the role the plainclothes policemen played in screening, identifying, and arresting many fans who showed sympathy to the legendary former player Aboutrika.

In both the flashlight gesture and the anti–Turki Alshikh chants, Ultra groups and pro-uprising football fans demonstrated their organizational strength and the fact that it is extremely difficult to completely erase their existence. Raymond Williams (1977) proposed that epochal historical analysis should recognize and account for the dynamism of cultural and social processes. He highlighted how focusing only on the dominant or hegemonic forms of culture might blind observers to the presence of two other forms: the residual and the emergent. The residual might be a social or cultural formation that was an alternative or even oppositional to the current form. The importance of the residual lies in the fact that it is still active in the present in a manner that reveals some characteristics of the dominant. The chants and flashlight gestures are not just mementos of a once strong social organization. Here, Ultra and Ultra-sympathetic oppositional chants and gestures expose the current oppressive and autocratic football administration and its true militaristic nature, and reveal the presence of the khaki-colored army uniform of the state, no matter how the regime tries to disguise itself in civilian dress.

Notes

1 For a list of the characters, plot, and synopsis, see *The Choice* 2020.
2 https://www.youtube.com/
  watch?v=1EYnkyhUT7M&ab_channel=WATCHiT%21
3 Sayed (a pseudonym), interview by the author, 2014.
4 Tamir Shawqi, interview by the author, July 5, 2019; and Mohamed Soliman, interview by the author, June 20, 2019.
5 Ahmed Hamed, interview by the author, June 25, 2019.
6 Anonymous, personal correspondence with the author, July 15, 2021.

7 In 2017, Cairo Criminal Court added his name to a terrorist list and he has been denied entry to Egypt since then. Even when his father died, he could not come back to bury him. The fans chanted his name at the twentieth minute of each game because 20 was the number on his shirt.

Works Cited

Amar, Paul. 2016. "The Street, the Sponge, and the Ultra: Queer Logics of Children's Rebellion and Political Infantilization." *GLQ* 22, no. 4: 569–604.

Bayat, Asef. 2013. *Life as Politics: How Ordinary People Change the Middle East*. 2nd ed. Stanford, CA: Stanford University Press.

The Choice. 2020. TV series directed by Peter Mimi. 90 episodes. https://www.imdb.com/title/tt12222224/

Clarke, K. 2011. "Saying Enough: Authoritarianism and Egypt's Kefaya Movement." *Mobilization* 16, no. 4: 397–416.

Close, R. 2019. *Cairo's Ultras: Resistance and Revolution in Egypt's Football Culture*. Cairo: American University in Cairo Press.

EG. 2019. "When Football Stadiums Become Military Zones." *African Arguments*, July 23. https://africanarguments.org/2019/07/egypt-when-football-stadiums-become-military-zones/

Egyptian Organization for Human Rights (Cairo). 2017. "Egypt: Referral of Ultras Fans to the Military Judiciary Violation of the Right to a Fair Trial." July 27. https://allafrica.com/stories/201707310850.html

Ennarah, K. 2017. "The Ultras Ahlawy: Football, Violence and the Quest for Justice." Arab Politics Beyond the Uprising Report, April 11. The Century Foundation. https://tcf.org/content/report/the-ultras-ahlawy/

Grix, Jonathan. 2012. "'Image' Leveraging and Sports Mega-events: Germany and the 2006 FIFA World Cup." *The Journal of Sport Tourism* 17, no 4: 289–312. https://doi.org/10.1080/14775085.2012.760934.

Hamam, Mohamed, and Rana Mamdouh. 2017. "Parliamentary Committees Approve Bill Stipulating Harsher Penalties for Sports Team Fan Associations." *Mada Masr*, March 12. https://www.madamasr.com/en/2017/03/12/feature/politics/parliamentary-committees-approve-bill-stipulating-harsher-penalties-for-sports-team-fan-associations/

Hassan, H.M. 2015. "Extraordinary Politics of Ordinary People: Explaining the Microdynamics of Popular Committees in Revolutionary Cairo." *International Sociology* 30, no. 4: 383–400.

Hassan, N. 2018. *Football, Capitalism and Militarization of the Public Space in Egypt*. Egyptian Institute for Political and Strategic Studies.

Ibraheem, D. 2015. "Ultras Ahlawy and the Spectacle: Subjects, Resistance and Organized Football Fandom in Egypt." Master's thesis, American University in Cairo. AUC Knowledge Fountain. https://fount.aucegypt.edu/etds/140

Jerzak, Connor T. 2013. "Ultras in Egypt: State, Revolution, and the Power of Public Space." *Interface: A Journal for and about Social Movements* 5, no. 2: 240–62.

Lim, M. 2012. "Clicks, Cabs, and Coffee Houses: Social Media and Oppositional Movements in Egypt, 2004–2011." *Journal of Communication* 62, no. 2: 231–48.

Linn, Emily Crane. 2015. "Egypt Names Hard-core Soccer Fans as Terror Group." *Al-Monitor*, March 26. https://www.al-monitor.com/originals/2015/05/egypt-football-ultras-zamalek-white-nights-fight-terrorist.html

Mikhail, George. 2019. "Who Controls Egypt's Sports Scene?" *Al-Monitor*, January 18. https://www.al-monitor.com/originals/2019/01/egypt-soccer-monopoly-state-presentation-caf-afcon-league.html

Moneim, Doaa A. 2020. "Egypt's Poverty Rate declines to 29.7%: CAPMAS." Al-Ahram Online, 3 December 2020. https://english.ahram.org.eg/NewsContent/3/12/396107/Business/Economy/Egypt%E2%80%99s-poverty-rate-declines-to--CAPMAS.aspx

ON TV. 2021. "The Terrorists Wanted to Bomb the Stadium during the Match, but Our Men Handled Them." YouTube video, May 11. Posted by #Al-Ekhteyar2. https://www.youtube.com/watch?v=BpcYSI6y_sA

Oweidat, N., Cheryl Benard, Dale Stahl, Walid Kildani, Edward O'Connell, and Audra K. Grant. 2008. *The Kefaya Movement: A Case Study of a Grassroots Reform Initiative*. Santa Monica, CA: Rand Corporation. https://www.rand.org/pubs/monographs/MG778.html

Rommel, Carl. 2016. "Troublesome Thugs or Respectable Rebels? Class, Martyrdom and Cairo's Revolutionary Ultras." *Middle East—Topics & Arguments* 6: 33–42. https://doi.org/10.17192/meta.2016.6.3788

Shafick, H. 2018. "The Return of Ultras Ahlawy?" *Open Democracy*, March 22. https://www.opendemocracy.net/en/north-africa-west-asia/return-of-ultras-ahlawy-egypt-football/

El-Sherif, Ashraf. 2012. "The Ultras Politics of Fun Confront Tyranny." *Jadaliyya*. https://www.jadaliyya.com/Details/25219

Shorbagy, M. 2007. "The Egyptian Movement for Change—Kefaya: Redefining Politics in Egypt." *Public Culture* 19, no. 1: 175–96. https://doi.org/10.1215/08992363-2006-029

Sika, N. 2012. "Youth Political Engagement in Egypt: From Abstention to Uprising." *British Journal of Middle Eastern Studies* 39, no. 2: 181–99. https://doi.org/10.1080/13530194.2012.709700

Singerman, Diane. 2009. "The Siege of Imbaba: Egypt's Internal Other, and the Criminalization of Politics." In *Cairo Contested*, edited by Diane Singerman, 111–43. Cairo: American University in Cairo Press.

Williams, R. 1977. *Marxism and Literature*. New York: Oxford University Press.

Zengin, A. 2019. "The Afterlife of Gender: Sovereignty, Intimacy, and Muslim Funerals of Transgender People in Turkey." *Cultural Anthropology* 34, no. 1: 78–102. https://doi.org/10.14506/ca34.1.09

10

URBAN (COUNTER)REVOLUTION AGAINST GENTRIFICATION
SHADOW SECURITY NETWORKS, *BALTAGIYA* SUBJECTIVITIES, AND COMMUNITY DENSITIES

OMNIA KHALIL

During the 2011 Egyptian revolution, the Bulaq Abu al-'Ila neighborhood of Cairo was a vital center of political activity. It is adjacent to Tahrir Square, which—as many authors in this volume point out—was often the epicenter of the revolutionary events in the Egyptian capital. Bulaq's residents were portrayed in the media and by state officials as either heroes of the revolution or revolutionary thugs, depending on the political perspective that prevailed at different moments of the uprising and in its aftermath. As Hassan, El Raggal, and Ahmed's chapters in this volume describe, the Egyptian state increasingly relied on a network of privatized enforcers—often called "thugs" *(baltagiya)*—to manage public space. This was particularly the case in the years leading up to the revolution. The present chapter traces one instance of the rise of this unofficial network of residents who work as a shadow security state, enforcing order and punishing residents whom they deem to be out of order. Importantly, this network does not operate simply for the state or for neighborhood residents: its role in the district is murkier and more complicated. As we shall see below, they play a paradoxical role, supporting residents against forced evictions but also sometimes engaging in violent counterrevolutionary action. To flesh out this argument, I first discuss the spatial practices of securitization that have surfaced recently, especially in the Maspero Triangle area of the district. I then locate this area within the wider political, economic, and social landscapes of Cairo, tracing the ways that violence and territorial control have been co-constitutive in the post-coup period. I conclude by explaining how the state deploys a form of governance in the neighborhood that paradoxically both instrumentalizes and criminalizes illicit practices and regularizes them at the center of governmentality.

Shadow Security Network

"We are the security arm of the state,"[1] Wael stated, referring to his and other residents' relationship with the neighborhood and the state. Wael, a man in his early forties, is generally very energetic and talkative. When I asked him to elaborate on that statement, he went on: "We, here at the Triangle, have Maspero and the ministry buildings; both are highly securitized. We [the residents] are always asked about what is going on in the neighborhood. The government is always afraid of any interference from unknown persons."[2] He explained how many residents work as informants for the police, which reflects how the neighborhood is being governed. This conversation took place in 2016, before the neighborhood's residents were dispossessed by the urban renewal projects which they were then opposing. I had entered the neighborhood from its southern entry and walked into an alley, where Wael had met me. As we walked, he repeatedly greeted other residents in the neighborhood, whether workers at a car workshop or neighbors. We sat in a café, where I was the only woman. Since strangers often came to the neighborhood because of its participatory planning project (Khalil 2019), my presence didn't raise questions. Wael introduced me to several people, saying I was an architect who wanted to learn about the neighborhood. All around us were four-story residential buildings with walls covered in graffiti and slogans against forced evictions.

The urban fabric of the neighborhood is reflected in the organized and unorganized histories of its urbanization processes, and it is not hard to follow its trajectory simply by looking at a map. However, the shadow security network constituted a group of people who were not readily visible while serving as an unofficial part of the securitization of the state. The state does not directly and officially hire informants for the police, and hardly anyone would describe themselves that way. There is an official government employee, called an "investigator" (*mokhber*), who is a graduate of the police academy and regularly receives his paychecks at the police station (SharafEldin 2007). "Informant" (*morshed*) is a different category, classified as an unofficial and unpublicized "volunteer" job for citizens. Wael was presenting the job in a neutral fashion, as if it were a common role in the regular power relations between the state and its citizens. This unofficial security system, running parallel to the more commonly recognized systems, has its own hierarchy. In the shadow security network, the informants are classified in accordance with the nature of the mission to which they will be assigned. Each police station has a database with details on all the residents who have committed so-called crimes. These people are labeled as dangerous, with criminal records that are classified as A, B, or C, depending on their history— categories that originate in Egyptian criminal law. Usually, most type A or B criminals have already been sentenced to a probationary period, to be served after their release from prison. They pay regular visits to the police station in their neighborhood, signing their names on attendance sheets and/or spending some hours there.

Wael clarified that the police station needed this parallel system due to its inability to deal with the large number of inhabitants in the neighborhood. Bulaq is home to 48,147 residents (CAPMAS 2017), and the maximum number of police staff at the station who must monitor them is thirty. Wael pointed out that police station personnel cannot operate without people like him: the support of guys on the street corner are a necessity for governing (Ismail 2006). After 1997, Minister of the Interior Habib al-Adli decided to use such neighborhood monitors to enhance the security system (Fact Finding Committee Report 2012; Dessouki 2012; Mansour 2013). Thus these personnel became the regime's shadow security network, who would help with elections, demonstrations, and activities in which the regime might not want to be directly involved. These groups have been socially defined as *baltagiya* (thugs)[3] (Iskandar 2013; Amar 2013; Ghannam 2012).

According to the police, Wael is considered *sha'i* (naughty or unruly). He served as a member of the National Democratic Party and participated in falsifying an election in a process called *al-wara'a al-dawara* (the rotating paper ballot). In this process, a voter would hide a blank white paper inside their pocket when entering the voting station. After being handed a paper ballot, they would switch the blank paper in their pocket with the official paper ballot. The voter then would walk out of the voting area and put the blank paper into the ballot box. Upon leaving the building, the voter would deliver the blank ballot to a member of his group and then received money in payment. The group would write the name of their candidate on the sheet and give it to another voter. The new voter would place the filled ballot into the ballot box and keep the new blank paper ballot. The process continued to rotate all day long and all the voters would get paid. While interviewing Wael, I created a time-line of political events in order to ask him where he was in the parliament elections of 2016 and the presidential elections since 2018. In April 2019, before the constitutional amendments had been made,[4] Wael told me that he had been planning to get a small truck with a microphone and songs, obeying an order from Bulaq's police to create a carnival in the streets to show that there were alliances who supported the regime. These trucks would drive around the area, playing loud chants and songs through megaphones. Posters would be printed and displayed with the president's image to remind residents to vote YES for the governing party (*Mostaa'bal Watan*, or the Nation's Future). Wael explained that in August 2020, he decided not to participate in the senate elections as they were only paying 50 Egyptian pounds per person ($3.30). Instead, he decided to wait for the November 2020 parliamentary elections, which would be more profitable.

Politicized Territoriality

In January 2020, while Wael and I walked through the Maspero con-struction site, he suddenly pointed to a lone palm tree and recalled, "This is exactly where my room was. It was my very personal space." He then pointed to a demolished wall and remembered: "Here is the loca-tion of the café where we first met." The scene was very different from before. Half of the land was now a construction site, filled with bulldoz-ers, cement, concrete, and a billboard with an illustration of how the project would look when completed. Another 30 percent of the land had already been turned into a parking lot.

The Maspero Triangle (Muthallath Maspero, in Arabic) is shaped like a triangle on the map (fig. 10.1). Before the demolition in 2018, most of the neighborhood consisted of old houses, three and four sto-ries tall. Most of these buildings had unique architectural features. But since 1992, when a strong earthquake hit Cairo, most of the old buildings badly needed repair and structural restoration. The Egyptian govern-ment decided not to issue restoration permits to the owners, instead pursuing a policy geared toward the depopulation of these old neigh-borhoods in unique, potentially valuable geographical areas in Cairo. Land was becoming expensive in Sayida Zeinab, al-Khalifa, Hattaba, and Bulaq Abu al-'Ila. The depopulation plan was not announced, and it resulted in a rapid deterioration of Cairo's urban core, which included many car repair workshops, distributed all across the neighborhoods, that provided income to their owners.

Beside these urban cores of deteriorated buildings, there is the façade of the neighborhood looking over the Nile, which still exists as it was originally built. This façade consists of seven high-rise residential and business buildings, just behind the Ramses Hilton Hotel and in front of the renowned Egyptian Museum, where Egypt's ancient heritage has long been on display. The Ramses Hilton is at the very south end of Maspero. North of it are seven residential buildings and the Maspero Building, housing the headquarters of Egypt's Television and Radio Ministry as well as the Ministry of Foreign Affairs. The Nile flows along the west edge of the Triangle, while the two other sides consisted of residential buildings of the urban core that was demolished.

Ali, another resident of the neighborhood, has a type A criminal record, indicating the most serious of crimes in his past. He prepared an area of one hundred square meters to be the gathering spot for the shadow security network at Maspero during the events of September 2019.[5] Throughout 2019 and 2020, the police called on residents like Ali to assist with each political event, which indicates that the security apparatus did not change their strategy during this period. Ali was a parking attendant: another layer of the security network. The shadow security network involves not only informants and thugs, but also includes many additional intersectional layers of doormen, parking attendants, cigarette kiosk vendors, and others classified as precarious laborers. Ali explained how the construction site of Maspero was turned into parking lots, which he partially manages. The Cairo Governorate decided to make that status official, renting the vacant land as a parking lot for LE 8,000 a month (approximately $500).

"Do you see this billboard?" Wael asked me. "The owners could not have it here without our permission."[6] The owners initially had constructed a concrete base with a metal stub to hold the vertical metal post. Wael and his friends decided to ruin the stub, which forced the owners to negotiate with them in order to be able to construct the billboard. Until today, the owners pay Wael and two friends monthly payments to guard the billboard. Wael claimed, "We forced them to pay us *(baltagna 'alihum)*."[7] I asked him, "What does *baltaga* mean?" to which he responded, "Someone takes something by force that is not his." Wael differentiates between a single act of *baltaga* (thuggery) and the subjectivity of *baltagiya* (thugs). He does not define himself within the class of *baltagiya*, instead using the action of *baltaga* to illustrate his powerful position for accumulating wealth.

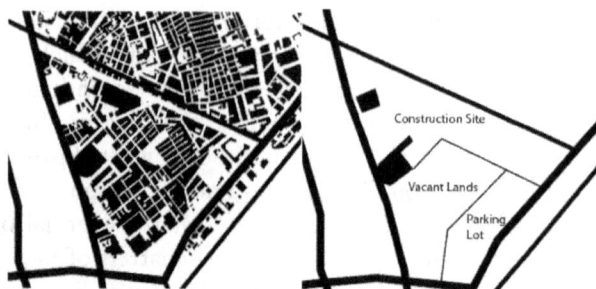

Figure 10.1. Maspero Triangle before the demolitions in 2018 (left) and after the demolitions in 2020 (right).

Neither Wael nor Ali would consider themselves thugs, *musaggal khatar* (high-profile criminals), or *sha'i* (naughty, referring to those who do not usually have a single profession). Instead, they describe themselves as "precarious labor." This precarity in work and living adds another dimension to the security network, which entails more than just those who have a criminal record. The connections between the beneficiaries of the neighborhood and the police can take many forms. Half of Maspero's residents were unemployed (CAPMAS 2017), working in various ways that constitute the so-called informal economy (Khalil 2014; Khalil 2019). This informality plays a key role in police work. Low-ranking policemen ask for bribes in exchange for not arresting workers. In return, precarious laborers cannot refuse to provide information to the police without risking being humiliated, tortured, and/or arrested. As an example, consider the parking attendant, who knows the car owners and the visitors to the neighborhood. Parking attendants bribe the police to overlook illicit activities (e.g., drugs) and, in return, provide information about the neighborhood. Security networks emerge in the form of doormen, parking attendants, and kiosk traders who are in regular communication with the local police, thereby constituting investigative territories and invisible networks of shadow security (Deleuze and Guattari 1989; Brenner 1999; Staeheli, Kofman, and Peake 2004).

Regime Puppets

The 2011 upheaval produced a revolutionary/counterrevolutionary binary. In the early days of January 2011, the two poles were obvious. February 1, 2011—the day of the Camel Battle[8]—was a day of counterrevolutionary actions. The word *baltagiya* was widely used to describe the paid thugs who came to Tahrir Square to initiate violence.[9] Within the eighteen days of the revolution,[10] a distinct counterrevolution emerged, composed of groups who supported and worked for Mubarak's regime. The accusations that people and groups were being counterrevolutionary ebbed and flowed between January 2011 and July 2013. The word *baltagiya* carried a very significant meaning that was also used by demonstrators to describe pro-regime individuals. At the same time, the Supreme Council of the Armed Forces[11] used the same word as an accusatory term for the demonstrators they arrested to socially shame them. When, during the occupation of Tahrir Square, a crowd of people suddenly caught and beat up a person, they shouted that they had caught a *baltagi* (thug), who was identified as a member of the National Democratic Party.[12] The shadow security network I describe obfuscates the line between revolutionary and counterrevolutionary, between the state and the people.

While walking with Wael in the neighborhood, I observed that everyone seemed to know him, and he seemed to know everyone. Usually, Cairenes would describe men like Wael as *gada'* (a good man) (Jacob 2011; Ghannam 2012; Elychar 2012). This is a form of masculinity and manhood that focuses on the collective good (Amar 2013; Ghannam 2013). Wael was first introduced to me as an organizer against forced eviction and gentrification. His police record did not include any explicit criminal convictions, which meant that the police could depend on him for state rallies. Wael was able to wear both hats: one as a mobilizer against the government evictions and simultaneously another as a counterrevolutionary during a revolutionary time. His political subjectivity supports this paradox.

Wael attempted to clear things up for me about the so-called revolution. He told me, "The people who believe in the revolution, like you, would never exceed 2 percent [of the population]. Everyone else has a *maslaha* (interest)."[13] Wael started his career by assisting tourists who came to the Abdel-Moniem Riad terminal looking for accommodations. He used to walk them to hotels and take a commission. As a teenager, he noticed the difference between himself, as a boy attending school, and others in the neighborhood who did not go to school. His father told him that he should be an educated person with a good job, but Wael decided to combine both ways of life. He liked his adventures with his neighborhood peers, who were street-corner guys. Stealing fruit was the first activity that he got away with, and that escalated to learning how to stab a person without killing them.

"We are the sons of the streets, not the sons of apartments,"[14] Wael informed me, claiming that he and his friends understand how their neighborhood is governed. This phrase touches on the difference between *effendiya* (educated) and *fahlawiya* (educated and precarious). Wael described professionals like me as *wilad nas*, referring to middle- and upper-middle-class people who are well educated. He meant that we were born in apartments, went to schools, and are hypothetically responsible for the process of (re)forming the world. The human rights narratives supported by many of the *effendiya* seem logical, but for Wael they are not applicable. Wael told me that human rights groups want police officers to deal with people while respecting their dignity, but he questioned how this could happen and what would then happen to their current method of governance, which is based on corruption. For Wael, being *baltagi* was logical and essential for him to survive and to make his way within the neighborhood.

Classifying Wael as counterrevolutionary would be a mistake, as would classifying him as a revolutionary: both are reductive ways of understanding his subjectivity. As El Raggal points out in their chapter in this volume, Islamists, thugs, and drug dealers exist in parallel coexistence and, as Hassan relates (also in this volume), their ethos is much more likely to be one of self-centered cost-benefit analysis. As such, Wael's decisions are highly situational; revolutionary and counterrevolutionary actions were both tools for his own interest and are correlated to political geography (Harvey 2009) and political governance within local neighborhoods in Cairo (Bayat 2013; Ismail 2006). Wael's loyalty goes first to his peers in the neighborhood, who are considered to be *gada'* (Ghannam 2012).

Conclusion

In understanding how political life is tied to the economic structure of the neighborhood and its subjectivities, and how modernity gave birth to law in that part of society that rendered me and my peers part of the *effendiya*, I ask: what do we mean by the law? This chapter considers the lives of people who were born in a society of informal codes of conduct that have sprung up between the state and its citizens. I contend that the state uses the shadow security network as a tool to secure its position. It is useful to have a group of people on hand who can commit crimes on the state's behalf, leaving state officials in the shadows. Political subjectivity is formed within paradoxes and contradictory actions. The hegemonic rule is: *"Illi tiksabbu, il'abbu"* (play to whatever makes you win).

This is the logic and value of neoliberalism. Wael's whole journey is premised on the idea of benefit. Any game he involves himself in needs to be a profitable game; it does not matter with whom or how. Counterrevolution, geography, and gentrification are in the hands of the ruling classes who manipulate the ordinary people. The word "agency" makes no sense to them in view of the power exercised over them by the police station or other governmental personnel. The relationship between revolution, urban geography, and anti-gentrification is a matter of a movement that does not have a fixed base or distinct allies.

Can we see someone like Wael as representative of ordinary people? Some might say "no." Wael asserted that all his actions, his precarious labor, were incentivized by compensation. He comes from what some would see as a class that represents a problem in terms of in its relationship to a neoliberal state through territorialities, parking lots, and election sites. This understanding of Wael's position constitutes the violence and labor of *baltagiya*. Violence is outsourced, on certain occasions, from official police to others. The binary of revolution and counterrevolution becomes an illusion if one criminalizes the regime that makes soldiers out of residents.

Notes

1 Wael (a pseudonym), interview by the author, June 14, 2016.
2 Wael (a pseudonym), interview by the author, June 14, 2016.
3 Thugs have a negative racial connotation in the United States, and the use of the word here is specific to Egypt. In this chapter, it has a very particular meaning and only refers to the closest English translation of the word (*baltagiya*), a member of the shadow security network.
4 The constitutional amendment in April 2019 was vital, as it changed the terms of the presidency, allowing al-Sisi to serve as the president until 2032.
5 During August 2019, an Egyptian contractor left Egypt for Spain, where he started live-streaming a series of videos defaming the military Engineering Committee that has taken over construction work in Egypt since 2014. Mohamed Ali had been a contractor for that committee and is related to al-Sisi's family. After his series of videos announcing specific details about construction projects of the government, he called for demonstrations to oust al-Sisi on September 20, 2019. The security network prepared itself to the maximum level, and more than four thousand persons were

arrested during the demonstrations and unrest, which continued for about twenty days. There were even rumors that a coup against al-Sisi might be launched from inside the army. Many activists have been arrested since then, including Alaa Abdel-Fattah, Mahinour El-Masry, Esraa Abdel-Fattah, and many others.

6   Wael (a pseudonym), interview by the author, February 17, 2020.

7   Wael (a pseudonym), interview by the author, February 17, 2020.

8   On February 1, 2011, Mubarak's regime paid thugs who rode horses and camels and initiated violence in Tahrir Square in order to suppress the demonstrations. The Muslim Brotherhood made up the front lines, and many revolutionaries joined them in order to kick the counterrevolutionaries out. The two days of clashes became known as the Battle of the Camels.

9   In 2005, during an event called "Black Wednesday," paid thugs were used to harass women and inflict violence during the elections.

10 From January 25 to February 12, 2011.

11 The SCAF officially ruled Egypt from February 11, 2011 to June 29, 2012, during a transitional period until a new president was elected.

12 The Mubarak regime's ruling party.

13 Wael (a pseudonym), interview by the author, March 10, 2019.

14 Wael (a pseudonym), interview by the author, March 10, 2019.

Works Cited

Amar, Paul. 2013. *The Security Archipelago: Human-security States, Sexuality Politics, and the End of Neoliberalism.* Social Textbooks. Durham, NC: Duke University Press.

Arendt, Hannah. 1970. *On Violence.* New York: Harcourt Brace & Co.

Bayat, Asef. 2013. *Life as Politics: How Ordinary People Change the Middle East.* Stanford, CA: Stanford University Press.

——. 2017. *Revolution without Revolutionaries: Making Sense of the Arab Spring.* Redwood City, CA: Stanford University Press, 2017.

Benjamin, Walter. 2004. *Walter Benjamin: Selected Writings,* edited by Marcus Paul Bullock and Michael William Jennings. Vol. 1, 1935–1938. Cambridge, MA and London: Belknap.

Bhan, Gautam. 2016. *In the Public's Interest: Evictions, Citizenship, and Inequality in Contemporary Delhi.* Athens: University of Georgia Press.

Bourdieu, Pierre. 1977. *Outline of a Theory of Practice.* Cambridge Studies in Social Anthropology 16. Cambridge: Cambridge University Press.

Bourdieu, Pierre, and Loic Wacquant. 2004. "Symbolic Violence. " In *Violence in War and Peace*, edited by Philippe Bourgois and Nancy Scheper-Hughes, 272–74. Malden, MA: Blackwell Publishers.

Brenner, Neil. 1999. "Beyond State-centrism? Space, Territoriality, and Geographical Scale in Globalization Studies." *Theory and Society* 28, no. 1: 39–78.

Bush, Ray, and Habib Ayeb. 2012. *Marginality and Exclusion in Egypt*. London: Zed Books.

Caldeira, Teresa. 2000. *City of Walls: Crime, Segregation, and Citizenship in Sao Paulo*. Berkeley: University of California Press.

CAPMAS (Central Agency for Public Mobilization and Statistics). 2017. CAPMAS reports of 2017. https://www.capmas.gov.eg

Castells, Manuel. 1983. *The City and the Grassroots: A Cross-cultural Theory of Urban Social Movements*. Berkeley: University of California Press.

Das, Veena. 1987. "The Anthropology of Violence and the Speech of Victims." *Anthropology Today* 3, no. 4: 11–13.

———. 2006. *Life and Words: Violence and the Descent into the Ordinary*. Berkeley: University of California Press.

Deleuze, Gilles, and Felix Guattari. 1989. *A Thousand Plateaus: Capitalism and Schizophrenia*. 2nd ed. Minneapolis: University of Minnesota Press.

El-Dessouki, Mustafa. 2012. "Qanun gadid li-muwagahat al-baltagiya fi Misr." *Al Majalla*. https://arb.majalla.com/taxonomy/term/67676

Elychar, Julia. 2012. "Before (and after) Neoliberalism: Tacit Knowledge, Secrets of the Trade, and the Public Sector in Egypt." *Cultural Anthropology* 27, no. 1: 76–96.

"Fact Finding Committee Report of the 18 Days of the Egyptian Revolution, 2012." Accessed May 19, 2023. https://rb.gy/xvzho

Ghannam, Farha. 2012. "Meanings and Feelings: Local Interpretations of the Use of Violence in the Egyptian Revolution." *American Ethnologist* 39, no. 1: 32–36.

———. 2013. *Live and Die Like a Man: Gender Dynamics in Urban Egypt*. Stanford, CA: Stanford University Press.

Hall, Stuart. 1980. *Policing the Crisis: Mugging, the State, and Law and Order*. Critical Social Studies. Houndmills, Basingstoke: Palgrave.

Harvey, David. 2003a. *The New Imperialism*. Oxford: Oxford University Press.

———. 2003b. *Urban Revolution*. Minneapolis: University of Minnesota Press.

———. 2009. *Social Justice and the City*. Rev. ed. Athens: University of Georgia Press. https://muse.jhu.edu/book/13205

——. 2012. *Rebel Cities: From the Right to the City to the Urban Revolution*. London and New York: Verso.

Iskandar, Adel. 2013. *Egypt in Flux*. Cairo: American University in Cairo Press.

Ismail, Salwa. 2006. *Political Life in Cairo's New Quarters: Encountering the Everyday State*. Minneapolis: University of Minnesota Press.

Jacob, Wilson Chacko. 2011. *Working Out Egypt: Effendi Masculinity and Subject Formation in Colonial Modernity, 1870–1940*. Durham, NC: Duke University Press.

Khalil, Omnia. 2014. "The People of the City, Space, Laboring and Power: In Quest of Unraveling the HOW in Ramlet Bulaq." Cairo: American University in Cairo Press. http://dar.aucegypt.edu/handle/10526/3959

——. 2019. "The State as an Urban Broker: Subjectivity Formation, Securitization, and Place-making in Post-revolutionary Cairo." *Urban Anthropology and Studies of Cultural Systems and World Economic Development* 48, no. 1/2: 85–128.

Lefebvre, Henri. 1996. "The Right to the City." In *Writings on Cities*, edited and translated by Eleonore Kofman and Elizabeth Lebas, 147–59. Malden, MA and Oxford: Blackwell.

Madd Platform. 2015. "Maspero Parallel Participatory Project, 2015." https://issuu.com/maddplatform/docs/maspero_parallel_participatory_proj

Mansour, Ahmed. 2013. "Sina'at al-baltaga fi Misr." *Shorouk News*, May. https://www.shorouknews.com/columns/view.aspx?cdate=21052013&id=aa1b8774-1b5d-4374-93b4-66dfc9ff6050

Radicati, Allesandra. 2020. "The Unstable Coastline: Navigating Dispossession and Belonging in Colombo." *Antipode* 52, no. 2: 542–61.

Ralph, Laurence. 2014. *Renegade Dreams: Living through Injury in Gangland Chicago*. Chicago: University of Chicago Press.

Riches, David. 1986. *The Anthropology of Violence*. Oxford and New York: Blackwell.

Roitman, Janet. 2005. *Fiscal Disobedience: An Anthropology of Economic Regulation in Central Africa*. Princeton: Princeton University Press.

Roy, Ananya. 2015. "Who's Afraid of Postcolonial Theory?" *International Journal of Urban and Regional Research* 40, no. 1: 200–209.

Selim, Gehan. 2017. *Unfinished Places: The Politics of (Re)making Cairo Old Quarters*. London and New York: Routledge.

SharafEldin, Nabeel. 2007. "Akthar min nisf million mukhbir fi Misr." *Elaph*,

Sharp, Deen, and Claire Panetta, eds. 2016. *Beyond the Square: Urbanism and the Arab Uprisings*. New York: Terreform.

Sharp, Deen, and Claire Panetta, eds. 2016. *Beyond the Square: Urbanism and the Arab Uprisings*. New York: Terreform.

Simone, Abdoumaliq, and Vyjayanthi Rao. 2012. "Securing the Majority: Living through Uncertainty in Jakarta." *International Journal of Urban and Regional Research* 36, no. 2: 315–35.

Singerman, Diane, and Paul Amar. 2009. *Cairo Cosmopolitan: Politics, Culture, and Urban Space in the New Globalized Middle East*. Cairo: American University in Cairo Press.

Smith, Neil. 2002. "New Globalism, New Urbanism: Gentrification as Global Urban Strategy." *Antipode* 34, no. 3: 427–50. https://doi.org/10.1111/1467-8330.00249

Staeheli, Lynn, Eleonore Kofman, and Linda Peake, eds. 2004. *Mapping Women, Making Politics: Feminist Perspectives on Political Geography*. 1st ed. New York: Routledge.

Tawakkol, Lama. 2020. "Reclaiming the City's Core: Urban Accumulation, Surplus (Re)production and Discipline in Cairo." *Geoforum* 126, no. 4: 420–30. DOI:10.1016/j.geoforum.2019.12.014.

11

URBANIZING DREAMS
THE STRUGGLES OF ATTAINING "NEW" SOCIAL CONTRACTS FOR THE MIDDLE AND UPPER MIDDLE CLASSES AT CAIRO'S DESERT EDGE

MOMEN EL-HUSSEINY

I'll begin with the following hypothesis: Society has been completely urbanized. This hypothesis implies a definition: An urban society is a society that results from a process of complete urbanization. This urbanization is virtual today but will become real in the future.

(Lefebvre 2003, 1).

On Agency, Urbanization, and the Egyptian Dream

As many other authors in this volume point out, the current drive toward a new urbanism in Egypt is based on a history of national aspirations toward modernity and civilization that, at varying moments in the past, have taken Europe or the United States as their guiding models (Hammad, Elsaket, this volume) and that today seems to be seeking inspiration in the new metropolises of the Persian Gulf (Sinno, this volume). One question that remains unanswered, however, in all these past and present attempts to achieve a "modern, civilized, urban" Egypt is whether these foreign models can or should actually be applied to Egyptian realities.

While Lefebvre hypothesizes that an "urban society" will be attainable in the future, the question of *how* remains unexplored. Achille Mbembe asserts that modernity has never been linear in the global south (2001). In fact, urbanization in the south is in constant re-formation toward developing an *urban society* with established relationships of citizenship. The middle-class struggle for citizen representation in their built environment is one example. The process of accommodating the middle class with their dreams for a modern society has never been linear in the context of postcolonial Cairo. The changing dynamics of attaining dignified housing have long shaped the surroundings of the city. Since 1952, the government has embraced a drive to modernize the built environment by extending the city outward into the desert, establishing Tahrir Province (El-Shakry 2007) and Nasr City (El-Husseiny 2015). This expansion was politically driven by Nasser's vision rather than people's aspirations; the people had no agency. Migrants inhabited the city slums, the upper class resided in khedivial colonial Downtown and in affluent neighborhoods, while the middle class were relegated to the new city expansions on the desert edge. Shaped by wide vehicular roads, Nasr City was built to accommodate the state's military parades, government buildings, stadiums, new university, and superblocks. It represented a modernist city, albeit a political one. At the outset, its detail-less aesthetics with dry façades and brutalist architecture resembled the international style. However, at its core was a political homage to secular society. It included a new university campus, intended for the relocation of the venerable Islamic al-Azhar University from historic Cairo, followed by a plan to restructure its curricula to encompass secular knowledge (El-Husseiny 2015; Zeghal 2009). Driven by the state's control and society's aspirations toward promoting the model happy Egyptian family, the middle class was driven to incubate in the apartments of Nasr City's superblocks.

From the 1952 coup d'état to the World Bank's 1991 economic adjustment program, the voices of the middle class were never urbanized in accordance with Western, liberal, and democratic models, and the dream of an urban society with citizen representation remained out of reach. The nation-state continued to be primarily characterized as a police state. Middle-class and upper-middle-class citizens in Egypt have never experienced the meaning of town halls, public hearings, neighborhood representations, collective gatherings, and a sense of community engagement. During many interviews conducted for fieldwork with residents in the eastern and western compounds outside of Cairo from 2008 to 2012 and 2017 to 2020, residents expressed a keen interest in escaping the existing urban conditions inside the city, which they characterized as patriarchally dominated and saturated by the police state and community oversight (Ismail 2014). One incident among many others took place in March 2021, when a doorman and three residents invaded the apartment of a thirty-three-year-old female doctor who lived alone in al-Salam district in Maadi, Cairo. Because they suspected the woman of committing adultery, they broke into her place and forced her to jump off her apartment's balcony (El-Din 2021). This event symbolizes the core matter of *why* an "urban society" is a long-deferred Egyptian dream. A rising sense of insecurity for women and families with regard to liberties, however, constantly reinforces the urgency of realizing this dream, of searching for new possibilities for a social contract.

During the 2000s, several Cairo urban scholars began to reflect on the mushrooming of gated communities at the city's desert edge (Mitchell 2002; Kuppinger 2004; Denis 2006; Ghannam 2014). As a new and growing phenomenon with still underdeveloped enclaves, most of the output from this suburban research relied on "the perspective from outside" the walls through quick visits and the reading of internet pages, advertisement brochures, design schemes, and so forth, except for a few attempts at ethnography (Marafi 2011; Arese 2018). Today, we are living in a complexly reconfigured suburban environment (Caldeira 2001; Herzog 2014; Berger and Kotkin 2017; Keil 2018), requiring sociocultural ethnographic analysis. The mushrooming of gated communities reflects the process of massive urbanization and outward internal migration of the middle and upper middle classes. Yet, after more than twenty years of such expansive mobilization, the "perspective of life experience in compounds" is still surprisingly understudied. Exploring the need to rethink the term "gated communities" as an outcome of global north theorization, and to reproduce epistemologies based on the global south's spatial dynamics and practices, is the principal theoretical drive of this chapter.

This chapter explores three modes of spatial development of the "Egyptian dream" at Cairo's desert edge: the rural second home, the totalizing experience, and the suburban world-city through the lens of dream-making and city-becoming. The chapter traces the expansion of *dreams* in space and time over thirty years of mass suburbanization, and how these dreams redefine new relationships of privatized citizenship. In doing so, the author deploys the portfolio of a real estate developer, Talaat Moustafa Group (TMG), to posit three paradigmatic practices of compound transformation: al-Rabwa (520 acres, 1994–2006), al-Rehab (2,500 acres, 1996–2017), and Madinaty (8,000 acres, 2006–23). These three enclaves reflect the transformative nature of compound development at Cairo's desert edge. Their massive rescaling has magnified internal frictions and contestations, exposing people's unsatisfied urge to draft a new social contract. The developer's growing spatial and social armature at the edge echoes a capital city in flux: nothing is determined, and accordingly, TMG leaves *things* indefinite, undefined, and subject to constant repurposing and simultaneous possibilities.

Methodologically, this chapter moves away from holistic metanarratives of the "global city" framework toward a "pluralistic simultaneity" of agency and considers how this helps us in understanding the city's transfigurations, through micro-narratives and the spatial experiences of everyday frictions toward a better form of inhabitation. First, I posit that the sociocultural notion of "embeddedness" (Polanyi 2001) is an operative tool used to analyze the "more-than-urban" process. The urban is a process, not a site (Harvey 1996, 52); it requires an intricate understanding of the situated politics of extended urbanization and its human ecology (Angelo and Wachsmuth 2015; Brenner 2019; Tzaninis et al. 2020; Keil 2020). Second, I build on the "worlding" practices of developers and transnational citizens with their frames of reference rooted in south-to-south circuits of city-becoming (Simone 2001; Roy and Ong 2011). Third, while the chapter invokes the work of a real estate developer as an entry point to analyze the planning schemes of mass suburbanization (Mitchell 2002; Sims 2014; Schmid 2019), I rely on the narratives of citizens, with their attendant frictions and struggles, in order to repurpose those schemes (Simone 2019; Hurley 2019). Lastly, the chapter joins with the calls of other postcolonial urban scholars to build a theory from within the global south, based on its historic-present contingencies (Roy 2018; Bhan 2019).

Building Dreams, Capitalizing on the Void

Cairo's gated communities provide an urban imaginary away from the state police control of every aspect of daily life experienced in the city center. They expand the possibilities for residents to engage, confront, contest, and produce nascent relationships between the governing (real estate developers, in this case) and the governed (homeowners and renters). One of the discernible characteristics resulting from compounds' embeddedness in densely populated Cairo is the process of their rescaling, leading to a variety of spatial articulations. Their exponential growth, developed through improvisation and diversification, incorporates more than merely residential houses. The compounds have morphed into mixed-use developments, with vacant structures and half-empty amenities; their walls have been transformed from single-layered fences to a buffer zone of recreational activities. In terms of scale, they have grown from small enclaves of 5,000 inhabitants, expanding to medium-scale enclaves of around 200,000 inhabitants, and in some cases have become large-scale enclaves of around 700,000 inhabitants. The transformative urbanization of these compounds has pushed a quasi-internal migration from the city center to what is no longer a periphery.

Real estate developers play a major role in reshaping the expansive landscape of gated communities (Yousry 2009). Developers acquire permits to build compounds from the New Urban Communities Authority (NUCA) through a rendered masterplan and land-zoning analysis, stipulating percentages of built-up areas and housing typologies. Every developer generates their sub/urban vision of inhabitation and frames of reference without the state's interference. The government's role is limited to oversight, ensuring that there are no drastic changes from the original masterplan after compounds are being built. The architectural character and spatial experience vary from one compound to another and are, essentially, unrestricted. Each compound's character emanates from the developer's portfolio. Cairo's real estate developers include Egyptians, Gulf Arabs, and the Engineering Authority of the Armed Forces. Their various developments have resulted in a diversified terrain of compounds serving a varied clientele.

The developer Talaat Moustafa Group (TMG) is one of the major players in the development of Cairo's compounds. Beginning in the 1970s, engineer Hisham Talaat Moustafa began his career in the construction business with his three sons. In the late 1980s, they moved into real estate investment on the outskirts of Alexandria, establishing al-Rawda al-Khadra' and Virginia Beach Village during a boom of beach resorts along the north coast. TMG's aspirations to expand were made possible after the group shifted to Cairo during the deregulation of desert lands in the 1990s, when the state housing authority decided to sell land at the outskirts of Cairo to private developers for the purpose of building gated communities. TMG was one of the first developers assigned to this mission, and in the 1990s, they started their endeavor with two small enclaves: al-Rabwa in Sheikh Zayed, thirty kilometers west of downtown Cairo, and May Fair in al-Shorouk City, forty-five kilometers east of downtown Cairo, both with target populations of some one thousand to two thousand residents. In the late 1990s, TMG acquired 2,500 acres of empty land to construct al-Rehab in New Cairo, thirty kilometers east of downtown Cairo, planned for 200,000 inhabitants. From the 1990s to the 2000s, targeted residency thus increased by

100 percent. During this period, TMG began experimenting with several new spatial configurations for outdoor life inside the compounds to serve as catalysts and energize New Cairo. In retrospect, they expanded their targeted pool of residents to incorporate the middle class by constructing four-story buildings. Furthermore, TMG dedicated a set of apartment buildings for the compounds' maintenance, cleaning, gardening, and security workers in al-Rehab, providing temporary residences for workers to stay overnight on the days they work in the compound. Moreover, TMG provided a private bus network connecting al-Rehab to downtown Cairo, making the city more accessible.

In the late 2000s, TMG secured a bigger plot of eight thousand acres forty-five kilometers east of downtown Cairo, close to May Fair, to build Madinaty, with a target population of 700,000 residents. The threefold growth of compounds during this period, in both scale and size, is quite striking. The Madinaty dream, however, came under threat after Hisham Moustafa was convicted of hiring a hitman in 2008 to kill his lover, the Lebanese pop singer Suzanne Tamim (Associated Press 2010). Ironically, the aftermath of 2011 and the geopolitical conflicts and civil wars across the MENA region saved the compound, with marketing teams explicitly offering security for the city's escaping middle and upper middle classes. Madinaty sought to become the destination of families seeking refuge in the crumbling political landscape.

The dream owes its existence to the middle classes, who lack both the social infrastructure and collective solidarity of the urban poor, and the power patronage of the upper social classes (Mitchell 2002; El-Shakry 2007). Most residents living in Cairo's gated communities are Egyptians with family members working abroad to help make ends meet. They also include middle-class Iraqis pushed out of their country as a result of the American invasion in 2003 and its 2011 aftermath. Finally, they include middle-class Syrians forced to migrate after their country's civil war in 2011. Neither of the latter two groups has the wealth to migrate to the United States, Canada, or Europe, or, if they do, they wish to avoid the humiliating conditions of refugee camps at the borders of Lebanon, Turkey, Jordan, and Europe. Multiple refugee families share a unit and distribute their resources, fading into Cairo's landscape of emerging compounds. They occupy a space of transience, an intermittent dream. Ultimately, these communities are not the Iraqi/Syrian's "dream," but rather a stopping point on the way to a destination. The promise of the gated community, for them, is only one of security rather than some utopian dreamland. Such dreams are interchangeable.

With the growing opportunities of retail shops inside compounds, many Iraqis and Syrians can own shops and businesses, enabling them to climb up the local social ladder. The transformative spatialities of compounds, with their diverse open-endedness, facilitate such unforeseen spatial and social mobility. Cairo compounds have become transformative in nature, acting as harbingers of opportunities through their well-defined configurations. In the following section, I draw on TMG's contemporary history of emergence and scalar development as one example of a developer's mindset that is reshaping Cairo's desert edge and its *new* social contract for the middle and upper middle classes.

Rescaling, Reshaping, and Reconfiguring

The extreme increase in scale of the production of compounds, from al-Rabwa to al-Rehab to Madinaty, illustrates the need to rethink the term "gated communities" as an outcome of global north theorization, creating epistemologies based on the global south's spatial dynamics and practices (Roy and Ong 2011). In Cairo, the city's extended urbanization embodies a process in the making that is accompanied with an unclear "social contract" between developers and the upper/middle-class residents. Expanding compounds produce friction, both between residents and between residents and developers. The moral code of conduct is in constant reformulation. While residents are embracing a dream of social mobility, real estate developers are reimagining cities in the form of compounds at a time of state withdrawal from urban governance. All of this (re)generates frictions and modes of conflict resolution between the diverse stakeholders involved in these processes. The sections below attempt to capture the frictions and collisions refiguring the three compounds that I analyze as they rescale Cairo's modes of inhabitation.

Al-Rabwa: A quest for self-representation

In 1995, TMG envisioned al-Rabwa as a closed, controlled, and low-density compound consisting of villas for single-family homes—970 villas in total, with pitched roofs of concrete-brick tiles. They mirrored the iconic Egyptian villas of the upper class, surrounded by garden space and grass lawns, as seen on agricultural land in the Saqqara area along Mariutiya Road. At al-Rabwa, there were organized services and vast greens, however, as well as a golf course, and infrastructure (e.g., telephone, internet, security, electricity, water, etc.) with medical services for ensuring the safety of the compound's residents. There was also a clubhouse with an upper floor organized around a library, and billiard and bridge rooms, mimicking the British colonial architecture of the elite Gezira Sporting Club in Zamalek.

In 2008, al-Rabwa witnessed an internal struggle between the real estate developer and residents over self-representation. A new law, No. 119/2008, granted the right to self-governance through the forming of neighborhood associations (NA). Residents requested elections in the compound to elect NA members, but TMG refused. Residents filed a lawsuit and tension grew. This moment demarcated a shift in the compound's structure, from being a community of consumers to a politically conscious enclave. Spearheaded by a resident governmental minister, the movement mobilized through the courtroom and eventually won the case, forcing TMG to step down from controlling the town hall and subcontracting services. There were consequences from the confrontation in the courtroom, however. In the determination of how to calculate the votes for elections, the compound's area was divvied up, with each section given a number of votes. Then there was a fight over calculating the votes regarding common amenities. According to the verdict, any house area translated into a certain number of votes. Owning a larger house yielded more votes per household. Meanwhile, the developer owned two main assets: the clubhouse and the shopping mall. The verdict ruled that the votes of commercial and administrative buildings are multiplied by two. The developer included the vast golf course as part of the clubhouse. The residents protested this decision and filed another lawsuit. The court ruled against TMG in favor of the residents, declaring the golf course to be common property, together with the streets and mosque. This resulted in TMG stopping any golf activities from taking place, and the course remains unused to this day.

Since 2008, there has been a constant swing between winners of the electoral contests. The verdict left the developer with 8 percent of the land (the clubhouse and the mall) and a 16 percent total voting share in any given election. Residents need to outnumber these voting assets. Moreover, a good number of TMG shareholders reside within the compound and have personal votes. In 2008, residents won the elections, but their victory did not last for long. In the 2014, 2017, and 2020 elections, the TMG shareholders won control of the compound's governance. Yet in the 2020 elections, these victories met with a rebuttal when a group of youth activists, graduates of private universities and inspired by the 2011 revolt, competed for the elections against TMG shareholders and independent businessmen. Regardless of the final result, the contestation over representation indicates that the *dream* behind the walls of al-Rabwa has yet to be realized.

Al-Rehab: Street politics inside the walls

The friction within a massively populated compound such as al-Rehab took a different direction. Representing itself as the future of Egyptian neighborhoods—reminiscent of Heliopolis, Maadi, Muhandisin, and Dokki—al-Rehab is a garden city of mixed-class housing with heterogeneous zoning and land use. There are nineteen gates, three of which are for visitors. It was the first compound to develop the half-closed/half-open, half-private/half-accessible, and half-quiet/half-jammed-with-activities approach. During the 2000s, hustle and bustle transformed the compound into the epicenter of New Cairo. Car-cleaning outlets, mechanic repair shops, car-battery and electrical stores, and food markets inside the compound attracted a pool of craftsmen and workers looking for jobs. These workers came from the first and third settlements of New Cairo, after being forced out of the city during the 1990s and 2000s without state planning to absorb them. They followed a path through the backyards of al-Rehab's *souk*, working late nights at coffee shops that replicated the everyday culture of Cairo—a reminder that one cannot entirely sanitize the characteristics of a city and its residents.

As al-Rehab grew significantly in its first decade, attracting a wide range of residents, from homeowners of villas and apartments to renters of all sorts, the compound's governance became a challenge to TMG's town-hall structure. In 2007, encountering difficulties in making their voices heard, a group of residents and realtors created a website, Rehaby, to act as a communication platform for residents to post complaints. It mobilized residents' demands for better services, representation, and governance. Tahrir Square was a source of inspiration for the formation of many independent youth coalitions in al-Rehab, who utilized Facebook for organizing protests in the *souk* and the compound. They protested peacefully against the massacres occurring in Maspero in the aftermath of 2011, directing their contestations against the privatized town hall's authority, as protesting against the state police would mean running the risk of getting arrested or even risking one's life. In the global south, contestations tend to occur through multiple representations, dubious meanings, and indirect masked representations (Mbembe 2001). The complaints of al-Rehab's residents therefore focused on the degradation of the built environment, inadequate garbage collection, and the presence of construction waste. Apartment residents denounced the inflated price of food in the markets, as well as of school fees that increased annually, the lack of security, and other negative aspects impacting their everyday lives.

The street contestations in the *souk* came into conflict with the class politics of the villa owners, who objected on the grounds that the confrontations would negatively affect the market value of the compound. For the homeowners, order and discipline were key values. They felt that the beautification of open spaces was more important than protesting food prices in the markets. On the other hand, the apartment residents concentrated their efforts on fighting for affordable everyday sustenance, reaffirming the significance of securing the means of inhabitation. These differences reflect the struggles and disappointments of urbanizing dreams and their class politics. The mixed-class approach instantiates structuring the use-value of dwellings for mass population, like multistory apartment buildings in the compound, more toward achieving equity across class and religious differences.

In the aftermath of the Arab Spring, an influx of Syrian families settled in al-Rehab, causing a significant surge in real estate values for both the residential units and the commercial shops. In an interview with TMG's marketing director, he shared internal research revealing that al-Rehab was a preferred choice in the region for Syrian women and children due to its reportedly tight social community, which they needed for living in solidarity and safety away from home. Moreover, the compound offers a critical mass of population for running a business in the market. Today, al-Rehab *souk* hosts eight large Syrian food outlets, including large restaurants and oriental pastry shops, as well as a furniture shop. There is also a real estate company called "Soryana" serving Syrian residents.

Madinaty: Arbitrary shades of visualization

Madinaty, with its 8,000 acres and intended 700,000 inhabitants, embodies what Marshall Berman describes in the phrase "all that is solid melts into air" (1984)—that is, it promises urbanity somewhere in the middle between open/closed, huge/confined, modern/desert, and city/compound. The compound's monumental entrance makes the gate almost too small to be seen. The effect of the gate is minimal, making it an open "gated community" with an influx of traffic. The sense of estrangement ascends as you cross its "wall of cascading water" in the hot desert climate. Madinaty is about this vast emptiness for the enclave yet to become. It represents a Dubai, of sorts, built in

Cairo: a city compound at the edge of a metropolis. The main road is about forty meters wide, leading to the open-air market and food court, with the "central park" beside the mosque. The compound's open-air mall and *souk* convey a sense of enormousness and an empty feeling, presenting viewers with a fake wind catcher, vacant scaffolding, and repeated arches with no clear function.

A local architectural firm reports that it prides itself on portraying the notion of Dubai-ness, a pride that is evident in its rendered night shots of Madinaty presented to Hisham Talaat Moustafa for a short-listed competition to build the compound. The firm claims these renderings got them hired, but the illustrations' perspective is imprecise and the compound's architecture was left undefined. This imprecision, uncertainty, hazy appeal, and open-endedness are what made the project attractive to the developer. It is a compound of possibilities, each creating its own narrative. Everyone can explore their own definition of Madinaty, an aspect communicated well in the project's ad campaign over Ramadan. The vagueness of the dream triggers the subconscious mind, epitomized by the slogan written underneath the renderings: "Madinaty: An International City on Egyptian Soil." There is a dual purpose here of belonging to Egypt while becoming international. The world reference was Dubai rather than Paris, London, or Los Angeles. The masterplan of Madinaty ended up with the stamps and signatures of US urban design firms. It is this internationalization and hybrid intermingling that TMG sought in their massive rescaling.

Open-ended Conclusion

Gated communities had their genesis in the dreams of an alternative to the state's authoritarian modernism. The efforts of real estate developers have created the illusion of an alternative urban imaginary at the edge of the city, but their creations are being continuously contested. Through the work of one of the leading developers, TMG, and their rationale for rescaling "gated communities" over three decades by doubling the population and tripling the size of the enclaves, we observe a resulting accumulation of capital via desert inhabitation. Al-Rabwa was modeled on upper-middle-class Egyptian mansions found in rural areas. Al-Rehab was inspired by the middle- and upper-middle-class Egyptian urban homes. Madinaty became an obscure simulacrum of Dubai.

These communities all represent dreams in the process of becoming. By considering the frictions and struggles described above, we can deepen a methodological approach that seeks to better configure the compounds' embeddedness and extended urbanization around Cairo. The tensions between residents and the developer reveal a disappointment in realizing dreams, and yet a perseverance in claiming them. The rescaling of the desert edge continues to mushroom, and the process of its inhabitation will continue evolving, emerging, and being repurposed, moving toward a new social contract of dreams and frictions.

Works Cited

Angelo, Hillary, and David Wachsmuth. 2015. "Urbanizing Urban Political Ecology: A Critique of Methodological Cityism." *International Journal of Urban and Regional Research* 39, no. 1: 16–27. https://doi.org/10.1111/1468-2427.12105.

Arese, Nicolas. 2018. "Seeing Like a City-state: Behavioural Planning and Governance in Egypt's First Affordable Gated Community." *International Journal of Urban and Regional Research*. https://onlinelibrary.wiley.com/doi/abs/10.1111/1468-2427.12601

Associated Press. 2010. "Egyptian Billionaire Convicted of Killing Pop Star Lover Spared Death Penalty." *The Guardian*, September 28. https://www.theguardian.com/world/2010/sep/28/egyptian-billionaire-spared-death-penalty.

Berger, Alan, and Joel Kotkin, eds. 2017. *Infinite Suburbia*. New York: Princeton Architectural Press.

Berman. 1984. *All that Is Solid Melts into Air: The Experience of Modernity.* New York: Verso.

Bhan, Gautam. 2019. "Notes on a Southern Urban Practice." *Environment and Urbanization* 31, no. 2: 639–54. https://doi.org/10.1177/0956247818815792.

Brenner, Neil. 2019. *New Urban Spaces: Urban Theory and the Scale Question.* New York: Oxford University Press.

Caldeira, Teresa P.R. 2001. *City of Walls: Crime, Segregation, and Citizenship in São Paulo.* 1st ed. Berkeley: University of California Press.

Denis, Eric. 2006. "Cairo as Neoliberal Capital? From Walled City to Gated Communities." In *Cairo Cosmopolitan: Politics, Culture, and Urban Space in the New Globalized Middle East,* edited by Diane Singerman and Paul Amar, 47–71. Cairo: American University in Cairo Press.

El-Din, El-Sayed Gamal. 2021. "3 Alleged Home Invaders Referred to Court for Causing Woman to Fall to Death from 6th-floor Balcony." *Ahram Online*, March 15. https://english.ahram.org.eg/News/406081.aspx.

Ghannam, Farha. 2014. "The Promise of the Wall: Reflections on Desire and Gated Communities in Cairo." January 3. https://www.jadaliyya.com/Details/30034/The-Promise-of-the-Wall-Reflections-on-Desire-and-Gated-Communities-in-Cairo

Guney, K. Murat, Roger Keil, and Murat Ucoglu, eds. 2019. *Massive Suburbanization: (Re)Building the Global Periphery*. Toronto, Buffalo, and London: University of Toronto Press, Scholarly Publishing Division.

Harvey, David. 1996. "Cities or Urbanization?" *City* 1, no. 1–2: 38–61. https://doi.org/10.1080/13604819608900022.

Herzog, Lawrence. 2014. *Global Suburbs: Urban Sprawl from the Rio Grande to Rio de Janeiro*. 1st ed. New York: Routledge.

Hurley, Amanda Kolson. 2019. *Radical Suburbs: Experimental Living on the Fringes of the American City*. Cleveland, OH: Belt Publishing.

El-Husseiny, Momen. 2015. "Compounds of Modernity: National Order and the Other in Egypt (1940–Present)." PhD diss., University of California, Berkeley. https://escholarship.org/content/qt7cc02032/qt7cc02032.pdf.

Ismail, Salwa. 2014. "The Politics of the Urban Everyday in Cairo: Infrastructures of Oppositional Action." In *The Routledge Handbook on Cities of the Global South*, edited by Susan Parnell and Sophie Oldfield, 291–302. New York: Routledge.

Keil, Roger. 2018. *Suburban Planet: Making the World Urban from the Outside In*. Cambridge and Medford, MA: Polity Press. https://onlinelibrary.wiley.com/doi/abs/10.1111/1468-2427.12668

———. 2020. "The Spatialized Political Ecology of the City: Situated Peripheries and the Capitalocenic Limits of Urban Affairs." *Journal of Urban Affairs* 42, no. 8: 1125–40. https://doi.org/10.1080/07352166.2020.1785305.

Kuppinger, Petra. 2004. "Exclusive Greenery: New Gated Communities in Cairo." *City & Society* 16, no. 2: 35–61. https://doi.org/10.1525/city.2004.16.2.35.

Lefebvre, Henri. 2003. *The Urban Revolution*. Minneapolis: University of Minnesota Press.

Marafi, Safaa. 2011. "The Neoliberal Dream of Segregation: Rethinking Gated Communities in Greater Cairo, a Case Study: Al-Rehab City Gated Community." Master's thesis, American University in Cairo.

Mbembe, Achille. 2001. *On the Postcolony*. Berkeley: University of California Press.

Mitchell, Timothy. 2002. *Rule of Experts: Egypt, Techno-politics, Modernity*. Berkeley: University of California Press.

Polanyi, Karl. 2001. *The Great Transformation: The Political and Economic Origins of Our Time*. 2nd ed. Boston: Beacon Press.

Roy, Ananya. 2018. "Urban Studies and the Postcolonial Encounter." In *The SAGE Handbook of the 21st Century City*, edited by Suzanne Hall and Ricky Burdett, 1st ed., 32–46. Thousand Oaks, CA: SAGE Publications Ltd.

Roy, Ananya, and Aihwa Ong, eds. 2011. *Worlding Cities: Asian Experiments and the Art of Being Global*. 1st ed. Malden, MA and Oxford: Wiley-Blackwell.

Schmid, Karl. 2019. "The Making of Cairo's Vast Planned Periphery: Particularities and Parallels Revealed through an Examination of Four Suburban Cultural Assemblages." In *Massive Suburbanization: (Re)Building the Global Periphery*, edited by K. Murat Guney, Roger Keil, and Murat Ucoglu, 303–19. Toronto, Buffalo, and London: University of Toronto Press, Scholarly Publishing Division.

El-Shakry, Omnia. 2007. *The Great Social Laboratory: Subjects of Knowledge in Colonial and Postcolonial Egypt*. 1st ed. Stanford, CA: Stanford University Press.

Simone, AbdouMaliq. 2001. "On the Worlding of African Cities." *African Studies Review* 44, no. 2: 15–41. https://doi.org/10.2307/525573.

———. 2019. "Maximum Exposure: Making Sense in the Background of Extensive Urbanization." *Environment and Planning D: Society and Space* 37, no. 6: 990–1006. https://doi.org/10.1177/0263775819856351.

Sims, David E. 2014. *Egypt's Desert Dreams: Development or Disaster?* Cairo: American University in Cairo Press.

Tzaninis, Yannis, Tait Mandler, Maria Kaika, and Roger Keil. 2020. "Moving Urban Political Ecology beyond the 'Urbanization of Nature.'" *Progress in Human Geography* 45, no. 2: 1–24. https://doi.org/10.1177/0309132520903350.

Yousry, Ahmed M. 2009. "The Privatization of Urban Development in Cairo: Lessons Learned from the Development Experience of al-Rehab Gated Community." Conference: "New Urban Communities Development: Issues & Priorities," Bibliotheca Alexandrina, March 28–30, 2009.

Zeghal, Malika. 2009. "Cairo as Capital of Islamic Institutions? Al-Azhar Islamic University, the State, and the City." In *Cairo Contested: Governance, Urban Space, and Global Modernity*, edited by Diane Singerman, 63–82. Cairo: American University in Cairo Press.

12

MILITARY CAPITALISM
THE ECONOMIC AND SECURITY LOGICS OF EGYPT'S NEW ADMINISTRATIVE CAPITAL

ROBERTA DUFFIELD

Introduction

By 2022, Egypt had hoped to join a group of more than thirty nation-states who have relocated their political seat of power to new-built capital cities. Under construction since 2015, the New Administrative Capital (NAC), some forty-five kilometers east of the existing metropolis of Cairo, is the centerpiece of the al-Sisi government's development vision. Although finding precedence in decades of state desert reclamation for ex-nihilo settlements, the magnitude of the NAC represents an unprecedented venture in modern Egyptian history, imposing an ambitious new structure and reality on society, rather than following conventional planning to modify the existing urban fabric. The lure of the capital megaproject is clear: for an aspirant metropolis that lacks the historical context that has produced global city status, this proposes a shortcut to success. The inhospitable desert landscape further enhances the project's symbolic attractiveness: man (and this is very much symbolically engendered) conquers nature in an indelible feat of ingenuity, power, and prestige.

This chapter joins Abul-Magd's analysis, in this volume, of the involvement of the Egyptian Armed Forces (EAF) in the country's new wave of urban development and securitization. It explores the reasserted economic and political role of the EAF in Egyptian society as demonstrated through the lens of their involvement in the NAC megaproject. The regime gives two primary justifications for the new capital's construction. First, it presents a solution to Cairo's rapidly expanding population, as a new settlement theoretically alleviates strain on the existing city by relocating citizens and workplaces away from the city's severe pollution and congested streets: "Cairo isn't suitable for the Egyptian people. . . . There's no humanity," says NAC spokesman Brigadier-General Khaled el-Husseiny Soliman (Michaelson 2018). Second, the NAC articulates the al-Sisi administration's ambitions for global city status and Egyptian prestige on the world stage. It is to be a powerhouse fit for modern government, business, and the good life.

The generative properties of the NAC's Dubai-inspired visual globality are evident. Prime Minister Mostafa Madbouly said of the project: "Egypt will enter the age of skyscrapers and high-rise towers" (Mukhtar 2018). Project chairman Major General Ahmad Zaki Abdin has stated, "Those who go shopping in Cyprus, Greece, or Dubai must come to us. All of Dubai is based on these malls and this is what we are planning in the administrative capital. The experience of Dubai is pioneering and has established a big place for itself in the global market" (*Sout al-Omma* 2018). The hypermodernity of the Gulf metropolises has thus come to represent the correct Middle Eastern response to globalization and modernity, as encapsulated by rapid economic growth and new-built urban development. Dubai's aesthetic of the superlative—the world's largest, tallest, and best—becomes an emulative model to reify success that focuses more on the visual trappings of cosmopolitan globality than the decades of infrastructural investment, economic diversification, and capture of human capital that has permitted the Emirati oil city to flourish. Accordingly, a run-down of the NAC's credentials is an exercise in excess, as outlined in Table 1 (MHUUC n.d.; *Mada Masr* 2016; Reuters 2019; *al-Araby al-Jadid* 2020). Amenities include 40,000 hotel rooms, a 5,000-seat conference center, 2,000 schools, 663 medical facilities, a new military headquarters named "the Octagon," and rumored reports of replicas of the Eiffel Tower and the Washington Monument (*Mada Masr* 2016; Amar 2018).

The Military in the Heart of the Regime

"There is no question that the military has returned in force to the heart of the regime," says Hazem Kandil of the current administration led by former general Abd al-Fatah al-Sisi (2016, 7). The Egyptian Armed Forces stand as one of the few national militaries to weather the instability of the Arab Spring, an untouchable "deep state" able to publicly present

Table 12.1. Proposed Projects and Credentials of the New Administrative Capital

Projects and Credentials	Details
715 km² total area	Roughly the same size as Singapore.
1.1 million residential units	Divided into 21 housing districts.
5 million target residential population	To be later increased to 6.5 million.
1.75 million permanent jobs	Includes an initial 50,000 relocated government employees, to be increased to 100,000 after three years.
5.6 km² Central Business District	Includes 20 skyscrapers and the Iconic Tower, Africa's tallest tower.
91 km² energy farms	Includes solar and wind power fields.
16 km² airport	Four-times larger than London Heathrow.
4 km² theme park	Seven-times larger than California's Disneyland.
More than 50 embassies	Around 20 embassies have agreed to transfer premises. As of October 2020 many others (including major European and Asian countries) continue to resist the move.
1,250 religious buildings	Includes the Nativity of Christ Cathedral, the Middle East's largest church and tallest steeple; and the 8,000-capacity al-Fattah al-'Alim Mosque.
35-kilometer Green River	The longest man-made river in the world. Surrounding parkland will be double the size of New York's Central Park.
Opera house	The largest opera house outside of Europe.
Presidential palace and government ministries	Relocated from Cairo.

itself as a hero of the nation, which refused to turn on civilian protestors in Tahrir (albeit after a careful period of watching to assess the shifting balance of power), distinct from Mubarak's repressive police force. Following the 2011 Revolution, the National Democratic Party of previous leaders Anwar al-Sadat and Hosni Mubarak was dissolved, with al-Sisi choosing to rule through the presidential office alone, alongside an executive inner circle of former servicemen. Twenty of Egypt's twenty-seven current provincial governors hail from military or police backgrounds, up from the twelve appointed by interim president Adly Mansour in 2013 (Iyhab 2018; *Middle East Eye* 2019; Batrawy 2013).

In April 2019, constitutional amendments removed the presidential term limits originally imposed in 2014, enabling President al-Sisi to theoretically remain in office until at least 2030 (*BBC News* 2019). The EAF's mandate was also extended, redefined as "preserving democracy and the Constitution, protecting the basic principles of the state and its civilian nature, and protecting people's rights and individual freedoms" (Mostafa 2019), breaking with previous interpretations of the military's singular role as protecting the country and defending its territorial integrity.

The seemingly deliberately vague nature of what may constitute a threat to civil freedom or democracy raises the potential for military intervention in election proceedings and other political affairs, or erosion of the balancing principles of the separation of powers by placing military generals as the final arbiters of the constitution. These changes also allow the president to exercise greater powers of patronage over senior state judiciary bodies and to extend military trials to civilians. Veto power has also been granted to the Supreme Council of the Armed Forces (SCAF) over the defense minister's portfolio (*BBC News* 2019; Cairo Institute of Human Rights Studies 2019). This reemphasizes the trope that the EAF is the only Egyptian entity capable of carrying out government functions beyond its responsibilities for national defense. The military is seen as the singular competent national institution, a view seemingly shared by Western and Arab governments and international investors alike, with financial aid flooding in from the United States, United Arab Emirates, and Saudi Arabia following its suspension during Mohamed Morsi's brief civilian presidency from 2012 to 2013 (Awad 2012; Topol 2014; Marshall 2015).

The EAF's economic dimension as both a public service provider and private-sector partner has been long established under Nasserite state-centric modernization drives (Gamal Abd al-Nasser was president of Egypt 1954–70) and, after that, the liberalization, trade "opening," and privatization waves, called *infitah*, implemented under the presidency of President Anwar al-Sadat (1970–81). Under the subsequent thirty-year rule of Hosni Mubarak, the polarization between state-centric and private-sector favoring roles were blurred by Mubarak's courting of wealthy civilian elites and bringing military and corporate leaders into circles of power. Under Mubarak, multimillionaire family conglomerates such as the Bahgat, Orascom, Mansour, Talaat Moustafa, and Seoudi Groups were favored with lucrative government contracts, stakes in real estate development, preferential tax breaks, and foreign partnerships. From the 2000s onward, NDP-affiliated businessmen were given ministerial appointments relating to their private business enterprises. Although Mubarak continued to appoint members of the military's (EAF's) upper cadres into government as a deterrent to possible leadership coups as he prepared his son Gamal—a former investment banker and confidant of Egypt's enterprise elites—to inherit the presidency, a new mixed business–political class of civilian and military power stakeholders emerged from this clientelism (Abul-Magd 2017; Marshall 2015).

Since 2014, however, military-affiliated institutions have increasingly taken over national development projects or partnered with ministries and state enterprises. Shana Marshall (2015) describes the EAF as "the primary gatekeeper for the Egyptian economy." The military now controls and coordinates an increasing number of major state-run projects, with ex-generals found in political appointments and company boardrooms. Its factories produce everything from ammunition to cutlery, washing machines, and olive oil. Its engineers build roads, bridges, malls, sports clubs, universities, and housing. Its agencies run banks, hotels, fish farms, beach resorts, water treatment facilities, and import-export companies (Abul-Magd 2017; Topol 2014). The boundary between what is "state" and what is "military" is thus porous and uncertain, shifting conceptions of Egypt's economy as a classic formation of free-market neoliberalism, despite its hallmarks of privatization, IMF-backed austerity, and the ingress of foreign capital.

The blurring of state and business interests permits worrying new economic paradigms to emerge. Since September 2013, due tender processes can be legally bypassed in cases of undefined urgency, guaranteeing preferential contracts for military entities. Companies owned solely by the military are exempt from taxes, regardless of function. Military personnel can collect profits from projects, and state entities can shift debt onto Egyptian taxpayers. Civilian partners and subcontractors also often harbor military connections; awarding lucrative state contracts to the firms of former officers is a common practice in the so-called republic of retired generals. With the EAF's budget unpublished, it is difficult to leverage accountability or to quantify how far its reach extends, but estimates suggest its control amounts to between 5 and 40 percent of the national economy (Marshall 2015).

Economic partisanship therefore takes precedence over principles of due process and transparency. This has allowed the military to function as the main speculative authority for new projects, empowering their political and economic capacities by fortifying and leveraging foreign partnerships for investment and establishing holds within global supply networks. As a result, Egypt's political economy is increasingly reliant on the EAF's strategic role as broker to the nation. This also includes domestic civilian elites; post-2014, the military has sought rapprochement with several wealthy businessmen with ties to former administrations, such as Naguib Sawiris, Ahmed Abou Hashima, and Ahmad Ezz (Marshall 2015; Attalah and Hamama, 2016).

Constructing the Capital: Who and How?

The New Administrative Capital illustrates the centrality of the military in Egyptian political and economic affairs. The project is overseen by the Administrative Capital for Urban Development (ACUD), jointly established by the New Urban Communities Authority (NUCA, part of the Ministry of Housing, Utilities and Urban Communities) and the EAF, with a 51 percent ownership majority by the latter (Magdy 2018). ACUD's chairman is Lieutenant General Ahmad Zaki Abdin, who has also served as minister for defense and military production since June 2018. ACUD will also take over the vacant premises of government offices after they have relocated to the new capital, generating further development opportunities on prime downtown real estate, likely to add to central Cairo's growing surplus of half-empty luxury hotels, as indicated by the agency (Michaelson 2018).

The EAF also owns the land upon which the NAC is being constructed. A 1997 presidential decree granted the EAF usage rights over all undeveloped nonagricultural land (comprising 87 percent of the country), concentrating power over one of the most profitable national resources in the hands of an absolute authority. Of the 490 km² available for private development within the NAC, plots will be leased rather than sold, retaining the military's land monopoly (Lindsey 2017). Military entities have been awarded significant tenders for the project, notably the Engineering Authority of the Armed Forces (EAAF), one of several military agencies used by the armed forces to conduct economic activities. The EAAF's construction, infrastructure engineering, and town planning capabilities have allowed it to increasingly come to function as a huge parastatal contractor for government development projects (Attalah and Hamama 2016; Abul-Magd 2017; Elshahed 2014). The military's profile is further raised by their partnerships with foreign investors, which constitute the backbone of the new capital's funding plan.

Despite the EAF's self-promotion as the singular bastion of national competence, both the NAC's construction timeline and cost projections have since been exceeded. Completion of the first building phase has been successively delayed since 2018 and the initial budget of $45 billion scrapped. "There is no total budget," admits ACUD spokesperson Brigadier-General Khaled el-Husseiny Soliman (Michaelson 2018). Financial uncertainty is compounded by broader trends that see Egypt struggle to attract major foreign investments outside of the oil and gas industries. Foreign direct investments (FDI) fell by $200 million in the fiscal year ending June 2018 (its lowest point since Egypt's adoption of the IMF austerity plan in 2016) and, despite a recovery in 2019, went into another sharp decline due to the 2020 COVID-19 pandemic. Egypt's external debt has also risen consistently in recent years, reaching an all-time high of $123.5 billion in June 2020 (Magdy 2018; CEIC Data 2020; *Power Technology* 2020). Indeed, many of the NAC's initial major investors have since dropped from the project, citing financial disputes and lack of progress. The list of retreating mega-investors includes the Capital City Partners Fund (established by Emirati real estate mogul Mohamed Alabbar), Alabbar's construction conglomerate Emaar, the China Fortune Land Development Company, and the China State Construction Engineering Corporation (CSCEC)[1] (Mukhtar 2018; *Global Construction Review* 2017, 2019; Magdy 2018).

Major work on the new capital has been largely undertaken by domestic entities including the EAAF, NUCA, and Egyptian companies such as Orascom, the Talaat Moustafa Group, and Arab Contractors. ACUD's chairman Ayman Ismail extolled the fact that "these huge real estate projects that are considered to be the future of Egypt will only be built by the hands of the nation's sons" (Abu Jabal 2017). The fact that the majority of the Egyptian populace will not be able to access the NAC's utopic suburbia is left unsaid, with its construction workers and conscripted corvée laborers disappearing from the site once development is finally completed. Meanwhile, the labor—domestic and otherwise—of the nation's daughters remains entirely invisible in this gendered narrative of national development.

The NAC's markers of globality and developmental success are thus revealed as hollow, devoid of both practicality and social provision. Despite boasting schemes for affordable residential areas, its houses are priced well above average Egyptian incomes. Even with a 25 percent discount for government employees, the average property cost of LE 8,000 to 9,000 per square meter, as quoted by Brigadier-General Soliman, outstrips the mean public sector monthly wage of LE 1,860 (ECES 2018; Michaelson 2018). Most government workers do not own cars, meaning accessing new workplaces will be challenging. The tariffs, commute time, and efficiency of the future Chinese-built railway connecting Cairo to the NAC are still unknown. However, recent rises in Cairo's inner-city Metro ticket pricing[2] do not indicate that social inclusion and equitable usability are top transport priorities. The purported relocation of government personnel also undermines justifications of de-densifying downtown Cairo: if workers do not own cars, then closing government offices is likely to have little impact on congested city center roads. Separate government plans to construct a new Central Business District in the Maspero area of Downtown (as detailed by Kahlil in this volume) also suggests increased traffic and visitation to the area, not less. Furthermore, cynics suggest that the resignation or early retirement of lower-middle-class government employees who cannot afford to travel to their new places of work in the NAC is the main point of all of this, cutting down a costly, swollen bureaucracy that increasingly cripples government coffers.

Political Security and Revolution

Utopian security logics are clearly expressed by the NAC's status as the new seat of national executive power. The movement of government agencies out of Cairo's crowded center is not a new idea, having been proposed in various forms by previous presidents Nasser, Sadat, and Mubarak, albeit with little practical implementation. Conversely, the al-Sisi administration has demonstrated the clear political will to refocus policy around regime security and self-preservation.

The legacy of 2011 cannot be ignored in this regard. The specter of the uprising runs throughout Cairo's urban development, whether consciously rationalized in the securitization of symbolic sites of revolution, or indirectly perpetuated through projects that promote a class-based usability based on politicized and moralized narratives of risk and identity regarding visibility in public spaces (Abaza 2016).

Although officially canonizing the Egyptian Revolution, the al-Sisi administration's overriding objective has been to prevent its repetition. During the uprising and subsequent years, government buildings in Tahrir Square and its surrounding streets became targets of revolutionary outrage, given their association with the repressive regime security apparatus (Omnia Khalil, Al-Samragy, this volume). The NDP headquarters behind the Egyptian Museum in Tahrir were set alight by protestors in January 2011, its ruins later demolished in 2015. In 2016 the Ministry of Interior relocated to the al-Tagammu' al-Khamis district of Misr al-Gadida, some twenty-five kilometers away from its original downtown location, where it faced repeated attacks from protestors. The Police Academy, Office of the Prosecutor-General, State Lawsuits Authority, and other state offices also moved in the same year (Eltohamy 2016). Only then were some of Downtown's security measures—walls, razor wire, police presence—relaxed.

Although Downtown's overcrowding is often cited as justification for relocation, in a 2016 interview, Police Academy director General Ahmad al-Badri stated that the transfer of government buildings was specifically informed by security concerns—namely, the targeting of state institutions by protesters who "strive to spread chaos throughout the country" (Eltohamy 2016). The removal of government offices thus effectively severs the physical and symbolic currency of Tahrir as a space of popular protest, in tandem with prohibitive legislative measures and security crackdowns that have made public political expression extremely risky. Downtown Cairo as a locus of regime power has thus been eroded, negating it as a target of civil dissent when those targets no longer exist, transformed into Hiltons, Four Seasons, and Steigenbergers under ACUD's direction. Once the apparatus of government is relocated to Cairo's wealthy suburbs and later to the new capital, its distance affords a measure of discretion from the public eye and disassociation from contested communal realms. Future NAC inhabitants become a de facto first line of defense for the state: monied elites who suffer the least from Egypt's ills of unemployment, poor housing, and social immobility, and therefore are less predisposed to anti-government activity. A double barrier, both material and social, has thus been constructed for the longevity of the regime. This is more critical now than ever before, when the military stands as the state and the state as the military to a degree unprecedented in recent years. Any new outbreak of revolution means that, unlike in 2011, the EAF itself as an institution is at stake.

Connected, Green, and Global in the Madina Dhakiya

Promotional material and press statements abound with descriptions of the NAC as Egypt's first "smart city" (*madina dhakiya*), to be coordinated by the EAF and ministries of Defense, Interior, and Communications and Information Technology. We are told it will be a "connected" and "integrated" sustainable knowledge hub "modeled on Dubai, Singapore, and China" (*Sout al-Omma* 2018). ACUD's project chairman, Major General Ahmad Zaki Abdin, stated that the city will be free from crime, as "all of the streets of the capital will be monitored through solar-powered cameras dispersed everywhere, which prevents the possibility of committing illegal acts" (Hammad 2018). Policemen will not even be needed for directing traffic; this can be achieved via electronic road sensors and streetside screens coordinated by a central control headquarters. These sensors can also monitor and respond to changes in energy usage and traffic flows in real time, boosting the city's environmental credentials. The NAC will also be the nation's first cashless city in order to "encourage e-commerce . . . and make Egypt a regional hub for such cross-world industry and the mounting global growth for these trade activities" (*Ahram Online* 2019). A "Knowledge City" within the new capital will support this, hosting centers for digital entrepreneurship to stimulate local enterprise with an international reach.

Smart city status captures a current, global zeitgeist in urban planning and governance practices. The marriage between neoliberal politics and global tech corporations presents a normative development model whereby digital innovations stand as the primary driver for twenty-first-century success. With the state as an arbiter of sound developmental practice, smart urbanism and its apparent amelioration of ecological and security concerns are weaponized as a method of spatial and population control. An elite-defined, irrefutable "need" to construct a clean, green, safe city subsumes not only the human concerns of the general populace, but their humanity itself, defined as destructive and ignorant, set against state paternalism's visionary foresight for the greater good.

Truth, reality, probability, and success thus become conceptually malleable within the techno-political frame of smart city rhetoric. Indeed, the failure of the digital-utopian vision is a distinct possibility if development is not grounded in local contingencies. For example, maintaining air-conditioned interiors for glass skyscrapers under the desert sun requires huge amounts of energy, and expansive green spaces need water to thrive. The city's location beyond the Nile Valley, which supplies 97 percent of the nation's drinking supply, means water will be diverted from Cairo and nearby satellite cities to serve it (Michaelson 2018), even as the United Nations predicts severe water shortages for Egypt by 2025. Chinese money to build pipelines able to monitor drainage flows is meaningless if no water will flow through them. Similarly, for all the digital connectivity of the *madina dhakiya*, Egypt experiences some of the slowest internet connection speeds in the world—according to a recent survey, it ranks 170th out of 200 nations (Dhiraj 2018)—and suffering further hindrance when the government shuts down internet service providers during periods of civil unrest. Egypt's existing homegrown technology initiatives are mixed, but all showcase the same themes of social exclusion built into their materiality. The Smart Village, a gated business park, lies half empty in the desert on Cairo's outskirts, and Downtown's GrEEK Campus is an elite space of security guards and higher education. A NAC Knowledge City will undoubtedly function along similar exclusive lines. Likewise, that a cashless economy precludes participation for those without access to digital technology—reinforcing class-based exclusionary networks of interaction and commerce—appears less important to urban planners and the ruling administration than the pursuit of techno-political indicators of global status.

Conclusion

Egypt's New Administrative Capital can be considered a culminative expression of dynamic local and global paradigms that have shaped modern Egypt and its urban policies. To understand the proclivity for building new settlements in the desert—an enduring principle of governmental development policy—Egypt must first be recognized as a militarized nation whose armed forces and associated, impenetrable state apparatus exploit significant inroads into the national economy and shape distributions of wealth. Emerging from this is a form of military capitalism, whereby the free-market principles of privatization and foreign investment are tempered by closed economic and political networks of elite military and business nepotism, blurring the line between public and private capital. These development logics should not be misread as merely a return to "Mubarak-era" politics following the uncertainty of the postrevolution period. Under President al-Sisi's rule, the EAF has captured the nation's political and economic apparatus to a greater degree than before. By moving beyond a primarily defense-focused mandate, the EAF has taken on new roles as investor, contractor, and developer of the natural and urban commons, distinct from the tempering of the military's economic and political role during the administration of Hosni Mubarak.

Mega-construction and urban development are central to the military capitalist model. They provide opportunities for profit and strategic foreign partnerships, combined with an abundance of land resources and the allure of prestigious megaprojects. The latter can also be recognized as a manifestation of state-propagated "global city" discourse, whereby the NAC is touted as a material assertion of Egyptian presence on the international stage and a destination for foreign capital. This is visually realized in dramatic architectures of scale and stature, drawing on Dubai's subjectivity as a successful Arab economic center of power, and on normative digital-utopian narratives of "smart" and environmentally cognizant urbanism, which function as a seductive shorthand for prosperity and modernity.

In reality, this project offers little social content for the majority of the population the NAC purports to serve. The techno-politics of the smart city provide a modern solution to overcrowding and pollution in the same breath that they condemn the old city (and those who inhabit it) as irredeemably ungovernable. Discussions of wealth redistribution and welfare provision are abandoned—rather than reform the old, simply build anew. The state thus ignores or renders invisible its previous failures to provide adequate urban solutions in the preexisting inhabited space. In doing so, the state doesn't just ignore or erase, it actively pathologizes the existing city and its population—depicting them as risky, suspicious, and deserving punishment.

A bunkerization of the symbols of government away from sites of public circulation such as downtown Cairo and, more specifically, Tahrir Square demonstrates the regime's intention for self-preservation in light of 2011's popular mobilization, which in turn strives to convince foreign partners that the EAF remains a stable business partner. While preventing a return of widespread anti-government protest continues to be a paramount concern, the regime has simultaneously appropriated both the EAF's revolutionary role as an ally of the people and the postrevolution legacy of political instability to amplify claims of their singular competence to govern and to the guardianship of the nation. Following the 2019 constitutional amendments to the role of the EAF, the military's influence has further expanded over civil society, building on platforms of control established by its expanding economic and urban activities. Given the security logics and lack of transparency inherent within a military-dominated political class, this does not bode well for a democratic and equitable Egyptian future.

Notes

1   CSCEC pulled out of its contract to build the NAC's government quarter in 2017, although it currently remains involved in the development of its Central Business District.

2   Metro fares pegged at a flat rate of LE 1 for many years have been raised several times since 2018, to much public outrage.

Works Cited

Abaza, Mona. 2016. "Violence, Dramaturgical Repertoires and Neoliberal Imaginaries in Cairo." *Theory, Culture & Society* 33, no. 7–8: 111–35.

Abu Jabal, Imad. 2017. "al-'Asima al-Idariya al-Gadida tunafis al-istithmar fi al-Sa'udiya wa-l-Imarat wa-l-Kuwait: tafra malhuza bi-l-a'mal al-munaffadha . . . ." *Veto*, September 10. https://www.vetogate.com/2864892.

Abul-Magd, Zeinab. 2017. *Militarizing the Nation: The Army, Business and Revolution in Egypt*. New York: Columbia University Press.

Ahram Online. 2019. "Egypt Plans to Make New Administrative Capital First Cashless City in the Country." *Ahram Online*, February 16. http://english.ahram.org.eg/News/325689.aspx.

Amar, Paul. 2018. "Military Capitalism." *NACLA Report on the Americas* 50, no. 1 (March 29): 82–89. https://doi.org/10.1080/10714839.2018.1448601.

al-Araby al-Jadid. 2020. "Ta'athur intiqal al-sifarat li-'asimat al-Sisi: 'aqabat iqtisadiya wa-i'tibarat siyasiya." *Al-Araby al-Jadid*, September 21. https://www.alaraby.co.uk/politics/%D8%AA%D8%B9%D8%AB%D8%B1-%D8%A7%D9%86%D8%AA%D9%82%D8%A7%D9%84-%D8%A7%D9%84%D8%B3%D9%81%D8%A7%D8%B1%D8%A7%D8%AA-%D9%84%D8%B9%D8%A7%D8%B5%D9%85%D8%A9-%D8%A7%D9%84%D8%B3%D9%8A%D8%B3%D9%8A-%D8%B9%D9%82%D8%A8%D8%A7%D8%AA-%D8%A7%D9%82%D8%AA%D8%B5%D8%A7%D8%AF%D9%8A%D8%A9-%D9%88%D8%A7%D8%B9%D8%AA%D8%A8%D8%A7%D8%B1%D8%A7%D8%AA-%D8%B3%D9%8A%D8%A7%D8%B3%D9%8A%D8%A9

Attalah, Lina, and Mohamed Hamama. 2016. "The Armed Forces and Business: Economic Expansion in the Last 12 Months." *Mada Masr*, September 9. https://madamasr.com/en/2016/09/09/feature/economy/the-armed-forces-and-business-economic-expansion-in-the-last-12-months/.

Awad, Marwa. 2012. "Special Report: In Egypt's Military, a March for Change." Reuters, April 10. https://www.reuters.com/article/us-egypt-army/special-report-in-egypts-military-a-march-for-change-idUSBRE8390IV20120410.

Batrawy, Aya. 2013. "Egypt's Leaders Name New Governors; Liberals and Islamists Say Many Are Mubarak Holdovers." *Star Tribune*, August 13. https://www.startribune.com/egypt-s-rival-sides-upset-with-new-governors/219402031/.

BBC News. 2019. "Egypt President Could Rule until 2030 as Constitutional Changes Backed." *BBC News*, April 24. https://www.bbc.com/news/world-middle-east-48035512.

Cairo Institute of Human Rights Studies. 2019. "Al-ta'dilat al-dusturiya al-muqtaraha tuhaddid al-istiqrar wa-tamnah al-ra'is al-hukm mada al-hayah." Cairo Institute of Human Rights Studies, February. https://cihrs.org/%D9%84%D8%A7-%D9%84%D9%84%D8%A7%D9%86%D9%82%D9%84%D8%A7%D8%A8-%D8%A7%D9%84%D8%AF%D8%B3%D8%AA%D9%88%D8%B1%D9%8A/

CEIC Data. 2020. "Egypt's External Debt." CEIC Data, October 11. https://www.ceicdata.com/en/indicator/egypt/external-debt.

Dhiraj, Amarendra Bushan. 2018. "Which Countries Have the Fastest (and the Slowest) Internet Connections, 2018?" CEOWorld Magazine, July 23. https://ceoworld.biz/2018/07/23/which-countries-have-the-fastest-and-the-slowest-internet-connections-2018/.

ECES (Egyptian Center for Economic Studies). 2018. "Egypt's Economic Profile and Statistics." Egyptian Center for Economic Studies, February 18. https://www.eces.org.eg/PublicationsDetails?Lang=EN&C=5&T=1&ID=675&Egypt%27s-Economic-Profile-and-Statistics---2018.

Elshahed, Mohamed. 2014. "From Tahrir Square to Emaar Square: Cairo's Private Road to a Private City." *The Guardian*, April 7. https://www.theguardian.com/cities/2014/apr/07/tahrir-square-emaar-square-cairo-private-road-city.

Eltohamy, Amr. 2016. "Al-sulta al-misriya tanqil maqar al-wazarat al-rasmiya ba'idan 'an marakiz al-ihtigagat." *Al-Monitor*, March 6. https://www.al-monitor.com/pulse/ar/contents/articles/originals/2016/05/egypt-cairo-move-ministry-buildings-away-protests.html.

Global Construction Review. 2017. "Chinese Firm CSCEC Pulls Out of Cairo Relocation Mega Project." *Global Construction Review*, February 14. http://www.globalconstructionreview.com/news/chinese-firm-cscec-pulls-ou7t-ca7iro-reloca7tion/

———. 2019. "'Talks Stopped' with Emaar over Egypt's New Capital Deal." *Global Construction Review*, January 3. http://www.globalconstructionreview.com/news/talks-stopped-emaar-over-egypts-new-capital-deal/.

Hammad, Muhammad. 2018. "Khutat misriya tamuha li-insha' 16 madina dhakiya." *Al-Arab*, July 16. . https://alarab.co.uk/%D8%AE%D8%B7%D8%B7-%D9%85%D8%B5%D8%B1%D9%8A

%D8%A9-%D8%B7%D9%85%D9%88%D8%AD%D8%A9-
%D9%84%D8%A5%D9%86%D8%B4%D8%A7%D8%
A1-16-%D9%85%D8%AF%D9%8A%D9%86%D8%A9-%D8%
Bo%D9%83%D9%8A%D8%A9

Iyhab, Fadia. 2018. "Mihan al-muhafizin al-gudud: liwa'at wa-atibba' wa-asatidhat gami'at." *El Watan News*, August 30. https://www. elwatannews.com/news/details/3625243.

Kandil, Hazem. 2016. "Sisi's Egypt." *New Left Review* 102 (November–December): 5–40. https://newleftreview.org/issues/ii102/articles/ hazem-kandil-sisi-s-egypt.

Lindsey, Ursula. 2011. "Neglected, Mismanaged Cairo Is Also Resourceful and Forbearing." *The National*, May 6. https://www.thenational. ae/uae/neglected-mismanaged-cairo-is-also-resourceful-and-forbearing-1.455006?videoId=5754807360001.

———. 2017. "The Anti-Cairo." *Places Journal*, March. https://placesjour-nal.org/article/the-anti-cairo/#0

Mada Masr. 2016. "Chinese Company Signs US$20 bn Agreement to Build New Administrative Capital." *Mada Masr*, October 4. https:// madamasr.com/en/2016/10/04/news/u/chinese-company-signs-us20-bn-agreement-to-build-new-administrative-capital/.

Magdy, Mirette. 2018. "China's $20 Billion New Egypt Capital Project Talks Fall Through." December 16. Bloomberg. https://www.bloomberg.com/news/articles/2018-12-16/ china-s-20-billion-new-egypt-capital-project-talks-fall- through.

Marshall, Shana. 2015. "The Egyptian Armed Forces and the Remaking of an Economic Empire." Carnegie Middle East Center, April 15. http://carnegie-mec.org/2015/04/15/egyptian-armed-forces-and-remaking-of-economic-empire-pub-59726%20.

MHUUC (Ministry of Housing, Utilities, and Urban Communities). n.d. "Al-'asima al-Idariya al-Gadida." Ministry of Housing, Utilities and Urban Communities. http://www.mhuuc.gov.eg/Programs/ Index/132.

Michaelson, Ruth. 2018. "'Cairo Has Started to Become Ugly': Why Egypt Is Building a New Capital City." *The Guardian*, May 8. https://www.theguardian.com/cities/2018/may/08/ cairo-why-egypt-build-new-capital-city-desert.

Middle East Eye. 2019. "Egypt's Military Expands Authority as General Named New Transport Minister." *Middle East Eye*, March 11. https://www.middleeasteye.net/news/egypts-military-expands-authority-general-named-new-transport-minister.

Mostafa, Randa. 2019. "The Armed Forces and the Constitution: Amendments Grant the Military Unchecked Powers." *Mada Masr*, February 28. https://madamasr.com/en/2019/02/28/feature/politics/ the-armed-forces-and-the-constitution-amendments-grant-the-military-unchecked-powers/.

Mukhtar, Hind. 2018. "Ra'is al-wuzara' fi gawla maydaniya bi-l-'Asima al-Idariya al-Gadida. Mostafa Madbouly: Misr satadkhul 'asr natihat al-sahab wa-l-abrag al-shahiqa . . . ." *Youm7*, November 24. https://bit.ly/2H389l8.

Power Technology. 2020. "The State of Play: FDI in Egypt." *Power Technology*, August 21. https://www.power-technology.com/fdi/ the-state-of-play-fdi-in-egypt/.

Reuters. 2019. "Egypt's Sisi Opens Mega-mosque and Middle East's Largest Cathedral in New Capital." Reuters, January 6. https://www.reuters.com/article/us-egypt-religion/ egypts-sisi-opens-mega-mosque-and-middle-easts-largest-cathedral-in-new-capital-idUSKCN1P00L9.

Sout al-Omma. 2018. "Madina dhakiyya 'ala ard misriya: al-'asima al-idariya tahmi al-amn al-qawmi (video)." *Sout al-Omma*, December 11. https://bit.ly/2LbCltI.

Topol, Sarah A. 2014. "In Egypt, the Military Means (Big) Business." *Bloomberg*, March 14. https://www.bloomberg.com/news/ articles/2014-03-13/in-egypt-the-military-means-big-business.

13

GULF INVESTMENT, MEGACONTRACTOR PROJECTS, AND URBAN ISOMORPHISM
THE IMPOSITION OF A NEW WAY OF LIFE

MAÏA SINNO

Gulf influence in Cairo's urbanization did not begin with the 2011 revolution, but it has dramatically increased since then, reinforcing the degree of foreign presence in this thousand-year-old city. Cairo has evolved through the centuries by depending on foreign support, which has shaped its urbanity into a multicultural urban identity. Since 2011, Gulf countries have become major stakeholders as geopolitical partners and privileged investors, particularly in the real estate and construction sectors in Greater Cairo. These economic and political actors largely support the Egyptian military, upon which real estate transactions in Cairo exclusively depend. Gulf countries' urban models are often created by international teams of architects, who forge "standardized" cities with a twist of orientalist fantasy following an internationally shared image of the ideal Arab desert city. The Gulf urban model adopted by Egypt is shaped by cultural symbols of success and modernity, much as earlier visions of Egyptian modernity were shaped by Europe (see Hammad, this volume) and the United States (see Elsaket, this volume). Today's goal is less about copying a religious Saudi Arabia and more about following the example of the prosperous United Arab Emirates.

The adaptation of Egyptian social norms and habitus to the Gulf way of life is influenced by Gulf-styled and -funded real estate projects. The building of compounds like Uptown Cairo within the city, as well as outside of it and in the new capital, imagined as a Gulf capital in Egypt (see

Duffield, this volume) aims to exclude those Egyptians who can't afford this lifestyle or who refuse to abide by its restrictions. This exclusion is both vertical, with golden towers representing unattainable wealth, and horizontal, as rich gated communities eat away at the spaces occupied by informal areas in an effort to ease fears of a new popular uprising (see Arese, El-Husseiny, Borham, O. Khalil, and Mohie, this volume). The increasing Gulf influence on Cairo's urbanization, and the resulting increases in exclusivity and unaffordability, mark important turning points in mentalities and social interactions within the city limits.

Emerging Partnerships in a Postrevolutionary Period

Prior to 2011, Saudi Arabia, Kuwait, Bahrain, Qatar, and the United Arabic Emirates were close friends of the former Egyptian regimes. Their partnerships shared multiple economic, financial, and political goals, built over many decades, thanks to bonds between wealthy and influential families. Important Gulf families became intrinsically linked to the Egyptian government, reinforcing the neoliberal system adopted by Egypt, characterized by a ruling *'asabiya* and corruption. *'Asabiya* is a concept of social solidarity with an emphasis on unity, group consciousness, and a sense of shared purpose and social cohesion, originally in a context of "tribalism" and "clannism." It was familiar in the pre-Islamic era and later became popularized in Ibn Khaldun's *Muqaddimah*, a historic work from the fourteenth century. Ibn Khaldun describes *'asabiya* as the bond of cohesion that forms a community. It often carries negative associations because it can sometimes suggest loyalty to one's group, or partisanship, regardless of circumstances. This was one factor that deterred a transition to a more democratic or inclusive political order, as the political-economic system continued to serve a small community of people belonging to either the ruling families or the army, as well as a handful of persons living in the main Gulf cities. The result was a two-track or severely class-segregating growth pattern that increased the socioeconomic gap between wealthy and poor. It was reinforced by the structural delay of Egypt's entrance into the international market as well as by a closed economic system mainly hinging on Egyptian rents: tourism, the Nile economy, Suez Canal, oil production, American aid donations intended to guarantee peace with Israel, and financial contributions from the Egyptian diaspora, working outside the country.

The support of the Gulf States remained relatively constant during the four years of instability following the expulsion of Mubarak.

For the fiscal year of 2013–14, the Egyptian Central Bank registered more than 11 billion dollars of Gulf aid. At the end of 2013, numerous conferences and economic agreements between Egypt and the Gulf coalition encouraged the reinforcement of economic and political partnerships. The goal was to erase accusations of corruption by the temporary regime against some Gulf investors, to offer investment opportunities, and to remove barriers to foreign investment in Egypt. Nonetheless, Gulf assistance dried up progressively from 2014 onward for both political and economic reasons. After being one of Egypt's most important partners during the Morsi presidency (2012–13), Qatar had to step aside when a coalition of Saudi Arabia, the United Arab Emirates, Kuwait, and Bahrain took the lead in supporting al-Sisi's subsequent regime before a global economic crisis forced a reduction of aid and loans. At that point, donations were replaced by direct foreign investments.

Gulf economic and political support comes with a very high economic and political cost: loans must be reimbursed, and preferential treatment must be given to Gulf investors over Egyptian contractors. According to Central Bank of Egypt data, around 20 percent of the county's external debt is due annually to Saudi Arabia, the United Arab Emirates, and Kuwait, which also represented 13.7 percent of the Egyptian volume of trade in July through December 2019. The same countries made up 34.5 percent of total foreign direct investments in Egypt in 2018–19, with an increase in investments by the United Arab Emirates, Qatar, and Kuwait, but a decrease in Saudi direct investments.

The economic and political influence of the Gulf countries has reinforced the neoliberal system established by Mubarak, which was disrupted during Tantawi's and Morsi's administrations, that shut down many business elites and militarized the economy. The neoliberal system was reinstituted in 2014, after the election of Abd al-Fattah al-Sisi as the new president of Egypt. At this point, the Gulf States became part of the new political regime, not only as its allies (as before the revolution), but also as key partners in maintaining Egyptian political and economic stability. While they previously had been part of the Egyptian 'asabiya, Egypt's growing dependence allowed the Gulf countries to wield even more control over the current Egyptian political scene, especially where the distribution of the resources is decided.

This outside influence also implies an unclear boundary between the private and public sectors. According to Ahmad S.,[1] a former manager at the GAFI,[2] it is impossible to launch a real estate project in

Egypt without distributing graft at every step of the process. Accordingly, a real estate company works with and pays a public sector company directly. According to Ahmad, Gulf companies must respect these same "rules," forcing international actors in Egypt to play the graft "game." Foreign companies need a locally influential figure to make a deal possible. For example, the political influence of Shafik Gabr, a billionaire industrialist and chairman of ARTOC,[3] facilitated Emaar Misr[4] to get authorization for its projects, which include the settlements of Marassi, Mivida, and Uptown Cairo, all built on strategic land owned by the Egyptian army. Gulf partners are also formulating new investment rules based on privilege and friendships on a regional scale, rather than relying on state regulation and free markets. Therefore, the leaders of several Gulf companies are part of a limited group of political elites in Cairo whose economic and political power is drawn from family, marriage, and friendship ties with the Egyptian ruling families. Moreover, the families at the head of Emaar and Majid Al Futtaim Group—two real estate corporations—were active participants in government even before the discovery of oil and gas in Egypt. Mohamed Alabbar (founder and chairman of Emaar) and Majid Al Futtaim, and their companies, are vectors of geopolitical influence in their countries as members of a public–private community on a regional level, with a defined hierarchy.

Since Abd al-Fattah al-Sisi's rise to power, he has initiated ambitious megaprojects, most notably building an entirely new capital city, as Duffield relates elsewhere in this volume. For Ahmad S., "Gulf companies were always present in Egypt—in particular UAE and Saudi Arabia—and since the revolution they have become preferential economic and commercial partners. This is due to a real rapprochement with their mentality and the weight of a common religion."[5] Thus the investments of Gulf companies in real estate have multiplied. For instance, Cairo Gate—a new LE 11.5 billion ($735 million) compound in Sheikh Zayed City, a suburb of Cairo located along the Alexandria Road—was launched at the beginning of 2020 by Emaar. The Dubai company's project follows the same urban direction as its other projects. Like Uptown Cairo and Mivida, it consists of a compound and a mall. For the last few years, they have worked closely with another well-known construction firm, Arabtec, despite the latter's possible bankruptcy. As another example, Majid Al Futtaim continues to invest in retail in Cairo, planning to open more Carrefour shops after completion of two main retail projects in Greater Cairo: Cairo Festival City and Mall of Egypt.

The Influence of the Gulf Model on Cairo's Urbanization

Such investments outside the city also influence urbanization processes inside Cairo. Most Gulf-funded projects are located somewhere in Greater Cairo, often in recently built desert cities (e.g., compounds, malls, hotels). Reflecting on the regional influence of the Gulf on Cairo, Abaza (2011) writes, "Nostalgia is coincidental with what is described here as the 'Dubaisation' of the city of Cairo, which is observed in three central zones. In using the term 'Dubaisation,' I refer to the next patterns of space segregation that have been created by developments advertised as 'islands of luxury' and using privatized security guards" (Abaza 2011, 1076). In a chapter in the present volume, Elshahed describes the almost hallucinatory way in which these projects are sold to their potential buyers.

Kareem, the director of an association working to promote "the right to the city," does not think that this urbanization model is specifically imported from the Gulf countries, insisting that he does not "believe in the Dubai model. When we talk about malls and gated communities, we talk about a global model."[6] Khaled, an architect involved in New Cairo's luxury compounds, claims that he does not find Dubai in Cairo—that it is

not just a question of an imported economic model, but also of way of life. The urban planning [around] Cairo 2050 is about gigantic projects, some of which need to erase entire neighborhoods, often poor, in a big "cleaning," which is a euphemism for mass eviction. And for that, Gulf money is essential. Working with the Gulf means to raise standards for the future. The model of modernity in Cairo is closer to Solidere in Beirut than Dubai for me. . . . I heard once that the Gulf pushes Egyptian companies to be better. One thing is sure: the quality is not the same as it is in Dubai, even with the Gulf projects in Egypt.[7]

So, what exactly is the origin of this model? What are the common cultural aspects between the Cairo and Dubai populations? For Mohammed, the director of an Egyptian real estate company, "The mall culture is coming from the Gulf. But the new generation is not coming from the Gulf."[8] He is referring here to the labor-related migration of middle-class and poor Egyptians in the 1960s, now returning to Egypt in waves, particularly from Saudi Arabia, bringing back a new vision of consumerism. Today, Egyptian businessmen often seek to mimic an imagined Gulf "way of life" that they have not experienced directly but have been exposed to through consumption. There is a difference between the Gulf influence on the former generations, which mostly followed a religious model, and the generations of today, who envy the consumerism of Doha or Dubai, relayed through social networks.

As in Gulf cities, malls and hotels have no single function, but host a large variety of activities. These are the meeting places of the wealthy classes in Egypt, and they are indeed almost the only places where they can meet, for pleasure or for business. They are used to moving from one place to another only by car, as the street is seen as the territory of the lower classes and, as such, is not considered safe or convenient. Malls and hotels are deemed safe semi-public areas open only to certain social categories. Security cameras and a police presence at the entrances filter the people allowed in, and if the *gallabeya* (the long robes of the Egyptian peasant and many urban workers and doormen) is commonly not accepted in these venues, the *dishdasha* (the similar robes worn by Gulf Arab men) is more than welcome. The internationalization of these spaces is not synonymous with global integration and harmony.

St. Regis on Cairo's Corniche

The Corniche in Cairo is bordered by many towers that face the Nile, hiding the Bulaq area and offering a window of verticality as international proof of success and modernity. The tower is a symbol of the standardization of globalized cities (Didelon 2010). It is a cultural implant, detached from the local surroundings. It also brings with it a strong cultural dimension of globalized civilizational values that serve several functions: presenting a window of power, increasing the accessibility of networks, creating hybrid and multifunctional buildings, and reducing new infrastructure costs while increasing profits by erecting towers within the already existing city core (Rossignol et al. 2013).

What differentiates the Qatari Diar's St. Regis Hotel from the rest of the towers along Cairo's Corniche? At first glance, not much. However, the opening of the hotel took place in summer 2020, in the midst of the pandemic, nine years after its construction began. The severance of diplomatic relations between Egypt and Qatar in 2017 delayed its realization. The urban evolution of Cairo remains dependent on regional geopolitical relations and crises. The golden façade of the St. Regis hides the Bulaq General Hospital, a public medical facility that the state has been desperately trying to close for many years, despite the opposition of the inhabitants of the Bulaq neighborhood. The state's aim is not so much to gain additional space as to encourage gentrification in this area and to glorify the aura of wealth that verticality projects.

The St. Regis Hotel was designed by the internationally famous architecture firm of Michael Graves. A fantasy image of the "Arab city" circulates among these international architecture firms, rapidly becoming a new standard of modernity. It is a postmodern vision (Harvey 1989, 66–98) of the Arab city, reproducing the classic lines of the orientalist imagined city while maintaining a contemporary look. The St. Regis Hotel is a good example of this tendency, along with the Sheraton Miramar Hotel and Resort in El Gouna, located on the Red Sea coast. On Michael Graves's website, the St. Regis's style describes its own décor as quintessentially Egyptian—"From the custom wallcoverings with subtle papyrus patterns and inlayed wood cabinets in the guestrooms to glass light fixtures and stone patterns in the public spaces, the interiors subtly refer to the Egyptian context"—while the style of the Sheraton is defined as "contemporary interiors inspired by tradition." It is, to say the least, paradoxical to call on American firms to find "traditional" lines in the architecture of glitzy buildings in the Middle East. Watered-down visions of cultural heritage are appropriated by directors of American companies. Choosing an international firm for the Gulf project of a luxury hotel on Cairo's Corniche is most appreciated in Cairo by affluent clientele, who are spectators of the frantic race for luxury at a cost in cultural reductionism and erasure.

Uptown Cairo: Tuscan Villas in a Gulf Project?

If the malls and hotels represent vertical spaces for Cairo's elites to gather, then the compounds on the edges of Greater Cairo represent horizontal spaces, as described by Elshahed and El-Husseiny in this volume. Uptown Cairo is an exception, offering a 5.4-million-square-meter residential complex comprising about fifteen high-security "villages," a golf course, mall, and clubhouse, all located in the middle of the old city, on the top of Muqattam Hill. This location is very convenient, since it is central, but separate and private—not even the inhabitants of the well-known neighboring "Garbage Village," primarily inhabited by impoverished Coptic Egyptians who recycle the city's garbage and live in horrific environmental conditions—can see behind the walls around the project. It was imagined in 2005 by Emaar Misr, a subsidiary company of Emaar, at a cost of $11 billion.

Designing a residential area as "villages," as often done by real estate and marketing agencies, reinforces a sense of security as well as of being separate from the rest of overcrowded Cairo, while remaining near the center of the city. "Villages" evoke escape and travel, while the feeling of being separate is encouraged through the creation of semi-public spaces restricted to "village" inhabitants, in a pleasant setting of "Tuscan" architecture. The Madinaty complex, built by Jumeirah in Dubai, resembles a small Venice, where visitors can get around on wooden motorboats. The appropriation of European architectural codes is common to this type of urbanization and evokes childhood games of creating visual stories on cardboard. The "Tuscan" model in Uptown Cairo stands in sharp contrast to the aesthetics of downtown Islamic Cairo and the numerous informal neighborhoods that fill the city. Likewise, the interiors of the enclave's houses reflect a specific type of elegance and a baroque style, since the houses are delivered already furnished by Emaar Misr. Buying a house or an apartment in Uptown Cairo seems to be the easiest way to forget about Cairo while continuing to reside in it. Unsurprisingly, then, the new neighborhood is a big hit with buyers, as confirmed by Randa A., an architect at a New Cairo compound: "There is hysterical speculation about this project; Emaar is deciding the prices."[9] The consumerist amenities and European-style standardized housing drive the fast sale of Uptown Cairo housing in the Egyptian market. Buyers see their purchases as investments, hoping to rent their villas to rich Gulf families looking for the same type of residences as in their own countries.

A Gulf Capital in Egypt?

President al-Sisi's administration has presented the new capital as an initiative that could solve most of the problems of an Egypt riddled with instability, including, but not limited to, a housing crisis, rising inflation and unemployment, and a depletion of global currencies spurred by divestment. The inefficiency of the Egyptian government has pushed it to repeat the same mistake, creating new cities in the desert, which represents a huge waste of land, resources, and money (Sims 2015). These are not long-term, data-driven projects, but are more indicative of a headlong rush to try to erase the recurring problems of Egypt, which remained unresolved after the revolution and include corruption, a widening gap between social classes, a rents-based economy, dependence on unstable political and economic partnerships, and much more. While they allow the sitting president to gain visibility, they also represent a massive land grab that marries the interests of the military and the economic and political elites (Abul-Magd 2017). Most worrisome, "the new capital of Egypt has no residents. It doesn't have a local source of water. It just lost a major developer, the Chinese state company that had agreed to build the first phase. You might say the planned city in the desert 45 kilometers east of

Cairo doesn't have a reason to exist" (Lindsay 2017). Emaar was indeed supposed to oversee the project, which was proposed as if the president were presenting the new capital of Egypt as a regional capital of the Gulf region, just in a hinterland. A few months later, the Dubai-based company stepped back from the project and was replaced by two Chinese state companies, of which only one remains involved in the project today. At this point, the Egyptian government has no other choice than to pursue the project and hope for the best to avoid losing an economic and political legitimacy already weakened by authoritarianism and economic crisis following the revolution.

The presence of new urban influences could mean the redefinition of a completely new way of life for Cairo inhabitants, as well as the partial deletion of hundreds of years of culture and patrimonial legacy. The implications for Egypt as a nation and for its population, if a Gulf presence continues to define its urbanization processes, are not only urban, but also structural. Desperately trying to reposition the center of the country in the barren desert rather than among the millennia of layers of history in Cairo, the government is turning its back on the violence and demands of the revolutionaries, whose echoes still resonate on Mohammad Mahmud Street, abandoning the popular classes to their dusty fates in the old capital. All of these sacrifices seem to be a small price to pay to mold a new capital, with the ultimate goal of Gulf acceptance. It is not certain that Cairo's poorest people, already weakened by ten years of demonstrations, authoritarianism, and inflation, will be able and willing to follow this new cultural way of life. It is also not certain that the upper classes will agree to leave the old capital to live in half-deserted towers and empty compounds, to embrace a Gulf dream which might never come true. By encouraging the population to adopt a new culture and to forget the old one, urban developers and state officials risk exacerbating a social gap in an already fragmented environment.

Notes

1   Ahmad S. (a pseudonym), interview by the author, Cairo, 2013.
2   General Authority for Investment and Free Zones.
3   ARTOC is an Egyptian conglomerate with interests in automobiles, real estate, and publishing.
4   Emaar Misr is the Egyptian subsidiary company of the UAE-based real estate company, Emaar.
5   Ahmad S. (a pseudonym), interview by the author, Cairo, 2013.
6   Kareem (a pseudonym), interview by the author, Cairo, 2014.

7   Khaled (a pseudonym), interview by the author, Paris, 2015.
8   Mohammed (a pseudonym), interview by the author, Cairo, 2014.
9   Randa A. (a pseudonym), interview by the author, al-Tagammuʻ
    al-Khamis, 2014.

Works Cited

Abaza, Mona. 2011. "Critical Commentary: Cairo's Downtonwn Imag-
    ined: Dubaisation or Nostalgia?" *Urban Studies* 48, no. 6: 1075–87.
Abul-Magd, Zeinab. 2017. *Militarizing the Nation: The Army, Business, and
    Revolution in Egypt*. New York: Columbia University Press.
Al-Aees, Shaimaa. 2016. "Construction Projects for New Administrative
    Capital in Full Swing." *Daily News Egypt*, June 12. https://dailynews
    egypt.com/2016/06/12/construction-projects-new-administrative-
    capital-full-swing/.
——. 2017. "10 Years Tax Exemption, Transfer of Profits Abroad Revive
    Egypt's Real Estate Sector." *Daily News Egypt*, May 15. https://www.
    dailynewsegypt.com/2017/05/15/10-years-tax-exemption-transfer-
    profits-abroad-revive-egypts-real-estate-sector/.
Alshahed, Mohammed. 2011a. "Cairo's Colonial Cities." *Cairobserver*,
    November 21. http://cairobserver.com/post/13081441926/cairos-
    colonial-cities#.WR1zjWjyjIU.
——. 2011b. "New Construction: St Regis." *Cairobserver*, December
    24. http://cairobserver.com/post/14738026127/new-construction-
    st-regis#.WI9vyvnhDIV.
——. 2014. "From Tahrir Square to Emaar Square." *Cairobserver*,
    February 23. http://cairobserver.com/post/77533681187/from-tahrir-
    square-to-emaar-square#.WTgiCmjyjIU.
Aman, Ayah. 2014. "Sisi Counting on Gulf Aid to Deal with Egypt's
    Economic Crisis." *Al-Monitor*, April 7. http://www.al-monitor.com/
    pulse/originals/2014/04/economic-crisis-egypt-influence-sisi-
    popularity.html.
Aveline-Dubach, Nathalie. 2008. *Immobilier: L'Asie, la bulle et la mondiali-
    sation*. Paris: CNRS Editions.
Didelon, Valery. 2010. "Dreamlands: des parcs d'attractions aux cités du
    futur." *Critique d'art*, September. doi:10.4000/critiquedart.1547
Farid, Doaa. 2015. "Businessmen and the State: A Confusing Relationship."
    Daily News Egypt, November 21. https://dailynewsegypt.com/2015/
    11/21/businessmen-and-the-state-a-confusing-relationship/.
El-Ghobashy, Tamer, and Esther Fung. 2016. "Soft Power: China Backs
    Egypt's New $45 Billion Capital." *The Wall Street Journal*, May 3.

https://www.wsj.com/articles/big-chinese-developer-pushes-overseas-ambitions-with-egypt-project-1462267802.

Hanieh, Adam. 2011. "Egypt's Uprising: Not Just a Question of 'Transition.'" *Monthly Review MRZine*, February 14. https://mronline.org/2011/02/14/egypts-uprising-not-just-a-question-of-transition/.

Harvey, David. 1989. *The Condition of Postmodernity: An Enquiry into the Origins of Cultural Change*. Cambridge, MA and Oxford, UK: Blackwell Publishers.

Kalin, Stephen. 2014. "Sisi's Economic Vision for Egypt: Back to the Future." Reuters, May 22. http://www.reuters.com/article/us-egypt-sisi-economy-idUSBREA4L0KL20140522.

Kamal, Ahmad. 2017. "Chinese Project to Build New Egyptian Capital Revived." *Asian Review*, May 26. https://asia.nikkei.com/Business/Companies/Chinese-project-to-build-new-Egyptian-capital-revived.

Lindsay, Ursula. 2017. "The Anti-Cairo." *Places*, March. https://places-journal.org/article/the-anti-cairo/#ref_3.

Prasad, Ananthakrishnan, Heba Abdel Monem, and Pilar Garcia Martinez. 2016. "Macroprudential Policy and Financial Stability in the Arab Region." IMF Working Paper. International Monetary Fund, May 20. https://www.elibrary.imf.org/view/journals/001/2016/098/article-A001-en.xml.

Rossignol, Claire, Leila Kebir, Vincent Becue, and Youssef Diab. 2013. "Tall Buildings as Urban Objects for Sustainable Cities? A New Approach to Characterise Urbanity of High-rises." Paper presented at the Annual Conference of the IGU Urban Commission, July 21–26, 2013, Johannesburg-Cape Town, South Africa.

Selim, Adham. 2015. "Capital Cairo: A Regime of Graphics." *Mada Masr*, August 5. http://www.madamasr.com/en/2015/08/05/feature/culture/capital-cairo-a-regime-of-graphics.

Sims, David. 2012. *Understanding Cairo: The Logic of a City Out of Control*. Cairo: American University in Cairo Press.

———. 2015. *Egypt's Desert Dreams: Development or Disaster?* Cairo: American University in Cairo Press.

14

CAIRO UP! INFRASTRUCTURES OF SECURITY AND DESIRE

AYA NASSAR

Vignette: The Makeshift Drone

A TikTok video zooms in on a cell phone taped to a kite, playing a *mahragan* song in the background: "This is Cairo, Cairo Up"![1] The kite is released by four young men. We might have expected a clear bird's-eye view, but initially it is dizzying, like a sudden twist on a roller coaster. Then the kite is stable, and we see rooftops, parking spots, and the four young men, growing smaller and waving to their TikTok camera before they reel the kite in. The TikTok video is called "Drone al-Ghalaba," or "our makeshift drone."[2] This is not a literal translation, which would typically mean "the poor or wretched drone," but rather is a reference to what this term inspires in this context. "Our makeshift drone" is the term kites have gained on social media as they lift their owners' cell phones to snap shots of Cairo—as well as other places in Egypt—from above.

As Elmeshad and Westmoreland have discussed in their chapters in this volume, the Egyptian population's ability to produce alternative news and images about their realities has historically been very fraught. The kite videos proliferated in the spring of 2020 and represented a new form of counter-hegemonic visualization of the city. That spring saw numerous phases and articulations of lockdowns, slowdowns, and interruptions as governments around the world tried to react to the COVID-19 global pandemic. In Egypt, the pandemic did not result in a total lockdown but, instead, ended up with a curfew that restricted movement at night. The time and scale of the curfew changed regularly to accommodate some semblance of normality. For example, during the month of Ramadan (April–May 2020), the curfew was relaxed to allow movement after breaking fast at sunset (Reuters 2020), when many would look forward to collective gatherings. A couple of hours before sunset, many Egyptians would raise kites up to the skies, with neighborhood teams of various districts competing with each other for the kite that flew highest or captured the most panoramic view. Easter passed, the pandemic continued, and so did the kites.

The kite contests fostered a kind of joy in Cairenes. Competitions were best spotted on al-Sahil Bridge, where there is a skyline and space to maneuver. It wasn't long before people commenting on the aforementioned TikTok video—released on Twitter and shared via Facebook—started asking if this drone-like view was a threat to national security. These comments turned into a briefing request in parliament about the potential national security threat of kites. At the time, no one took it seriously (*New Arab* 2020). But by July, kites had been banned and seized, and their flyers fined, both in Cairo and in Alexandria. The pretexts for the crackdown were personal safety as well as national security. The crackdown even made it into English-speaking newspapers—"Egypt Grounds Kites for 'Safety,' 'National Security'" (*Arab News* 2020)—making it another one of those things states do for security and to crack down on joy.

Rather than an analysis of this incident, this chapter is intended to provide a series of provocations that are inspired by this vignette. The use of a vignette here follows its use by various feminist thinkers as both methodology and form. In particular, I draw on Marysia Zalewski's "exquisite corpse" interventions (2013). For Zalewski, vignettes allow a writing that is disquieting, disorderly, and eclectic. It assembles a knowledge of politics from eccentric texts but also, importantly, from everyday experience as it encompasses contingent narratives and traces. Zalewski describes this methodology as foraging, collaging, and playing with poetic license and academic writing forms (Zalewski 2013, 3). Building on her work, I use vignettes as a way of resisting hygienic methods, extractivist field work, and masterful claim-making and generalization (Nassar 2019). In this sense, the vignette represents an entangled and poetic flash (Glissant 1997), not an empirical case or a showcasing of fieldwork. How can this ordinary practice of flying kites challenge our accepted understanding of the securitization processes of the city? Why pay attention to seemingly mundane instances situated within the spectacular moments of curfew and pandemic? I propose that this moment brings to light two important types of logic regarding security: aerial urbanism, and the entanglement of materiality and affect.

By "aerial urbanism," I refer to a recent and growing focus on understanding the geographies of cities and territories as anything but flat: as vertical, volumetric, and extending physically, financially, and imaginatively into the air (Chen 2020; Adey 2010; Adey 2015; McCormack 2015; Engelmann 2015; Squire 2016; Nieuwenhuis 2014; Nieuwenhuis 2018). From skyscrapers to elevated highways, from pollution to tear gas, from the extended steel rods of incremental urbanization to the monetization of air rights, the air is a register that is typically overlooked when discussing security and urbanization in the context of Cairo. This is a discussion in which something like a makeshift drone intervenes in a long and ongoing security anxiety about disclosing urbanity from a bird's-eye view, sometimes quite literally. The entanglement of materiality and affect is a discussion that is just starting to garner some attention with regard to Cairo. Here, I refer to the attention paid to the matter that makes up our cities as well as our embodied and emotional entanglement with the spaces in which we move and to which we relate. In the work of Timothy Mitchell (Abourahme and Jabary-Salamanca 2016; Mitchell 2002b), modern experiences of infrastructural materiality are analyzed in relation to urbanity. Scholarship on the geographies of emotion and affect have also started to gain momentum recently (see, for example, Abaza 2020; Prestel 2017; Pettit 2019). Within these two registers, I view the release of things—such as phones and the gaze of individuals—into the sky as forms of infrastructural extensions into the air.

These extensions are not just about verticality (see Weizman 2007; Graham 2016), although verticality is indeed central to that discussion, but also about a topological relationship with the city (Secor 2013). By referring to a topological relationship with the city, I follow Anna Secor's provocation. In this context, I mean the ways in which we can appreciate the affective life within the infrastructural glitch of a curfew. By drawing these two registers together, I push for a framework through which to think about urban (in)security in terms of infrastructure. Specifically, I consider air, skylines, bridges, and other "fantastic things" that populate Cairo's skies, and I question how social and material infrastructures extend, suspend, and respond to fantasies of (in)security. How do these types of infrastructure sit within ongoing and ordinary forms of inhabiting the city? By addressing that question through the material and affective life of infrastructure, I propose that we can work against urbanity's dualistic approaches (e.g., above/below, normality/exception) (Aradau 2013), which have been the dominant lenses through which to understand urban (in)security in the past decades. The first of the next two sections works with the temporal and affective frame of the pandemic's curfew, typically read as an obvious articulation of logics of exception. I approach it through the imagination of Lauren Berlant's (2016) conception of the glitch. The second section focuses on some of the competing fantasies and anxieties that populate Cairo's sky.

Infrastructures, Glitches, and Curfews

Thinking with and about infrastructures has become one of the most generative terrains in the social sciences. This is seen as largely due to the term's expansive definitions (Larkin 2013). Originally French, *infrastructure* migrated to the English language in the twentieth century to indicate the work required either beneath or prior to the construction of railroad tracks. In postwar discourse, the term made its way into the worlds of military cooperation and international development,[3] and by the late twentieth century retained only some of its original militaristic associations (Carse 2017). It is thanks to critical infrastructure scholarship that the entanglement of infrastructure, violence, and security remains a subject of scrutiny (Cowen 2014; Chua et al. 2018; Khalili 2020; Aradau 2013).

Infrastructure brings with it specific orientations to social phenomena, one being relationality. Far from immaterial, it forms the core of our meaning-making processes, since "individuals are sufficiently attuned to the ways in which buildings, roads, stairs, sidewalks, aisles, and rooms not only posit an infrastructure of everyday performance but possibilities of figuring new modes of witnessing and transacting, of call and response, deliberating, of saying something to each other" (Lancione and Simone 2020). By being a thing in itself as well as a relationship between things, infrastructure assembles material, social, and affective relations and, in the process, reconfigures spaces and subjectivities (Harvey, Jensen, and Morita 2019). It folds within it the spectacular and the mundane, what is at surface and what lies in depth and orients to logics of (in)visibility and inherent fragility (Harvey, Jensen, and Morita 2019; Larkin 2013). Methodologically, to decide to discuss something as infrastructure is a "categorical act" since it is not "in any positivist sense, simply out there" (Larkin 2013, 30) and therefore a critical study of infrastructure and security can start from anywhere (Aradau 2013). To call an infrastructure into being is "to draw attention to the complications of other-than-human dimensions of the political relations that join and divide us" (Harvey, Jensen, and Morita 2019, 7).

Infrastructure is not just about materiality, but also about relationships of finance, violence, racialization, nation building, and its promises of (and broken promises to) the future. Beyond the spectacular projects of the powerful, infrastructure is also about the mundane and ordinary patterns that keep life going. Articulations such as social infrastructure and people-as-infrastructure drawn from places like Cairo and Johannesburg (Elyachar 2010; Simone 2004) sometimes orient us toward an infrastructure beyond individual relations. This particular attention to infrastructure as social eschews the investment in thinking about it as totally regulated or as a site of governmentality. Instead, it becomes open to playful and unpredictable improvisation as well as ordinary affective relations.

This opening to ordinary inhabiting of the city (Stewart 2007; Berlant 2011; Berlant 2016) posits that infrastructures are simply (and not so simply) ongoing patterns that manage contingency and ambivalence. In other words, infrastructure keeps us bound to an awkward proximity to the world, as Lauren Berlant would argue. I am drawn to this articulation since it captures our affective investment in infrastructures as patterns that bind us to the world even if these patterns do not work for us in the ways we expect or want them to. These patterns get disrupted of course, and this interruption is what Berlant calls a "glitch." A glitch reveals a failure of infrastructure and "an interruption within a transmission" (Berlant 2016, 393). A glitch makes apparent a condition of ordinary infrastructural failure. The interruption of the glitch might be often addressed by sociality extending itself beyond the glitch. This is not to say that this extension is necessarily a repair or restoration, or that a glitch is not ordinary. It is also not to say that a glitch is only an articulation of arrest or stall; rather, it opens up space for alternative formation, speculation, forgetting, or even reinhabiting the ordinary.

Rather than an exception, I want to treat the pandemic's curfew as a "glitch" in this expansive sense. This treatment enables us to depart from the theoretical language that is invested in logics of exception and emergency when it comes to the question of urban security in Cairo. The aspects of logics of exceptions are manifold and theoretically rich, but here I am particularly imagining the privileging of an exception over normative binaries that rests on the decision-making of the sovereign. By contrast, a glitch attunes us to the ordinary relations that this interruption only makes apparent. Berlant's (2016) affective theoretical scaffolding enables us to think about urban space beyond the lens of the state of exception that has captivated the imagination of many commentators on Cairo over the past decade.

Let's return to the opening vignette about the pandemic curfew and flying kites to extend and change time, rhythm, and space. When young people took to flying kites to deal with the boredom of a curfew, it represented an expression of joy and conviviality. It is true that these moments also provoked security anxieties that called on the state to regulate this rhythm and space. The causes cited for banning and confiscating kites were citizens' safety and security, especially after some kite-flyers supposedly fell off roofs. This propelled commentators to call kites a "silent killer" (Shehta 2020). Lurking among these anxieties as well were the national security concerns of people apprehensive about the filming of the city from above. While kites were grounded in Cairo and Alexandria, to the great interest of Western media, the news of their banning was quickly swept under the carpet by the continued and ongoing highway and flyover construction in greater Cairo, which visibly progressed despite the effect it had on residents' livelihoods (Elshahed 2020; Dessouky 2020). This drive for infrastructural achievement is, of course, not novel. The way infrastructure captivates and holds attachments and desires is perhaps one of the enduring logics of government in Egypt (see, for instance, Barak 2013; Moore 1994; Mossallam 2014; De Coss-Corzo 2020). That said, infrastructure is never only the purview of the powerful (Elyachar 2010; Elyachar 2014). Our opening vignette is less about the grounding of kites and more about their extension. This is what thinking with kites, even if they have been grounded, enables us to do. Thinking with infrastructure enables one "to work with," "to attune to," and "to space out in ways that can contribute to a renewed sense of intimacy with and through the extended world we inhabit" (Lancione and Simone 2020). The forms of play that use rooftops, bridges, and phone cameras in kite wars offer a condition in which the city's infrastructure becomes an avenue of conviviality and improvisation. This noncommittal conviviality, or "people as infrastructure" (Simone 2004), tends to be missed if we approach it only through the logics of the state or of resistance to the state. This is how we can think of practices of coming together that play with logics of security even while inhabiting the time and space of a curfew. Nevertheless, these relationships are continuously performed, extended, and withdrawn in ways that make urban living possible even under conditions of emergency.

To See This Country from Above

Throughout the past decade (and even longer), life in Cairo was seen as insufferable and was sometimes made deliberately so through aggressive urban replanning and a chronic housing problem (Abaza 2020; Shawkat 2020). This visual and affective mode instigated a flight out of the city that has intensified over the past decade, with a new capital city becoming a national mission of the state (Selim 2015; Lindsey 2017; Duffield, this volume) and a migration of Cairenes to the city's extensions (Mitchell 2002a; Sims 2014; El-Husseiny, this volume). Expanding outward (to new satellite cities, summer houses, or the new capital) garners more attention than other forms of spatial and temporal extensions—namely, upward. This is despite the fact that rooftops, for instance, are fundamental to understanding the patterns of life and living in Cairo. Constant vertical extensions of reinforced concrete—always under construction—speak to a desire for future incremental building (Silver 2014) and convey intimate liveliness (Marji 2020). In films, the rooftop is the place from which the protagonist attempts to make sense of the city below and ahead (Nassar 2020). These vantage points have traditionally been spaces for snipers targeting official convoys but are also the stereotypical place of respite from the hustle and bustle of the city. In the case of our vignette, the rooftop becomes a playground when statesmen impose restrictions on possible street play.

In 2013, a stork was detained in Egypt under suspicion of spying through a tracking device. Again, news of this went viral in the foreign media as it picked up on the measures that emerge from within state-led security anxieties. A project by artist Heba Amin speaks of this story not only as one of the absurdities of paranoia and conspiracy, but also in order to unpack the ways in which birds, drones, and aerial surveillance have been entangled with a colonial gaze. Amin picks up on Adel Imam's line in the film *Birds of Darkness*: "To see this country from above is not the same as seeing it from below" (Amin 2020). In the film, Imam's character talks about the classed privilege of a gaze from a high-rise. Amin traces the stork, logics of surveillance, and drone warfare to convey a story that entangles the entire region. She situates this event within the historical and contemporary colonial and warfare technologies that have written the geopolitics of the region from above, as well as on the map (Amin 2020). Seemingly silly stories of arresting storks and grounding kites are, in actuality, implicated in the serious logics of geopolitics.

While the crackdown on kites is minor, it invokes the long-held anxiety regarding an aerial surveillant gaze, which finds echoes in the stork story. Amin reminds us that the scale and security logics "of above" and "of below" bear little fruit in the analysis of urbanity. It is not a coincidence that Adel Imam's casual sentence—rooted primarily within questions of class—refracts in contemporary academic literature about Cairo, which tends to be enamored with Michel de Certeau's *Practice of Everyday Life* (1988). De Certeau's seminal notes on seeing the city from above as opposed to knowing it from the ground seem to resonate with logics of understanding, knowing, and capturing the city. As inspiring as they are, we might want to question whether this logic of power and security from above, and resistance and messiness from below, actually holds true in spaces like Cairo. Beyond the city and the art world, Caren Kaplan (2018) has attempted to counter the idea that the aerial gaze is by default a modernist, powerful, and all-seeing mode and contends that it should be juxtaposed with subterranean/sideways modes of resistance. Here, alongside the playful but serious footage from our makeshift drone, I propose to take Kaplan's argument seriously when rethinking the imaginations of securitizing the city.

Conclusion by Suspension

Middle Eastern skylines are full of "security objects": bombs, fireworks, military jets, air raids, and drones, to name a few. Some of these cities have fantastic skylines that prompt Western and Arab commentators to look toward them as the next new thing in urbanism: skyscrapers, towers, and makeshift islands that, seen from outer space, have the shape of the globe (Graham 2016). Some of these cities captivate our imagination with claims of orientalist authenticity: minarets, domes, and ruined remains of some imagined past. The skies of our cities are a contested space that can render kites as unexceptional objects of (in)security.

I propose thinking of insecurity and the ordinary when flying a makeshift drone, which is illegal in Egypt except with permission from the Civil Aviation Authority. I am eager to stress, however, that I don't read the practice of a makeshift drone as response, resistance, or counter-conduct. My aim here was to dwell on the image of kites released as a convivial practice that extends to the sky within the emptiness of a curfew. This orients us to think of practices of release and suspension (McCormack 2018) as alternative approaches to comprehending the logics of security. I don't critique binary logics simply because they are binary. This tends to (re)create strawman complex theoretical traditions and dismisses generative research. My contention here has been more modest: to shift the theoretical lens to one that is not too hung up on the logic of a securitization theory of normality/exception, and power from above/tactics from below—that is, to allow ourselves to follow the playful and the ordinary and to be able to make sense of how urban living continues to pattern itself, even within emergencies, curfews, and lockdowns. This, I propose, might orient us to stay with the complexities of what tends to be subsumed under a state of emergency. In short, I propose working with entanglement and nonresolution. The aerial is a space of security and insecurity, the playful and the securitized, capture but also escape.

Notes

1   *Mahraganat* is a type of electro dance music relying on synthesized sounds. It started gaining attention as a genre in the 2010s (Diefallah 2020). "Cairo Up!" is the name of one *mahragan* track, which references Cairo's rivalry with Alexandria. https://www.youtube.com/watch?v=2AFqG8xXSSg.
2   While the TikTok video described here was also "released" in the public domain, I decided not to cite it, given that TikTok videos were interestingly entangled in moral panics and legal attention during the writing of this piece.
3   In 1949, the term was adopted simultaneously by NATO and in Truman's inauguration speech (Carse 2017).

Works Cited

Abaza, Mona. 2020. *Cairo Collage: Everyday Life Practices after the Event.* Manchester, UK: Manchester University Press.

Abourahme, Nasser, and Omar Jabary-Salamanca. 2016. "Thinking against the Sovereignty of the Concept: A Conversation with Timothy Mitchell." *City* 20, no. 5: 737–54. https://doi.org/10.1080/13604813.2016.1224486.

Adey, Peter. 2010. *Aerial Life: Spaces, Mobilities, Affects.* Chichester: Wiley-Blackwell.

———. 2015. "Air's Affinities: Geopolitics, Chemical Affect and the Force of the Elemental." *Dialogues in Human Geography* 5, no. 1: 54–75. https://doi.org/10.1177/2043820614565871.

Amin, Heba Y. 2020. *The General's Stork.* Edited by Anthony Downey. Research/Practice 02. Berlin: Sternberg Press.

Arab News. 2020. "Egypt Grounds Kites for 'Safety,' 'National Security.'" *Arab News,* July 11. https://www.arabnews.com/node/1703291/middle-east.

Aradau, Claudia. 2013. "Infrastructure." In *Research Methods in Critical Security Studies: An Introduction*, edited by Mark B. Salter and Can E. Multu, 181–85. 1st ed. London and New York: Routledge. https://doi.org/10.4324/9780203107119.

Barak, On. 2013. *On Time: Technology and Temporality in Modern Egypt.* Middle Eastern History. Berkeley: University of California Press.

Berlant, Lauren Gail. 2011. *Cruel Optimism.* Durham, NC: Duke University Press.

———. 2016. "The Commons: Infrastructures for Troubling Times*." *Environment and Planning D: Society and Space* 34, no. 3: 393–419. https://doi.org/10.1177/0263775816645989.

Carse, Ashley. 2017. "Keyword: Infrastructure—How a Humble French Engineering Term Shaped the Modern World." In *Infrastructures and Social Complexity: A Companion*, edited by Penelope Harvey, Casper Jensen, and Atsuro Morita, 27–39. London: Routledge.

Certeau, Michel de. 1988. *The Practice of Everyday Life.* Translated by Steven Rendall. Berkeley: University of California Press.

Chen, Hung-Ying. 2020. "Cashing in on the Sky: Financialization and Urban Air Rights in the Taipei Metropolitan Area." *Regional Studies* 54, no. 2: 198–208. https://doi.org/10.1080/00343404.2019.1599104.

Chua, Charmaine, Martin Danyluk, Deborah Cowen, and Laleh Khalili. 2018. "Introduction: Turbulent Circulation: Building a Critical Engagement with Logistics." *Environment and Planning D: Society and Space* 36, no. 4: 617–29. https://doi.org/10.1177/0263775818783101.

Cowen, Deborah. 2014. *The Deadly Life of Logistics: Mapping Violence in Global Trade.* Minneapolis: University of Minnesota Press.

De Coss-Corzo, Alejandro. 2020. "Patchwork: Repair Labor and the Logic of Infrastructure Adaptation in Mexico City." *Environment and Planning D: Society and Space* 39, no. 2: 237–53. https://doi.org/10.1177/0263775820938057.

Diefallah, Mariam. 2020. "I Come from El Salam: Mahraganat Music and the Impossibility of Containment." *Jadaliyya*, August 25. https://www.jadaliyya.com/Details/41601/I-Come-from-El-Salam-Mahraganat-Music-and-the-Impossibility-of-Containment.

Dessouky, Nermin. 2020. "Highway Mania: Snapshots of Cairo's Sociopolitical Contradictions." *Arab Urbanism*, January. https://www.araburbanism.com/magazine/highway-mania.

Elshahed, Mohamed. 2020. "Demolitions and the Urgency of Architectural History in Egypt." *Platform*, September 7.

https://www.platformspace.net/home/demolitions-and-the-urgency-of-architectural-history-in-egypt.

Elyachar, Julia. 2010. "Phatic Labor, Infrastructure, and the Question of Empowerment in Cairo: Phatic Labor." *American Ethnologist* 37, no. 3: 452–64. https://doi.org/10.1111/j.1548-1425.2010.01265.x.

———. 2014. "Upending Infrastructure: 'Tamarod,' Resistance, and Agency after the January 25th Revolution in Egypt." *History and Anthropology* 25, no. 4: 452–71. https://doi.org/10.1080/02757206.2014.930460.

Engelmann, Sasha. 2015. "Toward a Poetics of Air: Sequencing and Surfacing Breath." *Transactions of the Institute of British Geographers* 40, no. 3: 430–44. https://doi.org/10.1111/tran.12084.

Glissant, É. 1997. *Poetics of Relation.* Ann Arbor: University of Michigan Press.

Graham, Stephen. 2016. *Vertical: The City from Satellites to Bunkers.* London and New York: Verso Books.

Harvey, Penelope, Casper Jensen, and Atsuro Morita. 2019. *Infrastructures and Social Complexity: A Companion.* London: Routledge.

Kaplan, C. 2018. *Aerial Aftermaths: Wartime from Above.* Durham, NC: Duke University Press.

Khalili, Laleh. 2020. *Sinews of War and Trade: Shipping and Capitalism in the Arabian Peninsula.* London and New York: Verso.

Lancione, Michele, and Abdoumaliq Simone. 2020. "Bio-austerity and Solidarity in the COVID-19 Space of Emergency—Episode 2." *Environment and Planning D: Society and Space.* March. https://www.societyandspace.org/articles/bio-austerity-and-solidarity-in-the-covid-19-space-of-emergency-episode-2.

Larkin, Brian. 2013. "The Politics and Poetics of Infrastructure." *Annual Review of Anthropology* 42, no. 1: 327–43. https://doi.org/10.1146/annurev-anthro-092412-155522.

Lindsey, Ursula. 2017. "The Anti-Cairo." *Places*, March. https://places-journal.org/article/the-anti-cairo/.

Marji, Noor. 2020. "Extended Steel Reinforcement on Amman's Rooftops." *Arab Urbanism.* https://www.araburbanism.com/tafseela/en/extended-steel-reinforcement-on-ammans-rooftops.

McCormack, Derek P. 2015. "Envelopment, Exposure, and the Allure of Becoming Elemental." *Dialogues in Human Geography* 5, no. 1: 85–89. https://doi.org/10.1177/2043820614565875.

———. 2018. *Atmospheric Things: On the Allure of Elemental Envelopment.* Durham, NC: Duke University Press.

Mitchell, Timothy. 2002a. "Dreamland." In *Rule of Experts: Egypt, Techno-Politics, Modernity*, 272–304. Berkeley: University of California Press.

———. 2002b. *Rule of Experts: Egypt, Techno-Politics, Modernity*. Berkeley: University of California Press.

Moore, Clement Henry. 1994. *Images of Development: Egyptian Engineers in Search of Industry*. 2nd ed. Cairo: American University in Cairo Press.

Mossallam, Alia. 2014. "'We Are the Ones Who Made This Dam "High"!' A Builders' History of the Aswan High Dam." *Water History* 6, no. 4: 297–314. https://link.springer.com/article/10.1007/s12685-014-0114-6.

Nassar, Aya. 2019. "Spaces of Power: Politics, Subjectivity and Materiality in Post-independence Cairo." PhD diss., University of Warwick, Coventry.

———. 2020. "To Stand by the Ruins of a Revolutionary City." *International Journal of Middle East Studies* 52, no. 3: 510–15. https://doi.org/10.1017/S0020743820000689.

New Arab. 2020. "Egypt Parliament Ridiculed for National Security Debate about 'Kites' Being Potential Spy Equipment." *The New Arab*, June 28. https://english.alaraby.co.uk/english/news/2020/6/28/egypt-parliament-ridiculed-for-security-debate-on-kites.

Nieuwenhuis, Marijn. 2014. "The Terror in the Air." Open Democracy, December 21. https://www.opendemocracy.net/en/terror-in-air/.

———. 2018. "Atmospheric Governance: Gassing as Law for the Protection and Killing of Life." *Environment and Planning D: Society and Space* 36, no. 1: 78–95. https://doi.org/10.1177/0263775817729378.

Pettit, Harry. 2019. "The Cruelty of Hope: Emotional Cultures of Precarity in Neoliberal Cairo." *Environment and Planning D: Society and Space* 37, no. 4: 722–39. https://doi.org/10.1177/0263775818825264.

Prestel, Joseph Ben. 2017. *Emotional Cities: Debates on Urban Change in Berlin and Cairo, 1860–1910*. 1st ed. Emotions in History. Oxford and New York: Oxford University Press.

Reuters. 2020. "Egypt Loosening some Lockdown Restrictions for Ramadan; Coronavirus Toll Rises." Reuters, April 23. https://www.reuters.com/article/uk-health-coronavirus-egypt-idUKKCN2252BL.

Secor, Anna. 2013. "2012 Urban Geography Plenary Lecture Topological City." *Urban Geography* 34, no. 4: 430–44. https://doi.org/10.1080/02723638.2013.778698.

Selim, Adham. 2015. "Capital Cairo: A Regime of Graphics." *Failed Architecture*, October 29. https://failedarchitecture.com/capital-cairo-a-regime-of-graphics/.

Shawkat, Yahia. 2020. *Egypt's Housing Crisis: The Shaping of Urban Space.* Cairo: American University in Cairo Press.

Shehta, Alsayid. 2020. "Al-mawt 'ala ginah tayyara waraq." *Youm7*, July 4. https://www.youm7.com/story/2020/7/4/%D8%A7%D9%84%D9%85%D9%88%D8%AA-%D8%B9%D9%84%D9%89-%D8%AC%D9%86%D8%A7%D8%AD-%D8%B7%D9%8A%D8%A7%D8%B1%D8%A9-%D9%88%D8%B1%D9%82/4860382.

Silver, Jonathan. 2014. "Incremental Infrastructures: Material Improvisation and Social Collaboration across Post-colonial Accra." *Urban Geography* 35, no. 6: 788–804. https://doi.org/10.1080/02723638.201 4.933605.

Simone, Abdoumaliq. 2004. "People as Infrastructure: Intersecting Fragments in Johannesburg." *Public Culture* 16, no. 3: 407–29.

Sims, David. 2014. *Egypt's Desert Dreams: Development or Disaster?* Cairo: American University in Cairo Press.

Squire, Rachael. 2016. "Rock, Water, Air and Fire: Foregrounding the Elements in the Gibraltar–Spain Dispute." *Environment and Planning D: Society and Space* 34, no. 3: 545–63. https://doi.org/10.1177/0263775815623277.

Stewart, Kathleen. 2007. *Ordinary Affects.* Durham, NC: Duke University Press.

Weizman, Eyal. 2007. *Hollow Land: Israel's Architecture of Occupation.* London and New York: Verso.

Zalewski, Marysia. 2013. *Feminist International Relations: Exquisite Corpse.* Interventions. London and New York: Routledge.

15

THE CURIOUS CASES OF THE DISAPPEARING MAIDS
MOBILIZATION AND PRECARITY AMONG FOREIGN
DOMESTIC WORKERS IN CAIRO

SABRINA LILLEBY

Introduction

In an online forum where employers in Cairo discuss their former
and current domestic workers, yet another woman rants on about her
maid, who has seemingly vanished into thin air after being employed
by her mother for only a few weeks. Scornfully, she writes that "she
is very manipulative, and she lied. She told my mom she will leave
for thirty minutes and took her bag. She left all her clothes at home,
and the driver dropped her off at her building. One, she doesn't live
there. Two, she got in a car with a random man and left. Third, she
sent my mom a message saying she isn't coming back." The employer's daughter then shares a copy of a passport where we can read that
her mother's previous maid hailed from the Philippines, where she
was born in 1989. Her name is Joy, but she looks anything but joyful.
Later in the post, it is revealed that Joy arrived by way of a broker who
received $500 under the promise that Joy would stay for two years,
working for the family. Pondering her disappearance, an outsider
might have felt worried that the young woman's safety had been compromised, but this is a common story on this forum, and no one raises
any concerns in the ensuing discussion. Instead, the post simply joins
an archive of blurry passport snapshots and descriptions of maids who
have suddenly packed their bags and left, sometimes under the dark
of the night.

Another family struggling with a high turnover of maids is that of Rania's in-laws. They live in a large hillside mansion on the outskirts of Cairo.[1] When you sit by their pool, you can see the sprawl of the city all the way to the Pyramids. Rania and her husband live here with his parents while waiting for their new villa in Sheikh Zayed to be completed. Sipping fresh juice that arrived on a little tray, Rania describes how the family of four usually employs an even larger number of workers to cook, clean, garden, and drive them around town in one of their cars. Her mother-in-law is the one responsible for the management of the house and all its staff. Rania explains how several foreign maids have taken off in the middle of the night and left her mother-in-law "alone" to manage the massive house.

When discussing the most sought-after domestic workers in Cairo, "the Filipinas," Rania places the mystery of the disappearing maids in an economic language where the world is organized according to supply and demand. She suggests that "there is such a high demand for Filipinas that they quit all the time. They don't even bother to tell their employers." This economic rationalization would indeed have made sense had the change of employment been accompanied by a salary increase. Yet the labor market in Cairo is organized in such a way that these workers can rarely, if ever, expect a higher salary when they quit, and they usually lose several days or weeks of income in the process. Still, this endless dance continues, and as a relative outsider one is at a loss to understand why it endures. The question then becomes "Why do domestic workers leave at such a high rate?" Perhaps even more interestingly, why do the same employers hire new workers over and over again? The answer lies in the very fact that a certain way of life in middle- and upper-class homes in Cairo—a way of life celebrated as modern, civilized, and urban (see Elshahed's, El-Husseiny's, and Sinno's contributions to this volume)—is wholly dependent on these maids. Domestic workers are crucial components in assembling these family homes as sites of tradition and affection. When workers leave, their departure acts as an inaudible form of protest. This form of labor politics does not necessarily improve wages, but lays bare the reliance on a group of workers that effectively make everyday middle-class life function. Furthermore, a racialized hierarchy exists, in constant tension with these everyday labor protests. From the vantage point of domestic work—in this market organized according to racialized and gendered hierarchies—we can understand something about global economic processes and the ways in which workers practice labor politics within and against them (Singerman and Amar 2006).

Changing Labor Relations and the Arrival of "Modern-day Slaves"

These introductory paragraphs portray an emerging form of labor relations in Cairo very different from that of the past. Currently middle- and upper-class urban households are moving away from what was for centuries common practice. Earlier, the convention among the urban wealthy was to bring girls from the countryside, as young as seven or eight years old, to do domestic work in the city (Ahmed and Jureidini 2010). The arrival of these girls usually marked the beginning of lifelong relationships involving mutual responsibilities of unequal care for each other that extended beyond the mere exchange of money. Everyone involved was part of larger social networks, and roles were often implicitly understood. For instance, the cook who works for Rania's mother today began as a chambermaid for her at only ten years old. Today, she still travels several hours on crowded public transport all the way from Fayoum (an oasis outside of Cairo) once per week to cook for the family. She has now worked for that family in one capacity or another for over fifty years. Many urban families appreciated employing these young and inexperienced workers because they arrived on their doorsteps as "blank slates" ready to be molded into skilled and loyal workers. But this loyalty was expected to be reciprocal; it meant that it was also quite difficult to let someone go.

In Cairo today, these women are certainly still part of the workforce but find themselves competing with and complementing a whole set of new actors. With the intense rural–urban migration in Egypt over the last half a century and the urban sprawl of the city itself into previously rural land, most domestic workers today come from popular-class (*sha'bi*) neighborhoods. But now Cairene families do not only employ workers from Egypt but also from other African countries and Asia. The second-largest group of domestic workers after Egyptians are women who come from sub-Saharan Africa, while those coming from Asian countries such as the Philippines, Indonesia, and Sri Lanka constitute only a small portion (Thomas 2010). Unlike countries in the neighboring Gulf, Egypt is a sending country in the world of labor migration. Due to its sizable population and relatively high level of poverty, a significant proportion of Egyptian families include one or more men who work either seasonally or full time in the Gulf. While Egyptian migrants abroad are largely men, a very different group of migrants come to Egypt from other countries. Though Gulf countries and Lebanon are famous for their *kafala* (sponsorship) laws that facilitate the import of labor, the current legal framework in Egypt makes it almost impossible to obtain a work permit for foreign domestic workers. As a result, most workers operate on expired visas or refugee documents without a legal work permit. This means that these workers cannot rely on unions, organizations, or state institutions when negotiating salaries or work conditions, or appeal to them when they need protection. This inability to benefit from rights as citizens or workers ostensibly adds a certain level of precarity, yet it is not unlike many Egyptian domestic workers who also work without contracts or any legal protection. While non-Egyptian maids/domestic workers face many challenges, while working in Egypt they do not experience, in most cases, the kind of extremely limited mobility that their colleagues working in the Gulf experience. Employers in Egypt rarely hold onto passports of foreign domestics, as is commonly done in the Gulf.

Migrant domestic workers in the Arab world have received international media attention under headlines where the words "maids" and "slaves" appear on the same line. Human rights organizations also deploy this attention-grabbing strategy. In these articles and reports, countries, ethnicities, and religions tend to conflate; Saudi Arabia and Lebanon become the entire "Middle East" while state-sanctioned Hanbali jurisprudence turns into Islamic law. In a region already struggling with negative publicity, the effect is an oversimplification of a complex global division of labor that renders the Arab world an exception to a historical moment. This rhetoric makes it appear as if the conditions facing these workers belong to a bygone era where the Arab world is trapped in the Middle Ages. Accordingly, these countries simply need to "catch up" so that the exploitation and injustice may finally vanish. This obfuscates the various ways in which workers, despite living and working under highly precarious conditions, practice alternative labor politics (De Regt 2010). Of course, during my many conversations with domestic workers, I have also been privy to atrocious stories about violent and wretched conditions that cannot and should not be glossed over. However, these stories, I argue, do not belong to a feudal past, but are rather part and parcel of labor conditions contemporaneous with the rest of the world. Instead of assuming Cairo to be an exception in the contemporary world, I show how dynamics that can be observed here can also be observed elsewhere in the urban global south, particularly in regard to domestic work.

"They Are Here to Work"

Commonly, middle- and upper-class employers express a desire to hire "modern workers"—autonomous persons who can operate modern-day appliances without many directions or much oversight. However, they rarely pay workers in accordance with what one might expect in a modern meritocracy, if such a thing exists. The determining factor for someone's salary is *not* years of experience, education, skill level, or previous training. Instead, the domestic work market is one where pay is determined by nationality in a complex hierarchy. For example, a Ugandan woman can expect around $50 more per month than her Nigerian colleague, and both the Ugandan and Nigerian workers can expect more than those from Sudan. It is the workers from Asia that are paid the most while Egyptians and Sudanese are paid the least. This means that an inexperienced Filipina domestic worker can still expect to be paid hundreds of dollars more than her colleague from South Sudan with many years of experience under her belt. While much of the literature on domestic work in other locations depicts labor as being imported from other countries because of its relative cost effectiveness, it is interesting to note that in Egypt, workers from within Egypt receive the worst pay. This dynamic begs the question: why will employers go to such length to find and hire foreign workers when there are fewer of them, and they get paid more? Employers attribute this preference for foreign labor to what they claim to be divergent skill levels among the different nationalities. Although this racialization itself is itself quite striking, I wish to suggest an alternative analysis to explain this preference for foreigners.

What quickly became apparent through my research was that the employers who considered themselves "liberal" and "modern" were likely to feel incredibly uncomfortable with the daily disciplining of Egyptian workers, whether they hailed from popular-class neighborhoods in Cairo or the Egyptian countryside (Bhatt et al. 2010). Employers described them as unruly and unmanageable. For them, there is always that potential sick uncle in need of surgery or the son collecting money for his upcoming wedding. This negative view was causally expressed with the idiom *'uqdat al-khawaga* (foreigner complex), comparing them to subpar Egyptian merchandise. This expression is used when purchasing manufactured goods such as electric appliances. Retailers will claim that items assembled in other countries are superior to the domestic ones. Little explanation is given since seemingly everyone agrees that products assembled in Egypt are fundamentally unreliable. Just as many see domestically produced commodities as inherently defective, Egyptian workers are perceived as lazy and troublesome. Employers accuse them of sloppy cleaning practices and of cutting corners, preferring to drink tea and share gossip instead of working. Egyptian workers are understood as inhabiting a bygone mentality and unable to perform in an era governed by rationality and professionalism.

Among employers, when asked why they would rather employ Filipina workers instead of someone from Sudan or Egypt, they answer that "you don't have to tell them what to do" and "they are here to work." Both these statements were repeated during multiple conversations with employers, and they are indicative of the perceived difference between the groups. Filipina workers are perceived as the quintessential self-governing employees. Employers understand the relationship with them as different from the one described above, where one becomes entangled in long-term—even lifelong—relationships of obligation. It is not based on personal knowledge or trust, but instead on their skilled abilities to govern themselves, acquired through training. Interestingly, I was twice told that Filipina women even dust the leaves of plants without being asked. The image of the Filipina as someone who does not need to be disciplined, but rather someone who disciplines herself, is not only present in Cairo but belongs to a global trope. It is an "export commodity" partially created by the Philippine government, which has named their young women working abroad their "new national heroes" (Pande 2013). In the Philippines, the "Technical Education and Skills Development Authority," which operates under the Philippine government, gives licenses to training centers who certify young Filipina women in the skills required as maids.

But in Cairo, the preference for foreigners cannot only be attributed to a few weeks or months of this training in the Philippines since many Egyptian maids have decades of experience. Instead, I wish to draw attention to how Filipinas are assumed to be alone in Cairo; Egyptian workers, however, are deeply embedded in the local community (De Regt 2008). What I propose is that employers tend to covet those workers "marketed" as the least unruly. In effect, they are willing to pay a premium for an assumed docility—for the labor of women who are only "here to work." This view is amplified by media images of Asian workers in the Gulf and Lebanon, where human rights organizations and the media paint them as "modern-day slaves." This dynamic points to a particular racialization and feminization of labor where the young and docile, but also self-disciplining and self-managing, female body is highly sought after and worth an extra premium.

Labor Politics and Assembling Homes

I began this text with a tale of disappearing maids, but also promising a description of a precarious form of a labor politics. How do these domestic workers practice labor politics within the restrictive environment described here, and from where do they draw strength to carry on? The short answer lay in the simple words of Faith, a worker from Kenya, who one day stated bluntly, "They really need us, you know." This statement is reflected in the activity on the forum described in the introduction. For instance, after an employer "caught" a worker trying to take off without notice, she wrote in a comment aimed directly at African workers that "we hire you because we have no alternative, but most of you are lazy and have no idea about cleaning because you are used to live [*sic*] in tents." She and many of her fellow employers on the forum set lower salaries for African workers than Asian workers based on blatantly racist ideas such as the one laid bare in her statement. Yet despite this vulgar comment, the employer is also completely and fully reliant on these domestic workers to produce and maintain a home.

To meditate on this dependence, I use assemblage as a heuristic to move away from a description where the worker is simply understood as a "helper" of her female employer and completely at her mercy. Instead, I wish to rethink the site of the home and the crucial role the domestic worker plays in its composition as well as in middle-class identity construction. A home is constituted by a set of entities—humans, animals, and things—which may relate to each other through uneven relationships that make up this distinctive assemblage. Despite these uneven relationships of power, all agents participate in the creation of the assemblage, and it becomes more than merely the sum of its parts (Latour 2007). As such, the assemblage relies on all its parts in order to exist, and ceases to be once the parts are ejected. But the parts may be taken out of a given assemblage and function on their own or become parts of new assemblages (De Landa 2006).

In middle- and upper-class Cairene homes, the pivotal role the domestic worker plays in the making of homes becomes most apparent in her absence and from the vantage point of employers who are constantly searching for new workers. It is through "domestic work, homes are *made* and people *reproduced*" (Naïe 2009, 7). When a domestic worker leaves her job, she detaches from an assemblage, and every time she gets hired elsewhere, she joins in the creation of a new assemblage—a new home. Despite the constraints of the market and although they work without official documentation, workers' rapid change of employment demonstrates how they are not simply victims, but rather active subjects. When workers leave their jobs without warning, the employers do not lament the loss of that specific person, but rather feel frustrated over the fact that their homes cease to function. The departure of a worker causes a disruption in the everyday operation of the home. It is in this very important part she plays in the assemblage of the home that her power lies. Her labor power is revealed in the moment another home falls apart—is disassembled—by her departure. On the forum I refer to in this chapter, we see desperate employers daily looking for new workers as their previous ones have left. This is often, or usually, because their homes disintegrate without domestic workers. In her departure, the "subversive potential [that] is characteristic of the social force of all labor, ever indeterminate in its centrality—as a subject—within while yet against capital" becomes visible (De Genova 2009, 461). It is precisely here, in this navigation of everyday micropolitics, that we begin to see the contours of a different kind of labor politics suited specifically for these profoundly precarious labor conditions.

In this context, domestic workers are the crucial puzzle pieces that enable the production of the home and the stabilization of its function. In one household I visited, a divorced woman in her thirties chose to live with her own mother, who ostensibly helped her take care of her two children. But neither of the two women knew the kids' weekly school or homework schedules because this, like most child-rearing tasks, was performed by the nanny. One day the maid said she was leaving on vacation, going back to Uganda, but she never returned. When she failed to come back, the eight-year-old daughter began going to school without having completed her homework until the private tutor discovered it. Another example was provided by Faith, who described a home she had worked in where the maids frequently were tasked with checking the toilets for excrement to make sure they were always flushed. She laughingly added that "they don't even know how to go to the bathroom without us!"

In this study, men were conspicuously absent, and it was never even suggested that they might be involved with domestic work itself or with the management of domestic workers. Maids help middle- and upper-class households sustain a pretense of tradition and a notion of an Egyptian identity often embedded in a heteronormative division of labor. These are often the factors that distinguish a proper home. This construction of a traditional home is premised on the labor of women. Producing middle- and upper-class homes—particularly permeated by "Egyptian traditions" such as those exemplified by home-cooked and labor-intensive food and attentive care of children—is the job of women. However, in this case, the job is outsourced to other women from outside the family and often outside the country (Gutiérrez-Rodr guez 2010). As a result, domestic workers aid in the specific identity construction of middle- and upper-class women since the work of the former allows the latter the freedom to simultaneously inhabit "traditional" and "modern" roles, while women of other classes and races take care of many of the tasks that produce a traditional home.

The Egyptian family cannot be regarded as a bastion of "tradition" since many middle- and upper-class families do not in fact rely on "traditional forms" of labor organization. As previously mentioned, these employers attempt to avoid the explicitly intimate yet unequal relationships that were so prevalent in the recent past. Still, they value docile workers. That is why employers are willing to pay a premium for someone who can "manage their own docility." Thus, they willingly pay higher salaries to foreigners, and specifically Filipinas, because they are perceived to be the least "troublesome."

But interestingly, although they are described as the most compliant, Filipina workers are just as often—if not more often—attacked on the forum for leaving too quickly and without notice, even more often than their Sudanese, Ethiopian, and Nigerian colleagues. These frequent attacks verify that this racial hierarchy of supposedly skilled and unskilled workers based on nationality alone is mainly fictitious. Most employers do not seem upset that a specific worker quit after they had developed a personal relationship with that person. They rarely know their employees' family names or from which city or town they had come, but they are acutely aware of their nationality and race (if they come from the African continent). This, then, becomes a point of attack, as employers note that Filipinas are liars who claim to be docile only to leave without notice, or African workers are uncivilized and live in tents (reproducing memes that have been popular in Egyptian media and cinema since the mid-twentieth century, at least, according to Elsaket, this volume). The comments on the forum show how unimportant it is to employers whom they currently employ. Their concern is simply that someone is there to perform the function of care with the least possible opposition. That is perhaps why employers seem the most outraged when Filipina workers leave because, in the racial hierarchy, they are thought of as precisely the most docile, and therefore receive the highest salaries.

In contemporary Cairo, upper- and middle-class families prefer to hire female workers who they assume will manage themselves quietly and efficiently. Their hope is that these workers are sufficiently detached from the social fabric of Cairene society and less likely to stage outright forms of protest. The better a worker is thought to fit into perceptions about particular national groups, the more she is paid. The Filipina worker is paid the most because she is referred to as the "most skilled." What belies this description is the actual meaning of *skill*, because it refers to her apparent ability to manage herself without protest and belligerence. However, the Filipina is not actually docile. Her forms of protest merely take a different shape: an act of refusal. Just like her other foreign colleagues, she perpetually changes jobs and thus dissolves the assemblage that is her employers' home; she leaves in the middle of the night or when she goes out to buy groceries. Middle- and upper-class households in Cairo are completely reliant on domestic workers to sustain their homes as sites of both modernity and tradition. This can be heard from employers who say it is virtually impossible to "manage" without a maid and give excuses for why they hire new maids over and over again, although vexed by those who have already left. This is where the power of the worker can be found. When she leaves, she can break up a home and an entire way of life. This is labor politics under highly precarious conditions outside the purview of legality and legal rights.

Notes

1   I use pseudonyms throughout this chapter except for comments made on public forums.

Works Cited

Ahmed, Y., and R. Jureidini. 2010. "An Exploratory Study on Child Domestic Workers in Egypt." Cairo: Terre des Hommes, Cairo, and The Center for Migration and Refugee Studies, American University in Cairo.

Bhatt, A., M. Murty, and P. Ramamurthy. 2010. "Hegemonic Developments: The New Indian Middle Class, Gendered Subalterns, and Diasporic Returnees in the Event of Neoliberalism." *Signs* 36, no. 1: 127–52.

De Genova, N. 2009. "Conflicts of Mobility, and the Mobility of Conflict: Rightlessness, Presence, Subjectivity, Freedom." *Subjectivity* 29, no. 1: 445–66.

De Landa, M. 2006. *A New Philosophy of Society: Assemblage Theory and Social Complexity*. London: Continuum.

De Regt, M. 2008. "High in the Hierarchy, Rich in Diversity." *Critical Asian Studies* 40, no. 4: 587–608.

———. 2010. "Ways to Come, Ways to Leave: Gender, Mobility, and Il/legality among Ethiopian Domestic Workers in Yemen." *Gender and Society* 24, no. 2: 237–60.

Gutiérrez-Rodr guez, E. 2010. *Migration, Domestic Work and Affect: A Decolonial Approach on Value and the Feminization of Labor*. London: Routledge.

Latour, B. 2007. *Reassembling the Social: An Introduction to Actor-Network-Theory*. Oxford: Oxford University Press.

Naïe, L. 2009. "The Making of 'Proper' Homes: Everyday Practices in Migrant Domestic Work in Naples." *Modern Italy* 14, no. 1: 1–17.

"Maids Made into Slaves in the Middle East." n.d. http://www.huffington post.com/josie-ensor/maids-made-into-slaves-in_b_397648.html.

Pande, A. 2012. "From 'Balcony Talk' and 'Practical Prayers' to Illegal Collectives: Migrant Domestic Workers and Meso-level Resistances in Lebanon." *Gender & Society* 26, no. 3: 382–405.

———. 2013. "'The Paper that You Have in Your Hand Is My Freedom': Migrant Domestic Work and the Sponsorship (Kafala) System in Lebanon." *International Migration Review* 47, no. 2: 414–41.

Singerman, D., and P. Amar, eds. 2006. *Cairo Cosmopolitan: Politics, Culture, and Urban Space in the New Middle East*. Cairo: American University in Cairo Press.

Thomas, C. 2010. "Migrant Domestic Workers in Egypt: A Case Study of the Economic Family in Global Context." *American Journal of Comparative Law* 58, no. 4: 987–1022.

16

CRUISING ETHICS IN CAIRO
QUEER STREET SOCIALITIES AGAINST FEAR REGIMES

AHMED AWADALLA

"Can I borrow your lighter?" I asked him. "You can borrow the lighter and its owner too," he replied.

Standing anxiously on the pavement one late night, holding out my cigarette, I uttered this pickup line. I was reassured by the openly flirty response. These were the first lines exchanged between me and Ashraf, a man around my age, who became a sex partner. Hanging out in front of a street café in downtown Cairo, we had made eye contact, but I was not sure if the interest was mutual. As he began to leave, a surge of courage propelled me to approach him.

Through recounting my encounter with Ashraf, I aim to weave intersecting narratives. I tell the story of public spaces in Cairo and how they have been appropriated by queer people. I trace the shifts in public space as informed by policing and security regimes. I analyze how state and non-state actors enforce modes of policing, and how class difference is identified and perceived. I reveal how modes of queer sociality subvert norms imposed by these repressive environments. Finally, I propose an ethics of queer sociality as a way of rethinking fear regimes. I continue my exploration of queer identities and intimacies, building on queer and affect theories and my observations as a psychosocial worker, but most importantly, on the lessons that I have learned from Cairo's streets.

Downtown Cairo: Looking Back from a Position of Exile

Exile is a severe form of punishment. Faced with the fate of exile from Sodom, and in the act of fleeing, Lot's wife ignored her husband's warnings and looked back toward her city. She immediately paid the price for this act of disobedience by being transformed into a pillar of salt. This can be read as a cautionary tale, a warning against dwelling in nostalgic sentimentality or, as Edward Said (2000) warns, in the tendencies of exiles to hold onto nationalisms. Turning into a salt pillar could be a metaphor for stagnation. For exiles—whose contact with the physical space they yearn for is severed—time can stop.

Writing about Cairo from my place of exile in Berlin is rife with risks. One is the risk of memory distortion caused by not being able to access emotional registers stored in places, smells, and sounds. Or simply by forgetting. Will I risk inscribing feelings of loss and mourning? I know that for me, Egypt grows more and more abstract with time. While writing can be seen as a form of abstraction, writing from exile feels like a bid against abstraction. In this light, I see Lot's wife looking back as an act of defiance. I reclaim nostalgia and reminiscence as an antidote to loss and fragmentation.

Not least because it begins in downtown Cairo, I chose to narrate my encounter with Ashraf. It is the part of Cairo that I identified with the most—where I lived, hung out with friends, danced, demonstrated, cruised, and was brutalized by the police. Cairo's Downtown is a vast space, rife with contested and conflicting meanings, as O. Khalil's discussion about thuggery in this volume illustrates. It is the relic of a golden era, evidenced by the colonial architecture and streets commemorating Egypt's symbolic embrace of a certain notion of modernity in the late 1800s and early 1900s. But as Hammad's chapter on sex work in early twentieth-century Cairo demonstrates, even during that so-called golden age, Downtown was a contested space, occupied by a series of heterogenous actors. The nostalgia for this bygone era is contrasted with the 2000s-era image of an overcrowded commercial center, marred by chaos, sexual harassment, and traffic jams. Downtown is at once a historic haven for intellectuals and artists, the space that hosted the 2011 revolution, and a heavily securitized and gentrified target for projects of progress and "beautification," as Ahmad Borham's thoughts on the Haussmannization of the city reveal (this volume).

Mirroring these clashing social visions of what downtown Cairo means, my early memories of the zone are at odds with each other. When I was growing up in Minya (Upper Egypt, in the south of the country), my family would visit Cairo during the summer holidays. I remember being grumpy while my mother went on extended shopping sprees in downtown stores, and my excitement at going to the cinemas to watch foreign movies—a luxury that wasn't available in my hometown. It took years to finally leave my hometown. Once I graduated from university, I packed and left for Cairo. My degree in pharmacy was my visa, opening the door to finding a job fairly quickly. In the early years, I lived in a family apartment in Bulaq Abu al-'Ila, on the upper margins of Downtown. It would take years for me to start living in downtown Cairo itself. Moving from Minya to Cairo was a tradeoff. I replaced the comfortable yet suffocating provincial familiarity with anonymity, freedom, and independence. I left the middle-class bubble in Minya for a working-class neighborhood in Cairo.

Leaving a small town for the capital is a common story of queer social mobility. I was another small-town boy whose mother would never understand why he left, seeking answers and seeking love, although I found more questions and endless encounters. As I sat in front of my PC in Minya talking to other queer people in chatrooms, the city and its encounters had been calling me. I had been dreaming of becoming part of "the society," a word used for the gay scene. But wasn't that the point of urbanization and big cities anyway, maximizing interactions with strangers, enabling us to find our niche?

Years before the revolution, I arranged an online date with a guy who suggested we meet in Tahrir Square. Soon I realized we were not alone. Other guys would greet him, sometimes from a distance; others came closer to examine the newcomer, me. One of them, when he learned I was new, asked me if had a membership card. He ululated, adding, "That is our password," while disregarding passersby. I was both shocked and exhilarated. This corner of Tahrir served as a social club, one that won't go into queer history.

In Cairo, I met queer people who cruised downtown streets, others who watched Derek Jarman films in fancy Nasr City apartments, and those who went to public bathhouses and hosted rave parties secretly in villas on the outskirts of the city. I realized that several "societies" existed: in the neighborhoods of Zamalek, Maadi, and Heliopolis, among others. The scene was divided along class lines. Some more privileged men cruised in their cars while others were on foot. I found the downtown scene the most democratic, representing a cross-class community. It was also a particular refuge for those who had left their small hometowns all over Egypt to follow the city's calling.

In the decade I spent in Cairo, the downtown scene—and how it was navigated by queer people—changed dramatically. In the years preceding the revolution, queer presence and visibility increased. What I observed at Tahrir earlier multiplied into several pockets of safety and sociability for queers. In downtown cafés, this presence was felt as more businesses explicitly accommodated queer people. Some owners and workers at these spaces were oblivious to their clientele. In other cases, they were friendly or belonged to the spectrum of queerness themselves. I remember at one point, I used to hang out at a lesbian-run café. Following the 2011 revolution, this scene thrived, at least temporarily. The security vacuum caused by the disappearance of the police from public spaces—as an odd form of retaliation by the police state against the population for having dared to launch a revolution—offered fresh air for queers to be themselves in public.

Exiles are often burdened with redefining their roots, culture, and identity. I often wonder about my choices, why I changed my career and joined the revolution. I have no simple answer, but I know that Cairo politicized me. I observed stark class differences, whether by virtue of living in a working-class neighborhood or through the encounters within the queer community. But this politicization also had its costs. I had to leave Egypt in 2014, amid a crackdown on political opposition, activists, NGOs, and the queer community. At that point, I had to finally admit to myself that the revolution had failed.

When I saw photos on Facebook of the refurbished Tahrir Square after government-led "beautification," I felt pain shoot through my heart. Some of these changes had already been palpable before I left Cairo. Many downtown street cafés were closed, and police checkpoints and intrusive searches had become commonplace. Apartments in Downtown were raided on several occasions as a result of neighbors snitching on those affiliated with the revolution. In more recent crackdowns, police have searched mobile phone records and contact lists to investigate political orientations, defiance, and "deviant" tendencies. This naturally poses more risk for queer people. Gay dating apps have been used to entrap queers in Egypt in recent years. Alongside the possession of items such as makeup, feminine clothes, or even condoms, the presence of these apps on one's phone is used as proof of "debauchery," the vague legal term under which queer people are prosecuted.

I am often told that our Cairo no longer exists. The spaces changed and many friends left, remain in prison, or lost their lives. It is more difficult for me to trace the changes that Downtown endured after I left.

Yet I find hope in the least expected of spaces: secret online groups for Egyptian queer communities. "How is Downtown now?" is a recurrent question in these virtual spaces. Not only are queer people connecting, debating, and sharing memes, but they are also exchanging security tips and anecdotes, warning each other of police presence. Virtual spaces serve to develop safety strategies for navigating public space. "How is Downtown now?" was for me not only a safety strategy but a glimpse of hope. Queer people of younger generations are not demoralized by the narrative of failure and shrinking spaces. They continue to appropriate the corners of downtown Cairo to create queer encounters. I think of a new generation of children that were only starting to grow up as we were demonstrating in Tahrir in 2011.

Maspero Triangle: A History of Violence

A few months after my encounter with Ashraf, I ran into him near Tahrir Square. He was on his way to get some hashish and asked me if I wanted to chip in. His destination was the nearby Maspero Triangle, which was considered a slum and an informal urban settlement adjacent to Tahrir Square (see O. Khalil, this volume). I hesitated for a minute, then agreed. A voice in my head was telling me that it wasn't the safest idea. I had only met Ashraf once; could I trust him? I followed my gut feeling and went ahead. We walked into the narrow yet busy streets of the triangle. He called someone's name out loud. A young man appeared out of a first-floor window. Ashraf took the money and went into the building. Thoughts rushed through my head as I waited anxiously for him. He returned, a smile on his face, and winked at me.

From the Maspero Triangle, we took a taxi to my place in the neighborhood of Mounira, my last residence in Cairo. I sat next to the taxi driver to give him directions while Ashraf rode in the backseat. Before I had a chance to warn Ashraf, the taxi drove right into the checkpoint at Lazoghli Square, next to the Ministry of Interior. The car stopped and a police officer approached us. He peered in, examining the two of us. "Are you two together?" he began, trying to determine whether he should treat us individually or collectively, as it is not uncommon for people to share taxis in Cairo. "Yes, we are together," I responded. Displeased with the answer, the officer demanded we step out of the car and show our IDs. "You're a pharmacist. Do you have any Viagra on you?" he asked with a smirk on his face. I was used to this question. Living in Downtown, I had gotten quite used to stop-and-searches. My ID stated my original job as a pharmacist, while, in fact, I was working at an NGO at that time.

Despite the half-serious questions by the police about Viagra or tramadol, my "official job" came in handy. It gave me respectability.

Carefully examining our IDs, the police officer called on two low-ranking officers standing nearby and ordered them to perform a body search. Although this wasn't the first time, I hadn't seen it coming. I was used to better treatment, given a middle-class background that was supported by my education and job, as stated on my ID. I tried to remain calm as the officer performed a body search. My heart pumped as I watched Ashraf getting body searched, sensing impending doom. I had affirmed that Ashraf and I were together, and the hashish was somewhere on his body, which could land us both in jail.

I recount my story of that moment with Ashraf since it unleashes a set of narratives. The Maspero Triangle, the space we went together to buy hashish, no longer exists. It was demolished in 2018 and its eighteen thousand residents were evicted and displaced in a process described by O. Khalil in their contribution to the present volume. The name of the area is derived from its triangular shape on the map, and because it lies next to the Egyptian State Radio and Television headquarters, named Maspero after a famous French Egyptologist.

The Maspero Triangle was the southernmost part of Bulaq Abu al-'Ila, a district that occupies a unique location in the heart of Cairo. Its location on the eastern bank of the Nile gave it significance over different periods of time. The story of the district goes back to the Mamluk era in the fifteenth century, when it served as Cairo's main port on the Nile River's commercial shipping lane. In the period of the ambitious rule of modernizer and state-builder Mohammed Ali (the largely independent Ottoman governor of Egypt from 1805 to 1848), Bulaq became an industrial hub, hosting metal and transport industries that helped Mohammed Ali build Cairo as an important world capital. He also established the first printing house in that neighborhood. These developments drew migrant workers from all over Egypt to the factories and workshops. The period has shaped the character and occupations of Bulaq's working-class population up to the present. Bulaq continues to host the metal industry as well as several newspaper headquarters.

The demolition of the Maspero Triangle has a long history. Bulaq was largely demolished by French troops in retaliation for its residents' revolt against Napoleon's occupation. The neighborhood was also badly affected by the 1992 earthquake. However, a slower process of demolition has taken place over the last few generations. President Gamal Abd al-Nasser (president of Egypt 1956–70) ordered construction of the state media headquarters in the area, and this project began a process of displacing residents to other parts of Cairo. It is said that during one of subsequent president Anwar al-Sadat's visits to the state media headquarters in the 1970s, he felt the surrounding industrial and working-class neighborhoods were an embarrassment, particularly because of their location opposite the affluent island of Zamalek, which hosts numerous foreign embassies. A bid to "beautify" the area began, with investors replacing the Bulaq residential quarter with luxury hotels and high-rise buildings at the expense of the original residents. In the 1980s and 1990s, several more towers were built on the eastern bank of the Nile, including the Ministry of Foreign Affairs and the World Trade Center. The bridge that connected Bulaq to Zamalek was removed in 1998.

I witnessed some of these changes in the area during my early years in Cairo. I lived in a small apartment that belonged to my grandfather in Ramlat Bulaq, the northern part of the neighborhood. The specter of eviction and relocation was a recurrent theme. Only a few meters away from our working-class quarter, the Nile City Complex was launched, containing a top-notch hotel, mall, and high-rise business towers. I remember that I could hear the techno music in my room when parties were held there for Cairo's elite. I also remember how the area was teargassed for several days when riots broke out in 2012 after a police officer shot dead one of the slum residents. The neighborhood was collectively punished, and many residents were arrested and sentenced while the media portrayed them as thugs.

There are, however, other layers to the demolition of the Maspero Triangle and its surroundings. In her work on affect and political participation in revolutionary Egypt, Dina Wahba (2020) reveals that the state's relocation policies for the district originate not solely in economic interests. During the 1977 uprising, or "Anti-IMF Bread Riots," some protesters took shelter in 'Ishash al-Turguman, another quarter of Bulaq, which prompted Sadat to relocate its residents, bulldoze their homes, and replace the space with a parking lot. Wahba argues that the disciplining of political dissent in Cairo and its popular quarters is crucial to understanding the eviction and relocation policies. This process intensified after the 2011 revolution, where the Bulaq Abu al-'Ila quarters played a crucial part in defying the state, aiding protestors, and confronting security forces—a process that was repeated in many poor urban areas of Greater Cairo. Examining the workings of power in Egyptian politics as it operates through affect, Wahba suggests that the affective register of "the Midan" was conducive to transformative political engagement.

These affects include dismantling fear, whether of the police state or for one's own safety. In addition, affective solidarities between different political backgrounds, genders, and classes were made possible.

Counterrevolutionary agendas can be viewed not just as a reactionary movement, but as the systematic deconstruction of the emancipatory potential of the revolution through attacks on this affective register. In other words, "Egypt's post-colonial state inherited the colonial mechanism of affective governance, building on the narratives of the *'baltagi'* (the thug) to govern the unruly masses and to break emerging solidarities and alliances" (Wahba 2020; Hassan, El Raggal, this volume).

This history sheds new light on what happened to Ashraf and me at the police checkpoint. When the police officer posed the question, "Are you two together?" it served different purposes simultaneously. It projected the classist gaze on the body of Ashraf, a working-class man. This is made possible through the security's discriminatory profiling based on education, work, mannerisms, ways of dress, and language use. The question reinstated fear and encouraged the betrayal of the alliance and solidarity between Ashraf and me. This prohibition of cross-class solidarity or intimacy (and the assumption that such solidarity is queer or a sex crime) is embedded in histories of controlling subjects and populations—a contemporary variation on the logic of divide-and-conquer. The Maspero Triangle's history of resistance dates to the colonial era. Similarly, our policing at the checkpoint carried colonial features. This resonates with James Baldwin's observation that "people are trapped in history and history is trapped in them" (1955).

Cruising Ethics: Rethinking Securitization

My encounter with Ashraf ended happily, by some miracle of chance or because Ashraf was smart about hiding his hashish. When the invasive body search ended, the police officer told us to go home. I didn't understand how we were so fortunate to escape arrest, but I remained silent in the taxi. When we got home, Ashraf showed me the secret pocket where he hid the hashish. We spent a few hours of intense intimacy before he left, and we became strangers again.

There is an essential reason why I chose to tell this story: it embodies the queer practice of cruising. Cruising is simply the means of searching for a sex partner, usually of the anonymous, casual, and one-time variety. Encounters can happen in public spaces—on the street, on public transportation, and in public toilets and parks— but remain largely hidden from the public eye.

In the previous sections, I described how queer people appropriate public spaces such as downtown Cairo and engage in modes of queer sociality that blur the binary between public and private. I examine these practices as I share Foucault's (1997) mistrust of "the tendency to relate the question of homosexuality to the problem of 'Who am I?' and 'What is the secret of my desire?'" He proposes instead to ask oneself, "'What relations, through homosexuality, can be established, invented, multiplied, and modulated?' The problem is not to discover in oneself the truth of one's sex, but, rather, to use one's sexuality henceforth to arrive at a multiplicity of relationships" (Foucault 1997, 135–36). Foucault is asking us to imagine how relations could be generated through queerness.

For many queer and non-queer people, the practice of cruising entails notions of risk and evokes fear. But cruising is also driven by desire for, intimacy with, and access to the other. Examining these affects is compelling, since "we are not just talking about emotions when we talk about emotions. The objects of emotions slide and stick, and they join the intimate histories of bodies, with the public domain of justice and injustice" (Ahmed 2014). I discuss these emotions in order to develop a queer feminist ethic of engaging with the other.

Cruising is motivated by desire to be with the other. Desire can always be exclusionary, but in cruising—determined by the chances provided by the public space—we are more likely to step beyond the rigid boundaries of our desires and the class and other social boxes we are shaped in. In other forms of social networking and contact (such as dating apps), we are more likely to be bound by barriers of class, age, (dis)ability, and so forth. Cruising is a specific mode of queer sociality, from which everybody can find counsel and intimacy, with any other social subject. Cruising creates intimate encounters otherwise not possible. But what are the terms of endearment spoken?

The queer theorist Tim Dean (2009) asks, "Why can't the strangers be lovers and yet remain strangers?" Dean hails cruising as a way of life and proposes erotic risk as a relational ethic. Our fear of the stranger involves a fear of strangeness that is only inflamed by the rhetoric of safety and domestic security pervading official political discourse. An example of this is the thug rhetoric in Egypt. Dean argues that in cruising, the contact with the other is "capable of becoming a source of pleasure, not only traumatic disruption. There is pleasure and satisfaction in risking the self by opening it to alterity—pleasure and satisfaction quite distinct from those to be found in securing the self around its familiar coordinates" (Dean 2009, 176). A psychoanalytic ethic insists that the other's strangeness be preserved rather than annihilated through identification. In this light, cruising is "not a way of sociality or sexuality, rather a way of how to treat the other and how one treats their own otherness" (Dean 2009, 212).

While my encounter with Ashraf ended in pleasure, I remember I also felt fear. When Ashraf left me alone to buy the hash in the Maspero Triangle, I was afraid. Part of it was from not knowing if he would come back. This terror has a personal history for me. Right after I moved to Cairo, I arranged a date with a guy at an internet café. He borrowed my mobile phone to call his father, stepped out, and disappeared forever with my phone. In some of my other encounters, mugging was combined with physical and sexual violence.

Our encounter with the other, as discussed in the previous section, is mired in histories of power. How do we not let our encounters with the other be based on circumspection and fear? And if the worst happens, how do we guarantee accountability when consent is broken, and acts of violence are committed? And if we have a desire for the other, how do we ensure that our desire for them is not occurring at the expense of the other? That is, how do we steer clear from intimacy being strictly fetishistic and alienating the other rather than connecting and sharing with them?

Fear serves a purpose. It keeps us alive. Left unchecked, it can eat our souls. Standing there in the Maspero Triangle, waiting for Ashraf, I was having flashbacks. I was hypervigilant. Through my work as a psychosocial worker, I learned that hypervigilance is a trauma response. I also learned that our perception of the world is influenced by the ways in which we heal from trauma, and that healing from trauma includes not allowing these events to shape us or how we engage with the world. Violence against queer people begins at home and extends to the public realm. Despite traumatic experiences, I refuse to let these experiences shape me.

I often wondered about the meaning of that situation in the taxi with Ashraf. Despite the fragility of our bond, I responded to the police officer, "Yes, we are together." At some point I felt guilt: did I make him more vulnerable? Guilt is not a conducive affect. I know that my impulse was to not deny him. I refused to disavow him to the police officer, before even thinking we might be jailed for the possession of drugs. Fear did not break my temporary alliance with Ashraf. He also didn't need my protection. Ashraf had been prepared for this situation all along.

Treading the murky waters of these themes around trauma, class, and violence is no easy task. Sharing these narratives can trigger extreme reactions. This is a dynamic I have observed in several debates. For example, I refer to the testimony authored by Salma El Tarzi, which was published amid a renewed #metoo debate in Egypt. Salma survived rape by two young men who broke into her apartment and stole her belongings. One of them turned out to be the son of the building's doorman/superintendent. After the arrest of the perpetrators, she reflected, "I would also like to discuss how state justice is selective based on power dynamics of class and race . . . I would like to talk about how this latest incident was the ideal rape situation to guarantee support and 'approval'—I was alone, in my own home, upper middle class, and the perpetrators working class. It wouldn't be the case if I was raped in a club or at a friend's house, if I was working class, if my rapist was my husband, or worse if my rapist was a woman. I am not only talking about the state, but also society, community, and even friends" (El Tarzi 2020). Salma provides an intersectional perspective on sexual violence.

Salma's widely shared and debated testimony became polarizing. El Tarzi was praised for her bravery and brutal honesty. However, the testimony also triggered harsh responses including accusations of class guilt, fetishizing the poor, and romanticizing poverty. That is what is at stake when we share personal narratives that refuse to center trauma in our response to the world.

Salma El Tarzi's attempt to analyze power dynamics led to her dismissal by the press and public as "traumatized" and therefore incapable of making political claims. Indeed, trauma can lead to identifying with the perpetrator and taking the blame on oneself. I learned from my psychosocial work about a modality to heal from trauma called mentalization, developed by the psychotherapists Peter Fonagy and Anthony Bateman. *Mentalization* is an imaginative mental activity which enables us to understand the mental state of oneself or others and to perceive and interpret human behavior. Effective mentalization involves maintaining the balance between self and other. Finding the balance between the desire to contact the other and maintaining intact boundaries is a skill and a behavior code embodied in the sociability practices of street cruising. Seeking intimacy with a stranger does not allow us claim to assimilate or obliterate them. It is not driven by superiority or guilt, but rather by openness to pleasure and an appeal for solidarity.

We need to be cautious about how discussions of sexual violence can reinforce classphobic arguments. This is a recurrent theme in debates around sexual violence in the public space in Egypt. Discourses around sexual harassment in Cairo reproduce working-class men as hypervisible objects, furthering their demonization, as Paul Amar shows. Egypt's security state deploys and revives the classphobic metaphor of the Arab street/slum to manage public space and political participation (Amar 2013, 201). We need to steer clear of reproducing "carceral feminisms," or criminalizing perspectives that reinforce control and policing of the other and their removal from the public space. These feminisms echo with a vision of a segregated, gentrified, and gated-community Cairo. Amar proposes strategies of critical desecuritization "instead of engaging in respectability politics or liberal depoliticized forms of gender activism." Critical desecuritization entails "tactics that turn the gaze back on the state to reveal the interests, histories and power relations that generate certain race, sex, and moral subjects and metaphors" (Amar 2013, 231–33).

In sharing my story with Ashraf, I argue that cruising represents a model of relational ethics and cross-class sociability. My analysis reveals the intimate scale of power relations, historical entanglements, and political subjectivities. These confessionals relate untold stories of queer sociality in Cairo. I question securitization practices by way of interrogating fear itself. Cruising bridges the gap between the body and the mind. What we do with our minds—be it mentalization or reminiscence—cannot be separated from what we do with our bodies and how our bodies move within space. I propose a cruising ethics of contact that can forge new solidarities and alliances in the face of fear regimes.

Works Cited

Ahmed, Sara. 2014. *Cultural Politics of Emotion*. Edinburgh: Edinburgh University Press.

Amar, Paul. 2013. *The Security Archipelago: Human-security States, Sexuality Politics, and the End of Neoliberalism*. Durham, NC: Duke University Press.

Baldwin, James. 1955. "Stranger in the Village." In *Notes of a Native Son*. Boston: Beacon Press.

Dean, Tim. 2009. *Unlimited Intimacy: Reflections on the Subculture of Barebacking*. Chicago: University of Chicago Press.

Foucault, Michel. 1997. "Friendship as a Way of Life" In *Michel Foucault: Ethics: Subjectivity and Truth*, edited by P. Rabinow, translated by R. Hurley et al., 135–40. The Essential Works of Michel Foucault, 1954–1984, vol. 1. New York: The New Press.

Said, Edward. 2000. "Reflections on Exile." In *Reflections on Exile and Other Essays*, 173–86. Cambridge, MA: Harvard University Press.

El Tarzi, Salma. 2020. "Things I Want to Talk About." *Mada Masr*, August 22. https://www.madamasr.com/en/2020/08/22/opinion/society/things-i-want-to-talk-about/.

Wahba, Dina. 2020. "Affect and Emotions in Counterrevolutionary Egypt." PhD diss., Freie Universität.

17

SOUTH SUDANESE REFUGEES AND COMMUNITY SCHOOLS IN CAIRO
A HOME AWAY FROM HOME

AMIRA HETABA AND ELENA HABERSKY

Introduction

Due to the historical and geographical intimacy between Egypt and Sudan, Cairo has become host to a substantial number of migrants and refugees from sub-Saharan Africa. As of February 2021, a little over 260,000 refugees and asylum seekers have been registered with UNHCR in Egypt, with Sudanese (49,378) and South Sudanese (19,853) forming the second and third largest communities among them (UNHCR 2021). This chapter analyzes one of the most essential struggles faced by the Sudanese and South Sudanese refugee communities in Egypt: providing their children with good quality education. Many families face difficulties in accessing the Egyptian education system and sending their children to public schools in their respective neighborhoods. Because of racial and class divides with the host community that manifest as targeted harassment and bullying, Sudanese and South Sudanese parents are more likely to send their children to local community-based schools, which often organically develop within their own social networks. In this way, parents and caregivers provide a safe space for education to take place apart from students' homes, and children have a minimized exposure to the safety concerns they encounter whenever they enter the public space. Utilizing one-on-one and group interviews with refugees and migrants from Sudan and South Sudan—particularly teachers, students, and parents in the working-class neighborhood of

Ain Shams—this chapter shows how these two communities adapt to the challenges they face in navigating the city by creating safe spaces where their children can study in the comfort of a familiar environment. In addition, this chapter draws on legal research and focus-group discussions conducted as part of a report on refugee entitlements in Egypt, published by the Center for Migration and Refugee Studies in February 2020 (Hetaba, McNally, and Habersky 2020).

Enjoying the Right to Education

According to the 1951 Convention Relating to the Status of Refugees (Article 22), asylum seekers and refugees are entitled to the same treatment as nationals in accessing primary education and are to be treated no less favorably than foreigners in general with regard to secondary and higher education (United Nations 1951). Thus, Sudanese and South Sudanese asylum seekers and refugees should have the right to send their children to Egyptian public schools under the same conditions as Egyptian children. However, the Egyptian government appended a reservation to this provision of the Refugee Convention, stating that Egyptian authorities retain the right to grant these privileges on a case-by-case basis. Nevertheless, other international human rights treaties[1] can fill this gap, as they are applicable to everyone, including asylum seekers and refugees. Under these treaties, Egypt is obliged to provide all children with free access to primary schools regardless of nationality. In practice, however, this obligation is unfortunately not fully implemented.

Under Egyptian law, foreign children may not attend Egyptian public schools, and their access to education is limited to private schools, which impose very high tuition fees. This rule was most likely established to counter the overcrowdedness of public schools and their lack of financial means by prioritizing the free access to public schools to Egyptian nationals. Only certain nationalities are granted an exception from this rule: Sudanese, Libyan, Jordanian, and Saudi Arabian students are allowed to enroll in public schools, provided they pay a tuition fee that is higher than the nominal fee Egyptian students pay. Children of Palestinians employed in or retired from the government, public sector, or armed forces in Egypt are also included in this exception according to the Ministry of Education's Decree No. 284 of 2014 (Ministry of Education, Republic of Egypt 2014). In addition, school officials sometimes allow South Sudanese students, although not directly referred to in the law, to access public educational facilities under the same conditions as Sudanese, though again provided they pay higher tuition fees than Egyptian students. Not many can afford these higher tuition fees, much less the fees for private schools, while those who have the necessary financial means to enroll their children in Egyptian schools often face problems during the registration process if they are unable to provide the required documents, such as previous school transcripts or a valid residence permit. Another common obstacle during the registration process is that school officials often mistakenly refuse to accept refugees' UNHCR blue or yellow cards as valid identification, as they are unaware that these documents are an officially acknowledged alternative to lost identification papers or passports. Furthermore, some parents have recounted that they were asked to pay an additional fee to secure the registration of their children, which can only be interpreted as a request to pay a bribe (Hetaba, McNally, and Habersky 2020).

Creating Community

Due to constant legal roadblocks and administrative problems, as well as numerous cases of harassment experienced by sub-Saharan refugee communities in Cairene society, many refugee communities have come together to organically form community schools (*Egyptian Streets* 2019). These schools are mostly located in ordinary apartment buildings in working-class and informal neighborhoods of Cairo. In order to accommodate all the children wishing to attend, day and afternoon shifts based on grade level are often arranged by the school administrators, many of whom are refugees themselves. Instruction for many of the communities is in English, though local languages and Arabic are also used.

A leader of the South Sudanese community living in the area of Ain Shams in Cairo provides an example of how these schools operate, based on his personal experience. The community school he works at offers education from grades one to seven, and had ninety-five registered students in the academic year 2019–20. Surprisingly, the community schools show a high level of structure and organization considering how few resources they have at their disposal. They follow the South Sudanese curriculum and cooperate with the South Sudanese embassy about scheduling exams. Thus, the community schools can offer the official exam that students in South Sudan take after secondary school to be accepted into university. The exam is also accredited in Egypt and enables students to be accepted into Egyptian universities, should they be able to afford the tuition.

Nevertheless, the school faces many problems. Some parents are unable to afford the yearly school fee of about LE 2,800 (approximately

$180). Due to financial restrictions, the school can only afford to rent a small apartment, where they hold classes in shifts to fit all the students into the four available rooms. Grades one to four attend school in the mornings, while grades five to seven take their turn in the afternoons. The school administration urgently needs assistance with paying rent in order to be able to accommodate all students adequately. While some local NGOs, such as Catholic Relief Services, assist with the fees of community schools, they can only cover half of the annual fees. Another difficulty lies in the lack of quality control in community schools. New schools open on a regular basis, and those running them are not always qualified to do so. Activists and observers argue for the urgent necessity of creating a supervisory body representing all community schools which could ensure that all the schools follow basic quality standards and offer the same curriculum, and that those opening a school have the necessary qualifications to do so.

Through the creation and maintenance of these community schools, it is evident that the agency of migrant communities leads to the schools becoming a subaltern counterpublic in Cairene society. The subaltern, as coined by the Italian Marxist Antonio Gramsci, is a term for a group of individuals who are under the hegemonic power structures of a ruling class. As these refugee communities have been pushed to the margins of Cairene society, it is only logical that they create spaces of belonging and security in which they can live and also educate their youth in the hope of a more prosperous future. The term "subaltern counterpublic," as first used by Nancy Fraser, refers to spaces "where members of subordinated social groups invent and circulate counter discourses to formulate oppositional interpretations of their identities, interests, and needs" (Fraser 1992). They can be spaces to escape racism, harassment, and violence of all forms—physical, social, or mental.

Not surprisingly, Egypt's government does not formally recognize these schools, leading to fears of shutdowns and a future of uncertainty. However, because the state attempts to control the educational system while providing no affordable alternative solutions, members of the South Sudanese refugee community, among others, have taken issues into their own hands. In this way, a Cairo residential apartment building comes to accommodate families of students, teachers, and staff as well as the original residents. Just as a family apartment can provide safety from the chaotic and oftentimes violent urban space, the classroom apartment can provide safety to learn, develop, and grow, away from the harassment of the streets. Instead of marking milestones of first steps and words, the apartments-turned-classrooms mark educational milestones.

Journey to Ain Shams

Walking from the Ain Shams Metro down the roads of the crowded working-class neighborhood, the influence of sub-Saharan African culture is apparent—from street goods displayed for sale, placed on bed sheets on the ground that can be easily snatched up in a hurry if needed, to women walking in their traditional and often colorful attire.[2] Many Sudanese and South Sudanese refugees call Ain Shams home because of its lower rents and the cheaper prices of everyday commodities. After an approximately ten-minute walk from the Metro, one of the authors enters an average apartment building off a main road. No signs or posters mark its use as a school. One flight of stairs opens to a landing where parents of young children are waiting in the principal's office, apparently to register their children for the upcoming school year, in the hope it will happen at all due to the COVID-19 pandemic. The single fan blows the hot air of the dusty and hot early October day, a reminder that it is very much still summertime in Cairo. After playing peek-a-boo with one of the small children who is hiding behind her mother's legs and under her long dress, the author is led up two more flights of stairs. There is no electricity in the stairwell, and the heat of the afternoon sun clings to everything. This floor is home to the classrooms, marked by long wooden benches and desks, although nothing is displayed on the walls. A teacher from another community school—a refugee himself from the Dinka tribe of South Sudan and a local community leader—introduces the author to the students and explains why she has come to their school. The students want to talk to her, but not in a group, as they do not feel comfortable talking about their issues in front of their peers. A smaller classroom next door is used for the interviews, and older students are called in to discuss their lives in this South Sudanese community school.

Paul Miranda's chapter in this volume describes the racism and violence Sudanese can face in Cairo, even while doing such simple tasks as going to school. This violence is highly gendered, as quickly becomes apparent in the students' testimonies. The first student I interview is twenty years old and is, at first, very shy. She discusses how the route to and from this community school is fraught with harassment. As she is the only South Sudanese student in her area of Ain Shams and has no friends to walk with her, she walks to and from the community school, fifteen minutes each way, by herself. She reports that she has been verbally harassed and grabbed at by Egyptian men on the way to school. She believes women are at a distinct disadvantage because they are often unable to physically defend themselves against those who harass them, predominantly men. While she believes her home and school are safe spaces for her, the route in between causes her daily anxiety, and sometimes she wakes up not wanting to go to school.

Another female student, eighteen years old, has had dogs set on her on her way to the school in order to scare her. While she also echoes the belief that school is a safe space, the school is not located in a safe area. Previously, Egyptians who live across the street from the school where the author now conducts interviews have entered with knives, complaining that the school is too loud and the students are making too much noise for a residential area. This confrontation has led to physical altercations between the teachers, attempting to defend the students, and the perpetrators. While this confrontation has rattled the young woman, she claims that school is life and there is nothing that could happen to force her to not go to school. While she has been living in Cairo for the past seven years, her parents remained in South Sudan, and she is trying to make the best of her situation and eventually intends to go back to South Sudan to help her people with the education she receives in these small classrooms.

A twenty-year-old male student also believes the area of the school is unsafe. He claims that Egyptian "hooligans," or street children, constantly barrage him with questions to provoke him and others, repeatedly asking where he is from, if he speaks Arabic, and why he looks the way he does. He usually ignores their advances, though sometimes he snaps and responds. He acknowledges that the school administration tries their best to protect the students, but there is no actual security at the school. When the school was attacked by Egyptians who live across the street, he says the administration didn't even bother calling the police because they knew the police would be unwilling to help them. He does feel lucky, though, as he can at least protect himself because he is a male. He knows his South Sudanese sisters may not be as lucky. Usually, the Egyptians who harass them, especially the males, are only after money. "Money is everything," he explains. "If you don't have money, you may be beaten in the street and left to die. It doesn't matter how much money you have; they will take whatever you have."

Through the words of these three students, one can see how this community school acts as a subaltern counterpublic in the public sphere. While there is not a counter discourse being created in this space per se, it is utilized by the community to escape the difficulties they face on a daily basis in the urban space of Cairo—namely, racism, which oftentimes manifests itself in violence. The students, especially, utilize their time in school to escape from the outside world that continually marginalizes them, whether through verbal and physical harassment or racist tropes on their journeys to and from the school building. Even though problems may arise within the school, it is a space for community, fellowship, and learning for a marginalized community.

Without Neighborhood Security

While the students generally feel safe at home and inside the school, interviews with parents reveal that they live in constant fear for their families, which is one of the main reasons that they send their children to a school organized and run by the community. One mother, who came with her children to Egypt in 2016, has faced constant issues since arriving in Ain Shams. When she first arrived, one of her sons was beaten up in the streets, so she had her older son walk with him to school for protection and she called them every day on the way to make sure they did not face any additional problems. She has also had issues with her Egyptian neighbors. One poured water on her baby when they were having an argument, and another time, her neighbors forced themselves into her apartment and started breaking the lights and other things. She called the police, but because she had let her residence permit expire, they didn't do anything, further marginalizing her and her family. Daily harassment on public transport makes her trip to and from work unbearable, and her Egyptian employer regularly withholds her LE 4,000 (approximately $255) monthly salary. She has tried to find new employment as a domestic worker, but has not been successful (see Lilleby's chapter for more on the racial hierarchization of the domestic labor market and the relative disadvantages sub-Saharan African women face there). To improve the situation for her children, she has tried to send them to Saint Andrew's Refugee Services for schooling, where they would receive a free breakfast, which she is currently unable to provide for her children. However, her son failed his end-of-year exam, even though he had never failed at school before. In addition, she has developed diabetes and cannot afford her medication. She views her situation in Egypt as impossible and insufferable.

Another mother, who has been in Egypt for twenty years, says that South Sudanese people face many problems in Egypt. She lives alone with her children and says people always try to look into her apartment windows to see what she is doing, making her feel unsafe in one of the only spaces where she has some semblance of privacy. Someone once broke into her apartment through a window while she was in the shower. She immediately told the landlord, but even the landlord is afraid of the intruder and their family. Her five children face problems every day, and she wants to return home to South Sudan. After twenty years, she says there is no way for her or her family to integrate into Egyptian life. She explained that the entire community's focus in Ain Shams is on the children because there is no security in the neighborhood. She suspects that her children have even started picking up bad habits from the Egyptian children on the streets, though she thinks this happens unconsciously and that they do not do it purposefully to make their parents upset. She related a story about how once, while her child was walking home with groceries along a main road, a microbus sped up and tried to hit him. Her son dodged out of the way, but dropped the groceries on the street, and the bus ran them over, resulting in the loss of their weekly groceries. This is just one problem of many that her family has had to deal with since arriving in Cairo in 2000.

Another mother has had issues with people entering her home, pretending to work with UNHCR, causing the entire community to worry that someone would use the one agency they trust will assist them to potentially harm them. In one instance, she let a man who said he worked at UNHCR into her apartment. He kept asking her questions he should have known from her file—who lives at home, how many children she has, her marital status. He was rude and kept telling her to talk faster because he was in a hurry. She had a feeling he did not work at UNHCR because he had a "creepy vibe" and refused to show her documentation from UNHCR. Because she was alone and afraid, she told him there were men at home, but they were asleep. He then said a microbus would come and take her entire family to the office for registration between 3:00 and 4:00 a.m, but she knew this was a lie. Scared, she said she was going to get an Egyptian neighbor because she couldn't understand his Arabic accent. He quickly left and never came back to her house. When the woman called the UNHCR to report the situation, they told her she must be lying because the story was too far-fetched. She had felt helpless and explained to the interviewer that some of the Egyptians who operate at high-level positions within NGOs whose mission is to assist refugees, including UNHCR, are not helpful. "How are we supposed to get help if they always think we are lying about our daily situations, which are extremely difficult?" she ended, exasperated from her retelling of the story.

Students and parents face relentless harassment, racism, and government neglect. These daily occurrences speak to the marginalization of the South Sudanese within both the Ain Shams community and Cairene society as a whole. It is such stories as these that have spurred the movement and organization among the refugee communities to create their own spaces for their children to have safe access to learning. This network of safety depends on the creation of the many community schools situated all over Cairo.

Educators with Scarce Resources

Two teachers, who are both members of the South Sudanese refugee community, also described the daily difficulties they face as teachers and members of that community. One teacher explained that her students do not have enough money to buy books and barely manage to pay the school fees, even with assistance from local NGOs, who pay half the price. If the students cannot pay the fees, the teachers cannot get paid. In addition, the school does not have enough money to provide the students with breakfast or lunch, and some of the students come to school hungry because their families do not have enough money to feed them multiple meals per day. For her female students, she wishes the school could afford menstrual products for the bathrooms, because some of them skip school when they have their periods because they cannot afford sanitary pads. These issues make her sad on both a professional and a personal level.

Another teacher wishes that his colleagues from all the local community schools could receive training on how to become better educators. He is not an officially certified teacher; rather, he does it because he is educated and knows that giving his time helps his community sustain the space to help themselves. He believes that training in pedagogy would enable the students to receive a better-quality education.

Through the examples of these two teachers, we can see how the community was able to come together to organize a space for learning and also succeeded in creating an environment of solidarity with the best interests of the students in mind.

While the South Sudanese community schools, families, and students encounter daily harassment and racism, inadequate funding, overall safety issues, and mental health issues, the local community schools—as reported by all the interview participants—offer a safe haven away from these daily hassles. While school and residential spaces have organically developed to compensate for a public sphere made unsafe by racism in Cairo, this created community space is preferable to the alternatives of expensive private schools or overcrowded and often unwelcoming public schools.

The Sudanese and South Sudanese refugee communities face a two-fold problem when attempting to access quality education in Egypt. First, their children's right to free and compulsory education is not upheld by Egyptian legislation. Therefore, it is urgently necessary to reform the regulations and to give all refugee children the possibility to attend public primary schools under the same conditions as nationals. However, even if this free access to education could be realized, the second component of the problem remains: the risk of harassment and discrimination experienced by students both on their way to and inside of public schools. If this part of urban life cannot be enjoyed without such hazards, the right to education can never be fully realized by refugee children. Only when navigating these public spaces becomes safe for the students will it no longer be necessary to resort to the community schools, which create an alternative safe and private space apart from the students' homes.

Notes

1   The International Covenant on Economic, Social, and Cultural Rights (ICESCR) obliges states to provide free compulsory primary education to all, regardless of nationality, and to make secondary and higher education generally available and accessible for everyone (ICESCR, Articles 13–14). But once again, exceptions can be made to these rights, this time through the concept of "progressive realization," which means that the ICESCR acknowledges that not all states are financially able to realize the rights stipulated in the Covenant at once. In addition, The Convention on the Rights of the Child (CRC) confirms that primary education has to be free and compulsory for all children (CRC, Article 28). According to international law, Sudanese and South Sudanese children should therefore have the right to access primary schools under the same conditions as Egyptian students, while Egypt may impose some restrictions on their access to secondary schools and universities. Regional legal instruments mirror this framework. The African Charter on Human and People's Rights and the African Charter on the Rights and Welfare of the Child both confirm that children are entitled to free and compulsory primary education.

2   One-on-one and group interviews were conducted at a local South
    Sudanese community school in a working-class neighborhood of
    Ain Shams. In total, fifteen students, seven parents, and three
    teachers were interviewed by one of the authors.

Works Cited

Egyptian Streets. 2019. "Two Young Egyptians Slammed for
    Humiliating South Sudanese Refugee Student." *Egyptian
    Streets*, November 17. https://egyptianstreets.com/2019/11/17/
    video-showing-south-sudanese-refugee-student-humiliated-
    sparks-anger/.

Fraser, Nancy. 1992. "Rethinking the Public Sphere: A Contribution to
    the Critique of Actually Existing Democracy." In *Habermas and the
    Public Sphere*, edited by Craig J. Calhoun, 109–42. Cambridge, MA:
    MIT Press.

Hetaba, Amira, Claire McNally, and Elena Habersky. 2020. "Refugee
    Entitlements in Egypt." Cairo Studies on Migration and Refugees,
    Paper No. 14. The Center for Migration and Refugee Studies,
    American University in Cairo.

Ministry of Education, Republic of Egypt. 2014. "Ministry of Educa-
    tion Decree No. 284 of 2014 (Concerning the Rules of Incoming
    Students to Egyptian Universities, Scholarships for Incoming
    Students, and Egyptian Students Studying in Egyptian Schools
    Abroad)." *Al-Jarida al-Rasmiyya*, July 7.

Organization of African Unity, African Commission on Human
    and Peoples' Rights, African Court on Human and Peoples'
    Rights, and the African Union. 1981. "African Charter on Human
    and Peoples Rights, 27th June 1981 (1520 UNTS 217, OAU
    Doc CAB/LEG/67/3 rev.5, UN Reg No I-26363), OXIO 370."
    https://opil.ouplaw.com/display/10.1093/law-oxio/e370.013.1/
    law-oxio-e370?rskey=WJ2Bgl&result=1&prd=OPIL.

Organization of African Unity. 1990. "African Charter on the Rights
    and Welfare of the Child (1990)." OAU Doc. CAB/LEG24.9/49,
    entered into force November 29, 1999. https://www.ohchr.org/en/
    resources/educators/human-rights-education-training/2-african-
    charter-rights-and-welfare-child-1990.

UNHCR (United Nations High Commissioner for Refugees). 2021.
    "Egypt Fact Sheet." Monthly Statistical Report, February 28.
    https://www.unhcr.org/eg/wp-content/uploads/sites/36/2021/03/
    Monthly_Statistical_Report_February_2021.pdf.

United Nations. 1951. "Convention Relating to the Status of Refugees." July 28. 189 UNTS 137 (entered into force April 22, 1954).
https://www.ohchr.org/en/instruments-mechanisms/instruments/
convention-relating-status-refugees.
———. 1966. "International Covenant on Economic,
Social and Cultural Rights." December 16. 993 UNTS
3 (entered into force January 3, 1976). https://www.
ohchr.org/en/instruments-mechanisms/instruments/
international-covenant-economic-social-and-cultural-rights.
———. 1989. "Convention on the Rights of the Child." November
20. 1577 UNTS 3 (entered into force September 2, 1990). https://
www.ohchr.org/en/instruments-mechanisms/instruments/
convention-rights-child.

18

ENTANGLED IN THE CITY
INTERSTITIAL AND QUEER URBANISM THROUGH THE EYES OF A SECOND-GENERATION NUBIAN

YAHIA MOHAMED SALEH

He sees it as home, but also as a place of diaspora and exile. It is where he managed for twenty-two years or so with the struggle to navigate risks, indulge, find safety, fight oppression, and experience identity crises, pride, exclusion, and freedom. It is where he lost and rediscovered himself countless times. Cairo is the city where Dahab was born and raised. Through his story, he will accompany us through contested territories within the greater Cairo region from Maadi to Faisal—passing through downtown Cairo. I write about a raced and sexualized body, and about the embodied experience from a position of constant exposure to the racializing gaze (as analyzed by Yancy 2008, 65).

Maadi, Revelation of In-betweenness
Joyous music accompanied the voice of the Sudanese legend Mohammed Wardi singing his broken heart out. From the car window along Cairo's Nile, Dahab daydreamed and wondered how a song about heartbreak could be so full of elation. This was one of Dahab's "self-moments" that took place every Friday on the way home to Maadi from the weekly family gathering on the western bank of the glorious river. Dahab was born to a middle-class Nubian family with working-class origins. As early as the age of six, he realized that borders, limits, and in-betweenness were going to be central to the formation and negotiations of his personality, identity, and ideology.

In more than one way, listening to Nubian and Sudanese music from a young age provoked concern in Dahab that he didn't know where he belonged. Living in a working-class neighborhood while sustaining a middle/upper-middle-class lifestyle made him nervous in his daily interactions with neighbors, who questioned his softness as a boy as well as his well-matched outfits. His desire to seek refuge in books instead of playing football in the street with other boys never passed without commentary from his neighbors and peers. The geography and Dahab's behaviors were a convenient match for very protective parents who wanted to maintain a distance between their middle-class kids and their working-class milieu, but also didn't want to come across as classist.

And while behaviors in conflict with normative forms of masculinity in his neighborhood did serve to inform Dahab about himself, much of his analysis came from an ethnic perspective. The area of Maadi and Hada'iq al-Maadi has emerged as one of the major Nubian clusters in Cairo, along with the neighborhoods of Abdin and Imbaba. Since the beginning of the twentieth century, many Nubians have moved to Cairo from Upper Egypt in hopes of a better life in the face of national "development" projects destroying their ancestral homes. The grandiose initiatives destroyed the main sources of their livelihood in the form of inundations following the construction of the Aswan High Dam, especially in agriculture, fishing, and trade. Cairo's Nubian urban communities became homes for a growing diaspora that faced the dilemmas of cultural assimilation with Egypt's predominately Arab population. The neighborhood of Maadi emerged in the early twentieth century as a prosperous suburban district some twelve kilometers to the south of downtown Cairo, on the eastern bank of the Nile. Maadi railways connected the suburb of Helwan to the capital. The neighborhood flourished at the same time that Dahab's ancestors' land was being erased by the construction of the Aswan Dam.

In a rapidly changing neighborhood, Dahab was always allowed to visit relatives who lived in the same area. He enjoyed playing in the street with his relatives' children, since his parents prohibited him from roaming the streets otherwise. His parents encouraged him to form friendships with other Nubians and to spend time with them in order to guarantee a certain amount of Nubian-ness in Dahab's life in the midst of the Cairene surroundings. Dahab's non-Nubian friends lived in the same building, assuring a shared middle-class way of life. Like many kids in the 1990s, in the course of growing up, Dahab and one of his non-Nubian friends, Maher, began to investigate VHS films that represent a gateway to pornography, sex, and sexuality. Maher managed to find a videotape that he and Dahab watched together many times before they had the urge to imitate some of the sexual acts together, which they did repeatedly.

Dahab recognized his attraction to males from a very young age. From the age of six, while he could not put it into words, he knew that there was something queer about him. The older he became, the more he understood the importance of and the relationship between safe spaces and freedom. School was the place where Dahab felt the most vulnerable. There he was bullied and picked on because of his skin color, his big nose, and his feminine curves. He tried to be a perfect student but did not always succeed. He developed one-sided feelings for class-mates and had his heart crushed by their cruel comments. The hours he spent with Maher, his Nubian peers, or the middle-class neighbors were the only moments he could partially be himself and explore his various identities. The streets of Maadi and Hada'iq al-Maadi were the places he first experienced both hypervisibility and invisibility. His childhood neighborhood was where he first grasped the informal aspect of surveil-lance in the public space, when relatives formed a network of informants and security agents to control his behavior indirectly. Securitization and surveillance in public spaces would be his lifelong antagonists.

Downtown: The Playground of Identities

The screech of the Cairo Metro entering the tunnel to Downtown sounded like a battle to Dahab, but it also brought him much happi-ness. Downtown Cairo, like Maadi, was a product of the colonial era, emerging in the 1860s as a result of Khedive Isma'il Pasha's eagerness to imitate Paris and showcase the progress achieved during his reign. Downtown represented a modernized Cairo, distinct from the colonial stereotype of a backward Orient (Ryzova 2015, 7).

Dahab experienced his own un-becoming along with downtown Cairo as it became a commercial and entertainment hub for lower-mid-dle-class families (Ryzova 2015, 13). Dahab's explorations included visiting the museums in Downtown, Old Cairo, and al-Gezira. These trips were an important ritual curated by his mother to assure their proper mid-dle-class upbringing. Downtown meant freedom, knowledge, and excitement. The boy could disappear and be anonymous in that space, where he could experiment with different versions of himself. It allowed him to see himself as an independent being beyond his family-dependent identity. Dahab's mother was very authoritarian, even in her ideas of how leisure time should be spent. There were no chances for anyone to grow out of her box. She was the first to actively securitize Dahab's identity down to the smallest details of his clothing and temperament. Downtown's posh, sophisticated architecture and the presence of a so-called cultural elite gave Dahab the room to escape this familial control, and his relationship with the neighborhood matured with time, during which his family moved from Hada'iq al-Maadi to Faisal, a lower-middle-class neighborhood in Giza, on the west bank of the Nile.

By the age of eighteen, Dahab had already come a long way in understanding and exploring his sexuality. During his years at university in the early 2000s, he and his friends took spontaneous walks downtown to buy school supplies or visit galleries, and they usually would stop for a moment on Qasr al-Nil Bridge. Dahab felt safe, surrounded by his heterosexual friends, and enjoyed playing a game in his head, guessing who might actually be gay. Downtown and Qasr al-Nil Bridge were known for having a noticeable presence of the queer community. They frequented the adjacent cafés and bars, animated by late-evening walks and people cruising in their cars.

Dahab's many years at university, where he studied art, justified spending much of his time in the downtown area. He would occasionally walk alone, when he enjoyed flirtatious eye contact with other men. During that time, however, he didn't dare to escalate such interactions. Loneliness was not new to Dahab. Since childhood, he had managed to savor his loneliness by watching people from his balcony overlooking their little street in Hada'iq al-Maadi, and now he found himself two new vantage points for that activity: the bridge and Tahrir Square. He watched people, imagining their souls, feelings, and hidden dramas. He watched for a potential friend, ally, enemy, sexual liaison, or perhaps lover. He created imaginary lives where he and everyone could just be as they wanted to be. These worlds didn't remain imaginary for long. The virtual relationships he started to have on the internet gave him the chance to talk to other queer people. He knew that they existed and eventually became brave enough to meet some of them in a familiar setting where he felt anonymous enough to be safe.

Dahab spent the next ten years of his life walking from Tahrir Square to Talaat Harb, down through Mohammad Sabri Abu 'Alam Street to sit in one of the Boursa cafés with his queer friends, and walking down Mahmud Bassiuni to sit in al-Tak'iba Café. He also hung out at the Townhouse Gallery, one of Downtown's prominent cultural centers. Dahab didn't know then that one day all his worlds would melt together amid revolution and counterrevolution, and that he would see death in the streets of Downtown and run from it repeatedly. He didn't know that some of his queer and non-queer friendships that started there would cross international borders. To develop all these selves—political, Nubian, queer, sexual, and intellectual—separately and together, not only fostered his understanding of himself but established a continuity from his childhood.

Faisal: The Emotional Backyard

While stuck in one of Cairo's eternal traffic jams entering Faisal Street, one notices the complex identity of this geography. The street—which was named, according to the residents, after King Faisal of either Iraq or Saudi Arabia—runs parallel to al-Haram Street and cuts through a socioeconomically diverse part of the city. Like downtown Cairo, al-Haram Street was initially constructed by Khedive Isma'il in the late 1860s to connect the capital to the Giza Plateau and to encourage an influx of touristic and elitist country residents. Both the roads and their neighborhoods developed rapidly during the late 1950s, hosting nightclubs and cabarets (Amar 2013, 87).

In the early 2000s, two major changes took place in Dahab's life: he started art school and his family moved to a neighborhood on Faisal Street. Dahab describes this as a new era of his life in one of the late-formed Nubian communities where many of Dahab's relatives lived. While participating in these networks of safety and shared ethnicity reflected an imaginary village of black and brown faces, this same proximity constrained his social behavior. However, he continued to spend time in Downtown, Dokki, and Zamalek. Dahab didn't want to invest himself emotionally in this new neighborhood, which served as both a container and a window to the future. Faisal became a place of privacy, where Dahab could close his bedroom door and study, belly dance, read, hide, and dream of different realities. It was clear to him that he didn't need to struggle to try to belong to a place he never chose. He had spent much of his childhood and teenage years trying to navigate and negotiate these relationships to place. His emotional dissociation with Faisal allowed him to attach to other neighborhoods and to people other than his family. And as Dahab detached himself from Faisal, he also put an end to an era of familial authority and control.

One night, coming home alone from Downtown after hanging out with some queer friends, while waiting on the platform for the Metro, Dahab felt a gaze and returned the eye contact. Dahab was unsure of his desire, ambivalent about whether he should respond or flee home. In his head, it was just another moment of possible connection that might not lead to further interaction. To his surprise, they got off at the same station, Faisal, and took the same microbus from the Metro to his home neighborhood. At that point, Dahab had mixed feelings and couldn't decide what to do. It was too close to home, not where he wanted such activities to happen. While considering his options, he felt a hand grab his and his heart start to pound. They walked together, flirting, although Dahab remained unsure of what would come of this exceptional encounter. Faisal, for him, was an ephemeral station in his life that he planned to leave behind. His relationship to the neighborhood was, in his eyes, reaching an end. The excitement of meeting someone who lived close by was overpowered by Dahab's middle-class temperament. Ultimately, his class preferences, combined with his determination to compartmentalize Faisal from the rest of his social activities, made him end the encounter with the man on the Metro.

The Home, the Maze, and the Revolution

Dahab's detachment from the Faisal neighborhood grew during the January 2011 Revolution in Egypt. During this extraordinary moment, downtown Cairo felt even more familiar to him due to his political involvement. Except for some scattered days that he spent with some friends from college in a coffee shop and a few nights he spent with his family, Dahab's relationship to Faisal concluded when he moved into a shared apartment downtown.

For some in Cairo, self-actualization takes a certain amount of hustle to survive and thrive. This is a more challenging undertaking for someone who is Black, queer, and a political activist during uncertain times. Survival for Dahab required him to be alert at all times, questioning the intentions behind every look, the possibilities of being bullied in specific neighborhoods and streets, and of being seen by relatives or neighbors while committing some action they would deem unacceptable. The risk of being outed or detained had to be calculated within seconds during every interaction. Nevertheless, as Ahmed Awadalla relates in their chapter in this volume, the queer landscape of downtown Cairo flourished during this period and offered many opportunities for hitherto unheard-of sociability and expression for a young gay man.

While Dahab didn't have a large margin of freedom to navigate the maze of Cairo before the early 2000s, by the time he became eighteen, he was well prepared. Survival techniques, including hiding his various identities or learning quickly by experience, meant that Dahab had to engage in emotional work, detachment, heartbreak, and conflict. He didn't have the words for all of his experiences, but he was able to endure them throughout his early childhood. He needed to navigate his way to safety throughout his lifetime, armed with a daring instinct but still making mistakes, taking risks, and testing the limits of freedom in the face of dictatorship. Living in a massive metropolis gave him the privilege of anonymity in a context of oppression. As a boy in school he had been called a slave. As an adult (in 2013) he was called "zingy" (the n-word in Arabic) among other degrading words on the streets. Egypt has not changed much in terms of its anti-Blackness (which, as Elsaket's chapter in this volume points out, has a long history in Egyptian media and popular culture), but Dahab had changed. These experiences helped him recognize that he is not able to mask all of his identities. As a cis-gendered male he could camouflage his queerness, but his blackness was obvious, making race his strongest vulnerability.

Dahab had grown up during the Mubarak era, an era of false stability. He first felt the effect of contentious politics during the 1990s wave of terrorist attacks. At that point, the fear of being a victim destroyed his joyful love for Downtown. The pictures of massacred bodies followed him during his sleep and while he clung to his mother's hand. Dahab became more religious in a spiritual way during his teenage years, but he never allowed the Quranic anti-queer narratives of Sodom and Lot to define his piety. Although he accepted himself as "normal," this self-identity was first disrupted by the Queen Boat crackdown in 2001, when he saw that his "normal" was considered illegal. He realized that his queerness meant persecution after reading the vicious media reports against those on the Queen Boat and their alleged "sexual deviation." His existence, he now recognized, was inseparably linked to politics. A sociopolitical change for him was a necessity.

Dahab knew from a very young age that to survive he would have to endure structures of power even before he understood what politics was. Growing up in a neighborhood surrounded by relatives and family, in a sort of community, was a direct result of the securitization of race and ethnicity. His family needed to create an identity that presented as apolitical while maintaining a level of assimilation. In the middle of this process, Dahab was watched by his family and friends long before the state surveilled him. His realization of his sexuality was strongly attached to the fear of scandals and police. It always seemed bizarre to him that his skin color, mother tongue, favorite music, and natural desires could be matters of national security and family reputation. The politics of securitization of identities created informal structures of power where every oppressed group and individual needs someone to feel superiority over—in order to defend identity, safeguard morality, or stay in power. In this context, Dahab's family, friends, and the state were not so different from each other.

The securitization of minorities is a key tool used by the state to control them and create a forced sense of national cohesion, which depended on Nubians surveilling their own communities. When individuals act as guardians for the nation's morals and identity, there is no place for personal freedoms, private space, or differences. Dahab believed the revolution in 2011 was a very personal and collective act of survival—a moment of hope and despair—and the fact that it started in a place that had always implied freedom for him made it more personal. As a member of more than one minority, Dahab saw his political engagement in itself liberating and not just a way to freedom. He also believed that he needed to find a balance between representing a minority that he actively advocates for and identifying with the majority in its broader cause. In order to break the chain of securitization, he found it essential to have this intersectional perspective of politics, to allow a minority just the needed amount of specificity that does not create an "other" that is feared or oppressed.

Dahab used to walk the streets of downtown Cairo awestruck by the architecture, filled with joy, with a big ice cream cone in one hand and a bag of new clothes in the other. He walks the same streets now with tearful eyes, remembering the bravery of many revolutionaries running from and toward death with joyful hearts. Postrevolution Downtown became a spot where all his identities melted together and where he felt more whole. He came out to some of his Nubian comrades and discussed politics and Nubian issues with fellow queers. He finally walked the streets of downtown Cairo as free as he used to feel as a kid in a village in Aswan.

The freedom Dahab felt and shared with many others didn't guarantee safety. The risk of death, detention, or assault hovered over his head constantly. But he believed that being free implied repeatedly taking risks. It is in the core of oppression that he managed to liberate himself from his body and soul—even though public space remains policed and oppressive on many levels. This liberation would not be possible if it were coming from a place of individualism; it was embedded in building a community, a safety net that protects individuals from the collective act of surveillance supported by a police state. He finally grasped this when he compared himself to queer people born and raised in so-called free countries. There are many who, in those contexts, fail to liberate themselves or accept their sexuality. They take the very essence of freedom for granted. Navigating Cairo might be tiring and, at some times, frustrating. Still, Dahab managed to enjoy it, to feel enriched by it, even. He could be a different self every day, to sit in a corner of a coffee shop in Tahrir Square and watch a flowing humanity pass by, to learn and refine his knowledge and intellect through every interaction, and to reach the moment of liberation only when he felt ready.

Works Cited

Amar, P. 2013. *The Security Archipelago: Human-security States, Sexuality Politics, and the End of Neoliberalism*. Durham, NC: Duke University Press.

Ryzova, L. 2015. "Strolling in Enemy Territory: Downtown Cairo, Its Publics, and Urban Heterotopias." *Orient Institute Studies* 3: *Divercities. Contested Space and Urban Identities in Beirut, Cairo, and Tehran*. Beirut: Orient-Institut Beirut.

Smith, Elizabeth A. 2006. "Place, Class, and Race in the Barabra Café: Nubians in Egyptian Media." In *Cairo Cosmopolitan: Politics, Culture, and Urban Space in the New Globalized Middle East*, edited by Diane Singerman and Paul Amar, 399–414. Cairo: American University in Cairo Press.

Yancy, G. 2008. *Black Bodies, White Gazes: The Continuing Significance of Race*. Lanham, MD: Rowman & Littlefield.

19

SEEING LIKE A CITY-STATE
BEHAVIORAL PLANNING AND GOVERNANCE IN EGYPT'S FIRST AFFORDABLE GATED COMMUNITY

NICHOLAS SIMCIK ARESE

Introduction

A new class of gated community is taking form in Cairo's 6th of October satellite city.[1] Thirty-four kilometers from central Cairo—amid wide roads that were master-planned in the 1980s and 1990s, and between swaths of desert designated for gated communities and malls—rests Haram City. Established in 2007, it is Egypt's first and only private city that combines prices suitable for aspirational suburbanites while also professing to become a one-stop shop for the full urban management of resettled slum dwellers. Accordingly, it offers a new template for managing interactions between the middle classes and the urban poor. With a target population of 400,000, the development was built on land subsidized by the Egyptian government to fulfill its affordable housing targets while allowing it to reduce welfare provisions. The project's developer declares that its aim is to become fully "self-suffi-cient" from the state. It consists of privately constructed and managed infrastructure, policing, and healthcare, and eventually will also provide energy, education, and other social services. While for some, the development offers entry-level prices into a suburban middle-class lifestyle, social development and governance addressing inequality and class-based resource conflicts, nominally provided by the Egyptian state, are also effectively privatized by this city's management team. This chapter explores how private management codifies and governs fractured social relations at the city scale, occupying the space left by the Egyptian state's absence.

This ethnography is based on eleven months of living with residents, participating in Haram City's planning process, and conducting regular interviews with the individual exercising everyday planning authority. The purpose is to interpret the day-to-day constitution and implementation of a private management regime negotiating class vulnerabilities. This chapter forgoes a focus on subaltern resistance and instead highlights the intent, logic, and method of disciplinary governance, irrespective of its success. It proposes that Haram City's ambition to synthesize the gated-community model with poverty management imitates the Egyptian state's top-down attitude to social inequality—attitudes of "seeing like a state" (Scott 1998). However, it does so exclusively through bottom-up forums for social management in neighborhoods—forums for "seeing like a city" (Valverde 2011). In the process, city and state logics of governance intertwine and become indistinguishable in Haram City, resulting in a third logic of governance: "seeing like a city-state." As many authors in this volume have reported, urban growth in Egypt is largely being driven by expansion into the deserts surrounding the cities. So far, however, most of these new developments are heavily stratified by class, seeking to create highly surveilled, monopatterned, and "civilizing" spaces for the Egyptian masses removed from "dangerous" urban areas downtown (Mohie, O. Khalil, this volume) or hallucinatory mirages of an orientalized "good life" for the middle and upper classes (Elshahed, El-Husseiny, this volume).

Sitting in his office, Tarek, Haram City's manager and the sole on-site authority for all planning and community matters, describes his passion for being able to act as president, mayor, and therapist, simultaneously—the power to manage all construction, all governing rules of the community, and most day-to-day disputes between residents. Tarek, a middle-aged man with a background in tourism, describes his ability to govern at state, city, and household scales at once—to harmoniously implement top-down material plans and to adjudicate over people's bottom-up adaptation to them. He does so by reference to an unprecedented ability to rapidly zoom in and out of the community as though it is a computer game: "I love my job. It's like my favorite game: CityVille on Facebook." References to a simulated city-state are present throughout the city manager's discourse, framing unruly residents who circumvent the rules as "city hackers." According to Tarek, to prevent the poor from turning Haram City into the rest of Cairo, "hackers" must be "upgraded" in the same way as the city's pipes—master-planning behavior into what he calls "people infrastructure," toward programming a unified moral code for this nascent city.

When people buy into private spaces, management's accountability to a common citizenry is underwritten by their status as customers. When spaces occupied by the poor are wholly privatized as subjects of development, however, there is no such clarity. Mixing consumers with development subjects raises the question of who ought to be eligible for all the livelihood possibilities and services that a public city normally provides. As local battles over eligibility for resources combine with the attempts of Tarek and his team to define criteria for legitimate belonging to a new political community, class awareness between the resettled and home-buyers is laid bare. And as bottom-up neighborhood dispute resolution goes hand in hand with top-down technical interventions, customer biases are embedded in the discourse of routine company decisions. As the research will show, this combination of "seeing like a city" and "seeing like a state" manifests most clearly in management's imitation of legality to plan tribunals, codes, and new political subjects. Ritualized court-like deliberations define moral norms and the kinds of behavior that justify eligibility for resources or home modification. However, by supervising urban dispute resolution, managers design social and spatial hierarchies that self-fulfill as though preordained. In seeing like a city-state, the performance of law becomes an end itself: authoritarianism works through the appearance of consensus-based neutrality.

Haram City: Affordable for Whom?

Haram City was launched in 2007 by the developer Orascom Housing Communities (OHC), or Orascom li-l-Iskan al-Ta'awuni (literally "Orascom Cooperative Housing"). Since then, OHC has walked a fine line by promoting the development as affordable housing. While OHC stopped referring to the project as "low-income housing" in 2010, OHC's billionaire CEO Samih Sawiris continues to characterize it as "low-income" and "affordable" interchangeably. This reflects the fact that Haram City was constructed as part of former president Hosni Mubarak's LE 34 billion ($1.1 billion), six-year National Housing Program (NHP, or "Iskan Mubarak" of 2005–12), whose goal was to build half a million homes. This is one of several incomplete social-housing desert schemes proposed since 2006 (Egyptian Initiative for Personal Rights 2014). In the promotional literature, the exchange of cheap land for full private service and infrastructure in Haram City is described as a public–private partnership (UNDP 2011; World Bank 2013). As part of the NHP, potential home-buyers in Haram City are technically subject to Ministry of Housing upper income limits of LE 2,500 ($81) per month for couples and LE 1,750 ($56) per month for singles, and eligible for a World Bank–supported affordable mortgage initiative. Yet home payment-by-installment plans also require proof of regular employment, in accordance with World Bank affordable-mortgage recommendations, invariably excluding the 55 percent of Egyptian workers aged between fifteen and sixty-four whom the World Bank defines as informally employed (World Bank 2014). As a result, rows of identical semidetached homes with gardens, priced between LE 70,000 (for 48 square meters) and LE 110,000 (for 63 square meters) ($2,260–3,550) are purchased by the regularly employed middle classes.

Most clients are recently married salary earners between twen-ty-five and forty years old who are able to source funds from family irrespective of their own income. Other properties are simply purchased as second-home investments. The long commute is presented more as a mark of exclusivity tied to car ownership, and the distance from the congested city center enables the OHC to market itself to potential buy-ers as exclusive and safe. Since the original land subsidy, as Haram City has been joined by such famous upscale developments as Dreamland (Mitchell 2002; Denis 2006), affordability targets are being balanced by the values of "prestige" and "status" to attract clients.

In 2008, soon after Haram City's opening, a catastrophic rockslide killed about 119 people in Duwiqa, one of Cairo's poorest neighbor-hoods. This disaster led, in turn, to numerous evictions in areas hitherto categorized by the government as "unsafe" and located on valuable land (Amnesty International 2011; Rabie and Adam 2013). The Cairo Governorate then negotiated a resettlement scheme into Haram City, purchasing 1,300 smaller homes from OHC (which donated an addi-tional 600) in one quadrant of the site. While families evicted from adjacent sites settled in, Duwiqa victims organized prolonged protests, demanding new homes in Duwiqa itself. Their efforts were unsuccessful and, in 2010, the original 231 families who had been victims of the rock-slide finally agreed to resettle in Haram City. Tensions have since flared in the gated community between resettled urban poor and homebuyers over what state-subsidized but gated affordability ought to mean.

In 2014, Haram City had 28,000 residents, 12,000 of whom had been resettled from the dense popular districts of Manshiyat Nasir,

Dar al-Salam, Izbat Khairallah, Istabl 'Antar, Basatin, and Duwiqa. Resettlement homes are in subzones A1 and A2, a section of OHC land where tenure is not secured by deed but by a "letter of guarantee" for unspecified duration signed by the Cairo governor. This document was produced by officials to convince people to resettle, leaving many to erroneously believe that it constitutes proof of ownership of new homes. Additionally, during the 2011 uprising against Hosni Mubarak, the original 231 Duwiqa families began squatting in larger, vacant homes in a section of the adjacent A3 homeowner subzone. Most continue to do so, albeit under continuous pressure from management to move. This, in turn, fuels squatters' threats to blow up their homes using cooking gas canisters if evicted, something that would irrevocably damage Haram City's middle-class reputation (Simcik Arese 2018). Subzones A3–A4 and B1–B4 consist of neatly maintained homeowner properties and unsold houses in equal measure. Purchasing a home here entails ownership of the actual house and any walled construction, but not of the actual land or gardens. Homeowners are separated from the resettled population only by two perpendicular main roads that divide a two-by-one-kilometer site into quarters (subzones are referred to in residents' vernacular as A-areas for the resettled and B-areas for homeowners). Despite disputes over the meaning of affordability—and thus over legitimate belonging—Haram City is deemed a "best-practice" case study by UNDP and the World Bank for promoting a new trend in twenty-first-century urbanism.

Seeing at Scales: City and State Governance

As Haram City takes form in the desert ex nihilo, the problems of top-down planning become evident at the local scale. What is absent is a clear understanding of how a bird's-eye view and street-level scales of city management—generally treated as distinct domains by scholars—operate together in clean-slate settlements run by private companies, particularly when targeting thresholds between classes.

On the one hand, a rich body of research on governance and poverty management in Egypt emphasizes a very broad scale of social intervention, focusing for example on the state's desert conquest through "satellite cities." This governance-zoomed-out, from Scott's "seeing like a state" (1998) to Mitchell's "techno-politics" (2002), is a crucial logic characteristic of high-modernist and neoliberal regimes, involving expert-driven and bird's-eye-view enumeration, mapping, and disciplining of society, and particularly of society's most vulnerable. As both

Scott's and Mitchell's works show, technocratic projects reduce the everyday lives of the poor to numbers, facilitating the imposition of normatively driven solutions, and a corresponding extraction or allocation of resources. On the other hand, the day-to-day reality of governance at a smaller scale—the scale of the neighborhood—primarily involves the fine-grained work of mediating frictions between behavior and morality over the uses and abuses of a shared space. Criminologist and legal geographer Mariana Valverde defines this local politics approach to behavioral management as "seeing like a city," explicitly distinguishing it from Scott's "seeing like a state" (Valverde 2011). While commensurable with the vertical imposition of norms, "seeing like a city" describes the contested and improvisational ways in which urban-specific legal instruments—property entitlements, zoning, licensing, nuisance, and policing—work slowly to solidify deeply embedded moral biases. At this rescaled vision of governance, where a state's imposition of objective rules may falter, institutions work with communities to establish shared rules for local planning and urban life.

"Seeing like a city" acquires its normative power through a bottom-up framework, with neighborhood disputes resolved through deliberated consensus that can allow biases to acquire the status of common sense. When private management addresses such matters in developing "affordable" housing, prescriptive master-planning (i.e., "seeing like a state") and the incremental codification of local subjectivities and customs (i.e., "seeing like a city") become entwined. To understand how these two forms of governing populations meet—namely, in seeing like a city-state—one must also grasp how the Egyptian state facilitates Haram City's exceptionalism within a circumscribed territory.

Haram City and the Egyptian State

Everyday questions of "affordable for whom?" cannot be separated from the issue of how conditions of possibility for an autonomous city are designed by the state. OHC interprets the state's role as providing a one-off land subsidy to pursue "fully integrated self-sufficiency." This entails OHC construction of, and profits from, all infrastructure and services. The city's boss, Tarek (whose official title is Customer Services Manager), supervises seven assistants but has the final word in all urban decisions—from planning infrastructure (sewage, electricity, and water distribution) to settling protocol for services (policing, schooling, and healthcare). Like a judge, he spends hours intervening in people's neighborly relationships. He emphasizes that pursuing state channels will produce no immediate results in a setting where he is the official planner. He focuses the conversation on sustainability credentials, boasting about city-wide recycling, water management, a twenty-four-hour private health clinic, passive cooling of buildings, and plans for a 66-megawatt power plant—the alleged final step for ensuring total self-sufficiency.

The indeterminacy in OHC's public–private partnership is strategic: it allows flexible recourse to the state, yet leaves the company's powers open-ended. Strategic indeterminacy is supplemented by two important ambiguities. First, Haram City is at the forefront of Egypt's long history of structural adjustment. It was conceived of along with World Bank–sponsored affordable mortgages to push developers to build homes for non-elites (World Bank 2010). Proponents therefore frame Haram City as not only the socially aware evolution of a satellite city, invented to test further privatization, but as an experiment that must avoid state intrusion to be deemed replicable. Egypt's satellite cities are mostly populated by those who have found wealth under state privatization—who seek lifestyles, consumption, and a sense of personal autonomy beyond that deemed possible in traditional urban Egypt, an arena perceived to be plagued by intrusions on privacy, social disarray, and moral vulnerability, foreclosing on one's ability to plan a future (Ghannam 2002; Asad 2015). For Haram City to succeed in the market, it is necessary to protect this promise irrespective of diverse clientele.

Second, Haram City took form in a profoundly mutable Egypt. Amid scrapped constitutions, governments, and social unrest in the 2011–13 revolutionary period, the legitimacy of law and state were widely debated. Either because they could not afford to travel to Tahrir Square or because of political differences, most Haram City residents watched mass mobilizations through their flickering television screens. However, even at a distance, the indictment of numerous developers and the imprisonment of Egypt's former housing minister following Mubarak's fall inspired popular dialogue over who should benefit from land subsidies. Those who had been forcibly resettled cited each report of a major developer's corruption as justification for building modifications and squats. This debate transpired as suburbs were even further unmoored from law enforcement, which had become focused on containing the downtown Cairo protests. For example, the sporadic military curfews were not enforced within gated communities, including Haram City. These discrepancies in law between inside and outside were, for residents, an affirmation that in elite desert masterplans, the law never entirely applied to begin with, and presented staff with fertile conditions for governing this territory like both a city and a state.

City Hackers and Upgrading People

A frequent topic of conversation between homeowners and OHC staff involves articulating the profound sense of vulnerability of the middle class in view of the resettled poor's improvised building modifications. Tarek and his staff convene frequent meetings with homeowners and identify positions that unite the propertied. Mohammed, a thirty-two-year-old unmarried artist and recent homeowner, describes Haram City's A-areas as perpetuating the condition that motivated his abandonment of downtown Cairo's art scene. He emphasizes parallels between the commercial construction that resettled people undertake for their own purposes and Downtown's mushrooming street vendors. In Mohammed's words, "These places are not for them. You know? No, don't be a hacker of the road." After being asked for further explanation, Mohammed replied, "Hacker. Like computer hackers. Don't be a hacker of the shopping mall. You can sell, OK. But not in this area. . . . If someone dies in a car accident and the ambulance needs the road, it's a problem. Find solutions for your problems, but don't make problems for others in doing so." The English word "hacker" resonates with the etymology of the Egyptian term for "thug," *baltagiya* (literally, "axe-bearer"). Mohammed's use of the term "hacker" to refer to livelihood-based informality underlines competing values for getting by in the city. He believes that some needs are more just, and corresponding "solutions" should take priority. The masses appear to be hacking a new city before its codes are written.

Sherif—a single homeowner in his mid-forties, who quit working at a Giza bank to breed Labradors in his new garden—shares his own vulnerability by expressing a need to design new limits of freedom and therefore also to regulate private construction. He tells me that "many people don't understand the real meaning of freedom. They understand only 'I will fight everywhere. I will smoke drugs everywhere and be a *baltagi* (thug) because now I am free . . .' Here some people, like Duwiqa, [think], 'Because I am free to get naked, I will just do it . . .' Do you need to do this? No, but ah! It's my right!" Sherif hopes Haram City "will become more organized" so that it may protect his home and future, as "the level and quality of the people changes according to prices." He supports corrective action, observing that introducing disciplinary customs can target errant freedoms and class vulnerability more effectively than the law. For Mohammed and Sherif, resettlement into the private sphere engenders a distinct sense of collapse in not only the material order of things, but also an implicit social and moral order—a hacked code. Behind gates, Haram City is open to engineering customs against the "hacking" found within. OHC responds directly to this call—indeed, it sells it.

Ambition to develop people like infrastructure, or like the city itself, is a central managing principle for OHC staff. Intended literally, Tarek plans errant behavior the way he plans broken pipes, fixing things and people interchangeably. Staff contend that if behavior does not accommodate the customs required for self-sufficiency, then it can and must be "upgraded." In this sense, the staff describe their boss's job as dream manager and psychologist. When I point this out to Tarek and add that—given his strong personal approach—a more accurate job title could be *mohafez* (governor), he agrees: "That's right. I handle the residents. I try to handle Duwiqa, and I try to handle the waves [of new clients]. I try to put everything in its place." He stresses that a governor's duty is to "upgrade people," which amounts to psychology. He insists that "[Residents] bring their personal problems [to me] from inside their houses. They ask for our help because they trust us . . . this creates a mysterious link between us and residents." Desire to "put everything in its place" evokes more than social exclusion of the "out of place" (Sibley 1995) or the title of Constance Perin's classic ethnography on propertied order and social ideals in 1970s American suburbia (Perin 1977). It is evidence of an explicit imperative to rationalize space and lives according to behavior, discerned through dialogue and technical analysis of minds.

An Urban Repertoire

By trial and error, OHC staff invents nuanced governance practices tailored to a literal interpretation of psychology as infrastructure. These techniques adopt "seeing-like-a-city" as a means—dispute resolution appearing to inclusively define the appropriateness of certain behaviors—to achieve "seeing-like-a-state" as an end, imposing norms and categorizations of people by plan. While OHC refuses to sanction improvised construction in A-areas, sometimes Tarek turns a blind eye. Contracts specify that unit gardens—the site of most private construction—are technically the property of OHC, delegating restricted usufruct to a resident (e.g., limited wall heights, removable coverage, paint specifications, and prohibition of commercial use). However, OHC avoids provoking unrest through demolition of private construction, instead opting to withhold services such as rubbish collection and street maintenance from noncompliant homes. This passive approach is used selectively, however, in a manner reminiscent of the "privatized" law and enforcement structures Hassan and Shawkat describe (in two chapters in this volume) as being common in "Old Cairo." Surviving rooftop pigeon coops, for example, frequently correspond with the social influence of a particular resident. Nonintervention, as Tarek explains, amounts to de facto licensing of certain A-area residents' self-built commercial space, ensuring that they stay where they are.

With A-area influencers appeased, OHC opens its office to address service provision complaints as well as inter- and intra-household arguments. Due to the recombinant nature of resettlement, complaints over offensiveness are not only aimed at the urban poor but also occur among them. OHC encourages licensed influencers to refer disputing parties to management for personal consultation. Tarek assumes the role of therapist, and meetings require "direct eye contact, being a good listener, and replying to vital problems . . . [so that] other customers understand that [I am] on the same line." As Tarek welcomes parties into his office, arguments over reasonable behavior become official and part of professional duties, on a continuum from interfamilial connectivity to street connectivity. As the resettled residents acclimate to OHC's mediation, occasional conflict-resolution meetings become regular nuisance tribunals.

A disregard for suggestions may result in coercion, albeit indirectly administered to protect management's supposed objectivity. Persistent violations might lead to encounters with the state police over separate issues (police enter the city gates only by OHC's invitation). Punishment focuses on extracting admissions of impropriety, on setting examples for legitimacy of future behavioral norms. Tarek reports, "When we catch someone like this with what he stole [company land] . . . we send him to the police. They have their own ways to get a confession." Vacant home occupations are dealt with even more harshly. In such cases, OHC hires non-state, non-corporate security: Bedouins for whom "it is very easy to kill and walk away . . . so [squatters] respect them." Developers frequently confront Bedouin land claims on the Nile's desert fringes. OHC likely negotiated undisturbed construction by paying Bedouins to defend the development against attacks from the Bedouin themselves. Members of this extra-legal troop occasionally roam Haram City's cafés, smoking shisha and carrying large rifles.

Tarek maintains that homeowners eventually "want to be completely removed from [the resettled]," but he also considers home-owners' growing need for cheap labor. To reconcile these issues, he plans to repartition Haram City on behavioral grounds. It is a strat-egy that imitates zoning because, while it is a vertically imposed and future-oriented scheme, it is designed to self-materialize out of contin-ued public deliberation over past grievances. During one staff meeting, an employee produced a detailed map of Haram City. Pencil in hand, Tarek mapped how to incrementally install barriers to movement. The scheme operates like a self-fulfilling prophecy, accelerating as each intervention immediately seems to necessitate a subsequent, more severe one. It is designed in this way so that homeowners can easily argue it into existence in residents' debates. Tarek tells me, "We are starting to separate some areas as a pilot project. In subzone B4 you will find that we have closed some streets by putting [plants]. When this green grows, it will become a natural fence." Once shrubs become large bushes, he explains, they will require a metal fence for support. A fence will then require a gate to allow pedestrian passage. And once a gate is placed, a guard is needed to ensure that it functions. This pilot will be first in a series of similar projects. Tarek elaborates, "We will close B4, then all [other] B-zones by themselves, then A3, then A4, all away from A1 and A2. . . . We will take this part here, and here, and there, and fws-sht! It will be a closed community."

Based on this vision, Haram City is still in the process of becom-ing a closed community. Rather than simply walling off subzones A1 and A2, which could be interpreted as punishment, Tarek walls off upscale areas to reward residents for conforming with customs. Prop-erty rights and city beautification—"you dream to live in a closed community, a better community, and we have to provide it"—are used to incrementally rank and distinguish the most proprietary areas, following the logic of rules-as-goals, until only half of A-area remains "open." Subzones gradually become permanent sub-enclaves. Only at this point will OHC supply basic services, such as telephone access, to the leftover "open" resettlement areas. This frames exclu-sion (for homeowners) and basic rights (for the resettled) as rewards for behavioral compliance. Behavioral compliance and class remain tightly intertwined, and sub-enclaves are predetermined to mirror and manage the stratifications of the inner city. A final move inverts new fences, opening "closed" homeowner spaces to each other but leaving the remainder "open" only to itself, de facto isolating the resettled residents. The introduction of internal identification cards specifying sub-enclave would then fully inscribe behavioral rankings, not only into rezoned space, but into classes of citizenship.

Zoning has long been understood by legal scholars as the "codification of nuisance" (Valverde 2011, 292). Disputes over nuisance are solicited for the purposes of moral categorization, rule-as-goal-making, and reward-by-rezoning—a scheme that imitates urban law to naturalize difference in a hierarchy of sub-enclaves. Seeing like a city-state, then, means to plan, in a top-down way, the very realm of bottom-up decision-making. It also involves adapting top-down plans to bottom-up disputes to render permanent (physically or statutorily) the "consensual" outcomes of a rigged game. In other words, "seeing like a city" becomes an instrument to "see like a state," and vice versa.

Conclusion

In Haram City, the codification of behavior is managed through techniques that resemble urban law but that are planned through the technical imperative to "upgrade" behavior and pipes alike. Tarek's repertoire for enacting the "seeing-like-a-city" logic of governance aims to establish consensus over offensiveness and reasonableness, but is also utilized to stealthily impose grand plans, norms, and designs—similar to "seeing like a state." Under the full private management of the civic services upon which the poor's livelihoods depend, a politics of suggestion and distribution encourages preconceptions based on homeowners' vulnerabilities to self-fulfill. From this perspective, OHC's march toward gates within gates becomes immanent, not discernible as a top-down imposition but cast as "nothing but law adapting itself to life" (Valverde 2011, 288).

It is important to emphasize that, while cumulatively discernible as a variation on suburban authoritarianism, this perspective derives from the condensation of a year's participant-observation. Regrettably, this study privileges the voices of men. As a non-Egyptian male researching vulnerability at a time of political strife, prolonged contact with women would often jeopardize trust with key participants. Additionally, OHC's interventions work on a complaint-by-complaint basis, with an overriding preference for stability. As long as home sales endure, so could a kind of indeterminate status quo—a tacit, unsatisfactory, and laborious coexistence. In the long run, we cannot exclude the possibility that the urban poor and middle classes might overcome OHC's vision through the same organic accords that bind inner Cairo together every day.

This chapter, then, shows OHC's efforts at social engineering in a historical context where such projects have long framed configurations of power and privilege. It also shows how historical context blends with the moral framings that justify today's creation of public–private partnerships globally. Conceivably, "seeing like a state" and "seeing like a city" can be combined in any number of ways. However, under "full self-sufficiency" for the private sector—amid state turmoil and a combination of aspirational property ownership and slum resettlement—each vision fuses with and recursively validates the other in a mode of governance I term "seeing like a city-state."

Notes

1   This chapter is a revised version of an article previously published in the *International Journal of Urban and Regional Research* in 2018.

Works Cited

Amnesty International. 2011. "Egypt: 'We Are Not Dirt': Forced Evictions in Egypt's Informal Settlements." August 23. https://www.amnesty.org/en/documents/mde12/001/2011/en/.

Asad, T. 2015. "Thinking about Tradition, Religion, and Politics in Egypt Today." *Critical Inquiry* 42, no. 1: 166–214. https://doi.org/10.1086/683002.

Denis, Éric. 2006. "Cairo as Neoliberal Capital? From Walled City to Gated Communities." In *Cairo Cosmopolitan: Politics, Culture, and Urban Space in the New Globalized Middle East*, edited by D. Singerman and P. Amar, 47–72. Cairo: American University in Cairo Press.

Egyptian Initiative for Personal Rights. 2014. "Social Housing between Old Policies and Future Opportunities." Press release, December 7. http://eipr.org/en/pressrelease/2014/12/07/2296.

Ghannam, F. 2002. *Remaking the Modern: Space, Relocation, and the Politics of Identity in a Global Cairo*. Berkeley: University of California Press.

Mitchell, T. 2002. *Rule of Experts: Egypt, Techno-politics, Modernity*. Berkeley: University of California Press,.

Perin, C. 1977. *Everything in Its Place: Social Order and Land Use in America*. Princeton, NJ: Princeton University Press.

Rabie, D., and M. Adam. 2013. "Years after Deadly Rockslide, Duweiqa Residents Still Await Relocation." *Egypt Independent*, March 11. http://www.egyptindependent.com/news/years-after-deadly-rockslide-duweiqa-residents-still-await-relocation.

Scott, J.C. 1998. *Seeing Like a State: How Certain Schemes to Improve the Human Condition Have Failed*. New Haven, CT: Yale University Press.

Sibley, D. 1995. *Geographies of Exclusion: Society and Difference in the West*. London: Routledge.

Simcik Arese, N. 2018. "Urbanism as Craft: Practicing Informality and Property in Cairo's Gated Suburbs, from Theft to Virtue." *Annals of the American Association of Geographers* 108, no. 3: 620–37.

UNDP (United Nations Development Programme). 2011. "Growing Inclusive Markets Case Study: Orascom Housing Communities." http://growinginclusivemarkets.org/media/cases/Egypt_Orascom_2011.pdf. Viewed August 6, 2013.

Valverde, M. 2011. "Seeing Like a City: The Dialectic of Modern and Premodern Ways of Seeing in Urban Governance." *Law and Society Review* 45, no. 2: 277–312.

World Bank. 2010. "Systems of Cities: Harnessing Urbanization for Growth and Poverty Alleviation—the World Bank Urban and Local Government Strategy (English)." July 1. Washington, DC: World Bank Group. http://documents.worldbank.org/curated/en/784411468330978912/Systems-of-cities-harnessing-urbanization-for-growth-and-poverty-alleviation-the-World-Bank-urban-and-local-government-strategy.

———. 2013. "Affordable Housing Brings Hope for Low Income Egyptians." World Bank, December 6. http://www.worldbank.org/en/news/feature/2013/12/06/affordable-housing-brings-hope-for-low-income-egyptians.

———. 2014. "Informal Is the New Normal: Egypt's Informal Sector Is on the Rise, but Careful Regulatory Innovation Can Help Turn the Tide." Egypt World Bank Issue—Brief No. 2. http://www.world-bank.org/content/dam/Worldbank/Feature Story/mena/Egypt/Egypt-Doc/egy-jobs-issue-brief-2-ENG-ARA.pdf.

20

PERIPHERALIZATION AND INFRASTRUCTURAL VIOLENCE

"HAUSSMANNIZATION" IN MANAGUA, NICARAGUA AND CAIRO, EGYPT

AHMAD BORHAM

Peripherization versus Peripheralization

The bulldozer is making its way through the city, clearing boulevards, with the aim of improving traffic flow. With this clearing, the agents of the state claim that they are enhancing infrastructure. But actually, they are reconfiguring the city and forcing part of the population into developments out toward the periphery, including toward the New Administrative Capital and the Alamein and Mount Galala developments. The redirection of investment from the center to the periphery has resulted in a rapidly eroding urban fabric in the center (Sharp 2018). It has created an uneven geography of divestment and investment, as Guirguis, Elshahed, El-Husseiny, and Duffield, among others, have described in their chapters of this book.

The state has always played a central role in the internal migration process of Cairenes, especially its poor, to the city's peripheries. President Anwar al-Sadat managed to relocate part of the Bulaq Abu al-'Ila neighborhood to al-Zawiya al-Hamra'. His successor, Hosni Mubarak, continued the onslaught on Bulaq and similar areas. And in the post-Mubarak era, attempts at this redistribution of population continue. Most recently, we have witnessed the demolition of the Maspero Triangle in 2018 (see O. Khalil's chapter in this volume for further information).

Peripherization can be characterized as the "formation of low-income residential areas in the peripheral ring of the city" (Barros 2004,

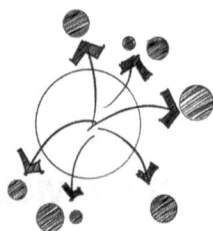

Figure 20.1. Peripherization.

Figure 20.2. Peripheralization.

314). Peripheralization, on the other hand, is the "process of becoming disconnected from and dependent on the centers" (Fischer-Tahir and Naumann 2013, 9). Figures 20.1 and 20.2 illustrate the correlation of the two terms. Peripherization, as shown in figure 20.1, is a process of growth and expansion of the city at the periphery in the form of residential settlements on former agricultural lands, labeled as "unplanned areas." These resettled areas were not state-initiated, but rather were mostly built by the people occupying that agricultural land. These *'ashwa'iyat* (unplanned, or informal, areas) are "islands" juxtaposed with the more elite *tagammu'at* islands in the desert (sometimes called gated communities or enclaves, as described by El-Husseiny and Sinno in their chapters in this volume), surrounded by commercial developments and shopping malls.

Peripheralization, as shown in figure 20.2, not only disconnects the city center from the desert cities, but in doing so, it also weakens the rural–urban relationship. Both diagrams serve as an organizing framework for the rest of the chapter, wherein I demonstrate how both processes—peripheralization and peripherization—are related to securitization. I relate the two terms to one other while considering the origin of Cairo's Ring Road *(Da'iri)* and how it acts as a catalyst for these dynamics, with the Ring Road's bridges and highways bisecting the city (see Elshahed in this volume for more details on this project and its successors). I also analyze how both processes focus on the ongoing evictions in the city's older neighborhoods in relation to a rapid transformation of infrastructure.

Securitization and Infrastructure

Securitization has been described as "a means of moving certain issues beyond the democratic process of government" (Vuori 2008, 66). But is securitization theory applicable in nondemocratic contexts (Pratt and

Rezk 2019)? This question raises a kind of violence currently being practiced by the state, which we can call infrastructural violence. Cities can generate systems of governance where power configurations take specific materialistic forms, such as infrastructural development (Rodgers 2012). Infrastructure studies is an approach through which to reflect upon rigorous forms of violence practiced by the current ruling regime in Egypt. Active infrastructural violence (Rodgers and O'Neill 2012) consists of a set of actions intended to regulate social and territorial relations. An example of this is the Haussmannization of Paris and its securitized boulevards during the nineteenth century.

Dennis Rodgers has compared and described the dramatic transformations of Managua, Nicaragua, and Paris in the nineteenth century. In this analysis, he explores Haussmannization as a paradigmatic example of planned urban change. The Haussmann project eliminated many medieval streets in Paris and replaced them with wider avenues, in times of political and economic contestation. Haussmann wrote in his memoirs that the principal aim of constructing these straight, wide boulevards was to ensure security and crush resistance, with improving traffic circulation as only a second priority. This planning scheme has been reproduced in Cairo, as it is being dissected by wide and dramatic highways that connect the peripheral developments around the city. Rodgers argues that this extreme makeover of the city is a result of market forces that have appropriated state power. In Nicaragua, the construction of Nueva Managua (New Managua) has been the product of disruptive infrastructural transformation. This transformation mainly focused on creating a road network that facilitated the urban elite's swift movement between the city's new malls, restaurants, villas, houses, and gated communities on the periphery of the city.

Securitization involves controlling and directing circulation within the city. Cairo's rapidly growing bridge infrastructure plays a central role in this process. Less than 14 percent of Cairo households own cars, so this entire investment in road networks and bridges is directed toward that privileged class (Sims 2011). Public transport users get stuck underneath these bridges, suffering from pollution and traffic jams worse than ever. Pedestrians, who were completely ignored by the design of these highways and overpasses, cannot find a safe way to cross these new widened thoroughfares cutting through the city and its satellites. In Managua, Nicaragua, the extension of a four-lane boulevard has sliced through a socioeconomically underprivileged neighborhood. In both Cairo and Managua, highways wall off, or detour around, neighborhoods deemed "unsafe" or simply "undesirable." Consequently, working-class residents and carless citizens experience a sense of being cut off and disconnected from the city. Car owners have drastically different criteria for assessing whether a city is "secure" or not.

As a reminder, peripheralization involves the disconnection of the periphery from the center. The same process applies to old neighborhoods, where residents are evicted and forced to relocate to the periphery, often to places with unstable housing conditions, to accommodate the roads. The subtext here is that securitization entails clearing space and increasing visibility. Officials in the security sector claim that the narrow streets of older Cairo's *sha'biya* neighborhoods are dangerous. Barrio Carlos, a small settlement to the southeast of Managua (Rodgers 2012), provides another example of disguised messaging. In April 2008, the municipality there began to work on extending a four-lane highway, renamed the Boulevard Miguel Obando, directly through the Barrio Carlos neighborhood. Officially, it was claimed that this would help reduce traffic congestion in the neighborhood, yet its primary functional outcome was to connect several gated communities from the periphery and to facilitate quick movement out of densely crowded areas near the city center. In Egypt, the case of Izbat Khairallah—where the Ring Road splits the neighborhood into two areas—reflects a similar trend.

Infrastructural violence is not something new, nor is it simply a result of the current regime of political authoritarianism. As Guirguis and Carreño's chapters on health and sanitation in Cairo (in this volume) point out, it is an inherent component of contemporary urban governance. The "Cairo 2050 Plan"[1]—temporarily halted after the turbulent years following 2011—envisioned slicing a wide thoroughfare through Greater Cairo, connecting Sphinx Square, in Agouza, near downtown Cairo, to al-Rimaya Square near the Giza pyramids. Infrastructural plans that assure safe elite and touristic experiences depend on forms of securitization. Likewise, peripheralization goes hand in hand with investment in infrastructure. During the Mubarak era, characterized by neoliberal urbanism, the Ring Road strategy was presented as a mechanism for limiting sprawl and containing the expansion of the city. We can now see, with two decades of perspective, that the Ring Road has actually facilitated expansion of the greater Cairo region and enabled accelerated development of unplanned housing on the periphery.

Peripherization grows by incorporating Cairenes of all classes. Authorities responsible for land governance have recognized that selling large chunks of land to developers—mostly from the Gulf region after the recession in 2008—would generate more revenue for the state and elites, quickly and easily. In this context, we have seen the emergence of such speculative settlements as Obour, New Cairo (including Rehab and Madinaty), and Shorouq. Simultaneously, low-income housing settlements surround Cairo on the urban–rural northern and western edges and in the southern sector of the Ring Road, and are being constructed alongside gated communities and upscale desert enclaves (Sims 2011). Investment in road networks is being directed toward gated communities where most of the residents own cars. Most of these gated communities attempt to be self-sufficient and completely isolated from the city. Such patterns of urban expansion include several separate, isolated, residential, private "islands," constructed in a sector dedicated as a business district. As with Managua, Nicaragua, the peripheral ring of Cairo consists mostly of low-income housing, including large spontaneously constructed settlements, which usually lack in-built urban infrastructure and services such as sewer, electrical grids, and trash collection. Thus, peripherization clearly constitutes a social problem, reaffirming extreme social inequalities that have been intentionally built into the fabric of the city through new infrastructural violence and profit-driven speculation.

Urban Activism

Political geographer Roman Stadnicki argues that the protests that broke out in Egypt in January 2011 unleashed new waves of urban activism in Cairo and in other Egyptian cities where struggles for spatial justice contested the physical fabric of the city itself. But this does not mean that before 2011 there was no urban activism. Since the 2000s, there have been protests against forced evictions in many neighborhoods, such as al-Qursaya and Bulaq-Maspero. The case of Maspero was particularly intriguing as it involved a coalition between the interests of the state and the real estate developers as forces of gentrification investing in high-rise buildings on the Nile waterfront. But who is an urban activist?

Stadnicki classifies urban activism into two types: first, urban professionals such as architects and urban planners, who may also be scholars or consultants; and second, politicized activists, who are concerned with urban issues but are not specialists in the field (Stadnicki 2015). In May 2013, a law was passed in Egypt that obliged urban activist NGOs to register with a new government body that would monitor their activities. This surveillance and the increase of direct state violence since 2013 have caused major setbacks to the efforts of Cairo's activists. Regarding evictions, the Maspero Triangle case, as described by O. Khalil in this volume, demonstrates the kind of activism that can occur in these cases as well as the rise of an interesting model of negotiation initiated by civil society in collaboration with community organization. The negotiations were later mediated by the government itself in order to generate a consensus among the stakeholders (including residents and investors); however, that model was eventually disrupted. I was personally involved in these experiments. They are just some examples among other parallel streams of urban activism that utilize different methods to deal with manifestations of peripherization and peripheralization.

Urban activism has been peripheralized by securitization just as much as urban city space. Urban activism in Egypt was peripheralized through the penetration of the state, which limited or paralyzed the actions of most activists, whether by passing laws, by monitoring activists' actions, or by arresting and torturing them. As a result of this kind of peripheralization, urban activists began to take refuge in academia or distance themselves from the violence of development. Many turned to theorizing and writing about these issues and discussing them in conferences among other scholars. Their studies are published in journals and proceedings that may only be read by fellow specialists.

Amid these gloomy and dark times, some spaces of hope appear. Stavros Stavrides reminds us of this as he discusses housing movements in Latin America that are confronting the policies of the official systems of urban governance that forcibly relocate huge numbers of people to city peripheries in a similar manner. Activists in such movements have created networks of autonomous settlements that form a city beyond the official city, where residents self-organize and collaborate with architects and activists who are providing different housing models based on sharing and negotiation (Stavrides 2020). In Berlin, an open collective of activists called Anarche, which includes PhD students and scholars with emancipatory ideas, hosts spontaneous demonstrations, and acts as a medium for social movements and in solidarity with squatter activists. These cases and conditions raise the need to redefine the term "urban activist." Are we specialized individuals and groups motivated by a belief in socio-spatial justice? Or are we city dwellers facing the threat of eviction and its consequences, and trying to resist in every aspect of everyday life?

Notes

1   The 2050 plan has since been restarted by Prime Minister Mostafa Madbouly (el-Mahdawy 2021).

Works Cited

Barros, Joana. 2004. "Simulating Urban Dynamics in Latin American Cities." In *GeoDynamics*, edited by P.M. Atkinson, G.M. Foody, S.E. Darby, and F. Wu, 313–28. New York: CRC Press.

Fischer-Tahir, Andrea, and Matthias Naumann. 2013. *Peripheralization: The Making of Spatial Dependencies and Social Injustice.* Wiesbaden: Springer.

el-Mahdawy, Hadeer. 2021. "Cairo Eye: Will the Great Wheel of History Keep Turning?" *Mada Masr*, February 11. madamasr.com/en/2021/02/11/feature/politics/cairo-eye-will-the-great-wheel-of-history-keep-turning/.

Pratt, Nicola, and Dina Rezk. 2019. "Securitizing the Muslim Brotherhood: State Violence and Authoritarianism in Egypt after the Arab Spring." *Security Dialogue* 50, no. 3: 239–56.

Rodgers, Dennis. 2012. "Haussmannization in the Tropics: Abject Urbanism and Infrastructural Violence in Nicaragua." *Ethnography* 13, no. 4: 413–38.

Rodgers, Dennis, and Bruce O'Neill. 2012. "Infrastructural Violence: Introduction to the Special Issue." *Ethnography* 13, no. 4: 401–12.

Sharp, Deen. 2018. "The Urbanization of Power and the Struggle for the City." *Middle East Report* 287: 2–5.

Sims, David. 2011. *Understanding Cairo: The Logic of a City Out of Control.* Cairo: American University in Cairo Press.

Stadnicki, Roman. 2015. "Urban Activism in Egypt: Emergence and Trajectories after the 2011 Revolution." *Orient Institute Studies* 3. https://shs.hal.science/halshs-01249910/document.

Stavrides, Stavros. 2020. "Reclaiming the City as Commons: Learning from Latin American Housing Movements." *Built Environment* 46, no. 1: 139–53. https://doi.org/10.2148/benv.46.1.139.

Vuori, Juha A. 2008. "Illocutionary Logic and Strands of Securitization: Applying the Theory of Securitization to the Study of Non-democratic Political Orders." *European Journal of International Relations* 14, no. 1: 65–99. https://doi.org/10.1177/1354066107087767.

21

STATIZING INFORMALITY AND UNBUNDLING RIGHTS
NEOLIBERAL INFRASTRUCTURE IN CAIRO'S *'ASHWA'IYAT*

DEENA MAHMOUD SOBHY KHALIL

Introduction

"Everybody in Cairo has equal access to water; the only difference is that some people pay for it, and others steal it."[1] This is what I was told when inquiring with the Greater Cairo Water and Wastewater Company (GCWWC) about water scarcity in Greater Cairo's informal areas. Residents of informal neighborhoods have been complaining about a lack of water for years. The official I spoke to was repeating a popular trope within the state's discourse about informal areas, which is that of widespread utility theft. Official spokespersons for the GCWWC, as well as the South and North Cairo Electricity Distribution Companies (SCEDC and NCEDC, respectively), have repeatedly highlighted in the media the extent to which water and electricity are being stolen through non-metered connections that are costing the companies millions of Egyptian pounds. These illegal connections are widely assumed to be concentrated within "unplanned areas."

In the mainstream media and often in official statements, non-metered connections and the *'ashwa'iyat* are often discursively conflated together, largely because the majority of buildings in unplanned areas are unlicensed.[2] Until recently, it was illegal for utility companies to connect any unlicensed buildings to public utility networks, and therefore many such buildings relied on unofficial connections. However, today many unlicensed buildings within Cairo's *'ashwa'iyat* are connected to the public networks through official metered connections, or have alternative arrangements with the utility companies to pay a fixed charge for their consumption (CAPMAS 2006). This change has occurred within the shadow of neoliberal reforms that have affected Egypt's water and electricity sectors since the early 2000s.

In this chapter, I am concerned with the impact that neoliberalism has had on Cairo's unplanned areas, particularly vis-à-vis the Egyptian state. Egypt is often depicted as the quintessential neoliberal state, and has been described as a "poster child for neoliberal reform" (Shenker 2009). Until recently, the water and electricity sectors were considered some of the least neoliberalized sectors in comparison to others, such as housing, healthcare, and education (Armbrust 2011; Marafi 2011). Neither sector had been privatized, and tariffs were described as "among the lowest in the world" and too low to cover even system operating and maintenance costs (Sims 2010). But more subtle forms of neoliberalism are becoming increasingly common within sectors considered to be part of the commons, such as water (Bakker 2009; Smith 2004). As opposed to full-fledged privatization or private sector participation, these less obvious forms of neoliberalism often include corporatization of state agencies. By 2004, Egypt's water and electricity agencies had been transformed into public holding companies with new mandates around cost recovery and financial sustainability.

The built environment within Cairo's 'ashwa'iyat is caught in a continual process of becoming, as many authors in this volume have demonstrated (Hammad, O. Khalil, Shawkat, and Hassan, among others). Supposedly unplanned neighborhoods embody the essence of securitized "illegality" while also being hypervalued as new geographies of capital accumulation and of state power and revenue. This securitizing and "othering" discourse of illegality and informality demands critical reconceptualization. We need to move beyond traditional conceptions of neoliberalism as a paradigm that prescribes state "rollback," and reinterpret it as a political rationality that seeks to reshape the effect of the state by producing new forms of the state–society relationship. This political securitizing neoliberal rationality generates new spaces and subjects of power while obscuring them, rendering them seemingly external to the state while subjecting its population to surveillance and policing. Guirguis's study (in this volume) of Cairo's lack of public hygiene infrastructure offers one excellent example of this process, but there are many more areas in which it needs to be revealed and interrogated.

In addition to focusing on the impact of neoliberalism, this chapter explores the way in which state-owned water and electricity companies have changed how they deal with non-metered connections, and the ways in which the *'ashwa'iyat* are implicated in the discourse surrounding these practices. The mainstream discourse around Greater Cairo's informal areas has often been laden with stigma, fearmongering, and legal ambiguity. In this sense, the securitization of urban space highlights the most illiberal tendencies in the so-called neoliberal regime form, identified by Paul Amar in *The Security Archipelago* (2013) as the criminalizing "human–security state," or described as "vernacular neoliberalism" and as forms of globally articulated and engineered class polarization in Singerman and Amar's *Cairo Cosmopolitan* (2006). I take these discourses and practices of stigma, fear, and (il)legality orbiting around the *'ashwa'iyat* as a starting point to explore what the sudden spread of numerical and prepaid technologies within utility infrastructure can suggest about urban citizenship within the context of Egypt, and within a broader context of ongoing sectorial neoliberal reforms.

Accommodating Informality?

In 2009, a spokesperson for the NCEDC claimed that although the *'ashwa'iyat* are consuming electricity, over 15 percent of their users engage in electricity theft (Yousif 2009). He claimed that people within the *'ashwa'iyat* prefer to steal electricity, even when there are legal provisions that allow them to connect formally, thereby repeating a common trope about informal area dwellers. His solution was to conduct an intensive campaign in cooperation with the Ministry of Interior to file reports against homes illegally tapped into the network and to impose fines. He insisted that "these fines are transferred to the prosecutor's office for either payment or jail time" (Yousif 2009).

As the utility companies increased their focus on cost recovery during the mid- to late 2000s, they began to devise arrangements that would enable them to collect payments including from non-metered connections in informal areas. One of the earliest commonly used methods to deal with such connections has been a system called *mumarsa*, still used in some areas today. Under this system, the company establishes a fixed charge that users then pay every month, based on the size of the home and the number of residents. If users feel this estimation is inaccurate or unjust, there is nothing they can do. Though *mumarsa* remained an unofficial policy for years, the company spokespersons denied its use. Then, in 2010, the Egyptian prime minister stated that he would be issuing a decree allowing unlicensed buildings to apply for a new type of temporary meter. These coded meters, known in Egyptian Arabic as ʿaddad cody, are prepaid meters that users can charge using a scratch card, and that would not carry the user's name, but rather the building's number—hence the name "coded meter." These meters would allow residents to bypass the municipality, which is legally responsible for dealing with unlicensed buildings, and interact directly with the utility companies.

After the surge in unlicensed construction after the 2011 revolution, the water and electricity companies complained of an unforeseen strain being placed on the networks, which were not built to serve the population sizes that were actually using them. They also complained of a surge in theft that was costing them millions. In 2014, the head of the Holding Company for Water and Wastewater (HCWW) stated that illegal connections were costing the company over LE 4.2 million every month (Alexandria Portal 2014). The electricity company has made similar complaints about the increase in illegal connections since 2011. Thus, they have confirmed in the media the use of mumarsa and have also formally institutionalized the temporary prepaid coded meters. The water company has stated that it will follow the model of the electricity company and purchase 6.2 million prepaid coded meters to contribute toward their cost-recovery efforts, considering it a necessary measure to recover these costs until the state decides to deal with these alleged transgressors. All of this points to the heightened importance placed on ensuring that unplanned areas are financially incorporated into utility companies' consumption monitoring and payment mechanisms.

The increased access that residents of such areas have today to formal, metered utility connections is often interpreted by donors and state agencies through a developmentalist narrative. It is true that coverage of informal areas by the public utility networks has increased over the past several years. But the belief that this development has been driven largely by neoliberal reforms has led to the curious situation where informal areas are incorporated financially but not legally. Residents of unplanned areas are, on the one hand, treated as clients who must pay for services just as all other citizens do. On the other hand, they continue to be portrayed as illegal occupants who have encroached on state land and have a natural proclivity toward theft and crime.

Increased "Statization" of Unplanned Areas

The 2011 revolution disrupted the clientelist networks that had revolved around the existence of the ruling National Democratic Party (NDP) and then dissolved along with the party. These channels had, for decades, been the primary means through which various state agencies monitored and intervened in informal areas. The dissolution of the networks has created a political vacuum, which is being filled by increasingly heavy-handed interventions by state institutions. The water company has sped up the process of installing pipes in the remaining unconnected areas and has been trying to simplify its procedures to allow applicants to receive meters even if they cannot provide the necessary paperwork. The electricity network is focusing its energies less on filing police reports against non-metered connections and more on creating institutional mechanisms to incorporate them. The natural gas company has, for the first time, begun installing its network in unplanned areas. These developments are taking place within a broader context of increased state attention toward unplanned areas, renewed by a president interested in making a mark on Cairo's "*'ashwa'iyat* problem." The Informal Settlement Development Facility, in cooperation with the Cairo Governorate, has been implementing upgrading and relocation projects in unplanned areas at an unprecedented pace. The 2014 national constitution was the first in Egyptian history to stipulate the commitment of the state to developing a national plan to address *'ashwa'iyat*. It is not coincidental that 2014 also saw the establishment of a new ministry for informal settlements, which lasted just over a year.

Such developments have led to what can be described as an increased statization of unplanned areas. Everyday life is permeated by the state through uneventful, mundane practices where citizens engage with the state on a regular basis (Painter 2006). These practices tend to revolve around the organization of space—urban plans, zoning laws, land use regulations, allocations of basic services, administrative spatial divisions and boundaries—essentially determining what citizens can and cannot do in a given area. The state invests a lot of time and effort into developing the rules, regulations, and procedures that together ensure it is "imagined in some ways rather than others" (Scott 1998; Ferguson and Gupta 2002). The degree to which state practices of order and regulation infiltrate into one's daily life reflects the degree to which they are "statized." Since such practices are often uneven, different social groupings—whether economic, political, spatial, or anything else—can be statized to different degrees. Far from representing conflict or disorganization, this "prosaic statization thus necessarily proceeds unevenly, and so geographical variations in the provision of health care, policing, education and so on are not 'aberrations' but integral to the operation of modern state institutions" (Painter 2006, 764).

Such a conception challenges the way in which the development literature discusses the existence of urban informality and informal areas as a process that exists outside or despite the state. One would expect, in this case, that such areas would see a lesser presence of state institutions and a weaker infiltration of regular state practice in their daily lives. But the exact opposite has been happening, with unplanned areas witnessing heightened processes of "statization." Moreover, this process has tended to take place in less obvious ways through the provision of infrastructure and services.

Unbundling of Rights

This situation of attention focused on informal areas also challenges scholars of neoliberalism, who have argued that neoliberal reforms necessitate a roll-back of the state, and that the state apparatus should be replaced with transnational bodies, such as the WTO and IMF. Quite the opposite is happening; alongside processes of globalization and neoliberalization, the everyday lives of people are becoming more intensely "statized" (Painter 2006) Some scholars have argued that the roll-back of the state has resulted in the destruction of the traditional social contract that has bound citizens and state. This assertion is often linked to the dismantling of welfare policies, instead placing citizens at the mercy of the market (Brown 2015). Others have found that neoliberal reforms did not lead to a dismantling of welfare policies but rather a compromise between existing welfare mechanisms and the more market-oriented policies being promoted by international discourse (Collier 2011). In Egypt, neoliberalism has resulted in increased state control rather than state roll-back. What is actually being dismantled is not the state, but rather the link between citizenship and a collection of rights.

Unbundling "involves the conversion of one property right into a bundle of separate instruments, each designed to pursue a different objective and, often, operate at different scales" (Young 2011, 20). The 2014 Egyptian constitution guarantees the right to adequate housing for all citizens. This bundles together the rights to water, sanitation, electricity, and secure tenure, among other things. While residents of unplanned areas continue to link metered utility connections with proof of tenure, the utility companies have stated that the temporary coded meters are to be used by illegal buildings that cannot apply for a formal connection. They insist that in no way should this be considered a form of proof of tenure (Ramadan 2015).

The water company spokesperson affirmed that these meters are given a number and not a name tied to a formal contract with the company, that they are not to be considered a proof of ownership or tenure, and that if the state decides to demolish these homes, they can demolish the meter along with it (Alexandria Portal 2014). Both companies have stated repeatedly that the incorporation of non-metered connections—whether through *mumarsa* or temporary meters—should not be misconstrued by residents as a sign of legality or proof of tenure. By 2015, the electricity company had only been able to install 163,000 coded meters (out of over 800,000 applicants), due largely to the municipal governments refusing to install them because they are worried the meters would be used as a proof of tenure (Alexandria Portal 2014). I interpret these statements by the utility companies as efforts to unbundle access to water from the broader questions of secure tenure and adequate housing that are constitutionally promised to all citizens.

Statizing Informality, Unbundling Rights

The neoliberal reforms implemented in Egypt's water and electricity sectors and the impacts they have had within Cairo's unplanned areas are causing rapid and unforeseen changes. Since the 2000s, the way in which informal areas have been accommodated financially, but not legally, combined with the way the right to adequate housing is being unbundled—for example, water and electricity can be addressed without needing to address tenure—has allowed the state to benefit from informality without having to deal with the many systemic issues supporting it. In unplanned areas, neoliberal reforms in the water and electricity sectors have had the dual effect of an increased presence of state institutions and an unbundling of rights guaranteed to all citizens.

These reforms are indicative of the unique vantage point offered by infrastructure from which to study neoliberalism and power. Neoliberalism should not be seen as an all-encompassing force that erodes all rights. Rather, its technologies have repeatedly unbundled sets of rights such that they promote certain rights while hindering others. The reform process also underscores the need to understand informality not as something that occurs outside the state. Rather than seeing informal connections to public utility networks as a fixed category, such as "illegal," the above analysis shows that a more processual analysis—one that considers informality as a transformation created just as much by the state as by informal area dwellers—is warranted. The built environment within Cairo's 'ashwa'iyat is thus caught in a continual process of becoming, whereby it is simultaneously reproduced as a manifestation of the "illegality" of these unplanned neighborhoods while also being reproduced as a terrain through which to create new geographies of capital accumulation. The process highlights the need to move beyond traditional conceptions of neoliberalism as a paradigm that prescribes state "roll-back," and to reinterpret it as a political rationality that seeks to reshape the effect of the state by producing new forms of the state–society relationship.

Notes

1 Nawal K., interview by author, March 29, 2014, Greater Cairo Water and Wastewater Company.
2 The term "unplanned areas" is part of official state terminology, defined by Law 119/2008 as "areas that emerged in contravention to the laws and procedures that regulate urban planning and construction" (Arab Republic of Egypt 2008). Colloquially—and in the mainstream media as well as some official documents, such as the 2014 national constitution—these areas are referred to using the Arabic Egyptian colloquial term 'ashwa'iyat, which roughly translates to "haphazard areas."

Works Cited

Alexandria Portal, Ministry of State for Administrative Development. 2014. "Sitta million 'addad bil-'ashwa'iyat li-man' sariqat al-miyah." http://www.alexandria.gov.eg/Lists/List5/DispForm.aspx?ID=4146.

Amar, Paul. 2013. *The Security Archipelago: Human-security States, Sexuality Politics, and the End of Neoliberalism*. Durham, NC: Duke University Press.

Arab Republic of Egypt. 2008. "The Official Gazette—Issue No. 19." Cairo: Office of the Presidency.

———. 2014. "The Official Gazette—Issue No. 29." Cairo: Office of the Presidency.

———. 2016. "The Official Gazette—Issue No. 13." Cairo: Office of the Presidency.

Armbrust, Walter. 2011. "Egypt: A Revolution against Neoliberalism?" *Al-Jazeera*, February 24. https://tinyurl.com/mh6qzwj.

Bakker, Karen. 2009. "Neoliberal Nature, Ecological Fixes, and the Pitfalls of Comparative Research." *Environment and Planning* A 41, no. 8: 1781–87.

Brown, Wendy. 2015. *Undoing the Demos: Neoliberalism's Stealth Revolution.* New York: Zone Books.

Callon, M. 1998. "Introduction: The Embeddedness of Economic Markets in Economics." *The Sociological Review* 46, no. 1 (S1): 1–57.

CAPMAS. 2006. "National Census." Cairo: Central Agency for Public Mobilization and Statistics (CAPMAS). https://egypt.opendata forafrica.org/EGSNS2006/egypt-census-2006.

Collier, S.J. 2011. *Post-Soviet Social: Neoliberalism, Social Modernity, Biopolitics.* Princeton, NJ: Princeton University Press.

Ferguson, J., and A. Gupta. 2002. "Spatializing States: Toward an Ethnography of Neoliberal Governmentality." *American Ethnologist* 29, no. 4: 981–1002.

Marafi, Safaa. 2011. "Neoliberal Policies, Urban Segregation and the Egyptian Revolution." Master's thesis, American University in Cairo.

Painter, Joe. 2006. "Prosaic Geographies of Stateness." *Political Geography* 25, no. 7: 752–74.

Ramadan, Rahma. 2015. "'al-Kahraba' tatalaqqa 36,000 talab tawsil tayyar li-l-'ashwa'iyat." *Youm7.* https://tinyurl.com/yxdmv4om.

Scott, James C. 1998. *Seeing Like a State: How Certain Schemes to Improve the Human Condition Have Failed.* New Haven, CT: Yale University Press.

Shenker, Jack. 2009. "And the Rich Got Richer." *The Guardian*, November 8. https://www.theguardian.com/commentisfree/2009/nov/08/egypt-imf.

Sims, David. 2010. *Understanding Cairo: The Logic of a City Out of Control.* Cairo: American University in Cairo Press.

Singerman, Diane, and Paul Amar. 2006. *Cairo Cosmopolitan: Politics, Culture, and Urban Space in the New Globalized Middle East.* Cairo: American University in Cairo Press.

Smith, Laila. 2004. "The Murky Waters of the Second Wave of Neoliberalism: Corporatization as a Service Delivery Model in Cape Town." *Geoforum* 35, no. 3: 375–93.

Young, Mike. 2011. "The Role of the Unbundling Water Rights in Australia's Southern Connected Murray Darling Basin." WP6 IBE EX-POST Case Studies, IBE Review Reports, December 19. Adelaide: University of Adelaide.

Yousif, Nadia. 2009. "Al-tala'ub fi al-'addad." *Al-Ahram.* April 1. http://www.ahram.org.eg/Archive/2009/4/1/Inve2.htm.

22

AL-ASMARAT
MANAGING INFORMALITY, REPRODUCING PRECARITY, AND DISLOCATING WORKERS

MOSTAFA MOHIE

On my way to al-Asmarat, I had to cut through twenty kilometers from the center of Cairo to al-Muqattam on the eastern side of the capital. As my car was approaching al-Asmarat, I started to see lines of residential buildings, all of the same height and design, boasting the same slogan in bold colors: "Long Live Egypt." This slogan has become famous since it was used by Abd al-Fattah al-Sisi's 2014 presidential campaign, later becoming the tag line and name for various construction projects. I entered al-Asmarat's gate, which had a noticeable security presence, with police trucks and security personnel in evidence. I wasn't stopped or asked about my destination, though. It was already evening, and the wide streets of the complex were illumined in strong artificial lights. I could see small groups of people hanging out, sitting on the corners, drinking tea and chatting. The area looked different from the last time I had visited in 2017. Back then, it was emptier, with almost no shops. The streets were dominated by pedestrians, and there were few public buses transporting the residents to the gates of the city so they could catch other forms of public transportation. Now, a few shops had opened here and there: groceries, bakeries, and one or two coffee houses—most of them owned by people who lived outside al-Asmarat. Private cars, microbuses, and minivans were transporting people in and out.

In June 2016, Egyptian president Abd al-Fattah al-Sisi inaugurated al-Asmarat as a relocation and rehousing project for the residents of informal districts in Cairo that had been designated as "unsafe" by the government. The total capacity of the project is more than eighteen thousand housing units, with a cost of almost LE 3.6 billion (Ministry of Housing n.d.). It was funded by the Cairo Governorate, the Informal Settlements Development Fund (ISDF), and the Long Live Egypt Fund. The project was described by pro-regime media as the government's solution to informal settlements *(ashwa'iyat)* and a war on "slums" (Hamza 2020). Al-Asmarat is not the only newly built complex for the residents of unsafe areas in Greater Cairo. There are also relatively smaller projects, such as al-Mahrusa, Ahalina, and Ard al-Khayala. In Alexandria, there is the Bashayir al-Khair housing project. All of these were built for the residents of "unsafe" areas. The government started to study the possibility of building cities similar to al-Asmarat in all of the governorates' capitals—a project that has no clear plan yet.

Urban expansion into the deserts surrounding Cairo has resulted in the construction of planned mega-communities for the upper and middle classes, as El-Husseiny and Borham have pointed out in their chapters in this volume. It has also become a means to enact the securitization and peripheralization of Cairo's "dangerous" poor masses through forced removal and resettlement, as O. Khalil's and D. Khalil's contributions illustrate. The current chapter looks at one of these new developments and how it often reproduces exactly the same problems it was supposed to solve, along with a host of new difficulties, in the name of "civilizing" the threatening poor.

Our study of government approaches to dealing with neighborhoods deemed unsafe ought to go back at least as far as September 2008, when a series of rockslides in Duwiqa smashed 166 houses, killing 119 people and injuring 55 others (Shawkat 2018). One month after the disaster, the ISDF was founded by presidential decree to fund and plan the development of informal neighborhoods, with an urgent focus on unsafe areas. According to the Central Agency for Public Mobilization and Statistics (CAPMAS), 38.6 percent of the urban areas in Egypt are informal. These areas are divided into two categories: unplanned neighborhoods, which don't follow the official planning and building conditions (constituting 97.2 percent of the informal areas), and unsafe neighborhoods, which constitute 2.8 percent of the informal areas (CAPMAS 2016). The ISDF has designated 357 areas around Egypt as "unsafe," encompassing 242,905 housing units *(Al-Masry Al-Youm* 2020). These areas were categorized into four degrees of threat: life-threatening housing, unsuitable shelter conditions, area health risks, and instability of tenure. The ISDF and government officials had such cases in mind when they referred to plans to "end the problem of informal settlements" by the end of 2020 (CAPMAS 2016). This project affects more than one million residents. It was even argued that the term "development of informal settlements" doesn't accurately describe government efforts to relocate residents, which includes forced evictions that lack any community participation (Khalil 2018).

In Cairo, there are fifty-seven unsafe areas, which host more than seventy thousand housing units. Only 32 percent of these units are considered life-threatening, and almost 50 percent of them are inadequate but could be improved sufficiently. However, the ISDF has built almost twenty-six thousand housing units in complexes[1] like al-Asmarat, and intends to add fifteen thousand more as relocation sites for Cairenes living in areas deemed unsafe. In most of these cases, these new complexes are located in remote areas in comparison with the informal neighborhoods being emptied. In media portrayals and official discourse, al-Asmarat is portrayed as "civilized housing" that promises not only to avoid the various threats of the unsafe areas, but also to provide a "civilized life" for its inhabitants. Most of the visuals that are used by the officials to show the progress of the project highlight two pictures representing the "before" and "after": the informal neighborhood and the newly built houses. While the former appears dense, irregular, and crowded, the latter looks spacious, uniform, and empty. The pictures produce binaries between the formal and informal, safe and unsafe, ordered and chaotic, and constructed and organic. The schema includes the IDSF projects, social housing,[2] new settlements, and the New Administrative Capital.

In this chapter, I argue that although al-Asmarat was built to provide the residents of neighborhoods deemed unsafe with allegedly safer houses, it imposes other forms of unsafety on these Cairenes. Because of several legal and economic reasons related to the act of relocation, the residents of al-Asmarat still live under precarious conditions. The constructed environment of al-Asmarat was used to control the residents' practices to prevent the emergence of any "informal behaviors"—that is, behaviors similar to those practiced in the informal neighborhoods. I have relied on informal, semi-structured interviews, conducted in 2017 and 2020, with thirteen respondents from the Maspero Triangle, Manshiyat Nasir, Duwiqa, and al-Madabigh neighborhoods after their relocation to al-Asmarat. In addition, in 2018, I interviewed the executive manager of the ISDF, Khalid Siddiq. My analysis follows two themes. The first focuses on how the process of formalizing housing has rendered the lives of al-Asmarat residents as precarious as they were before relocation (and sometimes more) through rental debts, outstanding bills, and lack of jobs. The second examines the different aspects of social control practiced on these residents through security checks and restrictive rules in al-Asmarat.

Reproducing Precariousness

Although fifteen thousand Cairene families had already been relocated to al-Asmarat city by the end of 2019 (al-Khalafawy 2019a), almost none of them had received any form of tenancy contract or deed. They signed contracts the moment they were assigned an apartment, but weren't allowed to take copies with them and didn't see those contracts again. The families were granted apartments through different arrangements. While the residents of the Maspero Triangle were granted deeds for their residential units in al-Asmarat for LE 300, paid in monthly installments, most of the families from other neighborhoods were just granted usufruct contracts, which cannot be passed on to one generation after the death of the main tenant, for a monthly rent of LE 300 (Mohie 2018a).

For Ibrahim, who originally came from Manshiyat Nasir, the shift from being a home "owner" to becoming a tenant in al-Asmarat gave him a sense of unease. His family, like most of the families in Manshiyat Nasir, had squatted on government-owned land and built their own house over decades as a life investment. For years, Cairo Governorate officials resisted any demands or suggestions to start land titling programs, with the assumption that it would encourage the growth of informal settlements, set precedents for other informal communities to demand public services and formalization, and allow newly titled residents to sell their property to real estate speculators (El-Messiri 1989; Tekçe, Oldham, and Shorter 1994; Dorman 2011, 281). Even when the governorate began a titling process as part of a USAID-funded project in Manshiyat Nasir in the 1980s, it set land prices at levels comparable to those in city-center neighborhoods. The project ultimately failed for this reason.[3] For the families of Manshiyat Nasir, the fact that the government had accepted their existence on this land for decades—providing infrastructure for their neighborhoods, installing electricity meters, and collecting real estate taxes from them—had created a sense of formalization. Nevertheless, this didn't help Ibrahim's family, who lost their house because of an illegal acquisition of land and the designation of the surrounding area as life-threatening. Yet even after moving to al-Asmarat, the family's legal position remains ambiguous due to the fact that they were denied copies of their contracts.

Some interlocutors aren't worried about the fact that they didn't receive copies of the contracts they signed. Husni, who was relocated to al-Asmarat from the al-Madabigh neighborhood in 2019, believes that the receipts of the LE 4,600 deposit and the monthly rent are enough proof of his legal right to his apartment. In addition, electricity and gas utilities are registered in his name now, which gives him more confidence. In other words, Hosni is still relying on the same legal grounds the families in informal neighborhoods used to claim the right to their houses, which eventually may leave him in the same precarious position they are currently in. This precariousness was experienced by dozens of families who received eviction notices in April 2018 after not paying their rent for just under two years. The families protested the eviction threat, asking to defer the debt. After negotiations with a minister of parliament, the protest ended. However, later in the same month, twelve of the al-Asmarat residents were arrested and accused of illegally protesting. Within one month, a court had sentenced them to two years in prison (Mohie 2018b). For the residents, not having copies of their contracts disrupts their ability to contest eviction orders.

For most of my interlocutors, the fact of moving from informal to formal housing increased the cost of living. Mahmud, for example, received one of the eviction notices. It was impossible for him to pay the LE 300 monthly rent out of his LE 2,000 salary, not to mention the LE 7,000 rental debt accumulated over almost two years. He was a vendor in a clothes shop and lived with his wife and five children in Manshiyat Nasir before the government demolished his house. Before their relocation, most of my interlocutors were either paying rent that didn't exceed LE 50 or were not paying any rent at all since they had built their own homes. Now, they are being asked to pay a monthly rent of LE 300, which will increase by 7 percent annually. What adds to the hardship of formalization is the new reality that electricity and gas are prepaid utilities in al-Asmarat, unlike in the informal neighborhoods, where utilities were paid after usage. For many al-Asmarat residents— especially those who depend on government pensions—the choice is between paying the rent or the electricity, gas, and water bills. And when it comes to prioritizing one thing over another, the utilities tend to take priority. Before the relocation, utility payments could be postponed or rescheduled. Even if they weren´t paid, it would be technically difficult for the utility companies to shut off the service to a specific house.

Furthermore, the meters did not always accurately reflect consumption. For instance, in informal neighborhoods where water meters weren't installed, consumption was decided based on estimates made by the water company. Every unit was charged a more or less fixed amount of money every month. According to my interlocutors, this estimated payment was significantly less than what is paid now in al-Asmarat.[4] Utility companies, which are owned by the government, make sure that consumption is counted and paid for by setting up prepaid utilities in all of the units of al-Asmarat, leaving the residents with no way to negotiate.

Moving to al-Asmarat from informal neighborhoods has also limited job prospects. Hussein, an unemployed young man originally from the Maspero Triangle, mentioned *marzaqa* (the first time I heard the term), which refers to an abundance of *rizq*, or means of livelihood. The term means more than having a good job. *Marzaqa* can be a permanent or temporary job or even a one-time transaction in exchange for financial compensation. But *marzaqa* vanished for Hussein after he moved to al-Asmarat. In the Maspero Triangle, he had been a street vendor, selling clothes in the nearby famous flea market *(wikalat al balah)*. He was able to store his merchandise in his house and take it in the mornings to the flea market. Calculating the costs of transportation, meals while working, and leasing a place to store his merchandise convinced Hussein that it wouldn't make sense to keep working in the flea market while living in al-Asmarat; the daily expenses would exceed half of the already small profit margin he would make. After that, he couldn't find any other means of livelihood in al-Asmarat.

One of the main tactics to sustain life in informal neighborhoods dominated by low-income families is to keep everything close by: house, work, and family. It makes life affordable by cutting transportation expenses and expanding the social network of the individual within the neighborhood. The demolition of a neighborhood ends this tightly woven life. These challenges are not only Hussein's. Another two interlocutors, Ashraf and Islam, lost their jobs due to their inability to pay transportation costs. Before moving to al-Asmarat, the former had been a tailor in the 'Ataba district and the latter had been employed in a clothing shop in Downtown. Both used to live in the Maspero Triangle, which was adjacent to their workplaces.

The story repeats itself throughout my interviews. Zeinab, for example, sustained herself by working at a grocery shop that is owned by her family back in Maspero. When the neighborhood was demolished, she wasn't compensated with a job in another shop in al-Asmarat and she lost her main source of income. After demolishing unsafe neighborhoods, the government didn't compensate the residents for the demolished shops or workshops, which left them in hardship. Ibrahim, to offer another example, was a mechanic in Manshiyat Nasir, where he also used to live. Since he relocated to al-Asmarat, his market has shrunk significantly, as he now works on the sidewalk without a proper workshop. Essam is a tanner who used to live and work in the tanneries neighborhood. In 2019, the government relocated 773 families from that neighborhood to al-Asmarat, and moved the tanneries to a bigger, well-equipped space sixty kilometers away from al-Asmarat (Mohie 2020). Essam has decided he needs to stay at his workplace during the weekdays and go back to his family in al-Asmarat only on weekends, to save on daily transportation costs.

In my 2018 interview with the executive manager of the ISDF, Khalid Siddiq, he told me that "it is not necessary for places of residence and employment to be in the same area. This is not how societies in the developed world work. There is low-cost transportation available between al-Asmarat, Manshiyat Nasir, Maspero, and other areas." But even with low-cost transportation, lengthy daily commutes strain the budgets of the residents. When I asked Siddiq about the 290 shops in al-Asmarat, which weren't yet open, he replied that they would be sold in a public auction, adding that "the main purpose of these shops is to pump new life into Asmarat, and for residents to be able to satisfy their needs." However, when these shops eventually were sold in public auctions, most of the residents of al-Asmarat weren't able to compete with other buyers and lost the chance to create jobs for themselves within the city where they live. It is true that in 2019, Cairo Governorate opened some workshops for small crafts, providing the residents with 1,400 job opportunities, according to governorate officials (al-Khalafawy 2019b). Yet this is still far from being enough, according to the residents.

Ironically, the main reason for building al-Asmarat, according to the government discourse, was to provide the residents of informal neighborhoods with safe housing. But precarious economic and domestic well-being cannot be considered safe. The lack of contract copies, the increasing cost of formalization, and decreasing opportunities to secure means for their livelihood have all intensified feelings of uncertainty among most of al-Asmarat's new residents.

Striving for Social Control

When 'Eid was relocated to al-Asmarat in 2017, he had already retired from his government job. Yet his monthly pension of LE 900 wasn't enough to pay for all his expenses. He decided to sell candy and groceries from the balcony of his ground-floor apartment. He didn't expect that the municipal employees, led by the head of the municipality, would raid his makeshift shop, confiscating his goods and threatening to evict him from his unit if he resumed his commercial activities. I was told a similar story by Nagat, another interlocutor who is also using her balcony to sell goods. She recounted how one of the residents started to sell fava beans on a cart only to have it confiscated by the municipal employees, who spilled the food onto the ground. The municipality doesn't tolerate any activity that alters the designated purpose of each place: the house shouldn't be turned into a shop. In the first two years of the city, only the government buses—not microbuses or minivans—were allowed to transport the residents within the city (a rule that was later abandoned). Furthermore, the municipality has opposed social gatherings of any sort in the streets of al-Asmarat. Unlike in their former neighborhoods, residents are not allowed to have funerals, weddings, *iftar* in Ramadan, or similar collective activities in the street (Wahba 2020). The message is that there is low tolerance for any activity that might lead to the reappearance of "informality": al-Asmarat must be a place for "civilized life."

Fighting informality and ensuring uniformity is evident in numerous regulations. Residents weren't allowed to bring their own furniture and household appliances to their new homes. Before relocation, families were told to sell or get rid of their furniture because the residential units in al-Asmarat were identically pre-furnished apartments. However, some items like an extra sofa or a refrigerator were smuggled in by the families without the knowledge of the municipal employees or after negotiations with them. This tendency to ensure uniformity is also evident in the way the apartments were designed. They are all identical: sixty-two square meters of apartment space, consisting of two bedrooms, one living room, a kitchen, and a bathroom. One bedroom has a large bed, and the other has two single beds. In the living room, there are four dining chairs. It is an apartment for a nuclear family of two parents and two children, regardless of the fact that this design doesn't match the reality of most of the families relocated to al-Asmarat.

Furthermore, in the first year of al-Asmarat, guests were stopped by the gates and asked to identify their hosts before they were allowed to enter. Sometimes guests were asked to call the host to come and escort them. Later, when more families moved in, it became difficult to maintain the same level of control, and these measures were abandoned.

However, the security presence didn't disappear, and a small police station was established inside the city. For Hussein, this security presence doesn't necessarily result in a feeling of safety. To the contrary: for young men, it means they can be stopped and their personal identification documents may be checked while going through the gate—something that often happens in other places in the city. These security checks can last for minutes, hours, or even a day. Husni believes this examination doesn't happen to everyone, but according to the officers' biases and discretion. Both of Husni's sons, who were students at technical schools, were stopped and had their IDs checked. When the police officer found out they were from the tanneries neighborhood, he insisted on keeping them until he checked their IDs on the computer to see if there were any legal cases against them. Fortunately, their records were clean, and they were let go. Their mother mentioned that they were smart enough to keep their heads down during this situation.

In general, there is a feeling among most of the residents that they have no control over their immediate environment, but, rather, they are being strictly controlled. They admit that the new houses are better and the buildings are safer, but life itself is neither easier nor less precarious. On the contrary, the state's vision for an "ideal and civilized society" has resulted in a more uncertain and punitive one. One of the most common complaints among al-Asmarat residents is that violent fights erupt repeatedly every week among young men who are originally from different neighborhoods. The fights reflect the feeling of unease among everyone caused by the forced neighborhood restructuring. It is ironic that the fights have increased, since they are part of what state officials describe as manifestations of life in informal neighborhoods. An urbanism constructed under authoritarian pretenses, like al-Asmarat, wasn't enough to mold residents into a government ideal. It might, instead, be a reason to inflame them.

Notes

1   Although most of the people refer to al-Asmarat as a city, I prefer to use the word "complex" since, legally, it is not a separate city.
2   I am referring to the government project, which started in 2011 and relaunched in 2014, to build one million subsidized housing units for low-income families. For more information, see "A Million Units for Whom? Six Facts about the Social Housing Project," published by the Built Environment Observatory on May 28, 2018, and available at https://tinyurl.com/3dfwh6yy.

3   In 2019, the parliament passed legislation allowing reconcilia-
    tions over building violations. The official discourse about the
    law portrayed it as a chance to legalize informal housing, once and
    for all. However, residents who own or live in houses on govern-
    ment-owned land are not being allowed to reconcile. Also, several
    accounts have criticized the vague law. It is unclear who is respon-
    sible for paying the reconciliation fee: the owner who built the
    unit or the tenant who lives in it. Another criticism highlighted the
    inflated reconciliation fees and the complicated bureaucratic pro-
    cess needed to finalize the reconciliation. Almost two years after
    issuing the law, the government announced that it had received 2.7
    million reconciliation requests. However, it is unclear how many
    of these requests were accepted and reached the final phase of
    reconciliation. See "Form 10: Climbing the Bureaucratic Ladder
    to Legalize Homes in Egypt's Countryside" at https://tinyurl.
    com/6xev9cwpfile:///Users/paulamar/Downloads/h

4   It is also important to mention that the government has raised
    the prices of electricity and natural gas multiple times since 2015
    as part of a plan to cut energy subsidies, supported by the Interna-
    tional Monetary Fund (IMF), which has resulted in a significant
    increase in energy prices. According to a report by the Egyptian
    Initiative for Personal Rights, electricity prices increased by 160
    percent between 2015 and 2018. See https://tinyurl.com/sbht9wrs.

Works Cited

CAPMAS (Central Agency for Public Mobilization and Statistics of
    the Arab Republic of Egypt). 2016. "Dirasat tatwir wa tanmiyat
    al-manatiq al-'ashwa'iya fi Misr. 2016–23423–81." May. Cairo:
    CAPMAS.
Dorman, W.J. 2011. "Of Demolitions and Donors: The Problemat-
    ics of State Intervention in Informal Cairo." In *Cairo Contested:
    Governance, Urban Space, and Global Modernity*, edited by Diane
    Singerman, 269–90. Cairo: American University in Cairo Press.
Hamza, Ayman. 2020. "Al-dawla tu'lin al-harb 'ala al-'ashwa'iyat."
    Al-Watan, October 20. https://tinyurl.com/y4y2ru9f.
al-Khalafawy, Sayed. 2019a. "al-Asmarat madina gadida khallasat
    al-'asima min al-'ashwa'iyat." *Youm7*, September 19. https://tinyurl.
    com/yaukxley.
———. 2019b. "Tahta shi'ar 'Suni'a fi al-Asmarat.'" *Youm7*, March 23.
    https://tinyurl.com/y2kpv424.

Khalil, Omnia. 2018. "From Community Participation to Forced Eviction in the Maspero Triangle." Tahrir Institute for Middle East Policy, June 14. https://tinyurl.com/y5sebsv3.

Al-Masry Al-Youm. 2020. "Ma hiya al-manatiq ghayr al-amina wa-igmali 'adaduha?" *Al-Masry Al-Youm*, July 12. https://tinyurl.com/y63cenxu.

El-Messiri, Sawsan. 1989. "Regularization of Land Title for Informal Communities in Cairo: An Analysis and Proposal Approach." Cooperative Housing Foundation for USAID, Cairo.

Ministry of Housing, Arab Republic of Egypt. n.d. "Mashru'at tatwir al-manatiq al-'ashwa'iya." Cairo: Ministry of Housing. https://tinyurl.com/y5qjyppj.

Mohie, Mostafa. 2018a. "Interview: On Developing the Maspero Triangle and the Future of the Asmarat Housing Project." *Mada Masr*, August 4. https://tinyurl.com/yyqdk3re.

———. 2018b. "Asmarat: The State's Model Housing for Former 'Slum' Residents." *Mada Masr*, June 18. https://tinyurl.com/y8wp57kz.

———. 2020. "'Ala anqad magra al-'uyun: mashahid min agmal madina fi al-'alam." *Mada Masr*, March 18. https://tinyurl.com/y3lvtbm3.

Shawkat, Yahia. 2018. "The Duweika Disaster Ten Years On—Part 1: Disaster and Aftermath." The Built Environment Observatory, September 7. https://tinyurl.com/y4otasxp.

Tekçe, Belgin, Linda Oldham, and Frederic Shorter. 1994. *A Place to Live: Families and Child Health in a Cairo Neighborhood.* Cairo: American University in Cairo Press.

Wahba, Dina. 2020. "Urban Rights and Local Politics in Egypt: The Case of the Maspero Triangle." Arab Reform Initiative, January 23. https://tinyurl.com/y5yeazua.

23

PACTA SUNT SERVANDA?
EXERCISING POSSESSION IN AN INFORMALIZED CAIRO

YAHIA SHAWKAT

On a windy October morning in 2000, Ms. Fulan and Mr. al-Sayid signed a contract of sale for an apartment from the latter to the former.[1] Handshakes and money were exchanged. Ms. Fulan was probably excited over her new purchase and relieved to have found a new home that she could afford after months of looking at dozens of overpriced and underwhelming properties. Sadly, her excitement was short-lived and quickly turned into confusion and shock, when she found someone already living in "her" apartment.

The police were called, and a report was lodged that an intruder was occupying Ms. Fulan's apartment. However, they were powerless to evict the alleged intruder as no signs of forced entry were visible. Only a court could decide on this horrid situation where the same property was apparently sold to two different buyers in an act of fraud.

This chapter examines this type of fraudulent activity in relation to the right to adequate housing, and its central component of security of tenure. I use Ms. Fulan's case as a real-life example that ran for close to two decades—from the date she signed the fateful contract in October 2000 until a final verdict was passed in May 2017 in one of the palatial courtrooms of Dar al-Qada' al-'Ali (High Court House) in downtown Cairo. It represents an evolution of previous work on the exploitation of tenure informality by the government against individuals and communities by manufacturing a gray spectrum of informality

339

(Shawkat 2020, 176, 195–96). This study aims to shed light on a lesser-known practice by individuals and small private enterprises targeting and taking advantage of other individuals, although still within the government's laws regarding "manufactured informality." And while an examination of the government's exploitation of informality shows how it gains by commodifying housing and then exploiting the rent gap, this chapter illustrates how the private sector—from individuals to large corporations—has been profiteering through fraud. Since three-quarters of urban Egyptians are homeowners, this profiteering also claims low-income victims.

Ms. Fulan's case has become less the exception and more the rule, as she is among many victims dispossessed of their homes every year by this informalization and a poorly enforced rule of law in Cairo—and the rest of the country—while the perpetrators thrive through fraud, administrative corruption, and violence. There are no statistics for this type of fraud, though some strong indications suggest that it is widespread. In the early 1990s, a "progressive increase in tenure disputes . . . catalyzed by the housing crisis" prompted the Shura Council (the upper house of Egypt's parliament) to amend the procedural code to reform how the prosecutor's office and courts deal with the mounting cases (Law 23/1992). Over the last five years, Egypt's highest appellate court, the Court of Cassation,[2] passed verdicts on twenty-three property dispute cases, including Ms. Fulan's.[3] Based on this table, one can infer that there are many more ongoing cases in the appeals and local district courts. In a recent case in Alexandria, case files indicated how a property development company made 350 sale contracts for only 177 units in one of its new buildings, leading to a torrent of cases against it as well as violent disputes between competing "owners" (*Youm7* 2018).

Another point of departure here depends upon reframing geographic informality. As Mohie, Nassar, and Duffield have illustrated in their contributions to this volume, much of the academic and state agency literature on urban Egypt considers informality a physical feature, drawing maps of areas deemed informal, unplanned, or even unsafe and in need of development, formalization, legalization, or demolition (De Soto 1998; Kipper and Fischer 2009; ISDF 2011). This approach has created a dangerous dichotomy based on geography, where the formal city is supposedly better off: well served with infrastructure and with property rights upheld.

Investigating Ms. Fulan's property dispute case—against the backdrop of a state that has a vast legal infrastructure and advertises the rule of law—reveals that informalization knows no physical boundaries, affecting most contracts of sale. In a country where most households (85 percent) are home "owners" (CAPMAS 2017, 166), millions have been forced to rely on their tenure alone, apart from any legal contract, in order to secure their right to housing, using forms of a semi-parallel customary system that entwines with the official one of the state.

Pacta Sunt Servanda

When the lock to the newly bought apartment's door refused Ms. Fulan's key, an ancient legal principle was instantly broken. *Pacta sunt servanda*— Latin for "agreements must be kept," which established the sanctity of contracts—can trace its origins to ancient Rome (c. 1–250 CE), and was formulated as such in thirteenth-century Europe (Hyland 1994). During the seventeenth century, French jurist Jean Domat embedded the *pacta* principle into his elaborate legal digest, *Lois civiles dans leur ordre naturel*, which France used as its main law for centuries (Aynes 2005). *Pacta* was then enshrined almost verbatim as Article 1134 of the Code Napoléon of 1804 (French civil code) as "Les conventions légalement formées tiennent lieu de loi à ceux qui les ont faites"[4] (Aynes 2005).

The French lineage of Roman law would regulate contracts in Egypt by the mid-twentieth century, when Article 1134 found itself translated yet again in the 1940s—this time into Arabic—by Egyptian jurist Abd al-Razzaq al-Sanhuri (1895–1971) and French jurist Édouard Lambert (1866–1947). The Ministry of Justice recommended al-Sanhuri for this task; he is seen as the "master rebuilder of Arab law in the twentieth century," and participated in penning not just the Egyptian but also the Iraqi, Syrian, and Libyan civil codes at the time, as well as Egypt's 1923 and Kuwait's 1961 constitutions (Shalakany 2001). Al-Sanhuri, in turn, recommended Édouard Lambert, who was the former director of the Khedivial School of Law at Cairo in 1906 and al-Sanhuri's mentor and doctorate supervisor throughout the 1920s (Hill 1988). Above all, Lambert was "the leading figure in comparative law in France" at the time (Kirat 2007). Together, they worked on a draft using comparisons of more than twenty modern codes, the jurisprudence of the Egyptian courts, and Islamic sharia (Hill 1988). But *pacta* was a direct translation of Code Napoléon, Article 1134 (*al-ʿaqd sharīʿat al-mutaʿaqidin*, or "the contract is the law of the parties") (al-Sanhuri 1952).

If there is one article of the Egyptian Civil Code's one-thousand-plus articles—indeed, of any law—that many Egyptians know by heart, it is *al-ʿaqd sharīʿat al-mutaʿaqidin*. It might be that it sounds Islamic, since the word "shari'a" means "law" and is commonly used to refer to Islamic law. Indeed, some scholars have shown how *pacta* is also a Muslim legal principle (Wehberg 1959; Zahid and Shapiee 2010). Over half a century of enforcement has also meant that Egyptians have become familiar with al-Sanhuri's explanation that in case of dispute, judges would apply the contract's terms as if they were the law, though maybe forgetting this is not in absolute terms but within a scope applicable by the law (al-Sanhuri 1952). When Mr. al-Sayid sat down with Ms. Fulan to sign the contract of sale to an apartment that he had already sold to someone else, he knew full well that he was breaking not just the secular law, but an ancient principle, and yet apparently he did not care. Or rather, Mr. al-Sayid took the step knowing that he was likely to succeed with impunity because he knew not only the law about contracts but also the way they are (not) enforced by current policing and judicial structures in Egypt.

Informalization *Legalis*

After filing the police report, Ms. Fulan took the step of taking the alleged intruder to court, filing for his eviction and access to her property. She duly presented her contract to the judges, while Mr. Ibrahim, to everyone's surprise, presented nothing. Apparently, while he claimed to have bought the apartment in 1998, he had supposedly lost the contract and could not produce any copies. According to this fact and the law, Mr. Ibrahim should have been evicted and Ms. Fulan should have had full access to her apartment, and her nightmare would have been over. But another unpleasant surprise awaited her: the local district court threw out her case. This outcome makes it seem as if Egypt does not protect property rights, even though an entire legislative arsenal exists to do so. The constitution recognizes the sanctity of private property, reflected in the 1971 version of Article 29 that "ownership shall be under the supervision of the people and the protection of the State" (Constitution of the Arab Republic of Egypt 1971). The 2014 version that oversaw the later trials promised much the same in Article 35, stating very succinctly that "private property is protected" (Constitution of the Arab Republic of Egypt 2014).

Al-Sanhuri's Civil Code also laid out property rights and their transfer in almost two hundred articles (Law 131/1948 of the Civil Code 2011, sec. 2, book 3, chap. 1). Another of his monumental works, *al-Wasit fi sharh al-qanun al-madani al-gadid*, was a ten-volume encyclopedia that he wrote between 1952 and 1970 to explain the Civil Code. Volume four deals with contracts of sale, volume eight covers property rights, and volume nine how they are transferred (al-Sanhuri 1952). However, there is one caveat that had little to do with the Civil Code itself, and more to do with the glacial machinations of property reform in Egypt. While al-Sanhuri was drafting the Civil Code, a new Notary Deed Registration Law 114/1946 (*qanun al-shahr al-'aqari*) was passed, stipulating that contracts—and not the property itself—should be registered at the notary public. In turn, the Civil Code stipulated that property rights over immovable property are not transferred unless the notary deed registration law is observed (Article 934). Under the old Civil Code of 1883, contracts only needed to be registered in special circumstances, while under Islamic shari'a, there was no requirement to register contracts (Debs 2010, 21, 132).

Confusingly, the registration system was changed again two decades later with the passing of the Real Register Law 142/1964 (*qanun al-sigill al-'aini*), which should have created a database of all immovable property by prompting owners with registered deeds to transfer them to the system, as well as initiating those without deeds to register exchanges. By 2005, the property registration database had only been used for around three-quarters of agricultural land, and with no application on urban land and property (Menelaws 2005, 33). The deed registration system also fell into disuse after the government used it as a de facto tax collection agency, imposing a 3 percent registration fee that has since been reduced to a flat rate, as well as levying a 2.5 percent real estate transfer tax from buyers in the likely case that sellers fail to pay (Menelaws 2005, 35). The system also sought to ensure compliance with building permits. Understandably, owners found the process complicated, time-consuming, and ultimately expensive, as court cases were sometimes also needed. Instead, the culture of '*urfi* (or customary) preliminary contracts, which existed before these laws were passed, prevailed for transferring ownership rights, though paradoxically by utilizing the formal judicial infrastructure.

One way of giving some formality to contracts is the *sihhat tawqi'* (signature validity), which is a simple and inexpensive court procedure that simply ensures the validity of the seller's signature without validating any of the contract's actual contents. Those that seek more assurance make out an irrevocable power of attorney at the notary public for a nominal fee, which gives buyers full rights of use over the property as a way of sale (Menelaws 2005, 36). These offices also come under the jurisdiction of the Ministry of Justice. Buyers may also initiate *sihha wa-nafadh* (contract validation) court procedures. This process can be much more expensive, requiring a payment up to 5.7 percent of the contract price as a judicial fee in addition to a 0.5 percent fee to the lawyers' syndicate (Egypt Lawyers' Syndicate 2020), and, of course, one's lawyer's costs that may take more than a year for a prolonged case. While judicially more robust than the other two forms of customary registration, this has been mostly used by those seeking to fully register their property (Menelaws 2005, 55).

Ms. Fulan had no intention, and very possibly no means, to fork out extra thousands in fees to buy her peace of mind, especially since Mr. al-Sayid probably seemed to her to be a trustworthy person. Everything seemed to be in order, but by choosing the most affordable and most popular option, *sihhat tawqi'* of a *'urfi* contract, she lost everything.

Probatio Diabolica

When Ms. Fulan brought the case against Mr. Ibrahim, the burden of proof of ownership lay squarely on her, one that al-Sanhuri saw as a "much heavier burden than proving mere possession" (al-Sanhuri 1952, 598). The "master rebuilder" of the law went on to elaborate that "the law does not recognize a title deed that directly and irrefutably proves ownership in this manner, except the real estate register. Once a property has been registered in someone's name in this register, it becomes irrefutable evidence of their ownership in front of all. And since the real estate register remains limited in Egypt till now [1967], at the moment, no irrefutable evidence of ownership exists." This candid statement from the most prominent Arab jurist of the time can only tell us one thing: that the law was too perfect—or too alien—for the reality it aimed to rule, and that ownership would not become an open and shut case, but would remain a contestable claim where buyers, sellers, and any number of other parties would have to depend on both customary law and the courts to do the simplest of things, such as transfer ownership.

Unsurprisingly, al-Sanhuri lays out the rules of battle where "indirect methods and evidence have to be used to prove ownership" (al-Sanhuri 1952, 602). He mentions how the courts in France and in Egypt have, throughout the nineteenth and early twentieth centuries, sought a chain of evidence and possibilities that, while not necessarily irrefutable, give "as much as possible on a case-by-case basis, an indication *(iha')* that the claimant is most probably the owner, or that they have produced the more likely possibilities and the stronger evidence than their opponents have" (al-Sanhuri 1952, 602). Clearly the "modern" law was being propped up by ancient practice.

Proving ownership itself became the cornerstone of property transfer claims. Here, only three methods were laid out that al-Sanhuri and his brethren, decades later,[5] saw as irrefutable evidence of ownership (al-Sanhuri 1952, 603–605). The first was the title from the real estate register, which some six decades from its inception is still largely inoperative. The second was squatting or adverse possession (Articles 968–969), where five to fifteen years of continuous, uncontested possession can be proven. The third, *hiyaza* (possession) in good faith (Article 964), is considered physical evidence of legal ownership although it is not entirely irrefutable, since a title from the real estate register, if available, may prove the contrary. Here again, we find that al-Sanhuri's modern code relies on ancient shari'a, which considers possession to be "the strongest indicator of one's ownership" (Cuno 1992, 78–79, 194–95).

At some distance from these three methods is the customary–judicial hybrid method of registered title deed—not property—registered either at the notary public or by *sihha wa-nafadh* court ruling (al-Sanhuri 1952, 605–607). While these registered deeds are official documents, they may be easily refuted due to fraud or informality where sellers may not have been rightful owners in the first place. Lastly comes proof of registration with the real estate tax office, or payment in a possessor's name as supporting evidence, but not direct evidence, and other lesser proofs.

In addition to explaining this hierarchy of proof, al-Sanhuri provided us with some examples of weighing proofs against one another (al-Sanhuri 1952, 610). Relevant to Ms. Fulan's case is that, where both the claimant and the defendant have contracts from the same seller, the court should prefer the registered one. If both are registered, then the first contract to be registered should take priority. In case both contracts are unregistered, then the first one made is to be recognized. Ms. Fulan was among the estimated 90 percent of buyers who chose the customary route to ownership, accepting a preliminary contract with only signature validation. When the judges in both the local court and, years later, in the Court of Cassation weighed the evidence presented to them, they were playing by al-Sanhuri's book. At the first step, Ms. Fulan's unregistered *'urfi* contract was given the same weight as Mr. Ibrahim's verbal one, which, while obviously unregistered, was proved with witnesses. Both the written and verbal contracts were made with

Mr. al-Sayid. At the second step, Mr. Ibrahim's contract was found to have preceded Ms. Fulan's by two years and was therefore accepted by the courts as the more valid of the two.

Even if the verbal contract could not be validated, Mr. Ibrahim had something that trumped the contracts both of them had: possession. We can find this resort of "modern" courts to customary law in many other ownership contestation cases. One claimant demonstrated how he had "exercised possession" by visiting the property from "time to time" (Court of Cassation 1969). Another stated how he has "appeared at the property in a manner that clearly and without a doubt reflected he was the owner" (Court of Cassation 1984). Mr. Ibrahim did the same by showing how he was the one who had physical ownership of the property, and the court ruled by customary law that Ms. Fulan was never in "physical possession of the property, and [she] has not executed her contract on the ground. Therefore the [appealed] judgement is compromised and must be annulled" (Court of Cassation 2017).

Coda: Complacency or Complicity?

After seventeen years in litigation, whom could Ms. Fulan blame for ending up without a home? Some would say herself. According to the latest estimate from the Ministry of Justice, which oversees the real estate register, only 10 to 15 percent of properties are registered (*al-Watan* 2020). Therefore, Ms. Fulan bought an apartment using the most common method, in a deregulated market where buyers are the weaker of the two parties and owners dictate the terms. It is, after all, the government's responsibility to uphold the modern law it expects its citizens to follow by maintaining the real estate register as well as by enforcing contracts. However, Egypt certainly fails at this responsibility, as it has recently ranked 130 and 166 out of 190 countries surveyed on property registration and enforcing contracts (World Bank 2020). On these counts, Ms. Fulan can blame the government for complacency in its role.

The study on property registration mentioned earlier hinted that the courts generate "substantial" revenue from the property disputes it rules over, and presumed that activating the real estate register would decrease the case load and rob the courts of this resource (Menelaws 2005, 49). Since the civil courts, the Real Estate Register, and the notary public are all under the jurisdiction of the Ministry of Justice, this is a logical assumption to make. A more ominous aspect to this has been the private interests from some low- and even high-level employees of the judicial system. In 2017, a newspaper report alleged that a judge had used his knowledge of a property dispute case, as well as his influence, to bribe a notary public employee to falsify documents and register a residential building in his name (Nijm al-Din 2017). These allegations were probably true: President Abd al-Fattah al-Sisi issued a decree three years later stripping the judge of his post (Presidential Decree 527/2020).

Case 5322/2020 (Misr al-Gadida Criminal Court) involves seventeen defendants who are alleged to have falsified not just contracts and property registration documents, but court verdicts as well, to usurp LE 500 billion worth of state-owned property over the course of eleven years (al-Minshawi 2020). Three of the defendants are court employees, and one is the head of the notary public office of a provincial town. Small wonder that official stamps keep disappearing from notary public offices on an almost regular basis.[6]

There have been official efforts to reform the real estate registry, whether to boost Egypt's international ranking or to kick-start the mortgage market; however, all have been undone. The slashing of real estate registration fees of the early 2000s was replaced with an amendment of the income tax law that stipulated that property cannot be registered until the transfer tax is paid (Law 51/2005, Article 42). In 2020, amendments to the Real Estate Registration law made it impossible to introduce utilities to new homes, or transfer existing ones to new owners' names, unless the property was registered first (Law 186/2020). However, the amendment proved strongly unpopular, with owners citing the high transaction costs, so much so that the changes were deferred for two years by presidential order to "allow a community discussion" around the law (Arab Republic of Egypt (ARE) Presidency 2021).

Over the last seven decades, attempts to achieve al-Sanhuri's "irrefutable evidence of ownership" have been scuttled by complacent authorities' gate-keeping antics seeking to exploit tenure security in order to rake in revenue. Complicit officials' outright fraud to make personal gains has also slowed the transition from customary to modern law. Informalization has allowed both the private sector and the government to rob Ms. Fulan and many other Cairo residents of their right to adequate housing: they are forced to navigate the gray zone created between the two legal paradigms, risking their life savings in order to find a home. Those luckier than Ms. Fulan were able to lay their hands on a home, which represented their only chance of gaining security of tenure.

Notes

1 Actual names have been used except where redacted from the court documents, such as Ms. Fulan's. For more information, see Court of Cassation (2017).

2 Egypt's court system is based on the French Civil Law structure that consisted of three courts. The judicial courts (those dealing with criminal and civil laws) go through three tiers: courts of first instance, courts of appeal, and the Court of Cassation (Supreme Court of Appeals). The administrative courts, which see cases that involve a state-affiliated person or body, also go through three tiers: local administrative courts, administrative courts of appeal, and the State Council (Supreme Administrative Court). A third branch of the judiciary, the Supreme Constitutional Court, decides on the constitutionality of laws and administrative legislation from cases that may be referred from either of the two main branches (Georgetown Law Library n.d.).

3 Mahkamat al-Naqd al-Misriya online database: http://www.cc.gov. eg/; work search "*al-mushtariyin li'aqar wahid.*"

4 Agreements lawfully entered into take the place of the law for those who have made them.

5 The Civil Code has seen little modification since it was passed in 1948, while a recent legal handbook on ownership, written by a head of an appeals court, lists almost word-for-word al-Sanhuri's grounds and methods of proving ownership (Tolba 2015, 52).

6 The "Official Gazette" regularly publishes *i'lanat faqd*, advertisements for lost items, usually official stamps, registers, and other papers by government agencies. In one of these, two stamps were reported "lost" and were annulled from the notary public office of Biba, and one from Ismailia. See "Official Gazette" (2013, 30).

Works Cited

Arab Republic of Egypt (ARE) Presidency. 2021. "President El-Sisi Meets with PM and Minister of Justice." March 1. https://www.presidency.eg/en//قسم-الأخبار/أخبار-رئاسية/ /الرئيس-عبد-الفتاح-السيسي-يجتمع-برئيس-مجلس-الوزراء-ووزير-العدل-2021-03-01.

Aynes, Laurent. 2005. "Le contrat, loi des parties." Constitutional Council of France. March. https://www.conseil-constitutionnel.fr/nouveaux-cahiers-du-conseil-constitutionnel/le-contrat-loi-des-parties.

CAPMAS. 2017. "Final Results of the General Census for Population and Housing Conditions for 2017." Cairo: Central Agency for Public Mobilization and Statistics (CAPMAS). http://www.capmas.gov.eg.

Constitute Project. 2022. "Egypt's Constitution of 2014 with Amend-
    ments through 2019." April 27. https://www.constituteproject.org/
    constitution/Egypt_2019.pdf?lang=en.
Constitution of the Arab Republic of Egypt. 1971. Including amend-
    ments until 1980. https://www.refworld.org/cgi-bin/texis/vtx/
    rwmain/opendocpdf.pdf?reldoc=y&docid=54917e9c4.
———. 2014. https://www.ilo.org/dyn/natlex/docs/ELECTRONIC/
    97325/11544/F281017262/EGY97325%20Ara.pdf. Accessed on Octo-
    ber 28, 2023
Court of Cassation. 1969. "Appeal 1756/38C." https://www.cc.gov.
    eg/i/H/111121103.pdf.
———. 1984. "Appeal 838/49C." https://www.cc.gov.eg/i/H/111122134.pdf.
———. 2017. "Appeals 3436,5081/86C." https://www.cc.gov.
    eg/i/H/111356982.pdf.
Cuno, Kenneth M. 1992. *The Pasha's Peasants: Land, Society and Economy
    in Lower Egypt, 1740–1858*. Cambridge: Cambridge University Press.
Debs, Richard A. 2010. *Islamic Law and Civil Code: The Law of Property
    in Egypt*. New York: Columbia University Press.
DeSoto, Hernando. 1998. *The Other Path: The Invisible Revolution in the
    Third World*. New York: Perennial Library.
Egypt Lawyers' Syndicate. 2020. "Min al-alif ila al-ya': iqra'at al-tasgil
    al-'aqari bi-naw'ayh, rida'i—sihha wa-nafadh." September 14.
    https://egyls.com/من-الألف-إلى-الياء-إجراءات-التسجيل-الع/.
Georgetown Law Library. n.d. "French Legal Research Guide."
    Georgetown Law Library. https://guides.ll.georgetown.edu/c.
    php?g=362135&p=2446075.
Hill, Enid. 1988. "Al-Sanhuri and Islamic Law: The Place and Signifi-
    cance of Islamic Law in the Life and Work of 'Abd al-Razzaq Ahmad
    al-Sanhuri, Egyptian Jurist and Scholar, 1895–1971 [Part II]." *Arab
    Law Quarterly* 3, no. 2: 182–218. https://doi.org/10.2307/3381872.
Hyland, Richard. 1994. "Pacta Sunt Servanda: A Meditation." *Vir-
    ginia Journal of International Law* 34, no. 2: 405–33. https://doi.
    org/10.7282/t3-67jr-np54.
ISDF. 2011. "National Map of Unsafe Areas 2011 (Internal Report)."
    Informal Settlements Development Facility (ISDF). Cairo.
Kipper, Regina, and Marion Fischer, eds. 2009. "Cairo's Informal Areas:
    Between Urban Challenges and Hidden Potentials." Cairo: GTZ
    Egypt Participatory Development Programme in Urban Areas (PDP).
    http://www.egypt-urban.net/publication-cairos-informal-areas-bet
    ween-urban-challenges-and-hidden-potentials-facts-voices-visions/.

Kirat, Thierry. 2007. "Lambert, Edouard (1866–1947)." In *Encyclopedia of Law & Society: American and Global Perspectives*, edited by David S. Clark, 909. London: Sage Publications, Inc. https://sk.sagepub.com/reference/law.

Law 23/1992. 1992. Shura Council Committee Report amending the Procedural Law 13/1968 (semi-official digital copy). Cairo: Shura Council. https://www.cc.gov.eg/legislation_single?id=398952.

Law 51/2005. n.d. Law on income tax, including amendments. Cairo: Shura Council. https://www.cc.gov.eg/legislation_single?id=406914.

Law 131/1948. 2011. Semi-official digital copy of the law, including amendments up to July 16, 2011. Cairo: Shura Council. https://www.cc.gov.eg/legislation_single?id=404569.

Law 186/2020. n.d. Amending Real Estate Register Law 114/1946. Cairo: Shura Council. https://www.cc.gov.eg/i/l/404665.pdf.

Menelaws, Dougal. 2005. "Property and Registration Law in Egypt: Current Operation and Practice—Task 2 Inception Report." Technical Report 3. June 1. Egypt Financial Services Project. United States Agency for International Development (USAID). http://pdf.usaid.gov/pdf_docs/Pnadg840.pdf.

al-Minshawi, Mostafa. 2020. "Qadiyyat al-nisf trillion ginih—halaqa 1." *Al-Shorouk*, September 20. https://archive.vn/YqfFl https://archive.vn/YqfFl.

Nijm al-Din, Tariq. 2017. "Misr: watha'iq taqdim qadi rashwa li-muwaz-zaf li-tasgil aradi ghayr qaunuiya." *Al Araby Al Jadeed*, October 27. https://archive.vn/rmuu6.

"Official Gazette." 2013. 285. *Al-waqa'i' al-Misriya*. Cairo: Al-Amiriya Press.

al-Sanhuri, Abdelrazaq. 1952. *Al-wasit fi sharh al-qanun al-madani al-gadid*. 10 vols. Beirut: Dar Ihya' al-Turath al-'Arabi. https://tinyurl.com/yxa6dwcv. Consulted July 21, 2021.

Shalakany, Amr. 2001. "Between Identity and Redistribution: Sanhuri, Genealogy and the Will to Islamise." *Islamic Law and Society* 8, no. 2: 201–44.

Shawkat, Yahia. 2020. *Egypt's Housing Crisis: The Shaping of Urban Space*. Cairo: American University in Cairo Press.

Tolba, Anwar. 2015. *Naz' al-milkiya li-l-manfa'a al-'amma*. Cairo: Sharikat al-Nas li-l-Tiba'a.

al-Watan. 2020. "Al-'adl: 'adad al-'aqarat al-musaggala fi Misr 15% min al-tharwa al-'aqariya." September 24. https://archive.vn/UjHNQ.

Wehberg, Hans. 1959. "Pacta Sunt Servanda." *American Journal of International Law* 53, no. 4: 775–86. https://doi.org/10.2307/2195750.

World Bank. 2020. "Doing Business 2020—Doing Business in
Egypt, Arab Rep." https://www.doingbusiness.org/en/data/
exploreeconomies.

Youm7. 2018. "Mutadarrir min waqi'at nasb fi wihda sakaniya bi-l-Iskan-
dariya." *Youm7*, February 20. https://archive.vn/sszzt.

Zahid, Md Anowar, and Rohimi Shapiee. 2010. "Pacta Sunt Servanda:
Islamic Perception." *Journal of East Asia and International Law*
3: 375. https://heinonline.org/HOL/Page?handle=hein.journals/
jeasil3&id=375&div=&collection=.

24

GESTURES OF TERRITORIALISM
BALTAGIYA, LAND ANXIETIES,
AND SECURITIZING SQUATTING

HATEM HASSAN

The period 2011–16 proved a watershed for the re-formation—not invention—of the imaginaries and social realities of Egyptian *baltagiya* ("thugs"), due to their centrality in public concerns as well as (and not merely in) state discourse. This period witnessed the circulation of a kaleidoscope of beliefs, language, images, habits, practices, reports, and governing techniques concerning *baltagiya* in the popular imaginary that helped make sense of desired political, moral, and cultural modes of being during a moment of legal instability and popular distrust. The following analysis captures some of the oral histories, debates, and government portrayals that contributed to forming the *baltagi* (singular) in the popular imaginary of the Cairo neighborhoods of Talbiya, Misr al-Qadima, and Ard al-Liwa', among others. Several stories of accused *baltagiya* concern situations where they act as occupying forces, or squatters. Further discussions on the *baltagi* can be explored in the exceptional work of the scholars Omnia Khalil, Aly El Raggal, Salwa Ismail, Paul Amar, Dina Wahba, and Farha Ghannam, among others.

This narrative describes the central regulatory power of the *baltagi*: the ability of the official discourse to reaffirm the importance of official/formal territory and to get accustomed to extralegal enforcement regardless of who the beneficiaries might be. The practice of sending out *baltagiya* (plural of *baltagi*) into tense situations both enforces and is a response to a fear of instability, leading to confrontation with varying forms of securitization—moral, political, economic, urban, and so forth. By *baltaga*, "thuggery," I refer to processes that "attempt to delegitimize, intimidate, and blur both the image and message" being communicated between social movements or practically any other opposition to top-down governance that extends beyond state actors and institutions alone. I also follow Amar's definition of *baltagiya* as "plain-clothes thugs, deputized by police and paramilitary security forces" (Amar 2013, 211). This intentional and ephemeral blurring and disguising has long-term consequences that have "not only terrorized . . . protesters but also generated new images for domestic and international media and criminological narratives for international security agencies and local law enforcement" (Amar 2013, 212). This effect intends to collapse the complexity of spontaneous and transformative political initiatives and inspiration, reformulating them through a process of securitization— that "reconfiguration of political debates and claims around social justice, political participation, or resource distribution into technical assessments of danger, operations of enforcement, and targeting of risk populations" (Amar 2013, 17). This is effective precisely because the *baltagi* is nonideological, disloyal to political agendas, especially as analysis moves beyond one specific event or neighborhood, as Omnia Khalil shows in this volume.

Residential Occupations as *Baltaga*

A budding visual artist in her mid-twenties narrates the story of a local strongwoman residing in Misr al-Qadima, the artist's hometown and one of Cairo's oldest neighborhoods, located only a few Metro stops from Wist al-Balad (downtown Cairo). My informant describes how she was recently and forcibly evicted from her apartment by the alleged female thug. She tells me, "They sent a *baltagi* to force me out of my home, so I was forced to get a *baltagi* to get my belongings out of [the apartment] because they wouldn't let me back in." Distressed while recalling the initial events, she continues, "I got my mom to ask someone for help. Of course, because it is a 'rough place' and is filled with thugs, my mom asked several people in our building about hiring someone. We found a person known to have killed the local strongwoman's son . . . He was really known as someone very tough . . . We called him, and he let us go into the apartment to get my things." Distinguishing who is responsible for what actions in the fight for this apartment, she makes clear, "But this [what I did] is not thuggery, because we went to retrieve something that was ours in the first place. Because when we went to the police originally, they refused to help us. The police superintendent [*amin al-shurta*] at first tried to give my mother a hard time, harassing her sexually." Notice that thuggery immediately surfaces its head here, revealing its systemic qualities. The young artist continues, "[My mother] told him to show respect [and] that she is a married woman. In response, he told my mother that there is nothing that they [the local police] can do about the thug and that they will not search or open a case for her. They made it seem like those people [thugs] were very difficult to control—even for them, the police. This is why we were forced to get someone. But we thought of him as more of a bodyguard. . . . We treated and paid him like a bodyguard."

On reviewing this account, one might ask a set of questions of the narrator: Is the thug here (1) the local strongwoman of Misr al-Qadima, who forcibly evicted our respondent from her home, (2) my informant's bodyguard, who forcibly entered a home to retrieve her possessions, or (3) my informant, who orchestrated the bodyguard's retaliatory efforts? Does this contentious episode revolve around local rivalries, or is it the byproduct of a failed, state-sanctioned conflict resolution process (i.e., of the sexually predatory male police officer and his refusal to help my informant's mother once she had deflated his ego)? Rather than "select our thug" and feel some empirical, ethical, and political resolution, we may take the narrative as an opportunity to untangle the thug's inextricable relationship to land, private property, and verbal or physical space.

In Dokki, I met residents who told me that they had discovered apartments that were left vacant in 2011 by older residents who had rented or purchased other apartments in Alexandria and other coastal areas and then had returned to their Cairo apartments, only to find them occupied by other people. This story was common, especially in middle-class neighborhoods, where such practices were quickly deemed acts of *baltaga*. Once labeled, the elusive *baltagi* were described as part of a growing phenomenon of lawlessness.

In Talbiya and Ard al-Liwa', two Giza neighborhoods, we encounter numerous instances of illegal occupation of spaces designated for nonresidential purposes. The fact that both neighborhoods are commonly associated with *'ashwa'iyat*—residential areas that do not formally conform to the city's zoning laws—suggests a certain degree of creativity or flexibility by inhabitants toward varied uses of the land. But from the perspective of the residents in both stories, "thuggery" refers to a very specific practice clearly deemed unjust: the privatization of the community for a resident's individual profit. Walking to one of many of the open-air parking garages with friends and interview participants, I was told that the "real thuggery" is on the part of those individuals who take possession of space for non-collective aspirations, rather than building more housing or schools for the residents. One man—originally from Aswan but who had migrated with his parents to Cairo from his Nubian hometown—tells me that the media has paid no attention to land conversion—into garages, for example—preferring to focus on how the informal settlements are encroaching on planned areas of the city. He insisted that there is also encroachment from within the *'ash-wa'iyat* of spaces that the whole neighborhood could use if it were not for such acts of "thuggery." For him, land ownership and the associated battles are understood through an ancestral struggle, since his migration to Cairo was due to generations of land encroachment by the Egyptian government onto indigenous Nubian territory. But land conflicts in these poorer neighborhoods remain contested due to their unique history. Despite their image as lower-class areas, informal neighborhoods host some wealthier residents. However, the complexity of these neighborhoods collapses when middle-class Cairenes in Dokki, Muhandisin, Maadi, and al-Tagammu' al-Khamis (the Fifth Settlement), among other neighborhoods, ignore the large populations of economically marginalized Egyptians and East African migrants that render Ard al-Liwa' distinct. These informal areas are viewed as sites of thuggery because of a perceived lack of concern for legality. During the rise of *ligan sha'biya* (popular committees, or neighborhood watch groups), outsiders from neighborhoods such as Imbaba and Bulaq were labeled as "thugs" after they had squatted on agricultural land along the banks of the Nile in Cairo. The association with this encroachment onto land deemed of value to the government and the circulation of a criminal discourse on thuggery only increased in speed and focus in the years following 2011.

The Occupation of Physical Space: Thug versus the Sacred

Moral-ethical frameworks are used by governing entities to manage economic behavior they deem worthwhile and virtuous, as was the case when sit-ins, strikes, and protests became a component of everyday life in Cairo between 2011 and 2013. This vignette addresses an anti-thuggery project directed against the physical occupation of apartments, main squares, and economic arteries in Cairo. Here I offer instances when the newspaper accounts of state-sponsored media outlets alleged encroachment of *baltagiya* onto state, public urban, agricultural, and sacred spaces—offering a snapshot of the anti-thuggery journalism and military-led projects that aimed to "clean up" the city and nation alike. Thugs are not simply characterized as disruptive to the economic cycle, but also immoral due to their "selfish, anti-patriotic" behaviors. The relationship between the public's daily interaction with alleged thugs and the latter's depiction in state-sponsored news sheds light on a unifying thug "attribute": the encroachment upon and subsequent protection of territory. Rather than take a moral position or political decision, the following opts to reveal the *baltagiya*'s place in the verbal and physical–spatial arena, for they became useful precisely at a time when state rulers sought to reclaim public territory that had been contested amid popular mobilization, when ordinary people desired economic stability regardless of the promulgating machineries of the state. Then the state resumed its remarkably persistent dream "of a market economy . . . envisaged only under authoritarian military rule, under which the army becomes the major manipulator of vast amounts of land and can market it as it wishes without providing any transparency in the transactions" (Abaza 2017).

The occupation of a *physical* space—one previously designated as "public"—is sometimes labeled an act of reappropriation, at least and in part because of its originally governed dimensions. Reshaping how urban dwellers interact with streets, squares, quasi-public areas such as football stadiums or malls, and other physical landscapes may also affect a city's economic, cultural, and political formations. Neighborhood segregation, for example, often reifies economic disparities, constrains the overall mobility of urban dwellers, and heightens tactics of policing against those who ignore such invisible boundaries (Khalil 2015; Hassan 2015). The creation of physical infrastructure commonly associated with the upward "progress" of a city reshapes perceptions of specific neighborhoods, their role in the urban economy, the subjectivities and life-chances of the individuals who inhabit them, and their relationship to the rest of the metropolis. Actors simultaneously reconsider the physical structures and sociopolitical relationships that constitute their quotidian structures of meaning. One does not cross, for example, the ostensibly "neutral" material structures (bridges, railroad tracks, college campus lines) of one's neighborhood without an understanding of the bodily and social repercussions involved in such an act.

Discussions in newspapers on the subject of the unofficial occupation of apartments and the spread of thuggery began *only* in 2011, with twenty-two front-page reports accusing thugs of illegally taking up residence in either state- or privately owned but momentarily unoccupied homes (not to mention encroachment in public parks, sidewalks, heritage sites, and agricultural lands). The unauthorized occupation of the Mubarak Housing projects[1]—in 6th of October (Giza Governorate), Damanhur (Beheira Governorate), Sidi Talha (Kafr al-Sheikh), and Suez—gained considerable attention after 2011 but was a process that began over a decade earlier. Occupation (whether in protest or for housing purposes) was perceived to be a quintessential thug activity by all the major media outlets and some ordinary people. Only ten days following Mubarak's removal, an *al-Ahram* front-page headline read: "Asking for Assistance from the Army to Evict Thugs from Apartments." In the article, former governor of Alexandria and minister of local development Mohammad Abd al-Salam Mahgub expressed clear reservations about the behavior of the alleged "thugs and prisoners"—another article discusses "thugs and rioters"—who "stormed hundreds of apartments reserved for eligible citizens." The reporter went on to dramatize an event unverified by most other major newspapers, stating that

in the broad daylight, they lift their daggers and swords and threaten, with acid, those who tried to resist them. They took over the apartments and turned the roofs of buildings into military arsenals equipped with bricks and Molotov cocktails in order to resist any intervention by the armed forces or police. Unfortunately, the guards of these buildings assisted the thugs in this conspiracy. They occupied vacant units, which are not known to others, with the hope that they will have a share of this cake. (Abd al-Salam 2011a)

Regardless of whether one could reliably fact-check the occupation itself, military solutions to the illegal occupation of private homes are quite uncommon. Previously, the military had only deployed its forces against civilians during the 1977 bread riots and following internal dissent within the Central Security Forces (*al-amn al-markazi*) in 1986. Still, it is more than predictable that a former military figure would call on his own forces to limit the negative consequences of the revolutionary moment. If this is what happened, then a direct association was being made between the effects of mass mobilization, the removal of a nation's leader, and the occupation of private property. This association was made explicit by another contributor, claiming that "a new phenomenon in the city of New Damietta, of 'occupying buildings,' refers to many properties being looted by a large number of people at the time of a security chaos that followed the January

25 revolution" (September 18, 2014). Years earlier, another journalist noted that "the state of chaos experienced by many Egyptian cities, including Alexandria, extended to the owners of villas and palaces," moving on and attempting to tie the narrative with "thugs [who] create wooden kiosks in public areas and main streets and sell them to peddlers" (February 26, 2011). The incidence of alleged thugs who occupied spaces unlawfully was explicitly associated with the security vacuum caused by the initial January mobilizations, suggesting an unexpected turn of far-fetched coordination.

The more explicit association—of thugs and unofficial occupation—occurred in the months and years between Mubarak's downfall and al-Sisi's rise, and it continues to this day. On April 20, 2011, a regular contributor to *al-Ahram* and *Youm7* asked why thugs had not been stopped in their plans "to terrorize the unsuspecting and to seize citizens' and the people's property. . . . Has this terrible silence not led to the destruction of our homeland's principles *(usul)*?" (Amr Abd al-Samih 2011). On the six-month anniversary of the revolution, *al-Ahram* once more interviewed Mohamed Abd al-Salam, who demanded that citizens "take charge of the capital in these difficult circumstances because the chaos of the streets and governorates comes at a time of a weak [national] budget. And thugs are seizing the apartments and, in governorates, burning neighborhood police stations" (Abd al-Salam 2011b). For the former colonel and governor, the illegal occupation of apartments is analogous to arson (especially of state-owned properties)—a dominant practice central to the initial mobilization of young Egyptians tired of draconian police forces (Ismail 2012). The immolation of police stations and illegal occupation of apartments are both seen as direct challenges to the state's monopoly on private property and violence.

Al-Ahram journalists 'Attia Abd al-Hamid, Ibrahim al-Ashmawi, Mohamed Mutawi', Nivin Mustafa, Hamada al-Said, Hassan al-Asmar, and Hassan Saad put forth a rather assertive conclusion in an article reporting on occupations of governorates across the entirety of Egypt, claiming "the information presented confirms that these encroachments on the land are always led by elites and is the [initial] boulder that shatters all laws in its path. Subsequently, ordinary people are encouraged to encroach upon the land, with some resorting to crooked tactics such as obtaining letters issued from the Agricultural Association by way of bribes" (Abdel-Hamid et al. 2014). The unofficial encroachment on land—as argued by reporters of the most widely circulated and explicitly state-endorsed newspapers—leads to a cascade of unlawful practices. Egypt's most politically and economically powerful groups commit the original sin and set a precedent of corrupt and informal practices. This tradition of circumventing legality, according to the reporters' explanations, is absorbed into everyday life and trickles down in the form of encroachment. The report finds its urgency by depicting thug-specific encroachment on land as a challenge to the modern state's fundamental building block: territory demarcations between the private and public, the personal and political. In the words of one reporter, some thugs "take over homes, while other thugs lay their hands on state land."

Not restricting themselves to private places of residence, the reports have also focused on occupations of both agricultural land and cultural landmarks (i.e., sacred places). A front-page article featured the takeover of a mosque in a small village northeast of Cairo, in the Sharqiya Governorate, detailing how alleged thugs converted the house of worship into an exclusive space of residence. *Al-Ahram* provides historical background by bringing in an "expert" to explain the events.

Dr. Abdullah Abu-l-Naga, a professor at Zagazig University and chair of the mosque's council, explained that the mosque was established in the 1970s through generous donations and through the self-drive efforts of the people from Qayrateen [a village in Sharqiya Governorate]. . . . In 1980 the mosque was renovated by a Kuwaiti institution. . . . The second floor consists of a nursery for the children of the village and a space for Qur'an memorization. Upon its completion, many were surprised by the fact that some people broke into the second floor and turned it into apartments. (Al-Shawadfi 2012)

Dr. Abdullah urged state officials that the "house of God" must be protected from the squatters who allegedly had committed this act. Suddenly and unexpectedly, we are told that an anti-occupation campaign is nothing less than an existential and spiritual project even bigger than the nation. The attention that such a case received—in a little-known village, about a mosque with a quite banal history—speaks to thug utility as a linguistic tool to catapult local land disputes onto a politico-moral plan of cosmic proportions. Here we observe how thug discourse is able to weave together a narrative of a nationwide occupation that is in direct and seamless response to a revolution-provoked security vacuum.

The cultural threat of such illicit occupations of property may be seen in another report titled "Oasis Heritage Museum in the Grips of

Thugs," where a journalist openly grieves the seizure of the renowned museum in al-Wadi al-Gadid (New Valley), a governorate in the southwestern region.

Dr. Alia Hassan, the director of a museum that is the only one of its kind, confirmed that a group of people took over the Ethnographic Museum for Cultural Heritage in the New Valley. They also confiscated its possessions, expelled tourist delegations, ignored the museum's president, and put their objects, furniture, and kitchen appliances inside the museum. . . . It was officially opened in 2002 according to the guidelines and supervision of the president of the Supreme Council of Antiquities. The museum has many rare items collected over the fifty years of scientific research on the oasis. It was confirmed that a group of people broke into the museum . . . [for the purposes of] exercising their normal home lives as if they own it. (Emran 2011)

The occupation of a heritage site—a site whose value is documented in a detailed historical report of the space—presents us with a group of alleged thugs who threaten the country's economic resilience (due to its touristic appeal) and national pride for Egypt's ancient civilizational legacy. Again, we are thrown into the cosmic importance of fighting these persistent thugs.

Systematic raids and the government's removal of Cairo's downtown and outdoor coffee shops, major art galleries, public housing projects, residential spaces on al-Warraq Island (see Amy Fallas's chapter in this volume), railways, and even alleged encroachments of protected ecological spaces become emblematic of a concerted "anti-thug" regime. These seemingly varied projects reflect an anxiety-ridden impulse by the state's security apparatus, that deems any non-corporate land their own (even if it is desert) and any contested places a security concern. In the northernmost Delta region, for example, post-Mubarak rulers have conducted a systematic campaign to "cleanse" Lake al-Manzala—what was once one of the largest wetlands in the entire Mediterranean coastal area and a source for seventeen thousand jobs in fisheries. Located between the Nile River and the Suez Canal in the northern Delta region—and along with Lakes Burullus and Idku—al-Manzala constitutes one of the most important natural habitats in the nation. The lake lost most of its freshwater due to the building of the Aswan High Dam in the 1960s and a subsequent increase in sedimentation, heavy metal accumulation, drainage (with hopes of converting the lake into agricultural land), and salinity levels since the 1930s. But somehow, the lake only became increasingly visible to the national population and reportedly

riddled with thug activity in the months following the initial revolutionary mobilization. Shortly thereafter, a report read: "Security services in
Dakahlia, in cooperation with the General Directorate of the Environment and police, prepared a large campaign aimed at the water levels of
Lake al-Manzala . . . and its aesthetic, to remove acts of encroachment
and control all fishing-related criminal activity" (Meleegy and Farouq
2011). In previous pre-revolution contexts, reporters blamed pollution
on major oil and gas companies, but since 2011, the regulation of uncon-
trolled fishing led reporters to claim that the lake had become a source
of "terrorism and thuggery" (Abdel-Hamid 2014) and "a breeding ground
for thugs, arms dealers, drainage of water banks, and the killing of fish"
(Al-Husseiny 2016). What was previously considered the work of an
oligarchy of energy firms—unofficially controlling the lakes' fish—was
actively recast as a narrative that posited as scapegoats an amalgamation
of alleged anti-regime criminals who had little official documentation
and illegitimately exploited the resources of the land.

Land Anxieties of a Hypersecuritized Regime

A lack of affordable housing since the 1970s—especially for young
newlyweds—and the continued failure of government-subsidized
accommodation in subsequent decades has fostered unregulated citi-
zen-led construction of "informal" residential buildings. State officials
have claimed that just between 2011 and 2014, there have been approximately 450,000 illegally constructed buildings, many of which are
subject to state demolition (Alsharif 2014). Simultaneously, private
contractors advertise an escape from the political "dangers" and incon-
venience of the downtown area by rampantly constructing new gated
communities that remain largely unoccupied (Bayat 2012). Since the
informal construction of buildings around Cairo's Ring Road is subject
to increasing surveillance by and suspicion from state officials (since
there have been police actions against such settlements in the past), it is
possible that those who cannot afford to pay for housing (or refuse to do
so) would rather occupy an apartment that has been neglected by owners
who live elsewhere or in housing yet to be occupied. This, of course, is
only speculative, as people generally are more likely to settle in places
that are also near convenient transportation, economic opportunities,
and basic services (access to water, electricity, etc.). Whether rumor or
exaggeration, *al-Ahram*'s reporting of thugs occupying apartments built
through the government-neglected National Housing Program (Iskan
Mubarak, sometimes referred to as Iskan al-Shabab, or Youth Housing)

reflects the government's anxiety—that Egypt's poor will find their own means to secure housing and to govern themselves.

The use of the term *baltagiya* to refer to those who squat in unoccupied homes, public gardens, and elsewhere is woven into a fabric larger than any interlocutor could ever individually plan. *Al-Ahram* reports:

in the absence of the state and its law, and with the collapse of security, thugs have emerged. . . . All [of them] agreed without exception to the destruction of our homeland's dreams and future through their encroachment [al-ta'addi] on its river, lakes, canals, and agricultural lands. Instead of planting these lands with fruits, crops, and food, they planted them with concrete blocks and entertainment projects opposed to [the] public . . . The number of infringements reached 876,000 feddans nationally. (Abdel-Hamid et al. 2014)

Consider how common it is for state-sponsored newspapers to sound as prescriptive as the aforementioned passage. The *baltagiya* are portrayed at once as particular and elusive, responsible for a phenomenon of encroachment, and somehow always out of reach in terms of both geography and identification.

The *baltagiya* disregard and actively break through spatial heuristics commonly imagined (in theoretical formulations) or experienced (and in the words of people who circulate this discourse): private and public, collective and personal. Since 2011, the *baltagiya* have at times been illustrated as an elusive amalgamation engaged in a determined search for property to illegally occupy. In this illustration, they are accused of dismissing the very notion of private property and of personal space, but of doing so with no particular ideological objective—they are neither anarchists nor adherents to accelerationism, but instead represent the crude terms of an entirely self-centered analysis of cost-benefit. The trend of moving into (and claiming ownership of) currently unoccupied apartments (including those purchased or rented by a family, but never used) was mentioned by my interviewees and news reports alike. Economic uncertainty galvanizes a population, as does class disparity.

Citizens wishing for a return to a stable economy have tended to view and label as *baltagiya* any obstacle to revolutionary moments. The argument was made that *baltagiya* claimed territory and citizens' private spaces unrightfully and sometimes unlawfully. Police and military campaigns have been the response to accusations of encroachment and usurpation, and the alleged thugs have been arrested while selling goods on public streets, protesting in main squares, or simply being residents of a stigmatized neighborhood. The *baltagiya* enter precisely through campaigns against occupation and are vilified by state officials, adherents of the old regime, demonstrators, and observers. The thug is an occupier without a political ideology—or, alternatively, without an impetus to reimagine land "occupation" altogether—a momentary disruption of a particular way of relating to the world, a way that provides boundaries between personal and collective rights as well as privatized domestic and public space. Its intensifying presence as a spoken, imagined, social and textual reality provokes an anxiety that a complete political and economic leveling of power will force those with accumulated resources to relinquish their possessions. That anxiety, in turn, fosters and fuels a logic, apparatus, and national campaign that proposes policing not simply as a solution to protect privatized land but as a campaign of moral and economic salvation. In this calculation, thugs represent the ever-greedy usurpers of physical property and space to which they have no right.

Notes

1   Efforts began in 1996 when the Ministry of Housing, Utility, and Urban Communities claimed that it would "provide 70,000 affordable dwelling units, in a healthy and productive residential environment," of which "beneficiaries were the youth who belong to the disadvantaged/low-income groups."

Works Cited

Abaza, Mona. 2017. "Cairo: Restoration? and the Limits of Street Politics." *Space and Culture* 20, no. 2: 170–90.

Abdel al-Salam, Mohamed. 2011a. "Al-isti'ana bi-l-gaysh li-tard al-baltagiyya min al-shuqaq." *Al-Ahram*, February 21.

———. 2011b. "Muhafiz al-Qahira: al-'ashwa'iyat qadiyyat hayah aw mawt." *Al-Ahram*, February 21.

Abdel-Hamid, Attia. 2014. "Ahali al-Matariyya yushayyi'un gathamin Badr al-Islam; ganazat al-dahaya tatahawwal ila muzaharat ghadiba wa-tutalib bi-tathir al-Manzala min al-baltagiya." *Al-Ahram*, December 16. tinyurl.com/53xy68jm

Abdel-Hamid, Attia, Ibrahim al-Ashmawi, Mohamed Mutawi', Nivin Mustafa, Hamada al-Said, Hassan al-Asmar, and Hassan Saad. 2014. "Bi-l-ihsa'iyat wa-l-watha'iq . . . aradi al-Nil wa-l-buhayrat wa-l-sarf al-sihhi taht saytarat al-baltagiya." *Al-Ahram*, February 5.

Alsharif, Asma. 2014. "Illegal Housing Boom Is Big Challenge for Egypt's Leader." Reuters, April 28. https://www.reuters.com/article/

us-egypt-election-housing/illegal-housing-boom-is-big-challenge-for-egypts-leader-idUSKBN0DE14O20140428.

Amar, Paul. 2013. *The Security Archipelago: Human-security States, Sexuality Politics, and the End of Neoliberalism.* Durham, NC: Duke University Press.

Amr Abd al-Samih, Essam. 2011. "al-Takhrib al-mumanhag." *Al-Ahram,* April 20.

Bayat, Asef. 2012. "Politics in the City Inside Out." *City & Society* 24, no. 2:110–28. https://doi.org/10.1111/j.1548-744X.2012.01071.x.

Emran, Ibrahim. 2011. "Mathaf al-turath al-wahati fi qabdat al-baltaga." *Al-Ahram,* June 9.

Hassan, Hatem M. 2015. "Extraordinary Politics of Ordinary People: Explaining the Microdynamics of Popular Committees in Revolutionary Cairo." *International Sociology* 30, no. 4: 383–400.

Al-Husseiny, Hijaz. 2016. "Buhairat Misr: marfu'a min al-khidma! Tahawwalat ila awkar baltaga badalan min intag al-asmak." *Al-Ahram,* August 6.

Ismail, Salwa. 2012. "The Egyptian Revolution against the Police." *Social Research* 79, no. 2: 435–62.

Khalil, Omnia. 2015. "The People of the City: Unraveling the How in Ramlet Bulaq." *International Journal of Sociology* 45, no. 3: 206–22.

Meleegy, Essam, and Ayman Farouq. 2011. "Al-baltagiya ya'taridun 'ala al-amn bi-l-shari'." *Al-Ahram,* March 1.

Al-Shawadfi, Nermin. 2012. "al-Istila' 'ala ghurfatayn bi-masgid wa tahwilahuma ila shaqqa sakaniya." *Al-Ahram,* July 11.

Singerman, Diane. 2007. "Youth, Gender, and Dignity in the Egyptian Uprising." *Journal of Middle East Women's Studies* 9, no. 3: 1–27.

25

CAIRO MILITARIZED
ARMY ECONOMIES, SECURITY INDUSTRIES, AND SURVEILLANCE GEOGRAPHIES

ZEINAB ABUL-MAGD

Egypt's urban spaces had already been deeply militarized for decades when President Hosni Mubarak, an ex-army officer himself, took power. While Cairo didn't have an ex-general serving as its governor then, ex-officers occupied numerous administrative positions as second- and third-tier rulers of the sprawling, populous city. In addition, the military institution owned gigantic business enterprises that sold almost every consumer good to the city's masses and offered them almost every service they needed. From bureaucratic offices and the premises of lucrative businesses, the officers securitized everyday life in the rich, middle-class, and poor neighborhoods across Cairo, and made sure that its population was constantly being watched and disciplined (Abul-Magd 2017). While Mubarak kept a civilian façade for his government, he allowed his fellow retired generals to function as de facto rulers of the country's surveilled urban spaces in and outside the capital. One of the main demands of Tahrir's revolutionaries was to "demilitarize" the nation.

In the decade that followed the 2011 Revolution, the exact opposite happened, as Abed, Duffield, and Elmeshad have pointed out in their contributions to this volume. For the first time in decades, Cairo is governed by a retired general, as are most major cities and small towns across the country. Cairo's main neighborhoods are similarly headed by ex-officers, and the main bureaus of the government authorities concentrated in the city are filled with retired generals and colonels. The city's urban planning is managed by military contractors, in charge of building upscale districts, multi-lane bridges that connect those districts, and toll highways. Cairo's population, now and more than ever, consumes food, medicine, cars, gas, home appliances, washing detergents, hand sanitizers, and COVID face masks produced in military-owned enterprises (Salim 2020; al-Lahuni 2020). The daily lives of the city's inhabitants are under constant surveillance, and the aim is clear: to never let 2011 happen again.

At last, the regime insists, the inhabitants of Cairo's slums have a decent place to live. They have been moved to hundreds of high-rise apartment buildings with thousands of flats and some green spaces around them. As El-Husseiny and Duffield attest (this volume), the Engineering Authority of the Armed Forces built these areas quickly as part of their more general responsibilities for enacting Cairo's new urbanism. As soon as the settlements were built, poor families were relocated to them—often forcibly—from their older neighborhoods. The army officers who led construction in the new areas took care of providing services—as ex-general Khalid Siddiq, the director of the state's Informal Settlements Development Fund, asserted. The governor of Cairo, ex-general Khalid Abd al-'Al, pointed out that the new buildings are exemplary models that allow a clean, safe, and dignified life. The minister of local development, ex-general Mahmud Sha'rawi, celebrated the fact that they had paid special attention to the needs of youth when designing them by making plenty of sporting activities and facilities available (Tallima 2020; al-Sharqawi 2020; al-Sharqawi 2018; Fayiz 2020). As Mohie has shown, also in this volume, these "civilizing" aspects of the new settlements were often of more concern to the authorities than guaranteeing their residents the means to make a living. While older parts of Cairo are being transformed through megaprojects and surveillance, military-run communities on the peripheries are creating a new reality for Cairo's poor and middle class (Hasan 2009).

If one considers the situation since 2013 as a war of repression or a counterinsurgency launched by the Egyptian armed forces against a disobedient segment in the society, then this perspective can be extended to posit that the Egyptian government is trying to turn the entire society into a military camp, where every rebellious or docile citizen is subjugated and watched. In a lesser-known treatise titled *Society Must Be Defended*, Michel Foucault wrote,

While it is true that political power puts an end to war and establishes or attempts to establish the reign of peace and civil society, it certainly does not do so in order to suspend the effects of power or naturalize the disequilibrium revealed by the last battle of war . . . the role of political power is perpetually to use a sort of silent war to reinscribe that relationship of force, and to reinscribe it in institutions, economic inequalities, language, and even bodies of individuals. (Foucault 2003, 15–6)

In another short treatise titled *Security, Territory, and Population,* Foucault asserted, "Defense of society is tied up with war by the fact that . . . it is thought of in terms of 'an internal war' against the dangers arising from the social body itself" (Foucault 2007, 489). In the same book, he indicated that the modern state aims at structuring its urban institutions in a "panoptic" shape, which "basically involves putting someone in the center—an eye, a gaze, a principle of surveillance—who will be able to make its sovereignty function over all the individuals [placed] within this machine of power" (Foucault 2007, 94). According to the governing logic of military rules and some portions of the population, Cairo, a city of twenty million inhabitants and the central command of the camp, undoubtedly needs special measures of surveillance that deeply penetrate the very homes and bodies of the city's population. This is facilitated in the age of information technology since the personal data of civilians is more easily accessible on smartphones and social media accounts.

Scenes from a Militarized City
In the past, the image of a militarized city was usually of streets full of tanks with armed soldiers standing atop them. This no longer seems to be necessary. Military economies and spaces have proliferated throughout the metropolis. For example, Cairo's Metro stations not only provide access to speedy transportation in the congested city, but also have grown into small, informal markets—military markets—for millions of daily riders. Since it was developed in the 1980s, the exit of the Maadi Metro station has always had street sellers from whom the Metro's passengers could purchase anything—from vegetables, fruits, and fish to cheap clothes and slippers. In the past few years, a new competitor has shown up next to them: military-owned trucks with large refrigerators that sell frozen beef and poultry. At the door of each truck, conscripted soldiers sell meat at affordable prices that has been raised and slaughtered in the military's vast commercial farms—hundreds of thousands of acres of cultivated lands with stockyards and food processing mills

attached. On the other side of the Metro station, there is a small kiosk where other soldiers sell light goods such as Coca-Cola, biscuits, chocolate bars, and other snacks.

Both individual army officers and military companies have shaped surveillance in recent years. In 2014, Falcon Group, a new "private security" firm, took charge of guarding Cairo University's gates (Ibrahim 2014). The new notion of "private security firms" became familiar after the US occupation of Iraq. There, a company called Blackwater, which hired ex-army officers, was contracted by the Pentagon to commit acts of violence considered unacceptable for the standing army to engage in (Wamsley 2020). In 2016, the Cairo Governorate issued a new decision that all shops must install security cameras. Stores are not allowed to obtain or renew their operation permit without several monitoring cameras installed in visible spots outside and inside the premises to allow a full view of the streets and shoppers. Owners who violate the requirement must pay a large fine. Cameras are also required at almost every other building in the city: mosques, schools, nightclubs, sporting clubs, shopping malls, manufacturing mills, and so forth (Abd al-Raziq 2017). After the parliament codified this decision into Law No. 151 of 2019, the military-owned electronics factory embarked on producing such cameras in order to help fulfill the increasing demand for them among civilians (Husni 2020).

Securing Cairo University—whose campus hosts tens of thousands of students across its colleges and departments—was among the early profitable contracts for the Falcon Group. The head of the large firm is an ex-military intelligence officer who recruits professional and highly trained guards from retired army and police officers (al-Bardini 2014). The company's uniformed guards have been stationed at every gate of the walled university to identify all who enter the campus; they are also responsible for breaking up protests (France 24 2014). Falcon went on to get other government contracts to secure Cairo's underground Metro stations, through which millions of riders pass every day, and Cairo International Airport, through which millions of travelers pass every year. Falcon is keen on delivering the best services to its client, the Egyptian state, by buying the newest surveillance technology for facial and audio recognition that functions well in "places of mass gatherings," such as football stadiums and entertainment sites (Mayhew 2016).

Falcon also offers its services to help the government with house inspections. In 2017, the Ministry of Electricity contracted Falcon to read residential electricity meters on the state's behalf, and the firm hired thousands of agents to fulfill the task in Cairo and other cities across the country. The Ministry of Electricity informed its customers—which include all Egyptian citizens, since the ministry is the only provider of electricity for homes in the country—that Falcon is a part of a "sovereign authority" (*giha siyadiya*), an expression usually used to refer to military or intelligence bodies. In 2020, with the increases in electricity bills and the difficult conditions induced by the COVID-19 pandemic, Falcon embarked on streamlining the work of both the ministry and the citizens by digitizing the collected information. They photograph the electricity meters and send the data to the ministry electronically. Meanwhile, all residential electricity meters are being replaced by smart ones (Salah 2017; al-Sawi 2020). Falcon represents just one example of the regime's larger commitment to digital and military-led securitization projects.

Launching a Digital Government

Previously, all citizens, at some point, had to visit Tahrir's Mugamma'—a government building in downtown Cairo and the paragon of Egyptian bureaucracy—to get necessary paperwork done (e.g., driver's and marriage licenses, passport services, and tax-related work). More recently, its offices were moved to Abbasiya. The government recently delivered the good news that they would be initiating a "Digital Egypt" project. The Ministry of Military Production (MoMP), headquartered in Khedival Cairo near Tahrir, is undertaking much of this project. The MoMP's Information Systems and Computers Center (ISCC) has already embarked on digitizing the records of the Ministry of Supply, responsible for providing low- and middle-class citizens with subsidized food and issuing them new electronic cards (*bitaqat tamwin*) to obtain their rations at state outlets. During the digitization process, the MoMP dropped millions of beneficiaries from their system, considering them unqualified to continue to receive the subsidies. Similarly, the MoMP has already digitized records for the Ministry of Health and issued new health insurance cards for the citizens who benefit from public health services (*kart al-ta'min al-sihhi*). The Ministry of Defense (MoD), head-quartered near Abbasiya Square, is taking care of securing the electronic files of the new health care system, as all the records will be eventually transferred to this ministry once completed (Zayn 2019). It is worth mentioning that MoMP has recently ventured into building new plants for producing and selling drugs and other medical supplies for profit. Moreover, in order to contribute to digitizing the electricity services, the

MoMP has started a new production line to make the aforementioned smart electricity meters for use by the Falcon security firm (Ramadan 2018). The MoMP, which also handles weapons manufacturing, and the MoD, whose job seems to be related to barracks, now have access to data on millions of civilians and their modes of consumption of public goods.

Data storage requires physical and secure spaces to function. According to President al-Sisi in a conversation with youth, Egypt's e-government exists "14 meters underground in some [hidden] place and it will be greatly secured" (Abul-Magd 2021). Some might assume that the unknown place is likely to be at the new administrative capital that is being lavishly constructed by military engineers in a desert area near Cairo ('Afifi 2019). The digitized records of all the ministries will be interconnected, and this artificial "brain" may include every little detail about the life of each citizen: their birth certificates and national ID cards, their photos from birth to old age, their contracts of marriage and divorce, food consumption, what type of medicine they take, how much they pay every month for electricity and water bills, their properties and taxes, how many times they have traveled abroad, whether they completed the compulsory military service, and much more. Digitization cannot be seen as a politically neutral initiative or a technocratic one proposed by a government that promotes technological innovation as the future of the nation. Rather, in this case, it must also be seen as a tool for the surveillance, governance, and control of the citizenry.

Passing through the Cairo–Ismailia Highway

Driving from Cairo to Suez to visit relatives or do business has gotten much easier lately. The new Cairo–Ismailia Desert Road is a smoothly paved toll highway with multiple lanes and barriers to collect passage fees. Above the toll stations, there is a large signboard bearing the logo of the Ministry of Defense, that reads "National (*Wataniya*) Company for the Construction, Development, and Management of Roads." This is one of a long chain of other companies that all carry the word *wataniya* in their names, and they are all owned, in turn, by the MoD (Abul-Magd 2017). They include, for example, Wataniya for Petroleum, which owns hundreds of gas stations, and the gigantic manufacturing plants of Wataniya for Steel in Suez; Wataniya for Cement in Sinai and Middle Egypt; and Wataniya for Granite and Marble in several provinces. All these government endeavors involve for-profit businesses of essential goods. The Cairo–Ismailia Road is only one of a large number of toll highways that the Wataniya for Roads has recently developed and is collecting daily fees from as millions of cars and trucks pass through. The same company owns the restaurants, cafés, stores, and billboards on these roads, extending for hundreds of miles (Ministry of Defense n.d.).

On the road to Ismailia, vehicles wait in a long line for their turn to reach the fee-collection booths. They pay a toll of LE 10 and take a ticket with a serial number that reflects the number of cars that have passed through at that point on any given day. Noncommercial drivers pay smaller fees than heavier vehicles, such as the trucks carrying basic goods that inhabitants of the city need daily. A young Egyptian military intelligence officer, whom I met while he was studying in the United States at the Marine Corps University, explained to me that the military has its own contracting companies to construct roads, and ex-officers in charge of public transportation, "so if the enemy invades, the army knows the entrances and exits of the country." His description of both simple and extremely complicated economic investments and incentives was reduced to a question of security.[1]

Leaving the Slums for al-Asmarat

The state-owned, televised celebrations of al-Asmarat's opening show-cased recently relocated families to the new housing project. The district, spreading over almost two hundred acres, includes high and colorful apartment buildings with thousands of flats to accommodate the inhabitants of Cairo's old "slums." The area has some green spaces in between the identical buildings, and a mosque, church, grocery store, bakery, schools, and football fields. As Mohie has described the settlement in this volume, al-Asmarat is surrounded by a long, guarded wall with a big gate guarded by police officers and patrol cars. To enter, one must know a resident or be authorized to conduct business within the area. The Engineering Authority of the Armed Forces built al-Asmarat to relocate residents from quarters in Islamic Cairo such as Fustat, Sur Majra al-'Uyun, and al-Sayyida Zaynab, and from the Maspero Triangle. After he assumed his position as the new governor of Cairo in 2018, ex-general Khalid 'Abd al-'Al pledged to declare Cairo a city free of the dirty, unsafe "slums" by 2020 and to provide their inhabitants with a more "civilized" life (al-Khalafawi 2020).

General 'Abd al-'Al is the first ex-officer to serve as governor of Cairo in at least three decades. The last retired general to run the city was hired by Mubarak in 1989. As stated previously, in the past few years, most of the country's provinces assigned ex-officers from the military and police as governors; an ex–police general was appointed to manage the city of Cairo. Under him, the heads of the large quarters of the city are mostly ex-army officers, including in the areas where the old slums are located. For example, ex-general Sami 'Allam, who is in charge of the Khalifa quarter, asserted that destroying the historic graveyards and fragile buildings in Fustat is a step toward developing this area. Ex-general Khalid Siddiq, the director of the state's Informal Settlements Development Fund, aids him in these efforts, claiming that the larger objective is to alleviate poverty and has nothing to do with potential foreign investments in the demolished areas for touristic purposes (Tallima 2020).

The policy of dislocating the inhabitants of the slums entails simultaneous projects of gentrification of Cairo's center and the securitization of the new periphery. Walking deeper inside al-Asmarat, one can notice a pack of stray dogs moving around bags of trash. There are few jobs available inside the area, since the inhabitants had to leave behind their shops and other sources of income, such as work as daily laborers, in their demolished neighborhoods. Mohie's chapter in this volume describes in depth what the resettlement has meant in terms of increasing the residents' economic precarity. Even driving a tuk-tuk (auto-rickshaw) to transport passengers across the widely stretched al-Asmarat is forbidden. Some of the families fail to pay the rent for their apartments, which they lease from the government, and don't own as they might have done with their previous houses and shops. The only places available for shopping for basic goods—vegetables, groceries, or bread—are military-owned stores. The residents of ground-floor apartments have iron bars installed on their windows and around their balconies in response to an uncertain environment. Taking a look at the neighborhoods from which they were displaced, one can see huge foreign investments translate into a growing skyline for residential and commercial purposes and lucrative touristic projects (Tallima 2020).

Cairo has become a laboratory of a totalizing regime, obsessed with profit-driven securitization that seeks to incorporate and control almost all aspects of public life. It wishes to have a hand in all newly built spaces and social worlds. While this may represent a state expanding its writ in an age of digitalization and counterinsurgency, perhaps we are witnessing the public sector asserting sovereignty in order to push a developmentalist agenda, in a context of global peripheralization or dependency. Is this *wataniya*? Or is this a vision of a megacity articulated by a small set of individual generals and security-industry titans, who extract wealth by force, degrading ecologies and resources, and marginalizing laboring bodies and the sovereignty of the people? Perhaps it would be useful to extend this question: has there *ever* been a pure, disinterested nationalism *(wataniya)* that can be separated from the individual and collective interests of the powerful who have seized control of the nation?

Notes

1   Personal communication, anonymous officer, Marine Corps University, Quantico, October 21, 2015.

Works Cited

Abd al-Raziq, Yasmin. 2017. "Al-Qahira tulzim ashab al-mahallat wa-l-mabani al-hayawiya bi-tarkib kamirat muraqaba." *Al-Shorouk*, January 19.

Abul-Magd, Zeinab. 2017. *Militarizing the Nation: The Army, Business, and Revolution in Egypt.* New York: Columbia University Press.

———. 2021. "Diaries of a Surveilled Citizen after a Failed Revolution in Egypt." *International Journal of Middle East Studies* 53, no. 1: 145–54. https://doi.org/10.1017/S0020743821000088.

'Afifi, Nirmin. 2019. "Al-Sisi: 'aql al-dawla li-manzumat al-raqmana mu'amman wa-madfun 'ala 'umq 14 mitr." *El-Watan News*, July 31.

al-Bardini, Ahmad. 2014. "Falcon al-wahida al-hasila 'ala rukhsat al-bunduqiya wa-ra'isuha wakil sabiq li-l-Mukhabarat al-Harbiya." *Al-Shorouk*, October 15.

Fayid, Muhammad Mahmud. 2019. "Kamil al-Wazir: tahadiyat wa-ingazat . . . ." *Akhbar el-Yom*, March 10.

Fayiz, Wa'il. 2020. "Al-Tanmiya al-Mahaliya: al-intiha' min naql 13 alf usra ila hayy al-Asmarat." *Al-Ahram*, December 18.

Foucault, Michel. 2003. *Society Must Be Defended.* Translated by David Macey. New York: Picador.

———. 2007. *Security, Territory, and Population.* Translated by Graham Burchell. Basingstoke: Palgrave Macmillan.

France 24. 2014. "Hal yatahawwal al-tawattur bayna al-hukuma al-misriya wa-tullab al-gami'at ila sira' maftuh?" October 17. https://f24.my/1Dib4.

Hasan, Sharif. 2009. "Al-amn yamna' dakhlat al-Ahly." *FilGoal*, February 3.

Husni, Samir. 2020. "Masna' al-iliktruniyat yabda' fi intag kamirat muraqaba." *Youm7*, October 8.

Ibrahim, Adli. 2014. "Al-gami'at tahta hirasat Falcon." *Al-Bawabh News*, October 9. https://www.albawabhnews.com/831436.

al-Khalafawi, Sayyid. 2020. "Muhafiz al-Qahira: al-'asima khaliya min al-'ashwa'iya nihayat 2020." *Youm7*, July 7.

al-Lahuni, Ahmad. 2020. "al-Intag al-Harbi . . . yadd tasna' al-dhakha'ir wa-l-asliha wa-ukhra tusa'id fi mustalzamat muwagahat kuruna." *Al-Mal News*, June 14.

Mayhew, Stephen. 2016. "STC Partners with Falcon to Increase Security in Egypt." *Biometric Update*, December 13. https://www.biometric update.com/201612/stc-partners-with-falcon-to-increase-security-in-egypt.

Ministry of Defense. n.d. https://www.mod.gov.eg/ModWebSite/ NProjectsAr.aspx?id=3.

Ramadan, Rahma. 2018. "Iftitah masna' intag al-'addadat al-dhakiya." *Youm7*, October 31.

Salah, Muhammad. 2017. "Al-kahraba' tata'aqad ma'a Falcon Group li-qira'at al-'addad." *Al-Shorouk*, August 22, 2017.

Salim, Maha. 2020. "Ayna wa kayfa tahsul 'ala kimamat wa-mutahhirat al-Intag al-Harbi?" *Al-Ahram*, June 14.

al-Sawi, Hanan. 2020. "Al-sura ma bitikdibsh . . . hal yunhi birnamig Shu'a' mashakil fawatir al-kahraba'?" *Akhbar el-Yom*, October 23.

al-Sharqawi, Amira. 2018. "Ta'arraf 'ala 5 mashru'at gahiza li-iskan al-'ashwa'iyat bi-l-Qahira qariban." *Al-Ahram*, October 27.

———. 2020. "Muhafiz al-Qahira: al-intiha' min izalat al-'ashwa'iyat al-khatira nihayat al-'am al-hali." *Al-Ahram*, June 3.

Tallima, Nisma. 2020. "al-Mudir al-tanfidhi li-sunduq tatwir al-'ash- wa'iyat al-muhandis Khalid Siddiq . . . ." *Al-Ahali*, March 11.

Wamsley, Laurel. 2020. "Shock and Dismay after Trump Pardons Blackwater Guards Who Killed 14 Iraqi Civilians." NPR Politics, December 23. https://www.npr.org/2020/12/23/949679837/ shock-and-dismay-after-trump-pardons-blackwater-guards-who-killed-14-iraqi-civil.

Zayn, Muhammad. 2019. "Hiwar ra'is ma'lumat al-Intag al-Harbi yakshif aliyyat hadhf ghayr al-mustahiqqin min al-tamwin." *Akhbar el-Yom*, September 12.

26

THUGGERY, URBANITY, AND ENFORCED SOVEREIGNTIES
COMPETING UNIVERSES OF THE *BALTAGA*

ALY EL RAGGAL

Seven social phenomena marked Cairo in the 1990s: police brutality; a huge public police presence; the expansion of informal housing settlements; the emergence and expansion of gated communities; the increasingly influential roles of lower-ranking police officers; various Islamist groups; and thuggery. Simultaneously, neoliberalization was intensifying. These phenomena are not the product of the 1990s itself, but during this time the subjects of securitization and the hyper-visibilization of "thugs, slums, Islamists, and popular districts" in Cairo had become a hegemonic discourse. Despite the inherent contradictions and animosities between these different phenomena, they coexisted, flourished, and were mutually constitutive. Their interconnections were channeled and infused through the media, police, political officials, real estate developers, cinema, and social media. Securitization is "the reconfiguration of political debates and claims around social justice, political participation, or resource distribution into technical assessments of danger, operations of enforcement, and targeting of risk populations," while hypervisibilization is "the spotlighting of certain identities and bodies as sources of radical insecurity and moral panic in ways that actually render invisible the real nature of power and social control" (Amar 2013, 17). These two concepts are central to this chapter, as they shed light on the issue of thugs, urbanism, and governance, helping to frame the issue of their interconnectedness theoretically and anthropologically.

The focus of this chapter is thugs (*baltagiya*, or *baltagi* in the singular) and thuggery (*baltaga*) and the roles they have played in reconstructing the imagination of the city and the practical aspects of its policing. The chapter argues, in tandem with Bassem Al-Samragy's chapter in this volume, that through the securitization of urban communities and social-political life through the cultivation of thug practices and networks, the whole set of security and police practices have come to function as a repressive web that imprisons most of Cairo's poor and middle-class population. Thuggery has become both territorialized and deterritorialized within the city. The former occurred through the occupation of public spaces, with physical presences established within different spots and areas of neighborhoods, using spatiality as territory for enforcing sovereignty. The latter occurred through the provision of thuggery services upon request—physical assaults, their role in influencing parliamentary elections, the destruction of property and morals, and the repression (physical and sexual) of opposition on behalf of the state. These permanent processes of territorialization and deterritorialization have transformed thugs into omnipresent ghosts of the city, located in slums and popular quarters, but capable of striking at any moment, in any place. This ghost occupies a huge place in the way different people imagine and visualize the city and govern movements within it.

I do not focus here on any particular event, but rather on the daily dynamics and articulation of security. In order to avoid the shortcomings of linguistic approaches, I do not limit my concept of "discourse" to language. Rather, I adopt Laclau's understanding of discourse as "not essentially restricted to the areas of speech and writing, but any complex of elements in which relations play the constitutive role. This means that elements do not pre-exist the relational complex but are constituted through it" (Laclau 2005, 68). The following chapter is the result of fieldwork that I have conducted, mainly in Cairo and Alexandria, from 2011 to 2019. I do not tackle all seven of the phenomena mentioned in my introduction above due to space constraints, but I draw links and bonds between them, as I strongly believe one cannot approach the topic of thugs without first situating these phenomena in the background.

The Rise of Thuggery in the Urban Scene

By the mid-1980s, Egypt had entered both a financial and a housing crisis (Soliman 2013). This was at the same time that the war on terrorism erupted and an informal economy had expanded within the country.

The financial crisis intensified the gradual retreat of the state from its social responsibilities. The state's ability to impose discipline and build stable relations with a wide-ranging variety of actors began to weaken, making way for the growth of an informal economy and limited state concessions, and further undermined the state's ability to enforce laws. While a lack of revenue had weakened the state's ideological apparatuses, the repressive ones grew stronger. In order to maintain its sovereignty and dominance, the state tolerated informality and illegality while publicly asserting power and control through violence and social repression. It delegated many of its roles to clientelist networks—among them, the *baltagi*. Simultaneously, and in response to the housing crisis, President Mubarak made an unwritten deal with the population, allowing informal housing to expand while the rise of real estate investments, both formal and informal, became marked by corruption, illegality, and the vast, concentrated accumulation of wealth (El Kadi 2009). Poorer residents of the new "informal" areas provided their own services (e.g., electricity, water pipes and drains, and so forth) by seizing the closest source available to them (Bayat 2009). This created a permanent state of illegality that transformed and conditioned the relationship between the state and the different independent-minded communities, which were categorized as poor, illegal, and dangerous. As we shall see with *baltagiya*, the state tried to fight informal housing by decree, "culminating in 1996 with the promulgation of two presidential decrees stipulating that any new construction on agricultural land and any urban construction without a valid building permit would be severely punished through military courts" (Sims 2012, 129). But the configuration of the political regime—the absence of alternatives and the expected social unrest in cases of prevention—allowed informal housing to expand rapidly. Both thugs and informal settlements began to play a strategic role within Egyptian society.

The internal dynamics of many new settlements were characterized by physical violence. Different groups, ethnicities, and new families fought over their safety, presence, sovereignty, and prestige (Al-Raggal 2022). New thugs were born or exiled to these new areas, and had to compete with those of the old city and within their areas to prove their own capacity for dominance. Some thugs from the new popular quarters succeeded in building their fame, but one of the main characteristics of the new areas was the absence of strong stakeholders in the universe of thuggery. Strong thugs and small gangs competed over the same areas and even over the same streets within a neighborhood.

The presence of strong thugs who could control their men and enforce and ensure discipline over wider territories thus became a source of security and stability. Strong and established thugs became part of the clientelist system of the Mubarak era. It is also important to note that *baltagiya* have existed and flourished as a social phenomenon—both urban and rural—since long before Mubarak, but his regime extensively invested in thuggery as a means of social control. By the 2000s, a lack of strong stakeholders and a fragmentation of thuggery marked the older city districts.

A decade of fieldwork in Cairo and Alexandria shows that drug dealing was part of a wide variety of thug activities on display in the cities. Small and young distributors took over the corners of inner-city streets, becoming a source of trouble. In describing the new quarters, a former drug dealer from Abdin—an old historical neighborhood in Cairo—told me that these thugs were "too many, too young, and too undisciplined. They form unstable and changeable small gangs. They fight with each other and with [thugs from] other streets. Sometimes the two ends of the same street fight against each other over drug dealing and dominance. The market is too big and less controlled."[1] Some residents of these streets fight constantly against the young gangs. Other thugs are sometimes called in to fight the particular thuggery of young drug dealers. Many women and girls feel intimated by the presence of the young gang members and dealers, fearing harassment and masculine violence. Despite a popular narrative claiming that thugs do not harass the girls of their own streets and neighborhoods, my fieldwork has shown the opposite, with many violent fights and severe injuries resulting from sexual violence. These young gangs also police morality and monitor women's movements, affairs, and dress codes.

Some Islamists living in the new quarters have tried to oppose street drug dealers (Ismail 2006), but the police have tended to ignore any petitions or complaints from Islamists against thugs and drug dealers. My fieldwork has shown that Islamists, thugs, and drug dealers have maintained a parallel coexistence, a state of affairs that can also be seen in O. Khalil's description of thugs in the Maspero Triangle, in this volume. They intentionally avoided each other while police made sure that they neither fought nor cooperated with one another. The police also made it clear to Islamists—particularly militants—that recruitment of thugs would constitute a red line that must not be crossed. The police have adopted the same strategy in prisons, as a Salafist from al-Matariya explained. He owned a shop in al-Matariya for a long time and was imprisoned between 2003 and 2008. In business, he argues, "it was good. Our properties were safeguarded by clear orders, not from the police station of the district, but from the state security apparatus itself. But we knew it was shaky and unstable state [sic] of safety. [Thugs] were spying on us from the '90s and we knew that the police could unleash them at any moment. But it was also a matter of a balance of power and physical capacities. This balance maintained that we both avoid [sic] each other."[2] Drug dealing accompanied thuggery while a larger, more business-oriented, and strategic type of thuggery was developing.

The new settlements, consisting of a mix of formal and informal housing and real estate investment projects, opened a new phase for thug networks to become established in different forms: being hired by others to seize a piece of land; harassing and exerting pressure on land owners; safeguarding construction equipment; acting as a land broker and real estate investor; helping other investors to bribe state officials; and obtaining needed papers from different state institutions (e.g., police station, local councils). Land investment projects created a strong and wide network among police, thugs, and the bureaucracy. Low-ranking police officers were a very strong node in this web. They had access to thug networks, local investors, and bureaucratic officials, and acted as the main social arm of the police stations in penetrating everyday life. They became more powerful and influential than senior police officers within the popular districts, and manipulated the illegalities of some of the informal neighborhoods. These conditions allowed these police officers to build their own sovereignty, engaging widely with all the informal activities and taking a share of the business profits, running their own informal businesses, or extorting residents.

Slums and new settlements in Cairo often surround or border posh, upper- and middle-class neighborhoods. The latter are not easily accessible and are enclosed by either roads—the Ring Road being a great example of this, as Elshahed has discussed elsewhere in this volume—bridges, the Nile, or the desert, while slums and new settlements are socially demarcated as dangerous. The presence of thugs and informality (of housing, businesses, and so forth) factor into this fear, but alone do not explain it. It is the lack of social or communal activities and spaces of mingling, urban conviviality, and trust building that intensify thuggery rather than the pre-existence of thugs in any given area. Through different interviews, I began to see that the presence of thugs was used to vilify new areas as insecure and chaotic.

Deinstitutionalization and Political Thugs

The war on Islamic terrorism by the Egyptian state was waged in part by the police "deinstitutionalizing" themselves, that is, outsourcing their "dirty work." The police (that is, for the most part, the Interior Ministry) since the 1980s came to rely increasingly on thug networks to combat, penetrate, and track different Islamist groups. This war on terrorism reinforced the presence of thugs in the security network and expanded their roles. The thugs were strategic tools of the state, but this does not mean that the police had an entirely cordial relationship with them. This war was always characterized by alternating violent confrontations and cooperation. By the end of the 1990s, thugs, low-ranking police officers harassing citizens in the streets, and the informalization of coercion had become features of urbanity. But by the late 1990s, this outsourcing and informalization dynamic started to get out of control and exceed the control of the state. Many thug groups became real threats and concerns for the state, sometimes working against the interests of the uniformed police or the state-allied elites. By 1998, the Law of Baltaga was instituted to help combat this phenomenon, taking aim at two alleged crimes: the public display of force and the obstruction of law enforcement by "thuggery" or *baltaga*. It became clear that the state's employing thugs as a tool to enforce its sovereignty had, at least in part, backfired.

The Egyptian state has used thugs as a political tool to intimidate and assault opposition parties and figures since at least the late 1970s and 1980s (Kandil 2012), but this method became commonplace in the 2000s. The year 2005 witnessed the widespread use of thugs (both male and female) in the parliamentary elections to attack opposition members, prevent voting, defame opponents, and block polls. Concurrently, the police used thugs to attack and sexually assault female protestors in downtown Cairo (Amar 2013). In the 2005 and 2010 parliamentary elections, thugs and police cooperated against opposition groups (Maadi 2011, 272–77). In 2010, after the opposition was completely excluded from traditional political avenues, thugs were used massively by Mubarak's National Democratic Party (NDP) members against each other. Thug networks were often employed by NDP members in their clashes against other members and in rivalries over land, business, and political hegemony. But 2010 marked a new horizon, where the outsourcing of violence became omnipresent. The increased pressure on the regime from national and international human rights organizations, as well as the structural contradictions within the economy and social fabric, produced outsourced violence at scale. Influential families in Egypt have a tradition of resorting to violence during parliamentary elections, but familial support was gradually replaced by hired thugs, who proved to be safer, more efficient, and less likely to be prosecuted.

Thuggery, Security, and Criminality

Some forms of thuggery have become a safe replacement and substitute for other criminal acts. Thuggery has become a way of making a living that may avoid imprisonment and police harassment. This has made thuggery visible and somewhat stable. A middle-ranking thug and his small gang took over an empty space in Misr al-Qadima (a historical popular neighborhood in Cairo) next to a cultural center. This thug worked for another higher-ranking thug. The space they occupied was supposed to be a parking place for visitors to the center. The thug's scheme was to make visitors pay him for parking and, in return, he safeguarded their cars from robbery and other potential threats. But this arrangement was not reached smoothly. In order to establish it, the thug himself robbed some of the cars, forcing the center to negotiate. By establishing his control over this unregulated territory, the thug secured several things for himself and his gang. He was able to run a small business that could, on the one hand, be legally met by police repression, but on the other hand, remained safer than more serious acts of thuggery. This opened a door for negotiations and safer arrangements with the police station of the district, since the crimes committed by the thug were less serious and local power had been established. Building up connections with low-ranking police officers by profit-sharing made him more desirable as a partner to other locally powerful thugs,

In addition to the parking arrangement, the endeavor allowed the thug to manage disputes in the area, such as visitors being exposed to any kind of physical annoyance, sexual harassment, residents expressing disdain for gender openness in parties, and noise complaints. Here the thug played two security roles: securing the center from any potential threats and establishing a buffer zone between visitors and locals. Another positive consequence of having a stable deal with a thug in the area, according to one of the center's workers, is that while this thug enforced a certain kind of sovereignty, workers were automatically included in these arrangements. The police station also enjoyed the buffer and did not have to secure the area as long as the thugs did not act politically or exceed the limits set by the state security apparatus to manage civil society. Still, the space is not particularly safe for the thug; it is contested by others who would like to take it over. The thug has to reconsolidate his power every now and then, and is constantly exposed to occasional police raids. An officer running an investigation regularly calls on the thug and threatens him in order to reestablish police sovereignty over the territory and over the thug himself.

Another case from Dar al-Salam shows similar dynamics between space management and thuggery. 'Attia al-Aqra', a famous thug in Dar al-Salam, used to control the microbus stops in one of the important streets of the district. 'Attia is a classic example of the thug: a young, fierce, and ruthless man who gained fame by killing another thug who came to kill him. Killing another locally influential thug is a rite of passage toward becoming a well-established name in that area. But after 'Attia took control of the microbus station, he had to secure the station and not cause trouble. He understood that the more security he could deliver, the more secure his own position would be. Over time, 'Attia was able to establish a stable relationship with the police station. He succeeded in avoiding the repeated raids and harassment that are often part of such relations. Meanwhile, 'Attia played several security roles: he kept the microbus drivers safe, resolved local conflicts, and defended the Dar al-Salam police station from attacks by protestors and other thugs during the January 28, 2011 "Day of Rage." After the fall of the police station, he was chased out by the revolutionaries and other thugs of the area and disappeared for some years. He reappeared after 2013 or 2014 and was killed in 2016 by another thug.

'Attia and hundreds of other similar cases have succeeded in positioning themselves within the equation of security and territory. On the one hand, they are sources of insecurity; on the other—through a kind of enforced sovereignty backed by the police—they become an unreliable, unstable means of delivering security. Other cases show that spatiality and contested spaces of business, when accompanied by networks of thugs, can lead to incidents of excessive violence and different forms of police intervention. The provision of informal and illegal satellite cable services used to be a flourishing business, but has begun to fade because of technological advancements and internet accessibility. This business attracted many young men from the popular districts seeking a source of income, particularly in the first decade of the century. Sometimes when conflicts erupted within the industry, they were not due to economic reasons but, rather, could be blamed on masculine paternalism—examples include a fight between two men, one of whom had harassed a sister of another thug; police sexually harassing a woman from the neighborhood, and so forth. Typically, once a conflict unfolds, the police wait until the fight is over to intervene. The common practice is to arrest as many people as possible in order to foster docility among rising thugs. However, if the fighting thugs are strong enough and have strong ties with the police station—and if prestigious members of the community get involved—the police can work as mediators to resolve the conflict.

Both thugs and the police in Egypt have had the same schizophrenic effects over time, particularly through the 1990s and into the new millennium. Thugs, in particular, have occupied a prominent space within the popular imagination as a source of terror and simultaneously as an indispensable source of security, safety, and the management of discipline and order. In some of the cases related above, the relationship between space and thuggery has inverted the logic of criminality and increasingly blurred the boundary line between police and thugs.

Thugs as Thick Signifier and Their Policing Practices

Security and acts of thuggery have become thick and floating signifiers, particularly in that they have taken hold of a wide range of urban conditions in the greater Cairo popular districts and *'ashwa'iyat*. By using the term *thick signifier*, I mean that "security" and "thugs" have "a more performative than a descriptive force. Rather than . . . picturing a condition, it [a thick signifier] organizes social relations into security relations." It "does not refer to an external, objective reality but establishes a security situation by itself" (Huysmans 1998, 232). The performative force of security discourse is an action itself; it is not just a description of a social reality. It includes both a fear produced through language and a security measure to be deployed. The term also triggers hypervisibilization of specific practices, from ruthless violence to social suppression, prestige, and masculine hegemony. The thug has also been sexualized and fantasized. The word triggers a fear of sexual assault and symbolically represents immorality, physical domination, and subordination. Any discourse that uses *thug* as a signifier becomes powerful and urgent. Thuggery and security are entwined in this instance, where "any discourse of security must always already, simultaneously and in a plurality of ways, be a discourse of danger too" (Dillon 1996, 121). The security discourse, adopted in Egypt by the state and its different organs, has used thugs to emphasize the social and political necessity of the police state and to help articulate heavy securitization processes. Security, then, can be perceived as "the move that takes politics beyond the established rules of the game and frames the issue either as a special kind of politics or as above politics" (Buzan et al. 1998, 23).

Thug has an earlier history that can be traced back to the 1930s and 1940s. Then it was used in opposition to *fatwana*, which carries positive connotations of masculine strength. When thugs reach a certain level of establishment, they are not called thugs, but rather *mi'allim* (master), *haj* (a man who has been to Mecca), or a "man who solves problems." But in the popular imagination, emphasized by the media, the thug is portrayed as a dark-skinned, vulgar, and ruthless individual. This chapter aims to demystify this stereotype. In reality, and anthropologically, the matter is much more complicated, specifically as it has evolved over the last thirty years. Thugs can be prestigious and educated men who work in different positions. They hold strong stakes in their districts and sometimes throughout the whole city. Young, vigorous men are definitely part of the phenomenon, but they represent the lower level of this universe and have nothing to do with the stereotypes presented in the media.

The securitization of bodies, a population, and entire poor neighborhoods takes place when thuggery comes to mean almost anything. But while the beneficiaries and victims may include a wide range of people, the problem of a thug administration is that it is inconsistent across neighborhoods and even within a single neighborhood. Security language organizes our relationships to other people via the logic of war (Wæver 1995). Most common in Cairo's securitization process is the massive installation of police checkpoints encountered on a typical Cairo night. The relationship between the checkpoints and thugs poses a serious question to everyday notions of safety, integrity, mobility, and accessibility for the urban poor. Officers check bodies for physical injuries, tattoos, and "white weapons" (knives, blades, and other non-firearm weapons). The police create borders and checkpoints, and resort to raids.

Several interviews with low-ranking police officers have revealed that through practice, shared experiences, personal experience, and reflection, they develop a sense of practicality, allowing them to easily recognize a thug. This explains why they gaze at faces so deeply, asking men to uncover their arms and shirts (checking for injuries and tattoos) and checking their neighborhood and profession on their state identification card. Other more militant and ruthless officers have frankly admitted, *it does not matter if you are a thug or not. People should be confronted and faced with security measures. They must fear the consequences of any unwelcomed actions. People from the slums and popular districts lack manners, morals and discipline. Students and middle-class citizens, as well, should know that they are under the hands and eyes of the police permanently. They all should know who is sovereign in the country.[3]*

The police deal with Cairo's poor not as a result of the poor's actions, but in reaction to their potential to act. Here, "the idea of dangerousness mean[s] that the individual must be considered by society . . . not at the level of the actual violations of an actual law, but at the level of the behavioral potentialities they represented" (Foucault 2001, 57). To this day, any discussion about poor districts transforms into a security debate: an ethical and political choice (Huysmans 1998). It is a choice that has been adopted by different sectors and classes of the society. One expert in peace, conflict, and democracy argues that the "security discussion is, above all, about the constitution of political order, about how our political identities are being constantly produced, reproduced, and transformed in discourses which legitimize the deployment of physical and political violence against the Other and against the traces of the Other in us" (Alvarez 2006, 81).

During Mubarak's thirty-year rule, security was transformed from a discourse into the regime's principal ideology: an ideology whose "function is to conceal the radical contingency of social relations and to naturalize relations of domination" (Howarth 2010, 310). This discourse was produced through a whole web of real estate developers, urban planners, media, police, and the judiciary system. The establishment of an elusive and generalized image of a dangerous component of the population—the thug—is what renders these floating signifiers of securitization so effective and desirable.

Notes

1   Former drug dealer from Abdin, interview by the author.
2   Salafist and shopkeeper from al-Matariya, interview by the author.
3   Police officer in Cairo, interview by the author.

Works Cited

Alvarez, Josefina. 2006. "Re-thinking (In)security Discourses from a Critical Perspective." *Asteriskos*, no. 1/2: 61–82.

Amar, Paul. 2013. *The Security Archipelago: Human-security States, Sexuality Politics, and the End of Neoliberalism*. Durham, NC: Duke University Press.

Bayat, Asef. 2009. *Life as Politics: How Ordinary People Change the Middle East*. Cairo: American University in Cairo Press.

Buzan, Barry, Ole Wæver, and Jaap de Wilde. 1998. *Security: A New Framework for Analysis*. Boulder, CO: Lynne Rienner Publishers.

Dillon, Michael. 1996. *Politics of Security: Towards a Political Philosophy of Continental Thought*. London: Routledge.

Foucault, Michel. 2001. "Truth and Juridical Forms." In *The Essential Foucault: Selections from Essential Works of Foucault 1954–1984*, vol. 3, edited by James D. Faubion, 1–90. New York: New Press.

Howarth, David. 2010. "Power, Discourse, and Policy: Articulating a Hegemony Approach to Critical Policy Studies." *Critical Policy Studies* 3, no. 3–4: 309–35. https://doi.org/10.1080/19460171003619725.

Huysmans, Jef. 1998. "Security! What Do You Mean? From Concept to Thick Signifier." *European Journal of International Relations* 4, no. 2: 226–55.

Ismail, Salwa. 2006. *Political Life in Cairo's New Quarters: Encountering the Everyday State*. Minneapolis: University of Minnesota Press.

El Kadi, Galila. 2009. *Spontaneous Urbanization*. Cairo: National Center for Translation and Eye Publishing House.

Kandil, Hazem. 2012. *Soldiers, Spies, and Statesmen: Egypt's Road to Revolt*. London and New York: Verso.

Laclau, Ernesto. 2005. *On Populist Reason*. London: Verso.

Maadi, Abd El Fatah. 2011. "Electoral Violence." In *The Parliamentary Election 2010*, edited by Amr Hisham Rabi, 253–93. Cairo: Al-Ahram Center for Political and Strategic Studies.

Al-Raggal, Ali. 2022. "Egypt's Informal Settlements: Soldiers, Gangs, Poverty, and Construction." Assafir Arabi and Rosa Luxemburg Foundation, May. https://assafirarabi.com/en/44982/2022/05/11/egypts-informal-settlements-soldiers-gangs-poverty-and-construction/.

Sims, David. 2012. *Understanding Cairo: The Logic of a City Out of Control*. Cairo: American University in Cairo Press.

Soliman, Samer. 2013. *The Strong Regime and the Weak State: The Management of Financial Crisis and Political Change in Mubarak's Era*. Cairo: General Authority for Culture Palaces.

Wæver, Ole. 1995. "Securitization and Desecuritization." In *On Security*, edited by Ronnie Lipschutz, 46–86. New York: Columbia University Press.

27

DECONSTRUCTING THUGGERY
RIOTS, PRISON BREAKS, AND THE CRIMINAL SUBJECT OF (NON)VIOLENT STREET POLITICS

MOHAMED AHMED

The Case of Izbat Abu Qarn

Based on field notes from ethnographic research conducted beginning in 2011, this chapter intends to deconstruct the permeating notions of nonviolence as a mantra of politics and effective mobilization, and to shift the analytical focus from middle-class protests in Tahrir Square to working-class mobilizations in the "slum" areas, known in Egypt as *'ash-wa'iyat*. As various other authors in this volume have attested (O. Khalil, Hassan, El Raggal, and Fallas, among others), politicians' statements, TV talk shows, newspaper columns, and popular discourse have stirred up a panic around thuggery (*al-baltaga*), described as exploding out of working-class slums and terrorizing the city. Reactionary commentators have framed the 2011 Revolution as a wave of chaos, looting, and indiscriminate violence ostensibly committed by irrational, criminal subalterns[1] and the residents of *'ashwa'iyat*. Here, I focus on Izbat Abu Qarn, a place which served as a projection screen for this discourse during the early twenty-first century. In this way, I will offer a new timeline for the revolution, locating its origin point in the policies of neoliberal governmentality of previous decades and exploring how these policies, in turn, produced a specific set of urban structures and criminalized social subjects. I also use this case to dismantle the instrumental understanding of urban violence that depoliticizes and reduces it to mere reaction to economic impoverishment, denying it any political significance or revolutionary potentiality. In this context, one could argue that the riots in the slums were not merely expressions of "depoliticized criminality." On the contrary, they included many examples of brave politicized activism, and they played pivotal roles in overthrowing Mubarak and his police regime.

Izbat Abu Qarn finds itself within the discourse of the 'ashwa'iyat in Cairo of the last twenty years—a discourse associated commonly with severe poverty, criminality, and moral decadence. The final scenes of two Egyptian blockbuster films, *Hina maysara* (2007) and *Dukkan Shihata* (2009), neatly exemplify the intellectual concern and fear of a violent change which seems inevitable thanks to corruption, dictatorship, and neoliberal policies (Hoad 2011; Khatib 2006, 60–83; Na'eem 2010). Izbat Abu Qarn emerged more than sixty years ago due to rural migration, especially from Upper Egypt, and simultaneous urban expansion during the Nasserist regime (1952–70). Immigrants moved to the city in search of jobs and a better standard of living, many settling in the area adjacent to what is known as Islamic Cairo. This residential area has grown dramatically and extended between Islamic Cairo (surrounding the 'Amr Ibn al-'As Mosque, the first mosque built in Cairo), Cairo's necropolis, and al-Muqattam. Abu Qarn gradually expanded to cover more than thirty feddans, where almost fifty thousand people live without legal contracts for rents or landownership. Due to the rural and southern backgrounds of the new inhabitants, most of their neighborhoods contained 'ezab ('ezba, singular)—family farmland plots or village collective plots. These 'ezab relied on communal and conventional codes. For instance, tribal affiliation and communal networks were used to organize issues of security, food supplies, and connection to electricity.

The police have typically operated in the area within these patterns of tribal affiliation and communal organization. But more centrally deployed and imposed policing strategies and criminalization apparatuses have increased since the 1980s as 'ashwa'iyat populations in Cairo multiplied rapidly in the previous decade due to housing shortages elsewhere and increased levels of rural–urban migration. Prior to that, Izbat Abu Qarn's location (relatively far from the middle- and lower-middle-class neighborhoods) distanced it from government control and prevented state-led development. But an eruption of moral panic around the expansion of these spaces resulted in Law 6, on thuggery, passed by the People's Assembly in 1998. This law grants police the power to arrest and detain citizens suspected of undermining public order through displays of aggression and physical strength, or on the mere suspicion that they will cause harm to others. These powers dramatically widened the scope of the repressive powers of the state's public order apparatus (Ismail 2006, 113).

The local economy in Izbat Abu Qarn depends basically on managing and selling off garbage and scrap steel, and supporting tannery, tin, and aluminum toolmaking and artisanal industries. The precarious economic and social conditions of these sectors, impacted by the restrictive policies of the 1990s, have led to the development of social practices of criminalized commercial activities and street vending. This informal business sector, which includes at least ten million people in the city of Cairo, does not contribute to state taxes or follow international financial regulations. In 2007, the nongovernmental organization Ala shanik ya baladi (literally translating to "For your sake, my country") started an initiative to modernize and develop Cairo's informal areas, and proposed seven programs to eliminate illiteracy, creating small business projects, teaching computer skills, and building teen centers, orphanages, and charity initiatives. The programs were not generated via local participation or independent investment; they depended on the charitable efforts of businessmen, graduate students, teachers, and physicians (Zaki 2013). The narrow scope of development—offering to paint houses and donating food and furniture to some residents—failed to deal with poverty and marginalization as structural problems.[2] During the 2000s, the ruling party (NDP) started to establish clientele networks in order to recruit supporters within the area. Their aim was to guarantee a wide voting base within the growing population and to facilitate the policing of these districts. Businessmen started to spend money in Izbat Abu Qarn, establishing NGOs to help educate children, support poor widows and divorced women, and incorporate residents into the formal economy (to pay taxes and serve national production) (Association for the Development and Enhancement of Women 2007; Magdy 2012; Abdel-Latif 2012).

The Mysterious Case of Khanufa

Ra'fat Abd al-Shakur, widely known as Khanufa, exemplifies the tragedy of Izbat Abu Qarn. He was first arrested at the age of twelve after a street brawl and served six months in a juvenile reformatory institution. This misdemeanor would mark the rest of his life. When he was released, he couldn't find a proper job and faced many economic hardships after the death of his father. Khanufa saw no other choice than to become a drug dealer, but decided not to get involved with the leading organized crime networks and instead launched his own business. The police targeted him to force him to serve as their informant. He refused and, consequently, the police investigators arrested him, charged him with drug trafficking, and sentenced him to seven years in prison. One of Khanufa's neighbors explained the nuances of his situation, arguing that Khanufa had wanted to take care of his family and that "he sold drugs, but refused to pay off the police or be a street dealer; he refused to coordinate with bigger, more corrupt drug dealers; he never stole from people" (Elmeshad 2011). Less than three months after being released, Khanufa determined he would change his life. Nevertheless, he was arrested once again and was sentenced to more than ten years for selling heroin, carrying a loaded weapon, and firing at the police.

He was eventually released from prison again, but this time along with thousands of other prisoners from Wadi al-Natrun prison on January 28, 2011 during the Interior Ministry's allegedly orchestrated prison emptying, which many have claimed was intended to spread chaos in the population (Wikileaks 2011a; Wikileaks 2011b; Fahmy 2010; Mohsen 2011a).[3] Khanufa recounted the incident, saying that he found the jail doors open and felt it was a divine intervention that had released him after being jailed unjustly. He recalled, "I prayed to God that he would save me from the injustice that happened to me, and God responded. I didn't escape, and anyone who says I escaped doesn't understand divine justice" (Elmeshad 2011). The police followed him and staged an ambush to arrest him. His "nothing left to lose" attitude made Khanufa not only decide to get married during his drama with the police, but also to have an audacious wedding out in the open, in the middle of his neighborhood (Al-Ahram 2011). When the police failed to arrest Khanufa after three raids and ambushes in his area, they arrested members of his family as hostages to force him to give himself up. His brother, Gameel, was beaten up, one of his sisters was sexually assaulted, his mother's house was destroyed, and she was taken to the police station. Khanufa responded by bringing bail money and supporters, friends from Izbat Abu Qarn, and organizing a protest in front of the police station. The situation got more complicated when the police clashed with the protestors, during which time a twelve-year-old boy was shot dead.

After this clash between community and police, Khanufa surprised the police, media, and TV audience when he called a live talk show on state TV and testified on air about the complications of the accident. He mentioned, "God granted me a release from the injustice that my brothers and I underwent . . . I was in jail no. 11, cell no. 9, and some

Figure 27.1. Khanufa's wedding picture.

people broke the windows and told me get out . . . I am not an escapee. I am innocent. The criminal who fled is Habib al-Adli [the Minister of Interior under Mubarak]. His men shot me in my leg and sentenced me to ten years."[4]

Khanufa accused police officers of blackmailing him for LE 1,000 each month when he didn't have even a few pounds in his pocket. After the police cracked down on his workshop and ruined his mother's house, another dramatic encounter took place when Khanufa and a large group of supporters blocked the Salah Salem highway. In the confusion, another boy, aged fifteen, was killed on his way home from selling scrap. Later on, a blogger followed Khanufa's story and convinced him to be interviewed in another video. Khanufa narrated his life drama, beginning with his first conviction at age twelve and continuing to recount the events of his life, half of which he had spent in prison. He denied and rejected the press's false accusations—that he was a drug dealer and the "most dangerous thug" in Cairo. He argued that the police chased him because he refused to be co-opted by the officers and drug kingpins who together dominate Izbat Abu Qarn.

Khanufa's video included a critique of the claims of police, generating a political and structural analysis. For example, Khanufa asked, "Why don't they utter a word about the big thieves outside the prisons? Why are they looking for us? They should go and look for the people smuggling arms and dealing heroin. Abu Alaa (Hosni Mubarak) 'ate' the country and murdered us. We are poor. Leave us, and search for Alaa and Gamal (Mubarak's sons)."[5] His final response to the accusation of thuggery framed the issue in moral terms: "Wherever we come from, we are Muslims, we are from this country, we are Egyptians. I am a Muslim man. I just want to feed my family. Leave me alone." He added eloquently that "Each action comes with a reaction . . . When they raided my home, when they wanted to kill me, I had all the surrounding neighborhoods supporting me . . . . Those who wanted to oppress me were sent to jail eventually for their injustices. Look at Habib al-Adli and Ismail al-Sha'ir (the head of Cairo's police); they are in court now. God is great and I don't worship any other." The police intensified its campaign against him and eventually arrested Khanufa using undercover police inspectors, who entered his neighborhood disguised as drug dealers. Khanufa was accused of killing the two boys during the two earlier incidents—one in front of the Manial police station and the other on the Salah Salem Highway—although the evidence pointed to police officers as the shooters. He was also accused of escaping from the prison during the revolution and evading justice, although the jailbreak had supposedly been orchestrated by the Mubarak regime (Abd al-Sami' 2011). The official media's headline read, "Egypt's Police Caught Cairo's Most Dangerous Thug among Ululation and Cheers of 'God Is Great.'" According to the police investigator, "honest citizens have cooperated with us to capture the vandal elements and the 'most dangerous thug' in Cairo." The file of Khanufa was sealed when he died in custody just two days after his capture. The police claimed the death was a suicide (Abdel Latif and Barakat 2011).

Revolution in Izbat Abu Qarn

The residents of Izbat Abu Qarn, like many other informal neighborhoods, responded in a variety of ways to activists' calls to join the protests on January 25, 2011. At the time, connections between the Tahrir Square activists and residents of informal neighborhoods hung in the balance. Many of those residents, especially daily workers and families with no savings, felt unsafe and worried about losing their livelihoods. While some blamed the protesters for disrupting their access to work, threatening their safety, and destabilizing the country (Ghannam 2012, 33), others sought to change the internal economy of violence and access to and distribution of resources within the slums and adjacent neighborhoods. Fathi Gleed, a parliamentarian representing District 21 of Cairo's Manial neighborhood, stated: "These people are very poor. As long as they have LE 10 [about $1.80] in their pockets to feed their families, they'll go home. They don't have much more far-reaching aspirations" (Elmeshad and Elwakil 2011). Because of government censorship, much of the public could only watch TV channels that presented the state media's perspective on the historic uprising. As Farha Ghannam (2012) noticed in another working-class neighborhood, many residents "thought poorly of the activists and repeated the lines offered by government propaganda, describing the protesters as troublemakers who were paid a daily allowance in Euros by outsiders and who were served free meals" (Ghannam 2012, 33).

Meanwhile, the ruling party tycoons, who had penetrated the informal neighborhoods and controlled their residents through drug rackets, arms, and thuggery, hired thugs to terrorize the protestors in Tahrir Square. Shukri Abd al-Qadir, a resident of Izbat Abu Qarn, got a call from Magdi 'Allam, the parliamentary representative of his district and a member of the ruling National Democratic Party. 'Allam asked him to attend a meeting close to the Faten Hamama Cinema in al-Manial district where the government's hired thugs were planning to attack Tahrir Square with guns, swords, knives, sharpened sticks, and clubs. The plan, according to Shukri's narrative, was to start by attacking anyone with a beard on their way to the square and to crack down on any group protesting, regardless of their cause. The purpose was clear, at the time: to intimidate citizens and to prove that, in the absence of the Mubarak regime, "we were a bunch of uncontrollable animals, desperate to kill each other," as Shukri states. He thought that the people in Tahrir were a bunch of "sissy kids" and privileged students who would flee once they were attacked, but his perception changed dramatically after the first confrontation with the people in Tahrir (Mohsen 2011b).

The complicated situation within the informal neighborhoods during the revolution can be further explained by the story of Yassir 'Ashur, another alleged thug from Izbat Abu Qarn. 'Ashur felt moved by Mubarak's speech on February 1, 2011, when Mubarak promised to hand over power after finishing his presidency and dissolving the cabinet. 'Ashur didn't deny the corruption of the Mubarak regime and was touched by the paternalistic tone that Mubarak used in his speech. He recalled that Mubarak looked like a "broken man, a fallen leader, and a mourning grandfather." 'Ashur affirmed that Mubarak was really a "criminal and stole the country," but 'Ashur insisted that he still had the right to a dignified exit from power instead of leaving the country for "spoiled young men." Accordingly, 'Ashur made his way to the state television building (Maspero), joining a group of Mubarak supporters there. The atmosphere among pro-regime protesters was not enthusiastic. He tried to break the ice by passing around strips of tramadol but realized eventually that the majority had been paid to attend this rally for Mubarak. His disillusionment was enough to send him back to Izbat Abu Qarn.

On Looting and Commodity Fetishism

During the days of the 2011 Revolution, when policing seemed to vanish from almost every neighborhood in Cairo, many incidents of organized and sporadic looting took place. Groups of people stormed into supermarkets, malls, banks, jewelry stores, electronics stores, and government buildings. One of the most famous looting incidents that took place near Izbat Abu Qarn was in al-Maadi, a wealthy district where groups of people believed to be from al-Basatin district broke into Carrefour Mall on the night of January 28. The incident was recorded by mobile-phone cameras that captured people running all over the mall, snatching all kinds of merchandise (International Crisis Group 2011). Conservative commentator and blogger Mohammad al-Naggar interpreted the mall looting in a different way, claiming that the video was recorded before the revolution, and that actually it was on the occasion of a big sale offering huge discounts. He insisted that the video had been uploaded on YouTube under the title "Carrefour: Egypt Racing for Sugar and Rice."[6] Subsequently he asserted that the women in headscarves, filmed in the video, were meant to stir sectarian resentment. Both the arguments were unsubstantiated by any credible evidence.

The International Crisis Group reported two types of looting across the country during the revolution. First, there was the organized looting that took place on the first nights of the uprising. Many of the neighborhood-watch groups told stories about "looters caught with police identification, or who confessed, when caught by neighborhood watches and turned over to the military, that they had been paid to wreak havoc" (*Huffington Post* 2011). The other type of looting took place on the so-called "Friday of Rage" (January 28). Witnesses said that looting started first with groups of individuals from poorer neighborhoods, but that at midnight, looters started to arrive in large numbers in trucks, carrying machine guns. According to some eyewitnesses, they broke into the mall and looted everything inside.

The scenes of looting and a corporate sale are strikingly similar. Looting during the revolt could be seen as a form of "do-it-yourself consumerism" (Ži ek 2014; Reynolds 2012), reflecting the intensive commodification of social relations and desires in the neoliberal era. Reynolds (2012) offers an interpretation of the Cairo Fire of January 1952, when consumer goods were targets for political agitation and protests. The rioters torched nightclubs, hotels, and cinemas, and set flames to the Barclay's Bank and other commercials centers. These were perceived as symbols of exploitation and foreign domination. They also attacked several British citizens, including high-ranking officers. As she concludes, the fire revealed the anxieties of mixed-up consumption that tended to defy the neat and binary categories on which colonial domination and nationalist revolt were based, and also revealed the echoes of the urban uprisings of the 1950s among those of 2012. While conservative critiques of the revolution highlighted the incidents of looting and thuggery, one could argue that the riots in the slums were not merely expressions of "depoliticized criminality." In fact, they included many examples of brave politicized activism, and they played a pivotal role in overthrowing Mubarak and his police regime.

Notes

1   The term "thug" carries colonial underpinnings, as the British authorities used the term "thuggee" to describe outlaws and bandits in India during the eighteenth and nineteenth centuries. The British launched massive campaigns to eliminate bandits and codified a notorious "criminal tribes law" in 1871 to criminalize certain tribes and outcaste groups that were thought to be habitual outlaws. Bandits, known in India as "thuggees," were defined in colonial discourse as "a fraternity of ritual stranglers who preyed on travelers along the highway" (Wagner 2007).

2   The management of poverty has shifted from public policies which deal with labor, investment, and subsidies, for instance, to the micro and individual levels, which cast the responsibility for poverty on personal faults. Salwa Ismail highlights the term "the deserving poor." As an object of "the scrutinizing eyes of charity activists, the poor must engage in public self-presentation that confirms their being worthy of assistance." She adds that "as the deserving poor, the successful supplicant may also qualify for integration into neoliberal plans of poverty relief" (Ismail 2006, 94).

3   See also "Hurub masagin min sign Wadi al-Natrun," video clip, YouTube, http://www.youtube.com/watch?v=8lW2JJRs_Co (this is a private video; advance authorization is required to view it); and map of "Wadi al-Natroun," Google Maps, https://www.google.com. eg/maps/place/Natrn+Valley,+El+Beheira+Governorate/@30.4370749, 29.9754148,10z/data=!3m1!4b1!4m6!3m5!1s0x1458b6a1400035d5: 0xe28a74cc61f24caa!8m2!3d30.4698437!4d30.2743484!16s%2Fm% 2F0276lnj?hl=en.

4   "Khanufa al-baltagi," video clip, YouTube, http://www.youtube. com/watch?v=8_lqaDu-yoE.

5   "Khanufa: Izbat Abu Qarn," video clip, YouTube, http://www.youtube.com/watch?v=ObpvJR6ZMbY.

6   Three YouTube videos clips: *Ta'awun al-haramiya fi sariqat Carrefour*, posted by MrBARBIDO, February 19, 2011, http://www.youtube.com/watch?v=_A3NPXwxpwU; *Sariqat Carrefour*, posted by m171982, February 5, 2011, http://www.youtube.com/watch?v=m MexIKc2tz0; *al-Sha'b yurid al-thawra*, posted by alsha3byorid, May 10, 2011, http://www.youtube.com/watch?v=TDxjvGDk_oE.

Works Cited

Abdel Latif, Mohammad, and Hani Barakat. 2011. "Suqut Khanufa." *Al-Ahram*, August 25. http://www.ahram.org.eg/archive/Incidents/News/97083.aspx.

Abdel-Latif, Noha. 2012. "Protocol ta'awun min agl al-fi'at al-muhammasha." *Nisf al-Dunia*, November 28.

Abd al-Sami', Mahmud. 2011. "Suqut Khanufa." *Al-Ahram*, August 24. http://digital.ahram.org.eg/articles.aspx?Serial=612513&eid=6076. Last accessed on July 12, 2021.

Al-Ahram. 2011. "Khanufa: akhtar baltagi." August 27. http://www.ahram.org.eg/Incidents/News/97561.aspx.

Association for the Development and Enhancement of Women (ADEW). 2007. "Annual Report, Cairo, 2007." http://www.adew.org/en/downloads/annualReport2007en.pdf. Last accessed on July 12, 2021

Elmeshad, Mohamed. 2011. "The Life and Death of Khanufa: A Personal Account of Cairo's Most Dangerous Thug." *Egypt Independent*, August 31. https://egyptindependent.com/life-and-death-khanoufa-person al-account-cairos-most-dangerous-thug/.

Elmeshad, Mohamed, and Mai Elwakil. 2011. "In the Shantytowns of Cairo, Mixed Feelings about Egypt's Uprising." *Egypt Independent*, February 6. http://www.egyptindependent.com/news/shantytowns-cairo-mixed-feelings-about-egypts-uprising.

Fahmy, Khaled. 2010. "When Historians Read WikiLeaks." *Egypt Independent*, December 26. https://khaledfahmy.org/en/2010/12/26/when-historians-read-wikileaks/.

Ghannam, Farha. 2012. "Meanings and Feelings: Local Interpretations of the Use of Violence in the Egyptian Revolution." *American Ethnologist* 39, no. 1 (February): 32–36.

Hassan, Lamia. 2011. "Class Struggle." A Voice from Cairo (blog), posted May 30. http://avoicefromcairo.wordpress.com/2011/05/30/class-struggles.

Hoad, Phil. 2011. "Will Egypt's Revolution Extend to the Cinema?" *The Guardian*, August 30. http://www.guardian.co.uk/film/filmblog/2011/aug/30/egypt-revolution-cinema-hollywood.

Huffington Post. 2011. "New Egypt Government to Be Appointed, but President Mubarak Refuses to Step Down." *Huffington Post*, January 29. http://www.huffingtonpost.com/social/Bolkonsky/new-egypt-government-to-b_1_n_815682_75618046.html.

International Crisis Group. 2011. "Popular Protest in North Africa and the Middle East (1): Egypt Victorious?" Report, February 24. https://www.crisisgroup.org/middle-east-north-africa/north-africa/egypt/popular-protest-north-africa-and-middle-east-i-egypt-victorious.

Ismail, Salwa. 2006. *Political Life in Cairo's New Quarters: Encountering the Everyday State*. Minneapolis: University of Minnesota Press.

Khatib, Lina. 2006. "Nationalism and Otherness: The Representation of Islamic Fundamentalism in Egyptian Cinema." *European Journal of Cultural Studies* 9, no. 1: 60–83.

Magdy, Omaima. 2012. "Samia: A Woman that Doesn't Take Vacations." *Shorouk News*, August 21.

Mohsen, Ali Abdel. 2011a. "Local Recounts Prisoners' Tales of Forced Escape from Wadi al-Natroun." *Egypt Independent*, March 3. http://www.egyptindependent.com/news/local-recounts-prisoners-tales-forced-escape-wadi-al-Natroun.

———. 2011b. "Thug Life: Pro-Mubarak Bullies Break Their Silence." *Egypt Independent*, March 18. http://www.egyptindependent.com/news/thug-life-pro-mubarak-bullies-break-their-silence.

Na'eem, Mohammad. 2010. "Rihab al-fawda." *el-Bosla*, October 4. http://elbosla.org/?p=1425.

Reynolds, Nancy Y. 2012. *A City Consumed: Urban Commerce, the Cairo Fire, and the Politics of Decolonization in Egypt*. Stanford, CA: Stanford University Press.

Sims, David. 2003. "Urban Slums Report: The Case of Cairo, Egypt." In *Understanding Slums: Case Studies for the Global Report on Human Settlements 2003*. London: University College London. https://www.ucl.ac.uk/dpu-projects/Global_Report/pdfs/Cairo_bw.pdf.

———. 2010. *Understanding Cairo: The Logic of a City Out of Control*. Cairo: American University in Cairo Press.

Wagner, Kim A. 2007. *Thuggee: Banditry and the British in Early Nineteenth-century India*. Houndmills, Hampshire, UK: Palgrave Macmillan.

Wikileaks. 2011a. "Research on Jail Breaks Saturday Night." January 31. https://wikileaks.org/gifiles/?q=egypt+jail&mfrom=&mto=&title=&notitle=&date=&nofrom=&noto=&count=50&sort=0&file=&docid=&relid=0#searchresult.

———. 2011b. "Re: Analysis for Comment—Egypt—Jail Break."
February 1. https://wikileaks.org/gifiles/?q=egypt+jail&mfrom=&m
to=&title=&notitle=&date=&nofrom=&noto=&count=50&sort=0&
file=&docid=&relid=0#searchresult.

Zaki, Amir. 2013. "Izbat Abu Qarn: 'ishash bigiwar buyut Allah."
Al-Shorouk, September 24. http://www.shorouknews.com/news/
view.aspx?cdate=24092012&id=9ca1a34d-3cec-4ac7–92c9–459
beb67616a/.

Ži ek, Slavoj. 2014. "Shoplifters of the World Unite." In *What Does
Europe Want? The Union and Its Discontents*, edited by Slavoj Ži ek
and Srecko Horvat, 104–12. New York: Columbia University Press.

28

SECTARIAN POLITICS?
SECURITIZATION, URBAN DEVELOPMENT, AND COPTIC ADVOCACY IN CAIRO

AMY FALLAS

The call of the 2011 revolution for "bread, freedom, and human dignity" remains unmet,[1] as state repression of Coptic activists and violent attacks by extremist groups against Coptic holy sites, parishioners, and neighborhoods have increased in the decade since the uprisings (Iskander 2012; Tadros 2013).[2] The Egyptian government under President Abd al-Fattah al-Sisi has responded to such incidents as the 2016 ISIS bombing of St. Mark's Coptic Cathedral in Cairo—the seat of the Coptic Orthodox Church—and the 2017 Palm Sunday suicide bombings in Tanta and Alexandria with enhanced security and surveillance. While al-Sisi claims these measures aid in the protection of Egypt's Christian citizens, these precautions rarely include Copts as part of the security apparatus or decision-making process and at times fuel their precarity (Hanna 2019; Ibrahim 2019).

The exclusion of Copts from the security sector underscores their vulnerability in postrevolutionary Egypt and imbricates them at the intersection of other civil liberties and human rights concerns, including freedom of speech and the press, of assembly, and of adequate housing. Human rights issues are usually considered separate from sectarian issues, but press censorship, activist repression, and politically motivated incarceration share securitization concerns with church building permits, discriminatory practices, and violence against Copts in Egypt (Fallas 2019). These social, economic, and political concerns are also reflected in the priorities of Coptic activists, from the formation of the Maspero Youth Union (Itihad Shabab Maspero) in 2010 to the ongoing work of Coptic advocates and researchers in 2020.

This chapter considers the relationship between securitization and advocacy through Coptic encounters with state intervention, security, and surveillance, with a particular focus on the neighborhood of al-Warraq in northern Cairo. In the aftermath of the high-profile attacks against Copts in 2017, churches in al-Warraq began to use their laity as security "scouts" to protect the Christian community from possible security threats (Roux 2018). More recently, the sizable Coptic community that resides in the area has been under threat of displacement due to a public–private development project seeking to transform the area's "informal settlements" into a new district of residential, commercial, and retail spaces, as described in the chapters by O. Khalil, Arese, and Borham in this volume. Resisting that development project, among other issues, contributed to the detention of Coptic activist and founder of the Maspero Youth Union (MYU) Ramy Kamel in 2019.[3] Such events underscore how social, economic, and political issues are central to Coptic advocacy priorities alongside religious concerns in the shadow of the state's growing security apparatus.

Advocacy and Lay–Church Tensions: Who Speaks for Copts?

On the eve of the eighth anniversary of the Maspero Massacre in 2019, the National Security Agency of the Egyptian Ministry of Interior requested that the Coptic Orthodox Church remove a memorial plaque of the "Maspero Martyrs" (al-shuhada maspero) due to claims that the memorial suggested the Egyptian army had perpetrated violence against Copts.[4] The plaque, located at the martyrs' final resting place on the grounds of a church in 6th of October City, commemorates those who "joined the heavenly altar on October 9, 2011 by the bullets and armored vehicles of the Egyptian Army . . . to call for a stop of the demolition of churches in Egypt."[5] The families of the martyrs, not the Coptic Orthodox Church, were primarily responsible for erecting the memorial. The incident in question occurred eight years before, during the events of 2011, when Egyptian security forces attacked hundreds of peaceful protesters in front of the Maspero state television building. The demonstrators were protesting the demolition of a church in Upper Egypt and on October 9 had embarked on a march from Dawaran Shubra to the Maspero building while chanting for "the fall of military rule."[6] Under SCAF direction, twenty-seven Egyptians were killed that day, most of them Copts, who at the time of writing remain largely unacknowledged as martyrs by the administration of the Egyptian state and the Coptic Orthodox Church.[7]

One of the tensions around the commemoration and remembrance of Maspero's martyrs centers on the question of who represents the Coptic community and speaks on behalf of its interests. Does this authority lie with the Coptic pope and the ecclesiastical establishment, or with its laity? These are enduring communal and national questions stemming as far back as the late nineteenth century, with contestation over communal authority between lay elites in the Coptic Communal Council (al-Maglis al-Milli) and the clerical establishment (Seikaly 1970). Although both groups appealed to and intersected with state power to legitimize their authority, a series of electoral crises for the Maglis during the late 1940s and 1950s—and its eventual dissolution by the Nasser regime in 1962—left the Church as the primary communal representative into the mid- and late twentieth century (Bland 2019).

Coptic activist groups emerged in response to this hegemonic role of the Church in intracommunal affairs during the charged years of 2010–11 (Sedra 2012). The MYU formed in November 2010 amid the rise of sectarian violence in Egypt and "promoted political secularism, or the separation of religion from politics, as a solution to inter-communal strife and as a remedy to intra-communal conflict over the position of the Coptic Orthodox Church as sole representative of the community" (Lukasik 2016, 111). This approach of the MYU to assert communal authority outside of ecclesiastical structures also troubles the prevalent position of the state, which invests in a narrative of Egypt's "unique" tradition of religious coexistence.[8] Some of the initiatives usually cited by politicians, government ministries, and President al-Sisi himself include legislation to streamline permits for church construction, mediating interfaith discourse, and building the largest cathedral in the Middle East (Kaldas 2019; Lukasik 2019). Yet even though many of these political and legal processes remain protracted, such as the slow process to approve church construction and renovation permits, al-Sisi continues to portray himself and the state as the protectors of Copts (EIPR 2017; Lukasik 2019).

One of the most tangible ways the al-Sisi regime exercises its guardianship of Copts is by appealing to recent ISIS-affiliated terror attacks against Christians to implement questionable security strategies, including retaliatory counterterrorism operations, the increased securitization of Coptic communal spaces, and an expansion of measures that restrict constitutionally guaranteed rights. In response to several visible and deadly attacks against Copts in 2017, the Egyptian government imposed a nationwide state of emergency, which has been in effect ever since and grants the president exceptional powers—monitoring of all forms of communication and correspondence, imposing curfews, and referring civilians to the State Security Emergency Court.

Under Coptic Pope Tawadros II, the church has openly held a pro-Sisi position and actively discourages Coptic participation in public protests and the kind of outspoken political activism advanced by the MYU. The Church's role, however, has come under criticism from Coptic youth and researchers. For example, Coptic activists expressed their disagreement with the patriarch in 2014 when he said that human rights should not take priority over the state's measures to address terror concerns (Fallas 2019). These isolated, but persistent, critiques from Coptic activists and researchers suggest a much wider range of communal priorities that intersect with human rights issues and expose intergenerational differences within the Coptic community. While a human rights discourse is more frequently utilized by younger generations, older generations are more likely to engage in discourses of citizenship and nationalism.

Development and Displacement: Ramy Kamel, al-Warraq, and Geographies of Violence

On November 23, 2019, Egyptian security forces invaded Coptic activist Ramy Kamel's home in al-Warraq. They confiscated his phone, camera, and computer, subsequently detaining him at the Supreme State Security Prosecution's headquarters in the Fifth Settlement neighborhood in greater Cairo. They beat and tortured him and charged him with "joining and financing a terrorist group and spreading false news."[9] Kamel was later transferred to Tora Prison in pre-trial detention, where he remains at the time of writing. As the founder of the MYU, Kamel has been a prominent figure in advocating for Coptic rights in Egypt since 2011.

Before he was detained, Kamel was working on several advocacy campaigns and especially monitoring sectarian incidents against Copts, opposing state securitization of Coptic religious complexes, and criticizing legal impediments to church building and renovation across Egypt. He was scheduled to participate in the United Nations Forum on Minority Issues in Geneva the last week of November before his arrest. While Kamel worked assiduously on sectarian issues, he also tied his communal activism to human rights more broadly and, in particular, to the housing rights of Copts facing intimidation and violence from militant groups or state-led investment projects.

According to the Cairo Institute for Human Rights Studies (CIHRS), Kamel was "one of the most committed activists" in tracking state violations against Coptic displacement due to security concerns or urban development initiatives by ensuring that residents received fair and timely compensation payments as well as secure alternative housing arrangements.[10] In September 2018, Kamel met with UN Special Rapporteur Leilani Farha to discuss adequate housing for "Christian families displaced in the contexts of state counter-terrorism operations or investment projects (such al-Warraq Island), or who were forced to leave their homes after repeated assaults and threats from militant groups."[11] Some of these recent displacements include Coptic flight from al-Arish following terror attacks in 2017, the ongoing relocation of Maspero Triangle residents with the intent to gentrify the area, and the forced evictions from state land in Ramy Kamel's own neighborhood of al-Warraq. Indeed, while the focus on Kamel's advocacy emphasizes his work on sectarian issues in Egypt, his activism was also directed toward his own living conditions and the circumstances that he and his neighbors faced as residents of al-Warraq—a neighborhood subject to speculation and development since the Mubarak era.

Al-Warraq is a primarily working-class neighborhood in northern Cairo, on the west side of the Nile Corniche, that encompasses the regions of Warraq al-'Arab, Warraq al-Hadar, al-Warraq Island, Mohammad Island, and Tanash. It has been targeted by both public and private development interests since the presidency of Hosni Mubarak. Al-Warraq Island, for example, was an important part of Mubarak's Cairo 2050 Plan that hoped to rebrand it as "Horus Island," "complete with glossy towers, wide boulevards and a marina" (Michaelson 2017). While the 2050 Plan crumbled alongside Mubarak's rule in the aftermath of the 2011 revolution, the island and its surroundings remained a focus of al-Sisi's development efforts, which included the elimination of Egypt's "slums" as part of his platform (*Egypt Today* 2020).

On July 16, 2017, residents and security forces engaged in violent clashes on al-Warraq Island following residential demolitions that were part of plans to build a bridge from the island to mainland east Cairo (El-Gundy and Gemeay 2017). The demolitions began in the morning when many of the residents were away at work, and demonstrations took place to deter construction workers from destroying homes. The clashes left dozens injured, one dead, and others in jail. This escalation occurred due to "a lack of transparency and community involvement" on behalf of state agencies, who ignored essential protocols on community dialogue that are required before initiating large-scale development projects (Khalil 2017).

These violent spatial transformations of al-Warraq's landscape are enmeshed in the very fabric of the neighborhood's sectarian histories and legacies of state intervention. In 2013, two assailants opened fire at guests attending a Christian wedding in al-Warraq's historic Church of the Blessed Virgin Mary. The incident left four dead and several injured amid a wave of anti-Christian sentiment following Coptic support for al-Sisi, who had come to power in Egypt by replacing his Islamist predecessor Mohamed Morsi in a coup (El-Dabh 2013). Despite requests for medical assistance and security during the incident, an ambulance arrived at the church almost an hour after the shooting and the police arrived much later. The delayed response, many observers noted, underscored state negligence and a failure to prioritize assistance for the injured and efforts to find the perpetrators. This slow reaction also did not align with the precedents of state intervention and security presence in the area.

Just four years earlier and 250 meters away from the Church of the Blessed Virgin Mary, the Church of the Virgin Mary and Archangel Michael had been the site of joint Muslim and Christian celebrations of a Marian apparition.[12] In fact, the first eyewitness reports of this "brilliant, panoramic burst of light" came from a local Muslim resident in December 2009 (Heo 2012, 372). Yet even this cross-confessional moment generated state regulation, as "all photographers, journalists and pilgrims alike, had to show a state-approved permit to enter [the church], and photographs of the apparition were confiscated" (Heo 2012, 373).

The very presence of the churches and the growth of the Coptic population in the neighborhood have generated ongoing spatial anxiety for the state, which is worried about altered Muslim–Christian social configurations, previously marked by coexistence and segregation in the neighborhood. The establishment of another church during the 1990s—the Church of Saint Mark, across the water on al-Warraq Island—demonstrates this tension. During the construction of Saint Mark's, Angie Heo notes that state officials "ordered the priests in charge to have tall, forbidding walls built that concealed the domes and steeples" in order to quell anxieties around the visibility of the cathedral (Heo 2012, 372).

In recent years, to cultivate trust and common cause between Copts and state security, local parishioners have been recruited by churches as scouts—volunteer security personnel to screen congregants entering Coptic religious complexes in al-Warraq. These roles are coordinated and managed by St. Mark's Coptic Orthodox Cathedral in Abbasiya and designed to supplement, not replace, the official police presence and control of religious complexes in al-Warraq (Roux 2018). Yet Copts continue to harbor misgivings about these measures that still put their congregants in potentially dangerous situations.

These interrelated experiences of state regulation and neglect, ubiquitous security forces, and the precarity of religious and residential spaces all undergird the suspicions of Coptic laypeople toward visible and direct government interventions in their churches and homes. More importantly, they demonstrate how basic human rights, like adequate housing, are a communal concern for Coptic advocacy in al-Warraq—a priority usually reserved for the safety of their houses of worship.

Coptic Activists and Human Rights Activism: What Is Sectarian?

While Ramy Kamel is one of the most notable Coptic activists, given his prominent career in advocating for Coptic rights, other Copts have received similar state accusations and charges for their activism. Just ten days before Kamel's arrest, labor activist Khalil Rizk was arrested by security forces at a café in downtown Cairo and accused of engaging in terrorist activities "after publishing pay hike demands by workers at a government-controlled pharmaceutical company" (Nader and Wirtschafter 2019). In February of the same year, Patrick George Zaki, a postgraduate student at the University of Bologna and researcher at the Egyptian Initiative for Personal Rights (EIPR), specializing in gender and human rights, was detained at Cairo International Airport and served with a list of charges, including "publishing rumors and false news that aim to disturb social peace and sow chaos; incitement to protest without permission from the relevant authorities with the aim of undermining state authority; calling for the overthrow of the state; managing a social media account that aims to undermine the social order and public safety; incitement to commit violence and terrorist crimes."[13] The arbitrary nature of the accusations and charges has become more commonplace since 2013 (Naji 2021).

These targeted arrests and trumped-up charges—especially those accusing Christians of terrorism—demonstrate how Copts are also engaged in a wide range of activist causes and research such as labor rights, adequate housing, and gender equality. They are engaged in these causes precisely because they affect everyday life for Copts, who need employment, a place to live, and equitable gender rights just as much as their Muslim fellow citizens. Although Egypt's Muslim majority comprises most of those who are imprisoned for their activism and political activities, Copts are also subject to the same security regime regardless of their Christian identity. Yet the persistent separation of "sectarian issues"—such as such church revolutions, communal security, and religious practice—from the human rights causes that Kamel, Rizk, and Zaki advance fails to account for the interwoven nature of these issues, and the church and state authorities that perpetuate this heavy-handed approach.

Anthropologist Mina Ibrahim poses compelling questions about the "unreconciled misfits" among the "everydayness of Coptic Christians in Egypt" (Ibrahim 2018). Ibrahim's research into forms of Coptic living in Egypt that occur outside the normative pious realms of the Church and intracommunal religious fellowship also considers what alternate spaces can tell us about Copts that fall outside these expectations of tradition. He considers how Copts in places like bars, coffee shops, PlayStation lounges, and prisons "wish or have to stay invisible" from the purview, prescriptions, and expectations of the Coptic Orthodox Church (Ibrahim 2019, 89).

I embrace this invitation to consider the "invisibility" of Copts by examining how Coptic activist commitments outside of religious issues are not as legible as those that are perceived as sectarian issues. The reasons for this fixation beyond religious issues are multifold, including the raison d'être of many international religious freedom organizations and the discursive focus of the Coptic Orthodox Church and the Egyptian government under al-Sisi. Yet this chapter argues that Coptic advocacy is neither one-dimensional nor exclusively dependent upon the leadership of the patriarch and the Church. I offer the case study of the neighborhood of al-Warraq to underscore how social, economic, and political issues are important to Copts alongside religious concerns, and how advocacy for issues such as housing rights contributed to the detention of activist Ramy Kamel. Further, I show how other Coptic activists are engaged in various strains of activism in contemporary Cairo. The state's growing security regime and its control over all forms of insecurity—from church protection to adequate housing—is at the fore of these concerns.

Notes

1   This chapter is dedicated to Ramy Kamel, Khalil Rizk, and Patrick Zaki, and to the thousands in Egyptian prisons unjustly detained for their social, political, and religious beliefs.

2   Copts represent Egypt's largest Christian denomination and claim indigenous origins in Egypt with the founding of their church by St. Mark in the first century. The appellation comes from the Arabic word "Qibt," derived from the Greek "Aigyptos," meaning Egyptian.

3   "Egypt: Immediately Release Coptic Activist Ramy Kamel," Cairo Institute for Human Rights Studies (CIHRS), http://tinyurl.com/ooxh7gze.

4   *Al-Araby al-Jadid*, https://tinyurl.com/ycqhk7ek.

5   Mina Thabet, Facebook post, October 5, 2019, https://tinyurl.com/y96x8d2e.

6   The Maspero Television Building and the surrounding area, known as the Maspero Triangle, has been a site of hyper-securitization for over a decade (see O. Khalil in this volume).

7   The publicly reported number of civilians killed that day varies from twenty-four to twenty-eight. I use the number most commonly referenced by news sites.

8   *The Egyptian Independent*, July 14, 2018, http://tinyurl.com/ooxh7gze.

9   "Egypt: Immediately Release Coptic Activist Ramy Kamel," Cairo Institute for Human Rights Studies (CIHRS), http://tinyurl.com/27mpbjjr.

10   "Egypt: Immediately Release Coptic Activist Ramy Kamel," Cairo Institute for Human Rights Studies (CIHRS), http://tinyurl.com/27mpbjjr.

11   "Egypt: Immediately Release Coptic Activist Ramy Kamel," Cairo Institute for Human Rights Studies (CIHRS), http://tinyurl.com/27mpbjjr.

12   A supernatural appearance of the Virgin Mary.

13   Egyptian Initiative for Personal Rights, "An Egyptian Human Rights Defender Disappeared and Tortured . . . ," EIPR press release, February 8, 2020, https://tinyurl.com/y7ejt5ax.

Works Cited

Bland, Weston. 2019. "Copts, the State and the 1949–1950 al-Majlis al-Milli Electoral Crisis: Articulating Community in a Time of Anxiety." *Islam and Christian–Muslim Relations* 30, no. 3, 303–22.

El-Dabh, Basil. 2013. "Investigations into Church Shooting Begin." *Daily News Egypt*, October 21, 2013. http://tinyurl.com/48bop8ql.

Egypt Today Staff. 2020. "Egypt's Prime Minister Follows Up Development Works of Maspero Triangle, Tahrir Square." *Egypt Today*, April 27. https://www.egypttoday.com/Article/1/85153/Egypt-s-Prime-Minister-follows-up-development-works-of-Maspero.

EIPR (Egyptian Initiative for Personal Rights). 2017. "Closed on Security Grounds: Sectarian Tensions and Attacks Resulting from the Construction and Renovation of Churches." Report, November 20. http://tinyurl.com/6vucrsrl.

Fallas, Amy. 2019. "Ramy Kamel, *Mada Masr*, and Seeing Coptic Issues as Civil Liberties in Egypt." Tahrir Institute for Middle East Policy, December 12. http://tinyurl.com/yl6g5rpf.

El-Gundy, Zeinab, and Passant Gemeay. 2017. "Anger on Warraq Island after Government Demolishes Homes." *Ahram Online*, July 17. http://tinyurl.com/b99so331.

Hanna, Michael. 2019. "Excluded and Unequal: Copts on the Margins of the Egyptian Security State." The Century Foundation, May 9. https://tcf.org/content/report/christian-exclusion-from-egypts-security-state/?session=1.

Heo, Angie. 2012. "The Virgin Made Visible: Intercessory Images of Church Territory in Egypt." *Comparative Studies in Society and History* 54, no. 2: 361–91.

Ibrahim, Ishak. 2019. "The Reality of Church Construction in Egypt." Tahrir Institute for Middle East Policy, June 27. http://tinyurl.com/qu343ssl.

Ibrahim, Mina. 2018. "Christmas Misfits: Ethnographic Notes on the Coptic 'Waguihs.'" Coptic Canadian History Project, December 30. https://egyptmigrations.com/2018/12/30/christmas-misfits/.

———. 2019. "The Invisible Life-worlds of a Coptic Christian." *Middle East—Topics and Arguments* 13: 89–94.

Iskander, Elizabeth. 2012. *Sectarian Conflict in Egypt: Coptic Media, Identity and Representation*. London: Routledge.

Kaldas, Timothy. 2019. "Egypt's Sectarian Committee to Combat Sectarianism." Tahrir Institute for Middle East Policy, January 28. http://tinyurl.com/1l6vj1av.

Khalil, Omnia. 2017. "Visions or Illusions? State Development Plans and Violence in al-Warraq." Tahrir Institute for Middle East Policy, August 3. http://tinyurl.com/yrfwqvdx.

Lukasik, Candace. 2016. "Conquest of Paradise: Secular Binds and Coptic Political Mobilization." *Middle East Critique* 25, no. 2: 107–25.

——. 2019. "Copts, Church, and State: Egypt's Christians Frustrated with Lack of Protection." Tahrir Institute for Middle East Policy, February 15. http://tinyurl.com/2rnazqkm.

Michaelson, Ruth. 2017. "Island v Megacity: The Cairo Islanders Fighting Violent State Evictions." *The Guardian*, July 21. http://tinyurl.com/eo7tbf1z.

Nader, Mina, and Jacob Wirtschafter. 2019. "Egypt Arrests Coptic Community Rights Activist amid Heightened Surveillance Measures." *Religion News Service*, December 5. http://tinyurl.com/arh2406t.

Naji, Ahmed. "Reading and Writing in an Egyptian Prison." *The Believer*, February 1. https://ahmednaji.net/2021/03/25/reading-and-writing-in-an-egyptian-prison/.

Roux, Martin. 2018. "Securing Coptic Churches: The Necessary Role of the Scouts." *Mada Masr*. https://www.madamasr.com/en/2018/04/08/feature/society/securing-coptic-churches-the-necessary-role-of-the-scouts/

Sedra, Paul. 2012, "The Church, Maspero, and the Future of the Coptic Community." *Jadaliyya*, March 19. http://tinyurl.com/aatie3p1.

Seikaly, Samir. 1970. "Coptic Communal Reform: 1860–1914." *Middle Eastern Studies* 6, no. 3: 247–75.

Tadros, Mariz. 2013. *Copts at the Crossroads: The Challenges of Building Inclusive Democracy in Egypt*. Cairo: American University in Cairo Press.

29

SECURITY FROM WITHIN
THE CASE OF THE INFORMAL POLICING OF AL-MATARIYA NEIGHBORHOOD

BASSEM AL-SAMRAGY

Whichever way you try to cross al-Masalla Square, one of the main squares within the neighborhood of al-Matariya, you can never escape the sight of the al-Nur al-Mohammadi complex, which consists of a big mosque, a charity hospital, and a large town hall. The complex is managed by al-Gam'iya al-Shar'iya, one of the biggest Islamic charitable organizations in the world. If you happened to be passing by the al-Nur al-Mohammadi complex in the evening of March 17, 2011, you would have noticed people overflowing from the town hall. The people were receiving a retired high-ranking police officer, the chief of one of the largest clans of the neighborhood—the clan of Abou-Eida—and a sheikh from al-Azhar to initiate reconciliation between the police and the people of al-Matariya.

Al-Matariya is one of the popular quarters at the northeastern border of the capital. On January 28, 2011, its residents, like the residents of all other popular quarters in Cairo, made their way to the police station. The encounter between Cairo's popular quarters and the Egyptian state, airing the people's grievances with the regime, took a distinctive form. While most of the population had suffered from police brutality, among other grievances, it was the intrusion of policing practices into the everyday lives of the people of the popular quarters that made the police station the main locus of people's anger. By the dawn of January 29, almost all the police stations in the popular quarters of Cairo had been burnt down and the police had withdrawn from the entire area of the capital. Hence, the town hall meeting was an attempt to prepare for the return of the al-Matariya police. The organization of that meeting illustrates the interlinkages of the hybrid network of control in al-Matariya, which connects the formal police with criminal networks. Through an examination of the public space of al-Matariya, this chapter explores the making and workings of this hybrid network, arguing against a specific and popular framework: security from above and criminality from below.

March 17, 2011 proved too early to initiate a return of the police to al-Matariya. While a police officer spoke about how police restoration was necessary for the people, the audience interrupted him, yelling that reconciliation could not be established before police officers were punished for all their past crimes. The sheikh tried to calm the people down by preaching about the virtue of tolerance. He was interrupted again by the youths, recalling their brothers killed a couple of months before. Finally, the chief of the Abou-Eida clan started to talk, trying to calm the youths, which outraged all the attendants. The people shouted, "Enough, enough with your lies. Don't you ever change?" Then they walked out of the meeting, which promptly ended.

Our examination of the securitization of neighborhood space should not be limited to the official role of the police fighting crimes. Rather, we should broaden our perspective to see how the police station and the other forms of power in the neighborhood are intertwined, creating a pervasive structure of discipline and governance. In this, we follow some of the same lines of investigation explored in the chapters of O. Khalil, Ahmed, and El Raggal, elsewhere in this volume. This chapter will start by situating the neighborhood of al-Matariya within the context of modernizing Cairo's public spaces. Then it will move to explain the specific effects of neoliberal policies on al-Matariya. Lastly, the chapter will explain the rise of the prominent clans of al-Matariya and how woven together clan and police politics have become.

Maze, Barracks, and Public Space

In the nineteenth century, Khedive Isma'il took over the project of modernizing Cairo, aiming to build a city reflecting the values of rationality and order (Lockman 2010, 64). Previously, there were neither signs nor names marking streets as distinct, with some deeming Cairo a maze (Mitchell 1988, 33). Thus, Isma'il tried to transform Cairo along the lines of its European counterparts whereby the "transformation of the city of Cairo from an aesthetic point of view required the filling in and leveling of the waste land around the city, the opening up of main streets and new arteries, the creation of squares and open places, the planting of trees, the surfacing of roads, the construction of drains, and regular cleaning and watering" (Mitchell 1988, 65).

Transforming the city required planners to reckon with the military's legacy in the city. Muhammad Ali Pasha's national army was the nucleus of the governing projects that affected much of Egyptian life (Fahmy 2002, 12). The government kept records of its citizens in order to transform the maze-like city of Cairo into a preplanned and more easily controlled and surveilled space. This was mirrored in the efforts of minister of education Ali Pasha Mubarak, who, after returning from his mission to Paris, established the Bureau of Public Works and the Bureau of Endowments. Both bureaus were responsible for reshaping the space of Egypt, especially that of the city of Cairo, so that the city could shed its premodern characteristics and better resemble the organization of the army, with wide streets and roundabouts (Mitchell 1988, 33–35).

During the nineteenth and early twentieth centuries, well-cultivated land occupied most of the space of what is now al-Matariya, with housing estates and rest houses belonging to members of Muhammad Ali Pasha's family. Hence, the neighborhood was not considered as a potential space for the project of "modernity from above." It was not until the mid-twentieth century that al-Matariya was considered by the government as a potential site for a barracks-like space. From 1952 to 1960, during the Nasser era, more than thirty-two thousand homes were built by the state at a cost of LE 24 million (Fahmy 2002, 68). This housing took the form of the popular *al-masakin al-sha'biya*, which consisted of uniformly constructed buildings, five or six stories high. There were public gardens, which were taken care of by government workers, and sports arenas where youth played football and other sports.

All the neighborhoods subjected to government spending were either located at the outskirts of the city, like Helwan, al-Matariya, and al-Zawiya al-Hamra', or adjacent to older and more urbanized areas, like Ramlat Bulaq (across the Nile from Zamalek). Developments were constructed on the outskirts of the city to accommodate peasants moving from rural areas to Cairo for work. The transformation of the city also offered a new generation, born in the heart of the city, mobility away from the center (Ghannam 2002, 38).

From Care to Policing

The government planning of al-Matariya did not encompass the entire area of the neighborhood, resulting in formal barracks-like structures adjacent to informal maze-like spaces. While the urban, formal barracks and the rural, informal maze-like spaces continued to grow and encroach upon one another, it was not until the 1970s that a surge of informal urbanization fused the two spaces into one (in)formal space. This expansion came in response to Sadat's (1970–81) open-door policy, which resulted in a noticeable rise in informal housing, leaving 60 percent of Cairo's inhabitants occupying houses built on former agrarian land without government permits (Malterre-Barthes 2016, 1), especially in the popular quarters of Cairo (e.g., al-Matariya). This encroachment of informal housing, alongside the retreat of the welfare state, brought with it a rise of "informal life" in the labor market — an eruption of spontaneous, unregulated business — challenging even further the boundaries of the barracks-like spaces.

The encroachment of the people from rural areas into al-Matariya occurred through family migration. Al-Matariya's spatial layout stood in sharp contrast to Khedive Isma'il's Downtown and Nasser's public housing projects. Instead of the planned wide streets, the space of al-Matariya was occupied by small houses lining narrow streets, forming blocks of territories for the different families in the neighborhood. Further expansion of informal housing offered opportunities for new generations born in the center of the city or in Nasser's housing projects. For example, my grandparents, who were born in the center of the city, moved to two separate popular housing projects in the 1960s where both were raised. For most of my life, I was raised in an apartment in a ten-story building informally built on agrarian land, located about three meters from a small farm and a farmers' market. These were later informally transformed into a parking lot in response to the increase in car owners in the area, itself a result of the expansion of informal construction. This family story has been repeated tens of thousands of times across the city, concomitant with the retreat of the welfare state, resulting in formal planned spaces being absorbed into the informal mazes. It is important to note that informal spaces did not replace formal ones. A hybrid, heterogenous, maze-like space was created that incorporates characteristics of both the formal and informal spaces. For example, buildings that were erected without government permits do not have access to government services — i.e., water and electricity — hence, people resort to informal ways of obtaining them. However, when a building is occupied, the government is incentivized to formalize the situation in order to be able to extract revenue from the usage of water and electricity.

Al-Matariya developed its own internal logic of transportation parallel to the one developed by the government, connecting the neighborhood to the rest of the city. The neighborhood can be accessed through three main points: al-Matariya square, the Metro station, and the bus station of al-Masalla. In order to move beyond these three points into the depths of the neighborhood, one must ride an auto-rickshaw (tuk-tuk) or a microbus, neither of which is legally authorized. Such transportation methods, however, are under informal surveillance by the police.

After the popular quarters—formerly areas designated as spaces for popular housing—were absorbed by the informal housing, any uniformity was lost. Instead of its planned five- or six-story buildings, al-Matariya now has structures up to fifteen stories high, built without permits on former agrarian land. The public gardens of *al-masakin al-sha'biya* were destroyed by both government negligence and residents' commercialization of the space into parking lots and small shops. Hence, people living in popular quarters acquired relative independence from the government, except in terms of their relationship with the police.

The logic of neoliberal production and exchange extends beyond the traditional economic spaces (factories and designated markets). There has been a well-documented and noticeable rise in the use of the street as a space of production and exchange, especially in the popular quarters. In addition to the elimination of public gardens, sidewalks have been occupied by street vendors and coffee shops. The neoliberal city is "the city inside-out, where a massive number of inhabitants become compelled by the poverty and dispossession to operate, subsist, socialize, and simply live a life in the public spaces" (Bayat 2010, 12). In the case of Cairo, this phenomenon is not limited to the popular quarters, but repression and surveillance of markets in informal neighborhoods remain noticeably higher. For example, in 2016, the police raided coffee shops in Heliopolis that had sprawled onto the sidewalks, while coffee shops in al-Matariya were left intact—the latter usually belonging to prominent, influential families, serving an important function in weaving together the threads of the hybrid control and surveillance network of the public space.

The Rise of the Urban Clans of al-Matariya

Al-Matariya has an ancient history. The city of Iunu, or On, which is the ancient Egyptian name for the city known as "the city of sun" during the Greek period, was situated on the northeastern borders of the city of Cairo, below the hill of al-Hisn (Tall al-Hisn), which is part of the neighborhood of al-Matariya. The granite obelisk erected by Pharaoh Senwosret the First of the Twelfth Dynasty (1971–1926 BCE) is still at its ancient position in the area of the Obelisk (Masalla). During the nineteenth and early twentieth centuries, the main population of the neighborhood consisted of the families of farmers and workers on the estates of members of the Egyptian royal family.

As an effect of the 1952 coup, the royal family's properties were nationalized. The agrarian lands were given to the farmers and to people who had worked for the royal family, either as part of the land reforms or after the royal family had fled the country. Many of the new owners of the royal family properties sought to grow wealth by demolishing the existing buildings and erecting tall residential buildings. This was also the case with agrarian lands that were converted for residential purposes. New clans emerged in al-Matariya and acquired capital and power through this process. For example, a member of the clan of Gizawi had worked for one of the pashas and was given a piece of land, where he built his first six-story residential building. His children and grandchildren, from the 1960s to the present, have continued to expand their real estate activity. The Gizawi Towers—the name used to describe the ten- to twelve-story buildings owned by the Gizawi family members—have spread all over the neighborhood.

Another dynamic through which the clans of al-Matariya have emerged was immigration from the rural governorates surrounding the city of Cairo. It is noteworthy that large, well-established clans in the rural areas rarely immigrate to the capital; in general, anyone who immigrates from his original space to the capital is someone who is searching for an opportunity to prosper. Al-Matariya has offered this opportunity for many people from the rural governorates next to Cairo, mainly Qalyubiya. The neighborhood included deserted agrarian land, away from the center of the capital, offering protection from government supervision. Hence, it was a place suitable for informal money-generating activities that entailed destroying agrarian land and erecting tall buildings. Such was the case with the Abou-Eida, al-'Umda, and al-Taweel clans, among others.

Between Clans and Police

Between the clans, with their rising power in al-Matariya, and the police there emerged (in)formal power networks in the neighborhood. The police station and the major clans joined to exercise power over the spaces of the popular quarters (Singerman 2011, 207). Most of the big clans of al-Matariya work in construction; however, their economic activities are not limited to that. They also deal in antiquities, which are frequently found while digging foundations for buildings. While most of the construction is done without permits, such activity cannot be accomplished completely outside the supervision of the government. This is especially true if this construction takes place in Masalla, which is less than one kilometer away from the local police station of al-Matariya.

Police involvement in the activities of construction and dealing in antiquities was exposed after the 2011 uprising by people who had worked for various clans. The local police station involvement was two-fold. When one of the big clans started digging, the police station would send a low-level officer *(amin al-shurta)* to sit in a location with a vantage point over the site—or, in the exact words of the people who told the story, "The officer constable used to sit on the head of the dig *(a'la ras fi-l-hafr)*"—in order to supervise the extraction of antiquities. By the end of the working day, the police constable would go back to the police station with a record of every item of antiquity found during the day. The police chief and other high-ranking officers in the station arranged with whoever had found the antiquities to share in a percentage of the profits they brought. This percentage varied depending on the power of the clan involved in the construction project. In return, the police station turned a blind eye to the entire criminal activity. The local chief of police was often given an apartment in any building he wished, either for free or for 10 percent of its market price. In return, he would turn a blind eye to construction projects without permits. Whoever refused to take part in these arrangements was denied any involvement and was subject to punishment. In 2004, one resident—an engineer who owned a two-story building built during the 1970s—decided to build a third story. The fact that this engineer was not a member of one of the big families with connections to the police station led to the demolition of this third floor during the process. Police officers and their accomplices from the big clans—who are not family members, but work for them—have further shared interests when regulating al-Matariya's internal transportation networks. The unauthorized microbuses are, in many cases, owned by police officers, while small-time accomplices from the big clans drive these vehicles. The drivers also agree to play a surveillance role in their communities, acting as informants to the police (Wahdan 2012, 130). Moreover, officers are also involved in small-scale drug distribution to dealers.

In addition to the monthly bribes (shahriya) paid by the big clans to the local police station, these exchanges of favors benefited police personnel in both their personal and professional capacities. As a bureaucratic state institution, the local police station continued to benefit from relations with the big clans, who would agree to send over some of their accomplices for small crimes like theft and small-scale drug dealing. They turned them over to the local police station on a monthly basis so that the station could keep up the appearance of enforcing laws in the neighborhood. Accordingly, the clans would take care of the accomplices' families financially while they were in jail. A first-hand witness reported one incident of a man in al-Matariya who was famous for violence. He did some of the dirty work for the neighborhood's big families. In fact, he was formally registered as a dangerous criminal (musaggal khatar), and therefore was a regular visitor to the police station. However, after a few years, he decided to quit that work and to just take care of his wife and his children. After not visiting the police station for few months, the police chief summoned him and asked, "Are you upset with anything? Has anyone done you any harm?" The police chief assumed that if this guy was not practicing violence for a few months, he must have been threatened by someone more powerful than him. When the guy responded that nobody could do him any harm, the police chief responded, "So, how can this police station survive if you quit?" This type of relationship is further illustrated in cinematic representations such as the film The Land of Fear (Ard al-khuf, 2000).

This relationship of mutual exchange between a police station and some of the big clans is no secret to be exposed through investigative journalism or works of art. It is a part of the city's fabric, woven through the everyday lives of the people in areas like al-Matariya. For example, one common scene is that, when a member of one of the big families has a wedding party, he might block a main street to set the stage for the massive ten-hour wedding party. The preparation for such weddings takes days, during which the street is closed. During the street party itself, illegal drugs and illegally imported alcoholic beverages are served. While blocking the street and serving illegal substances are both punishable by law, one can observe police officers—sometimes in uniform—enjoying the show, sharing happiness and substances with the families of the newly wedded couple.

Informal Securitization

The role of al-Matariya police station, in the eyes of the police, was not to impose "security from above." Rather, it was to foster liaisons and sustain "criminality from below." Hence, securitization and criminality were fused together under the false pretense that such a network is the only way to ensure the security of the neighborhood, considering its expansion beyond the state's reach. This entwined relationship is obvious and pervasive. Hence, we can understand why some of the people of al-Matariya did not rush to Tahrir Square to demand reforms. Instead, they chose to encounter the immediate manifestation of the state in their everyday lives by burning down the police station, where alleged security merged with criminality to impose a rather hybrid mesh of control over that sector of the population.

After the people of al-Matariya managed to disrupt that power structure on January 28, 2011, the people began to reclaim public space. By the end of March 2011, the al-Matariya Youth Coalition—a group of enthusiastic youth from the neighborhood, who had gotten together during the days of the 2011 uprising—decided to host an event to honor the mothers of the martyrs on Mothers' Day and to introduce the Coalition to the people. Although some of the powerful clans offered to sponsor it and some others threatened to not let the event take place, the youth refused to respond to either proposition. The event was completely self-funded and was successfully and safely held. One of the interesting questions people asked at the time was whether the event was sponsored by a big family or by the Muslim Brotherhood. This question reveals that, in the people's minds, these are the only groups entitled to access to the public space.

Works Cited

Abu-Lughod, Janet L. *Cairo: 1001 Years of the City Victorious*. Princeton, NJ: Princeton University Press, 1971.

Bayat, A. 2010. *Life as Politics: How Ordinary People Change the Middle East*. Stanford, CA: Stanford University Press.

Fahmy, Khaled. 2002. *All the Pasha's Men: Mehmed Ali, His Army, and the Making of Modern Egypt*. Cairo: American University in Cairo Press.

Ghannam, F. 2002. *Remaking the Modern: Space, Relocation, and the Politics of Identity in a Global Cairo*. Berkeley: University of California Press.

Lockman, Z. 2010. *Contending Visions of the Middle East*. Cambridge: Cambridge University Press.

Malterre-Barthes, C. 2016. "Housing Cairo: From Small-scale Informal Housing Construction to Semi-professional Speculative Urban Schemes." Paper presented at a Low/No Cost Housing Conference in June 2016. Zurich: Department of Architecture, ETH Zurich.

Mitchell, T. 1988. *Colonising Egypt*. Berkeley: University of California Press.

Singerman, D. 2011. *Cairo Contested: Governance, Urban Space, and Global Modernity*. London: I.B. Tauris.

Wahdan, Dalia. 2012. "Transport Thugs: Spatial Marginalization in a Cairo Suburb." In *Marginality and Exclusion in Egypt*, edited by R. Bush and H. Ayeb, 1st ed., 112–32. London: Zed Books.

30

CHALLENGING URBAN MILITARIZATION IN POST-2011 DOWNTOWN CAIRO
WALLS AND CHECKPOINTS

LAURA MONFLEUR

Introduction

As I was walking through downtown Cairo for the first time, in 2014, I encountered a street blocked by a huge cement wall. I tried to bypass this wall, taking another street, but found it also cut off. Policemen at a nearby checkpoint were regulating pedestrian and car traffic. What was supposed to be a ten-minute walk became thirty minutes. My tourist map was no help, and I began to add the street blockages to my map in order to help me move around Downtown more effectively.

The Egyptian regime has reinforced its authoritarianism through a set of legislations and repressions. Since 2013, a law has forbidden any protests not previously authorized by the Ministry of Interior. Additionally, this law permits security forces to use lethal force against any protest that is disturbing public order. This Terrorist Entities Law uses a broad definition of "terrorist entities," which can apply to political dissidents. These laws criminalize a wide variety of actions: mundane and peaceful gatherings, individual expressions of political frustration . . . almost anything, in short, can be interpreted as illegal activism or terrorism. These laws represent a counterrevolution that regularly mobilizes a set of government actions that employ a repertoire of violence (Abaza 2016). This repertoire is composed not only of laws and the practices of the police, but also of material security infrastructures and a set of spatial practices and tactics to control urban spaces. The present chapter tackles this securitization of urban spaces through material and militarized infrastructures in Cairo's Downtown since 2011.

As many of the authors of the present volume attest, the 2011 revolution led to a massive intensification and transformation of ongoing processes of securitization in Cairo. Although this is perhaps most obvious in slum resettlement and urban renewal plans (see Arese, D. Khalil, and Mohie in this volume), the re-statization of the media (Elmeshad, this volume), the precarization of health and sanitation infrastructure (Guirguis and Carreño, this volume), the "hygienization" of Egyptian football (Ahmed, this volume), and even the attempt to build an entirely new capital city intended as an untouchable enclave of the state bureaucracies (Duffield, this volume), these trends can also be seen in the physical barriers that have sprung up around Cairo.

Occupation and control of the downtown area has been a major issue at stake for the regime. In her personal account of the revolution, *Cairo, My City, My Revolution*, Ahdaf Soueif, an Egyptian novelist and political commentator, pointed out that controlling Tahrir is equivalent to controlling Cairo and, through this, to controlling Egypt (Soueif 2012). More broadly, because of its centrality in the media (Bayat 2009) and in the touristic circuits, downtown Cairo became the main stage of the competition between revolutionaries and the regime. Since 2011, and in a more visible and strengthened way since 2013, the regime has sought to regain control of this area to demonstrate a restoration of order and stability in the country in the eyes of both the national and international communities. Downtown has thus become one of the most securitized neighborhoods in Cairo. The first part of this chapter will analyze the urban and material *dispositif* of securitization in downtown Cairo between 2011 and 2020, based on qualitative fieldwork conducted in Downtown between 2014 and 2020 (including observations and semi-directed interviews). I use the term *dispositif* (dispositive) here, following Foucault (Frost 2020), to signify an array of physical and conceptual structures that support existing power relations in society. The second and third parts of the chapter will focus respectively on the discourses and practices of revolutionaries who are challenging and bypassing this urban militarization. When we speak of revolutionaries here, we are talking about liberal revolutionaries, as opposed to the revolutionaries from the Muslim Brotherhood, who are not among my interlocutors. Most of my interviewees are between twenty and forty years old, participated in the revolution, and do not hold any affiliation to a political party or institutions. They live or work in downtown Cairo and visit the streets, cafés, and cultural places of Downtown on a daily basis.

Militarization of Downtown, 2011–20: Urban and Material *Dispositif* of Control

The nature of the security forces, among them the army, and of their strategies for spatial control, including limiting demonstrations to specific places to prevent them from spreading across the entire city, testify to a militarized logic of control of political practices and public spaces. This militarization became more tangible when the Supreme Council of the Armed Forces built walls around such institutions as the Ministry of Interior and the parliament. The first wall was erected during the clashes on Mohammad Mahmud Street in November 2011. Since then, these walls have multiplied, especially around Downtown's ministries and Tahrir Square. In February 2012, there were eight walls in Downtown that were constructed as a frontline between the revolutionaries and security forces during clashes. They thus contributed to displacing demonstrations and sit-ins to more peripheral neighborhoods, as was the case in 2013 with the Muslim Brotherhood sit-ins in Rabaa al-'Adawiya and Nahda squares (Stadnicki 2014). In 2014, the army tore down some of the walls because the closure of the streets was disrupting the city's normal traffic flow. Those walls were replaced with sliding metal gates, either black or painted in the colors of the Egyptian flag. Between 2011 and 2016, this securitization was reinforced at night and between January 25 and June 30. This security infrastructure was also systematized around embassies in Garden City, such as the American Embassy after demonstrations against the United States in 2013. These walls and gates were accompanied by fortifications of the political institutions made with smaller cement blocks, curved cement blocks, and checkpoints. The last of these were composed of barbed wire, armored police vehicles, tanks, barriers, and dogs.

These measures are interconnected with the practices of repression and legislative decisions mentioned above. Along with laws and practices of repression, they are part of a militarized *dispositif*, "a thoroughly heterogeneous ensemble consisting of discourses, institutions, architectural forms, regulatory decisions, laws, administrative measures, scientific statements, philosophical, moral, and philanthropic propositions—in short, the said as much as the unsaid" (Foucault 1994, 98). The *dispositif* is a tool deployed to control protests, to prevent them, and to protect the political institutions representing an authoritarian military regime.

Since 2018, only the walls and metal gates around the US Embassy and the metal gates on Falaki Street (which now remain open) remain. The removal of the permanent security infrastructure followed the relocation in 2016 of the main security institution in Downtown—namely, the Ministry of Interior. This institution, responsible for the police and tasked with the repression of popular uprisings, had been the main target of the revolutionaries. As Elmeshad relates in their chapter in this book, it has been removed from Downtown and relocated in New Cairo.[1] Nonetheless, the regime still occupies Downtown through temporary checkpoints whose presence is more pervasive during commemorations of the revolution and after demonstrations, as was the case during September 2019 and September 2020.[2]

Clearly, walls, gates, and checkpoints are vital tools in securitized spaces. It is still important to trace the territorial logics of control that evolved between 2011 and 2020. The walls were initially reactionary, but the gates were maintained long after the revolution, becoming an effective tool for "a teichopolitic" (a politic of partitioning public spaces) (Ballif and Rosière 2009). They were progressively reified and became fortifications at some political institutions such as the Ministry of Interior, the Ministry of Justice, and the US Embassy, extending their presence to the streets surrounding the buildings and creating no-man's-lands around them. With the gates, the presence of security infrastructure gradually became normalized and eventually regarded as "urban furniture." Contrary to other studies of militarization that emphasize the technologization of security (Graham 2011), this incidence of securitization operates through material objects and territorialization (Ritaine 2009; Bou Akar 2018). Downtown was thus divided into two spaces: securitized areas that are controlled and occupied by the security forces, and spaces that are considered contested and dangerous. The walls define a protected inside for the regime and an unsafe outside composed of activists, political opponents, and terrorists. Theses labels and cartographies, created by authoritarian practices and imaginaries, are producing clear socio-spatial binaries in urban spaces, a fracturing of spaces and flows that threatens real violence to bodies.

Checkpoints are more flexible than walls, as they can be put up and removed easily and at any time. They are adaptable and responsive to the intensity of the political situation and of perceived political risks (Razac 2009). They allow normal traffic to proceed, but impede the progress of those who are considered to be suspicious. Rather than establish a binary distinction of two kinds of spaces, territorialization of security with checkpoints establishes "a multiplicity of points of control" (Graham 2011). Downtown becomes an archipelago of securitized places, inundated with the police officers who check state identification cards, phones, and bags. Such securitization, while more beneficial for the regime, is also more volatile: it's more difficult for the inhabitants to know where police are posted. The militarized logic of identification and targeting of particular "suspicious" populations permeates everyday life for those who live and pass through Downtown.

Challenging the Discourse of (In)Security

Civil society and some individuals have tried to challenge the militarization of Downtown by criminalizing the military infrastructure. In January 2012, the Egyptian Center for Economic and Social Rights and the Egyptian Initiative for Personal Rights filed a suit before an administrative court, arguing for the desecuritization of streets. One month later, inhabitants of Garden City protested in front of the parliament in Downtown. But after 2013, political voices and judicial resistance against the walls disappeared due to increased repression and the transformation of the walls into gates that appear more "normal" and "urban" (Monfleur 2017). This appearance of normality is a goal of the regime, trying to present an image of a modern, global, and touristic city center.

Nonetheless, everyday representations and discourses show that inhabitants of Downtown criminalize and delegitimize those military infrastructures. The walls were compared to the Green Zone of Baghdad or the Berlin Wall during the Cold War. The first comparison shows that the power that securitizes urban spaces and fortified institutions is associated with colonial power, in this case unlawfully occupying a space ostensibly belonging to the Egyptian people. One resident spoke of the process in terms of "occupation" and "monopolization." The second comparison equates walls with social and geopolitical borders. In this representation, inhabitants seem to reproduce the binary created by the walls, but in this case, it is seen as a binary not between spaces at risk and safe spaces, or between good and bad citizens, but more between the people who have legitimacy to occupy the downtown streets versus a political power that is illegitimate because it doesn't represent the people. Walls protect power, not the population. Political institutions are thus compared to "barracks" or "blockhaus."[3] Those representations mostly concern the Ministry of Interior, one of the most securitized buildings in Downtown.

While representing security for the government, walls, barbed wire, and checkpoints are a source of insecurity and violence for the inhabitants of Downtown. The infrastructure manifests itself materially, in an urban landscape "saturated by political violence" (Gregory and Pred 2006). Military infrastructures are physical reminders of repression and of the possibility of being arrested and suffering violence. Many interviewees mentioned the fact that they are afraid to walk in front of institutional buildings in Downtown. Yet some former revolutionaries have mocked and belittled the capacity of the walls and checkpoints to contain the populace. For most of them, it's a question of the government's image and of "acting as if." In both cases, interviewees opposed the arguments of security of the regime and safety of individuals. Securitization could well be the wrong answer to threats; security is a strategy that reflects the interests of a political power removed from civil society and individuals and that doesn't create tangible safety for people (Marcuse 2006).

Those discourses were used during the interviews that I personally conducted. Some of the interviewees mentioned how discourses against and critics of securitization can only be expressed in private circles and spaces due to political repression. Voices opposing the walls and the security forces have been raised publicly by some artists in exhibitions—for example, "Tank Girls" against the army by Nadine Hammam at the Gallery Misr in March 2012, and "Asa7by" about the protests and the police by Hany Rashed at the Mashrabia Gallery in November 2012. Nonetheless, recent fieldwork conducted between October 2020 and January 2021, and since 2015, reveals growing constraints on free expression by artists.

Challenging and Bypassing Urban Militarization

During the first days that the walls went up, the demonstrators tried to tear them down, and managed to remove some of the cement blocks to create a passage.[4] The revolutionaries thus competed with the security forces to occupy Downtown in a game of alternating construction and destruction (CEDEJ 2013). Nonetheless, removing a single cement block could take several hours, and the security forces won that game, building and rebuilding walls faster than the revolutionaries could topple them.

These "hard interventions" against walls were therefore gradually replaced by "soft interventions" (Nagati and Stryker 2013), one of which was graffiti (Abaza 2013; Karl, Hamdy, and Soueif 2014). The "No Walls" project was launched in 2012 by the artist and filmmaker Salma El Tarzi, aimed at recreating the continuity of the streets by painting optical illusions on walls. There were collective organized events near the newly painted walls, inviting people to gather for music and celebration to dispute the occupation by the security forces and by the regime. The graffiti contributed to the everyday memory and representations of less securitized times. One of the residents of Downtown extolled the ability of graffiti "to tell the government that our imagination and our dreams are beyond the walls. It's not the physical or material space that ends our dreams."[5] Another example was seen on the walls on Mohammad Mahmud Street, covered with pink camouflage in 2013. By painting one of the most militarized streets in pink, artists wanted to denounce the army's efforts to maintain a strong, positive image among the population and to monopolize the romantic memory and heritage of the revolution. They mocked the institution's paternalistic, authoritarian values by characterizing it with a color considered to be more feminine.[6]

As tangible and enduring infrastructures, the cement walls were the main canvas for these popular representations and artistic practices. Critics leaned on the walls to diffuse (in)security. With the walls' removal, those tactics evaporated. The pervasive use of movable tools like checkpoints (Razac 2009) to securitize urban spaces does not enable similar practices of resistance, especially because it is more difficult to predict their presence. The movable tools reinforce the presence of the police in the streets and their arbitrary exertion of control. Since 2016, street artists have stopped doing graffiti on the walls of Downtown after experiencing arrests and surveillance. While the relocation of the Ministry of Interior seems to have led to a less fragmented and militarized Downtown area, less tangible and less permanent types of infrastructure have established a more effective method of control.

Nonetheless, practices of mobility can be analyzed as a fluid response to this more flexible *dispositif* of control. Inhabitants and workers in Downtown have revealed their own spatial capacities and knowledge in the course of their everyday mobility. Most of the interviewees

Figure 30.1. Ammar Abo Bakr's graffiti representation of Khaled Said, one of the martyrs of the revolution. Pink camouflage is used to ironically denounce the militarization of political and urban life.

mentioned a precise geography of the checkpoints—they know where they will be, and when there will be moments of increased securitization—since even the police and army's repertoire can be learned to some degree. It allows them to avoid the checkpoints, to bypass them when they want to move around Downtown. An urban planner in the area mentioned an affective framework that Egyptians have developed, explaining "We know well enough now, we have a kind of detector. We can feel if it looks very intense. And if something is happening, you avoid ... you just take another route . . . . You can't take it for granted. There is no rule. So you have to really feel. Of course, if you live in the city and you grow up in the city, you can read it, it's easier, it's a culture."[7] They also demonstrate abilities to negotiate at checkpoints: walking or driving at a certain speed that is not suspicious, or turning off their cell phones to avoid its inspection. Everyday mobility becomes a set of "tactics" (Certeau 1990), with residents bypassing the checkpoints or negotiating a way out. Those tactics are ways to ensure their own safety, as one of the interviewees expressed: "If you don't find a checkpoint, you will find an officer. I'm always trying to find my ways to be safe, even if I will take a longer road."[8] Those tactics are also a way to challenge material and temporary control by the regime, as the interviewees often claimed a right to move around the city and to be in the streets that they consider to be theirs (Lefebvre 1971).

While the interviewees acknowledged the constraints and difficulties of expressing political views and of demonstrating against the government, securitization in Downtown since 2013 hasn't prevented protest altogether.[9] The more visible forms of opposition must now be informed by more popular practices and discourses with their own political dimension. From graffiti and artistic events to mobility strategies and other representations, those everyday practices and discourses can be analyzed as challenges to the urban militarization of Downtown, demonstrating a tactical purpose and intention to regain appropriation and control of the streets from the authoritarian regime. This "art of presence" (Bayat 2009) remains strong within the city despite repressive control and militarized *dispositif*, and offers a more fluid process of continuity and discontinuity, and of interacting with securitizing infrastructures.

Notes

1   The relocation of ministries and political institutions from downtown Cairo to the peripheries concerns not only the Ministry of

Interior. In the long term, ministries and embassies will be relocated to the New Administrative Capital, located in the desert on the
road between Cairo and Suez.

2   In September 2019, demonstrations against the government of
al-Sisi took place in Tahrir Square, following the airing of YouTube
videos of an Egyptian contractor who denounced the corruption
in the economy and real estate sectors. In September 2020, a new
call for demonstrations was launched throughout the country to
sustain the claims of the demonstrations of September 2019, as if
to commemorate them in a new revolutionary moment.

3   A fortified defensive structure often in cement, allowing soldiers to
fire in various directions. The people interviewed used this term in
reference to the *blockhaus* used during the Second World War.

4   Videos of those actions can be found in the video archive of the
Egyptian revolution "858": https://858.ma/.

5   An unnamed resident, interview by the author, April 1, 2015.

6   An unnamed street artist, interview by the author, March 21, 2015.

7   An unnamed urban planner working in Downtown, interview by
the author, February 11, 2015.

8   An unnamed worker in Downtown, interview by the author, March
19, 2015.

9   In September 2019, people demonstrated in the streets of Cairo
and several other cities after the publication of a YouTube video
made by an entrepreneur, Mohamed Ali, who denounced the corruption in the regime.

Works Cited

Abaza, Mona. 2013. "Walls, Segregating Downtown Cairo and the
    Mohammed Mahmud Street Graffiti." *Theory, Culture & Society* 30,
    no. 1: 122–39.

———. 2016. "Violence, Dramaturgical Repertoires and Neoliberal
    Imaginaries in Cairo." *Theory, Culture & Society* 33, no. 7–8: 111–35.
    https://doi.org/10.1177/0263276416670729.

Ballif, Florine, and Stéphane Rosière. 2009. "Le défi des 'teichopoli-
    tiques': Analyser la fermeture contemporaine des territoires."
    L'Espace géographique 38, no. 3: 193. https://www.researchgate.net/
    publication/277988127_Le_defi_des_teichopolitiques_Analyser_la_
    fermeture_contemporaine_des_territoires.

Bayat, Asef. 2009. *Life as Politics: How Ordinary People Change the Middle
    East.* Stanford, CA: Stanford University Press.

Bou Akar, Hiba. 2018. *For the War Yet to Come: Planning Beirut's Frontiers.*
    1st ed. Stanford, CA: Stanford University Press.

CEDEJ. 2013. "Murs." Billet. Les Carnets du CEDEJ (blog), posted May 26.

Certeau, Michel de. 1990. *Invention du Quotidien tome 1: Arts de faire.* Paris: Editions Gallimard.

Foucault, Michel. 1994. "Le jeu de Michel Foucault." In *Dits et Ecrits* (1976–1979), vol. 3, no. 206, 836. Paris: Gallimard.

Frost, Tim. 2020. "The Dispositif between Foucault and Agamben." *Law, Culture, and the Humanities* 15, no. 1: 151–71. https://journals.sagepub.com/doi/pdf/10.1177/1743872115571697

Graham, Stephen. 2011. *Cities under Siege: The New Military Urbanism.* London and New York: Verso.

Gregory, Derek, and Allan Pred, eds. 2006. *Violent Geographies: Fear, Terror, and Political Violence.* 1st ed. New York: Routledge.

Karl, Don Stone, Basma Hamdy, and Ahdaf Soueif. 2014. *Walls of Freedom: Street Art of the Egyptian Revolution.* Berlin: From Here to Fame.

Lefebvre, Henri. 1971. *Le droit à la ville.* Paris: Points.

Marcuse, Peter. 2006. "Security or Safety in Cities? The Threat of Terrorism after 9/11." *International Journal of Urban and Regional Research* 30, no. 4: 919–29.

Monfleur, Laura. 2017. "À l'épreuve des murs: Sécurisation et pratiques politiques dans le centre-ville du Caire postrévolutionnaire (2014–2015)." *Égypte/Monde arabe,* no. 16: 39–56.

Nagati, Omar, and Benedicte Stryker, eds. 2013. *Archiving the City in Flux: Cairo's Shifting Urban Landscape since the January 25th Revolution.* Cairo: Cluster.

Razac, Olivier. 2009. *Histoire politique du barbelé.* Paris: Flammarion.

Ritaine, Evelyne. 2009. "La barrière et le checkpoint: Mise en politique de l'asymétrie." *Cultures et Conflits* 73: 13–33.

Soueif, Ahdaf. 2012. *Cairo: My City, Our Revolution.* London: Bloomsbury Publishing.

Stadnicki, Roman. 2014. "Le Caire: Territoires de révolte." *Carto* 21: 32–33.

31

BECOMING A MAN IN CAIRO
SUDANESE AND SOUTH SUDANESE REFUGEES, GANGS, AND STRUCTURAL VIOLENCE

PAUL MIRANDA

Experiences of Anti-Black Racism and Structural Violence in Egypt

Santino, a South Sudanese man in his twenties who fled to Egypt when he was a child, explained "It's not just words, it's everything . . . your skin color, clothes, food, music . . . they [Egyptians] make racist comments about everything we do." He is referring to the constant racism that makes it impossible, he reports, for Sudanese and South Sudanese young people to attend Egyptian public schools, a situation that has also been detailed in the chapter on Sudanese refugees by Hetaba and Habersky in this volume. In the course of my work in Cairo, Sudanese and South Sudanese refugees often discussed the myriad ways racism, socioeconomic exclusion, physical violence, and other forms of structural violence impact their lives. Many have described the variety of contradictory ways Sudanese and South Sudanese gangs impact their neighborhoods and communities. Structural and intra-communal violence are linked by masculinity, patriarchy, and young men's pursuit of manhood. This chapter aims to explore how structural violence has influenced the development of masculinities among young Sudanese and South Sudanese in Cairo, how those masculinities influence the reproduction of violence and gangs, and how they relate to hypermasculine and patriarchal norms from Sudan and South Sudan, drawing on ethnographic research I conducted from 2017 to 2019.

I focus on the role of gender norms, but I do not intend to reduce the complex process of gang emergence to a simple causal chain of structural violence, racism, and the pursuit of manhood. Rather, I hope to highlight the role masculinity plays and emphasize the need to consider it in analyses of gang dynamics in Cairo. However, economic incentives, social isolation, and childhood trauma, among other factors, are crucial to consider, and further research is needed to analyze these factors simultaneously. Lastly, I use the term "gang" analytically to refer to a street-based group with a strong youth identity, composition, and territorial identification rather than to evoke the racist connotation the word often carries. In Cairo, people refer to these groups differently. Many members and former members call them "groups," but others use the Arabic word for gang, *'isaba*. Some community members say "groups," others say "gangs," and some pejoratively refer to them with an Arabicized pronunciation of the English n-word.

Egypt has a history of hosting specific refugee and migrant communities. Sudanese populations started to arrive in 1955 after the outbreak of the First Sudanese Civil War. Another wave of migration began in 1983, after the outbreak of the Second Sudanese Civil War (1983–2005). From the 1990s, continued conflict in the Horn of Africa led large numbers of Sudanese, South Sudanese, Ethiopian, Eritrean, and Somali refugees to arrive in Egypt. Most refugees and asylum seekers live in Greater Cairo and are spread out in twenty to thirty neighborhoods, where they live among other migrants (Miranda 2018). They also tend to subdivide and cluster together by identity group. Many of these neighborhoods are informal, and some are on the physical margins of the city. Black African refugee communities—Sudanese and South Sudanese in particular—have been living in Cairo for a prolonged period in what is officially termed "protracted displacement." While the United Nations High Commissioner for Refugees (UNHCR) doesn't release statistics on the average length of stay in Egypt, a 2012 study found that 40 percent of its Sudanese respondents had been in Cairo for five to eight years and 25 percent for eight or more years (Jacobsen et al. 2012). In my own experience, it was common for me to meet Sudanese and South Sudanese who had been living in Cairo for ten or more years.

Numerous forms of structural violence, including anti-black racism and xenophobia in addition to periodic physical violence, affect Sudanese, South Sudanese, and other African refugees in Cairo. Many of them are frequently referred to by Egyptians in the street as *dalma* (darkness), *samara* (black), or *chocalata*. Many mentioned experiences of Egyptians throwing trash or stones at them or their children in the street, as Hetaba and Habersky have also related in their chapter in this volume. Deng and Choul, two young South Sudanese men who grew up in Cairo, asserted that Egyptians "look at you like you're an alien." They noted, "it's very difficult to grow up [in Egypt] as a Sudanese or South Sudanese person . . . you have to learn how to survive." The racism Black African refugee women experience is strongly gendered, as their bodies are highly sexualized. They're referred to as prostitutes in the street, while Black African domestic workers are portrayed as "sexual beings" who are "willing to do anything" (Ahmed 2010). This sexualization of black women is the continuation of a long historical trend of the intersection of race, gender, and coloniality, which Hammad's chapter (in this volume) explores in greater depth.

Physical violence is also common. In one report, 82 percent of Sudanese respondents reported facing harassment from the local community, 40 percent experienced robbery, and 36 percent faced physical assault in the previous year alone (Jacobsen 2012). While some of this violence is related to petty street crime, some of it is also connected to racist harassment. In 2016, a Nuba Sudanese man told me that "our kids get stoned when we send them to the shop. When I intervene, they beat me, too."[1] In 2018, Sudanese and South Sudanese in the al-Hayy al-'Ashir neighborhood recounted an incident of group-level violence. After a fight broke out between a small group of Sudanese and Egyptian teenagers, a large group of young Egyptian men gathered and beat the group of Sudanese teenagers, and then went through the streets, assaulting any Black African they encountered. In February 2017, an Egyptian man who had been harassing Sudanese children for years in the neighborhood of Ain Shams murdered a South Sudanese teacher in the courtyard of a local Sudanese school.

Anti-Black racism has a long history in Egypt. In the Egyptian "jungle films" of the 1940s that Elsaket analyzes in another chapter of this book, Black Africans were depicted as silent and servile, Africa as a place of inferiority, and blackness represented violence and irrationality. Black Africans were then juxtaposed to Egyptians to affirm the latter's modernity. These depictions were rooted in Egyptian histories of slavery, racial superiority, and claims to empire (Elsaket 2017). In the present, hiring Black African domestic workers remains a marker of social class in Egypt because these "women continue the legacy of black slaves and 'honest black' Nubians who served in the households of Egyptian elites" (Ahmed 2010). Sudanese, South Sudanese, and other African refugees face numerous other challenges. Restrictions, exploitation, discrimination, and violence are common experiences for refugees in accessing healthcare and education, pursuing livelihoods, creating and running businesses, renting apartments, moving around the city, and accessing the judicial system. Most of the Black African refugee population lives under conditions of severe economic deprivation. Much of the existing research on Cairo's African refugees documents these challenges. But it is crucial to note that, despite the many problems refugees face in Cairo, Black African refugee communities are not passive victims. They actively organize themselves for the betterment of their communities and find ways to resist and sometimes overcome the challenges and abuses they face (usually) without any outside assistance, as Hetaba and Habersky have shown in their chapter (this volume) on Sudanese communities and schools.

Sudanese and South Sudanese Gangs: Becoming a Man in the Face of Structural Violence

Due to prolonged displacement, many young Sudanese and South Sudanese migrants were born in Cairo or arrived when they were children, which means that many have limited memories of their home countries, and their proficiency in their tribal languages varies. For example, Santino told me that he only understands Dinka when it's spoken to him, although he speaks Egyptian Arabic fluently. Santino explained that he occasionally attends meetings of his Dinka sub-tribe. These are held in Dinka, but when Santino speaks, he usually switches into Arabic or English, at which point one of the elders may scold him and remind him to practice his Dinka.

Generational differences extend beyond language. There is often a disconnect due to differences in lived experiences between the older generation—who came of age in Sudan and South Sudan—and Santino's generation in Cairo. Despite the challenges the youth face, Santino explained that some of the older men criticize young people, saying that "We studied by candlelight in South Sudan, your life here is easy . . . you have cellphones and houses you live in." In Santino's view, the older generation doesn't engage with young people in a nurturing way. "[They] don't share with the youth," he said, "they don't encourage us or hang out with us at all."

Generational differences can range from tensions to outright social exclusion, and previous research on Sudanese and South Sudanese gangs concluded that young men are often marginalized and excluded by the adults in their communities (Forcier 2009). For example, American hip-hop culture and rap are popular among Sudanese and South Sudanese youth. However, according to Santino, if a young person in the community listens to rap or dresses with a hip-hop aesthetic, some in the older generation "will look at you in a bad way." He added that "they think we're all gangsters unless we act exactly like them." Sudanese and South Sudanese community organizations, at one point, even refused to serve or interact with young men who dressed in any way associated with hip-hop culture.

Patriarchy and social expectations demand that boys and men must achieve and continually re-achieve the status of "being a real man," while others contest and police their manhood based on performances of masculinity (Heilman and Barker 2018). Manliness is a constant process of performing and fulfilling the contradictory roles and expectations associated with manhood, while defending against anything emasculating (Baird 2018; Heilman and Barker 2018). While boys and young men are obligated to seek out pathways to manhood, contexts of structural violence, anti-Black racism, socioeconomic deprivation, and extreme inequality often block off traditional routes to hegemonic masculinity for young men. These factors generate feelings of emasculation in young people, as they prevent them from achieving societal expectations. Sometimes local gangs can provide an alternative route to manhood, offering a space to accumulate "masculine capital" (respect, power, money, or whatever the markers of manhood may be) when other options are unattractive or nonexistent (Baird 2018). Joining a gang, then, may not represent deviant behavior, but rather a practical and logical reaction to young people's circumstances and societal pressures facing them to be "real men" (Baird 2012).

The first Sudanese and South Sudanese "gangs" existed as early as 2003–2004, but many agree that it was only in 2006 that the number of groups, sub-groups, and affiliated young people rose dramatically. This was also around the time of the Mustafa Mahmud Park protest—when approximately 2,500 Sudanese and South Sudanese carried out a four-month sit-in in front of the UNHCR office. The protest was sparked by the UNHCR's decision to halt its asylum process due to the signing of the Comprehensive Peace Agreement (CPA) in Sudan, but it was also very much a reflection of the community's long simmering frustration with their situation in Cairo. The protesters challenged not only the UNHCR, but also traditional Sudanese conceptions of authority and patterns of masculinity. The protest leaders were not traditional leadership figures, tribal leaders, elders, or religious figures, but primarily young, single men who circumvented them, which was previously unheard of (Lewis 2011; Rowe 2006). The protest leaders' subversion of authority figures provided an example of the potential to develop alternative structures within the Sudanese and South Sudanese communities. The protest also highlighted the inability of the UNHCR, the Egyptian state, and traditional Sudanese authority structures to materially impact people's lives for the better, leaving a gap for Sudanese and South Sudanese gangs to flourish. Six months after the protest, there were "hundreds of gang affiliates in Cairo, representing a substantial number of Sudanese youths" (Lewis 2011).

Two primary groups emerged in the mid-aughts: the Lost Boys and the Outlaws. Each claimed several neighborhoods as their territory and there was a degree of centralized leadership. However, the groups fractured over time, and now many areas have their own group that identifies with the neighborhood as well as different neighborhood subgroups. Fragmentation can go down to the street level. In Ain Shams, one street is claimed by two sub-groups with each controlling half the street. While leadership in the early years strongly resisted the formation of sub-groups, the "system of gang leadership isn't [exactly] working any more," according to one former gang member. He pointed out that some groups and sub-groups don't have formal leaders.

At first, these groups emerged primarily to serve social purposes. Young people built cooperative networks to pool resources to throw parties and host social events in order to "escape reality" for an evening (Forcier 2009). In 2019, a former gang member told me that early gang life was about being "cool and fancy" and going to "nice places, organizing parties, and drinking fancy alcohol." Gangs were not only spaces for socializing and community building: they also provided member support—money for rent, medical treatment, or other needed expenses—and a feeling of collective solidarity (Lewis 2011). Gangs also play contradictory roles for communities. Some members see themselves as protectors of their neighborhoods. For example, individuals explained to me that some group members escort youth when they go to play a football match in another neighborhood to ensure they don't face difficulties in the street. Others in my research noted that some families indirectly support their children's involvement because if their sons are gang-involved, other young men will be less likely to seek a premarital relationship with their daughters. Previous research argued that people involved in these groups rejected their tribal affiliation and primarily identified with their group, a point which is touched on below. But in my research, community members also explained that some tribal elders have on occasion instrumentalized gangs and encouraged members to "overwhelm the streets" as a sign of power against other tribes.[2] Not only do Sudanese and South Sudanese boys and young men face structural violence similar to other contexts of gang formation, but their displacement further complicates their pursuit of manhood. Displacement is a transformative experience for people: gender roles and livelihood systems often change, which can invert household relations and lead to conflict. In Cairo, domestic work is the most readily available livelihood for Black African refugees, and while some men work as cleaners, the majority are women. "The women have opportunities," a female Sudanese community activist told me. "But the men don't, so women have control of the money, which can lead to problems." Santino also expressed his frustration with the employment opportunities available, saying even if he "studied hard and finished school in Egypt," then the "only job [you] can get is in cleaning, and people are racist to you at every turn."

Gangs became spaces where young people redefined conceptions of Sudanese and South Sudanese masculinity to fit their circumstances and stake a claim to manhood. They rejected traditional Sudanese masculinity, societal norms, and rites of passage into manhood (evidenced by their resistance to and rejection of traditional Sudanese "elder" authority structures and social rules) while they also disassociated themselves from conservative Egyptian culture. In Sudan and South Sudan, there is a wide tapestry of identities influenced by tribe, region, sociopolitical history, and dozens of other factors. For the communities included in my research, traditional markers of masculinity can include fulfilling the role of protector of the family, homestead, cattle herd, marriage, and having children (Hutchinson and Jok 2002). For some boys, traditional passage into manhood may involve herding cattle for an extended period away from the family or undergoing scarification ceremonies. Despite the ways in which tribal identity can influence gang dynamics, many members outright reject tribal identification. In Forcier's research, one member emphasized that "the things that happen in Sudan, those aren't our problems any more. Our problems are here. North, South, tribes, religion, that is not who we are. We are [Group A]. We are [Group B]" (Forcier 2009). In 2019, some members continued to emphasize this notion when talking to us. The gangs and identities they developed provided conspicuous markers of masculinity and an alternative avenue to project power and public postures of strength (Lewis 2011). For example, young people, gang affiliated or not, often hang out in the street in the evenings in large groups. But many affiliated youths also drink alcohol, smoke hash, and hang around with young women in the street in a defiant rejection of Egyptian societal norms. A Sudanese teacher explained to me that a colleague of his once scolded a gang-affiliated student for sleeping in class, but the student saw this as an insult and called his fellow members, who came into the school brandishing weapons. The teacher brokered an apology, which crucially acknowledged the importance of respect to avoid a conflict. The episode, however, highlights the way in which members will use public postures of strength to stake or reaffirm their claim to manhood in response to anything they perceive as emasculating.

While validating the findings of my research with Sudanese and South Sudanese community workers, participants—many of them men and women in their twenties and thirties who have also spent considerable time in Cairo—spoke of how youth are stuck between worlds. They said that many don't feel entirely Sudanese, but they also can't identify as Egyptian either because of the many ways by which they are rejected by Egyptian society, racism included. Anti-Black racism is only one factor, but it is an important one that contributes to feelings of marginalization, hopelessness, and perhaps even emasculation. For example, after explaining that people are "racist to you at every turn," Santino said to me that "dealing with this life, it makes you frustrated and angry." This was a sentiment we heard often during my research.

Masculinity and Violence among Gang-affiliated Sudanese and South Sudanese Youth

Over the past decade, research has explored how masculine and patriarchal norms are linked to young men joining gangs or armed groups and helped explain why the use of violence is concentrated among young men globally. In the words of a former gang member, "we never fought because we believed in something; we only did it to gain power, respect, and to protect the area from other gangs." Research bears out the strong link between patriarchal and rigid masculinities and engagement in sexual and physical violence against women, and violence between men (Heilman and Barker 2018; UN Women 2013). Here, the objective is to understand what exactly it means to be a "real man" to young Sudanese and South Sudanese and how this connects to the use of violence.

The community members we spoke with voiced some universal themes regarding masculinity: having and projecting power, showing dominance over others, being strong and tough, not going back on your word, enjoying respect and reputation, and defending honor. Others emphasized economic and material markers, including "fancy clothes," expensive phones, and disposable income. However, due to the complete lack of job opportunities and severe economic marginalization affecting Black African refugees, in which multiple forms of structural violence and anti-Black racism play a key role, most boys and young men are unable to afford the conspicuous material markers of masculinity. Many noted that young men feel the need to continually "show" or "prove" their manhood in public, particularly if it is challenged or called into question by slights or insults. Riak, a community activist and schoolteacher in his early thirties in Cairo's Abbasiya neighborhood, noted that "If someone challenges you, proves he's a man to you, you have to show you're a man back to him. Showing cowardice is the worst thing for us." Bol, a former gang member from Abbasiya, explained that while the immediate reason for a conflict between two neighborhood sub-groups may be minor, "like girls or money," the "overarching goal is domination." The sub-group members "want to be the king of Maadi [or their neighborhood]. They want to show the others, 'I'm powerful and you're nothing,'" according to a female community activist in Maadi. The desire for young people to project power and continually prove and re-achieve their manhood is especially pronounced for those involved in gang life.

The immediate causes of violence in the street are critical to understanding motivations to participate in gangs and are reflective of the patriarchal and hypermasculine norms present in gang spaces. Riak explained that while gang leaders sometimes order their members to target individuals or to "go out and 'collect' ten phones" to generate money for their group, it is usually "trivial things like anger, jealousy, and rivalries" between individuals that lead to outbursts of violence. The interpersonal nature of violence was a common theme in interviews across Cairo's neighborhoods. In al-Hayy al-'Ashir and Arba'a wa Nus, two Nuba community leaders explained that the younger teenagers "get upset about something and create conflicts or disputes, which then drags in the older boys, who create more violence." But once the community leaders get involved, they "realize the original problem was something simple. It's always about a girl or something [small] like this." Competition over women and girls was one of the most cited sources of violence.

Boys and young men justify the use of violence in response to perceived advances on "their" women. In a telling example, a former gang member in Maadi explained that it was common for violence to break out when gang members uploaded pictures on social media of themselves with girls from a rival territory. Riak and others also highlighted how the desire for revenge leads to escalations in the severity and frequency of violence. Riak explained that for people in his community, "If you get stabbed, all that runs in your mind is revenge. But, in the end, you may not find the exact guy who stabbed you, so you'll do the same thing to someone else."

In his work on gangs in Cairo, Lewis (2011) explained the importance for young people to stake a claim to manhood amid racism, structural violence, and prolonged displacement. But violence and harassment from gangs themselves are another factor. Many of the people we spoke with in 2019 explained that as teenage boys begin to experience the ill effects of gangs—robbery, emasculating insults or threats, or physical attacks (targeted or mistaken)—they feel ashamed and powerless. To regain their sense of manliness, they joined a group: "the teenagers, they have a mentality, if they get beaten, they'll want to join a group. If the gangs beat an older person, he'll just ignore them. But a teenager, if he's beaten, he'll want revenge. He can't ignore what happened." Salwa and Mariam, two Nuba Sudanese women with teenage sons, explained how gang members use emasculating insults to engage youth. Members invite teenage boys who pass them on the street to hang out with them. If the boys ignore them, the members say things like "You're a pussy *(nyao)*" or "You're scared and not a man." While the gangs that young Sudanese and South Sudanese men formed in 2006 were created to serve social purposes and to provide a haven from the structural violence, anti-Black racism, and disrespect affecting their lives, the forms of masculinity that developed in these later groups came to resemble what are often considered hypermasculine norms to "escape reality for an evening" (an important function they still serve).

Sudanese Civil Wars and Inherited Masculine Norms

Gender research tells us that gender norms are passed on to children by their families, peer groups, social institutions, and other sociohistorical processes. These norms are interpreted and internalized by individuals, but individuals also "reconstruct" these norms by putting their own subjective interpretation on them (UN Women 2013). This means that boys and young men are likely to become men in a way that mirrors the older men around them (Baird 2012). While young Sudanese and South Sudanese men were able to claim respect and project power in an alternative way to traditional Sudanese masculinity, their versions of masculinity did not emerge out of a vacuum. They are inherently shaped by the masculine practices of previous generations, which means that the wars in Sudan and South Sudan have important implications.

Decades of conflict and militarization in the Nuba Mountains and South Sudan have produced and reproduced constructions of hypermasculinity and patriarchal norms that are connected to the use of violence against women and men (Hutchinson 2000). For example, the Sudan People's Liberation Army (SPLA) instilled in recruits a hypermasculine ideology which "glorified the raw of power of guns." The SPLA trainees' graduation song includes the line "your gun is your food; your gun is your wife" (Hutchinson and Jok 2002). During the Second Sudanese Civil War, SPLA commanders used gifts of bride wealth and wives to generate loyalty and consolidate power within the SPLA (Pinaud 2014), and commanders in South Sudan have given soldiers and militias license to loot, pillage, and rape whereby sexual slavery and abduction are accepted as compensation for those participating in the conflict (United Nations 2019). Generally, militarization relies on aggression being connected with performances of masculinity where "being a man" is equated with the willingness to kill (Heilman and Barker 2018). Recurrent violence leads to the construction and reconstruction of more patriarchal and violent masculinities, which then leads to further violence in a mutually reinforcing process (Taylor et al. 2016). Sudanese and South Sudanese men in Cairo raised similar ideas and linked them to the use of violence by gang-affiliated young men. For example, some told me, "We have to acknowledge how the violence we grew up in affects the youth . . . the war becomes part of you," and "[in South Sudan and the Nuba Mountains] if someone doesn't have a gun, he's not a man." Others we interviewed also noted the influence of Egyptian patriarchal norms on constructions of masculinity. They pointed out that men in Egypt "have to be loud," "take what's theirs," and be *gada'*.[3]

Masculinity does not solely account for violence or the social reproduction of gangs. Structural violence and marginalization play a crucial incipient role, as does the need for a source of income, protection, and childhood and adolescent trauma, among many other factors. But the role of masculinity and patriarchal norms is clear. As some boys try masculinizing, they will respond to their circumstances of structural violence and the societal expectation to become "real men" with one of the few choices available to them—gang membership. But due to the ways in which some Sudanese and South Sudanese masculinities, including those present in gang spaces, are connected to the need to project power and dominate, the likelihood of interpersonal violence between individuals associated with these groups remains. While gang violence has tragic effects on Sudanese and South Sudanese refugee communities in Cairo, it is these same communities who are at the forefront of preventing violence. In my research, we documented the extensive grassroots efforts of Sudanese and South Sudanese pastors, community leaders, former gang members, activists, and ordinary people to prevent and interrupt cycles of violence whereby they also demonstrate a different version of manhood to some extent—one that does not require the use of force or the projection of dominance (Miranda and Jacobsen 2020).

But these actions do not exist in a vacuum; they are merely one of the multitude of ways refugee communities organize themselves to resist the various forms of structural and interpersonal violence they face. There is an extensive network of Sudanese community schools that serve Sudanese and South Sudanese students. While families are theoretically entitled to enroll their children in Egyptian public schools, many are reluctant to do so due to racist bullying and abuse, and prefer the community schools despite the challenging conditions of many of them. Between 2017 and 2019, the UNHCR attempted to "mainstream" the Sudanese school population into Egyptian public schools, which included cutting UNHCR support to the Sudanese schools. The communities, however, resisted, and many continued to enroll their children in the Sudanese schools.

Examples of intra- and inter-refugee community support are endless. Community groups, church congregations, and social networks often raise funds to pay for medical expenses or help house individuals and families after they've been evicted, sometimes violently and without justification. A Nuba tribal association runs an after-school football league for youth in its neighborhood, which includes mentorship for teenagers to help them navigate the challenges of growing up in Cairo, that is self-funded through community donations. Despite the structural roadblocks facing refugees trying to open businesses, many find a way, and dozens of cafés, restaurants, grocery stores, and clothing and barber shops are immediately visible in their neighborhoods. The Nuba association puts on periodic cultural events to strengthen community interconnectedness and preserve a cultural renaissance that began in the 1990s as a tool of popular resistance against the brutal onslaught of the regime in Khartoum. Individual acts of solidarity between refugees occur daily. An Eritrean colleague described to me how he and his friends heard an Egyptian taxi driver was harassing an Eritrean woman in the street. They intervened and then arranged temporary free accommodation for the woman, as she had just arrived from Eritrea the same day. Through providing their own community services and daily acts of solidarity, refugee communities find ways to defend themselves against the structural and interpersonal forms of violence affecting their lives. These are not perfect institutions. They often carry with them the contours of the conflicts and gender norms they fled from, but despite their flaws, it is these efforts that we should look to and promote if we're to consider ways to support displaced communities striving to overcome the structural issues affecting their lives.

Notes

1   Anonymized interview with author conducted in June 2016.
2   It is crucial to contextualize tribal conflicts. Conflicts and rivalries are the not the result of "primordial" hatreds. Ethnic identities were quite fluid and, until the 1980s, Dinka and Nuer were heavily intermarried and bound together by a shared ancestry and an agro-pastoral economy (Hutchinson and Jok 2002). However, continued conflict and militarization have hardened identities and fostered extreme polarization. More crucially, "ethnic difference" has continually been exploited and instrumentalized by political–military "entrepreneurs" throughout the wars in Sudan and South Sudan in order to recruit and mobilize support (DeWaal 2015).
3   *Gada'*, when it refers to a man (it can also be used to refer to a woman), means a man who will always be there for his friends, defends them without question at a moment's notice, is honorable and respected, and protects his sisters, wife, and other female relatives.

Works Cited

Ahmed, A. 2010. "'I Need Work!': The Multiple Roles of the Church, Ranking and Religious Piety among Domestic Workers in Egypt." *Asia Pacific Journal of Anthropology* 11, no. 3–4: 362–77.

Baird, A. 2012. "The Violent Gang and the Construction of Masculinity among Socially Excluded Young Men." *Safer Communities* 11, no. 4: 179–90.

———. 2018. "Becoming the 'Baddest': Masculine Trajectories of Gang Violence in Medellín." *Journal of Latin American Studies* 50, no. 1: 183–210.

De Waal, A. 2015. *The Real Politics of the Horn of Africa: Money, War, and the Business of Power*. Cambridge, UK: Polity.

Elsaket, I. 2017. "Jungle Films in Egypt: Race, Anti-Blackness, and Empire." *Arab Studies Journal* 25, no. 2: 8–32.

Forcier, N.I. 2009. *Divided at the Margins: A Study of Young Southern Sudanese Refugee Men in Cairo, Egypt*. Cairo: Center for Migration and Refuge Studies, American University in Cairo.

Heilman, B., and G. Barker. 2018. *Masculine Norms and Violence: Making the Connections*. Report. Washington, D.C.: Promundo-US.

Hutchinson, S.E. 2000. "Nuer Ethnicity Militarized." *Anthropology Today* 16, no. 3 (June): 6–13.

Hutchinson, S.E., and J.K. Jok. 2002. *Gendered Violence and the Militarization of Ethnicity: A Case Study from South Sudan in Post-colonial Subjectivities in Africa*. London and New York: Zed Books.

Jacobsen, K., M. Ayoub, and A. Johnson. 2012. "Remittances to Transition Countries: The Impact on Sudanese Refugee Livelihoods in Cairo." Working Paper No. 2, Center for Migration and Refugee Studies. Cairo: American University in Cairo.

Lewis, T. 2011. "'Come, We Kill What Is Called "Persecution Life"': Sudanese Refugee Youth Gangs in Cairo." *Oxford Monitor of Forced Migration* 1, no. 1: 78–92.

Miranda, P. 2018. *Getting by on the Margins: Sudanese and Somali Refugees in Cairo. A Case Report of Refugees in Towns*. Boston: Feinstein International Center, Friedman School of Nutrition Science and Policy, Tufts University.

Miranda, P., and K. Jacobsen. 2020. "The Cowardly Man Raises His Children: Refugee Gang Violence and Masculine Norms in Cairo." Report, Refugees in Towns Project. Boston: Feinstein International Center, Tufts University.

Pinaud, C. 2014. "South Sudan: Civil War, Predation and the Making of a Military Aristocracy." *African Affairs* 113, no. 451: 192–211.

Rowe, M. 2006. "Performance and Representation: Masculinity and Leadership at the Cairo Refugee Demonstration." Paper presented at the 4th Annual Forced Migration Postgraduate Student Conference, University of East London, March 18–19, 2006.

Taylor, A.Y., T. Moura, J.L. Scabio, E. Borde, J.S. Afonso, and G. Barker. 2016. "'This Isn't the Life for You': Masculinities and Nonviolence in Rio de Janeiro, Brazil." Results from the International Men and Gender Equality Survey (IMAGES) with a focus on urban violence. Washington, D.C. and Rio de Janeiro: Promundo.

United Nations. 2019. "Report of the Commission on Human Rights in South Sudan." A/HRC/40.CRP.1. February 20. United Nations Human Rights Council.

UN Women. 2013. "Making Women Count: An Annual Publication on Gender and Evaluation." UN Women Multi Country Office for India, Bhutan, Sri Lanka, and Maldives.

32

POLICING WOMEN'S SEXUAL ECONOMIES IN DOWNTOWN CAIRO
STUDENTS AND THEIR BROTHEL FRIENDS IN COLONIAL TIMES

HANAN HAMMAD

On April 2, 1915, twenty-eight-year-old Mohammad Effendi Khalil arrived in Cairo from his hometown al-Mansura to stay in the al-Mu'ayyid Hotel on Clot Bey Street in downtown Cairo. Despite his choice to stay in the heart of the entertainment and commercial sex district, Khalil did not make the trip to enjoy himself with the leisure opportunities that downtown offered. Khalil came to Cairo to kill Sultan Hussein Kamil (r. 1914–17), whom the British had installed as a sultan under their protectorate. In the late afternoon of April 8, Khalil approached the sultan's parade on 'Abdin Street. Khalil pretended to throw a bunch of red roses toward the sultan while shooting bullets from his pistol, aiming at the sultan's heart. The first shot hit the sultan's vehicle's tire, causing the car to veer off the road and saving the sultan's life. Khalil was arrested and confessed that he believed that Sultan Hussein Kamil had betrayed Egypt when he accepted the British protectorate and praised the British occupation, despite all the injustices the British had inflicted on Egyptians (al-Kilani 1963, 118). On the same day that Khalil's shots missed Sultan Hussein Kamil, a violent confrontation broke out a few meters from the incident among Australian soldiers in the brothel area in Wagh al-Birka Street. The violence expanded and the police couldn't restore order. The Australian soldiers resisted the Egyptian police and fired several shots. They injured four policemen, among other citizens, and burned several properties. With additional forces from firefighters and police, the Cairo authorities arrested fifty soldiers. In July of that same year, drunken British soldiers entered a brothel on Wagh al-Birka in the daytime. Following an argument with sex workers, the soldiers threw a few women through windows and set the brothel on fire (al-Kilani 1963, 172). Between politically motivated violence and overwhelming foreign imperial forces, policing downtown Cairo proved a challenging task that the authorities, I argue, pursued on the backs of working women's bodies.

This chapter focuses on policing downtown Cairo against the backdrop of hosting both the country's largest brothel industry and the political turmoil of the first half of the twentieth century. Downtown Cairo—namely, the triangle encompassing today's 'Ataba, Tahrir, and Ramses Squares (also known as Khedival Cairo)—was the first part of the capital city that newcomers saw upon arrival from all the provinces of Upper and Lower Egypt. The area housed 80 percent of Cairene commercial sex work and hosted the types of entertainment venues that provincial Egyptians might not have seen in their hometowns and villages. Expensive sex workers—licensed and unlicensed, European and Egyptian—were concentrated along the upscale and European-influenced Wagh al-Birka Street. Meanwhile, local licensed sex workers offered their services on al-Was'a and Clot Bey Streets. Both commercial sex districts were in downtown Cairo and came under the authority of the Azbakiya, al-Darb al-Ahmar, and al-Muski police stations.

When we discuss Egyptian moralities and their ties to national myths of family and purity—as Abed, Rigot and Noralla, Carreño, and Awadalla do in their chapters in this volume—it is worth remembering that Cairo, in particular, has a very sexualized and eroticized past that informed the intersecting identities of many of the first generation of its postcolonial national "fathers" whom the al-Sisi regime references in its propaganda. Far from being morally pure family men and unambiguously upright Muslims, many of the protagonists of Egyptian nationalism's early struggles had their understandings of the "proper" role of the masculine state vis-à-vis "improper" women formed by their interactions with sex workers and the mix of modern and traditional contra-hegemonic practices that grew up in downtown Cairo during the waning years of British rule.

Downtown Cairo emblematized colonialism. The area housed large numbers of European civilians and occupation forces in addition to foreign businesses, the Mixed Court, British military camps, British clubs, and the stores that their soldiers frequented. It should be no surprise, then, that the area witnessed much politically motivated violence and suffered a state of disorder caused by drunken young foreign soldiers, particularly during the First and Second World Wars. For example, a young effendi attempted to assassinate the minister of endowments (*awqaf*), Ibrahim Fathi Pasha, in Cairo Station on September 5, 1915. Sultan Hussein Kamil faced another assassination attempt in downtown Cairo on December 20, 1914. Students of the law school demonstrated against the sultan's visit to their campus in the downtown area on February 17, 1915. The school expelled fifty-four students, banned thirty-one from attending their final exams, and moved its campus to Giza in the following year. Throughout the twentieth century, downtown Cairo evolved as a site of moral and national clashes, a stage for competing nationalist moral ideals and pleasure-seeking habits of consumption. In the process, the authorities intensified the policing of working-class women in that sleepless triangle in order to "contain deviant behaviors" while ignoring the women's need for public safety.

State regulation of commercial sex, following the British invasion in 1882, designated certain spaces in downtown Cairo—including in Azbakiya, al-Darb al-Ahmar, and al-Muski—as red-light districts. Two particular places became known as brothels: al-Wasʿa and Wagh al-Birka. Those particular areas had a more extended history of commercial sex before regulation emerged. Colonial authorities increased the number of police stations in Cairo from eleven to fourteen in the 1890s and designated most of the new stations to serve the downtown area. For example, one police section served the al-Muski area, which was about half of a square kilometer. Another section served the Azbakiya area, which did not exceed two square kilometers. A third section served the adjacent neighborhood of al-Darb al-Ahmar. The latter did not exceed 2.8 square kilometers (see table 32.1). The dense population and many European businesses and residents provoked heavy policing directed primarily at Egyptians from the working classes and national activist backgrounds.

The British officials controlling the Cairo police adopted criminalizing discourses against the Egyptian working classes, particularly those engaged in commercial sex. They also expressed racist moralistic views against middle-class men. Russell Pasha, the head of the Cairo police, suggested that 99 percent of middle-class Egyptian men consorted with clandestine sex workers and that working-class men used licensed sex workers. He favored the closing of the licensed quarter downtown and moving the brothel area to the outskirts of the city. He wrote, "I would

Table 32.1. The distribution of police sections in Cairo in the 1920s

Station	Population	Size in Km²	Density in 1 Km²	Inhabited houses
Azbakiya	69013	1.9	36323	3148
al-Darb al-Ahmar	80676	2.8	28813	6371
Bab al-Sha'riya	76943	1.1	4504	4194
'Abdin	78974	17.1	4618	4617
al-Muski	2577	.5	51552	1894
al-Sayyida Zeinab	103135	4.1	25155	6914
al-Gammaliyya	74731	4.2	17793	5465
Bulaq	121656	14.3	8507	8724
Misr al-Qadima	43703	12.8	3414	2790
al-Wayli	131138	68.6	1912	6354
Shubra	140026	19.1	7331	7471
al-Khalifa	68465	15.2	4504	4194
al-Ahram	—			
Helwan	44155	12.4	3561	—

Source: Wazarat al-Dakhiliya 1928.

Table 32.2. Major sex-work establishments in Azbakiya in 1940

Establishment	Number	Business	Number
Private club	40	Print house	67
Bar	129	Café	210
Pension (lodging)	30	Hotel	62
Theater	4	Cinema	14
Dancing hall	6	Dancing school	1
Pharmacy	37	Medical clinic	221
Hospital	5	High school	6
Elementary school	14	Ilzami school	4

Source: Sharif al-Din 1941, 33

Table 32.3. Registered sex workers and licensed brothels in Azbakiya

Year	Sex workers	Brothels	Year	Sex workers	Brothels
1928	495	88	1935	472	90
1929	532	99	1936	458	90
1930	656	99	1937	399	90
1931	344	98	1938	365	90
1932	478	98	1939	275	50
1933	495	73	1940	335	38
1934	472	73			

Source: Sharif al-Din 1941, 25.

maintain a purely native licensed prostitution quarter on the outskirts to meet the demand of the native population until the time that education and civilization make it possible to do away with licensed prostitution altogether" (Russell Pasha 1927). Nevertheless, downtown Cairo kept its brothels until an official decision abolished sex work altogether in 1949.

Policing the downtown continued to pose a challenge to authorities, residents, and visitors alike. While colonial administrators did not miss an opportunity to complain about the problem while linking disorder to the brothels, everybody in the brothel area took security seriously and took their own safety into account when visiting it, including customers and sex workers. I focus here on security and public order in downtown Cairo's red-light district, noting that I will not discuss state regulation of sex work, such as registration and health inspection procedures. I do not discuss the power hierarchy or give the area's social history but, rather, pay particular attention to attempts at securitizing the area in order to attract enough customers. Security of the brothel area became a concern of customers who cared about receiving service for a fair price in a safe place, sex workers who cared about continuing their businesses and maintaining safety, and the state, whose primary concern was public security and order (but which increasingly became preoccupied with morality and social control).

Effendiya in the Land of Students' Friends

Few Egyptian intellectuals dared to speak openly about their firsthand experiences and the lore of the red-light district that had attracted them in their youth. Notable playwright Tawfiq al-Hakim (1898–1987) opened up about the moral dilemma of his generation of nationalist effendis coming of age and formulating their world views about women, love, and sex in the early twentieth century. Effendis, or *effenddiya*, is a social category that emerged in the early twentieth century meaning educated Egyptian middle-class men. The group incorporated a wide range of modern men from various socioeconomic backgrounds: those who were literate and wore European clothing, and well-educated members of the intelligentsia and bourgeoisie, working as bureaucrats, technocrats, teachers, journalists, professionals, and public intellectuals. In his lengthy interviews with novelist Gamal al-Ghitani, published in the *Akhir sáa* and *al-Sharq al-Awsat* periodicals in 1983, al-Hakim talked about his sexual experiences in the brothels when he was in high school. He wrote, "We started to know women who were available to us in those dark places in Wagh al-Birka and Clot Bey Streets whenever we managed to save ten piasters on Friday night. . . . Since we went to those licensed houses, we learned about real sexual contact with women. We used to sneak in [those houses], lest our disciplining supervisors or those who were willing to disgrace us see us" (al-Ghitani 1998, 47). Al-Hakim acknowledges the contradicting emotions experienced by his generation of young effendis. Their feelings fluctuated between romantic love, desires for masturbation, frequenting the brothel, reading serious literature with public pride, and exchanging pornographic texts in secret.

Maintaining secrecy and fearing social exposure were not the only concerns of those young men. They also needed to feel safe in the brothels. One year before his death in 1990, the prominent Egyptian intellectual Dr. Louis 'Awad published his memoir *Awraq al-'umr* (Papers of Lifetime). In a shocking confession, 'Awad gave a detailed account of his periodic visits to the brothels in downtown Cairo after arriving from his hometown al-Minya as a college student in the 1930s. Awad wrote, "Just crossing the doors of one of these licensed houses triggered fear, anxiety, and terror. I needed strong encouragement from my companions." 'Awad spoke of a generation of provincial effendis, coming to the capital city for education, who could not resist the lure of downtown Cairo and its red-light areas. Young effendis who frequented the area adopted certain practices to assure themselves safe visits. They went to brothels in groups and avoided dark alleys. 'Awad continues, "We were reluctant to go to these places individually; one or two experienced students would lead us. We roamed the area in a group and went only into well-lit sections."

Sex workers took it upon themselves to encourage young effendis to try their services. Native, licensed sex workers who followed official regulations (e.g., registration, periodic health examinations) were mostly concentrated in the al-Was'a area and catered to clients with limited financial capacity. Sex workers' keenness to sustain business while maintaining security and order contradicted the moralist discourses that depicted sex workers as dangerous, mysterious women and the brothel as a wild place. They catered to a growing number of young effendi customers who had limited experience, limited financial means, and lots of hesitation. Sex workers in the licensed brothels provided their services in shops whose doors opened to the street. They dropped a curtain for privacy during the encounters. That spatial structure provided the customer with a sense of security since patrolling policemen and others could hear him easily if he screamed for help. That spatial structure did not start with state regulation in the 1880s. The French introduced it during Napoleon's campaign in Egypt (1798–1801) with the intent to protect French soldiers who patronized local sex workers.

Sex workers catered to the growing market of effendi customers. Some of them promoted their businesses by posting written signs outside the brothels, proclaiming themselves as *sadiqat al-talaba* (students' friends). In commercial sex, publicity entailed conveying a bargain: good service for a low price in a safe place. Friendship was also meant as a gesture at the inexperienced young men's anxiety and fears, as al-Hakim and 'Awad confessed. Fatima Rushdi, the theater star, used the same phrase when she provided students with discounted tickets for her matinée shows.

Aside from native Egyptians, imperial soldiers (including the British) frequented the area and did not restrict themselves to the European sex workers in Wagh al-Birka. Soldiers also used the cheap sex workers who offered their services in lower-class brothels in small shops that opened onto alleyways. The shops' doors were covered with curtains, behind which sexual encounters took place. Since sitting down compromised clients' privacy, they had sex standing. The curtains permitted a quick escape and, should they face an unsafe situation, allowed them to scream for help and be heard. Prices were posted outside the shop to minimize bargaining and misunderstandings due to language barriers. The British imperial soldiers flocked to the brothels, although the British military authorities tried to keep them away from the area. To contain the spread of venereal diseases among the imperial troops, the British headquarters in Egypt banned their soldiers from going to the native brothels in al-Was'a, which received mostly Egyptian clients. The British also banned imperial soldiers from frequenting particular areas of the Europeanized section, Wagh al-Birka. British authorities installed street signs marking the line beyond which soldiers were not allowed to go and expelled some sex workers from the downtown area. After the Second World War broke out, the number of registered brothels in Azbakiya dropped from ninety houses in 1937 to only thirty-eight in 1940. The number of registered sex workers in the area dropped from 399 to 335 during the same period. Abolitionist campaigns adopting moral and nationalist discourses against licensed sex work intensified in the late 1930s. However, wartime brought more imperial forces to Cairo and expanded the market for commercial sex work despite frequent curfews. The decrease in the number of licensed brothels and registered sex workers during those years may reflect the expansion of clandestine commercial sex following the decision of the Health Department on March 26, 1938 not to register new sex workers and brothels (Sharif al-Din 1941, 24). Secret brothels may have kept customers from public scrutiny while sex workers escaped registration.

The colonial military authorities' challenge was to keep soldiers healthy while maintaining local women available to serve their sexual desires. Venereal diseases (VD) were the excuse for the policing of working women rather than soldiers. During the Second World War, the British stationed 127,000 soldiers in Cairo and established seven medical clinics to treat VD. Members of the British Medical Brigade would sit outside pubs and brothels in downtown Cairo to hand soldiers prophylactics, boxes of ointment, and booklets containing information on the danger of VD, with instructions on medical protections (Bakr 2001 [1900–51], 34). The British army headquarters designated a specific section of the brothel area in Wagh al-Birka to serve soldiers during the Second World War, which consisted of ten houses managed by twenty-nine madams (Sharif al-Din 1941, 22). In one year, 623 soldiers reported that they had contracted VDs due to their encounters with sex workers in the area.

The reports triggered the intensive regulation of women's health, including subjecting women working in cafés and bars to health examinations. Investigations revealed that 164 sex workers and fourteen waitresses had VDs, yet there was no evidence indicating whether the women had transmitted to soldiers or vice versa. To appease the British officials' complaints, the Egyptian police launched a campaign in 1939 that led to raids on twenty unlicensed houses and the arrest of 371 women for streetwalking. When the military authorities issued martial law to shut down the brothels in Wagh al-Birka in 1942 and 1943, sex workers kept plying their trade and provided services to soldiers and others in the backseats of carriages (Bakr 2001 [1900–51], 34–35).

The Colonial State and Policing Women

Under the city's colonial administration, the Cairo police adopted discourses that dehumanized sex workers. Russell Pasha described the al-Wasaʿa brothel area as composed of "narrow and crowded lanes [which] reminded one of a zoo, with its painted harlots sitting like beasts of prey behind the iron grilles of their ground-floor brothels, while a noisy crowd of low-class natives, interspersed with soldiers in uniform and sight-seeing tourists, made their way along the narrow lanes" (Russell Pasha 1949 [1902–46], 179). When Cairo became packed with thousands of troops during the First World War, the police launched campaigns in the poor neighborhoods of downtown Cairo. In one set of raids over a couple of nights, police rounded up about one hundred men, whom Russell called "pests" (Russell Pasha 1949 [1902–46], 180). Police took advantage of the state of emergency and martial law declared during wartime to imprison "suspicious-looking" Egyptian men and women. According to Russell Pasha, his boss Harvey Pasha decided to "take drastic action to clear up outside the scores of free-lance girls and catamite boys who had sprung up outside the licensed quarters. One of his first orders under martial law was to establish an internment camp in Hilmiya [area] and to throw into it any of these long-haired degenerates that we could find" (Russell Pasha 1949 [1902–46], 180). We find at least one press report complaining that police arrested women randomly, assuming they were sex workers. According to the report, policemen lacked proper training, arresting women walking with their husbands and brothers and eavesdropping on people in their homes (al-Watan 1916). Police anxiety over women in downtown Cairo led to frequent arrests. In 1932, for example, police arrested 2,497 women in Azbakiya for allegedly streetwalking and urging the public to commit adultery (fisq) (Wazarat al-Dakhiliya 1933 [1932]).

Staffing police in downtown Cairo became a priority to protect imperial soldiers during wartime and to criminalize local women. For example, eleven Egyptian officers, four European and five Egyptian constables, forty-seven sergeants, and 282 rank-and-file soldiers served under the sheriff's command of the Azbakiya Police Section. Two of the officers served as vice police, eighty-four soldiers served as night patrolmen, while seventy-six did so during the day (Sharif al-Din 1941, 4). Additionally, the authorities established a police station and an office for the Vices Police Squad inside the brothel area in Wagh al-Birka in November 1940. The squad force included two European female constables (Sharif al-Din 1941, 20). The police station included fifty rank-and-file patrol soldiers and three on-duty officers under the command of a police chief.

Beginning in 1935, special police forces were designated to monitor commercial sex with the intention of protecting public morality and fighting vice. In 1937, those forces became a police department known as the Morality Police (al-Adab) (Ansari 1990, 16). Azbakiya's vice squad consisted of one officer, one European head constable, two European women ranking constables, one clerk, two soldiers, and one informant *(mukhbir)*. Staffing Cairo police with Europeans during the colonial period was common, as the commander of the Egyptian police was the British Russell Pasha. Having European women in the Vice Police Department and in the Azbakiya Police Section, in particular, responded to practical needs such as linguistic skills. Encouraged by the Capitulation protections (specially negotiated laws protecting European residents of Egypt), Europeans operated and worked in clandestine brothels in downtown Cairo. The Squad Police Office took care of their registration and the granting or canceling of sex work permits. Sex workers paid fees to obtain these licenses, and their fees formed a substantial financial resource for the Cairo Police (see table 32.4). From the table, we find that fees for issuing licenses continued to bring in income to the Cairo police even after the government suspended issuing licenses to new brothels in 1939. In 1942, moralist campaigns seeking the abolition of commercial sex resulted in a decision to shut down brothels outside Cairo and the capital cities of the provinces.

The vice police targeted mostly native Egyptian women rather than unlicensed Europeans. Police arrested 4,083 women, all locals, for

Table 32.4 Fees collected by the police from licensed sex workers

Year	Amount in LE	Year	Amount in LE
1933	2,698.755	1939	4,023.9
1934	3,497.72	1940	847.949
1935	4,680.339	1941	4,592.535
1936	4,567.827	1942	2265.51
1937	3,455.7	1943	7,283.32
1938	4,6882.71		

Source: Wazarat al-Dakhiliya 1944.

working without a license and sent them for medical examinations in which 1,175 women tested positive for VD. The Squad Police also handled the registration of women working in bars (277 women, all locals), arrested the unregistered ones, and sent them for medical checkups in which ninety-seven waitresses were reported to have VD. Heavy policing and the suspension of any application for new brothel licenses did not deter women from pursuing sex work due to wartime circumstances. Ninety more women applied for waitress licenses in Azbakiya, yet Azbakiya policemen still urged the government to move the brothel to Cairo's peripheries to maintain public security and morality until sex work could be abolished altogether. Police officers in Azbakiya adopted the same moral argument that abolitionists had used in the press and public discourse since the turn of the century. In his annual report, Azbakiya police officer Mikkawi Sharaf al-Din wrote: "We urgently press for the abolition of prostitution or moving those prostitutes from the area to protect family honor and protect the eyes of male and female youths and even the eyes of adults from seeing these terrible, disgusting images moving around streets" (Sharif al-Din 1941, 26).

The government was not open to the idea of moving the brothels because a previous experience of moving the quarter of Zinhum (not far from downtown) to the peripheries in Abbasiya had led to the emergence of illegal brothels around both the old and the new areas. Police discourses expressed organizational anxiety over maintaining security and public order while not getting involved in high politics. Local police served mostly to appease the colonial authorities' concerns over the safety and health of their troops, thus criminalizing more native working-class people. The area continued as a hotbed for protest, and politically motivated violence intensified in the 1940s. Among many examples, on March 22, 1948, Ahmad Bey al-Khazindar, chief of the Cairo Criminal Court, was assassinated on his way to the morning court. In the following month of April 1948, there were two attempts to bomb Mustafa al-Nahhas's house. Another assassination attempt on al-Nahhas and Fu'ad Sirag al-Din Pasha took place on November 11, 1948.

Amid political unrest, the government abolished commercial sex work and ordered the closing of all brothels in Cairo in 1949. Two years later, the law criminalized sex work. Thus, the postcolonial order ushered in the criminalization of sex workers, with intensive scientific discourses to medicalize sex workers as emotionally, mentally, and psychologically abnormal and perverted. Azbakiya continued to be an unofficial center for commercial sex, and police continued criminalizing working women, raiding their homes, and arresting them for streetwalking. A police report in 1952 depicted the population of the area in the following terms: "Parts of Azbakiya that used to be designated for prostitution before abolition continued to be a home for pimps, thugs, and fallen women who used to be registered sex workers and now continue their trade secretly" (Wazarat al-Dakhiliya 1953). Two years later, Cairo police used the power of martial law (order no. 15, March 1952) to send eighteen men and thirteen women into permanent detention without a trial, intending to isolate individuals with too large a criminal record to hope to reintegrate them into society after temporary imprisonment.

The January 2011 uprising reminded us that the criminalization of women's bodies has long been ingrained in the Egyptian security regime. Cases of virginity screening, among other horrific forms of sexual violations of female protestors, proved that policing women's bodies goes beyond preserving moral ideals—no matter how conservative these might be—toward preserving the security regime itself.

Works Cited

Ansari, Nasir. 1990. *Tarikh anzimat al-shurta fi Misr*. Cairo: Dar El Shorouk.

Bakr, Abd al-Wahab. 2001. *Mugtama' al-Qahira al-sirri: 1900–1951*. Cairo: al-'Arabi li-l-Nashr wa l Tawzi'.

al-Bigha' fi al-Qahira: Mash igtima'i wa-dirasa iklinikiya. 1961. Cairo: al-Markaz al-Qawmi li-l-Buhuth al-Igtima'iya wa-l-Gina'iya.

al-Ghitani, Gamal. 1998. *Tawfiq al-Hakim yatadhakkar*. Cairo: al-Maglis al-A'la li-l-Thaqafa.

al-Kilani, Muhammad Sayyid. 1963. *Al-Sultan Husayn Kamil fatra muzlima fi tarikh Misr: 1914–1917*. Cairo: Dar al-Qawmiya al-'Arabiya li-l-Tiba'a.

Russell Pasha, Thomas. 1927. *Cairo City Police Annual Report 1926*. Cairo: Government Press.

———. 1949. *Egyptian Service: 1902–1946*. London: John Murray.

Sharif al-Din, Mikkawi. 1941. *Taqrir 'an halat al-amn al-'am fi qism al-Azbakiya sanat 1940*. Cairo: Matba'at al-Ma'arif wa-Maktabat Misr.

al-Watan. 1916. "Al-Bulis wa al-adab al-'umumiyya." August 14.

Wazarat al-Dakhiliya (Ministry of Interior). 1927. *Al-taqrir al-sanawi li-bulis al-Qahira 'an 'am 1926*. Cairo: al-Matba'a al-Amiriya.

———. 1928. *Bulis madinat al-Qahira: al-taqrir al-sanawi li-sanat 1927*. Cairo: al-Matba'a al-Amiriya.

———. 1933. *Bulis madinat al-Qahira: al-taqrir al-sanawi li-'am 1932*. Cairo: al-Matba'a al-Amiriya.

———. 1944. *Bulis madinat al-Qahira: al-taqrir al-sanawi li-sanatayy 1942 wa 1943*. Cairo: al-Matba'a al-Amiriya.

———. 1953. *al-Taqrir al-sanawi li-bulis madinat al-Qahira 'an 'am 1952*. Cairo: al-Matba'a al-Amiriya.

INDEX

Note: Page numbers in italics indicate illustrations; those with a *t* indicate tables.

Abaza, Mona 225
Abd al-ʿAl, Ali 119–20
Abd al-ʿAl, Khalid 368, 373–74
Abd al-Hafiz, Shadi 133
Abd al-Hayy, Usama 135
Abd al-Qadir, Shukri 395
Abd al-Shakur, Raʿfat (aka Khanufa) 391–94, *393*
Abd al-Tawwab, Mohammad Ayman 148
Abdel-Fattah, Alaa 186n5
Abdel-Fattah, Esraa 186n5
Abdelrahman, Dina 63
Abdin, Ahmad Zaki 206, 210, 213–14
Abdul-Magd, Zeinab 24–25, 205–206
Abed, Sara Soumaya 15, 35–48, 97
Abo Bakr, Ammar *429*
"abolitionist desecuritization" 5, 9–11, 26–29, 456, 459
abortion, 16, 125–28, 131–34, 137–38
Abou-Eida clan 413–14, 418

Abou Hashima, Ahmed 63
Abourahme, Nasser 127
Aboutrika (soccer player) 171–72
Abu Khaled, Maryam 69
Abul-Magd, Zeinab 24–25, 100–101, 205, 367–75
Abu-l-Naga, Abdullah 360
Abu Qarn *see* Izbat Abu Qarn
activism 11, 29n1; queer digital, 95–106; urban, 22, 313–14, 401–408, 424–25
ACUD *see* Administrative Capital for Urban Development
ʿaddad cody (prepaid utility meters) 320, 323
al-Adham, Mawada 37, 39–40, 43–48, 49n18, 105
al-Adli, Abd al-Wahab 100–101
al-Adli, Habib 393, 394
Administrative Capital for Urban Development (ACUD) 210, 211, 213–14

African Charter on Human and People's Rights 282n1
African Charter on the Rights and Welfare of the Child 282n1
African Cup of Nations (2019) 119–20, 159, 160, 165–68, 170–72
agrarian urbanism 10
Ahmad, Wa'il 133
Ahmed, Mohamed 25, 389–97
Ahmed, Rania 159–72
AIDS 16, 111, 125–27, 129–31
Ain Shams neighborhood 272–73, 277–82, 435, 438
Alabbar, Mohamed 211, 224
Alexander, Jacqui 4
'Allam, Magdi 395
'Allam, Sami 374
Alshikh, Turki 164–65
alternative families 162
Amar, Paul, 1–29, 270; on *Cairo Cosmopolitan* 3, 248; on classphobia 171, 270; on desecuritization 270; on feminism and revolutionary feminism 134; on "human security states" 42, 118–20, 126, 270, 319; on hypervisibility 42, 354, 377; on "infranationalism" 134; on masculinity 185; on military capitalism 205; on moral panic 42; on moral securitization or moral cleansing 49, 119, 134, 270; on neoliberalism, 319; on nightlife economies and geographies 289; on Queen Boat case 44; on "queering" 47; on sexual harassment or assault 42, 382; on thug discourse 179, 354; on unruly children and youth 12, 126, 165
Amin, Heba 239–40
Amon, Joseph 126
Anarche collective 314
Anti-Cyber and Information Technology Crimes Law (2018) 105
antiquities market 419

antiretroviral treatments (ARVs) 16, 125–27, 129–31
Arab Spring (2011) 64–65, 161–62, 167, 200, 206–207, 313; *see also* January 25, 2011 Revolution
Arefin, Mohammed Rafi 116–17
Arese, Nicholas Simcik 21–22
'asabiya (social solidarity) 222
'Ashur, Yassir 395
'ashwa'iyat (informal communities) 23, 310, 379; infrastructure in 109, 116, 317–24; nonviolent politics in 389, 394–97; relocation projects for 327–35, 368; "statization" of 321–22; translation of 324n2; zoning laws and 355
Askar Kazibun 84
al-Asmarat, 327–35, 373–75
assemblage 253–56
Aswan High Dam 21, 286, 361
'Awad, Louis 454, 455
Awadalla, Ahmed 20
awqaf (religious endowments) 110, 117–18
al-Azhar Islamic Research Academy 125–26
al-Azhar University 110, 192

al-Badri, Ahmad 213
Bahgat, Ahmed 57–58
Bahgat, Hossam 62, 63
Bahrain 222–23
Baldwin, James 266
baltaga ("thuggery") 354–56, 377–87; benefits of 383–85; deconstructing of 389–97; definitions of 181, 354; informal policing by 186n9, 413–21; laws against 390–91; nonviolent politics versus 389, 394–97; police control of 379, 381, 384–85; rise of 378–81
baltagiya ("thugs") 9, 24–25, 266, 353–64, 377–87; definitions of 183, 185n3, 354; etymology of 397n1; extortion

by 182; hackers as 302; looting by 396–97; "manhood" of 436–45; political 382–83; as privatized enforcers 177, 353–54, 378, 382–83; soccer fans as 169, 171; stereotypes of 386; subjectivities of 177–85

El-Baradei, Mohamed 161

Bateman, Anthony 269

Battle of the Camels (2011) 182–83, 186n8

Bayat, Aset 165

Bedayaa (NGO) 99, 105

Bedouins 304

behavioral planning and management 295–305

Bell, Jennifer 116–17

Berlant, Lauren 236–38

Berman, Marshall 200

binary 4, 14; non-binary methodology 4, 14; crime vs security 9, 26, 240; informal vs planned 8, 22; public vs private 7, 267; revolution vs counterrevolution 183–85; slum vs enclave 17, 23; thugs vs police 24, 397, 426; victimhood vs agency 45; virtual vs real 15

blackface 69, 73, 78

Black Lives Matter (BLM) movement 69; see also racial issues

Blackness and Antiblackness 2, 15, 21, 28, 69–78, 291, 435

Blackwater 370

bodily integrity and autonomy 38–39, 48, 99, 117, 247, 357

Borham, Ahmad 22, 309–14

"broken window" crime theory 115

Bulaq Abu al-'Ila district 18, 264–65, 309

Bulaq General Hospital 226

Cairo 52 Legal Research Institute 97

Cairo Gate compound 224

Cairo Institute for Human Rights Studies (CIHRS) 405, 409n37

Cairo–Ismailia Desert Road 372–73

Cairo Ring Road 144, 151, 310, 312, 362, 381

Cairo 2050 Plan 151–52, 153n2, 225, 312, 314n1, 405

Camel Battle see Battle of the Camels

Capital City Partners Fund 211

capitalism, military 19, 205–16, 367–75

Catholic Relief Services 276

censorship 59, 61, 64, 117–18, 394–95, 428

Central Agency for Public Mobilization and Statistics (CAPMAS) 328–29

Central Security Forces 358

Certeau, Michel de 240, 430

Cheri Media company 64

children and resistance 165

China State Construction Engineering Corporation (CSCEC) 211, 216n1

Christians see Coptic Christians

Civil Code 341–43, 348n4

class issues 46, 170, 239, 264; "ecological sanitization" and 145–48; intersectionality of 40–42; LGBTQ+ community and 261, 266–70; "new" social contracts and 191–202; nonviolent politics and 389, 394–97; sex workers and 453–57; TikTok women and 47; urbanism and 191–94

clientelism, 195, 209, 321, 379–80, 391

Code Napoléon 341

Cold War 427

colonialism 28, 70, 77

commodity fetishism 396–97

community schools 273–82

Confederation of African Football (CAF) 160

consumerism 225–26, 396

contract law 23–24, 339–47

Convention on the Rights of the Child (CRC) 282n1

convivial sociabilities 19–21
Coptic Christians 9, 26, 227, 401–408
court system 23–24, 340, 343–47, 348n2
COVID-19 pandemic 19–20, 233–38,
    277; social media and 45, 46; sports
    events during 170
Crenshaw, Kimberlé 41
criminalization 4–5, 12, 28, 43, 390; of
    sexuality and health 46, 96–103,
    131–34; of slum populations 360; of
    women 29, 114–15, 459–60
critical security studies 5
cybercrime law (2018) 105; TikTok
    women and 36–40, 43

Dean, Tim 267–68
de Certeau, Michel 240, 430
"decrim" 29
deed registration 343–47
"densityphilia" 7, 17–19
"depoliticized criminality" 26, 397
Digital Egypt project 371–72
digital securitization 95–106
Dillon, Michael 385
dispositif 27, 424–27, 429, 430
domestic workers 20, 211, 247–56,
    279, 439
"Dubaisation" 19, 225; see also real
    estate developments
Duffield, Roberta 18–19, 118, 149,
    205–16, 368

EAAF see Engineering Authority of
    the Armed Forces
"ecological sanitation" 145–48
Economic Reform and Restructuring
    Programme (ERSAP) 55
effenddiya (middle-class men) 184,
    453–57
Egyptian Center for Economic and
    Social Rights 427
Egyptian cinema 69–79, 143–44,
    239, 390

Egyptian Football Association (EFA)
    165, 169
Egyptian Initiative for Personal
    Rights (EIPR), 96, 101, 132, 134,
    407, 427
Egyptian Media Group 56–57, 63
Egyptian Medical Syndicate 135
Egyptian Radio and Television Union
    (ERTU) 56–57
Eisenhower, Dwight D. 145
electric companies 22–23, 317–24,
    331, 417; increased rates by 336n4;
    meter readers of 370–72
elite enclaves 17–19
Elmeshad, Mohamed 15, 55–65, 87
Elostaz, Noha 39
Elsaket, Ifdal 15, 69–79, 144
Elshahed, Mohamed 3, 16–17,
    143–53, 227
Emaar Misr (real estate company) 224,
    227–29
"enforced sovereignties" 24–26,
    377–79, 382–84
"enforcement sovereignties" 24–26
Engineering Authority of the Armed
    Forces (EAAF) 210, 368, 373
entrapment 97–98
environmentalism 4, 146; 'ashwa'iyat
    communities and 116–17; ecolog-
    ical sanitization and 145–48; real
    estate development and 13, 110,
    116–17, 214, 216
Eritrean migrants 434, 445
Ethiopian migrants 434
exile 102, 260–62, 285

Facebook see social media
Fahmy, Khaled 87
Fairmont Hotel incident (2014) 35, 39,
    41–43
Falcon Group International 64,
    370–72
Fallas, Amy 26, 401–408

family values 7, 19–21, 45; cybercrime law on 37–38; Hanem on 48; Tik-Tok women and 105
Fawaz, Mona 8
feminisms 267, 459, 460; "carceral" 270; history of 38, 48n7, 450; Me Too Movement and 269; *see also* gender issues
Filipina workers 211, 248–56
films 69–79, 435; *Birds of Darkness* 239; *Dukkan Shihata* 390; *Hina maysara* 390; *Naduga* 70–79; *Road to the Future* 143–44; *Wadi al-nugum* 70–79
Floyd, George 69
Fonagy, Peter 269
football 159–72, 370, 424
Forcier, N. I. 439
Foucault, Michel 267, 368–69, 387, 424, 425
Fouda, Yosri 60–61
Fraser, Nancy 276
Fuentes Carreño, Miguel A. 16, 125–38
futurity, participatory 21–24

Gabr, Shafik 224
gada' (good man) 183, 184, 443, 445n3
Gaines, Jane 85
al-Gamʻiya al-Sharʻiya (NGO) 413
gangs 433–45; *see also baltagiya*
gender issues 38, 48n7, 129, 267–70, 450; domestic workers and 211, 247–56, 279, 439; educational system and 277–78, 282n1; gang manhood as 436–45; human rights and 407–408; intersectionality of 40–42; racism and 435; sexual harassment as 39, 277–78, 385; sex workers and 28–29, 449–60; *see also* sexual violence
gender reassignment surgery 125–26, 129, 134–37
General Authority for Investment and Free Zones 57, 223–24

gentrification 112, 177–85, 226, 313; "densityphilia" and 17–18; securiti-zation and 116, 374
Gizawi clan 418
Gleed, Fathi 394
Gohar, Mohamed 63
Gomaa, Mohamed Mokhtar 117–18
Gramsci, Antonio 276
Graves, Michael 227
Guirguis, Tina 16, 109–21, 318
Gulf way of life and investments 19, 191, 221–29; *see also* real estate developments

Habersky, Elena 20–21, 77, 273–82
Habil, I. 131–32
Haikal, Usama 62
al-Hakim, Tawfiq 453–55
Hamed, Ahmed 164
Hammad, Hanan 28, 260, 449–60
Hammam, Nadine 428
Hanem, Sherry 47–48
Haram City 295–307
Harb, H. 131–32
Harb, Talaat 73
Harris, Angela 41
Hashim, Mahmud 129
Hashim, Nora 47–48
Hassan, Alia 361
Hassan, Hatem 24, 184, 353–64
Hassan, Islam Khalid 130
Hassan, Wessam 129
"Haussmannization" 22, 260, 311–14, 414–15
health care system 371
Hegazy, Sarah, 35, *101*, 102–103
Hetaba, Amira 20–21, 77, 273–82
hip-hop culture 437
HIV 16, 111, 125–27, 129–31
homophobia 98, 100, 102–106; *see also* LGBTQ+ people
hormone therapy 17, 125–27, 134–37
Hossam, Haneen 37, 48, 105

human rights 168, 184, 250, 427;
censorship and 59; of Coptic
Christians 401, 404–405, 407–
408; domestic workers and 20,
252; LGBTQ+ people and 38, 101;
of refugees 274
"human trafficking" 40, 46
El-Husseiny, Momen 18, 144, 191–202,
227, 368

Ibn Khaldun 222
Ibrahim, Amani 148
Ibrahim Fathi Pasha 451
Ibrahim, Mina 408
Idris, Razan 70
image cycles 81–90
Iman, Adel 239–40
incarceration *see* prison and
imprisonment
Indonesian workers 249
infantilization (political) 173
Informal Settlement Development
Facility 321
Informal Settlements Development
Fund 328–29, 368, 374
Information Systems and Computers
Center 371
"infranationalism" 134
infrastructural violence 22, 309–14
infrastructure 233–41; etymology of
236; neoliberal 317–24; of public
health 126–38; road construction
and 143–53; securitization and
310–13
infrastructure studies 3
International Covenant on Economic,
Social, and Cultural Rights 282n1
International Crisis Group 396
International Monetary Fund (IMF)
13, 55, 322; austerity program of
209, 211; protests against 265;
utility prices and 336n4; *see also*
neoliberalism

internet service 214–15; *see also* social
media
intersectionality 4, 12; of HIV treatments 130; of queer-identified
youth 21; of respectability politics
37; of security network 181; of
sexual violence 269; of TikTok
women 40–42
intersex people 129
Interstate Highway System (US) 145
Iraq War 427
Ismail, Ayman 211
Isma'il Pasha, Khedive 287–89, 414–15
Ismail, Salwa 397n2
Izbat Abu Qarn 26, 389–97

January 25, 2011 Revolution 1–2, 55,
183, 367–68; feminism and 38, 460;
looting during 358–59, 396–97;
Maspero Massacre of 83–84, 199,
402–403; media coverage of 61;
urban activism after 313; urban
militarization after 423–30; *see also*
Arab Spring
Jarman, Derek 261
justice urbanism 10–11

Kabbash, Ibrahim A. 130
kafala (sponsorship) laws 249–50
Kamel, Ramy 26, 402, 404–408
Kamil, Abbas 63
Kamil, Hussein (sultan) 449, 451
Kandil, Hazem 206
Kaplan, Caren 240
Kefaya Movement 161
Kenyan domestic workers 253
Khafaga, Amr 57–58
Khalil, Deena Mahmoud Sobhy 22,
317–24
Khalil, Omnia 17–18, 177–85, 260, 264,
313–14
Khanufa (aka Abd al-Shakur) 391–94,
393

kite flying 19–20, 233–38
Kuwait 222–23; Gulf way of life and 19, 221–29; real estate investors of 24–25, 152

Laclau, Ernesto 378
Lambert, Édouard 341
Lebow, Alisa 91n5
Lefebvre, Henri 191
Leonardo, Zeus 41
Lewis, T. 442
LGBTQ+ people 13, 20–21, 95–106, 259–70; alternative families of 162; class issues and 261, 266–70; criminalization of 104; cruising ethics of 20, 259–70; homophobic attacks on 98, 100, 102–106; human rights of 38, 101; police harassment of 44–46, 97–100; queer theory and 47; Rainbow Flag incident and 101–103; Saleh on 287–93; *see also* transgender people
ligan sha'biya (neighborhood watch groups) 356, 396
Lilleby, Sabrina 20, 247–56, 279
Local Development Ministry 144
Long Live Egypt Fund 328
Lorde, Audre 37, 48

Madbouly, Mostafa 153n2, 206, 314
Madinaty development 193, 197, 200–202, 313
Mahgub, Mohammad Abd al-Salam 358
Majid Al Futtaim Group 224
Managua, Nicaragua 22, 311–12
manhood 436–45; *see also* gender issues
Mansour, Adly 117, 207
"manufactured informality" 23–24, 340, 343–44, 346–47
al-Manzala, Lake 361–62

Marian cult 406
Marshall, Shana 209
marzaqa (livelihood) 332
masculinity 24, 28, 76, 183, 286, 433, 442; and hypermasculinity 42, 443
Mashrou' Leila concert *101*, 101–102
Maspero Massacre (2011) 83–84, 199, 402–403
Maspero Triangle 177–82, *182*, 199, 212, 263–68, 309; gentrification protests at 313–14; Kuwaiti investments in 152; land deeds and 330; relocation project of 329, 405; securitization in 178–80; street vendors of 332–33
Maspero Youth Union (MYU) 26, 402–404
El Masri, Sama 35, *40*
El-Masry, Mahinour 186n5
al-Matariya neighborhood 27, 413–21
al-Matariya Youth Coalition 421
al-Matini, Mahmud 147
megaproject 18, 21, 57, 149–50, 205–15, 224, 368
Mehleb, Ibrahim 153
Me Too Movement 269; *see also* feminisms
middle class *see* class issues
midwives 128
mifepristone 133, 138n2
Mikhail, George 171
militarization, urban 425–30, *429*
military capitalism 19, 205–16, 367–75
Military Production Ministry (MoMP) 371–72
Miranda, Paul 28, 77, 277, 433–45
misoprostol 125, 133
Misr Company for Acting and Cinema 73
Mitchell, Timothy 235, 299–300, 414
modernism 201, 206, 260
Mohammed Ali Pasha 264, 415
Mohie, Mostafa 23, 327–35, 368, 373

Monfleur, Laura 27–28, 423–30
morality police 36, 96, 458
moral panic 36, 42–46, 127
Morsi, Mohamed 60, 208, 223, 406
Mosireen's revolutionary archives
    81–90
Moustafa, Hisham Talaat 195–96, 201
Mubarak, Alaa 393
Mubarak, Gamal 58, 161, 209, 393;
    Vision Cairo 2050 plan of 151–52
Mubarak, Hosni 149, 186n8, 208–
    209; Abed on 49n8; Bahgat and
    57; counterrevolutionaries of 183,
    395; coup of 367; housing projects
    of 358, 379; National Housing
    Program of 297–98; neoliberalism
    of 223; Queen Boat police case
    and 99–100
multiculturalism 221
mumarsa (fixed utility charge)
    319–20, 323
Mursi, Sally 129
Muslim Brotherhood 60–63, 87–88,
    421; Aboutrika and 171; Mansour
    and 117–18; urban activism of
    424–25
Mustafa, Niazi 74, 77
Muthallath Maspero *see* Maspero
    Triangle

NAC *see* New Administrative Capital
Naduga (film) 70–79
al-Naggar, Mohammad 396
Nassar, Aya 19–20, 233–41
Nasser, Gamal Abdel 13, 57, 110,
    192; Coptic Christians and 403;
    housing projects of 264–65, 415;
    modernization under 208
National Association for Change 161
National Council for Women
    (NCW) 40
National Democratic Party (NDP)
    49n8, 382; Bahgat and 58;

dissolution of 207, 321; Vision
    Cairo 2050 plan of 151–52
National Housing Program (NHP)
    297–98, 362–63
Nation's Future Party *(Mostaa'bal
    Watan)* 180
Negritude movement 4
neighborhood groups 198, 356, 396,
    444
neoliberalism 18, 184, 206, 223; com-
    modification of 396; definitions
    of 318; globalized values of 226; of
    Gulf families 222; informal econ-
    omy and 417; infrastructure and
    317–24; military interests and 209;
    securitization and 23, 377; unbun-
    dling of rights by 322–24; urbanism
    and 312; World Bank and 55, 147,
    192, 298–301; *see also* International
    Monetary Fund
New Administrative Capital (NAC)
    18, 205–16, 239, 391; budget for 211;
    plans for 206, 207t, 221–22, 229;
    workforce of 211
New Cairo 195–97, 199–201
New Urban Communities Authority
    (NUCA) 195, 210
Nicaragua 22, 311–12
Nigerian domestic workers 251, 255
Nile City Complex 265
nonviolent politics 389, 394–97
Noralla, Nora 16, 95–106
No Walls project 428–29
Nubians 21, 76–77, 285–93
n-word 291, 434

October Bridge 148–50
Olympic Games 118, 146, 166
Operation Anti-Sexual Harassment
    39
Orascom Housing Communities
    (OHC) 297–307
Ottoman Empire 48n7, 264

pacta sunt servanda (agreements must be kept) 341–42
Palestinians 274
paramilitary forces 8, 10–12, 354; *see also baltagiya*
"participatory futurity" 21–24
Perin, Constance 303
peripheralization 22, 309–14; peripherization versus *309*, 309–10; relocation projects and 328
Persian Gulf investors *see* Gulf way of life
Philippines *see* Filipina workers
"pill politics" 16
police harassment 335, 377, 382, 392–94, 413; social media and 36, 96; of transgender people 98
police informants 178–82, 392–93, 420; *see also* surveillance
policing, informal 186n9, 413–21
pornography 287, 454
Port Said massacre (2012) 160, 163, 168–69, 171
postcolonialism 15, 71, 194, 450, 459–60
precariousness 330–35
Press Regulation Laws (2018) 65
prison and imprisonment 40–47, 64, 87, 102, 104, 114, 161, 163–64, 179, 262, 301, 331, 358, 378–83, 389–93, 404–408, 457–60
property rights 339–47
prostitution 435, 449–60; legal definitions of 44, 45; penalties for 103–104; public toilets and 113; *see also* sex workers
public health 109–21, 318; infrastructure of 126–38

Qatar 171, 222–23, 226
Queen Boat case (2001) 44, 99–101, 291
queer digital activism 95–106

queer socialities 259–70
queer theory 47
queer urbanism 285–93; *see also* LGBTQ+ people
Qursaya Island 152–53

Rabaa Square massacre (2013) 61, 88
al-Rabwa development 193, 195, 197–99, 201–202
racial issues 15, 71, 285, 285; blackface as 69, 73, 78; educational system and 276, 282n1; Egyptian cinema and 69–79; intersectionality of 40–42; Negritude movement and 4; n-word slur as 291, 434; Sudanese and 20–21, 28, 277–79, 433–45; *see also* intersectionality
El Raggal, Aly 25, 184, 377–87
rape *see* sexual violence
rap music 437
Rashed, Hany 428
real estate developments 19, 193–202, 221–29, 379, 381; Emirati 24–25, 152, 195, 200–201, 206, 221–22, 225; graft and 223–24; Kuwaiti 24–25, 152; relocation projects and 327–35, 368, 404–405
refugees *see* South Sudanese
al-Rehab project 193, 195–97, 199–201, 313
respectability politics 6, 15, 16, 270; class issues with 42, 46, 170, 264; family values and 45; migrants and 20–22; social media and 37
Reynolds, Nancy Y. 396–97
Rigot, Afsaneh 16, 95–106
Ring Road *see* Cairo Ring Road
Rio de Janeiro 118–19
Rizk, Khalil 407, 408
Rubin, Gayle 42, 43
Rushdi, Fatima 455
Russell Pasha, Thomas 451–53, 457, 458

Sabahy, Hamdeen 61
al-Sadat, Anwar 100, 208, 265, 416
Sadiqu, Nabil Ahmed 102
Said, Edward 260
Saleh, Tania 69
Saleh, Yahia Mohamed 21, 285–93
Al-Samragy, Bassem 27, 378, 413–21
al-Sanhuri, Abd al-Razzaq 341–45, 347, 348n4
sanitation systems 109–21, 145–48, 318
Saudi Arabia 222–24, 274; Gulf way of life and 19, 221
Sawiris, Naguib 60
Sawiris, Samih 297
Sayigh, Yazid 63, 64
al-Sayyid, Nuha 133
SCAF see Supreme Council of the Armed Forces
Scott, J. C. 296, 299–300
sectarian politics 401–408; and sectarianized sovereignty 26
securitization 212–13, 292; cruising ethics and 266–70; definitions of 4–5; digital 95–106; dispositif of 424–27, 429, 430; etymology of 11; gentrification and 116, 374; informal 421; infrastructure of 233–41, 310–13; neoliberalism and 23, 377; "queering" of 11–12; of red-light districts 453–60; of relocation projects 328, 333–35; of squatting 353–64; territorialism and 426–27; of urbanism and 27, 401–408
security discourse 427–28
security firms 370, 375
security logic 118–19
security states 118–20
Selim III (sultan) 128
Senwosret Obelisk 418
sex reassignment surgery see gender reassignment surgery
sexual harassment 39, 277–78, 385; see also gender issues

sexuality infrastructures 125
sexual violence 385, 460; Fairmont Hotel incident of 35, 39, 41–43; intersectionality of 269; legal definition of 44; movement against 35, 38, 39, 43; El Tarzi on 269
sex workers 28–29, 449–60, 452t; criminalization of 29n1, 459–60; demographics of 453t, 456; fees paid by 458t; history of 260; racism and 435; Nicola Smith on 45; social media and 35–48; see also prostitution
shadow security networks 178–83
al-Sha'ir, Ismail 394
shamelessness 35–48
Sha'rawi, Mahmud 368
shari'a contracts 341–47
Sharp, Deen 3
Shawkat, Yahia 23–24, 339–47
Shawqi, Tamir 167
Shihata, Ibrahim 146
Siddiq, Khalid 329, 333, 368, 374
sifr al-mondial scandal 119–20
sihhat tawqi' (signature validity) 343–46
Sims, David 8
Singerman, Diane 14, 168
Sinno, Ma a 19, 144, 221–29
al-Sisi, Abd al-Fattah 62–63, 146; al-Asmarat relocation project of 327–28; Coptic Christians and 401, 403–404, 406, 408; Gulf aid for 223; Ministry of Endowments and 117–18; New Administrative Capital project of 18–19, 205–16; populism of 19; as presidential candidate 60–61; protests against 185n5; securitization efforts of 212–13, 215–16
Smith, Nicola 45
Sobhy, Ashraf 120
soccer 159–72, 370, 424
social cleansing 16, 112–21

sociality, 259–68; and alternative kinship 162; and interrupting infrastructure 237; and racial solidarity 8
social media 35–48; COVID-19 pandemic and 45, 46; cruising and 261–62; cybercrime law for 36–38; gang members on 442; internet accessibility and 214–15; morality police on 36, 96; prostitution laws and 45; queer activism on 95–106; respectability politics and 37; surveillance of 369; *see also* YouTube
social networks 226, 332, 417; domestic workers and 249; of LGBTQ+ people 16; of refugees 21, 273, 444
Soliman, Khaled el-Husseiny 206
Soliman, Mohamed 167
Somali migrants 434
Soueif, Ahdaf 424
South Sudanese 20–21, 433–45; community schools of 273–82; domestic workers from 251–52, 255, 279; Egyptian education system and 273–82; *see also* Sudan
squatters 299, 304, 314, 353, 360
Sri Lanka 249
Stadnicki, Roman 313
Stavrides, Stavros 314
street politics 15, 90, 199–200, 389
St. Regis Hotel 226–27
structural violence 28, 433–37
"subaltern counterpublic" 276–79
Sudan 28, 76–77, 433–45; civil wars of 434, 442–45; *see also* South Sudanese
Sudan People's Liberation Army (SPLA) 443
Suez 372
Supreme Council of the Armed Forces (SCAF) 59–60, 208, 403
surveillance 213–14, 368–70, 377; Foucault on 369; police informants for 178–82, 392–93, 420; rationales for 386–87; shops' security cameras for 370; of soccer fans 159–72; of social media 38; tree removal for 147–48
surveillance geographies 367–75
Syrian immigrants 200

Tahrir Square 212, 216, 395, 424, 425; cruising in 261–62; protests in 6, 84–85, 149, 163, 177, 394; public toilets in 112–13
Talaat Moustafa Group (TMG) 193–202, 211
Tamim, Suzanne 196
Tantawi, Muhammad Hussein 223
Tarzan films 72, 77–78, 435
El Tarzi, Salma 269, 428–29
Tawadros II (Coptic Pope) 404
al-Taweel clan 418
Tazkarti (ticket agency) 169–70
"teichopolitic" 426
Telecommunication Regulation Law (2003) 104
"terraform" 151
territorialism 18, 353–64, 378; securitization and 426–27
terrorism, war on 378–79, 382, 403–405
Terrorist Entities Law (2013) 423
"thick signifier" 385–87
"thugs" *see baltagiya*
TikTok women 35–48, 105, 247; Berlin demonstration for 39–40, *40*; intersectionality theory and 40–42; moral panic over 36, 42–46; *see also* social media
transgender people 98; gender reassignment surgery for 125, 126, 134–37; hormone therapy for 17, 125–27, 134–37; *see also* LGBTQ+ people
Transport Ministry 144

UAE *see* United Arab Emirates
Ugandan workers 251, 254
Ultras (soccer fans) 159–72
al-'Umda clan 418

unbundling rights 322–24
United Arab Emirates (UAE) 211, 222–24; Dubai real estate model of 24–25, 152, 195, 200–201, 206, 221–22, 225; foreign domestic workers in 250; Gulf way of life and 19, 221–29
"unsafe areas" 328–30, 333, 373
urban activism 22, 313–14, 401–408, 424–25
urbanism 27, 191–94; aerial 235; agrarian 10; family mobility and 19–21; Gulf way of life on 19, 221–29; "Haussmannized" 22, 260, 311–14, 414–15; "informal" 317; justice 10–11; Lefebvre on 191; multicultural 221; neoliberal 312; "new" 145–46, 368; queer 285–93
urban militarization 425–30, 429
urban studies 3, 125
'urfi (customary) contracts 343–44

Valverde, Mariana 296, 300
"vernacular mediascaping" 15–16
violence: masculinity and 440–42; structural 433–45
viral visualities 81–90
Vision Cairo 2050 see Cairo 2050 Plan
Voluntary and Confidential Counseling and Testing Centers (VCCTs) 131

voter fraud 179–80

Wadi al-nugum (film) 70–79
Wahba, Dina 265
al-wara'a ak-dawara (paper ballot) 179
Wardi, Mohammed 285
al-Warraq Island 152–53, 404–407
water companies 22–23, 317–24, 332, 417
Wazir, Abd al-Azim 119
Westmoreland, Mark 15–16, 81–90
Williams, Raymond 161, 172
working class see class issues
World Bank 298–301; economic adjustment program of 192; environmental projects of 55, 147; see also neoliberalism
World Cup 118, 119, 166
Wynn, L.L. 6

YouTube 37, 84, 86, 114, 398; Egyptian military on 143; Maspero Massacre on 83; al-Sisi protests on 431n2, 431n9; see also social media

Zaki, Patrick George 407, 408
Zalewski, Marysia 234
Zomorroda 47–48
zoning laws 303–306, 355

www.ingramcontent.com/pod-product-compliance
Lightning Source LLC
Chambersburg PA
CBHW051707020426
42333CB00014B/883